SECOND EDITION

AN ANTHOLOGY OF LIVING RELIGIONS

MARY PAT FISHER

LEE W. BAILEY

PRENTICE HALL
Upper Saddle River, N.J. 07458

Cataloging-in-Publication Data available from the Library of Congress

Editor in Chief: Sarah Touborg
Senior Aquisitions Editor: Mical Moser
Editorial Assistant: Carla Worner
Assistant Marketing Manager: Andrea Messineo
Managing Editor: Joanne Riker
Buyer: Sherry Lewis

Credits and acknowledgments of material borrowed from other sources and reproduced, with permission, in this textbook appear on pages 376–8.

Pearson Education Ltd.
Pearson Education Australia PTY, Ltd.
Pearson Education Singapore, Pte. Ltd.
Pearson Education North Asia Ltd.
Pearson Education, Canada, Ltd.
Pearson Educación de Mexico, S.A. de C.V.
Pearson Education–Japan
Pearson Education Malaysia, Pte. Ltd.

This book was designed and produced by Laurence King Publishing Ltd., London
www.laurenceking.co.uk

Every effort has been made to contact the copyright holders, but should there be any errors or omissions, Laurence King Publishing Ltd. would be pleased to insert the appropriate acknowledgment in any subsequent printing of this publication.

Commissioning Editor: Melanie White
Editor: Ursula Payne
Literary permissions: Nick Wetton
Cover and type design: Andrew Shoolbred
Typesetting and layout: Fakenham Photosetting, Norfolk
Map: Eugene Fleury

Front cover: Charlotte Johnstone, detail of *Fan Fire*, 1997. Oil and glaze on gesso board. Private collection/The Bridgeman Art Library, London.

1 0 9 8 7 6 5 4 3 2
ISBN-13: 978-0-13-206059-2
ISBN-10:   0-13-206059-0

CONTENTS

CHAPTER 2
INDIGENOUS SACRED WAYS
page 37

CHAPTER 3
HINDUISM
page 62

CHAPTER 5
BUDDHISM
page 113

CHAPTER 9
CHRISTIANITY
page 223

CHAPTER 10
ISLAM
page 268

CHAPTER 12
NEW RELIGIOUS MOVEMENTS
page 330

TEACHING AND LEARNING RESOURCES

Prentice Hall is proud to provide a second edition of *An Anthology of Living Religions* which integrates a wealth of valuable resources. Besides those cited at the ends of chapters, the following resources can enhance understanding of, and appreciation for, the world's living religions by connecting students to audio-visual media and further printed information as well as to valuable research material on the Internet. Please contact your local Prentice Hall sales representative for details of how to obtain or use the items listed below.

The Sacred World: Encounters with the World's Religions CD-ROM

This useful CD-ROM is Prentice Hall's multimedia exploration of the rituals, beliefs, art, and key personalities in the world's major faiths. The religions covered are Judaism, Christianity, Islam, Hinduism, Buddhism, Confucianism, Daoism, Sikhism, Jainism, and Shinto. Clips include a tour of Jerusalem, a feature on the Cathedral of St. John the Divine and its involvement in the New York community, an architectural look at Islamic mosques, an experience of the color and sound of Buddhist festivals, and visits to Sikh and Jain temples. Readers are directed to the CD-ROM by a disk icon which appears over 40 times within the book, calling out audio-visual clips that complement the content of the text.

TIME Special Edition: World Religions Magazine TIME

In partnership with TIME magazine, Prentice Hall can make available with its new texts *TIME Special Edition: World Religions* magazine. This includes over 20 articles on major world religions and topics in religious studies. Among them is material on the significance of Abraham for Judaism, Christianity, and Islam; Muslim thinkers' reflections on war; discussion of Buddhism in America; and essays on religious pluralism.

The Prentice Hall Atlas of World Religions

This atlas, produced in conjunction with Laurence King Publishing, contains 30 excellent, multi-dimensional maps which provide global, regional, chronological, and thematic perspectives on the world's living religions.

Companion Website™: *www.prenhall.com/fisher*

The Companion Website for *An Anthology of Living Religions'* partner book, *Living Religions,* is a powerful study tool. Organized by chapter, it provides multiple-choice, true/false, and essay questions to help students review the text and check their comprehension.

Research Navigator™

Prentice Hall's *Research Navigator*™ has been created to help students use their research time well, from finding relevant articles and journals to citing sources, writing effective papers, and completing research assignments. It includes Ebsco's *ContentSelect, The New York Times,* and Best-of-the-Web *Link Library.*

PREFACE

Religious points of view underlie the thinking and behavior of the majority of the world's citizens. As we enter the twenty-first century, a deeper understanding of these perspectives is a necessity in our increasingly interwoven, pluralistic cultures. To enhance understanding and perhaps appreciation of each religion, we offer here a selection of interesting and significant texts explaining each religion from the inside, as its founders and practitioners have explained it and as people are trying to live by its precepts today. Our book gives the major world religions—as well as a sampling of local and new religions—the opportunity to explain themselves in their own terms.

We have tried to open many windows to understanding. We offer excerpts from each religion's original inspired writings or oral traditions, exemplary stories about the founders, significant later elaborations of the teachings, and recent articles showing each religion grappling with contemporary issues. These include environmental decay, women's issues, social injustice, the relation between religion and politics, and tensions between fundamentalist and liberal interpretations of the faith. We have included women's voices and histories throughout the anthology. We believe that these excerpts old and new illustrate that religions are dynamic and relevant in today's world.

To guide readers through this wealth of material, we first introduce the founder, history, and basic principles of each faith. Each excerpt or group of excerpts is preceded by a brief introduction to the context and significance of the material. Unfamiliar terms are defined in a glossary at the end of the chapter. For each religion, we also offer a list of holy days, a historical outline, questions for review, and a list of further resources such as books, periodicals, and Internet websites. Although this anthology thus stands on its own, it follows the organization of Mary Pat Fisher's bestselling textbook, *Living Religions*, and can be used with that text for deeper understanding.

Additions to the Second Edition

In this second edition we have added many new pieces to bring the book up to date and to meet reviewers' requests for both historical and contemporary materials. In the first chapter, there is a new introduction to the academic study of world religions, a new article on the Darwinian account of religion, more experiential material such as a college girl's dream, a Greek myth of a virgin birth, and Judith Plaskow's feminist critique of the image of God as a dominating patriarchal male.

In chapter 2, on Indigenous Sacred Ways, there is a new article on an African goddess who can be seen as a patron of feminine leadership, a piece on Aboriginal women's health rituals, a northern Pacific coast Native American legend about the theft of light, and Thomas Banyacya's classic message from the Hopi Nation to the United Nations.

In chapters 3 to 7, on Eastern religious traditions, we have added new translations and selections from the *Upanishads,* the *Bhagavad Gita,* the *Dhammapada*, *The Book of Mencius*, and the *Dao de jing,* an article by a major contemporary Hindu woman guru, an analysis of non-exclusivism in Hindu tradition, a piece on first principles from a Jain perspective, an article outlining the history of Buddhism in the United States, and two new articles by contemporary Chinese scholars.

In the Judaism chapter we have added Psalm 23, the Shema prayer, new material on three major branches of modern Judaism, a new article on women in Jewish life, and a re-interpretation of the Ten Commandments as the "Ten Commitments." In the Christianity chapter, we have added a selection from the Gospel of Mary from the Nag Hammadi Library and ritual material from each of the three major branches of the faith. New articles by evangelicals focus on global warming and religion in politics. There is a piece on the rise of megachurches, and Roman Catholic struggles with ordination of women and priestly sex abuse are covered.

Chapter 10 includes a discussion of the Hajj's effect on asceticism and social leveling, a new article by Riffat Hassan on the rights of women in Islam, an interview with Samuel Huntington on his theory of the conflict of civilizations, and a positive personal testimony on relationships between Christians and Muslims. We add the Mormons to the chapter on New Religious Movements, with a scriptural passage from *The Book of Mormon* and an extract from the *Testimony of the Prophet Joseph Smith*.

A completely new final chapter, "Religion in a New Era," explores major contemporary themes in religious studies: globalization, ecology, violence, fundamentalism and universalism, and interfaith initiatives. We have added a new global map and a timeline of world religions, new discussion questions at the end of each chapter, and icons in the text that refer the reader to similar sections of the CD-ROM *Sacred World: Encounters with the World's Religions*. Lee Bailey selected the video segments for this CD-ROM, which can be used by students individually and in classes. In articles using Chinese language, we have switched wherever possible to the modern Pinyin system of transliteration to English, so, for example, Tao is now written Dao. We hope that these additions and changes will make the study of world religions more accessible in historical context and more relevant to today's situations.

Acknowledgments

Many people around the world helped in gathering materials for the first edition and are gratefully acknowledged therein. For this new edition, the authors want to express special gratitude to Randall Nadeau for preparing new translations of the *Dao de jing* and *The Book of Mencius*, to Serinity Young and Ellen Umansky for contributing new original articles on Buddhism and Judaism, and to Celeste Federico for sharing her dream. Mary Pat Fisher wants especially to thank David Vandiver for help in locating materials on contemporary Progressive Christianity. The constructive criticisms of our reviewers have been of great help in preparing this second edition, and for this we want to thank Athena DeGangi at New Hampshire Community Technical College, Nashua, Lisa Sargese at Montclair State University, Albert Terrillion at Loyola University New Orleans, and Mark O. Webb at Texas Tech University.

At Laurence King Publishing, our beloved editor Melanie White has been patient and wise in guiding our process and Ursula Payne painstaking and brilliant in copyediting, and at Prentice Hall Mical Moser has been very supportive.

Lee Bailey expresses his special thanks to the many thoughtful students, devoted collegial scholars, professors, clergy, friends, spiritual seekers, retreat guides, and conference presenters who have contributed to this vision of living world religions. For Mary Pat Fisher, its preparation has been particularly inspired by His Holiness Baba Virsa Singh, patron of the Gobind Sadan Institute for Advanced Studies in Comparative Religion, who generously shares his profound appreciation and understanding of the world's sacred scriptures with people of all faiths. May our readers also grow in understanding and appreciation, for the sake of us all.

Mary Pat Fisher, Gobind Sadan Institute for Advanced Studies in Comparative Religion, Delhi
Lee W. Bailey, Department of Philosophy and Religion, Ithaca College, New York (retired)

The predominant forms of religions in the world today

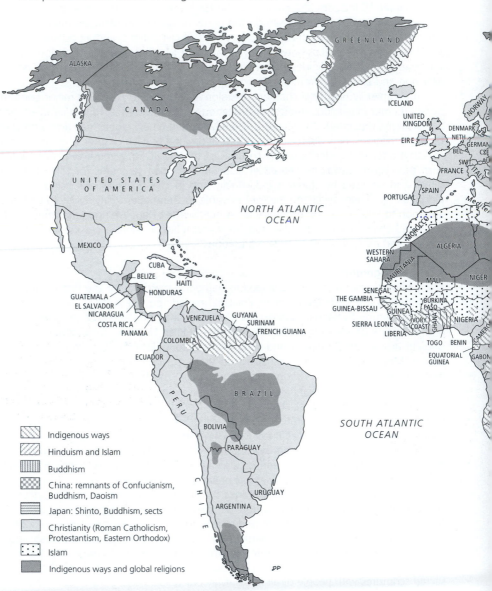

- Indigenous ways
- Hinduism and Islam
- Buddhism
- China: remnants of Confucianism, Buddhism, Daoism
- Japan: Shinto, Buddhism, sects
- Christianity (Roman Catholicism, Protestantism, Eastern Orthodox)
- Islam
- Indigenous ways and global religions

MAP XIX

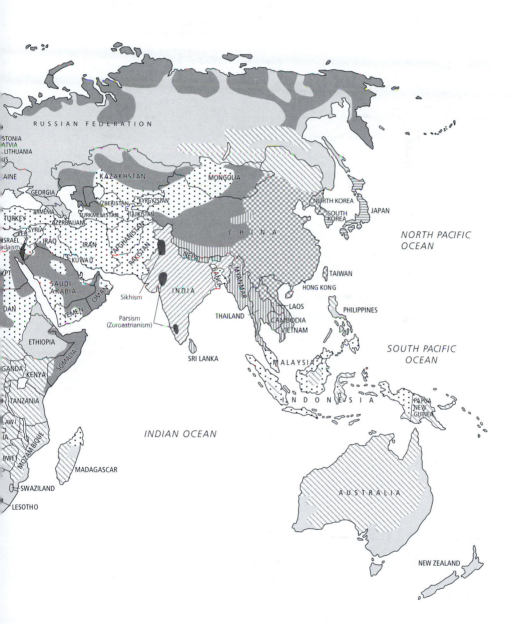

RUSSIAN FEDERATION

ESTONIA
ATVIA
LITHUANIA
US

AINE

GEORGIA

KAZAKHSTAN

MONGOLIA

NORTH KOREA

TURKEY

ARMENIA
AZERBAIJAN
ZER

ISRAEL
daism

IRAQ

UZBEKISTAN

TURKMENISTAN

KYRGYZSTAN

TAJIKISTAN

AFGHANISTAN

C H I N A

SOUTH
KOREA

JAPAN

NORTH PACIFIC
OCEAN

PT

KUWAIT

PAKISTAN

NEPAL

MYANMAR

TAIWAN

HONG KONG

Sikhism

INDIA

SAUDI
ARABIA

OMAN

YEMEN

BANG

LAOS

THAILAND

PHILIPPINES

Parsism
(Zoroastrianism)

CAMBODIA
VIETNAM

DAN

ETHIOPIA

SRI LANKA

SOUTH PACIFIC
OCEAN

GANDA
KENYA

SOMALIA

M A L A Y S I A

TANZANIA

I N D O N E S I A

LAWI
IA

INDIAN OCEAN

PAPUA
NEW
GUINEA

BWE

MOZAMBIQUE

MADAGASCAR

A U S T R A L I A

SWAZILAND

LESOTHO

NEW ZEALAND

	← 2000 BCE	1500	1000	500	0	300 CE
Indigenous	Neolithic reverence for ← nature, mother goddess, ancestors					
Hinduism	Indus River cultures with goddess and ← indigenous religions c. 2500 BCE	*Vedas* first written c. 1500 BCE	Vyasa systematizes *Upanishads* c. 1000–500 BCE	*Ramayana* and *Mahabharata* in present form 400 BCE–200 CE Patanjali systematizes *Yoga Sutras* by 200 BCE		*The Laws of Manu* compiled by 100–300 CE
Jainism	23 Tirthankaras ← before c. 777 BCE			Mahavira, last Tirthankara, c. 599–527 BCE Some *Agam Sutras* written down c. 300 BCE Svetambaras and Digambaras diverge after 300 BCE		
Buddhism				Gautama Buddha c. 563–483 BCE King Ashoka spreads Buddhism c. 258 BCE Theravada Buddhism develops 200 BCE–200 CE		Mahayana Buddhism develops c. 100 CE Asvaghosha writes *Acts of the Buddha* 2nd c. CE
Confucianism and Daoism			Laozi c. 600–300 BCE Confucius c. 551–479 BCE Liezi c. 475–221 BCE	Mencius c. 390–305 BCE Zhuangzi c. 365–290 BCE Educational system based on Confucian Classics from 206 BCE		Ge Hong on alchemy 200–300 CE
Judaism	Abraham c. 1900–1700 BCE?	Exodus from Egypt led by Moses c. 1250 BCE King David c. 1010–970 BCE King Solomon builds First Temple c. 950 BCE	First Temple destroyed; Jews exiled 586 BCE	Jerusalem falls to Romans; Jewish Diaspora begins 70 CE Canon of Tanakh agreed c. 90 CE Rabbinical tradition develops 1st–4th c. CE	Mishnah c. 200 CE	
Christianity				Jesus c. 4 BCE–30 CE Letters of Paul 48–64 CE Gospels written down c. 70–95 CE		Athanasius 296–373 CE Council of Nicaea: divinity of Jesus 325 CE Augustine 354–430 CE Official religion of Roman Empire 392 CE
Islam						
Sikhism						
New Religious Movements						

600	900	1200	1500	1800	2000
	Viking invasions carry Norse religion into northern Europe 800–1100		European colonialists invade indigenous cultures in Americas from 1492	Slave trade introduces African religions into Americas from 1550	Hopi Message to the U.N. General Assembly 1992
Puranas written down 500–1500					Mahatma Gandhi 1869–1948
Bhakti movement 600–1800					Paramahansa Yogananda 1893–1952
	Sankara organizes Vedanta school c. 788–820		Kabir c. 1440–1518		V. D. Savarkar, "Hindutva" 1923
			Mirabai c. 1500–50		
Division of Svetambaras and Digambaras formalized c. 450			New orders under Mughal rule 1526–1818	Jain teaching spreads out from India from 1818	Jain monks establish centers outside India 1970s–80s
	Buddhism declared national religion of Tibet 700s		Chan Buddhism to Japan as Zen 13th c.		Buddhism spreads in the West 20th c.
	Persecution of Chinese Buddhists begins 845				
Emperor declares Daoism official religion c. 400–448	Song dynasty: Neo-Confucianism 960–1279 Zhou Dunyi 1017–73 Zhang Zai 1020–77 Zhang Boduan, Awakening to Perfection 1075–8				End of Confucianism as state ideology in China 1911
Japan imports Confucianism c. 500–600					Cultural Revolution attacks religions 1966–76 Confucian and Daoist revival in East Asia from 1980s
Jerusalem Talmud c. 500	Maimonides c. 1135–1204			Baal-Shem Tov begins Hasidism c. 1700–60	Nazi Holocaust 1933–45 Independent state of Israel 1948
Babylonian Talmud c. 600			Mass expulsion of Jews from Spain 1492		Six-Day War 1967 Conflict between Hezbollah and Israel 2006
Canon of Bible set c. 400	Consolidation of papal power 800–1300	Anselm of Canterbury 1033–1109 Western and Eastern churches split 1054	Monastic orders proliferate 14th c. Spanish Inquisition established 1478 Protestantism begins with Martin Luther's "95 Theses" 1517 Council of Trent 1545–63	Methodism: John Wesley 1707–88	Mother Teresa 1910–97 Martin Luther King 1929–68 Vatican II 1962 Pope Benedict XVI elected 2005
Muhammad 570–632 Spread of Islam begins 633 Canon of Qur'an set 650	Islam's cultural peak under Abbasids 750–1258 Sahih Bukhari by 870 Sahih Muslim by 875 Ibn Sina 980–1037	Al-Ghazali 1058–1111 Ibn Rushd 1126–98 Ibn 'Arabi 1165–1240 Turks conquer Constantinople 1453	Akbar becomes Mughal emperor 1556	Sufi Order of the West 1910 Muslim-majority Pakistan separates from Hindu-majority India 1947 OPEC; Muslim resurgence 1970s	9/11 attacks in U.S. 2001 U.S. and allies invade Iraq 2003
		Guru Nanak 1469–1539	Guru Gobind Singh initiates Khalsa 1699 Guru Granth Sahib installed as Guru 1708	British massacre Sikhs in Amritsar 1919 Sikhs demand separate state 1984	Celebration of 300th anniversary of Khalsa 1999
			Bahá'u'lláh 1817–92 Mormon Church founded 1822 Jehovah's Witnesses established 1872 Theosophical Society starts 1875	Sun Myung Moon founds Unification Church 1954 Parliament of the World's Religions 1993, 1999, 2004	

CHAPTER 1
RELIGIOUS RESPONSES

Religious affiliations are sources of both comfort and conflict. Religions provide important guides to meaning and consolation in difficult times. But globally increased religiously supported violence, coupled with powerful new weapons, has intensified the urgency of understanding others' beliefs. Global religions and new religious movements are vibrant in many regions, often playing a significant role in public events as well as people's personal lives. For great numbers of people around the world, religion is a central aspect of life's patterns and meanings. Religious experiences may inspire courage, patience, tolerance, charity, morality, acts of extreme altruism, and selfless love. They may have a healing, transformative effect. They may reveal unseen dimensions of existence. Religious experiences and training unfortunately may also frighten, oppress, and breed violence and hatred of others, if the teachings have been misunderstood or distorted by religious "authorities" acting in their own self-interest.

There is no one pattern that can be universally termed "religion." Many prophets, teachers, and gurus have offered what is understood by their followers as enlightened wisdom. Institutions have been built around their teachings and, with them, somewhat different understandings of life and different methods of approaching the truth of existence. To many people, "religion" refers to reverence for and communication with the supernatural, but certain "religions" such as branches of Buddhism refer only to the material world and liberation from worldly sufferings, without explicit reference to deity.

In subsequent chapters, we will offer a wealth of primary source material giving intimate glimpses into each world of faith as the faithful understand it. However, before doing so, in this chapter we will approach religions from a distance, trying to gain a critical basis for understanding the many perspectives from which religious phenomena have been studied.

Some readers coming to the study of world religions from a traditional religious background may react with discomfort as they encounter new ideas and new religions. Others more skeptical or critical of traditional religions may be uncomfortable with certain practices, such as some authors' use of the masculine pronouns or expressions such as "man" meant to include both genders. We hope that readers will maintain both a sympathetic respect and a critical eye, and strive to understand the historical background and personal diversity for the colorful variety of human religious expressions. The best reasons for maintaining or changing religious practices come from understanding them.

The academic study of world religions

As modern technologies accelerate the globalization of culture, believers of the world's religions have come into contact with each other and compared their experiences of the **sacred**. As a consequence, the "comparative" study of religion has blossomed. It has become difficult for educated people to assume that their religion has the privilege of being the single absolutely valid religion. Interpretation, experience, and participation are now combined with a neutral, non-judgmental, respectful stance toward the richness of the world's spiritual traditions.

The Study of World Religions   by Lee W. Bailey

The study of world religions today is engaged in a conflict between the expansion and the reduction of understanding religion. In the past, many early world travelers could not resist trying to evaluate newly uncovered religions as inferior or superior to familiar faiths at home. Missionaries also judgmentally reduced other religions to "idol worship" and "devil worship." Many still see their own religion as the only absolutely true guide to life and read religious language with a naïve literalism. But today increased education and travel have stimulated more openness to other religions.

Can religion be defined globally? There are many possible universal definitions: "the way things are," belief in God or gods, **creedal statements**, the **ground of Being** (foundation of existence), obedience to laws, belonging to an institutional religion, what one does in one's private inwardness, social norms for ethical behavior, meditative experience of a nameless cosmic presence, participation in awesome natural wonders, gratefulness for existence itself, and belief that goodness ultimately overcomes suffering and evil. Often religions get tangled up with nationalism and are used to justify prejudices, hate, oppression, and violent atrocities. But from an expanded view of religion, cruelty shrouded in piety is a narrow corruption of religion that the study of world religions can help deconstruct.

In the nineteenth century, the comparison of world religions and search for common themes grew into an academic project in the West. F. Max Müller (1823–1900) at Oxford University translated numerous sacred texts into English for the first time in the late nineteenth century, preparing the 50-volume *Sacred Books of the East,* including Hindu, Buddhist, Chinese, and Muslim texts. Müller advocated the "scientific" study of world religions through a detached understanding, seeking "objective" knowledge outside the lens of Western **monotheistic** categories. Müller analyzed **myths** as rationalizations of natural events, a "proto-science" in cultural evolution. He sought to explain Indo-European religions as a widespread family of linguistically related strands (presenting, for example, the Indo-European word "Dyaus"—"shining"—as the root of the widespread Indo-European gods Zeus, Jupiter, Dyaus, and Pita, and the generic terms for god "deva," "deus," and "theos"). Simultaneously, he reduced religion to natural evolutionary causes.

In comparative studies there should be no talk of "idols" or "devils," "pagans," "barbarians," or "heathens." New cross-cultural categories such as myth, magic, mysticism, and **ritual** were developed for comparison. Some authors showed the strong influence of Darwinian theory and its offspring cultural evolution, with its effort to schematize world cultures into a developmental pattern that ended up with Christianity or Western scientific cultures on top. The "scientific" method seemed to offer a neutral stance, but perhaps exaggerated its ability to transfer the scientific study of nature to religion. Comparative studies pulled the mantle of scientific authority over themselves partly to defend against strong traditions of church influences that rejected the neutral stance.

From 1890 to 1937, James Frazer (1854–1941) wrote 13 volumes entitled *The Golden Bough,* an extensive, though not fully accurate, encyclopedia of world myths, rituals, and religions. He opened up a new study of cross-cultural themes such as magic, divine kingship, and the dying and rising god or goddess of vegetation. He put them into the era's popular schema of an historical evolution from magic through religions, giving way to science. Religions were thus interpreted as backward, unsuccessful, primitive sciences—a theory that anthropologists disproved by observing, for example, South Pacific island cultures that could make large boats and navigate effectively.

As the social sciences developed their application of scientific methods to the study of society, many theories unfolded interpreting religion as social rather than **transcendent**. The anthropologist Emile Durkheim (1858–1917) in France published the widely influential *Forms of the Religious Life* (1912). He saw religion as the most characteristic element of the collective mind of each society, the "glue" that held it together, expressed in rituals about gods, totems, taboos, and ancestor spirits. He sought to explain away transcendence by reducing it to the level of a social force.

Max Weber (1864–1920) in Germany developed the sociology of religion, arguing that economic forces directly influence concepts of gods and demons. In his *Protestant Ethic and the Spirit of Capitalism* (1905), he stressed the affinity between the Puritan spirit and the rise of middle-class capitalism. Combined with increased rationalism, he argued, Protestant Christianity's work ethic—notably in Calvinism—promoted greed for profit (the "prosperity gospel"), as successful pursuit of gain was seen as God's blessing.

The psychology of religion became another major approach. Early in the twentieth century, Sigmund Freud (1856–1939) in Austria showed the meaningfulness of the unconscious psyche, expressed in dreams, errors, and symptoms. In that late Victorian atmosphere, he stressed sexual instincts, notably the Oedipus Complex, in which a child is unconsciously in love with its father or mother. In *The Future of an Illusion* (1927) Freud argued reductively that religion is an infantile illusion based on the elevation of a beloved father figure to a divinity. Carl Jung (1875–1961) in Switzerland in the early twentieth century built on Freud's thought that the unconscious is meaningful and expressed in dreams and myths. But he rejected Freud's view of the centrality of sex in the unconscious and saw religion as a meaningful psychological reality, symbolized in many ways.

Rudolf Otto (1869–1937) in Germany wrote *The Idea of the Holy* (1917), arguing against the idea that the naturalistic sciences could reduce religion to a natural or social force. Conversant with the new mechanistic view of the world and Darwinism, he opposed their neglect of the autonomy of the human spirit. A world traveler, he argued that the rational attempts to explain religions were inadequate to comprehend the larger reality of the sacred. Otto advocated the *sui generis* nature of religion—religion as a category unto itself, not reducible to others. Behind creeds, **dogmas**, and religious institutions, Otto stressed the reality of the holy phenomena described as the awesome **numinous** experience of the sacred, essential to true religious understanding. Felt in the wonder of life in the cosmos, the numinous evokes the presence of a transcendent and present power outside oneself, a fascinating, tremendous mystery *(mysterium tremendum)*.

From 1925 to 1950, Gerardus van der Leeuw (1890–1950) in the Netherlands was formative in shaping the **phenomenology** of religion. His influential work *Religion as Essence and Manifestation* (1933) explored the intuitive "essences" of many phenomena such as sacred time, mysticism, compassion, obedience, and love, without reducing them to natural categories. He also built on the idea of **hermeneutics** (critical awareness of one's basic interpretive principles and methodological assumptions).

Mircea Eliade (1907–86) led the history and phenomenology of religion movement at the University of Chicago after World War II. Although he welcomed the input of the social sciences, he would not reduce religion to conscious experience and the natural world. Following study in India, where many Eastern religious traditions had developed, he wrote numerous influential books. He stressed the *sui generis*, non-reducible quality of religious experiences, viewing them as often not conscious or not thought about, and also emphasized the importance of the history of the factual aspects of religions. His books, such as *Patterns in Comparative Religion* (1958), are encyclopedic outlines of major phenomenological themes with many historical examples from world religions. He explored hierophanies[1] in the cosmos, nature, and human culture. He developed a theory of myth and ritual as ways of re-experiencing the ultimate powers of existence expressed in past stories

---

1 Hierophany—a manifestation of the sacred in a limited earthly form.

and events. According to Eliade, sky, sun, stone, fertility, vegetation, and temple all disclose sacred powers in the human thirst for primordial ultimate reality. He edited the first edition of the major *Encyclopedia of Religion* (1987, 2004).

Wilfred Cantwell Smith (1916–2000) at Harvard University, also familiar with India, argued that discrete "religions" do not exist, but only people who practice various versions of traditions. Comparative themes can however be traced. Smith also rejected the claim to objectivity in scientific methods of studying religion, since humans are so involved in it.

Following the dominance of Eliade, the rise of post-modernist thought raised criticisms of the phenomenological method—mainly that it sought to link too many divergent religious elements and neglected the specific historical details of various traditions. Post-modernists such as Jacques Derrida (1930–2004) and Michel Foucault (1926–84) rejected the authority of the meta-narratives of religious cosmic stories such as creation and historical dramas of salvation, as well as the claims to rational certainty about the natural world of some scientific thinkers.

Feminists such as Mary Daly joined the deconstruction of sacred authorities such as patriarchy in religion. Phyllis Trible exposed the "texts of terror" in sacred books that justify the abuse of women. Other feminist scholars explored worship of the goddess and witchcraft.

Jonathan Z. Smith at the University of Chicago leads the contemporary argument that comparative religion lacks the necessary scientific method. He warns against assuming that the same symbols mean the same things in various cultures, and rejects the phenomenological effort to find the "essences" of religious patterns. He rejects any view of the sacred if it is not a theoretical, conscious object or term (such as "projection of subject onto object"). He welcomes statistical studies as more objective.

Many scholars of world religions still seek to find common interfaith ground in a rapidly growing global culture. Examples are: Huston Smith's *Forgotten Truth: The Primordial Tradition* (1976), Raimon Panikkar's *The Intra-religious Dialogue* (1978), John Hick's *God Has Many Names* (1980), Thich Nhat Hanh's *Living Buddha, Living Christ* (1995), and Matthew Fox's *One River, Many Wells* (2000).

Other religious scholars now are finding a middle ground between broad generalizations about common patterns and careful attention to local cultural differences. Diana L. Eck at Harvard, for example, says that we must be careful in comparisons. In her study of Hinduism in Benares, for example, she found that the English term "worship" overlaps only slightly with the Hindu experience of *darshan* as "seeing" or "beholding" a divine presence. However, she writes, "the so-called scientific study of religion and its notions of purely 'objective' scholarship with no authorial viewpoint is increasingly understood to be intellectually naïve. . . . even the most 'secular' of social scientists write out of a set of premises. . . ."[2] Kimberley C. Patton,

---

2 Kimberley Patton and Benjamin Ray, *A Magic Still Dwells: Comparative Religion in the Postmodern Age*. Berkeley, CA: University of California Press, 2000, p. 141.

also at Harvard, stresses that post-modern scholars are themselves typically committed to meta-narratives such as social justice, anti-racism, women's rights, and opposition to imperialism and colonialism.

Clearly there is a variety of approaches to the study of religion today, as there has been in the past. Many voices are represented within this volume; we let them speak for themselves and encourage readers to examine them from various perspectives. One can look at them independently side by side, or seek common themes and compare the way each tradition has developed them. Images of transcendence, law, compassion, war, social justice, and inner peace, for example, take innumerable local religious forms.

Some stick to one-sided methods of study, such as a literal, or historical, or **empirical** approach, or an opposite: a faith, or intuitive, or comparative approach. Others combine intuitive and scientific, expansive and reductive, comparative and culturally specific methods. This uniting of opposites, rather than seeing them as conflicting extremes, is the best way of approaching world religions.

SOURCE: Original article for this book by Lee W. Bailey, 2006

The Sacredness of Nature and Cosmic Religion
by Mircea Eliade

Shinto—Nature and Ancestor Spirits

Mircea Eliade (1907–86) of the University of Chicago was a pioneer in the historical and phenomenological approach to the study of religion. He blended two major methods in his approach: first, the history of religions, in order to clarify the factual side of religions, such as the dates, places, historical contexts, and texts; and second, the phenomenology of religions, in order to reflect intuitively and symbolically on the "essences" of religions by comparing archetypal themes such as the sacred and the **profane** in space, time, nature, and human existence. He was a major contributor to a renewed understanding of myth and ritual as worldwide religious phenomena, highly symbolic and meaningful. Eliade's multi-cultural analysis of the "sky gods" from his classic 1957 book *The Sacred and the Profane* is an example of this approach.

For religious man, nature is never only "natural"; it is always fraught with a religious value. This is easy to understand, for the cosmos is a divine creation; coming from the hands of the gods, the world is impregnated with sacredness. It is not simply a sacrality *communicated* by the gods, as is the case, for example, with a place or an object consecrated by the divine presence. The gods did more; *they manifested the different modalities of the sacred in the very structure of the world and of cosmic phenomena.*

The world stands displayed in such a manner that, in contemplating it, religious man discovers the many modalities of the sacred, and hence of being. Above all, the world exists, it is there, and it has a structure; it is not a chaos but a cosmos, hence it presents itself as creation, as work of the gods. This divine work always preserves its quality of transparency, that is, it spontaneously reveals the many aspects of the sacred. The sky directly, "naturally," reveals the infinite distance, the transcendence of the deity. The earth too is transparent; it presents itself as universal mother and nurse. The cosmic rhythms manifest order, harmony, permanence, fecundity. The cosmos as a whole is an organism at once *real*, *living*, and *sacred*; it simultaneously reveals the modalities of being and of sacrality. Ontophany[3] and hierophany meet.

In this chapter we shall try to understand how the world presents itself to the eyes of religious man—or, more precisely, how sacrality is revealed through the very structures of the world. We must not forget that for religious man the supernatural is indissolubly connected with the natural, that nature always expresses something that transcends it. As we said earlier: a sacred stone is venerated because it is *sacred*, not because it is a *stone*; it is the sacrality *manifested through the mode of being of the stone* that reveals its true essence. This is why we cannot speak of naturism or of natural religion in the sense that the nineteenth century gave to those terms; for it is "supernature" that the religious man apprehends through the natural aspects of the world.

The Celestial Sacred and the Uranian Gods   Simple contemplation of the celestial vault already provokes a religious experience. The sky shows itself to be infinite, transcendent. It is pre-eminently the "wholly other" than the little represented by man and his environment. Transcendence is revealed by simple awareness of infinite height. "Most high" spontaneously becomes an attribute of divinity. The higher regions inaccessible to man, the sidereal zones, acquire the momentousness of the transcendent, of absolute reality, of eternity. There dwell the gods; there a few privileged mortals make their way by rites of ascent; there, in the conception of certain religions, mount the souls of the dead. The "most high" is a dimension inaccessible to man as man; it belongs to superhuman forces and beings. He who ascends by mounting the steps of a sanctuary or the ritual ladder that leads to the sky ceases to be a man; in one way or another, he shares in the divine condition.

All this is not arrived at by a logical, rational operation. The transcendental category of height, of the superterrestrial, of the infinite, is revealed to the whole man, to his intelligence and his soul. It is a total awareness on man's part; beholding the sky, he simultaneously discovers the divine incommensurability and his own situation in the cosmos. For the sky, *by its own mode of being*, reveals transcendence, force, eternity. It *exists absolutely* because it is *high, infinite, eternal, powerful*.

This is the true significance of the statement made above—that the gods manifested the different modalities of the sacred in the very structure of the

---

3 Ontophany—a manifestation of being or sacred ultimate reality.

world. In other words, the cosmos—paradigmatic work of the gods—is so constructed that a religious sense of the divine transcendence is aroused by the very existence of the sky. And since the sky *exists* absolutely, many of the supreme gods of primitive peoples are called by names designating height, the celestial vault, meteorological phenomena, or simply Owner of the Sky or Sky Dweller.

The supreme divinity of the Maori is named *Iho*; *iho* means elevated, high up. Uwoluwu, the supreme god of the Akposo [Africans], signifies what is on high, the upper regions. Among the Selk'nam of Tierra del Fuego God is called Dweller in the Sky or He Who is in the Sky. Puluga, the supreme being of the Andaman Islanders, dwells in the sky; the thunder is his voice, wind his breath, the storm is the sign of his anger, for with his lightning he punishes those who break his commandments.

SOURCE: Mircea Eliade, *The Sacred and the Profane: The Nature of Religion*, trans. W. R. Trask, New York and London: Harcourt Brace Jovanovich, 1959, pp. 116–20

Materialistic perspectives on religion

In recent centuries, the point of view of people of faith has often given way to a more materialistic point of view, which suggests that only the quantifiable material world is real and the sacred reality which most people have not seen is just a figment of human imagination. The following three excerpts give Freud's and Marx's interpretations that humans invented religion and then Nietzsche's charge that "God is Dead."

The Future of an Illusion by Sigmund Freud

Sigmund Freud, a Viennese physician, founded the widely influential psychoanalytic movement. He demonstrated, through the interpretation of dreams, errors, and physical symptoms, the reality and meaningfulness of the unconscious mind. Sexuality and distorted relationships with one's parents, Freud thought, were the central dynamics of the unconscious psyche. Religion, he charged, is an infantile illusion, an unconscious search for security in a father figure, projected into the heavens.

When the growing individual finds that he is destined to remain a child forever, that he can never do without protection against strange superior powers, he lends these powers the features belonging to the figure of his father; he creates for himself the gods whom he dreads, whom he seeks to propitiate, and whom he nevertheless entrusts with his own protection. Thus his longing for a father is a motive identical with his need for protection against the consequences of his human weakness. . . .

Religious ideas . . . are not precipitates of experience or end-results of thinking: they are illusions, fulfillments of the oldest, strongest and most urgent wishes of mankind. The secret of their strength lies in the strength of those wishes. As we already know, the terrifying impression of helplessness in childhood aroused the need for protection—for protection through love—which was provided by the father; and the recognition that this helplessness lasts throughout life made it necessary to cling to the existence of a father, but this time a more powerful one. Thus the benevolent rule of a divine Providence[4] allays our fear of the dangers of life; the establishment of a moral world-order ensures the fulfillment of the demands of justice, which have so often remained unfulfilled in human civilization; and the promulgation of earthly existence in a future life provides the local and temporal framework in which these wish-fulfillments shall take place. Answers to the riddles that tempt the curiosity of man, such as how the universe began or what the relation is between body and mind, are developing in conformity with the underlying assumptions of this system. It is an enormous relief to the individual psyche if the conflicts of its childhood arising from the father-complex—conflicts which it has never wholly overcome—are removed from it and brought to a solution which is universally accepted.

An illusion is not the same thing as an error. . . . What is characteristic of illusions is that they are derived from human wishes. In this respect they come near to psychiatric delusions . . . For instance, a middle-class girl may have the illusion that a prince will come and marry her. This is possible; and a few such cases have occurred. That the Messiah will come and found a golden age is much less likely . . . Thus we call a belief an illusion when a wish-fulfillment is a prominent factor in its motivation, and in so doing we disregard its relations to reality, just as the illusion sets no store by verification.

SOURCE: Sigmund Freud, *The Future of an Illusion*. New York: Doubleday, 1961, pp. 35–49

Religion as the Opium of the People   by Karl Marx

Karl Marx (1818–83) was a German philosopher who founded Communism. With Friedrich Engels (1820–95), he developed the theory that class struggle is the primary mover of history, and posited that the working class would lead society from democratic bourgeois capitalism to a socialist, then a communist state. His analyses of the alienation of workers from industrialism and of the unjust and destructive effects of capitalism still influence many thinkers. Marx proclaimed "dialectical materialism"—the material interchange between human economic arrangements and the natural world—to be the guiding force in history. His view of religion is similar to that of Ludwig Feuerbach (1804–72), who in 1841 charged that religion is an illusory psychological projection of human emotions into the heavens. Marx added that this process is more social than psychological, with religion sanctioning and blessing the unjust status quo.

4 Providence—God's care and guidance through inward inspiration and outer events.

For Germany the *criticism of religion* is in the main complete, and criticism of religion is the premise of all criticism.

The *profane* existence of error is discredited after its *heavenly* speech for the altars and hearths has been rejected. Man, who looked for a superman in the fantastic reality of heaven and found nothing there but the *reflexion* of himself, will no longer be disposed to find but the *semblance* of himself, the non-human where he seeks and must seek his true reality.

The basis of irreligious criticism is: *Man makes religion,* religion does not make man. In other words, religion is the self-consciousness and self-feeling of man who has either not yet found himself or has already lost himself again. But *man* is no abstract being squatting outside the world. Man is *the world of man,* the state, society. This state, this society, produce religion, *a reversed world-consciousness,* because they are a *reversed* world. Religion is the general theory of that world, its encyclopaedic compendium, its logic in a popular form, its spiritualistic point of honor, its enthusiasm, its moral sanction, its solemn completion, its universal ground for consolation and justification. It is *the fantastic realization* of the human essence, because the *human essence* has no true reality. The struggle against religion is therefore mediately the fight against *the other world* of which religion is the spiritual *aroma.*

Religious distress is at the same time the *expression* of real distress and the *protest* against real distress. Religion is the sigh of the oppressed creature, the heart of a heartless world, just as it is the spirit of a spiritless situation. It is the *opium* of the people.

The abolition of religion as the *illusory* happiness of the people is required for their real happiness. The demand to give up the illusions about its condition is the *demand to give up the condition which needs illusions.* The criticism of religion is therefore *in embryo the criticism of the vale of woe, the halo of which is religion....* Religion is only the illusory sun which revolves round man as long as he does not revolve round himself.

SOURCE: Karl Marx and Friedrich Engels, *On Religion.* Moscow: Foreign Languages Publishing House, 1955, pp. 41–2

God is Dead by Friedrich Nietzsche

The maverick German intellectual Friedrich Nietzsche (1844–1900) was one of the most influential of modern thinkers. Highly iconoclastic, he challenged many social and intellectual conventions. He said: "Morality is nothing else . . . than obedience to customs." He took the implications of industrial culture a step further than many dared, charging that "God is Dead," thereby strengthening modern atheism and clearing the way for science. Nietzsche also foreshadowed other important themes of the twentieth century, such as the Will to Power, soon unleashed in new wars of unimagined destruction, and in technologies applied with minimal ethical restraint. But Nietzsche did not cling to consistency. He was skeptical about the certainty of accepted truths, so his madman's proclamation of the death of God also expresses his fear of the consequences.

The Madman Have you not heard of the madman who lit a lantern in the bright morning hours, ran to the market-place and cried incessantly: "I seek God! I seek God!"—As many of those who did not believe in God were standing around just then, he provoked much laughter. Why, did he get lost? said one. Did he lose his way like a child? said another. Or is he hiding? Is he afraid of us? Has he gone on a voyage? or emigrated?—Thus they yelled and laughed. The madman jumped into their midst and pierced them with his glances.

"Whither is God?" he cried. "I shall tell you! *We have killed him,*—you and I. We are all his murderers! But how have we done this? How were we able to drink up the sea? Who gave us the sponge to wipe away the entire horizon? What did we do when we unchained this earth from its sun? Whither is it moving now? Whither are we moving now? Away from all suns? Are we not plunging continually? Backward, sideward, forward, in all directions? Is there any up or down left? Are we not straying as through an infinite nothing? Do we not feel the breath of empty space? Has it not become colder? Is not night and more night coming on all the while? Must not lanterns be lit in the morning? Do we not hear anything yet of the noise of the gravediggers who are burying God? Do we not smell anything yet of God's decomposition? Gods too decompose. God is Dead. God remains dead. And we have killed him. How shall we, the murderers of all murderers, comfort ourselves? What was holiest and most powerful of all that the world has yet owned has bled to death under our knives. Who will wipe this blood off us? . . . Must we not ourselves become gods simply to seem worthy of it?"

SOURCE: Friedrich Nietzsche, *The Gay Science*, repr. in *The Portable Nietzsche*, ed. and trans. Walter Kaufmann. New York: Viking Press, 1968, pp. 95–6

Religious points of view

Even the faithful do not necessarily share the same point of view. In the following three extracts, we see contemporary statements of faith in the monotheistic oneness of divinity, in the **polytheistic** plurality of divinities, and in no-divinity, concentrating instead upon human consciousness as part of the ground of Being.

The Oneness of the Divine by Abraham Heschel

Abraham Heschel (1907–72) was born into the Jewish mystical tradition of Hasidism in Warsaw, and educated in the mysticism of the Kabbalah. He studied in Berlin, but in 1938 he was forced out of Germany and escaped to England, then to New York, where he taught for many years at New York's Jewish Theological Seminary and wrote several influential books, including *Man is not Alone* (1951) and *The Prophets* (1962). He spoke for civil rights and interfaith co-operation. He blends the traditional Hasidic yearning for spirituality with the modern taste for free inquiry and impartial truth.

How do we identify the divine? . . . The notion of God as a perfect being is not of Biblical extraction. It is the product not of prophetic religion but of Greek philosophy; a postulate of reason rather than a direct, compelling, initial answer of man to His reality.[5] In the Decalogue,[6] God does not speak of His being perfect but of His having made free men out of slaves. Signifying a state of being without defect and lack, perfection is a term of praise which we may utter in pouring forth our emotion; yet for man to utter it as a name for His essence would mean to evaluate and to endorse Him.

There is, however, one idea that carries our thoughts beyond the horizon of our island; an idea which addresses itself to all minds and is tacitly accepted as an axiom by science and as a dogma by monotheistic religion. It is the idea of the one. All knowledge and understanding rest upon its validity. In spite of the profound differences in what it describes and means in the various realms of human thought, there is much that is common and much that is of mutual importance.

The perspective on which we depend in science and philosophy, notwithstanding all specialization and meticulousness in studying the details, is a view of the whole, without which our knowledge would be like a book composed exclusively of iotas. Accordingly, all sciences and philosophies have one axiom in common—the axiom of *unity* of all that is, was and will be. They all assume that things are not entirely divorced from and indifferent to each other, but subject to universal laws, and that they form, by their interaction with one another or, as Lotze put it, by their "sympathetic rapport," a universe. However, the possibility of their interaction with each other is conditioned upon a unity that pervades all of them. The world could not exist at all except as one; deprived of unity, it would not be a cosmos but chaos, an agglomeration of countless possibilities. . . .

Knowledge is at all possible because of the kinship of the knower and the known, because man's intelligence seems to correspond to the world's intelligibility. But over and above that there is another kinship: the kinship of being. We are all—men, stars, flowers, birds—assigned to the same cast, rehearsing for the same inexplicable drama. We all have a mystery in common—the mystery of being.

SOURCE: Abraham Heschel, *Between God and Man: An Interpretation of Judaism*. New York and London: Simon and Schuster, 1998, pp. 98–100

5 Heschel presented his position in a traditionally masculine voice. Jewish feminists (including Heschel's daughter) have subsequently presented another view.
6 Decalogue—the Ten Commandments.

The New Polytheism by David Miller

David Miller is a comparative mythologist (emeritus) at Syracuse University whose book *The New Polytheism* (1974) showed the growing impact of the study of world religions. He argued that monotheism—a belief in only one deity—may suffer from industrial culture's critique, but under the surface, polytheism—belief in a plurality of deities—has always been at work.

The death of God was in fact the demise of a monotheistic way of thinking and speaking about God and a monotheistic way of thinking and speaking about human meaning and being generally. The announcement of the death of God was the obituary of a useless single-minded and one-dimensional norm of a civilization that has been predominantly monotheistic, not only in its religion, but also in its politics, its history, its social order, its ethics, and its psychology. When released from the tyrannical imperialism of monotheism by the death of God, man has the opportunity of discovering new dimensions hidden in the depths of reality's history. He may discover a new freedom to acknowledge variousness and many-sidedness. He may find, as if for the first time, a new potency to create imaginatively his hopes and desires, his laws and pleasures. . . .

The death of God gives rise to the rebirth of the Gods. We are polytheists.

Polytheism is the name given to a specific religious situation. The situation is characterized by plurality, a plurality that manifests itself in many forms. Socially, polytheism is a situation in which there are various values, patterns of social organization, and principles by which man governs his political life. These values, patterns, and principles sometimes mesh harmoniously, but more often they war with one another to be elevated as the single center of normal social order. Such a situation would be sheer anarchy and chaos were it not possible to identify the many orders as each containing a coherence of its own. Socially understood, polytheism is eternally in unresolvable conflict with social monotheism, which in its worst form is fascism and in its less destructive forms is imperialism, capitalism, feudalism, and monarchy. There is an incipient polytheism always lurking in democracy. This polytheism will surface during the history of democracies if the civilization does not first succumb to anarchy. In calling our time polytheist, we are saying something about the state of democracy in our time.

Polytheism is not only a social reality; it is also a philosophical condition. It is that reality, experienced by men and women when Truth with a capital "T" cannot be articulated reflectively according to a single grammar, a single logic, or a single symbol-system. It is a situation that exists when metaphors, stories, anecdotes, aphorisms, puns, dramas, and movies, with all their mysterious ambiguity, seem more compelling than the rhetoric of political, religious, and philosophical systems. They seem more compelling than tightly argued and logically coherent explanations of self and society because they allow for multiple meanings to exist simultaneously, as if Truth, Goodness, and Beauty can never be contained in a logic that allows for only one of the following: good versus evil, light versus dark, truth versus fiction, reality versus illusion, being versus becoming. In a philosophically polytheistic situation the "new science" of the time will break forth with principles of relativism, indeterminacy, plural logic systems, irrational numbers; substances that do not have substance, such as quarks; double explanations for light; and black holes in the middle of actual realities. . . .

Religiously, polytheism is the worship of many Gods and Goddesses. Though monotheism in its exclusive forms—say, in Christianity, Judaism, and Islam—rules out the possibility of polytheism in religion, polytheism, in a curious way, includes a monotheism of sorts. The great polytheist cultures—Greek, Hindu, Egyptian, Mesopotamian, American Indian—have in actual practice been composed of communities of men and women who worship one God or Goddess, or at least they worship one at a time— Athena, Vishnu, Ra, Baal, Wakan Tanka. The *theologies* of these peoples, however, affirm the reality and the worship of many. This implies that a polytheistic religion is actually a polytheistic theology, a system of symbolizing reality in a plural way in order to account for all experience, but that the religious practice is composed of consecutive monotheisms. Similarly, it would seem possible that one might profess a monotheistic faith, but need a polytheistic theology to account for all of one's experiences in the life-context of that faith. . . .

What does this mean about theological explanations, about the nature of the Gods and Goddesses? It means that the Gods and Goddesses are the names of powers, of forces, which have autonomy and are not conditioned or affected by social and historical events, by human will or reason, or by personal and individual factors. This is one meaning of our use of the word "Immortal" as it is applied to divinities. The Gods are not contingent upon the conditions of mortality. Insofar as they manifest themselves in life they are felt to be informing powers that give shape to social, intellectual, and personal behavior. The Gods and Goddesses are the names of the plural patterns of our existence. Their stories are the paradigms[7] and symbols that allow us to account for, to express, and to celebrate those multiple aspects of our reality that otherwise would seem fragmented and anarchic.

SOURCE: David L. Miller, *The New Polytheism: Rebirth of the Gods and Goddesses*. New York and London: Harper and Row, 1974, pp. 3–7

---

7 Paradigm—a model of reality, such as the materialistic or idealistic model.

The Ground of Being   by Tarthang Tulku

Religion can exist without reference to any deity, as it does in some forms of Buddhism. Here the object of contemplation is consciousness itself. Tarthang Tulku is a contemporary Buddhist teacher in California, one of the first refugees from Tibet who began to explain to Westerners the insights of Tibetan Buddhism. In this selection from his book *Openness Mind* (1978), he discusses meditation as a process of discovering various levels of the workings of the mind in search of peace, the resolution of conflicting emotions, and, ultimately, the ground of Being. Is this "open ground" that which monotheists call God? This question is much debated today.

All of us are part of being; we *are* being. Our total life experience is this being, this ground, which embraces all of existence. *Nirvana*[8] and *samsara*[9] are both manifested within this ground level. The more we understand this, the more life becomes rich and fulfilling. We see that this ground of being is totally open; everything is manifest there. Nothing can destroy this openness.

Meditation enables us to remain at this ground state for long periods of time. Because it is a very peaceful state, free from desires and conflicting emotions, some of the Buddha's disciples stayed on this level for hundreds of years. However, this ground level is only an initial stage; nothing can actually be realized there. The mind naturally moves from this ground level to a second stage, which is a more conscious level, similar to recognition. This second stage is not actually sense perception, but rather an intuitive, seeing quality, a lightness and clarity. By very sensitively developing our awareness, we touch this intuitive second level directly.

The first stage of experience is like touching the ground, the second stage is like looking around, and then the third stage occurs, which is like surveying the horizon—observing with more precision and perceptivity. What we usually refer to as "experience" is produced on the second and third levels. We can learn to recognize these three levels of experience in each thought: first, the ground state; then we recognize the quality of the experience; finally we learn to extend the experience as long as possible.

As we become more familiar with the distinctions and qualities of each of these levels of experience, we are able to appreciate the subtle complexities and the more inward workings of the mind. Until our perception has developed in this way, we are like someone who has never eaten an apricot: we cannot imagine the taste. But once we are skilled at perceiving the arising and flowing of thought, we are able to go beyond this level of perception, to experience a level that is similar to the fresh perception of childhood. We are able to directly experience mind as a process. When we can soar, when we can transmute the quality of the mind, then we approach genuine freedom.

SOURCE: Tarthang Tulku, *Openness Mind*. Berkeley, CA: Dharma Publishing, 1978, pp. 92–4

8 *Nirvana*—in Buddhism, the cessation of suffering, attained through spiritual awakening.
9 *Samsara*—the endless round of bodily reincarnations in this world, with all its illusions.

Scientific perspectives on religion

After the eighteenth-century Enlightenment, science and religion seemed to go separate ways. Scientists placed their faith in that which could be observed and quantified, so leaving out explanations of reality which rest on the unseen and unquantifiable. However, twentieth-century scientific advances revealed that the universe is not as it appears on the surface, and that the tiny components of any apparently solid object seem to be racing through space behaving somewhat like energy and somewhat like matter. Probing the limits of human reason and mechanical measurements, some scientists have admitted the possibility that what religions are indicating is actually real. In the following two passages, the so-called **anthropic principle** is an example of the growing closeness between scientific research and religious belief.

A Not-So-Random Universe by Patrick Glynn

Patrick Glynn is a writer who explores the anthropic principle in his 1997 book *God: The Evidence*. This theory is based on mathematical analyses by scientists of the basic constants of the physical structure of the universe, from atoms to gravity. Were they ever so slightly different, the universe might be only dark, lifeless clouds of hydrogen or helium. This raises religious questions such as: is the universe a brutally absurd, meaningless chance accident, or a meaningful, even a caring spiritual structure?

The anthropic principle says that all the seemingly arbitrary and unrelated constants in physics have one strange thing in common—these are precisely the values you need if you want to have a universe capable of producing life.

This discovery, already percolating among physicists in the early 1970s, came as something of a surprise, to put it mildly. For centuries, scientific exploration seemed to be taking us down precisely the opposite road—toward an ever more mechanistic, impersonal, and random view of the cosmos. Twentieth-century intellectuals had commonly spoken of the "random universe." The predominant view of modern philosophers and intellectuals was that human life had come about essentially by accident, the by-product of brute, material forces randomly churning over the eons. The conclusion seemed to follow naturally from the two great scientific revolutions of the modern era, the Copernican and the Darwinian. . . .

The philosophical, cultural, and emotional impact of this conclusion could hardly be overstated. It explained the tone of despair and angst that came to characterize modern culture, the desperate feeling that humankind was alone and without moorings, and above all without God. It was this random universe cosmology that underpinned all the atheistic modern philosophies—from [Bertrand] Russell's own **positivism**, to **existentialism**, Marxism, even Freudianism.

But then the unexpected occurred. Beginning in the 1960s, scientists began to notice a strange connection among a number of otherwise unexplained coincidences in physics. It turns out that many mysterious values and relationships in physics could be explained by one overriding fact: Such values had been necessary for the creation of life. . . .

The Cambridge astrophysicist Brandon Carter presented some of these points in his 1973 lecture. Any tinkering with the gravitational constant in relation to electromagnetism, he pointed out, would have resulted in a universe with no middling stars like our sun, but only cooler "red" or hotter "blue" ones—incapable of sustaining life's evolution. Any weakening of the nuclear "strong" force would have resulted in a universe consisting of hydrogen and not a single other element. That would mean no oxygen, no water, nothing but hydrogen. . . .

Even the most minor tinkering with the value of the fundamental forces of physics—gravity, electromagnetism, the nuclear strong force, or the nuclear weak force—would have resulted in an unrecognizable universe: a universe consisting entirely of helium, a universe without protons or atoms, a universe without stars, or a universe that collapsed back in upon itself before the first moments of its existence were up. Changing the precise ratios of the masses of subatomic particles in relation to one another would have similar effects. Even such basics of life as carbon and water depend upon uncanny "fine-tuning" at the subatomic level, strange coincidences in values for which physicists had no other explanation.

To take just a few examples:

- Gravity is roughly 10^{39} times weaker than electromagnetism. If gravity had been 10^{33} times weaker than electromagnetism, "stars would be a billion times less massive and would burn a million times faster."
- The nuclear weak force is 10^{28} times the strength of gravity. Had the weak force been slightly weaker, all the hydrogen in the universe would have been turned to helium (making water impossible, for example).
- A stronger nuclear strong force (by as little as 2 percent) would have prevented the formation of protons—yielding a universe without atoms. Decreasing it by 5 percent would have given us a universe without stars.
- If the difference in mass between a proton and a neutron were not exactly as it is—roughly twice the mass of an electron—then all neutrons would have become protons or vice versa. Say good-bye to chemistry as we know it—and to life.
- The very nature of water—so vital to life—is something of a mystery. . . . Unique among the molecules, water is lighter in its solid than liquid form: Ice floats. If it did not, the oceans would freeze from the bottom up and earth would now be covered with solid ice. This property in turn is traceable to unique properties of the hydrogen atom.
- The synthesis of carbon—the vital core of all organic molecules—on a significant scale involves what scientists view as an "astonishing" coincidence in the ratio of the strong force to electromagnetism. This

ratio makes it possible for carbon-12 to reach an excited state of exactly 7.65 MeV at the temperature typical of the center of stars, which creates a resonance involving helium-4, beryllium-8, and carbon-12—allowing the necessary binding to take place during a tiny window of opportunity 10^{-17} seconds long.

The list goes on. A comprehensive compilation of these coincidences can be found in John Leslie's book *Universes*.

The depth of the mystery involved here has been captured best by astronomer Fred Hoyle, the former proponent of the steady state theory:

> All that we see in the universe of observation and fact, as opposed to the mental stage of scenario and supposition, remains unexplained. And even in its supposedly first second the universe itself is acausal. That is to say, the universe has to know in advance what it is going to be before it knows how to start itself. For in accordance with the Big Bang Theory, for instance, at a time of 10^{-43} seconds the universe has to know how many types of neutrino there are going to be at a time of 1 second. This is so in order that it starts off expanding at the right rate to fit the eventual number of neutrino types.

Hoyle's notion of the universe needing to "know in advance" later outcomes captures the depth of the mystery. The fine-tuning of seemingly heterogeneous values and ratios necessary to get from the big bang to life as we know it involves intricate coordination over vast differences in scale— from the galactic level down to the subatomic one—and across multi-billion-year tracts of time. Hoyle, who coined the term "big bang," has questioned the very legitimacy of the metaphor of an initial "explosion." "An explosion in a junkyard does not lead to sundry bits of metal being assembled into a useful working machine," he writes. The more physicists have learned about the universe, the more it looks like a put-up job....

The great modern era—spanning the nearly 350 years between the trial of Galileo and the 500th birthday of Copernicus—is at an end. It is truly justifiable to speak of our current period as the "postmodern age." And there is every reason to suppose that this postmodern age will also be postsecular, since the original philosophical assumptions underpinning the modern secular worldview have been shattered—ironically enough, by science itself....

The barrier that modern science appeared to erect to faith has fallen. Of course, the anthropic principle tells us nothing about the Person of God or the existence of an afterlife; it has nothing to say about such issues as right or wrong or the "problem of evil." But it does offer as strong an indication as reason and science alone could be expected to provide that God exists.

SOURCE: Patrick Glynn, *God: The Evidence*. Rocklin, CA: Prima Publishing, 1997, pp. 21–55

The Darwinian Account of Religion by Mikael Stenmark

A major scientific effort to explain religion without reference to any transcendent source, completely within a naturalistic framework, is the Darwinian theory of evolution. Recent studies, led by Edward O. Wilson at Harvard, have developed the field of sociobiology. Originally a specialist in ants, Wilson first argued in *Sociobiology: The New Synthesis* (1975) that human behavior can be studied using an evolutionary framework. For him human nature can be explained through the study of genetic patterns of mental development, from fear of snakes to appreciation of art and religion. This involves what he terms "the selfish gene," which means the survival of an organism and its species is its highest priority. Religious practices are explained as part of that instinct. Wilson has been accused of being reductivist, ignoring larger cultural realities, such as self-sacrificial behavior.

Mikael Stenmark teaches philosophy of religion at Uppsala University in Sweden. His book *Scientism* (2001) argues that Wilson's "scientism" is not science, but a disguised materialism or a naturalism that makes excessive claims about the capabilities of science to solve a broad range of problems.

Wilson maintains that "we have come to the crucial stage in the history of biology when religion itself is subject to the explanations of the natural sciences" (Wilson 1978: 192).[10] But he also admits that religion constitutes the greatest challenge to evolutionary biology. The reason for this is that "religion is one of the major categories of behavior undeniably unique to the human species" (175). We cannot find any parallel to it in wild nature. Whereas in morality we can find some similarities between animal behaviour and moral behaviour (for instance in respect to reciprocal cooperation), this is not true when it comes to religious behaviour. There exist no prayers, religious rituals or beliefs in God among members of other species living on this planet. Religion is a truly unique phenomenon. But the ability to be religious somehow emerged out of nature, where before there was no such ability. Can evolutionary theory explain this phenomenon and in such a way that any other kind of explanation becomes superfluous?

The strategy evolutionary biologists use for explaining religion is the same as the one they use to explain morality. Wilson writes, "When the gods are served, the Darwinian fitness of the members of the tribe is the ultimate if unrecognized beneficiary" (Wilson 1978: 184). Religion has high survival value in the same way as morality and that is the reason for its existence. Again,

> The highest forms of religious practice, when examined more closely, can be seen to confer biological advantage. Above all they congeal identity. In the midst of the chaotic and potentially disorienting

---

10 Edward O. Wilson, *On Human Nature*. Cambridge, MA: Harvard University Press, 1978.

experiences each person undergoes daily, religion classifies him, provides him with unquestioned membership in a group claiming great powers, and by this means gives him a driving purpose in life compatible with his self-interest. (Wilson 1978: 188)

So the thesis and explanatory scheme are basically the same as before:

(T$_1$) The most dominant determinant in religious behaviour is maximizing fitness, that is, the production of the most offspring in the following generations.

(E$_1$) Religious belief p, religious behaviour q or religious institution A exists and continues to exist because it emerged and continues to function as a strategy (or part of a strategy) adapted to secure the fitness of the individuals and their genes.

(E$_1$) does not attempt to explain merely this or that religious phenomenon, allowing that other religious phenomena might have a different explanation, but rather attempts to explain religion as such. The idea is that beliefs, myths, rituals and the institutional structures of the religions may differ greatly, but this does not matter because the function of religions is ultimately the same, and it is to protect the genes and secure the fitness of the individual.

The question we have to address is whether this explanation is more successful in the case of religion than it was in the case of morality. Again, (T$_1$) and (E$_1$) claim more than what the scientific expansionists can deliver. This is something they are also willing to admit. What Wilson and others attempt to do instead is to assemble more and more examples of religious belief, rituals and activities that can be successfully explained as fitness-maximizing strategies and in this way build an inductive case for the truth or likelihood of (T$_1$) and (E$_1$). This means, however, that (T$_1$) and (E$_1$) can be disconfirmed if we can find examples of religious belief, rituals and activities that cannot successfully be explained as fitness-maximizing strategies. Religious belief and behaviour could exist that do not favour, and may even hinder, the survival and reproduction of the individuals and their genes.

As I said before, once we take seriously that human beings are a part of the evolutionary scheme, we cannot deny the legitimacy of trying to explain why we have certain religious ideas or behave religiously by relating them to our evolutionary history. The crucial question is, however, *how much* of religion can be explained in this way. Can evolutionary theory offer us a complete explanation of religion in such a way that it excludes other scientific as well as theological and philosophical explanations?

It is quite reasonable to think, as Wilson does, that religion contributes to reproductive success. It provides people with an identity and affinity with the group as well as loyalty towards it. Religion sanctions morality and gets people to cooperate for their mutual good and therefore puts people in a better position to leave more offspring than they would have otherwise done. Fertility is a fundamental feature of religion. Religious believers worship the sun, pray for rain, seek cures for diseases and so on. Wilson's conclusion based upon observations like these is that "elementary religions seek the supernatural for the purely mundane rewards of long life, abundant land and food, the avoidance of physical catastrophes, and defeat of enemies" (Wilson 1975: 561). But he also maintains that the "ultimate, genetic motivation" for religious behaviour is

> probably hidden from the conscious mind, because religion is above all the process by which individuals are persuaded to subordinate their immediate self-interest to the interest of the group. Votaries are expected to make short-term physiological sacrifices for their own long-term genetic gains. Self-deception by shamans and priests perfects their own performance and enhances the deception practiced on their constituents. (Wilson 1978: 176)

. . . But, of course, religions are not a unified phenomenon; thus, we can find religious movements that emphasize chastity and poverty rather than fertility and prosperity. There are many different ways in which one can be religious.[11]

Nevertheless, religious believers are often aware that religion can offer mundane rewards. What they would contest is, rather, that this is all religion does. That is the crucial point, namely Wilson's claim that religion can be explained as *nothing but* a fitness-maximizing strategy. On this point surely religious believers would disagree. They do not believe that religion simply offers fertility. For many of them religion is primarily a response to life, to fertility and to what they experience as a divine presence within or beyond our world. All things are in some way an expression of this ultimate reality, and it can be sensed in the beauty of the world and the awe which it engenders. Some of these people also claim that they have directly encountered this reality, while others have merely experienced glimpses of something transcendent, something beyond limitation and imperfection. Worship and prayer are for them ways of deepening this awareness of the divine and not strategies to secure the production of the most offspring in the next generation, although that could be a spin-off. . . .

From a religious perspective there is therefore nothing surprising if religion offers mundane rewards and is compatible with religious people's own understanding of their religious behaviour. But Wilson's claim that science can explain traditional religion "as a *wholly* material phenomenon" in the sense that it can establish that religion offers "purely mundane rewards" is incompatible with what we can call a *theological explanation* of religion (Wilson 1978: 192; 1975: 561, emphasis added). The theological explanation of the phenomenon of religion is that people actually have experienced a divine presence within or beyond the physical world.

SOURCE: Mikael Stenmark, *Scientism: Science, Ethics and Religion*. Aldershot, Hampshire: Ashgate, 2001, pp. 80–3

11 See Dale Cannon, *Six Ways of Being Religious*. Belmont, NY: Wadsworth, 1966.

Ritual, symbol, and myth

Whereas some branches of every religion have interpreted their faith's stories, scriptures, and rituals as literally true, others have embraced them as symbols and metaphors for spiritual realities that cannot be described in literal language. Two leading figures in the study of religions from the latter point of view have been Carl Jung and Joseph Campbell.

Mandalas: Deity Unfolding in the World

by Carl G. Jung

Christianity—
The Living
Cathedral: St.
John the Divine

Carl Jung was a Swiss psychologist who developed archetypal psychology, which is the psychology most open to religious understanding. Jung built on Freud's demonstration of the meaningfulness of the unconscious psyche, while rejecting his views on the centrality of sex and the illusory nature of religion. Jung saw images from all religions as meaningful expressions of the "collective unconscious" of humanity. He spoke of "archetypes," meaning unconscious collective psychological instincts or patterns. The "Self" for Jung is the central, regulating archetype, the "God within" that guides and heals. It may be symbolized in many ways, not just as a heavenly old man on a throne. In dreams and myths, rituals and theologies, the ineffable depth called "God" may appear as a crystal, a goddess, a star, a tree, an animal, or even a geometric form— most notably the *mandala*, a circular design, such as a cathedral's round "rose" window, focusing on the "center": the center of the universe, the center of one's life.

The Sanskrit word *mandala* means "circle" in the ordinary sense of the word. In the sphere of religious practices and in psychology it denotes circular images, which are drawn, painted, modeled, or danced. Plastic structures of this kind are to be found, for instance, in Tibetan Buddhism, and as dance figures these circular patterns occur also in Dervish monasteries. As psychological phenomena they appear spontaneously in dreams, in certain states of conflict, and in cases of schizophrenia. Very frequently they contain a quaternity or a multiple of four, in the form of a cross, a star, a square, an octagon, etc....

In Tibetan Buddhism the figure has the significance of a ritual instrument (*yantra*), whose purpose is to assist meditation and concentration.... Its spontaneous occurrence in modern individuals enables psychological research to make a closer investigation into its functional meaning. As a rule a mandala occurs in conditions of psychic dissociation or disorientation, for instance in the case of children between the ages of eight and eleven whose parents are about to be divorced, or in adults who, as the result of a neurosis[12] and its treatment, are confronted with the problem of opposites in human nature and are consequently disoriented; or again in schizophrenics whose view of the world has become confused, owing to the

---

12 Neurosis—a mild form of mental illness.

invasion of incomprehensible contents from the unconscious. In such cases it is easy to see how the severe pattern imposed by a circular image of this kind compensates the disorder and confusion of the psychic state—namely, through the construction of a central point to which everything is related, or by a concentric arrangement of the disordered multiplicity and of contradictory and irreconcilable elements. This is evidently an *attempt at self-healing* on the part of Nature, which does not spring from conscious reflection but from an instinctive impulse. Here, as comparative research has shown, a fundamental schema is made use of, an archetype which, so to speak, occurs everywhere and by no means owes its individual existence to tradition, any more than the instincts would need to be transmitted in that way. Instincts are given in the case of every newborn individual and belong to the inalienable stock of those qualities which characterize a species. What psychology designates as archetype is really a particular, frequently occurring, formal aspect of instinct, and is just as much an *a priori* factor as the latter. Therefore, despite external differences, we find a fundamental conformity in mandalas regardless of their origin in time and space.

The "squaring of the circle" is one of the many archetypal motifs which form the basic patterns of our dreams and fantasies. But it is distinguished by the fact that it is one of the most important of them from the functional point of view. Indeed, it could even be called the *archetype of wholeness*. Because of this significance, the "quaternity of the One" is the schema for all images of God, as depicted in the visions of Ezekiel, Daniel, and Enoch, and as the representation of Horus[13] with his four sons also shows. The latter suggests an interesting differentiation, inasmuch as there are occasionally representations in which three of the sons have animals' heads and only one a human head, in keeping with the Old Testament visions as well as with the emblems of the seraphim which were transferred to the evangelists, and—last but not least—with the nature of the Gospels themselves: three of which are synoptic and one "Gnostic.". . .

As is to be expected, individual mandalas display an enormous variety. The overwhelming majority are characterized by the circle and the quaternity. In a few, however, the three or the five predominates, for which there are usually special reasons.

Whereas ritual mandalas always display a definite style and a limited number of typical motifs as their content, individual mandalas make use of a well-nigh unlimited wealth of motifs and symbolic allusions, from which it can easily be seen that they are endeavouring to express either the totality of the individual in his inner or outer experience of the world, or its essential point of reference. Their object is the *self* in contradistinction to the *ego*, which is only the point of reference for consciousness, whereas the self comprises the totality of the psyche altogether, i.e., conscious *and* unconscious. It is therefore not unusual for individual mandalas to display a

---

13 Horus—an ancient Egyptian divinity, son of Isis and Osiris.

division into a light and a dark half, together with their typical symbols. An historical example of this kind is Jakob Böhme's mandala, in his treatise *XL Questions concerning the Soule*. It is at the same time an image of God and is designated as such. This is not a matter of chance, for Indian philosophy, which developed the idea of the self, Atman or Purusha, to the highest degree, makes no distinction in principle between the human essence and the divine. Correspondingly, in the Western mandala, the *scintilla* or soul-spark, the innermost divine essence of man, is characterized by symbols which can just as well express a God-image, namely the image of Deity unfolding in the world, in nature, and in man.

The fact that images of this kind have under certain circumstances a considerable therapeutic effect on their authors is empirically proved and also readily understandable, in that they often represent very bold attempts to see and put together apparently irreconcilable opposites and bridge over apparently hopeless splits.

SOURCE: Carl G. Jung, "Mandalas," in *The Archetypes and the Collective Unconscious*, vol. 9, part 1 of *The Collected Works of C. G. Jung.* 2nd ed. Princeton, NJ: Princeton University Press, 1968, pp. 387–90

The Ominous Sphere: A Transforming Dream
by Celeste Federico

This account by a student illustrates Jung's theory of the archetypal *mandala*, which appeared to her in a dream after a year of college doubting God and criticizing religious institutions. The dream *mandala* takes the form of an energetic ominous sphere, pulsating with stormy electricity like lightning. Unlike many *mandalas* that are static visual pictures portraying a balanced harmony of psychological energies, this sphere was at first evil, tormenting and chasing her violently—an example of the shadow side of an archetypal image, which Jung proposed has a treasure within. This apparently evil sphere did have a positive intent, and it achieved a healing change of consciousness in her. Such a therapeutic effect is a classic part of the dynamics of the *mandala*, and it illustrates the dramatic numinous forces of the psyche moving in unexpected ways to achieve the self-healing that Jung perceived in the *mandala*.

After her studies, Federico moved to Colorado, worked in college administration, traveled extensively, and she is now a writer envisioning a career as a psychotherapist.

The dream It was a cloudy afternoon, and I felt normal: sullen, numb, and sad. I was walking through a field of tall grass when I happened upon a curiously beautiful ball, about three inches wide, nestled innocently in bent grass on the ground. I reached down, feeling drawn to it. The moment my fingers made contact, the sphere came alive. It pulsated with an evil current, undulating with lightning bolts. Its skin looked like an ominous storm. The ball took to the sky with a potent, killer quality, driven by dangerous electricity.

Within seconds, the sky changed. The clouds, low and dark, charged forward like tanks going to war, with thunderous intention. The ball swooped and dove wildly through the sky, in violent pursuit of me. "This ball is going to kill me," I thought. So I ran. And I ran.

I ran into a bar that teetered, unsteadily, in the hayfield. It resembled something like a Southern juke joint, tucked into the corner of a remote cotton field, its heels dug in since the days of Prohibition. I entered the bar, breathless and terrified. But my search for safety put me in harm's way. All the glass in the building shattered and a torrent of shards flew at me.

Out of the bar I ran, stumbling toward the banks of a pond that cradled an empty canoe in the middle. I thought I might swim to the canoe or hide from the wicked ball by submerging my body under water. But I could not hide. A menacing wave formed, threatening to overcome me. There, in the hayfield, scared and alone, haunted by something that wanted my blood and hunted my death, I seized. Looking to the sky and screaming with purpose, I offered one last soulful cry. "I do believe in God. I do believe in God. I do believe in God." My inflections mimicked Dorothy's "There's no place like home" in *The Wizard of Oz*.

The sky parted, the clouds diffused, and a balmy breeze ran over me. The sun came out and I took a deep breath. The ball had dropped to the ground at my feet. It was inanimate, powerless now. The overgrown hayfield was now a field of wild flowers. The howls and groans of the storm turned to the sound of chirping birds. Around me I saw something that looked like peace of mind. I was safe.

I jolted in my bed and awoke, sweaty and stiff. The dream had coursed through me with a power I had not known before. I was traumatized and afraid. I had just outrun death. What did this dream mean? And why me? Although I trembled inside, I was also certain. I had spent the past year in college doubting God and criticizing religion as a collection of mind-warping people and institutions. But now I did believe in God. And it was this that God wanted me to know. I became a Religious Studies major.

SOURCE: Original article for this book by Celeste Federico, 2006

The Hero with a Thousand Faces by Joseph Campbell

At Sarah Lawrence College, Joseph Campbell (1904–87) expanded Jung's archetypal theory of myth as a meaningful story, rather than a fictional error. He proposed a theory of the "monomyth," a pattern found, sometimes fragmentarily, in myths worldwide. The pattern follows the hero's journey into the mystical underworld, where various powers are met for struggles and learning. After the re-ascent to ordinary life, the hero can use the new powers to aid his or her people. As Campbell developed his theory of myth, he integrated more anthropological and historical themes.

Myth is the secret opening through which the inexhaustible energies of the cosmos pour into human cultural manifestation. Religions, philosophies, arts, the social forms of primitive and historic man, prime discoveries in science and technology, the very dreams that blister sleep, boil up from the basic, magic ring of myth. . . .

The bold and truly epoch-making writings of the psychoanalysts are indispensable to the student of mythology; for, whatever may be thought of the detailed and sometimes contradictory interpretations of specific cases and problems, Freud, Jung, and their followers have demonstrated irrefutably that the logic, the heroes, and the deeds of myth survive into modern times. In the absence of an effective general mythology, each of us has his private, unrecognized, rudimentary, yet secretly potent pantheon of dream.[14] The latest incarnation of Oedipus, the continued romance of Beauty and the Beast, stand this afternoon on the corner of Forty-second Street and Fifth Avenue[15] waiting for the traffic light to change. . . .

The unconscious sends all sorts of vapors, odd beings, terrors, and deluding images up into the mind—whether in dream, broad daylight, or insanity; for the human kingdom, beneath the floor of the comparatively neat little dwelling that we call our consciousness, goes down into unsuspected Aladdin caves. There not only jewels but also dangerous jinn abide: the inconvenient or resisted psychological powers that we have not thought or dared to integrate into our lives. And they remain unsuspected, or, on the other hand, some chance word, the smell of a landscape, the taste of a cup of tea, or the glance of an eye may touch a magic spring, and then dangerous messengers begin to appear in the brain. These are dangerous because they threaten the fabric of the security into which we have built ourselves and our family. But they are fiendishly fascinating too, for they carry keys that open the whole realm of the desired and feared adventure of the discovery of the self. Destruction of the world that we have built and in which we live, and of ourselves within it; but then a wonderful reconstruction, of the bolder, cleaner, more spacious, and fully human life—that is the lure, the promise and terror, of these disturbing night visitants from the mythological realm that we carry within. . . .

It has always been the prime function of mythology and rite to supply the symbols that carry the human spirit forward, in counteraction to those other constant human fantasies that tend to tie it back. In fact, it may well be that the very high incidence of neuroticism among ourselves follows from the decline among us of such effective spiritual aid. We remain fixated to the unexorcised images of our infancy, and hence disinclined to the necessary passages of our adulthood. . . .

The first work of the hero is to retreat from the world scene of secondary effects to those causal zones of the psyche where the difficulties really reside, and there to clarify the difficulties, eradicate them in his own

14 Campbell's 1940s masculine view has stimulated feminist and African versions of his theory of myth. See Maureen Murdock, *The Heroine's Journey*. Boston: Shambhala, 1990. Also, see Clyde Ford, *The Hero With an African Face*. New York: Bantam, 1999.
15 A central street crossing in New York City.

case (i.e., give battle to the nursery demons of his local culture) and break through to the undistorted, direct experience and assimilation of what C. G. Jung has called "the archetypal images." This is the process known to Hindu and Buddhist philosophy as *viveka*, "discrimination."

The archetypes to be discovered and assimilated are precisely those that have inspired, throughout the annals of human culture, the basic images of ritual, mythology, and vision.

Dream is the personalized myth, myth the depersonalized dream; both myth and dream are symbolic in the same general way of the dynamics of the psyche. But in the dream the forms are quirked by the peculiar troubles of the dreamer, whereas in myth the problems and solutions shown are directly valid for all mankind.

The hero, therefore, is the man or woman who has been able to battle past his personal and local historical limitations to the generally valid, normally human forms. Such a one's visions, ideas, and inspirations come pristine from the primary springs of human life and thought. Hence they are eloquent, not of the present, disintegrating society and psyche, but of the unquenched source through which society is reborn. The hero has died as a modern man; but as eternal man—perfected, unspecific, universal man—he has been reborn. His second solemn task and deed therefore . . . is to return then to us, transfigured, and teach the lesson he has learned of life renewed. . . .

Furthermore, we have not even to risk the adventure alone; for the heroes of all time have gone before us; the labyrinth is thoroughly known; we have only to follow the thread of the hero-path. And where we had thought to find an abomination, we shall find a god; where we had thought to slay another, we shall slay ourselves; where we had thought to travel outward, we shall come to the center of our own existence; where we had thought to be alone, we shall be with all the world. . . .

The standard path of the mythological adventure of the hero is a magnification of the formula represented in the rites of passage: *separation–initiation–return*: which might be named the nuclear unit of the monomyth.

> A hero ventures forth from the world of common day into a region of supernatural wonder: fabulous forces are there encountered and a decisive victory is won: the hero comes back from this mysterious adventure with the power to bestow boons on his fellow man.

Aeneas[16] went down into the underworld, crossed the dreadful river of the dead, threw a sop to the three-headed watchdog Cerberus, and conversed, at last, with the shade of his dead father. All things were unfolded to him: the destiny of souls, the destiny of Rome, which he was about to found, "and in what wise he might avoid or endure every burden." He returned through the ivory gate to his work in the world. . . .

---

16 Aeneas—legendary founder of the Roman race, whose journey is described by Virgil in the *Aeneid*.

A comparable vision is described in the apocryphal[17] Gospel of Eve. "I stood on a lofty mountain and saw a gigantic man and another a dwarf; and I heard as it were a voice of thunder, and drew nigh for to hear; and He spake unto me and said: I am thou, and thou art I; and wheresoever thou mayest be I am there. In all am I scattered, and whensoever thou willest, thou gatherest Me; and gathering Me, thou gatherest Thyself."

The two—the hero and his ultimate god, the seeker and the found—are thus understood as the outside and inside of a single, self-mirrored mystery, which is identical with the mystery of the manifest world. The great deed of the supreme hero is to come to the knowledge of this unity in multiplicity and then to make it known.

SOURCE: Joseph Campbell, *The Hero with a Thousand Faces*. 2nd ed. Princeton, NJ: Princeton University Press, 1968, pp. 3–40

Myths as Symbols of Religious Beliefs: The Greek Virgin Birth of Perseus by Apollodorus

Many myths worldwide echo similar themes about sky gods, nature spirits, ancestors, moral reformers, healing, virgin births, and returns from death. One old Greek myth is a version of the virgin birth theme. The grown Perseus was a popular Greek hero who decapitated the dangerous snake-headed Gorgon Medusa, using a mirror to avoid looking directly at her (which would have turned him to stone). Then he saved the life of the princess Andromeda, chained to a seaside rock as a sacrifice to a sea monster sent by the ocean god Poseidon. Here is the record of his birth as told by Apollodorus, who wrote in the second century BCE.

The Birth of Perseus When Acrisius inquired of the oracle how he should get male children, the god said that his daughter would give birth to a son who would kill him. Fearing that, Acrisius built a brazen chamber under ground and there guarded Danae. However, she was seduced, as some say, by Protetus, whence arose the quarrel between them; but some say that Zeus had intercourse with her in the shape of a stream of gold which poured through the roof into Danae's lap. When Acrisius afterwards learned that she had got a child Perseus, he would not believe that she had been seduced by Zeus, and putting his daughter with the child in a chest, he cast it into the sea. The chest was washed ashore on Seriphus, and Dictys took up the boy and reared him. Polydectes, brother of Dictys, was then king of Seriphus and fell in love with Danae, but could not get access to her, because Perseus was grown to man's estate.

SOURCE: *Apollodorus: The Library*, II.iv.1–2, trans. James Frazer. Loeb Classical Library. Cambridge, MA: Harvard University Press, 1976, vol. 1, pp. 153–5

---

17 Apocryphal—relating to unofficial, uncanonical ancient texts considered sacred by some.

Women and the feminine in religion

During the twentieth century, extensive research was begun in order to discover and restore women's leadership in religions, to reconsider patriarchal language and assumptions found in scriptures, and to explore situations in which the deity is known as Goddess. In all religions, women are demanding access to religious education and opportunities to serve in significant roles, and the important spiritual contributions of individual women are being brought to light.

The Image of God as Dominating Other by Judith Plaskow

One of the influential feminist scholars of religion has been Judith Plaskow. She teaches Religious Studies at Manhattan College and is co-founder of *The Journal of Feminist Studies in Religion* and past president of the American Academy of Religion. Her classic book on Jewish feminism, *Standing Again at Sinai* (1990), includes a strong critique of domineering patriarchal images of God as a male.

It is not simply male metaphors for God that need to be broken, however, but also the larger picture of who God is. . . . The God of Jewish liturgy is a king robed in majesty, a merciful but probing father, and master of the world. His sovereign Otherness is elaborated extensively: his dominion over creation, his control of history past and future, his revenge against his enemies, his power over the human soul. The purpose of prayer is to establish a relationship between the Jew and God, but this relationship is never balanced: The intimacy of the "you" addressed to a listening other is overshadowed by the image of the lord and king of the universe who is absolute ruler on a cosmic plane.[18] Next to this God, human beings are as nothing, "men of renown as though they never existed, the wise as if they were without knowledge."[19] The prayerbook as a paean to God's glory and daily wonders, as a plea for his forgiveness and mercy, presents an image of God's power as "power over" others, a power that is partly defined through the contrast with human weakness and dependency.

This understanding of divine power as domination, crystallized and promulgated by the liturgy, is also amply attested by other sources, so that it can be specified and elaborated in broader terms. God's power as dominance means, first of all, that the relation between God and human beings is profoundly asymmetrical.[20] God's maleness connotes power, and God's power is an extension of his maleness, but God is not powerful in the same

---

18 Alan Mintz, in "Prayer and the Prayerbook" (in *Back to the Sources: Reading the Classic Jewish Texts*, ed. Barry Holtz. New York: Summit Books, 1984, p. 407), implies that the experiences of intimacy and might are balanced. It seems to me this is rather like saying that God's masculine and feminine qualities are balanced. See Ellen Umansky, "(Re)Imaging the Divine," in *Response* 41–2, Fall–Winter 1982, p. 111.
19 Philip Birnbaum, *Daily Prayer Book: Ha-Siddur Ha-Shalem*. New York: Hebrew Publishing Company, 1949, p. 24.
20 Gordon Kaufman, *Theology for a Nuclear Age*. Manchester: Manchester University Press/Philadelphia, PA: Westminster Press, 1985, p. 39.

sense as ordinary men. His power is supreme, absolute, infinite, completely Other than human authority. God created the world through his word and continues to rule over it, so that all that happens in the universe is the result of his sovereign will and action.[21] To him, "The nations are but a drop in a bucket" (Isaiah 40:15); he brings their counsels to nothing (Psalm 33:10)....

Second, this utterly Other God is a being outside and over against the world who controls the world "in a way that inhibits human growth and responsibility."[22] Unlike the wise parent who encourages children to develop autonomy and self-reliance, God insists that humans obey him, and they concede their limits and God's overwhelming superiority....

The notion of God as dominating Other finds quintessential expression in the image of the holy warrior who punishes the wicked with destruction and death. The God who hears the groaning of his people in Egypt is a fighter more powerful than all the armies of Pharaoh, a God whose army can destroy the Egyptians, drowning them in the seas (Exodus 15). When Israel enters the promised land, God is present in his ark at the head of its marching armies, giving military victory over city after city (Joshua). Hardening the hearts of the local people, God ensures that they "should receive no mercy" but be "utterly destroyed" (Joshua 11:20)....

Metaphors of sovereignty, lordship, kingship, and judicial and military power evoke images of arbitrary and autocratic rule that have been rejected in the human political sphere at the same time they live on in religious language.[23] If the image of God as male provides religious support for male dominance in society, the image of God as supreme Other would seem to legitimate dominance of any kind. God as ruler and king of the universe is the pinnacle of a vast hierarchy that extends from God "himself" to angels/men/women/children/animals and finally the earth. As hierarchical ruler, God is a model for the many schemes of dominance that human beings create for themselves.

SOURCE: Judith Plaskow, *Standing Again at Sinai: Judaism from a Feminist Perspective*. San Francisco: HarperSanFrancisco, 1990, pp. 128–33

The need for religion today

At the dawn of the twenty-first century, many thoughtful people are asserting that religion is a necessity today, not just an historical artifact. However, they are redefining what is meant by "religion." The extract that follows from Paul Tillich is an example of fresh ways of thinking about religion and its place in modern life.

---

21 *Ibid.*, p. 38.
22 Sallie McFague, *Models of God: Theology for an Ecological, Nuclear Age*. Philadelphia, PA: Fortress Press, 1987, p. 68.
23 For a discussion of the religious use of political metaphors, see Davis Nicholls, "Images of God and the State: Political Analogy and Religious Discourse," in *Theological Studies* 42, June 1981, pp. 195–215, especially sections 2 and 4.

The Lost Dimension in Religion   by Paul Tillich

Paul Tillich (1886–1965) was a German Protestant theologian who emigrated to the United States. He developed many original themes for twentieth-century religions, such as "ultimate concern" as a definition of religion, "the ground of Being" as a way of discussing "God," and "the new being" as a new way of viewing Christ. Religious institutions, he envisioned, are "emergency" institutions, only made necessary by our forgetfulness of Being. He urged industrial culture to overcome its anxiety and despair due to its estrangement from the depths, from the ground of Being.

Being religious means asking passionately the questions of the meaning of our existence and being willing to receive answers, even if the answers hurt. Such an idea of religion makes religion universally human, but it certainly differs from what is usually called religion. It does not describe religion as the belief in the existence of gods or one God, and as a set of activities and institutions for the sake of relating oneself to these beings in thought, devotion and obedience. No one can deny that the religions which have appeared in history are religions in this sense. Nevertheless, religion in its innermost nature is more than religion in this narrower sense. It is the state of being concerned about one's own being and being universally.

There are many people who are ultimately concerned in this way who feel far removed, however, from religion in the narrower sense, and therefore from every historical religion. It often happens that such people take the question of the meaning of their life infinitely seriously and reject any historical religion just for this reason. They feel that the concrete religions fail to express their profound concern adequately. They are religious while rejecting the religions. . . .

If we define religion as the state of being grasped by an infinite concern we must say: Man [sic] in our time has lost such infinite concern. And the resurgence of religion is nothing but a desperate and mostly futile attempt to regain what has been lost.

How did the dimension of depth become lost? . . .

Modern man is neither more pious nor more impious than man in any other period. The loss of the dimension of depth is caused by the relation of man to his world and to himself in our period, the period in which nature is being subjected scientifically and technically to the control of man. In this period, life in the dimension of depth is replaced by life in the horizontal dimension. The driving forces of the industrial society of which we are a part go ahead horizontally and not vertically. In popular terms this is expressed in phrases like "better and better," "bigger and bigger," "more and more." One should not disparage the feeling which lies behind such speech. Man is right in feeling that he is able to know and transform the world he encounters without a foreseeable limit. He can go ahead in all directions without a definite boundary. . . .

The predominance of the horizontal dimension over the dimension of depth has been immensely increased by the opening of the space beyond the space of earth.

If we now ask what does man do and seek if he goes ahead in the horizontal dimension, the answer is difficult. Sometimes one is inclined to say that the mere movement ahead without an end, the intoxication with speeding forward without limits, is what satisfies him. But this answer is by no means sufficient. . . . He transforms everything he encounters into a tool; and in doing so he himself becomes a tool. But if he asks, a tool for what, there is no answer.

One does not need to look far beyond everyone's daily experience in order to find examples to describe this predicament. Indeed our daily life in office and home, in cars and airplanes, at parties and conferences, while reading magazines and watching television, while looking at advertisements and hearing radio, are in themselves continuous examples of a life which has lost the dimension of depth. It runs ahead, every moment is filled with something which must be done or seen or said or planned. But no one can experience depth without stopping and becoming aware of himself. Only if he has moments in which he does not care about what comes next can he experience the meaning of this moment here and now and ask himself about the meaning of his life. As long as the preliminary, transitory concerns are not silenced, no matter how interesting and valuable and important they may be, the voice of the ultimate concern cannot be heard. This is the deepest root of the loss of the dimension of depth in our period—the loss of religion in its basic and universal meaning.

When in this way man has deprived himself of the dimension of depth and the symbols expressing it, he then becomes a part of the horizontal plane. He loses his self and becomes a thing among things. He becomes an element in the process of manipulated production and manipulated consumption. This is now a matter of public knowledge. We have become aware of the degree to which everyone in our social structure is managed, even if one knows it and even if one belongs himself to the managing group. The influence of the gang mentality on adolescents, of the corporation's demands on the executives, of the conditioning of everyone by public communication, by propaganda and advertising under the guidance of motivation research, et cetera, have all been described in many books and articles.

Under these pressures, man can hardly escape the fate of becoming a thing among the things he produces, a bundle of conditioned reflexes without a free, deciding and responsible self. The immense mechanism, set up by man to produce objects for his use, transforms man himself into an object used by the same mechanism of production and consumption.

But man has not ceased to be man. He resists this fate anxiously, desperately, courageously. He asks the question, for what? And he realizes that there is no answer. He becomes aware of the emptiness which is covered by the continuous movement ahead and the production of means for ends which become means again without an ultimate end. Without knowing what has happened to him, he feels that he has lost the meaning of life, the dimension of depth. . . .

What we need above all—and partly have—is the radical realization of our predicament, without trying to cover it up by secular or religious ideologies. The revival of religious interest would be a creative power in our culture if it would develop into a movement of search for the lost dimension of depth.

This does not mean that the traditional religious symbols should be dismissed. They certainly have lost their meaning in the literalistic form into which they have been distorted, thus producing the critical reaction against them. But they have not lost their genuine meaning, namely, of answering the question which is implied in man's very existence in powerful, revealing and saving symbols. If the resurgence of religion would produce a new understanding of the symbols of the past and their relevance for our situation, instead of premature and deceptive answers, it would become a creative factor in our culture and a saving factor for many who live in estrangement, anxiety and despair. The religious answer has always the character of "in spite of." In spite of the loss of dimension of depth, its power is present, and most present in those who are aware of the loss and are striving to regain it with ultimate seriousness.

SOURCE: Paul Tillich, "The Lost Dimension in Religion," in *The Essential Tillich*, ed. F. Forrester Church. New York: Macmillan, 1987, pp. 1–8

GLOSSARY

Anthropic principle The new scientific hypothesis that the structure of the universe is so precise that its origin could not have been random.

Creedal statement Confession of faith that identifies a religious group, such as the Christian Nicene Creed: "I believe in one God, the Father, the Almighty. . . ."

Dogma A statement of beliefs considered authoritative or absolute truth.

Empiricism Philosophical view that experience, especially of the senses, is the only valid source of knowledge.

Existentialism A disparate mid-twentieth-century philosophical movement emphasizing issues such as death, experience, and life's meaning.

Ground of Being An image of ultimate reality used by Paul Tillich.

Hermeneutics The study of methodologies of interpretation, originally of religious scriptures, now of any principle of interpretation, such as literalism.

Monotheism Belief in one supreme god only, in contrast with polytheism.

Myth A religious and literary language

expressing not factual error, but symbolic images of psychological and transcendent meanings.

Numinous From the Latin *numen*, the uniquely religious experience of awesome mystery, tremendous and fascinating, beyond reason, goodness, and beauty.

Phenomenology Study of appearances of religious manifestations, seeking the "essence" of religion, and focusing on themes such as myth, ritual, shamanism, and the sacred/profane.

Polytheism Belief in many gods, in contrast with monotheism.

Positivism Philosophical doctrine limiting truth to sensory and logical data.

Profane Opposite of sacred, literally "outside the temple," whatever is considered impure or rejected by a community's sense of the sacred.

Ritual Repeated actions with symbolic significance, such as religious services (Roman Catholic Mass, Buddhist meditation) or social drama (football as refined combat).

Sacred Opposite of profane, the realm of ultimate reality, the appearance of the infinite.

Transcendent Rising above common thought; exalted, mystical, ultimate.

REVIEW QUESTIONS

1   What are the effects on the study of religions when the world's diverse cultures come into closer contact with each other?
2   What effect would acceptance of the anthropic principle have on the relationship between science and religion?
3   How do we understand myth and ritual in the comparative study of religion? Give examples.
4   How has the "ultimate concern" of religion been affected by industrial society?

DISCUSSION QUESTIONS

1   Discuss the two major different methods for studying religion that cluster around the scientific/historical and the phenomenological/intuitive extremes. Which authors use them? What differences do the methods make?
2   What differences in the use of language do the two major different methods (literal and symbolic) show? Give examples.
3   What implications for social and personal issues do various views of religion have? Give examples.

INFORMATION RESOURCES

Adams, Charles J. *A Reader's Guide to the Great Religions.* New York: Macmillan, 1977.

Anthropic Principle
<http://en.wikipedia.org/wiki/Anthropicprinciple>

Bailey, Lee W., general ed. *Introduction to the World's Major Religions.* 6 vols. Westport, CT: Greenwood Press, 2006.

Barbour, Ian. *When Science Meets Religion.* San Francisco: HarperSanFrancisco, 2000.

Barrow, John, and **Frank Tipler.** *The Anthropic Cosmological Principle.* Oxford: Oxford University Press, 1986.

Beliefnet
<http://www.beliefnet.com>

Bowker, John, ed. *Oxford Dictionary of World Religions.* Oxford: Oxford University Press, 1997.

Brasher, Brenda, ed. *Encyclopedia of Fundamentalism.* New York: Routledge, 2001.

Comparative Religion
<http://www.comparative-religion.com>

101 Cults and Sects
<http://www.religion-cults.com>

Films for the Humanities and Sciences/Religion
<http://www.films.com/ffhpr>

Gonzalez, Guillermo, and **Jay W. Richards** *The Privileged Planet: How Our Place in the Cosmos is Designed for Discovery.* Washington, DC: Regnery/Eagle, 2004.

Internet Sacred Text Archive
<http://www.sacred-texts.com/world.htm>

Johnston, William M., ed. *Encyclopedia of Monasticism.* Chicago and London: Fitzroy Dearborn Publishing, 2000.

Jones, Lindsay, ed. *Encyclopedia of Religion.* 15 vols. 2nd ed. New York: Macmillan, 2005.

Nation and World Religion Statistics
<http://www.adherents.com>

Palmer-Fernandez, Gabriel, ed. *Encyclopedia of Religion and War.* New York: Routledge, 2004.

Religion Facts
<http://www.religionfacts.com>

Religion and Philosophy
<http://www.insight-media.com>

Religious Tolerance
<http://www.religioustolerance.org/var_rel.htm>

Smart, Ninian. *Atlas of the World's Religions.* Oxford: Oxford University Press, 1999.

Swatos, William, ed. *Encyclopedia of Religion and Society.* Walnut Creek, CA: Alta Mira Press, 1998.

Van Huytssteen, J., and **Wentzel Vrede,** eds. *Encyclopedia of Science and Religion.* New York: Macmillan, 2003.

The Virtual Religion Index
<http://virtualreligion.net/vri>

Wabash Center Guide to Internet Resources
<http://www.wabashcenter.wabash.edu/internet/front.htm>

Walker, Barbara. *The Women's Encyclopedia of Myths and Secrets.* San Francisco: Harper and Row, 1983.

Ward, Peter, and **Donald Brownlee.** *Rare Earth: Why Complex Life is Uncommon in the Universe.* New York: Copernicus/Springer Verlag, 2000.

World Religions
<http://www.mnsu.edu/emuseum/cultural/religion>

World Religions Photo Library
<http://www.worldreligions.co.uk>

The WWW Virtual Library: International Affairs Resources
<http://www2.etown.edu/vl/worldrel>

Young, Serinity, ed. *Encyclopedia of Women and World Religion.* New York: Macmillan, 1999.

CHAPTER 2

INDIGENOUS SACRED WAYS

In pockets of the world remote from industrial culture, traditional small-scale societies still exist. Although they are increasingly being drawn into the global economy, some have managed to maintain part of their traditional religious ways. In these **indigenous** religions, the sacred and the profane are not separate; religious understanding pervades everyday life and every aspect of the environment.

Despite great differences from one indigenous culture to the next, certain common themes can be found. One is the concept of sacred relationship to all that exists. One's individuality is of less importance than one's kinship with the whole natural system. All beings are interrelated, and shaking the cosmic web at any point affects all things. Such relationships are described in myths and symbols.

Another common indigenous belief is that the natural world is pervaded by living, thinking presences, which should not be ignored even if one cannot see them. There are spirits in trees, in rocks, in rivers, in mountains, in the elements, and one should stay in proper spiritual relationship with them. The appropriate human attitude toward these spirits may be a certain fear or awe, and it may be necessary to make offerings to the spirits or carry out certain divinations or other rituals to keep them happy. Often these spirits are seen as the souls of dead **ancestors**. In addition to a plurality of spiritual beings, there may also be a belief in an underlying cosmic force which creates and sustains the natural world.

Although such awarenesses are incumbent on everyone in traditional indigenous cultures, there are also specialists who deal with the spirit worlds. By enduring great hardships, they develop communication with the spirits and thus can act as go-betweens on behalf of the people.

These ancient spiritual ways have typically been handed down and added to orally over the millennia within the local communities. But now that these small-scale societies have been marginalized, oppressed, or brought into industrial society, there are few people left to carry on the rituals and retell the stories. However, people both within and outside these ancient ways are learning to cherish them again as containing valuable instructions for living in harmony with the cosmos.

African sacred ways

Sub-Saharan Africa is home to at least 742 tribes, each with its own religious patterns and understandings. Nevertheless, some patterns, such as worship of ancestors, are widespread. The incursions of Christianity and Islam have stimulated new thinking within the indigenous religions, particularly with regard to the belief in a single High God. Initiation, drumming, and prayer are dramatic ceremonies that give an African flavor to universal themes, such as ritual awakening to the spiritual realm, celebrating it, and seeking its blessings.

Of Water and Spirit: An African Boy's Initiation
by Malidoma Patrice Somé

Malidoma Somé, born in Burkina Faso, West Africa, is an initiated **shaman** in his Dagara culture. He also holds three master's degrees and two doctorates. This selection from his 1994 book *Of Water and Spirit* tells of his initiation into his tribal wisdom after several years in a French missionary school. It describes the ritually altered states of consciousness through which he grasped the transcendent mysteries of his ancient people's traditions.

"So my initiation begins tomorrow—and I am not the least prepared for it."

"Your not knowing is your being prepared.". . .

I walked out of my room into the inner yard, where Father was waiting for me. He held ash in one hand and a bowl of water in the other. He handed me the water and I followed him into the **medicine** room.

We knelt down and he began. "*Walai!*" he said, saluting the spirits. "To the rising of the sun, to the powers of life. To you who established the directives and the meaning of crossing the bridge from nonperson to person through the hard road of knowledge. Here is another one who leaves his warm home and comes to you seeking the path of memory. The road is dangerous, the process uncertain, but with your protection, upon which we rely, he will return to us a man. Let him come back alive."

Father motioned to me to hand him the water, which he sprinkled onto the spirits, the statues of the male and female ancestors. He had already done the same with the ash in his hands. Then he continued, "Take this ash and give him the power of his ancestors. Take this water to seal the contract between us that he will return from his journey with a heart turned toward his tribe and a soul toward his ancestors."

He then turned to me and said, "The time has come. I will not have much to say to you again until . . . I may never say anything to you again unless you come back. I have done what a father should do, the rest is in your hands. Please come back to us."

The whole family was outside watching. When I followed Father out into the compound, everybody looked at me with sympathy. My younger brothers were staring at me as if I were going on a long journey with no specific time of return. I had no idea how long I was going to be absent. We all walked away from the house toward the outskirts of the village. As we neared the bush, more and more people joined us. There was a large group of young adolescents, maybe 13, maybe 14 years old packed together at the end of the bush. They looked so young that I felt out of place. They were all naked.

Nakedness is very common in the tribe. It is not a shameful thing; it is an expression of one's relationship with the spirit of nature. To be naked is to be open-hearted. Normally, kids stay naked until puberty and even beyond. It was only with the introduction of cheap cloth from the West, through Goodwill and other Christian organizations, that nakedness began to be associated with shame.

The naked kids were singing. As I came closer I could hear their words.

My little family I leave today.
My great Family I meet tomorrow.
Father, don't worry, I shall come back,
Mother, don't cry, I am a man.

As the sun rises and the sun sets
My body into them shall melt,
And one with you and them
Forever and ever I shall be . . .

As the candidates for initiation passed through the crowd, they took off their shirts and shorts. Their families embraced them. Some family members grabbed their hands and sobbed with them; perhaps they were saying goodbye for the last time. There were so many young men that I could not count them all. Many of them were strangers to me. My father asked me to take my clothes off. I obeyed him, but I felt ashamed. No one paid any attention to my nakedness, however. In the village clothing attracts more attention than nakedness. My sister was weeping . . .

We sang as we walked into the belly of the bush, swallowed by the trees. . . .

In the middle of the circle that we had instinctively formed, the coach was directing the singing. The song got inside of you, burning your heart like fire. I was quickly caught up with its rhythms, words, melody. We held each other's hands and swayed in cadence. It was intoxicating to sing in the middle of the bush at night—even on an empty stomach . . .

The elders chose this time to make a dramatic entrance. They looked like living skeletons, half naked and covered with white lines painted on their faces, necks, bellies, and backs. Each elder wore ritual cotton shorts. They were voluminous and looked from afar like bags. Their thin black bodies were not visible in the dark, just the white, almost phosphorescent lines painted on them. In addition each elder was carrying his medicine bag, made of feline skin. They walked in a line; slowly, quietly, and imperturbably. When shrouded in the darkness, far away from the fire, their bodies were luminescent, but as they came closer, into the light, the luminescence disappeared.

Their presence intensified the song. We sang more furiously as if the force of the elders, suddenly available, were a gift that flowed from the power of being old. Our teachers walked around the fireplace in the center of the circle—three times clockwise and three times counterclockwise. They did not sing with us. When they stopped their procession the song stopped as if by enchantment. Nobody asked us to stop singing—we simply lost the song. It departed from us as if a force had removed it from our lips as a calabash of water is removed from the thirsty lips of its drinker. The silence that followed was as thick as the darkness behind us in the bush.

One of the elders pulled something out of his bag, a pouch with an end like a tail. One could see long, mysterious, stiff hairs sprouting from the pouch as if they grew there. He brought the thing to his mouth and said something silently. Only his lips moved. Then he directed the tail end of the pouch toward the fire and uttered something in primal language. The color of the fire changed to violet and increased its roar. We still held each other's hands. The elder moved close to the fire, speaking again in primal tongue. With each of his movements, the fire grew taller and taller until the violet flame stood almost six meters in the air. From then on I heard nothing and thought nothing. . . .

The fifth elder, the one responsible for the initial experience, still stood in the middle of the circle next to the fireplace. Walking slowly around the circle, he spoke incessantly and breathlessly . . .

What he said was this: The place where he was standing was the center. Each one of us possessed a center that he had grown away from after birth. To be born was to lose contact with our center, and to grow from childhood to adulthood was to walk away from it.

"The center is both within and without. It is everywhere. But we must realize it exists, find it, and be with it, for without the center we cannot tell who we are, where we come from, and where we are going."

He explained that the purpose of Baor[1] was to find our center. . . .

All around me and underneath me I could feel life pulsating, down to the smallest piece of dirt on the ground. The way this life expressed itself was otherworldly: sounds were blue or green, colors were loud. I saw incandescent visions and apparitions, breathing color and persistent immobility. Everything seemed alive with meaning. Even the stonelike circle of people partook of the same cacophony of meaning. Each person was like the sum total of all the emanations taking place. The people, however, were not in charge of the operation of the universe around them—they were dependent on it and they were useful to it as well.

---

1 Baor—a boys' initiation into manhood ritual for the West African Dagora people.

The elder in the center of the circle was the most intriguing to watch. He looked like an impalpable being in fusion, an amalgamation of colors, sounds of varying pitch, and innumerable forms. All of his smallest constituent parts—his cells and bacteria in his body, even the tiniest atomic particles of his being—had come alive. He was not moving, but the colors, the sounds, and the life forms were. Without being able to put it into words, I understood what was happening, for at that stage of consciousness there is no difference between meaning and being. Things had become their meaning and I knew that was the lesson for the evening. I also understood that this was the kind of knowledge I was going to become gradually acquainted with—not by going outside of myself, but by looking within myself and a few others. For now, all I could do was to feel and honor the effects of the subtle invisible world breaking through my own blindness and preempting my perceptions. How acquiescent one becomes when face to face with the pure universal energy! . . .

I thought about the hardships of the day—the baking heat of the sun and my sweat falling into my eyes and burning them like pepper. I had lost all sense of chronology. I told myself that this is what the world looked like when one had first expired. I felt as if I were being quite reasonable. I could still think and respond to sensations around me, but I was no longer experiencing the biting heat of the sun or my restless mind trying to keep busy or ignoring my assignment. Where I was now was just plain real.

When I looked once more at the yila, I became aware that it was not a tree at all. How had I ever seen it as such? I do not know how this transformation occurred. Things were not happening logically, but as if this were a dream. Out of nowhere, in the place where the tree had stood, appeared a tall woman dressed in black from head to foot. She resembled a nun, although her outfit did not seem religious. Her tunic was silky and black as the night. She wore a veil over her face, but I could tell that behind this veil was an extremely beautiful and powerful entity. I could sense the intensity emanating from her, and that intensity exercised an irresistible magnetic pull. To give in to that pull was like drinking water after a day of wandering in the desert.

My body felt like it was floating, as if I were a small child being lulled by a nurturing presence that was trying to calm me by singing soothing lullabies and rocking me rhythmically. I felt as if I were floating weightless in a small body of water. My eyes locked on to the lady in the veil, and the feeling of being drawn toward her increased. For a moment I was overcome with shyness, uneasiness, and a feeling of inappropriateness, and I had to lower my eyes. When I looked again, she had lifted her veil, revealing an unearthly face. She was green, light green. Even her eyes were green, though very small and luminescent. She was smiling and her teeth were the color of violet and had light emanating from them. The greenness in her had nothing to do with the color of her skin. She was green from the inside out, as if her body was filled with green fluid. I do not know how I knew this, but this green was the expression of immeasurable love.

Never before had I felt so much love. I felt as if I had missed her all my life and was grateful to heaven for having finally released her back to me. We knew each other, but at the time I could not tell why, when, or how. I also could not tell the nature of our love. It was not romantic or filial; it was a love that surpassed any known classifications. Like two loved ones who had been apart for an unduly long period of time, we dashed toward each other and flung ourself into each other's arms.

The sensation of embracing her body blew my body into countless pieces, which became millions of conscious cells, all longing to reunite with the whole that was her. If they could not unite with her, it felt as if they could not live. Each one was adrift and in need of her to anchor itself back in place. There are no words to paint what it felt like to be in the hands of the green lady in the black veil. We exploded into each other in a cosmic contact that sent us floating adrift in the ether in countless intertwined forms. In the course of this baffling experience, I felt as if I were moving backward in time and forward in space.

While she held me in her embrace, the green lady spoke to me for a long time in the softest voice that ever was. She was so much taller than I was that I felt like a small boy in her powerful arms. She placed her lips close to my left ear and she spoke so softly and tenderly to me that nothing escaped my attention. I cried abundantly the whole time, not because what she told me was sad, but because every word produced an indescribable sensation of nostalgia and longing in me.

Human beings are often unable to receive because we do not know what to ask for. We are sometimes unable to get what we need because we do not know what we want. If this was happiness that I felt, then no human could sustain this amount of well-being for even a day. You would have to be dead or changed into a something capable of handling these unearthly feelings in order to live with them. The part in us that yearns for these kinds of feelings and experiences is not human. It does not know that it lives in a body that can withstand only a certain amount of this kind of experience at a time. If humans were to feel this way all the time, they would probably not be able to do anything other than shed tears of happiness for the rest of their lives—which, in that case, would be very short.

Human beings never feel that they have enough of anything. Ofttimes what we say we want is real in words only. If we ever understood the genuine desires of our hearts at any given moment, we might reconsider the things we waste our energy pining for. If we could always get what we thought we wanted, we would quickly exhaust our weak arsenal of petty desires and discover with shame that all along we had been cheating ourselves.

Love consumes its object voraciously. Consequently, we can only experience its shadow. Happiness does not last forever because we do not have the power to contain it. It has the appetite of a ferocious carnivore that has been starved for a long time—this is how much love and bliss and happiness there is in nature, in the place that was there before we existed in it.

I cannot repeat the speech of the green lady. It lives in me because it enjoys the privilege of secrecy. For me to disclose it would be to dishonor and diminish it. The power of nature exists in its silence. Human words cannot encode meaning because human language has access only to the shadow of meaning. The speech of the green lady was intended to stay alive in silence, so let it be.

I loosened my grip, lifted my wet face up to hers, and read departure in her eyes. I did not know where she was returning to, but wherever it was I did not want her to go without me. My feelings for her were so strong I felt that I would be able to brave anything to stay with her, nor did I think there was any reason we should part after having been separated for so long. Her face, however, said I could not go where she was going and that this was one of those imperatives that one had to respond to without negotiation. Things had to stay as they were. In despair I clung harder to her soft body, unable to do anything else. My eyes closed as my grip tightened, and the soft body under my hands became rough.

When I opened my eyes I realized I was desperately hugging the yila tree. It was the same as it had been before. Meanwhile, the elders had moved closer to me, obviously watching everything I had been doing. I heard one of them say, "They are always like this. First they resist and play dumb when there are a lot of things waiting to be done, and then when it happens, they won't let go either. Children are so full of contradictions. The very experience you rejected before with lies, you are now accepting without apology."

This seemed to have been directed at me. I looked up at the elder who spoke. He met my eyes, and I felt no further need to be holding on to the tree.

"Go find something to eat, and make your bed for the night," he said gently.

It was then that I noticed that the sun had set. My experience had lasted several hours, but the time had felt so short!

When I arrived back at the camping circle, the students were almost done making up their sleeping places. Nyangoli in his faithfulness was discreetly waiting for me. He looked relieved when I appeared, so relieved that, for the first time since we had arrived at the camp, he spoke to me first. "You're still alive! *Walai*."...

Nature looks the way it looks because of the way we are. We could not live our whole lives on the ecstatic level of the sacred. Our senses would soon become exhausted and the daily business of living would never get done. There does, however, come a time when one must learn to move between the two ways of "seeing" reality in order to become a whole person.

Traditional education consists of three parts: enlargement of one's ability to see, destabilization of the body's habit of being bound to one plane of being, and the ability to voyage transdimensionally and return. Enlarging one's vision and abilities has nothing supernatural about it, rather it is "natural" to be a part of nature and to **participate** in a wider understanding of reality.

SOURCE: Malidoma Patrice Somé, *Of Water and Spirit: Ritual, Magic, and Initiation in the Life of an African Shaman*. New York: Penguin Books, 1994, pp. 192–226

The Talking Drum: African Sacred Liturgy
by Georges Niangoran-Bouah

Georges Niangoran-Bouah, at the University of Abidjan in Ivory Coast, West Africa, brings to life the deeper meanings of the African drum's sacred messages. The drums' ancient poetry, carrying in rhythm far across African plains, praises God the Creator, Goddess Earth, and beautiful Moon. This primal discourse carries the sacred consciousness of ancient ways, he says, much as holy books do for other faiths.

Generally speaking, the outsider who comes to Africa for the first time is surprised by the omnipresence of the drum in both religious and profane ceremonies. The drum is an instrument that everybody hears and sees; it is the instrument of kings. . . .

The Sacred According to religious anthropology, the Sacred is that which is connected to religion and that which inspires respect and deep veneration. The Sacred is whatever goes beyond man and inspires his respect, his admiration. From the Sacred generally emanates a particular fervor, coupled with an element of fear of an absolute power and an element of mystery. The sacred being or object enjoys a fascinating power, often presented as being the locus of energy able to manifest itself at any moment and anywhere.

For the traditional African, the Sacred is an organized and hierarchized universe filled with invisible beings which include God, spirits, the spirits of the ancestors, myths, legends, ceremonies, elaborate rituals, and cult objects.

It is this universe of absolute power, of mystery, of fascinating might, that we are trying to reconstitute through what the African drums say.

The texts chosen to illustrate the point in this paper will not be followed by commentaries, in order to allow the reader to find for himself their philosophical, religious, or theological importance. The poet is not wrong in saying:

Contemporary drum
Of founding ancestors,
Messenger coming
From the beginning of time;
Drum, wherever you are
And whatever your state,
Drum word,

Memory of the Ancients,
We implore you, speak,
Talk to us in the African way
Of immemorial times,
Speak, speak to us
Of deep Africa
Of true Africa!

In black Africa, the talking drum is in fact a precious element of communication. In the highlands, with a favorable direction of the wind, the language of a drum can be heard at a distance of 40 kilometers.

For the Akan [tribe], the drummed documentation is serious; it is sacred and respected by the whole population. This is the reason that it is the preferred method of communication with gods, the spirits, and the ancestors....

Among the Akan in Côte d'Ivoire and Ghana, the drum defines its origin itself by saying:

God in creating the world
Has suffered to create.
What did he create?
He created the Drum.
Divine Drum,
Wherever you are
In nature,
We call upon you,
Come.
(Abron[2] drum text)

The drum is an animated being In this chapter, the drum is no longer only perceived as a material object of human conception and fabrication but also as an animated being endowed with a vital force and spiritual principle.

While organizing the world,
God-the-Creator
Has suffered to create.
What did He create?
He has created the Word
And the Word-carrier,
Has created the drum and
The drummer....
Divine drum,
Wherever you be
In nature,
We call upon you, come!

---

2 Abron—West African tribe in Ghana and Ivory Coast.

Divine drum,
We shall wake you up
And make you heard.
(Abron drum text)
I am coming from my dream
And find myself
In the hands
Of the drummer.
(Abron drum)

The Creation according to the drum

God-the-Creator
Has created Heaven,
And he has created the Earth.
He has created the night,
And has created the day,
Alone
Absolutely alone.
God has created the water
And has created the crocodile.
(Agni[3] drum)

Attitude and behavior of humans towards the Eternal One

Great God
Infinitely mighty
You who give us life
We glorify you,
Bless us!
(Agni drum)

Goddess Earth

Oh you good earth
Who nourishes us
The year has come to its end.
We glorify you,
Bless us!
(Agni drum)

Goddess Moon

Beautiful moon
Who brings together
The joyful troupes
Give me the strength
To sing to you all the years!
(Agni drum)

---

3 Agni—West African tribe in Ivory Coast.

Conclusion It is customary when talking of the religious thoughts of the ancient people of the Middle East to refer to the Bible or the Qur'an. In the same way the Akan refer themselves to the talking drum in order to quote any discourse related to the sacred. Bible, Qur'an, and Drum have the same vocation; these are fundamental sacred "books" venerated by their respective peoples. They are monuments of the human spirit because they are timeless. The drum is a tool and an appropriate instrument of knowledge which for a long time was considered as not being accessible to the universe of African traditional beliefs. The discourse of the drum, unchangeable and conventional, is not a discourse of an isolated wise man, but a real ideology of several thousand years which the memory of a whole people preserves with piety from generation to generation.

SOURCE: Georges Niangoran-Bouah, "The Talking Drum: A Traditional African Instrument of Liturgy and of Mediation with the Sacred," in *African Traditional Religions in Contemporary Society*, ed. Jacob Olupona. New York: Paragon House, 1991, pp. 81–92

Oya, Patron of Feminine Leadership by Judith Gleason

Priestess Judith Gleason has for decades been researching traditional African religions in Nigeria, Mali, and Lagos, as well as Caribbean countries, where they were carried by slaves and merged with other traditions. Her book *Oya: In Praise of the Goddess* (1987) is a personal exploration of the complexities of the deity in cultural context.

The goddess Oya, of African origin, manifests herself in various natural forms: the river Niger, tornadoes, strong winds generally, fire, lightning, and buffalo. She is also associated with certain cultural phenomena among the Yoruba people . . . notably with masquerades constructed of bulky, billowing cloth—ancestral apparitions—and with funerals. To the leader of the market women in Yoruba communities she offers special protection and encouragement in negotiation with civil authorities and arbitration of disputes. Thus, one may speak of Oya as patron of feminine leadership, of persuasive charm reinforced by *aje*—an efficacious gift usually translated as "witchcraft." Although Oya is associated with pointed speech, most of what she's about is highly secret. Always vanishing, she presents herself in concealment. More abstractly, Oya is the goddess of edges, of the dynamic interplay between surfaces, of transformation from one state of being to another. She is a jittery goddess, then, but with a keen sense of direction.

To describe and elaborate upon Oya's various manifestations is inevitably to present an idea not commonly thought of when the word "goddess" is mentioned. Oya's patterns, persisting through many media—from air to the human psyche—suggest something like a unified field theory of a certain type of energy that our culture certainly doesn't think of as feminine. . . .

Old women, the grandmothers are a strong, affecting presence in religious places all over the world. They light the candles. They arrange the flowers. They sew the altar cloths, the vestments, the shrouds. When speaking of the Yoruba system of belief, it is important to point to the predominance of feminine symbolism as well ... a succession of opaque containers rounded about hidden matrices. The feminine is primary to the Yoruba imagination. Womankind, therefore, is regarded with ambivalence. Female passion, potentially overwhelming, in turn is contained by male structures of thought and language ... which then by their own logic exclude women, except for occasional grandmothers, from enclaves and conclaves of authority. Even grandmothers are suspect.... A woman who has *aje* won't admit it.... In true womanly fashion, she'll contain it. Secrecy is feminine....

What is especially interesting about Oya in human context is her refusal to stay out of the enclaves of cult and culture preempted by male authority. She has, potentially, a sharp tongue, which occasionally she wields like a sword. Now and again her mouth spits fire. Furthermore, though she's rounded, though she might stay for a time in her corner (which is where her altars are always placed), suddenly she's storming all over the place, a revolutionary. So she has to be made part of the picture.... If excluded altogether, Oya turns unimaginably violent. She has whirled her way into the Yoruba pantheon (she isn't natally Yoruba). She has even managed to set herself indispensably in the midst of the male ancestral cult....

Oya is her simplest name. It is a verb form conveying her passage as an event with disastrous consequences. *O-ya*, meaning "She tore" in Yoruba. And what happened? A big tree ... getting in the way of the storm, wildly agitated its branches. Perhaps its crown got lopped off. She tore. A river overflowed its banks. Whole cloth was ripped into shreds. Barriers were broken down. A tumultuous feeling suddenly destroyed one's peace of mind. *"Eeepa!"* one exclaims, by way of homage. *"Eeepa Heyi!"* What a goddess!

SOURCE: Judith Gleason, *Oya: In Praise of the Goddess.* Boston: Shambhala, 1987, pp. 1–11

Aboriginal sacred ways

Only a century ago, hundreds of Aboriginal bands were scattered across great areas of Australia, sustaining themselves by ancient subsistence techniques. Now they no longer have access to such vast hunting grounds, and their traditional lives have been greatly changed by roads, towns, animal grazing, missionaries, and settlements.

Women's Health Rituals by Diane Bell

Anthropologist Diane Bell lived on settlements in central Australia from 1976 to 1982, studying the rituals of women.

When we consider the wide range of women's involvement in the maintenance of health, it becomes impossible to discuss women's activities as merely "growing up" children and applying a few herbal remedies. Women, in order to maintain good health, are staging ceremonies which focus on health at the cosmic level of restoration of harmony and happiness.

This is because women have rights in the country from which they derive power and for which they hold a sacred trust. . . .

All women's group ritual curing activities have to do with giving—with the infusing of the body with strength. Women attempt to restore a person to health by the gift of blood, fat or bodily secretions from underarm or eyes. In giving, women are once again acting out their nurturance role where love, care and power are freely given. *Ngangkayi* [traditional healers'] practice on the other hand is essentially an individual activity concerned more with the removal of foreign objects and alien forces from a person.

The role of women in the domain of health in Aboriginal society has been rendered almost invisible by the focus upon the healer and not the healed, the disease and not the context of the ill health, the magico-religious practices and not the relationships of health to other aspects of the culture. However, I suggest that women are acutely aware of the decline in physical health and the breakdown in social relationships. Fighting and drunkenness now disrupt their lives in a fashion unknown several generations ago. Women are aware that in the shift from the hunter-gatherer mode of subsistence to settlement life they have suffered. Daily they are presented with tensions and sorcery accusations on a scale which could not have been sustained in the past. They have sought to repair and restore damaged bonds through their most powerful and spectacular rituals.

This resurgence in women's ritual activity has not been accompanied by a concomitant increase in the status of women: their autonomy has been fundamentally eroded and their relationship to land dislocated. Women's contribution to the maintenance of health in the past was within the small family group and focused upon life-crisis ceremonies. It was in these rituals that women stated their importance as the makers of adult women and in their control over their own bodies. Here, then, is the physiological basis for their nurturance roles: women do give birth, they do menstruate. This power and the nurturance roles associated with birth and growth are symbolized in *yawulyu* [women's ceremonies and designs] rituals.

SOURCE: Diane Bell, *Daughters of the Dreaming*. 2nd ed. Minneapolis, MN: University of Minnesota Press, 1993, pp. 160–1

Native North American sacred ways

The Americas have been home to a great variety of ancient indigenous ways. In North America alone, there were at least two thousand different languages being spoken before the European settlers arrived. Many aspects of the indigenous religions are specific to the local environment, but some are now spreading throughout the region, such as the sacred pipe, sweat lodge, and **vision quest**. After centuries of oppression by people of European origin, the remaining indigenous tradition-carriers are being carefully studied and valued for their spiritual wisdom and ecological example. Some groups are seeking to regain ancestral lands.

That Mountain Has Spirit   by Southwest Indigenous Peoples

You go out and get a certain piece of rock. It's not just a rock. It's got energy forces in it; it's a living thing, too. . . .

You look at that mountain, that mountain has spirit, that mountain has holiness. There's a quiet there and yet there's a fervor there. And if you've ever seen clouds there you see that mountain like a hand grasping those clouds. There's life up there. That's why it's sacred. . . .

Before you go hunting the important thing is that you are going to have a little prayer . . . to the Mother Nature, the nature of the sky, and then the animal, and then you more or less cry a little bit, and ask Mother Nature to spare you some meat. When you went into that forest, you had to be that deer. . . .

We must try and worship the land, the ground and the stars and the skies, for they are the ones that have spirit. They are the mighty spirits which guide and direct us, which help us to survive.

SOURCE: Stephen Trimble, ed., *Our Voices, Our Land.* Flagstaff, AZ: The Heard Museum, Northland Press, 1986, pp. 24–47

The Theft of Light   by the Tsimshian Nation

This folktale is a traditional story from the Tsimshian people of the Northwest coast of North America, where the year has a long period of dim Arctic night. Its themes include that of the divine child, the presence of transcendent beings in animals, and the theft of light from the gods to grant clarity of conscious knowledge to uncom- prehending humans.

The whole world was covered with darkness. The people were distressed by this. Then Giant remembered that there was light in heaven, whence he had come. On the following day Giant put on his raven skin, which his father the chief had given to him, and flew upward. Finally he found the hole in the sky, and he flew through it. He took off the raven skin and put it down near the hole in the sky. He went on, and came to a spring near the house of the chief of heaven.

Then the chief's daughter came out, carrying a small bucket in which she was about to fetch water. When Giant saw her coming along, he transformed himself into the leaf of a cedar and floated on the water. The chief's daughter dipped it up in her bucket and drank it. After a short time she was with child, and not long after she gave birth to a boy. Then the chief and the chieftainess were very glad.

Now the child was strong and crept about every day. He began to cry *"Hama, hama!"* The great chief was troubled, and called in some of his slaves to carry about the boy, but he kept on crying, *"Hama, hama!"* Therefore the chief invited all his wise men, and said to them that he did not know what the boy wanted and why he was crying. He wanted the box that was hanging in the chief's house. This box, in which the daylight was kept, was hanging in one corner of the house. Its name was *mā*. Giant had known it before he descended to our world.

One of the wise men, who understood him, said to the chief, "He is crying for the *mā*." Therefore the chief ordered it to be taken down. They put it down near the fire, and the boy sat down near it and ceased crying, for he was glad. Then he rolled the *mā* about inside the house. Sometimes he would carry it to the door. Now the great chief did not think of it. Then the boy really took up the *mā*, put it on his shoulders, and ran out with it. While he was running, someone said, "Giant is running away with the *mā*! He ran away, and the hosts of heaven pursued him. He came to the hole of the sky, put on the skin of the raven, and flew down, carrying the *mā*.

At that time the world was still dark. Giant had come down near the mouth of Nass River. He went up the river in the dark. A little farther up he heard the noise of the people, who were catching *olachen* in bag nets in their canoes. Giant, who was sitting on the shore, said, "Throw ashore one of the things that you are catching, my dear people!" Those on the water scolded him, "Where did you come from, great liar...?" Then Giant said again, "Throw ashore one of the things that you are catching, or I shall break the *mā*!"

Giant repeated his request four times, but those on the water refused what he had asked for. Therefore Giant broke the *mā*. It broke, and it was daylight. The north wind began to blow hard, and all the fishermen, the Frogs who had made fun of Giant, were driven away down river until they arrived at one of the large mild tenderness islands. Here the Frogs tried to climb up the rock; but they stuck to the rock, being frozen by the north wind, and became stone. They are still on the rock ... and all the world had the daylight.

SOURCE: Abridged from Tsimshian Nation, "The Theft of Light," a Raven's Adventure story collected by Franz Boaz, in the Report of the Bureau of Ethnology of the Smithsonian Institution. Washington, DC: Smithsonian Institution, 1916, vol. 31, p. 60

The Great Vision by Black Elk, Lakota shaman

In the Plains area around the Black Hills (in what is now called South Dakota), a nine-year-old Lakota (Sioux) boy with virtually no contact with European culture had an unsought visionary experience. He fell deathly ill and had an intense vision in which he was carried up to a sky full of horses and a cloud tipi (Native American conical tent of animal skins) with a rainbow door. Entering the sky lodge, he sat with six cosmic Grandfathers who gave him powers to understand and to heal. He grieved for his nation's suffering at the hands of the oncoming invasion of European immigrants. He sought strength from the Great Mystery behind his vision, called **Wakan Tanka**, the spiritual power present in all the world—in blood, thunder, birds, and buffalo—saying: "I was seeing in a sacred manner the shapes of all things in the spirit." This boy grew up to become Black Elk (1862–1950), a shaman. Later Black Elk told his life story to John Neihardt, a poet, who in 1932 edited it, condensed it, and added a few poetic elaborations. The resulting book, *Black Elk Speaks*, has become a classic. In 1984 Raymond DeMallie published the original manuscripts of Neihardt's interviews as *The Sixth Grandfather* with editorial notes, from which the following extract is taken.

We stopped at a creek to get a drink. When I got off my horse I crumbled down, helpless, and I couldn't walk. The boys helped me up and when the camp camped again, I was very sick.... Both my legs and arms were swollen badly and even my face. This all came suddenly....

As I lay in the tipi I could see through the tipi the same two men whom I saw before and they were coming from the clouds.... They came and stood off aways from me and stopped, saying: "Hurry up, your grandfather is calling you." When they started back I got up and started to follow them. Just as I got out of the tipi I could see the two men going back into the clouds and there was a small cloud coming down toward me at the same time, which stood before me. I got on top of the cloud and was raised up, following the two men, and when I looked back, I saw my father and mother looking at me. When I looked back I felt sorry that I was leaving them....

I followed those men on up into the clouds and they showed me a vision of a bay horse standing there in the middle of the clouds....

I looked over there and saw twelve black horses toward the west, where the sun goes down. All the horses had on their necks necklaces of buffalo hoofs.... I was very scared of those twelve head of horses because I could see the light[ning] and thunder around them....

When I had seen it all, the bay horse said to me: "Your grandfathers are having a council, these shall take you; so take courage."...

I followed the bay horse and it took me to a place on a cloud under a rainbow gate and there were sitting my six grandfathers, sitting inside of a rainbow door, and the horses stopped behind me....

One of the grandfathers said to me: "Do not fear, come right in" (through the rainbow door). So I went in and stood before them. The horses in the four quarters of the earth all neighed to cheer me as I entered the rainbow door.

The grandfather representing where the sun goes down said: "Your grandfathers all over the world and the earth are having a council and there you were called, so here you are. Behold then, those where the sun goes down; from thence they shall come, you shall see. From them you shall know the willpower of myself, for they shall take you to the center of the earth, and the nations of all kinds shall tremble. Behold where the sun continually shines, for they shall take you there."

The first grandfather then showed me a wooden cup with water, turning it toward me. He said: "Take courage and be not afraid, for you will know him. And furthermore, behold him, whom you shall represent. By representing him, you shall be very powerful on earth in medicines and all powers. He is your spirit and you are his body and his name is Eagle Wing Stretches."

When I looked up I saw flames going up from the rainbow. The first grandfather gave me a cup of water and also a bow and arrow and said: "Behold them, what I give you shall depend on, for you shall go against our enemies and you shall be a great warrior." Then he gave me that cup of water and said: "Behold, take this, and with this you shall be great." (This means that I should kill all sickness on earth with this water.)

After this he got up and started to run toward where the sun goes down and as he ran he changed into a black horse as he faced me. The five men left said: "Behold him." And this black horse changed into a poor [emaciated] horse.

The second grandfather rose and said: "Take this and make haste." So I took an herb out of the second grandfather's hand. And as [*I turned to the dying horse*] I held it toward the black horse [*and this holy herb*] cured the black horse, making him strong and fat once again.

The second grandfather represented the north. He said: "Behold the mother earth, for you shall create a nation." (This means that I am going to cure lots of sickness with this herb—bring children back to life.) The bay horse stood with the black horse and said to me: "Father, paint me, for I shall make a nation on the earth." [The] second grandfather of the north said again: "Take courage and behold, for you shall represent the wing of the great giant that lives." The second grandfather stood up and ran toward the north and as he turned around he changed himself again into a white goose. I looked toward where the black horses were and they were thunders and the northern white horses turned into white geese. The second grandfather said: "Behold then, your grandfather, for they shall fly in circles from one end of the earth to the other." [*Through this power of the north I will make everybody cry as geese do when they go north in the spring because the hardship is over*.]

First grandfather's song:

> They are appearing, may you behold.
> They are appearing, may you behold.
> The thunder nation is appearing, may you behold.

Second grandfather's song:

> They are appearing, may you behold.
> They are appearing, may you behold.
> The white geese nation is appearing, may you behold.

The third grandfather, where the sun continually shines, says: "Younger brother, take courage, for across the earth they shall take you. Behold them" (pointing to the morning star and below the star there were two men flying), "from them you shall have power. All the fowls of the universe, these he has wakened and also he has wakened the beings on the earth" (animals, people, etc.). As the third grandfather said this, he held in his hand a peace pipe, which had a spotted eagle outstretched on the handle of the pipe; apparently the eagle was alive for it was moving. He said: "Behold this, for with this you shall walk across the earth. Behold this, for with this whatever is sick on this earth you shall make well."

Then the third grandfather pointed to a man who was solid red in color and said: "Behold him." Then the red man lay down and changed into a buffalo before he got up. When he was standing up, the third grandfather said "Behold him" again. The buffalo ran back to the east and when he looked at the horses in this direction they all turned into buffalo.

The fourth grandfather said to me: "Younger brother, behold me; a nation's center of the earth I shall give you with the power of the four quarters. With the power of the four quarters like relatives you shall walk. Behold the four quarters." And after he said this I looked and saw that at each of the four quarters there was a chief. . . .

The fifth grandfather represented the Great Spirit above. He said: "Boy, I sent for you and you came. Behold me, my power you shall see." He stretched his hands out and turned into a spotted eagle. Then he said: "Behold them; they, the fowls of the universe, shall come to you. Things in the skies shall be like relatives" (meaning stars). "They shall take you across the earth with my power. Your grandfathers shall attack an enemy and be unable to destroy him, but you will have the power to destroy. You shall go with courage. This is all." Then the eagle flew up over my head and I saw the animals and birds all coming toward me to perform a duty.

Then the sixth grandfather said: "Boy, take courage, you wanted my power on earth, so you shall know me. You shall have my power in going back to the earth. Your nation on earth shall have great difficulties. There you shall go. Behold me, for I will depart." (The sixth grandfather was a very old man with very white hair.) I saw him go out the rainbow gate. I followed him out the rainbow gate. I was on the bay horse now that had talked to me at the first. I stopped and took a good look at the sixth grandfather and it seemed that I recognized him. I stood there for awhile very scared and then as I looked at him longer I knew it was myself as a young man. At the first he was an old man, but he got younger and younger until he was a little boy nine years old. This old man had in his hand a spear.

I remembered that the grandfather of the west had given me a wooden cup of water and a bow and arrow and with this bow and arrow I was going to destroy the enemy with the power of the fearful road. With the wooden cup of water I was to save mankind. This water was clear and with it I was to raise a nation (like medicine). . . .

I could see nothing but dust flying on the four quarters of the earth. I looked up and could see right above me a spotted eagle hovering over me and this was evidently who had told me to look back. I started back to the camp with the eagle guarding me. No one was with me then but the eagle, but I knew that I was coming back to the center of the nation's hoop by myself. I could see the people following me. Soon I saw my own tipi at

home and I walked fast to get there. As I entered the tipi I saw a boy
lying there dying and I stood there awhile and finally found out that it
was myself.

The next thing I heard was somebody saying: "The boy is feeling better
now, you had better give him some water." I looked up and saw it was my
mother and father stooping over me. They were giving me some medicine
but it was not that that cured me—it was my vision that cured me. The first
thought that came to me was that I had been traveling and my father and
mother didn't seem to know that I had been gone and they didn't look glad.
I felt very sad over this.

SOURCE: Raymond J. DeMallie, ed., *The Sixth Grandfather: Black Elk's Teachings Given to John G.
Neihardt.* Lincoln, NE: University of Nebraska Press, 1984, pp. 111–42

The Essence of Cosmic Man by Tlakaelel

Tlakaelel is a Mexica-Tolteca elder, from near Mexico City. He is a teacher, heir and
guardian of the **oral tradition**, and spiritual guide. He explores the meanings
of his ancestors' monumental pyramids and hidden caverns, and is the author of
the book *Nahui Mitl: The Journey of the Four Arrows* (1998). He says: "Brethren:
Mexicayotl (the essence of cosmic man) will never die." But to keep this essence in
our hearts, we must come closer to the Creator.

How can we come closer to the Creator? For us Indigenous People,
communication is not only realized through the use of our five senses.
There also exists the sense of direction, of balance, of time, of panic, and
many more. For us to communicate with the different people, we must
bond with their different sensitivities.

To communicate with the Creator, we have various ceremonies like the
ceremony of initiation, which is done when we are born. This ceremony
opens our road to life. With it, we receive the sensibility that with time
develops as it is impulsed by our teachers.

When one of our children is born, we dedicate him to the sun. We raise
him up over our head and offer him to the sun by saying, "You gave the
energy so that this child would reach the world. Give him strength, continue
giving him life, nourish him." Then we present him to the south. We ask
that "Omeyotl," the great spirit of the south, Ketzalkoatl, take possession of
his body and participate in his knowledge, and grant him the universal
wisdom, the cosmic knowledge that is manifested through movement. Then
we turn him to the place where the sun sets, and we invoke the forces that
one day gave life to our ancestors. We present him to our ancestors, the ones
who formed this world, the ones who with their existence and their work,
have made this moment and the existence of this new being possible. We
thank them and ask them that wherever they are and whatever form they
now have, they manifest their love and give their strength to this new child.
And we continue turning towards the north where a great force exists. This

is the synthesis of all the forces. This is death, this is "Miktlan," the place where all the forces that exist converge. All that was, is, and will be rests here. We come to this place to participate with the forces that are here at that moment of creation. We call for rest here, so that later, we can resurge in a more energetic way.

Death signifies the union of the dual energy of the principal Creator. We will know that when we exhale for the last time, we have an internal force that maintains our lives within our bodies. We will know that we are no longer in this body, that we leave this place to return to the place from where we came to integrate ourselves to the "all." Because we are part of the energy of the Great Spirit, we will be in the west where the sun sets, in the red place. When we leave the earth, our bones will be clean, they will become ashes. But we will continue having a consciousness and we will go where the Great Spirit is. This is the place where black, white, red, and yellow are concentrated. This is where the four cardinal points are reunited. We will realize that we are a bird, a tree, a star, a cloud, and that we are free. We will find that we are the spirit and that we will continue the great work of the Creator.

This ceremony of the life/death cycle is a petition to all of the creative forces so that the new being, the new child, this new balance, be in equilibrium with life and death. When the child grows, he is taught to share everything, respect everything, and to create and be happy creating. The child learns to pray in sweat lodges (*temazcales*), in the mountains, and during the night, while gazing at the stars. He is taught to pray for every act of his life. He is taught to give thanks to the Creator for the favors that were granted to us. There are more ceremonies such as: the acquisition of a sacred pipe (*chanupa*), vision quests, and the culmination: the Sun Dance.

SOURCE: Tlakaelel, *Nahui Mitl: The Journey of the Four Arrows*. Chaplin, CT: Mexicayotl Productions, 1998, pp. 144–5

Seeing with a Native Eye by Barre Toelken

Barre Toelken, an anthropologist at Utah State University, lived with the southwestern Navajo people for two years, during which his "adopted Navajo father" helped him to see with a native eye, rather than with the eye of industrial culture. The immense gap between cultures and religious attitudes becomes evident in their discussion of a tall building, a jet bomber, and springtime.

In Western culture, religion seems to occupy a niche reserved for the unreal, the Otherworld, a reference point that is reached only upon death or through the agency of the priest. Many native American tribes see religious experience as something that surrounds man all the time. In fact, my friends the Navajos would say that there is probably *nothing* that can be called nonreligious. To them, almost anything anyone is likely to do has some sort of religious significance, and many other tribes concur. Procedurally, then, our problem is how to learn to talk about religion, even in preliminary ways, knowing perfectly well that in one society what is considered art may in another be considered religion, or that what is considered as health in one culture may be religion in another. Before we can proceed, in other words, we need to reexamine our categories, our "pigeonholes," in order to "see" things through someone else's set of patterns. This is the reason for the odd title: "Seeing with a Native Eye."

Through our study of linguistics and anthropology we have learned that different groups of people not only think in different ways, but that they often "see" things in different ways. Good scientific experiments can be provided, for example, to prove that if certain ideas are offered to people in patterns which they have not been taught to recognize, not only will they not understand them, they often will not even see them. We see things in "programmed" ways. . . .

If we talk about native American religions using the categories of Western religions, we are simply going to see what *we* already know is there. We will recognize certain kinds of experiences as religious, and we will cancel out others. To us, for example, dance may be an art form, or it may be a certain kind of kinesis. With certain native American tribes, dance may be the most religious act a person can perform. . . .

We might consider the Pueblo view that in the springtime Mother Earth is pregnant, and one does not mistreat her any more than one might mistreat a pregnant woman. When our technologists go and try to get Pueblo farmers to use steel plows in the spring, they are usually rebuffed. For us it is a technical idea—"Why don't you just use plows? You plow, and you get 'x' results from doing so." For the Pueblos this is meddling with a formal religious idea. Using a plow, to borrow the Navajo phrase, "doesn't hold any sheep." In other words, it does not make sense in the way in which the world operates. It is against the way things really go. Some Pueblo folks still take the heels off their shoes, and sometimes the shoes off their horses, during the spring. I once asked a Hopi whom I met in that country, "Do you mean to say, then, that if I kick the ground with my foot, it will botch everything up, so nothing will grow?" He said, "Well, I don't know whether that would happen or not, but it would just really show what kind of person you are."

One learns slowly that in many of these native religions, religion is viewed as embodying the reciprocal relationships between people and the sacred *processes* going on in the world. It may not involve a "god." It may not be signified by praying or asking for favors, or doing what may "look" religious to people in our culture.

SOURCE: Barre Toelken, "Seeing with a Native Eye: How Many Sheep Will it Hold?" in *Seeing with a Native Eye*, ed. Walter H. Capps. New York: Harper and Row, 1976, pp. 11–14

The Hopi Message to the United Nations General Assembly
by Thomas Banyacya

In his historic 1992 speech to the United Nations in New York, this Hopi chief sketches an indigenous people's warnings about the dangers present in the current world.

My name is Banyacya of the Wolf, Fox and Coyote clan and I am a member of the Hopi sovereign nation. Hopi in our language means a peaceful, kind, gentle, truthful people. The traditional Hopi follows the spiritual path that was given to us by Massau'u the Great Spirit. We made a sacred covenant to follow his life plan at all times, which includes the responsibility of taking care of this land and life for his divine purpose. We have never made treaties with any foreign nation including the United States, but for many centuries we have honored this sacred agreement. Our goals are not to gain political control, monetary wealth nor military power, but rather to pray and to promote the welfare of all living beings and to preserve the world in a natural way. We still have our ancient sacred stone tablets and spiritual religious societies which are the foundations of the Hopi way of life. Our history says our white brother should have retained those same sacred objects and spiritual foundations. . . .

Nature itself does not speak with a voice that we can easily understand. Neither can the animals and birds we are threatening with extinction talk to us. Who in this world can speak for nature and the spiritual energy that creates and flows through all life? In every continent are human beings who are like you but who have not separated themselves from the land and from nature. It is through their voice that Nature can speak to us. You have heard those voices and many messages from the four corners of the world today. I have studied comparative religion and I think in your own nations and cultures you have knowledge of the consequences of living out of balance with nature and spirit. The native peoples of the world have seen and spoken to you about the destruction of their lives and homelands, the ruination of nature and the desecration of their sacred sites. It is time the United Nations used its rules to investigate these occurrences and stop them now.

This rock drawing [he holds up picture] shows part of the Hopi prophecy. There are two paths. The first with high technology but separate from natural and spiritual law leads to these jagged lines representing chaos. The lower path is one that remains in harmony with natural law. Here we see a line that represents a choice like a bridge joining the paths. If we return to spiritual harmony and live from our hearts we can experience a paradise in this world. If we continue only on this upper path, we will come to destruction.

SOURCE: Thomas Banyacya, from "The Hopi Message to the United Nations General Assembly," Kykyotsmovi, Arizona, December 10, 1992
<http://www.alphacdc.com/banyacya/un92.html>

GLOSSARY

Ancestors Indigenous ancestors, who created the world and founded clans, need to be fed and honored. They continue to give guidance through divination and are reborn in new bodies.

Indigenous First nations native to a region.

Medicine Since indigenous cultures participate fully in the environment, healing partakes of several factors: physiological, astronomical, behavioral, and spiritual. Good medicine may include herbal mixtures, songs to ancestors or divinities, art, good social co-operation, family counseling, or sacrificial offerings.

Oral tradition Storytelling and singing are the vehicles for teaching and passing on sacred knowledge among indigenous peoples with no books.

Participation Indigenous people cultivate a deep sense of integration with a dependence upon the powers of the environment, and this is central to indigenous sacred ways. Any star, plant, or animal could be a cosmic or natural power, or a deceased ancestor who must be honored.

Shaman An indigenous people's medicine healer and leader of sacred ways; an inspired, ecstatic, and charismatic man or woman with the power to control spirits, often by incarnating them or making out-of-body journeys.

Vision quest Visions, whether during sleep or awake, are revelations of ultimate reality for indigenous people. Some come unsought, as Black Elk's, others are sought in a vision quest.

Wakan Tanka For the Lakota (Sioux), the ultimate power of the universe present in all the world, "the center of everything."

TYPICAL HOLY WAYS

Corroboree An Australian Aborigine dance festival held at special ceremonial grounds to celebrate events such as the gathering of clans, a battle victory, marriages, and initiations.

Divination An indigenous ritual for uncovering the spiritual cause of a problem and how to solve it, by indicators such as dreams, ordeals, reading bones, or animal behavior.

Kwanzaa An African-American and Pan-African holiday for family, community, and culture. Celebrated from December 26 through January 1, its origins are in the first harvest celebrations of Africa. The name Kwanzaa is derived from the phrase *matunda ya kwanza*, which means "first fruits" in Swahili, the most widely spoken African language. Kwanzaa was created by an African-American to introduce and reinforce the Nguzo Saba (the Seven Principles): *Umoja* (unity), *Kujichagulia* (self-determination), *Ujima* (collective work and responsibility), *Ujamaa* (co-operative economics), *Nia* (purpose), *Kuumba* (creativity), and *Imani* (faith). Kwanzaa is a cultural holiday, not a religious one, thus available to and practiced by Africans of all religious faiths.

Sacred pipe ceremony As a ceremonial, long, wood-stemmed pipe with a bowl made of pipestone, common in North American Plains tribes, is filled with sacred tobacco, all the world, including the ceremony's participants, identify with it as their own center and the center of the universe. Its smoke is an offering to the powers of the universe.

Sun dance A Lakota (Sioux) summer full-moon ceremony where men pierce their chest or back skin and dance around a central sacred tree or drag buffalo skulls until the skin rips, as an offering to the great sacred power, Wakan Tanka.

Sweat lodge A purification ceremony in a domed lodge of skins; a group of participants sit inside, while a central hole is filled with hot rocks and water is poured over them, making steam; prayers are offered to the powers of the universe present in the earth, stone, water, and all beings.

HISTORICAL OUTLINE

c. 5 million BCE—evolution of human ancestors in Africa

c. 200,000 BCE—*Homo sapiens* appears in Africa

c. 70,000 BCE—Neanderthals bury dead with red ocher, food, and tools, suggesting belief in afterlife

c. 30,000 BCE—migration of Aborigines from Asia to Australia

c. 22,000 BCE—possible date for migration of Native Americans across the Bering Strait from Asia

c. 1200–400 BCE—Olmec civilization in Meso-America

c. 1st century CE—hunter-gatherer Bantu people start migration to central and southern Africa

250–900 CE—Classic Maya civilization in Meso-America

5th century–1076—empire of Ghana in Africa

800–1100—Viking invasions carry Norse religion into northern Europe

from 12th century—Benin civilization in Nigeria

1100–1400—empire of Mali in West Africa

1300–1600—empire of Songhay in West Africa

1325–1521 Aztec Empire in Meso-America

early 15th century–1531—Inka Empire in South America

from 1492—European colonialists invade indigenous cultures in Americas

from 1550—slave trade introduces African religions into Americas

1992—Hopi Message to the U.N. General Assembly

REVIEW QUESTIONS

1   What do you think is meant by the Dagara song: "My little family I leave today./My great Family I meet tomorrow"?
2   Who were the six grandfathers and what powers did they give Black Elk?
3   What is Tlakaelel's view of life, death, and ancestor spirits?

DISCUSSION QUESTIONS

1   Describe how basic assumptions of industrial society's worldview differ from indigenous sacred ways worldviews.
2   Do you think visions such as those of Malidoma Somé and Black Elk are "real"?
3   Do the sacred ways of indigenous people have anything of value to offer to modern society?

INFORMATION RESOURCES

AFRICAN SACRED WAYS

Isizoh, Chidi Denis, ed. "African Traditional Religion."
<http://www.afrikaworld.net>

Karenga, Maulana, ed. "Kwanzaa."
<http://www.OfficialKwanzaaWebsite.org>

Lawson, E. Thomas. *Religions of Africa: Traditions in Transformation*. Prospect Heights, IL: Waveland Press, 1985.

Mbiti, John S. *African Religions and Philosophy*. New York: Praeger, 1969.

Middleton, John, ed. *Encyclopedia of Africa South of the Sahara*. 4 vols. New York: Scribner, 1987.

Murray, Larry, et al., eds. *Encyclopedia of African American Religions*. New York: Garland, 1993.

Ray, Ben C., *et al.*, eds. "African Religions," in *Encyclopedia of Religion,* ed. Lindsay Jones. 2nd ed. Vol. 1, pp. 83–119. New York: Macmillan, 2005.

Wilson, Monica. "Southern African Religions," in *Encyclopedia of Religion*, ed. Lindsay Jones. 2nd ed. Vol. 13, pp. 8655–88. New York: Macmillan, 2005.

Zahan, Dominique. *The Religion, Spirituality, and Thought of Traditional Africa.* Chicago: University of Chicago Press, 1979.

Zuesse, Evan M. *Ritual Cosmos: The Sanctification of Life in African Religions.* Athens, OH: Ohio University Press, 1979.

ABORIGINAL SACRED WAYS

Aboriginal Studies WWW Virtual Library
<http://www.ciolek.com/WWWVL-Aboriginal.html>

Australian Indigenous Spirituality and Sacred Sites
<http://www.trinity.wa.edu.au/plduffyrc/indig/sites.htm>

Berndt, R. M., and **C. H. Berndt**. *The Speaking Land: Myth and Story in Aboriginal Australia*. Ringwood, Victoria: Penguin Books, 1989.

Breeden, Stanley, and **Belinda Wright**, dirs. *Australian Aborigines*. Videorecording. National Geographic Society, 1988; distributed by Warner Brothers Home Video, a Time Warner Entertainment company.

Charlesworth, M., *et al.*, eds. *Religion in Aboriginal Australia*. St. Lucia, Queensland: University of Queensland Press, 1984.

Eliade, Mircea. *Australian Religions: An Introduction*. Ithaca, NY: Cornell University Press, 1973.

Fergie, Deane, *et al.* "Australian Indigenous Religions," in *Encyclopedia of Religion*, ed. Lindsay Jones. 2nd ed. Vol. 2, pp. 634–92. New York: Macmillan, 2005.

Lambert, Johanna, ed. *Wise Women of the Dreamtime: Aboriginal Tales of the Ancestral Powers*. Rochester, VT: Inner Traditions, 1993.

Lawlor, Robert. *Voices of the First Day: Awakening in the Aboriginal Dreamtime*. Rochester, VT: Inner Traditions, 1991.

NATIVE AMERICAN SACRED WAYS

Campbell, Joseph. *Historical Atlas of World Mythology*. 4 vols. San Francisco: Harper and Row, 1989.

Chapman, Abraham. *Literature of the American Indians*. New York: Signet New American Library, 1975.

Drury, Nevell. *Shamanism*. Shaftesbury, Dorset: Element Books, 1996.

Eliade, Mircea. *Shamanism: Archaic Techniques of Ecstasy.* Princeton, NJ: Princeton University Press, 1951/1964.

Gill, Sam D. *Native American Religions*. Belmont, CA: Wadsworth, 1982.

Halifax, Joan. *Shamanic Voices: A Survey of Visionary Narratives*. New York: Viking Penguin Arkana, 1979.

Hirschfelder, Arlene, and **Paulette Molin**. *Encyclopedia of Native American Religions.* New York: Facts on File, 1992.

Hoxie, Frederick E., ed. *Encyclopedia of North American Indians*. Boston: Houghton Mifflin, 1996.

Hultkrantz, Åke, *et al.* "North American [Indian] Religions," in *Encyclopedia of Religion,* ed. Lindsay Jones. 2nd ed. Vol. 10, pp. 6658–730. New York: Macmillan, 2005.

Indians
<http://www.indians.org>

Kehoe, Alice. *North American Indians: A Comprehensive Account.* Upper Saddle River, NJ: Prentice-Hall, 1981.

Mails, Thomas, E. *The Mystic Warriors of the Plains*. Garden City, NY: Doubleday, 1972.

Malinowski, Sharon, *et al.*, eds. *Encyclopedia of Native American Tribes*. Detroit: Gale Research, 1988.

Mann, Charles C. *1491: New Revelations of the Americas Before Columbus*. New York: Knopf, 2005.

Native America
<http://www.nativeweb.org>

Native Peoples Magazine
<http://www.nativepeoples.com>

Sturtevant, William, ed. *Handbook of North American Indians*. 20 vols. Washington, DC: Smithsonian Institution, 1988.

Weatherford, Jack. *Native Roots: How the Indians Enriched America*. New York: Fawcett Columbine, 1991.

CHAPTER 3

HINDUISM

The label "Hinduism" has been applied to a great variety of practices, beliefs, and scriptures which seem to have originated in the Indian subcontinent at least five thousand years ago and which are continuing to evolve today. This term is disputed by contemporary scholars who question the idea that "Hindu" refers to any particular institutionalized religion. They prefer the term "**Sanatana Dharma**," meaning the ageless way of moral order, duty, and natural law in the cosmos. At the same time, the term "Hindu-ness" is being waved as a banner by those using "Hindu" identity as a political rallying point.

Sanatana Dharma encompasses ancient mystical texts referring to the formless and transcendent Self, abstract philosophical treatises that disagree with each other about the truth of existence, and a wealth of ascetic meditation practices for realization of the eternal. It also includes a large pantheon of deities, many of whom may be individually worshipped as the totality of divinity and yet may coexist with other deities, even in the same temples. Devotees are free to choose their own favorite manifestations of the Divine. Today, as from ancient times, deities are worshipped with offerings of grains and clarified butter placed in sacred fires, with the waving of oil lamps, with fragrances and flowers, and with song and chants. In addition, villagers worship their local goddesses and gods, many of whom are unknown elsewhere.

Despite its great diversity, Sanatana Dharma has certain underlying themes. One is a belief in **reincarnation**: the idea that we are born again and again. Our lives are molded by our **karma**: the positive or negative effects of our previous thoughts and actions. Human life should reflect the order of the cosmos, and thus one has social obligations and a certain social standing defined by one's hereditary **caste**. Through good actions, lofty thoughts, detachment from the illusory and ephemeral material world, and profound meditation on the Absolute or self-surrendering love for any one of its divine manifestations, one may gradually achieve enlightenment, merge with Ultimate Reality, and escape from the karmic wheel of rebirths.

"Hinduism" has spread far beyond India, initially carried by emigrants and more recently by growing Western interest in its ancient wisdom and spiritual practices. It is currently undergoing a vibrant renaissance, with many new temples being built around the world and staffed by a growing number of **brahman pandits** (those of the hereditary priestly caste who are learned in the ancient ways and scriptures). Issues that are being disputed today include the politicizing of "Hinduness," the status of women, and the traditional system of castes which is still deeply entrenched in India.

Sruti texts

Sacred Texts

According to orthodox Hindu scholarship, the ancient scriptures of Sanatana Dharma are divided into two categories. One is the **sruti** texts which were "heard" by ancient **rishis** (enlightened sages) in profound and ascetic meditation, after they had so thoroughly cleansed their minds that they were transparent to eternal truth. The other category is the subsequent **smrti** texts, which explain the hidden meanings of the *sruti* texts for wider audiences in later, less enlightened ages.

The foundational *sruti* texts for most forms of Sanatana Dharma are the **Vedas.** Scholars think that they were written down by about 1500 BCE but represent a much older orally transmitted tradition. According to Hindu belief, the *Vedas* were heard by the *rishis* and then written down in 3102 BCE at the beginning of **Kali Yuga**, the current dark age, by the sage Vyasa. The language is terse poetic **Sanskrit**, whose sounds are said to evoke the realities to which they refer but whose deep meanings are not easily translated or fully understood.

Hymn to Agni, God of Fire from the *Rig Vedas*

The oldest of the *Vedas* are the *Rig Vedas*. They consist largely of invocations of different gods or goddesses, such as Usha, goddess of dawn, or Agni, the god of fire, which have been used since ancient times to carry offerings to the Unseen. These deities have also been understood metaphysically as abstract forces within the oneness of Creation. The extract below, a hymn to Agni, comes from Book 4 of the *Rig Vedas*.

Your envoy who possesses all, Immortal, bearer of your gifts,
Best worshipper, I woo with song.
He, Mighty, knows the gift of wealth, he knows the deep recess of heaven:
He shall bring hitherward the Gods.
He knows, a God himself, to guide Gods to the righteous in his home:
He gives e'en treasures that we love.
He is the Herald: well-informed, he doth his errand to and fro,
Knowing the deep recess of heaven.
May we be they who gratify Agni with sacrificial gifts,
Who cherish and enkindle him.
Illustrious for wealth are they, and hero deeds, victorious,
Who have served Agni reverently.
So unto us, day after day, may riches craved by many come,

And power and might spring up for us.
That holy Singer in his strength shoots forth his arrows swifter than
The swift shafts of the tribes of men.

Hymn on Creation   from the *Rig Vedas*

This hymn is from Book 10 of the *Rig Vedas*. It illustrates the philosophical sophis-
tication of the realization of ancient *rishis*. They sat in profound meditation to
explore the mysteries of primordial time before anything existed in the material universe. It is interesting to compare this passage with the theories of modern science
about the origins of the cosmos.

Then was not non-existent nor existent: there was no realm of air, no sky
    beyond it.
What covered in, and where? and what gave shelter? Was water there,
    unfathomed depth of water?
Death was not then, nor was there aught immortal: no sign was there, the
    day's and night's divider.
That One Thing,[1] breathless, breathed by its own nature: apart from it was
    nothing whatsoever.
Darkness there was: at first concealed in darkness this All was
    indiscriminated chaos.
All that existed then was void and formless: by the great power of Warmth
    was born that Unit.
Thereafter rose Desire in the beginning, Desire, the primal seed and germ of
    Spirit.
Sages who searched with their heart's thought discovered the existent's
    kinship in the non-existent.
Transversely was their severing line[2] extended: what was above it then, and
    what below it?
There were begetters, there were mighty forces, free action here and energy
    up yonder.
Who verily knows and who can here declare it, whence it was born and
    whence comes this creation?
The Gods are later than this world's production. Who knows then whence it
    first came into being?
He, the first origin of this creation, whether he formed it all or did not form
    it,
Whose eye controls this world in highest heaven, he verily knows it, or
    perhaps he knows not.

SOURCE: *The Hymns of the Rgveda*, trans. Ralph T. H. Griffith. New rev. ed. Delhi: Motilal Banarsidass,
1973, pp. 206, 633–4

---

1 That One Thing—the single primordial substance out of which the universe was made.
2 Severing line—a line drawn by the *rishis* to divide the upper world from the lower, to bring duality
out of unity.

Realise the Brahman   from the *Upanishads*

Brahma and Tolerance

Probably the latest of the *Vedas* are the **Upanishads**. Scholars think that they were recorded perhaps around 1000 to 500 BCE. They are profound and haunting reflections on ultimate truth as realized by the *rishis* and transmitted to their students. The extract below is from chapter 2 of *Mundaka Upanishad*. It describes the method of attaining the goal of spiritual striving: the **Brahman**, the undifferentiated, nonmanifest Being, the essential underlying Reality. **Om** is considered the primordial sound vibration by which everything was created; the **atman** is the individual soul.

The wisdom of the Upanishads is like a powerful bow. Make your intelligence a sharp arrow. Concentrate. Use the bow and the arrow to find your mark, the *Brahman*.

The syllable *om* is the bow, the *atman* is the arrow. It is said that the *Brahman* is the object of the bow and the arrow. Do not hesitate in trying to achieve your aim. Be as unmoving as the arrow and attain your target.

Realise the *Brahman* in whom can be found heaven, the earth, and the atmosphere. In him reside your senses and your heart. Forget everything else and attain the one and only *Brahman*. That is the way to salvation.

The spokes of a wheel surround the nave. Like that, the veins surround the heart. And in the heart is the being with many forms. He is the *Brahman*. Meditate on him, meditate on his symbol, the syllable *om*. May you be blessed so that you may cross the ocean of ignorance.

He is the fount of all wisdom; he is omniscient. The *Brahman* resides in the radiance of the heart. He rules over the mind and life. He is bliss. He is immortality. The learned ones are those who can visualise the *Brahman* in their own *atmans*.

He is the cause. He is action. When an individual visualises the *Brahman*, his heart is freed from all bondage. All his doubts are dispelled. He rises above the confines of mere action.

The *Brahman* is supreme and radiant. He has no form and he banishes all ignorance. He is like a sword in a scabbard. He is pure and full of energy. It is he who makes all objects shine. It is only the learned ones who know of the *Brahman*.

The sun cannot manifest the *Brahman*, nor can the moon or the stars. Lightning cannot make him manifest. How can the fire possibly manifest him? It is because the *Brahman* is radiant that the entire universe shines. All other objects draw their radiance from him.

The *Brahman* is in the forefront and he is everything. The *Brahman* is to the back, he is to the north and the south. He is above and below. This universe is nothing but the supreme *Brahman*.

SOURCE: *Mundaka Upanishad*, in *The Upanishads*, trans. Bibek Debroy and Dipavali Debroy. 2nd ed. Delhi: Books for All, 1995, chapter 2, pp. 64–6

Smrti texts

According to classical Hindu thought, the sublime realizations recorded in the *Upanishads* cannot be understood by the masses. In the current long period of darkest ignorance and irreligion, Kali Yuga, more popular scriptures and forms of worship are needed. Thus great epic poems, lengthy descriptions of the gods and goddesses, and codes of moral conduct have been added to the scriptural treasury of Sanatana Dharma.

I am the Beginning and the End

from the *Bhagavad Gita*

Benares and
Reincarnation

One of the two greatest Indian narratives is the *Mahabharata*, a lengthy semi-historical depiction of events thought to have taken place in approximately 1000 BCE, as two rival branches of a great family both laid claims to a kingdom near what is now Delhi. Its one hundred thousand verses depict all that is noble and ignoble in human nature. They include a major text of Hindu philosophy, the *Bhagavad Gita*. In it, Krishna, one of the major Hindu deities, gives spiritual instruction to Arjuna on the threshold of a great battle. Here, Krishna reveals the "most profound secret"—personal knowledge of God. In Hinduism, any one deity may be understood as the totality of divinity. Thus Krishna describes himself as all-pervasive creator of all that is, the "eternal source of all," and also as the One Being who can say, "I am what is and what is not."

I pervade the entire universe in my unmanifested form. All creatures find their existence in me, but I am not limited by them. Behold my divine mystery! These creatures do not really dwell in me, and though I bring them forth and support them, I am not confined within them. They move in me as the winds move in every direction in space.

At the end of the eon these creatures return to unmanifested matter; at the beginning of the next cycle I send them forth again. Controlling my *prakriti*,[3] again and again I bring forth these myriad forms and subject them to the laws of *prakriti*. None of these actions binds me, Arjuna. I am unattached to them, so they do not disturb my nature.

Under my watchful eye the laws of nature take their course. Thus is the world set in motion; thus the animate and the inanimate are created.

The foolish do not look beyond physical appearances to see my true nature as the Lord of all creation. The knowledge of such deluded people is empty; their lives are fraught with disaster and evil and their work and hopes are all in vain.

But truly great souls seek my divine nature. They worship me with a one-pointed mind, having realized that I am the eternal source of all. Constantly striving, they make firm their resolve and worship me without wavering. Full of devotion, they sing of my divine glory.

---

3 *Prakriti*—the basic energy from which the mental and physical worlds take shape.

Others follow the path of *jnana*,[4] spiritual wisdom. They see that where there is One, that One is me; where there are many, all are me; they see my face everywhere.

I am the ritual and the sacrifice; I am true medicine and the *mantram*.[5] I am the offering and the fire which consumes it, and he to whom it is offered.

I am the father and mother of this universe, and its grandfather too; I am its entire support. I am the sum of all knowledge, the purifier, the syllable *Om*, I am the sacred scriptures, the *Rik, Yajur,* and *Sama Vedas.*

I am the goal of life, the Lord and support of all, the inner witness, the abode of all. I am the only refuge, the one true friend; I am the beginning, the staying, and the end of creation; I am the womb and the eternal seed.

I am heat; I give and withhold the rain. I am immortality and I am death; I am what is and what is not.

Those who follow the rituals given in the *Vedas,* who offer sacrifices and take *soma*,[6] free themselves from evil and attain the vast heaven of the gods, where they enjoy celestial pleasures. When they have enjoyed these fully, their merit is exhausted and they return to this land of death. Thus observing Vedic rituals but caught in an endless chain of desires, they come and go.

Those who worship me and meditate on me constantly, without any other thought, I will provide for all their needs.

Those who worship other gods with faith and devotion also worship me, Arjuna, even if they do not observe the usual forms. I am the object of all worship, its enjoyer and Lord.

But those who fail to realize my true nature must be reborn. Those who worship the *devas*[7] will go to the realm of the *devas*; those who worship their ancestors will be united with them after death. Those who worship phantoms will become phantoms; but my devotees will come to me.

Whatever I am offered in devotion with a pure heart—a leaf, a flower, fruit, or water—I partake of that love offering. Whatever you do, make it an offering to me—the food you eat, the sacrifices you make, the help you give, even your suffering. In this way you will be freed from the bondage of *karma,* and from its results both pleasant and painful. Then, firm in renunciation and **yoga**, with your heart free, you will come to me.

I look upon all creatures equally; none are less dear to me and none more dear. But those who worship me with love live in me, and I come to life in them.

Even a sinner becomes holy when he worships me alone with firm resolve. Quickly his soul conforms to **dharma** and he attains to boundless

---

4 *Jnana*—higher wisdom.
5 *Mantram*—a Holy Name or spiritual formula.
6 *Soma*—an intoxicating drink used by worshippers in Vedic India.
7 *Devas*—gods or goddesses, divine beings.

peace. Never forget this, Arjuna: no one who is devoted to me will ever come to harm.

All those who take refuge in me, whatever their birth, race, sex, or caste, will attain the supreme goal; this realization can be attained even by those whom society scorns. Kings and sages too seek this goal with devotion. Therefore, having been born in this transient and forlorn world, give all your love to me. Fill your mind with me; love me; serve me; worship me always. Seeking me in your heart, you will at last be united with me.

SOURCE: *Bhagavad Gita*, trans. Eknath Easwaran. Delhi: Arkana/Penguin Books, 1986, chapter 9, pp. 132–6

Rama, Sita, and Lakshman Enter the Forest

from the *Ramayana*

The greatest examples of noble human conduct which continue to inspire Hindus today are Rama and his wife Sita. They are central characters in a long epic poem, the *Ramayana*, which was compiled in its present form approximately 400 BCE to 200 CE. In brief, Rama, noble son of King Dasaratha by one of his three wives, Kausalya, was about to be crowned king. But instead, Rama was banished to the forest for 14 years by the king, due to the machinations of an evil friend of his stepmother Kaikeyi. Rama's wife Sita and his stepbrother Lakshman, son of Kaikeyi, nobly insisted on accompanying him. During their sojourn in the forest, Sita was kidnapped by the king of the demons. A terrific battle ensued in which Rama was at last victorious, and he and Sita returned to the capital, Ayodhya. In some parts of India, Lord Rama is worshipped as the Lord Incarnate. The following excerpt (from chapter 19 of the *Ramayana*), in which Prince Rama first enters the forest to live as an ascetic, illustrates his exceptionally noble qualities.

The chariot reached the bank of the Ganga. They proceeded along the bank, admiring the beauty of the river. Finding a spot of surpassing charm, Raama [Rama] said: "We shall spend the night here."

Untying the horses, they sat under a tree. Guha, the chief of the region, having learnt already from his men that Raama would be coming there, came forward with his retinue to greet Raama and Lakshmana [Lakshman].

He had unbounded love for the Royal family and for Raama. Being the chieftain of the tribes who dwelt on the banks of Ganga, he was a man of great prestige and power. Raama and Lakshmana rose to greet Guha, even while the latter was still at some distance from them. Guha welcomed them with a hearty embrace, saying: "Regard this land as your own. This place is as much yours as is Ayodhya. Who can hope to have a guest like you? It is indeed my good fortune."

Guha had prepared a lavish entertainment. He said "Feel perfectly at home and happy in my kingdom. You may spend all the fourteen years with us here. You will not lack anything, I assure you. Looking after you will be a pleasure and privilege to me. Be gracious enough to accept my hospitality."

Warmly embracing Guha again, Raama said: "Brother, I know how deep is your love for me. Your wish is itself as good as hospitality rendered. I am bound by my vows and must refuse anything more. I have come to dwell in the forest and not to enjoy life as a chieftain's guest. These horses are my dear father's favourites. Pray feed them well. We shall be content with simple food and rest for the night."

They lay under the tree for the night. . . .

Early next morning, Raama told Lakshmana: "We must now cross the river. Ask Guha to make ready a boat big enough for crossing this broad river." Guha ordered his men to get this done and informed Raama.

Sumantra bowed low and stood before Raama seeking his further commands.

Raama understood Sumantra's unuttered grief and, laying his hand on Sumantra's shoulders, said: "Sumantra, return to Ayodhya with all speed and be at the side of the King. Your duty is now to look after him."

"O Raama," exclaimed Sumantra, "rectitude, learning and culture seem to be of no value. You and your brother and Vaidehi are going to live in the forest. What is going to be our lot? How are we going to fare under Kaikeyi's rule?" He now wept like a child.

Wiping the tears from Sumantra's eyes, Raama said: "Our family has known no nobler friend than you. It will be your task to console my father. His heart is riven by grief. Whatever his commands, carry them out dutifully. Do not ask yourself whether he wants a thing for himself or with a view to pleasing Kaikeyi. Avoid giving him any pain of mind. Have no anxiety about us.

"You should say this on my behalf to my aged father who is stricken with a grief he never knew before. Clasp his feet as you have seen me do, and assure him from me that none of us—not I nor Lakshmana, nor Seeta—feel injured or sorry at having been sent away from Ayodhya. We look forward to fourteen years of forest life which will speed on happy wings, and then surely we shall return to his feet for blessings. Give our love to my mother Kausalya, and tell her that protected by her blessings we are well and give a like message to my stepmothers, specially to Kaikeyi, lest she should think we have parted in anger. Tell the Mahaaraaja that it is my earnest prayer that he should hasten with the installation of Bharata, so that he may be a comfort to him in our absence."

But Sumantra, unable to restrain his grief, burst out: "How am I to return and with what words can I give comfort?" And when he looked at the empty chariot, he wept and said: "How shall I drive this chariot that stands desolate without you?"

Once again Raama spoke words of comfort and courage to Sumantra and urged on him the duty of patience, and sent him home.

"Guha," said Raama, "I could indeed spend fourteen years in your kingdom as you desire. But would that be fulfilling my vow? I have left Ayodhya to fulfil my father's pledge. I must therefore lead the life of a *tapasvi*.[8] I must not touch dishes daintily cooked and served. We have to live only on fruits, roots and permissible kinds of meat such as we offer in the sacrificial fire."

Comforting Guha thus, the brothers got their locks matted with the milk of the banyan. They helped Seeta into the boat and then got into it themselves. Guha bade the boatmen to row it across.

The boatmen took them quickly across the river. At midstream Seeta offered a prayer to the goddess of the river: "Devi, help us fulfil our vow and return safe to our homeland."

They talked as they went on. They reached the farther bank of Ganga. And there, for the first time, the three stood alone, unattended by friends!

"Lakshmana, you are my sole armed guard now," said Raama. "You will go first. Seeta will follow. And I shall walk behind you both. We must save Seeta as far as possible from the hardships of forest life. Hereafter there will be none to keep us company and no fun or amusement."

Raama's thoughts went to his mother Kausalya.

"Lakshmana," he said, "should you not go back to Ayodhya and look after mother Kausalya and Sumitra Devi? I shall manage my forest stay somehow."

Lakshmana replied: "Forgive me, brother; I am not going back to Ayodhya." Raama indeed expected no other answer.

SOURCE: *Ramayana*, trans. C. Rajagopalachari. 27th ed. Mumbai: Bharatiya Vidya Bhavan, 1990, pp. 86–9

Caste

Duties of the Four Castes from the *Manu smrti*

Hindu legal and social mores are codified in *The Laws of Manu*, or *Manu smrti*, compiled into 12 books by 100 to 300 CE. These codes are regarded by some as propaganda by the priestly *brahman* caste, for they give divine authority for the division of humanity into four castes: the priestly *brahmans*, the warrior *kshatriyas*, the merchant *vaishyas*, and the servant class, *shudras*. The extract below, from *Manu smrti* chapter 1, describes how the castes were assigned different duties.

For the sake of the preservation of this entire creation [Purusha],[9] the exceedingly resplendent one, assigned separate duties to the classes which had sprung from his mouth, arms, thighs, and feet.

Teaching, studying, performing sacrificial rites, so too making others perform sacrificial rites, and giving away and receiving gifts—these he assigned to the brāhmans.

Protection of the people, giving away of wealth, performance of sacrificial rites, study, and nonattachment to sensual pleasures—these are, in short, the duties of a kshatriya.

8 *Tapasvi*—renunciate.
9 Purusha—the Self, Brahman, the all-pervading Supreme Being.

Tending of cattle, giving away of wealth, performance of sacrificial rites, study, trade and commerce, usury, and agriculture—these are the occupations of a vaishya.

The Lord has prescribed only one occupation for a shūdra, namely, service without malice of even these other three classes.

Man is stated to be purer above the navel than below it; hence his mouth has been declared to be the purest part by the Self-existent One.

On account of his origin from the best limb of the Cosmic Person, on account of his seniority, and on account of the preservation by him of the Veda—the brāhman is in respect of dharma the lord of this entire creation. . . .

Of created beings, those which are animate are the best; of the animate, those who subsist by means of their intellect; of the intelligent, men are the best; and of men, the brāhmans are traditionally declared to be the best . . .

The very birth of a brāhman is the eternal incarnation of dharma. For he is born for the sake of dharma and tends toward becoming one with the Brahman. . . .

SOURCE: W. Theodore de Bary, ed., *Sources of Indian Tradition*. New York and London: Columbia University Press, 1958, vol. 1, pp. 220–1

The Faithful Wife from the *Manu smrti*

Manu smrti also justifies the subjugation of women to men. In this extract, from *Manu smrti* chapter 5, the virtues of the faithful wife are described.

The husband who wedded her with sacred texts, always gives happiness to his wife, both in season and out of season, in this world and in the next.

Though destitute of virtue, or seeking pleasure (elsewhere), or devoid of good qualities, (yet) a husband must be constantly worshipped as a god by a faithful wife.

No sacrifice, no vow, no fast must be performed by women apart (from their husbands); if a wife obeys her husband, she will for that (reason alone) be exalted in heaven.

A faithful wife, who desires to dwell (after death) with her husband, must never do anything that might displease him who took her hand, whether he be alive or dead.

At her pleasure let her emaciate her body by (living on) pure flowers, roots, and fruit; but she must never even mention the name of another man after her husband has died.

Until death let her be patient (of hardships), self-controlled, and chaste, and strive (to fulfil) that most excellent duty which (is prescribed) for wives who have one husband only.

SOURCE: Serinity Young, ed., *An Anthology of Sacred Texts by and about Women*. New York: Crossroad, 1995, p. 278

Desire to Know the Brahman   by Sankara

The *Vedas* gave rise to a number of different schools of Hindu philosophy, which sought to explain the texts according to human logic. One of the major ones was that of Sankhya, classically attributed to the sage Kapila, who made clear distinctions between spirit and matter. An opposing school is that of Advaita Vedanta, whose greatest teacher was the highly influential Sankara (c. 788–820 CE or earlier). In his nondualistic philosophy, the absolute ground of being is Brahman, the eternal and unchanging that lies within the world of changing appearances. According to Advaita Vedanta, realization of this eternal undifferentiated Self within oneself is the greatest goal of human life and the means to liberation from illusion. This perspective became predominant in Hindu philosophy.

Superimposition is the seeing of a thing in something which is not that; thus, when son, wife, etc., are all right or not, one considers one's own self as all right or not, one superimposes external attributes on the self even so does one superimpose on the self the attributes of the *body* when one considers that "I am corpulent, I am lean, I am fair, I stand, I go, I jump"; similarly attributes of the *senses* when one says, "I am dumb, one-eyed, impotent, deaf, blind"; and in the same manner the properties of the *internal organs*, e.g., desire, volition, cogitation, and resolution. Even so, man superimposes the self[10] presented in the cognition of "I" on the inner Self which is the witness of all the activities of the internal organ; and that inner Self, the very opposite and the witness of all, on the inner organ.

Thus without beginning or end, existing in the very nature of things, this superimposition which is of the form of a knowledge that is subject to sublation and is responsible for the agency and experience of man, is something which the whole world knows. It is for casting away this superimposition which is the cause of evil and for gaining the knowledge of the oneness of the Self that all the Upanishads are begun. . . .

The Brahman's existence is well known, because it is the Self of all; everyone realizes the existence of the Self, for none says, "I am not"; if the existence of the self is not well known, the whole world of beings would have the notion "*I* do not exist." And the self is the Brahman.

It may be contended that if the Brahman is well known in the world as the Self, it has already been known, and again it becomes something which need not be inquired into. It is not like that, for there are differences of opinion about its particular nature. Ordinary people and the materialists are of the view that the self is just the body qualified by intelligence; others think that it is the intelligent sense-organs themselves that are the self; still others, that it is the mind; some hold it as just the fleeting consciousness of the moment; some others as the void; certain others say that there is some entity, which is different

---

10 Self—the individual soul, which is ultimately one with the universal Self, or Brahman.

from the body, etc., and which transmigrates,[11] does and enjoys; some consider him as the enjoyer and not as the doer; some that there is, as different from the above entity, the Lord who is omniscient and omnipotent. According to still others, it is the inner Self of the enjoyer. Thus, resorting to reasonings and texts and semblances thereof, there are many who hold divergent views. Hence one who accepts some view without examining it might be prevented from attaining the ultimate good, and might also come to grief. Therefore, by way of setting forth the inquiry into the Brahman, here is begun the discussion of the meaning of the texts of the *Upanishads*, aided by such ratiocination[12] as is in conformity to Scripture and having for its fruit the Supreme Beatitude....

It is by the examination of the meaning of the scriptural texts and determining it exactly that Brahman-realization is achieved, not by inference and other sources of knowledge.

SOURCE: W. Theodore de Bary, ed., *Sources of Indian Tradition*. New York and London: Columbia University Press, 1958, vol. 1, pp. 313–17

Yoga Sutras by Patanjali

Om

A third major philosophical system based on the *Upanishads* is the school of Yoga, traditionally thought to have been given organized form by the sage Patanjali by 200 BCE. The Yogic system combines ancient meditation practices with a philosophy which is similar to that of Sankhya, but asserts the existence of a supreme God. These excerpts are from Patanjali's *Yoga Sutras*, 196 *sutras* or sayings methodically delineating a system for attaining the highest state of consciousness.

Now Yoga is explained.

Yoga is restraining the activities of the mind.

At that time, the perceiver rests in his own true nature.

When the mind is not concentrated, the perceiver identifies with its modifications.

There are five types of thought waves, some of which are painful and some of which are not.

The five kinds of thought waves are correct knowledge, erroneous understanding, verbal delusion, sleep and memory....

Their control is brought about by practice and non-attachment.

Abhyasa is the continuous effort towards firmly establishing the restraint of thought waves.

Practice becomes firmly grounded on being continued over a long period of time without interruption and with sincere devotion.

Vairagya, or non-attachment, is that state of consciousness in which the cravings for objects both seen and unseen is controlled through mastery of the Will.

---

11 Transmigrates—the soul passes into a different body after death.
12 Ratiocination—logical reasoning.

The highest state of non-attachment stems from awareness of Purusha; it renounces even the three qualities of nature.

Samprajnata samadhi (*samadhi*[13] with consciousness) is accompanied by reasoning, discrimination, bliss, and an awareness of individuality....

Asamprajnata samadhi (seedless state) is reached when all mental activity ceases and only unmanifested impressions remain in the mind.

Liberation comes quickly when the desire for it is intense....

[Success is swift for those who are] devoted to Ishwara.[14]

Ishwara is that particular center of Divine Consciousness that is untouched by misery, Karma, or desires.

In Him lies the seed of omniscience.

Unlimited by time, He is the Teacher of all other teachers, from the most ancient of times.

He manifests in the word OM.

Constant repetition of OM and meditation on its meaning lead to enlightening introspection and elimination of all obstacles.

The obstacles to Realization are disease, mental torpor, doubt, indifference, laziness, craving for pleasure, delusion, inability to practice and maintain concentration, and restlessness of mind due to distractions.

Mental pain, depression, physical nervousness, and irregular breathing are the symptoms of a distracted state of mind.

In order to remove these obstacles one should meditate on one aspect of Truth.

The mind becomes clear through the cultivation of friendliness, kindness, contentment, and indifference towards happiness, vice and virtue.

[Regulated] expulsion and retention of the breath [also clear the mind].

Steadiness of the mind is easily established when the higher senses come into operation,

Or the state of luminescence which is beyond sorrow,

Or by fixing the mind on one who has transcended human passions and attachments,

Or knowledge gained in dreams or deep sleep,

Or by meditation on what is agreeable.

Mastery extends from the smallest atom to infinity.

For the person who has controlled the waves of the mind through meditation, there is a merging of the perceiver, perceived, and perception, just as a crystal assumes the color of the background.

SOURCE: Swami Vishnu Devananda, ed., *Meditation and Mantras*. New York: Om Lotus Publishing, 1975, pp. 133–54.

---

13 *Samadhi*—the superconscious state of spiritual absorption.
14 Ishwara—God with manifest attributes, such as omniscience, mercy, kindness, and love, as opposed to Purusha or Brahman—God as pure, abstract essence.

In Praise of Durga   from the *Siva Purana*

Whereas philosophical texts were for the highly learned, a much more widespread form of *smrti* scriptures are the **Puranas**. These are Sanskrit poetic texts which were probably set down in written form between 500 and 1500 CE, although they contain material which is much older. This popular devotional literature gives elaborate depictions of various gods and goddesses and their miraculous powers and exploits, as known to their devotees. Excerpted first here is a passage from the *Siva Purana*, in which the powers of the goddess Durga are briefly described. Seated on her lion, she defeated the demons who were threatening to overrun the world. She is also known as the consort and spiritual power of the god Siva.

I began a continuous laudatory prayer of the Goddess Durgā, the beloved of Śiva, the creator of the universe, of the nature of Vidyā and Avidyā[15] and identical with the pure supreme Brahman.

I salute the Goddess who is omnipresent, eternal, for whom there is no support, who is never distressed, who is the mother of the three deities, who is the grossest of the gross and yet has no form.

O Goddess of the devas, you are Perfect Knowledge, Supreme Bliss, identical with the supreme Soul. Be pleased. Grant me the fulfilment of my task. Obeisance to you.

O celestial sage, on being thus lauded Candikā,[16] the mystic slumber, appeared before me.

Her complexion had the glossy hue of collyrium. She had comely features. She had four divine arms. She was seated on a lion. She showed the mystic gesture of granting boons by one of her hands, and pearls adorned her dishevelled hair.

Her face shone like the autumnal moon, the crescent moon bedecked her forehead. She had three eyes, looked beautiful and the nails of her lotus-like feet glistened.

O sage, seeing her who was Śiva's Energy herself, directly in front of me, my lofty shoulders bent down with devotion and I eulogized her after due obeisance.

Obeisance, obeisance, to Thee, who art in the form of Pravṛtti (Action) and Nivṛtti (Abstinence); who art in the form of creation and sustenance of the universe. Thou art the eternal Energy of the movable and the immovable beings capable of enchanting everyone.

Thou hast manifested thyself as Śrī, a garland round Keśava's form, who in the form of Earth holdest everything within, who art of yore the great Goddess causing creation and the destruction of the three worlds and art beyond the three Gunas.[17]

---

15 Vidyā and Avidyā—knowledge and ignorance.
16 Candikā—another name for Durga.
17 Gunas—the three attributes of material nature (passionate activity; darkness and inertia; and pure intelligence).

Thou art present in everything even in the essential atom and who art charmingly honoured by Yogins;[18] who art perceivable in the hearts of the Yogins purified by restraints, as well as in the path of their meditation.

Thou art the Vidyā of diverse sorts. Thou art endowed with illumination, purity and detachment. Thou assumest Kūṭastha (perpetually immovable), Avyakta (unmanifest) and Ananta (infinite) form and Thou art the eternal time holding all the worlds.

SOURCE: *Śiva Purāna*. Delhi: Motilal Banarsidass, 1970, pp. 320–1

Gods and Goddesses

The Way of Devotion from the *Bhagavata Purana*

The *Puranas* also contain instructions for worship of the gods and goddesses, according to the growing **bhakti** tradition of ecstatic devotion to one's favorite incarnation of the Divine. The feeling is that the Divine takes on human form for the sake of helping humanity, but remains pure in the midst of material life. Most popular of the *Puranas* is *Bhagavata Purana*, which describes the incarnations of the Lord in forms such as Krishna, the cowherding boy. This excerpt from the *Bhagavata Purana* describes ways of worship which are pleasing to the Lord incarnate.

One should therefore resort to a teacher, desiring to know what constitutes the supreme welfare. . . . Taking the teacher as the deity, one should learn from him the practices characteristic of the Lord's devotees. . . . First detachment from all undesirable associations, then association with the good souls, compassion, friendliness, and due humility toward all beings, purity, penance, forbearance, silence, study of sacred writings, straightforwardness, continence, nonviolence, equanimity, seeing one's own Self and the Lord everywhere, seeking solitude, freedom from home, wearing clean recluse robes, satisfying oneself with whatever comes to one, faith in the scriptures of devotion and refraining from censure of those of other schools, subjugation of mind, speech, and action, truthfulness, quietude, restraint, listening to accounts of the Lord's advents, exploits, and qualities, singing of the Lord, contemplation of the Lord of wonderful exploits, engaging in acts only for His sake, dedicating unto the Lord everything—the rites one does, gifts, penance, sacred recital, righteous conduct and whatever is dear to one like one's wife, son, house, and one's own life—cultivating friendship with those who consider the Lord as their soul and master, service to the Lord and to the world and especially to the great and good souls, sharing in the company of fellow devotees the sanctifying glory of the Lord, sharing with them one's delight, satisfaction and virtues of restraint, remembering oneself and reminding fellow-worshipers of the Lord who sweeps away all sin; bearing a body thrilled with devotion and ecstatic experience of the Lord, now in tears with some

18 Yogins—practitioners of yoga.

thought of the Lord, now laughing, now rejoicing, now speaking out, now dancing, now singing, now imitating the Lord's acts, and now becoming quiet with the blissful experience of the Supreme—such are the Lord's devotees, who behave like persons not of this world.

SOURCE: W. Theodore de Bary, ed., *Sources of Indian Tradition*. New York and London: Columbia University Press, 1958, vol. 1, pp. 333–4

Songs of the saints

Despite the wealth of ancient Sanskrit scriptures, Jainism and later Buddhism—Indian religions that were not based on the *Vedas*—gained many adherents. But with the flowering of the *bhakti* tradition, saintly devotees of the Hindu deities began to sing of their ecstatic realization of the Divine, in their own languages. The tremendous attraction of their songs in the vernacular[19] and the strength of their love, which the common people could understand, brought an upsurge of devotional worship of the Hindu deities. These saints came from all classes and were both women and men, unlike those of the classical Sanskrit tradition, which was controlled by *brahman* men.

Ravi Das was a fourteenth- to fifteenth-century shoemaker, whose occupation meant that he was considered of extremely low caste. However, his poetry reveals the heights of his realization.

The World of Illusion by Ravi Das

There is but One God. He is obtained by the True Guru's[20] grace.
When there was egoism in me, Thou wert not with me.
Now that Thou art there, there is no egoism,
As huge waves are raised by the wind in the great ocean, but are only water
     in water.
O Lord of wealth, what should I say about this delusion?
What we deem a thing to be, in reality it is not like that.

It is like a king falling asleep on his throne and becoming a beggar in dream;
His kingdom is intact, but separating from it, he suffers pain. Such indeed,
     has been my condition. . . .
Amidst all, the One Lord has assumed many forms
And He is enjoying within all hearts.
Says Ravi Das, the Lord is nearer to us than our hands and feet.
So let it happen as will naturally happen. . . .

Tell: Of what account are kingly mansion and throne without devotional
     service of the Lord?

---

19 Vernacular—the language of the people, as opposed to a classical language such as Sanskrit which was not understood by everyone.
20 True Guru—a perfectly enlightened spiritual teacher who can lead one to God-realization.

Thou hast not thought of the relish of the Lord King's Name, a relish in
    which all other relishes are forgotten.
We have become mad, we know not what we ought to know, and consider
    not what we ought to consider.
Like this our days are passing away. . . .

Lord of wealth, if Thou breakest not with me, then I will not break with
    Thee.
For if I break with Thee, with whom else shall I join?
If Thou art an earthen lamp, then I am Thy wick.
If Thou art a place of pilgrimage, then I am Thy pilgrim.
In true love I have joined with Thee, O Lord.
Attaching myself to Thee, I have broken with all others.
Wherever I go, I perform Thy service.
There is no other lord like Thee, O God. . . .

The skeleton is of bones, flesh and veins; within it abides the poor soul
    bird.
O mortal, what is mine and what is thine?
As a bird perches on a tree, so does the soul in the body.
Thou layest foundations and buildest walls.
Three and a half cubit measure of place is for thee in the end.
Thou beautifully dressest thy hair and wearest slanting turban on thy head,
But this body shall be reduced to a heap of ashes.
Lofty are thy palaces and beauteous thy brides,
But without the Lord's Name, the game is lost.

My caste is low, my lineage is lowly, and mean is my birth.
I have entered Thy sanctuary O my Luminous Lord king, says the cobbler
    Ravi Das.

SOURCE: *Guru Granth Sahib*, pp. 657–9, adapted from English translation of Manmohan Singh. 3rd ed.
Amritsar, Punjab: Shiromani Gurdwara Parbandhak Committee, 1989, pp. 2157–62

Worship Him in Silence by Lalla

Lalla was a mystic of Kashmir, so devoted to Lord Siva and detached from the world
that she forsook her brahmanic family, her marriage, and her clothing.

I, Lallā, went out far in search of Shiva [Siva], the omnipresent Lord; after
wandering, I, Lallā found Him at last within my own self, abiding in His
own home.

   Temple and image, the two that you have fashioned, are not better than
stone; the Lord is immeasurable and consists of intelligence; what is needed
to realize Him is unified concentration of breath and mind.

   Let them blame me or praise me or adore me with flowers; I become
neither joyous nor depressed, resting in myself and drunk in the nectar of
the knowledge of the pure Lord.

With the help of the gardeners called Mind and Love, plucking the flower called Steady Contemplation, offering the water of the flood of the Self's own bliss, worship the Lord with the sacred formula of silence!

SOURCE: W. Theodore de Bary, ed., *Sources of Indian Tradition*. New York and London: Columbia University Press, 1958, vol. 1, p. 355

Without Krishna I Cannot Sleep by Mirabai

Mirabai (c. 1500–50) was a princess of Rajasthan, but she was far more devoted to Lord Krishna than to her husband. When her husband died, she defied her in-laws' desire that she immolate herself along with her husband (throw herself on his funeral pyre), and instead became a wandering mendicant (beggar).

Without Krishna I cannot sleep.
Tortured by longing, I cannot sleep,
And the fire of love
Drives me to wander hither and thither.
Without the light of the Beloved
My house is dark,
And lamps do not please me.
Without the Beloved my bed is uninviting,
And I pass the nights awake.
When will my Beloved return home?
The frogs are croaking, the peacock's cry
And the cuckoo's song are heard.
Low black clouds are gathering,
Lightning flashes, stirring fear in the heart.
My eyes fill with tears.
What shall I do? Where shall I go?
Who can quench my pain?
My body has been bitten
By the snake of "absence,"
And my life is ebbing away
With every beat of the heart.
Fetch the herb quickly.
Which of my companions
Will come bringing the Beloved to meet me?
My Lord when will you come
To meet your Mīrā?
Manamohan [a generic term meaning "one who attracts minds"], the
    Charmer of Hearts,
Fills me with delight. When, my Lord,
Will you come to laugh and talk with me?

SOURCE: *The Devotional Poems of Mīrābāī*, trans. A. J. Alston. Delhi: Motilal Banarsidass, 1980, pp. 64–5

Three Poems by Kabir

Kabir (c. 1440–1518) was a weaver whose hymns are still greatly loved today by Muslims and Sikhs as well as Hindus, for they describe inner experiences that are common to mystics of all religions.

I.13 *mo ko kahāṉ ḍhūṉṟo bande*

O servant, where dost thou seek me?
Lo! I am beside thee.
I am neither in temple nor in mosque: I am neither in Kaaba[21] nor in
   Kailash:[22]
Neither am I in rites and ceremonies, nor in Yoga and renunciation.
If thou art a true seeker, thou shalt at once see Me: thou shalt meet Me in a
   moment of time.
Kabir says, "O Sadhu![23] God is the breath of all breath."

II.61 *grah candra tapan jot varat hai*

The light of the sun, the moon, and the stars shines bright:
The melody of love swells forth, and the rhythm of love's detachment beats
   the time.
Day and night, the chorus of music fills the heavens; and Kabir says
"My Beloved One gleams like the lightning flash in the sky."

Do you know how the moments perform their adoration?
Waving its row of lamps, the universe sings in worship day and night,
There are the hidden banner and the secret canopy:
There the sound of the unseen bells is heard.
Kabir says: "There adoration never ceases; there the Lord of the Universe
   sitteth on His throne."

The whole world does its works and commits its errors: but few are the
   lovers who know the Beloved.
The devout seeker is he who mingles in his heart the double currents of
   love and detachment, like the mingling of the streams of Ganges and
   Jumna;
In his heart the sacred water flows day and night; and thus the round of
   births and deaths is brought to an end.

Behold what wonderful rest is in the Supreme Spirit! and he enjoys it, who
   makes himself meet for it.
Held by the cords of love, the swing of the Ocean of Joy sways to and fro;
   and a mighty sound breaks forth in song.

---

21 Kaaba—holiest of Muslim shrines, at Mecca.
22 Kailash—legendary mountain abode of Lord Siva.
23 Sadhu—Hindu ascetic.

See what a lotus blooms there without water! and Kabir says
"My heart's bee drinks its nectar."

What a wonderful lotus it is, that blooms at the heart of the spinning
wheel of the universe! Only a few pure souls know of its true
delight.
Music is all around it, and there the heart partakes of the joy of the Infinite
Sea.
Kabir says: "Dive thou into that Ocean of sweetness: thus let all errors of life
and of death flee away."

I.36 sūr parkāś, tanh rain kahā_n pāïye

Where is the night, when the sun is shining? If it is night, then the sun
withdraws its light.
Where knowledge is can ignorance endure? If there be ignorance, then
knowledge must die.
If there be lust, how can love be there? Where there is love, there is no
lust.

Lay hold on your sword, and join in the fight. Fight, O my brother, as long
as life lasts.
Strike off your enemy's head, and there make an end of him quickly: then
come, and bow your head at your King's Durbar.[24]
He who is brave, never forsakes the battle: he who flies from it is no true
fighter.
In the field of this body a great war goes forward, against passion, anger,
pride, and greed:
It is in the kingdom of truth, contentment and purity, that this battle is
raging; and the sword that rings forth most loudly is the sword of His
Name.

Kabir says: "When a brave knight takes the field, a host of cowards is put to
flight.
It is a hard fight and a weary one, this fight of the truth-seeker: for the vow
of the truth-seeker is more hard than that of the warrior, or of the
widowed wife who would follow her husband.
For the warrior fights for a few hours, and the widow's struggle with death
is soon ended:
But the truth-seeker's battle goes on day and night, as long as life lasts it
never ceases."

SOURCE: *Songs of Kabir*, trans. Rabindranath Tagore. New York: Samuel Weiser, 1977, pp. 45–86

---

24 Durbar—court.

Modern texts

Vision of the Mother by Paramahansa Yogananda

One of the modern saints who has contributed to the global spread of Hindu principles and practices is Paramahansa Yogananda (1893–1952). His *Autobiography of
a Yogi*, first published in 1946, has awakened keen interest in the miraculous
aspects of Sanatana Dharma among people outside India.

I proceeded alone to the portico that fronts the large temple of Kali (God in
the aspect of Mother Nature). Selecting a shady spot near one of the pillars,
I sat down and assumed the lotus posture. Although it was only about seven
o'clock, the morning sun would soon be oppressive.

The world receded as I became devotionally entranced. My mind was
concentrated on Goddess Kali. Her statue in this very temple in
Dakshineswar had been the special object of adoration by the great master,
Sri Ramakrishna Paramahansa. In answer to his anguished demands, the
stone image had often taken a living form and conversed with him.

"Silent Mother of stone," I prayed, "Thou didst become filled with life at
the plea of Thy beloved devotee Ramakrishna; why dost Thou not also heed
the wails of this yearning son of Thine?"

My aspiring zeal increased boundlessly, accompanied by a divine peace.
Yet, when five hours had passed, and the Goddess whom I was inwardly
visualizing had made no response, I felt slightly disheartened. Sometimes it
is a test by God to delay the fulfilment of prayers. But He eventually appears
to the persistent devotee in whatever form he holds dear. A devout
Christian sees Jesus; a Hindu beholds Krishna, or the Goddess Kali, or an
expanding Light if his worship takes an impersonal turn.

Reluctantly I opened my eyes, and saw that the temple doors were
being locked by a priest, in conformance with a noon-hour custom. I rose
from my secluded seat on the portico and stepped into the courtyard. Its
stone surface was scorched by the midday sun; my bare feet were
painfully burned.

"Divine Mother," I silently remonstrated, "Thou didst not come to me in
vision, and now Thou art hidden in the temple behind closed doors. I wanted
to offer a special prayer to Thee today on behalf of my brother-in-law."

My inward petition was instantly acknowledged. First, a delightful cold
wave descended over my back and under my feet, banishing all discomfort.
Then, to my amazement, the temple became greatly magnified. Its large
door slowly opened, revealing the stone figure of Goddess Kali. Gradually
the statue changed into a living form, smilingly nodding in greeting, thrilling
me with joy indescribable. As if by a mystic syringe, the breath was
withdrawn from my lungs; my body became very still, though not inert.

An ecstatic enlargement of consciousness followed. I could see clearly
for several miles over the Ganges River to my left, and beyond the temple
into the entire Dakshineswar precincts. The walls of all buildings glimmered

transparently; through them I observed people walking to and fro over distant acres.

Though I was breathless and though my body remained in a strangely quiet state, I was able to move my hands and feet freely. For several minutes I experimented in closing and opening my eyes; in either state I saw distinctly the whole Dakshineswar panorama.

Spiritual sight, X-ray-like, penetrates into all matter; the divine eye is centre everywhere, circumference nowhere. I realized anew, standing there in the sunny courtyard, that when a man ceases to be a prodigal child of God, engrossed in a physical world indeed dream, baseless as a bubble, he reinherits his eternal realms. If escapism be a need of man, cramped in his narrow personality, can any other escape compare with that of omnipresence?

SOURCE: Paramahansa Yogananda, *Autobiography of a Yogi*. 2nd ed. Mumbai: Jaico Publishing House, 1975, pp. 207–9

Contemporary issues

Sanatana Dharma has given birth to many reformers who warned against practicing the ancient rituals without inner engagement, or who protested what they regarded as social injustices institutionalized by brahmanic Hinduism. Among these are the deeply embedded caste system and the subordination and abuse of women (which persists side by side with worship of the goddess).

Untouchability by Mahatma Gandhi

The father of the Indian independence movement, Mahatma Gandhi (1869–1948), was a vehement critic of the caste system, which causes some people to be considered "untouchable" by those of higher castes. He also fought against Hindu exclusivism[25] in a country that is home to large numbers of people from other faiths, trying to establish the principle of secularism,[26] meaning that the government would not favor any one religion and all would enjoy equal privileges.

Gandhi, Women and Untouchability

There is an ineffaceable blot that Hinduism today carries with it. I have declined to believe that it has been handed down to us from immemorial times. I think that this miserable, wretched, enslaving spirit of "untouchableness" must have come to us when we were at our lowest ebb. This evil has stuck to us and still remains with us....

Untouchability as it is practised in Hinduism today is, in my opinion, a sin against God and man and is, therefore, like a poison slowly eating into the very vitals of Hinduism. In my opinion, it has no sanction whatsoever in

25 Exclusivism—belief in the validity of only one religion.
26 Secularism—although usually meaning a non-sacred perspective, in modern India "secularism" means governmental non-preference for any religion.

the Hindu *Shastras*[27] taken as a whole. . . . It has degraded both the untouchables and the touchables. It has stunted the growth of nearly 40 million human beings. They are denied even the ordinary amenities of life. The sooner, therefore, it is ended, the better for Hinduism, the better for India, and perhaps better for mankind in general.

So far as I am concerned with the untouchability question it is one of life and death for Hinduism. As I have said repeatedly, if untouchability lives, Hinduism perishes, and even India perishes; but if untouchability is eradicated from the Hindu heart, root and branch, then Hinduism has a definite message for the world. I have said the first thing to hundreds of audiences but not the latter part. Now that is the utterance of a man who accepts Truth as God. It is therefore no exaggeration. If untouchability is an integral part of Hinduism, the latter is a spent bullet. But untouchability is a hideous untruth. My motive in launching the anti-untouchability campaign is clear. What I am aiming at is not every Hindu touching an "untouchable," but every touchable Hindu driving untouchability from his heart, going through a complete change of heart.

It is bad enough when dictated by selfish motives to consider ourselves high and other people low. But it is not only worse but a double wrong when we tack religion to an evil like untouchability. It, therefore, grieves me when learned pundits come forward and invoke the authority of *Shastras* for a patent evil like untouchability. I have said, and I repeat today, that we, Hindus, are undergoing a period of probation. Whether we desire it or not, untouchability is going. But if during this period of probation we repent for the sin, if we reform and purify ourselves, history will record that one act as a supreme act of purification on the part of the Hindus. But if, through the working of the time spirit, we are compelled to do things against our will and Harijans come into their own, it will be no credit to the Hindus or to Hinduism. But I go a step further and say that if we fail in this trial, Hinduism and Hindus will perish.

Harijan means "a man of God." All the religions of the world describe God preeminently as the Friend of the friendless, Help of the helpless, and Protector of the weak. The rest of the world apart, in India who can be more friendless, helpless or weaker than the 40 million or more Hindus of India who are classified as "untouchables"? If, therefore, any body of people can be fitly described as men of God, they are surely these helpless, friendless and despised people. Hence . . . I have always adopted Harijan as the name signifying "untouchables." Not that the change of name brings about any change of status but one may at least be spared the use of a term which is itself one of reproach. When caste Hindus have of their own inner conviction and, therefore, voluntarily, got rid of the present-day untouchability we shall all be called Harijans, for, according to my humble opinion, caste Hindus will then have found favour with God and may, therefore, be fitly described as His men.

SOURCE: Mahatma Gandhi, "For the Well-Being of the Nation," in *The Message of Mahatma Gandhi*, ed. U. S. Mohan Rao. Delhi: Ministry of Information and Broadcasting, 1968, pp. 90–2

27 *Shastras*—Hindu law books, such as *Manu smrti*.

Hindu-ness by V. D. Savarkar

The exclusivist movement has increased in recent times and has gained considerable political power. A major document encouraging Hindu exclusivism and nationalism was written in 1923 by V. D. Savarkar (1883–1966), who was opposed to harmonious coexistence with Muslims and to Gandhian principles. Many contemporary scholars, however, refute the idea that Sanatana Dharma supports any exclusive claims to truth. They argue that "Hindu-ness" is being used as a political rallying point, for there is no single Hindu religion but rather a multiplicity of ways to the Truth. This essay, "Hindutva" ("Hindu-ness"), and Savarkar's subsequent ideas have considerably influenced those who have promoted Hinduism as the national tradition of India in opposition to the claims of the non-Hindu minorities in India.

A country, a common home, is the first important essential of stable strong nationality: and as of all countries in the world our country can hardly be surpassed by any in its capacity to afford a soil so specially fitted for the growth of a great nation; we Hindus, whose very first article of faith is the love we bear to the common Fatherland, have in that love the strongest talismanic tie that can bind close and keep a nation firm and enthuse and enable it to accomplish things greater than ever.

The second essential of *Hindutva* puts the estimate of our latent powers of national cohesion and greatness yet higher. No country in the world, with the exception of China again, is peopled by a race so homogeneous, yet so ancient and yet so strong both numerically and vitally. . . . Mohammedans are no race nor are the Christians. They are a religious unit, yet neither a racial nor a national one. But we Hindus, if possible, are all the three put together and live under our ancient and common roof. The numerical strength of our race is an asset that cannot be too highly prized. . . .

The ideal conditions, therefore, under which a nation can attain perfect solidarity and cohesion would, other things being equal, be found in the case of those people who inhabit the land they adore, the land of whose forefathers is also the land of their Gods and Angels, of Seers and Prophets; the scenes of whose history are also the scenes of their mythology.

The Hindus are about the only people who are blessed with these ideal conditions that are at the same time incentive to national solidarity, cohesion, and greatness. . . .

Thus the actual essentials of *Hindutva* are, as this running sketch reveals, also the ideal essentials of nationality. If we would we can build on this foundation of *Hindutva*, a future greater than what any other people on earth can dream of—greater even than our own past; provided we are able to utilize our opportunities! . . .

Thirty crores[28] of people, with India for their basis of operation, for their Fatherland and for their Holyland, with such a history behind them, bound

---

28 Crore—10 million.

together by ties of a common blood and common culture, can dictate their terms to the whole world. A day will come when mankind will have to face the force.

Equally certain it is that whenever the Hindus come to hold such a position whence they could dictate terms to the whole world—those terms cannot be very different from the terms which [the] *Gītā* dictates or the Buddha lays down. A Hindu is most intensely so, when he ceases to be a Hindu; and with a Kabir claims the whole earth for a Benares[29] ... or with a Tukaram[30] exclaims: "My country? Oh brothers, the limits of the Universe— there the frontiers of my country lie."

SOURCE: V. D. Savarkar, "Hindutva" (1923), in *Sources of Indian Tradition*, ed. S. Hay. New York: Columbia University Press, 1988, vol. 2, pp. 292–5

The Secular Face of Hinduism   by Joseph Vellaringatt

According to the Indian Constitution, India is to be a secular country, meaning that no particular religion is to be favored by the government. However, the ideals of Hindutva have been promoted by some political groups in the name of Hinduism, creating an exclusivist, fundamentalist approach that many observers feel is alien to Sanatana Dharma. Joseph Vellaringatt, a Jesuit scholar, explains the tolerance, flexibility, and sense of the sacredness of everything that many feel is the true face of Hinduism.

In trying to understand any religion one should distinguish between its essence (*svarupa*) and its outward manifestations, between what is perennially valid and what is transitory and historically conditioned. Thus, for example, some of the characteristics that one attributes to modern-day Hinduism are, in fact, the creation of socio-political and economic factors. It is true that some of these historical and accidental accretions have received religious sanction. The caste system, with its resultant discrimination based on birth, is a case in point. Hindu fundamentalism of the present day has to be looked upon as the cumulative effect of various historical, socio-political and economic factors. In itself, the Hindutva ideology is a deviation from the true spirit of Hinduism. Such deviations have, from time to time, made their appearance in Christianity and Islam and other major religions of the world. The essentially liberal and secular core of Hinduism is, in course of time, bound to re-assert itself and disown its fundamentalist and ugly caricature. . . .

In political parlance "secularism" is usually taken to mean the strict separation of state and religion. If one were to take *dharmanirapeksata* ("secularism") in this limited sense, one would run the risk of concluding that the state has nothing to do with religion or religious values. The prevalent use of the term "secularism" has thus become a tool in the hands

---

29 Benares—Varanasi, a sacred place of pilgrimage.
30 Tukaram—seventeenth-century Hindu poet who believed in the equality of all humankind.

of the protagonists of Hindutva to brand their opponents as pseudo-secularists, who allegedly try to keep God and religion out of the lives of the people. According to genuine Hinduism religious and moral values do play an important role in nation building. A socio-political system which ignores or negates truly religious and moral values is alien to the true spirit of Hinduism. The "Ramrajya" ["Kingdom of Rama"] of Gandhiji's dreams is to be built on solid religious and moral foundations and is, therefore, akin to the "Kingdom of God" which Jesus came to announce.

A strict separation of the sacred and the profane/secular is alien to the spirit of Hinduism. Religion is an integral and inalienable part of Indian culture. The impact of religion is found in every sphere of human life. From birth to death religious rituals, feasts and other observances surround a person's life. . . .

For the reasons mentioned above the word *dharmanirapeksata*, in the sense of a strict separation of state and religion, is wholly inadequate to bring out the full implications of genuine secularism. *Sarvadharma-sambhava* and *sarvadharma-sadbhava* seem to be better options. The first phrase has the meaning of equal treatment of all religions. This would reject all theocratic systems, which uphold one particular religion as state religion and give it preferential treatment. But to make full sense *sarvadharma-sambhava* has to go hand in hand with and should be founded on *sarvadharma-sadbhava*, or positive and harmonious relationship between all religions. Such an attitude not only does not give any preferential treatment to any particular religion, but also promotes genuine respect and honour towards all religions. This spirit of openness and tolerance towards all religions is central to Hinduism and is based on some of its cardinal tenets, as we shall attempt to show in the following paragraphs.

Tolerance and Flexibility Hinduism allows the widest freedom in matters of faith and worship. Therefore we come across a wide variety of beliefs and practices, various philosophical systems dealing with the nature of God, man and the world, and various ways to God-realization. "Let good thoughts come from all sides" has always been the guiding principle. In India a prophet or a religious teacher never lacked a receptive audience. Even though some of the medieval saints came from the lower strata of society, they too found respectability and following among people of all castes. This spirit of openness has been of great help to Hinduism in withstanding the onslaughts of other religions and keeping its own separate identity. Hinduism has stood its ground by accepting and assimilating some of the positive elements found in them. . . .

The concept of Hinduism as a separate religion is a latter-day development. In the Hindu religious scriptures we do not come across the use of the term Hindu *dharma* to designate a separate religious identity. *Dharma* generally stood for moral conduct or the performance of each one's duty following the prescribed socio-ethical norms. It is only with the advent of religions of foreign origin that Hinduism came to assume a separate identity. It will not, therefore, be far from the truth to assert that "Hinduism" as a concept is largely the invention of foreigners, which gradually came to be accepted by Indians themselves. Hinduism does not have one single founder, or one single date and place of origin, or one single Scripture which is considered authoritative and binding on all. What we call Hinduism today is in fact the meeting point of various religious traditions that took birth and developed in various parts of India in different epochs of its history. . . .

Since the Hindu religion did not have a stereotyped form to which all were bound to conform, people could pick and choose according to each one's likes and temperaments. . . . One's understanding of God and the choice of one or other of the various ways of worshipping God are by and large determined by one's aptitudes, learning, level of enlightenment and personal preference. Thus, for instance, a man of intellectual and mystical bend of mind might find it easy to conceptualize and enjoy union with a God who is without name or form. Such a person may not feel the need of temples, rituals and symbols in worship. Another person might feel at home with a God whom he can lovingly call Rama or Krishna and one whom he can touch and see in the form of an idol. For such a person religious rituals and symbols are a great help in expressing the inner sentiments of the heart. Hinduism gives due respect and recognition to both forms of worship. . . .

Sense of the Sacred or the Divine This whole universe is the dwelling place of God. The Transcendent One, who is greater than the greatest . . . is also smaller than the smallest . . . as he is intimately present in the heart of every being. . . . There is the touch of the divine in every fibre of being. Creation is a theophany, a revelation, a presence of God. Every thing in creation, every flower, every leaf, is charged with the grandeur of God and can, therefore, lead us to communion with him. . . .

Sacredness of the Human Being If every thing is sacred and divine, the most sacred of all God's creatures is undoubtedly the human being who is created in the very image and likeness of God. Both God and the human being are in essence spirit (*atman*), pure awareness. . . . Not only are they of the same nature, but there is also an intimate relationship between them.

The affirmation of the fundamental divinity of the human being makes it the object of special reverence and respect. All forms of violence towards human beings, therefore, go against the true spirit of Hinduism. Fundamentalism and religious intolerance, leading to atrocities committed against others in the name of God and religion, thus are a negation of one of the cardinal principles of Hindu religion.

SOURCE: Joseph Vellaringatt, "The Secular Face of Hinduism," in *Vidyajyoti Journal of Theological Reflection*, September 2001, vol. 65, no. 9, pp. 645–50

Awakening of Universal Motherhood

by Mata Amritanandamayi

Women

In traditional Indian society, women are secondary to men. However, there are now strong movements supporting women's liberation from oppression. The contemporary guru Mata Amritanandamayi ordains women as priests, contrary to *brahmin* male domination of religion, and she argues for more recognition for women's important contributions even within the context of the traditional division of labor, in which the woman's place is in the home, defined by family relationships. "Amma" herself is considered a divine mother by her many followers around the world.

Woman is the creator of the human race. She is the first Guru, the first guide and mentor of humanity. Think of the tremendous forces, either positive or negative, that one human being can unleash into the world. Each one of us has a far-reaching effect on others, whether we are aware of it or not. The responsibility of a mother, when it comes to influencing and inspiring her children, cannot be underestimated. There is much truth in the saying that there is a strong woman behind every successful man. Wherever you see happy, peaceful individuals; wherever you see children endowed with noble qualities and good dispositions; wherever you see men who have immense strength when faced with failure and adverse situations; wherever you see people who possess a great measure of understanding, sympathy, love, and compassion towards the suffering, and who give of themselves to others—you will usually find a great mother who has inspired them to become what they are.

Mothers are the ones who are most able to sow the seeds of love, universal kinship, and patience in the minds of human beings. There is a special bond between a mother and child. The mother's inner qualities are transmitted to the child even through her breast milk. The mother understands the heart of her child; she pours her love into the child, teaches him or her the positive lessons of life, and corrects the child's mistakes. If you walk through a field of soft, green grass a few times, you will easily make a path. The good thoughts and positive values we cultivate in our children will stay with them forever. It is easy to mold a child's character when he or she is very young, and much more difficult to do so when the child grows up.

Once, when Amma was giving *darshan* [visual contact with the divine through encounters with Hindu images or gurus] in India, a youth came up to her. He lived in a part of the country that was ravaged by terrorism. Because of the frequent killings and lootings, the people in that area were suffering a great deal. He told Amma that he was the leader of a group of youngsters who were doing a lot of social work in that area. He prayed to Amma, "Please give those terrorists, who are so full of hatred and violence, the right understanding. And for all those who have faced so many atrocities and have suffered so much, please fill their hearts with the spirit of forgiveness. Otherwise, the situation will only deteriorate, and there will be no end to the violence."

Amma was so glad to hear his prayer for peace and forgiveness. When Amma asked him what made him choose a life of social work, he said, "My mother was the inspiration behind this. My childhood days were dark and terrifying. When I was six years old, I watched with my own eyes as my peace-loving father was brutally murdered by terrorists. My life was shattered. I was filled with hatred, and all I wanted was revenge. But my mother changed my attitude. Whenever I would tell her that I was going to avenge my father's death one day, she would say, 'Son, will your father come back to life if you kill those people? Look at your grandmother, how sad she always is. Look at me, how difficult it is to make both ends meet without your father. And just look at yourself, how sad you are, not having your father with you. Would you want more mothers and children to suffer as we do? The intensity of this pain would be the same for them. Try to forgive your father's killers for their terrible deeds, and spread the message of love and universal kinship instead.' When I grew up, people tried to get me to join different terrorist outfits to avenge my father's death. But the seeds of forgiveness sown by my mother had borne fruit, and I refused. I gave some of the youngsters the same advice that my mother had given me. This changed the hearts of many people who have since joined me in serving others."

The love and compassion, rather than hatred, that this boy chose to pour into the world stemmed from the wellspring of love in his mother.

It is thus, through the influence she has on her child, that a mother influences the future of the world. A woman who has awakened her innate motherhood brings heaven to earth wherever she is. . . . And so it is that the one who rocks the cradle of the babe is the one who holds up the lamp, shedding light upon the world. . . .

The essence of motherhood is not restricted to women who have given birth; it is a principle inherent in both women and men. It is the attitude of the mind. It is love—and that love is the very breath of life. No one would say, "I will breathe only when I am with my family and friends; I won't breathe in front of my enemies." Similarly, for those in whom motherhood has awakened, love and compassion for everyone is as much part of their being as breathing. Real leadership is not to dominate or to control, but to serve others with love and compassion, and to inspire women and men alike through the example of our lives. Amma feels that the forthcoming age should be dedicated to reawakening the healing power of motherhood. This is crucial. May all nations, all people, and their leaders realize that we do not have a choice. It is vitally important that we restore the lost balance in our world for the sake of humanity and Mother Earth, who sustains us all.

SOURCE: Mata Amritanandamayi, from "The Awakening of Universal Motherhood," an address to A Global Peace Initiative of Women Religious and Spiritual Leaders, Geneva, October 7, 2002

GLOSSARY

Atman In Hinduism, the soul.

Bhakti Popular devotion to a god/goddess or guru, with love and adoration.

Brahman The impersonal ultimate principle; also, one of the priestly, aristocratic caste.

Caste A social organization by hierarchy of occupations, sanctified by Hinduism.

Dharma In Hinduism, the universal cosmic law, duty; in Buddhism, cosmic law, the teachings of the Buddha, and the realization and practice of truth (the second of the Three Jewels: Buddha, *dharma*, *sangha*).

Kali Yuga The contemporary era, a dark age, one of many cycles (*yugas*) of a vast cosmic time.

Karma In Hinduism, the cosmic moral law of consequences for ethical actions and their effects on social and personal well-being or suffering that are seen as rewards and punishments for prior incarnations; the goal of religion is liberation from karmic cycles.

Om In Hinduism, the primordial sound vibration.

Pandit One of the hereditary priestly caste learned in ancient texts, customs, and rituals.

Puranas Mythological texts of ancient days; popular devotional texts.

Reincarnation After death, rebirth in a new body higher or lower in the caste system, according to one's *karma*.

Rishi (seer) A poetic sage; *rishis* are visionary authors of Vedic hymns heard within in meditation.

Sanatana Dharma The ageless way of moral order, duty, and natural cosmic law.

Sanskrit The ancient language of the holy scriptures.

Smrti texts Great epic poems, descriptions of gods and goddesses, codes of moral conduct, such as the *Mahabharata*.

Sruti texts "Heard" by ancient sages in meditation, mostly the *Vedas*.

Upanishads Philosophical reflections on ultimate reality, a oneness in which we all participate.

Vedas Foundational scriptures for Hindu tradition, written down c. 1500 BCE; oldest are the *Rig Vedas*.

Yoga (yoking [to divinity]) Techniques for transforming consciousness and attaining liberation; there are many forms, such as guru yoga, devotion, work, study, asceticism, physical exercises, *mantra* repetition, visualization, meditation.

HOLY DAYS

Hindu holy days are numerous and varied across India. Times are calculated variously by region, astrological sign, sun, and moon. Most communal religious celebrations are held during the bright half of the lunar months, for the full moon is sacred.

Domestic rites Conception, wishing for a son, and birth are surrounded with rituals (*pujas*) using food, fire, and prayers. Between the ages of 8 and 12 an upper-caste boy can be initiated into being a "twice-born." At weddings the bride and groom walk around the sacrificial fire in seven stages, solemnizing their union.

Fall renewals Gods' birthdays are celebrated as overcoming the hot summer (monsoons included). The birthdays of Krishna, avatar of Vishnu, and Vamana, dwarf avatar of Vishnu, signal a restored, auspicious time of year. The goddess Durga kills a buffalo demon in fall. In some parts of India late fall is seen as the time of the awakening of Vishnu, who has been asleep on the cobra Ananta for four months. Divali is a celebration of Lakshmi, the goddess of prosperity, and the victory of gods over evil forces.

Festivals

Pilgrimages These usually take place in summer, especially to sacred rivers such as the Ganges, where bathing (despite its current physical pollution) is ritually purifying. The dying are taken to Benares to be cremated. Other pilgrimages are taken to temples, for the sake of ancestors and worldly rewards, or for spiritual purification and rebirth in Heaven instead of earth.

Spring Holi For the lower castes a boisterous celebration, throwing colored powder and

water and celebrating Kama, god of sexual desire; the past year's evils are symbolically thrown into bonfires. In Bengal, associated with Krishna.

Spring New Year Soon after Holi the New Year is celebrated near the spring equinox, a time of cosmic balance and beginning/ending.

HISTORICAL OUTLINE

c. 2500 BCE—Harappan city civilization with goddess and indigenous religions in Indus valley, now in Pakistan

c. 2000–900 BCE—Aryan invasions of northern India

c. 1000–500 BCE—*Upanishads* systematized by Vyasa

c. 900–700 BCE—*Brahmanas* recorded

200 BCE—*Yoga Sutras* organized by Patanjali

400 BCE–200 CE—*Ramayana* recorded

400 BCE–400 CE—*Mahabharata* recorded

100–300 CE—*The Laws of Manu* compiled

c. 300 CE—Tantric texts recorded

500–1500 CE—*Puranas* recorded

600–1800 CE—*bhakti* movement strong

711 CE—Muslim invasions begin

c. 788–820—Vedanta school organized by Sankara

1556–1707—Muslim Mughal Empire

1836–86—Ramakrishna

1857–1947—British rule in India

1893–1952—Paramahansa Yogananda

1947—formation of Pakistan and East Pakistan (now Bangladesh)

1948—assassination of Mahatma Gandhi

1992—destruction of Babri mosque by extremist Hindus

REVIEW QUESTIONS

1   Why is the term "Sanatana Dharma" preferred to "Hindu" by scholars?
2   How would a believer respond to the monotheistic charge of idolatry for worshipping statues?
3   How did Yogananda's meditation "reinherit his eternal realm" at the temple of the goddess Kali?
4   How did Gandhi argue against untouchability, against Hindu tradition and law? What did he rename untouchables and why?

DISCUSSION QUESTIONS

1   What in human nature makes possible Hinduism's refined, universalist spirituality and simultaneously, its caste system, treatment of women, and exclusivist nationalism?
2   How can Hinduism embrace the extremes of severe *sadhu* asceticism and elaborate, imaginative, sensuous images of gods and goddesses?
3   What themes in Hinduism do you think might offer positive alternatives for monotheism's insistence on one god, which leaves out women, nature, and other areas?

INFORMATION RESOURCES

Alston, A. J. *The Devotional Poems of Mirabai.* Delhi: Motilal Banarsidass, 1980.

De Bary, W. Theodore. *Sources of Indian Tradition.* New York: Columbia University Press, 1958.

Devananda, Vishnu, Swami. *Meditations and Mantras.* New York: Om Lotus Publishing, 1975.

Gandhi, Mahatma. *The Message of Mahatma Gandhi,* ed. U. S. Mohan Rao. Delhi: Ministry of Information, Government of India, 1990.

Hawley, John S., *et al.* "Hinduism" in *Encyclopedia of Religion,* ed. Lindsay Jones. 2nd ed. Vol. 6, pp. 3988–4021. New York: Macmillan, 2005.

Hindu Resources
<http://www.hindu.org>

The Hindu Universe
<http://www.hindunet.org>

Hinduism Today, 107 Kaholalele Road, Kapaa, Hawaii 96746–9304, U.S.A.

Jayakar, Pupul. *The Earth Mother.* Delhi and Harmondsworth, Middlesex: Penguin Books, 1980/1989.

Kabir. *Songs of Kabir,* trans. R. Tagore. New York: Weiser, 1981.

Kinsley, David. *Hindu Goddesses.* Delhi: Motilal Banarsidass, 1986.

Prabhupada, A. C. B., Swami. *Bhagavad-Gita As It Is.* Los Angeles, London, Mumbai: Bhaktivedanta Book Trust, 1976.

Purohit, Shree, Swami, and **W. B. Yeats**, trans. *The Ten Principal Upanishads.* Calcutta: Rupa Co., 1992.

Rajagopalachari, C., trans. *Mahabharata.* Mumbai: Bharatiya Vidya Bhavan, 1994.

——. *Ramayana.* Mumbai: Bharatiya Vidya Bhavan, 1990.

——. *The Siva Purana.* Delhi: Motilal Banarsidass, 1990.

Shastri, J. L., ed. *Hymns of the Rgveda,* trans. Ralph T. H. Griffith. Delhi: Motilal Banarsidass, 1986.

Smith, Brian K., *et al.* "Hinduism," in *Encyclopedia Britannica.* Vol. 20, pp. 519–58. London, 1997.

Stutley, Margaret, and **James Stutley**. *Harper's Dictionary of Hinduism.* New York: Harper and Row, 1977.

Vivekananda, Swami. *Karma-Yoga and Bhakti-Yoga.* New York: Ramakrishna-Vivekananada Center, 1982.

Yogananada, Paramahansa. *Autobiography of a Yogi.* Los Angeles: Self-Realization Fellowship/ Mumbai: Jaico Publishing House, 1974.

CHAPTER 4

JAINISM

In addition to the Vedic religions of ancient India, another path evolved independently. This is Jainism (from *jina*, winner over passions), an extremely ascetic path. Its goal is liberation from the soul-tarnishing negative effects of one's actions, thoughts, and speech—one's **karma**. In Jain teaching, this liberation comes only through one's own strenuous and mindful efforts not to do wrong in any way. Jains reject the Hindu caste system and the idea of a creator God, but, like Hindus and Buddhists, believe in reincarnation.

The teachers of this path are called **Tirthankaras** ("bridgebuilders"). According to tradition, there have been 24 Tirthankaras during the current era. There is historic evidence of the existence of the three most recent teachers. The last is the best known: Mahavir (c. 559–527 BCE), who had been a prince but renounced his life of pleasure and power at the age of 30 to become a homeless ascetic. His austerities were so extreme that people thought him mad and tormented him. But he endured all hardships with equanimity, achieved perfect liberation, and taught others the way to liberation from *karma*. In order to increase sensitivity toward non-human life forms, he made detailed studies and gave insights into the categories and qualities of all that exists. A large community of monks, nuns, and laypeople gathered around him, and he gave them minute instructions on how to live without accumulating negative *karma*.

Today there is renewed interest in this ascetic way of life, for its basic principles are antidotes to modern problems. For example, Mahatma Gandhi's assertion of the power of non-violent resistance to oppression was strongly influenced by the Jain principle of **ahimsa**, or non-violence, based on reverence for all life. Jain precepts of non-violence, the interdependence of all life forms, compassion, non-acquisitiveness, and relativity are also being invoked as correctives to environmentally destructive modern lifestyles and to conflicts of dogma.

Teachings of Mahavir

The teachings of Mahavir did not necessarily originate with him but are part of a much more ancient tradition. They were transmitted orally by his followers for several centuries, along with the commentaries of learned teachers. The literature to be remembered was quite vast, and during 12 years of famine about 300 BCE, many monks died who had

Soul in the World, Mahavira

been carrying the teachings in their memory. Little had been written down, for books were considered possessions and causes for attachment, and were re-nounced by Jain ascetics like other possessions. At that time, books were written out by hand and were rare in any case.

The compilation of teachings and commentaries formed a **canon** called the *Agam Sutras*. After the famine, one group of Jain ascetics, the **Svetambara** sect, maintained that they had managed to remember most of the major texts. They held three conferences to compile and preserve what was available. Another even more ascetic sect, the **Digambara**, claimed that the entire canon had been lost. Today, the sects still disagree about the validity of the Jain Agamic scriptures. The Digambaras use scriptures written by great teachers from 100 to 800 CE which are thought to have been based on the earlier texts.

Mahavir's Stoicism from the *Akaranga Sutra*

Mahavir's own life is cited as a perfect example of the Jain teaching of self-mastery and non-aggressiveness toward all beings. The ideal is to bear both pleasure and pain with equanimity and compassion for other beings. Many stories of the tor-ments endured by Mahavir with great **stoicism** appear in the classic *Akaranga Sutra*, an excerpt from which is here retold by Shashi Ahluwalia. Before his libera-tion, Mahavir is referred to by his worldly name, Vardhaman.

Vardhaman left the palace and started his long journey like an ascetic. He had only a piece of cloth on his body and gave even that to a beggar. He became completely naked—*Digambara*. As Vardhaman was about to start from the Jnatri-sanda park on a wandering career, a Brahman named Soma approached him with a prayer for help. But Vardhaman had hardly anything worthwhile to give. So he shared half of his garment with the beggar and placed the other half on his shoulder.

The Brahman took the garment to a tailor to have the hem bound. The tailor advised him to get the other half, so that the two pieces together, duly repaired, would fetch him a handsome amount in the market. So the Brahman started at once and followed Vardhaman like his shadow, and waiting for a chance to get it. The chance came after 13 months. When Vardhaman was going from South Vacala to the North Vacala the piece on his shoulder was caught in a thorny bush and remained there. It was picked up by Brahman Soma.

At this point, Vardhaman took five resolutions which were

1   I shall not stay at an uncongenial place;
2   I shall meditate all the time in a statuesque posture;
3   I shall generally maintain silence;
4   I shall use the hollow on my palm as begging bowl; and
5   I shall not humble myself to any householder.

These resolutions became his guidelines throughout his life.

The famous "Ohana-Sutra" in the *Akaranga* contains the following account of his soul-stirring *sadhana*:[1]

Many living beings gathered on his body, crawled about it, and caused pain. Then he meditated, walking with his eye fixed on a square space before him of the length of a man. Many people who were shocked at the sight struck him and cried. He shunned the company of the female sex and of all householders. Asked, he gave no reply. He did not even answer those who saluted him. He was beaten with sticks and struck by sinful people. He wandered about disregarding all slights, not being attracted by any worldly amusement.

For more than a couple of years he went without using cold water. He realized singleness, guarded his body, obtained intuition and became calm. He carefully avoided doing injury to the meanest form of life. He did not use what was specially prepared for him. He used to eat only clean food. He did not use another man's robe, nor did he eat out of another man's vessel. He observed moderation in eating and drinking. He neither rubbed his eyes nor scratched his body.

He sometimes took shelter in workshops, sometimes in factories, sometimes in garden houses, sometimes in a cemetery, in deserted houses, or at the foot of a tree. In such places he sought shelter for 13 years. He meditated day and night, undisturbed, unperturbed, exerting himself strenuously. He never cared for sleep for the sake of pleasure. He waked up himself and slept only a little, free from cares and desires. Waking up again, going outside for once in a night, he walked about for an hour.

At his resting places, crawling or flying animals attacked him. Bad people, the guard of the village, or lance-bearers attacked him. Well-controlled, he bore all dreadful calamities and different kinds of feelings and he wandered about, speaking but little. Ill-treated, he engaged himself in his meditations, free from resentment. He endured all hardships in calmness. Well-guarded, he bore the pains caused by grass, cold, heat, flies and gnats.

He travelled in the pathless country of *Radha*—in *Vajrabhumi* and *Svabhrabhumi*, where he used miserable beds and seats. The rude natives of the place attacked him and set dogs to bite him. But he never used the stick to keep off the dogs. He endured the abusive language of the rustics, being perfectly enlightened. The inhabitants of the place caused him all sorts of tortures. Abandoning the care of his body, he bore pain, free from desire.

---

1 *Sadhana*—spiritual practice.

He abstained from indulgence of the flesh, though he was never attacked by diseases. Whether wounded or not, he did not desire medical treatment. In the cold season he meditated in the shade. In summer he exposed himself to the heat. He lived on rough food like rice, pounded jujube, and jujube. Using these three kinds of food, he sustained himself for eight months. Sometimes he did not drink for half a month or even for a month. Sometimes he did not drink for more than two months, or even six months. Sometimes he ate only the sixth meal, or the eighth, the tenth, the twelfth. Sometimes he ate stale food. He committed no sin himself, nor did he induce others to do so, nor did he consent to the sin of others.

He meditated persevering in some posture, without the smallest motion. He meditated in mental concentration on the things above, below, beside. He meditated free from sin and desire, not attached to sounds and colours, and never acted carelessly.

Thus, as a hero at the head of a battle, he bore all hardships, and remaining undisturbed, proceeded on the road to deliverance. Understanding the truth and restraining the impulses for the purification of soul, he was finally liberated.

SOURCE: "Ohana Sutra, Akaranga," in Shashi Ahluwalia, *Spiritual Masters from India*. Delhi: Manas Publications, 1987, pp. 4–6

Harmlessness

The Temple of 1,000 Pillars

Whatever their historicity, the Jain scriptures comprise a vast body of wisdom. Some of the literature concerns intricate scientific systems for classifying all aspects of living and non-living beings, space, and time. Minute sentient life-forms are said to exist in the earth, in fire, in air, and in water, in addition to the more visible plants and "movable beings." Many Jain *sutras* concern precepts for doing as little harm as possible to other beings.

On Non-Violence from the Jain Sutras

Know other creatures' love for life, for they are like you. Kill them not: save their life from fear and enmity.

All living beings desire happiness, and have revulsion from pain and suffering. They are fond of life, they love to live, long to live, and they feel repulsed at the idea of hurt and injury to or destruction of their life. Hence, no living being should be hurt, injured, or killed.

All things breathing, all things existing, all things living, all beings whatsoever, should not be slain, or treated with violence, or insulted, or tortured, or driven away.

He who hurts living beings himself, or gets them hurt by others, or approves of hurt caused by others, augments the world's hostility toward himself.

He who views all living beings as his own self, and sees them all as being alike, has stopped all influx of karma; he is self-restrained, and incurs no sin.

On Self-Restraint from the *Jain Sutras*

The painful condition of the self is the result of its own action; it has not been brought about by any other cause.

The soul is the maker and the unmaker, the doer and undoer; it is itself responsible for its own happiness and misery, is its own friend and its own foe; it itself decides its own conditions, good or evil.

Wealth and property, movable or immovable, cannot save a person from the sufferings he or she undergoes on account of the fruition of his or her own karma.

Greater is the victory of one who conquers his own self than that of him who conquers thousands of thousands of formidable foes in a valiant fight.

Fight with yourself; why fight with external foes? Happy is he who conquers his self by his self.

Conquer yourself, for difficult it is to conquer the self. If the self is conquered, you shall be happy in this world and hereafter.

All the creatures of the earth look for happiness outside of themselves, but real happiness must be sought inside the depths of their own hearts.

SOURCE: *Jain Sutras*, trans. Dr. Jyoti Prasad Jain, in *Religion and Culture of the Jains*. 3rd ed. Delhi: Bharatiya Jnanpith, 1983, pp. 187–8

Respect for Life from the *Akaranga Sutra*

Earth is afflicted and wretched, it is hard to teach, it has no discrimination. Unenlightened men, who suffer from the effects of past deeds, cause great pain in a world full of pain already, for in earth souls are individually embodied. If, thinking to gain praise, honor, or respect, . . . or to achieve a good rebirth, . . . or to win salvation, or to escape pain, a man sins against earth or causes or permits others to do so, . . . he will not gain joy or wisdom. . . . Injury to the earth is like striking, cutting, maiming, or killing a blind man. . . . Knowing this a man should not sin against earth or cause or permit others to do so. He who understands the nature of sin against earth is called a true sage who understands karma. . . .

And there are many souls embodied in water. Truly water . . . is alive. . . . He who injures the lives in water does not understand the nature of sin or renounce it. . . . Knowing this, a man should not sin against water, or cause or permit others to do so. He who understands the nature of sin against water is called a true sage who understands karma. . . .

By wicked or careless acts one may destroy fire-beings and, moreover, harm other beings by means of fire. . . . For there are creatures living in earth, grass, leaves, wood, cowdung, or dustheaps, and jumping creatures which . . . fall into a fire if they come near it. If touched by fire, they shrivel up, . . . lose their senses, and die. . . . He who understands the nature of sin in respect of fire is called a true sage who understands karma.

And just as it is the nature of a man to be born and grow old, so is it the nature of a plant to be born and grow old. . . . One is endowed with reason, and so is the other; one is sick, if injured, and so is the other; one grows larger, and so does the other; one changes with time, and so does the other. . . . He who understands the nature of sin against plants is called a true sage who understands karma. . . .

All beings with two, three, four, or five senses, . . . in fact all creation, know individually pleasure and displeasure, pain, terror, and sorrow. All are full of fears which come from all directions. And yet there exist people who would cause greater pain to them. . . . Some kill animals for sacrifice, some for their skin, flesh, blood, . . . feathers, teeth, or tusks; . . . some kill them intentionally and some unintentionally; some kill because they have been previously injured by them, . . . and some because they expect to be injured. He who harms animals has not understood or renounced deeds of sin. . . . He who understands the nature of sin against animals is called a true sage who understands karma. . . .

A man who is averse from harming even the wind knows the sorrow of all things living. . . . He who knows what is bad for himself knows what is bad for others, and he who knows what is bad for others knows what is bad for himself. This reciprocity should always be borne in mind. Those whose minds are at peace and who are free from passions do not desire to live [at the expense of others]. . . . He who understands the nature of sin against wind is called a true sage who understands karma.

In short he who understands the nature of sin in respect of all the six types of living beings is called a true sage who understands karma.

SOURCE: *Akaranga Sutra*, in *Sources of Indian Tradition,* ed. W. Theodore de Bary. New York: Columbia University Press, 1958, vol. 1, pp. 59–60

Perfection of the soul

If one compassionately avoids harming all forms of life, one may gradually free the soul or **jiva** from its karmic accretions and entanglements with material things, thereby achieving perfection and liberation of the *jiva*. The **Five Jain Vows** are made to help achieve this aim.

The Five Great Vows   from the *Akaranga Sutra*

The first great vow, Sir, runs thus:

I renounce all killing of living beings, whether subtle or gross, whether movable or immovable. Nor shall I myself kill living beings. As long as I live, I confess and blame, repent and exempt myself of these sins, in the thrice threefold way [acting, commanding, consenting, either in the past or the present or the future], in mind, speech, and body.

There are five clauses:

A Nirgrantha[2] is careful in his walk, not careless. The Kevalin[3] assigns as the reason, that a Nirgrantha, careless in his walk, might hurt or displace or injure or kill living beings.

2 Nirgrantha—a person without attachments, impurities, or possessiveness.
3 Kevalin—omniscient one.

A Nirgrantha searches into his mind. If his mind is sinful, blamable, intent on works, acting on impulses, produces division and dissension, quarrels, faults, and pains, injures living beings, or kills creatures, he should not employ such a mind in action.

A Nirgrantha searches into his speech; if his speech is sinful, blamable, intent on works, acting on impulses, produces division and dissension, quarrels, faults, and pains, injures living beings, or kills creatures, he should not utter that speech.

A Nirgrantha is careful in laying down his utensils of begging; he is not careless in it. The Kevalin says: A Nirgrantha who is careless in laying down his utensils of begging might hurt or displace or injure all sorts of living beings.

A Nirgrantha eats and drinks after inspecting his food and drink; he does not eat and drink without inspecting his food and drink. The Kevalin says: If a Nirgrantha would eat and drink without inspecting his food and drink, he might hurt and displace or injure or kill all sorts of living beings.

The second great vow runs thus:

I renounce all vices of lying speech from anger or greed or fear or mirth. I shall neither myself speak lies, nor cause others to speak lies, nor consent to the speaking of lies by others. I confess and blame, repent and exempt myself of these sins in the thrice threefold way, in mind, speech, and body. . . .

The third great vow runs thus:

I renounce all taking of anything not given, either in a village or a town or a wood, either of little or much, of small or great, of living or lifeless things. I shall neither take myself what is not given, nor cause others to take it, nor consent to their taking it. . . .

The fourth great vow runs thus:

I renounce all sexual pleasures, either with gods or men or animals. I shall not give way to sensuality. As long as I live, I confess and blame, repent and exempt myself of these sins, in the thrice threefold way, in mind, speech, and body. . . .

The fifth great vow runs thus:

I renounce all attachments, whether little or much, small or great, living or lifeless; neither shall I myself form such attachments, nor cause others to do so, nor consent to their doing so. As long as I live, I confess and blame, repent and exempt myself of these sins, in the thrice threefold way, in mind, speech, and body.

There are five clauses:

If a creature with ears hears agreeable and disagreeable sounds, it should not be attached to, nor delighted with, nor desiring of, nor infatuated by, nor covetous of, nor disturbed by the agreeable or disagreeable sounds.

If a creature with eyes sees agreeable and disagreeable forms, it should not be attached to, nor delighted with, nor desiring of, nor infatuated by, nor covetous of, nor disturbed by them.

If a creature with an organ of smell smells agreeable or disagreeable smells, it should not be attached to them. . . .

If a creature with a tongue tastes agreeable or disagreeable tastes, it should not be attached to them. . . .

If a creature with an organ of feeling feels agreeable or disagreeable touches, it should not be attached to them. . . .

He who is well provided with these great vows and their 25 clauses is really Houseless, if he, according to the sacred lore, the precepts, and the way correctly practices, follows, executes, explains, establishes, and according to the precept, effects them.

SOURCE: *Akaranga Sutra*, Book II, Lecture 15, trans. Hermann Jacobi in *The Sacred Books of the East*, ed. F. Max Müller. Delhi: Motilal Banarsidass, 1964, vol. 22, pp. 202–10 (first published by OUP, 1884)

The principles of anekantavada and syadvada

A central Jain principle is that of the multiplicity (**anekantavada**) and relativity (**syadvada**) of all points of view. The total of all perspectives can only be seen by the perfected soul whose clear vision encompasses the entire universe. If we grasp this teaching, we are less likely to fight to defend our own point of view, and thus we will be less violent and more tolerant in our relationships with others. This important teaching is explained elegantly and simply by L. M. Singhvi, former Ambassador of India to England, as part of a statement about Jain principles presented to Prince Philip in 1990, marking the entry of the Jain faith into the Network on Conservation and Religion of the World Wide Fund for Nature.

Anekantavada (The Doctrine of Manifold Aspects)
by L. M. Singhvi

The concept of universal interdependence underpins the Jain theory of knowledge, known as *anekantavada* or the doctrine of **manifold aspects**. *Anekantavada* describes the world as a multifaceted, everchanging reality with an infinity of viewpoints depending on the time, place, nature and state of the one who is the viewer and that which is viewed.

This leads to the doctrine of *syadvada* or relativity, which states that truth is relative to different viewpoints. What is true from one point of view is open to question from another. Absolute truth cannot be grasped from any particular viewpoint alone because absolute truth is the sum total of all the different viewpoints that make up the universe.

Because it is rooted in the doctrines of *anekantavada* and *syadvada*, Jainism does not look upon the universe from an anthropocentric, ethnocentric or egocentric viewpoint. It takes into account the viewpoints of other species, other communities and nations and other human beings.

SOURCE: L. M. Singhvi, "The Jain Declaration on Nature," pamphlet published privately and presented to Prince Philip on October 23, 1990, at Buckingham Palace, London

The Blind Men and the Elephant A traditional Jain fable

The principle of relativity of viewpoints is so important to Jain understanding that it is explained by way of numerous fables, such as the traditional Indian story of the blind men and the elephant.

As a joke, a king sent six blind men to feel an elephant and describe its nature. Each approached the elephant from a different direction, seized a different part, and, being blind, assumed that what he perceived was the whole elephant. One grasped the ear and declared, "Elephant is like a large fan." Another grasped a leg and declared, "Elephant is like a great pillar." Another blind man found the trunk, and feeling it, proclaimed, "Elephant is like the branch of a tree." Another grasped the tail and declared, "Elephant is like a rope hanging from the sky." A fifth encountered the side of the elephant and maintained, "Elephant is like a wall." The sixth insisted that the others were all wrong, for he had grasped the tusk. He proclaimed, "Elephant is not any of those; elephant is like a spear." Each being certain of the truth of his own experience, they began to fight.

A person who could see chanced to come by and found them quarreling. After listening to their individual perceptions from their different points of view, he gently explained that there was no need for fighting over the issue, for each was partially right. But to have complete knowledge of the nature of the elephant, he said, one would have to be able to be aware of and combine all the different aspects of the creature.

Renunciation

Another major Jain principle is that of **renunciation**: one should reduce one's desires and keep consumption to a minimum, thus freeing the soul from karmic entanglements with the material world and minimizing one's destruction of the planet. To overconsume, to misuse or pollute natural resources, are considered acts of violence.

There are degrees of harmfulness, corresponding to the karmic density of the soul. An example often used is ways of obtaining fruit. The most densely stained black soul uproots the whole tree to get its fruits. The blue-stained soul cuts the tree down for its fruit. The grey-stained soul cuts off a fruit-bearing branch. These three types of souls are all heavily karmically laden. Three other categories represent successively lighter karmic burdens. The yellow-stained soul cuts off a bunch of fruit. The lotus-pink soul picks ripe fruit from the tree. The sixth and most pure, the luminous white soul, simply picks up ripe fruit that has fallen to the ground.

Today voluntary simplicity and abstinence are being widely hailed as necessary for preservation of the environment. But Jains have always tried to live thus. A Jain fable traditionally used to inculcate this principle follows.

Forsaking Eternal Bliss for a Drop of Honey

A traditional Jain fable

Again and again, the gods and goddesses call out to a person, "Come—leave these earthly attachments and we will show you eternal bliss." At first the person says, "Not yet—let me first get married and raise a family." They call to him again, but he says, "Not yet—let me become financially well-off." And so it goes, year after year, and he remains entangled in worldly life.

One day the man is wandering through the jungle, whereupon a mad elephant begins to charge at him. From another direction, a repulsive demoness brandishes her sword at him with a dreadful cackle. Seeking refuge, he runs to a banyan tree and, unable to climb it, grasps a vine hanging from its branches. Clinging to the vine, he finds that he is suspended over a pit in which five snakes are hissing. Beneath them, a huge python awaits. Two mice, one white and one black, begin gnawing on the vine from above. The enraged elephant grabs the banyan tree with his trunk and shakes it, while the man maintains his perilous hold. As the elephant shakes the tree, a honeycomb on a branch above starts to fall; angry bees swarm out and begin stinging the man as he clings to the vine which is being eaten by the mice, with snakes hissing in the pit below.

The gods appear again, calling to the man that they are ready to free him from his miseries. But at that moment, a drop of honey from the comb falls into his mouth. Tasting its sweetness, he is oblivious to the elephant (death), the demoness (old age), the mice (the diminishing of one's lifespan through the inexorable procession of days and nights), the snakes (the treacherous lure of the five senses), the terrible python (hell that a person who is attached to sensual pleasures will suffer), the pit (human life), and the bees (diseases which torment a person). He says, "Not yet. I long for one more drop of this honey!" If a person were wise and fully aware of the perilous and tenuous nature of his existence, how could he prefer such fleeting pleasures to eternal liberation?

SOURCE: Traditional story as told by Swami Dharamananda to Mary Pat Fisher

The Renunciate Life of Sādhvi Vicakṣaṇa by N. Shanta

Although all Jains follow a path of renunciation and austerity, monks and nuns do so to an extreme degree. They have only a few possessions, which they carry with them, including a broom to sweep insects aside before inadvertently treading on them as they walk. Many wear a cloth over their mouth to avoid inadvertently inhaling any minute living beings. In winter they tolerate cold without heavy blankets; Digambara monks in fact never wear any clothing. In summer the monks and nuns tolerate intense heat without fans. This life is so arduous that one might imagine few would undertake it, but in fact there are large communities of Jain monks and nuns in India, even today. Many of them radiate an inner happiness which is the paradoxical result of extreme self-discipline.

The following story of a Jain nun who lived from 1912 to 1980 illustrates the particular difficulties for a woman choosing the path of renunciation, and also the liberating effects of doing so. It is noteworthy that Svetambara Jains have long believed that women are capable of a strict renunciate life, capable of fully understanding the teachings, and capable of helping both men and women to find the way to liberation.

.... The horoscope of the child revealed, so it was said, an unusual degree of courage and predicted that she would become an ascetic of great renown. In the meantime, she was an affectionate, friendly and intelligent child. They called her Dākhi, from *drākṣā*, bunch of grapes. In accordance with the custom of the day, she was affianced in childhood and up to the age of eight she knew the life of a happy family. The sudden death of her father was a terrible shock for her, for not only did she now lack his parental affection, but she began to ask the reason for her father's being so abruptly snatched from her. Life changed for her. Having neither brothers nor sisters, she remained alone with her mother, a young widow who was obliged to yield to the customs of her community. After many enquiries, this latter managed to trace the whereabouts of her cousin Sādhvi Suvaraṇa and, taking Dākhi with her, stayed with her several times. Thus Dākhi came into contact with the *sādhvis*[4] whom she proceeded to astonish by the liveliness of her intelligence. The mother of Dākhi had decided to receive *dikṣā*[5] when[ever] her daughter married the young man to whom she had been betrothed. This, however, was not Dākhi's desire. She felt an attraction for the ascetic life and to fulfil this aspiration, she carried on a tenacious struggle with her paternal grandfather, who loved her dearly and refused to give his consent to the *dikṣā*. The young man's family, perturbed and unhappy, also applied pressure. Dākhi struggled alone with a grandfather whom, at the same time, she loved—alone, as neither could her mother or the *sādhvis* help her in any way, for the grandfather would have accused them of bringing influence to bear upon the child.

Dākhi was kept at home and forbidden to go out to visit the temple or the *upāśrayā*.[6] Dākhi replied that she would obey, [but], as she was being forbidden to go to the temple, she would fast. This, then, is what she did. In the evening of the first day of the fast, her grandfather, softened at heart, offered her a cup of milk, but Dākhi refused. Softened still further, the grandfather gave her permission to attend the temple, but re-affirmed stoutly that he would never give his consent to her receiving *dikṣā* and that Dākhi must needs get married. To this she replied that she would not disobey, so, said she, she would wait for *dikṣā* but would never on any account marry! Confrontations of this sort continued for one week. The grandfather, realizing his powerlessness to persuade Dākhi and despairing of

---

4 *Sādhvi*—a Jain nun.
5 *Dikṣā*—consecration as a member of an ascetic Jain order.
6 *Upāśrayā*—community of renunciates.

the affair, lodged an appeal with the civil authorities. He informed them that the *sādhvis* had brought pressure to bear upon his 13-year-old granddaughter and were desirous of admitting her to *dikṣā* against the will of her guardian (himself); that they should be so good as to help him prevent Dākhi from joining the *sādhvis*. A *ṭhākura*, a type of magistrate of the district, was appointed to study the case and administer justice.

Here, now, are her chief replies in her dialogue with the magistrate:

Ṭhākura: "Do you really, my child, desire to embrace the ascetic life?"
Dākhi: "Yes, sir."
Ṭhākura: "Why?"
Dākhi: "It is an inner call."
Ṭhākura: "Why do you not wish to marry?"
Dākhi: "I have no desire for it."
Ṭhākura: "Do you know what the ascetic life means?"
Dākhi: "Without a knowledge of the ascetic life it is not possible to experience its attraction. I do know what is meant by both life in the world and by asceticism."
Ṭhākura: "Is not obedience to one's parents also part of the *dharma*?"
Dākhi: "Yes, indeed, but if it is clear that one's parents' demands are an obstacle to the full realization of human life and of the *ātman*, respectfully to oppose these demands is not contrary to the *dharma*."
Ṭhākura: "Do you see, my child, what is in front of you?"
Dākhi: "Yes, it is a rifle."
Ṭhākura: (to test her) "Leave aside all these arguments of yours and do as your grandfather tells you. If not, I'm going to use this rifle."—and with that he grasped the rifle.
Dākhi: "If it is your duty to do so, use the rifle. I have no fear of death; one must die some day. It's all the same, whether I die today from a gunshot or tomorrow from some illness. It is a great thing to die for one's ideal."...

Finally, after all these painful contretemps, the mother and her daughter received *dikṣā*; Rūpāmadevi became Sādhvi Vijñāna Śri and Dākhi, Sādhvi Vicakṣaṇa Śri, *vicakṣaṇa* meaning the one who is farsighted, wise, intelligent, who has discernment.

[After the *dikṣā*, the young Sādhvi Vicakṣaṇa] became a disciple of Sādhvi Jatana Śri. Her two first *cāturmāsyas* were spent in Rājasthāna, at Baḍalū and at Javapura where she gave evidence of her capacity for study. Then, to her great joy, she was summoned to Delhi to the side of the *pravartini*,[7] Sādhvi Suvaraṇa. She stayed there until the latter's Great Departure, that is to say, about seven years. These years of training were thus passed under the direction of a remarkable *guruni*. Sādhvi Suvaraṇa attached prime importance to *dhyāna*, *svādhyāya* and *adhyayana*.[8] She was

7 *Pravartini*—spiritual mother.
8 *Dhyāna*—mental concentration; *svādhyāya*—reflective reading of scripture; *adhyayana*—general studies.

herself the example and also the inspiration of her disciples. For her, *dhyāna* did not consist solely in a technique that one followed for a limited time; *dhyāna* was, as it were, the breathing of her whole being. Her depth of contemplation, people say, was most striking. She habitually remained for six to seven hours in deep concentration, in which *japa*[9] alternated with long moments of silence. Whoever her interlocutor might be, she brooked no idle talk. During the last years of her life, her concentration intensified and she was used to remain thus silent and absorbed for about 12 hours.

Viśvamitrā: **The universal Friend** After the years of training in Delhi, Sādhvi Vicakṣaṇa began her *vihāras*[10] up and down the country. We find her in the North, in the West, in the Centre and in the South. Her ardour is diminished by no obstacle or difficulty.

They have called her: *jaina kokitā*, the Jaina cuckoo, on account of her melodious voice, the sincerity and convincingness of her words, which, like the cuckoo's song, have enchanted all hearts. Of what does Sādhvi Vicakṣaṇa speak? Why do the crowds flock to hear her? The answer is simple: her language is direct, without pomposity or the slightest affectation; she goes straight to the essentials. It is her deep sincerity, her love for all living beings and the clarity with which she expresses herself that not only captivate all hearts, but transform them, removing both barriers and prejudices and lessening or even completely obliterating all enmities. . . .

In the presence of Digambaras, Sādhvi Vicakṣaṇa, herself a Śvetāmbara, attacks neither party, but rather seeks that which may unite them. At Hastināpura, a pilgrimage-place venerated by both traditions, but where the Digambaras are more numerous and more firmly entrenched, she broached the subject of the principal causes of dispute between them: can women attain *mokṣa*?[11] Do the *kevalins* take nourishment or not? The Digambaras answer both questions in the negative, the Śvetāmbaras in the affirmative. Addressing the whole assembly, she told them: "Do we not believe, you and I, that the *ātman*[12] is neither male nor female, that it is subject to no change and that male-ness and female-ness are due to the mode of *karman* relative to the body? But is *mokṣa* attained in the *ātman* or in the body?. . ." In the same vein, she said: "Do the *kevalins* take nourishment or not? Does that really affect the state of *kevāla-jñāna*? *Jñāna*[13] appertains to the *ātman*; nourishment is for the body. It is of little concern to us whether the *kevalins* take nourishment or not. Our aim is to believe in the state of being of the *kevalin* and to strive towards it. These useless quarrels are damaging and lead nowhere." Thus she exhorts them all, as disciples of Mahāvira, to drop these

---

9 *Japa*—recitation of a *mantra*.
10 *Vihāra*—movement from one location to another.
11 *Mokṣā*—liberation of the soul from accumulated *karma*.
12 *Ātman*—soul.
13 *Jñāna*—knowledge.

scholastic disputes inherited from the past, to come to a brotherly understanding and demonstrate *viśvamaitri*[14] instead of reviling one another.

SOURCE: "The Renunciate Life of Sādhvi Vicakṣaṇa," in N. Shanta, *The Unknown Pilgrims: The Voice of the Sādhvis: The History, Spirituality and Life of the Jaina Women Ascetics*, trans. from French by Mary Rogers. Delhi: Sri Satguru Publications, 1997, pp. 585–96

The Righteous Path for Laity and Ascetics

by Acharya Kund-Kund

Acharya Kund-Kund (c. 18–12 BCE) was a revered ascetic and teacher.

Conduct of laymen is eleven-fold, and of ascetics, ten-fold Lord Jinendra who enjoys Supreme Bliss ordains an eleven-fold code of conduct for laymen and ten-fold for ascetics. This is based on right perception.

Code for the laity The stage of the right view, of vows, of attaining equanimity, of fasting on certain holy days, of purity of nourishment, of not consuming food at night, of celibacy or absolute continence, of giving up occupation, of giving up possessions, abstinence from approving household activities, and renunciation of specially prepared food or lodging: These are the eleven stages of the conduct of renunciation for laymen.

The ascetic's code of conduct Supreme forgiveness, humility, uprightness, truthfulness, purity, restraint, austerity, renunciation, non-attachment, and celibacy: These are the ten forms of righteousness of the ascetics.

Supreme forgiveness One who does not feel angry in the least, even while there are direct extraneous reasons for provocations to anger, observes the virtue of forgiveness.

Supreme humility The ascetic who does not in the least feel proud about his ancestry, appearance, birth, wisdom, austerity, scriptural learning, and conduct, observes the virtue of humility.

Supreme uprightness An ascetic, who abstaining from thoughts of deceit follows the code of conduct with a pure heart, observes the virtue of uprightness as enjoined.

Supreme truthfulness An ascetic who abstains from speech that torments others and speaks what does good both to oneself and to others observes the fourth virtue of truthfulness.

Supreme purity An ascetic in the highest stage who has freed himself of desires and conducts himself with aversion for them is endowed with the virtue of purity.

Supreme restraint An ascetic who gives up the afflictions of mind, speech, and body, overcomes all sensual desires, and evolves himself by observing the vows and regulations, is endowed with the virtue of restraint.

Supreme austerity A saint who through meditation and scriptural study realizes the consummation of the subjugation of sensual desires and passions

14 *Viśvamaitri*—universal friendship.

and is devoted to contemplation of Self, truly practices the virtue of austerity.

Supreme renunciation The ascetic who has abjured the desire for all objects and is imbued with the three-fold detachment (from the mundane world, his own body, and pleasures) is endowed with the virtue of renunciation; so have the Jinendras declared.

Supreme non-attachment The homeless ascetic who has forsaken all possessions, has subdued his thought impulses for pleasure and pain and acts with equanimity, is endowed with the virtue of non-attachment.

Supreme celibacy The ascetic who on seeing all parts of women's body refrains from excitement with passion about them is really able to practice the rigorous virtue of celibacy.

[Explanation: Sex, in fact, has no meaning to a saint who views the physical body as inert and extraneous matter.]

Only those who observe the ascetic's code attain liberation The soul that discontinues the laymen's path to follow the ascetic's righteous path cannot fail to attain emancipation. This ought to be the incessant contemplation on righteousness.

Contemplation of Self with equanimity From the real standpoint, the soul stands distinct from the vows of both the householder and the ascetic. The pure soul should therefore be contemplated upon constantly with equanimity.

[Explanation: With due consideration of practical norms, different codes of conduct have been prescribed for the pious householders and the ascetic. But this distinction is purely conventional.

From the strictly real standpoint, it is the pristine purity of the Soul that is to be contemplated upon. Self-realization is the ultimate goal of the householder and the ascetic alike. The layman in his spiritual quest adopts the ascetic's vows as he advances spiritually. His aim is to liberate himself from the karmic bondage.]

SOURCE: Acharya Kund-Kund, *Barasa Anuvekkha*. Delhi: Kund-Kund Bharati, 1990, pp. 76–86

Jain ethics today

Remembering our own First Principles by Michael Tobias

Jains are a highly respected and economically successful community within India and in other countries where they have settled. It seems that their success has something to do with their strict principles. Michael Tobias, a global ecologist, author of 35 books, filmmaker, professor of environmental studies, and president of the Dancing Star Foundation in California, which is dedicated to animal and habitat preservation, has done research into Jain ethics and finds them a viable basis for a sustainable future.

Jainism is a momentous example to all of us that there can, and does, exist a successful, ecologically responsible way of life which is abundantly non-violent in thought, action and deed. We might misread our history, go forward confusedly to perpetrate other follies, but we will do so knowing that there is a viable alternative. . . .

According to Jainism, animals will eventually be reborn as human animals, at which time they will have to choose: empathy, peace, compassion—*ahimsa*—or perpetual degrees of violence. Humanity is the launching site for this choice. We have it in our power to reverse an evolutionary masterplan that is brutal, that needs fixing. The Jains have modeled themselves after a vision of nature that favors peace and love over war and hatred, and they have envisioned—indeed, realized—a major world religion whose guiding tenet is this heartfelt aspiration. The reader is likely to stop here and declare, "But all religions—or certainly most of them—are about love. What's the big deal?" Jainism departs from this theoretical norm in one striking and all-important manner: it has never deviated from its original pledge. If we can understand how an ancient, seemingly uncomplicated ethical position can continue to flourish in a more complex modernity, we will have accomplished a critical hurdle. . . .

Contrary to evolutionary expectation, the elephant, the gorilla, the rhino, the hippo, the megamouth shark (the largest shark in the world) are all vegetarians, in spite of their size and the human presumption that the mighty need meat . . . Others will argue that they simply *crave* the taste of a hamburger once in a while. And since there's no law preventing it, and nobody's looking over their shoulder, they can afford to ignore their conscience for the few minutes that it takes to devour a fast-food lunch. Jains have analyzed those "few minutes" and worked out various meditations and disciplines to avoid such temptation. . . . Killing, directly or indirectly, is the worst of all toxins. Not only does it kill a living being, but it inflicts enormous damage on one's own soul, which is the quintessence of all life. The soul itself, say the Jains, is not the one eating the hamburger. The soul is pure. But the physical body and its complex of desires and neuroses attach themselves to the soul, weaken it, obscure its nascent purity, and this process thickens with each needless moment of oblivion, until the soul is virtually snuffed out, mumbling in perdurable [eternal] darkness, with no one to hear it, and no hope of ever making beautiful music.

Those "few minutes" of psychological impasse, passion, disinterest, oblivion, appetite, are the same few moments that it takes to vent rage, to murder someone, to inflict every pain known to the human arsenal. Those few moments—repeated in so many variations—caused World War I—with its 20 million dead, 50 million injured; and nearly every other violent tantrum and disorder known to the brain. To temper that killer in man, and the subsequent killing fields, is to grope with those few moments where conflict begins.

Two minutes of unthinking, unfeeling behavior: Whether in the eating of a hamburger, the casting of a fishing line, or, more subtly, the habit of taking one's children to a circus to view animals who in fact have been reduced to insanity and pain. Two minutes of our own insanity, in the breeding of captive animals who were meant to be free, or worse—the abandoning of those pets to certain death; in the reining, or worse, the racing of horses; the killing of bugs in a frenzy of vindictiveness, as opposed to more patiently removing them without injury. The litany of transgressions cascades with numbing ubiquity. And it all comes down to the collaboration—mindful or not—with atrocity carried out by, or on behalf of, humans, and committed against other living creatures—whether around the dinner table, on the job, on the farm, the ranch, in the street, at the grocery store, in one's financial investments, in the donations one makes (many medical foundations, for example, put their charity dollars towards animal research—animal torture, in other words), in the clothes one wears, and so on....

Jains are accountable to nature, and thus to themselves, to their families, their community, and to the vast menageries of life forms which co-inhabit this planet with them. Jainism's accessible genius is this total embrace of the earth—so ancient, so contemporary....

Everyone I have ever known who has taken the time to learn about Jainism has become something of a Jain. I truly believe such conversion is unavoidable, not because the Jains teach anything we don't already intimately understand, at least in our hearts, but precisely because they remind us of our own first principles in such a way that we can no longer deny the urgency and beauty of such remembrance.

SOURCE: Michael Tobias, *Life Force: The World of Jainism.* Berkeley, CA: Asian Humanities Press, 1991, pp. 5–16

GLOSSARY

Ahimsa Principle of non-violence, based on reverence for all life.

Anekantavada The principle of manifold aspects, or the relativity of knowledge.

Canon The official list of books with authority in a religion, either because they are believed to be inspired or revealed, or have been so designated.

Digambara (atmosphere-clad) A nude Jain sect.

Five Jain Vows Non-violence, truthfulness, non-stealing, continence, and non-possessiveness.

Jiva Soul; every soul is potentially divine, and greatly influenced by *karma*.

Karma In Jainism, the cosmic moral law of consequences for ethical actions and their effects from prior incarnations; it appears as subtle particles that accumulate on the soul as a result of one's thoughts and actions, and is to be avoided by ascetic self-restraint.

Manifold aspects The multiplicity and relativity of all points of view, visible to perfected souls, promoting tolerance and non-violence.

Renunciation Reducing desires and minimizing consumption to free the soul from karmic entanglements and lessen earthly pollution.

Stoicism Impassive indifference to pleasure or pain (Greek word).

Svetambara (white-clad) A Jain sect that wears white clothing.

Syadvada The relativity of truth to different points of view.

Tirthankara (bridgebuilder) The 24 great enlightened Jain teachers.

HOLY DAYS

Most Jain festivals celebrate events in the lives of the Tirthankaras. Scriptures about their lives are read during the festivals.

Diwali A celebration to commemorate Mahavira's attainment of liberation.

Paryushana The custom of wandering monks staying in one place during the rainy season, when they meditate and teach

ocal Jain householders the principles of *dharma*.

Pratikramana A meditation for reflecting on one's spiritual journey and renewing the faith; it may be daily, monthly, or annual.

Samet Sikhar Yatra A popular pilgrimage to Samet Sikhar in Bihar, India, where 20 Tirthankaras attained *nirvana*.

HISTORICAL OUTLINE

c. 900 BCE—life of 22nd Tirthankara, Arishtameni, who renounced the cruelty of society to become a wandering ascetic

c. 900–800 BCE—life of 23rd Tirthankara, "Beloved Parshva," a saintly teacher for 70 years

c. 599–527 BCE—life of Mahavira, greatest Jain saint and 24th Tirthankara

c. 300 BCE—some *Agam Sutras* written down

after 300 BCE—division of Jains into Svetambara (white-clad) and Digambara (atmosphere-clad, i.e. naked) sects

c. 450 CE—division of Svetambaras and Digambaras formalized

1526–1818—new orders emerge under Muslim Mughal rule

1818 onward—Jain teaching spreads out from India

1970s–80s—Jain monks establish centers outside India

REVIEW QUESTIONS

1   Explain how Jains practice *ahimsa*, how it has influenced the wider world, and your opinion of its origin and effectiveness.
2   Contrast Western consumerism with Jain asceticism and evaluate each.
3   Does the Jain principle of manifold aspects of the relativity of truths have a place in religion, which usually stresses orthodoxy?

DISCUSSION QUESTIONS

1   What do you think would motivate a person to become a Jain monk or nun?
2   What three different reactions to Jains do you think would come from people of three major different personality or social types?
3   Do you think that the Jain religion is too passive and individualistic, or that it does have an impact in changing society?

INFORMATION RESOURCES

De Bary, W. Theodore. *Sources of Indian Tradition*. New York: Columbia University Press, 1958.

Dundas, Paul. "Jainism," in *Encyclopedia of Religion*, ed. Lindsay Jones. 2nd ed. Vol. 7, pp. 4764–72. New York: Macmillan, 2005.

Introduction to Jainism
<http://www.cs.colostate.edu/~malaiya/jainhlinks.html>

Jain Holy Days
<http://www.cs.colostate.edu/~malaiya/paryushan.html>

Jain, Surender K., ed. *Glimpses of Jainism*. Delhi: Motilal Banarsidass, 1997.

Jain Words Glossary
<http://www.cs.colostate.edu/~malaiya/jaingloss.html>

Kund-Kund, Acharya. *Barasa Anuvekkha*. 2nd ed. Delhi: Kund-Kund Bharati, 2003.

Müller, F. Max, and **Hermann Jacobi**, eds. *Jaina Sutras in Two Volumes: Sacred Books of the East Volumes 22 and 45*. Delhi: Low Price Publications, 1996.

Sangave, Vilas A. *Aspects of Jaina Religion*. Delhi: Bharatiya Jnanpith, 1990.

Shah, Unmakant, and **G. Ralph Strohl**. "Jainism," in *Encyclopedia Britannica*. Vol. 22, pp. 247–53. London, 1997.

Tobias, Michael. *Life Force: The World of Jainism*. Berkeley, CA: Asian Humanities Press, 1991.

CHAPTER 5

BUDDHISM

Siddhartha Gautama, it is told, was born prince of the Sakya clan in northeastern India, and probably lived 563–483 BCE. He renounced his comfortable life to seek the solution to suffering. He first sat with famous gurus, and practiced severe austerities, almost starving himself to death. Unsatisfied, he meditated, awakened to his true nature, then taught a "middle way" between luxury and austerity.

Having become a **Buddha**, or Awakened One, he taught a practical way of escaping from suffering and achieving liberation. Monks and then nuns whom he trained were organized into orders, and the teachings spread throughout Asia, south into Sri Lanka and southeast Asia, north into Tibet and China, and east into Korea and Japan. Three major historical traditions developed: the **Theravada**, the **Mahayana**, and the **Vajrayana**. Contemporary Buddhism, as it spreads across the globe, is strengthening an earlier theme: Engaged Buddhism.

To become a Buddhist is to adopt the Three Refuges: "I take refuge in the Buddha, the **dharma**, and the *sangha* [community of practicing Buddhists]." It is not the Buddha who saves. It is by living by the *dharma* which the Buddha taught that one achieves liberation from the continual painful round of births and deaths into the blissful state known as **nirvana**. The techniques for becoming conscious of the workings of the mind and for bringing it under control have become highly appealing to contemporary citizens of industrial societies who are seeking peace of mind.

Buddha taught the Four Noble Truths: (1) Life inevitably involves suffering; (2) Suffering originates in desires for transient things; (3) Suffering can be ceased by the eradication of desires; (4) The path to liberation from desires is the Eightfold Path: (a) Right understanding, (b) Right thoughts or motives, (c) Right speech, (d) Right action, (e) Right livelihood, (f) Right effort, (g) Right mindfulness, and (h) Right medita-

Basic Principles: The Four Noble Truths

tion. Buddhists may undertake a further set of basic obligations or precepts (*sila*): (1) Not harming living beings; (2) Not taking anything not given; (3) Not misusing sensual pleasures; (4) Not speaking falsely or abusively; (5) Not taking intoxicating drinks or drugs; (6) Not eating solid food after midday; (7) Not engaging in frivolous amusements; (8) Not adorning one's body; (9) Not sleeping in a high or luxurious place; and (10) Not being involved with money.

The Awakened One

Several elaborated traditional texts about the Buddha's life have been preserved and revered, notably the account told by Asvaghosha, who lived during the second century CE. In his Sanskrit epic *Buddhacarita*, or *Acts of the Buddha*, Asvaghosha shows a deep reverence for the Buddha.

Defeat of Mara and Enlightenment by Asvaghosha

The enlightenment of the Buddha is described in detail in Asvaghosha's *Acts of the Buddha*. Here Sakya Gautama, at age 35, meditating at the foot of a *bodhi* tree, is tempted by Mara, Hindu personification of evil. His temptations, such as sensual gratification and wantonness, are resisted by the Buddha, whose steadfast tranquillity defeats all of Mara's beastly lures and transforms his thunderous wrath into harmless flowers. Similarly, Jesus defeats Satan's temptation during his desert retreat. Thus, enlightenment blossomed and Gautama became the Buddha.

When the great sage, the scion of a line of royal seers, sat down there, after making his vow for liberation, the world rejoiced, but Mara, the enemy of the good Law, trembled. . . .

His three sons, Caprice, Gaiety and Wantonness, and his three daughters, Discontent, Delight and Thirst, asked him why he was depressed in mind, and he answered them thus:

"The sage, wearing the armour of his vow and drawing the bow of resolution with the arrow of wisdom, sits yonder, desiring to conquer my realm; hence this despondency of my mind." . . .

Then as soon as Māra thought of his army in his desire to obstruct the tranquillity of the Sākya sage, his followers stood round him, in various forms and carrying lances, trees, javelins, clubs and swords in their hands;

Having the faces of boars, fishes, horses, asses and camels, or the countenances of tigers, bears, lions and elephants, one-eyed, many-mouthed, three-headed, with pendulous bellies and speckled bellies; . . .

Then Māra gave orders to his raging army of demons for terrifying the sage. Thereon that army of his resolved to break down his steadfastness with their various powers.

Some stood trying to frighten him, their many tongues hanging out flickering, their teeth sharp-pointed, their eyes like the sun's orb, their mouths gaping, their ears sticking up stiff as spikes.

As they stood there in such guise, horrible in appearance and manner, he was no more alarmed by them or shrank before them than before over-excited infants at play. . . .

Some lifted up rocks and trees, but were unable to hurl them at the sage. Instead they fell down with the trees and rocks, like the spurs of the Vindhyas when shattered by the levin.[1] . . .

---

1 Levin—lightning.

Thereon others spat out snakes from their mouths as from rotten treetrunks; as if bound by spells, they did not hiss or raise themselves or move in his presence.

Others transformed themselves into huge clouds, accompanied by lightning and the fearsome crash of thunder-stones, and let loose on the tree a shower of stones, which turned into a pleasant rain of flowers. . . .

The less the sage was afraid of the fearsome troops of that array, the more was Māra, the enemy of the upholders of the Law, cast down with grief and wrath.

Then a certain being of high station and invisible form, standing in the sky and seeing that Māra was menacing the seer . . . addressed him with imperious voice:

"Māra, you should not toil to no purpose, give up your murderous intent and go in peace. For this sage can no more be shaken by you than Meru, greatest of mountains, by the wind. . . .

For such is his vow, his energy, his psychic power, his compassion for creation, that he will not rise up till he has attained the truth, just as the thousand-rayed sun does not rise without dispelling the darkness. . . .

His purpose is to deliver creation which is bound fast in mind by the snares of delusion." . . .

And when Māra heard that speech of his and observed the great sage's unshakenness, then, his efforts frustrated, he went away dejectedly with the arrows by which the world is smitten in the heart. . . .

The heavens shone with the moon like a maiden with a smile, and there fell a rain of sweet-smelling flowers filled with water. . . .

Then, after conquering Māra's host by his steadfastness and tranquillity, he, the master of trance, put himself into trance in order to obtain exact knowledge of the ultimate reality. . . .

As though living them over again, he recalled thousands of births, that he had been so-and-so in such-and-such a place and that passing out of that life he had come hither.

Then the compassionate one was filled with compassion for all living beings. . . .

Then with that completely purified divine eyesight he beheld the entire world, as it were in a spotless mirror.

His compassionateness waxed greater, as he saw the passing away and rebirth of all creatures according as their acts were lower or higher.

Those living beings whose acts are sinful pass to the sphere of misery, those others whose deeds are good win a place in the triple heaven.

The former are reborn in the very dreadful fearsome hell and, alas, are woefully tormented with sufferings of many kinds. . . .

Thus with the divine eyesight he examined the five spheres of life and found nothing substantial in existence, just as no heartwood is found in a plantain tree when it is cut open. . . .

"Alas! Living creatures obtain but toil; over and over again they are born, grow old, die, pass on and are reborn.

Further man's sight is veiled by passion and by the darkness of delusion, and from the excess of his blindness he does not know the way out of this great suffering." ...

Penetrating the truth to its core, he understood that old age and death are produced, when there is birth. ...

Then he saw rightly that birth is produced from existence due to the power of the act.

With his divine eyesight he saw that active being proceeds from the act, not from a Creator or from Nature or from a self or without a cause. ...

Then this conclusion came firmly on him, that from the annihilation of birth old age and death are suppressed, that from the destruction of existence birth itself is destroyed. ...

Further the latter is suppressed through the suppression of thirst; if sensation does not exist, thirst does not exist. ...

Similarly if name-and-form is rightly suppressed, all the six organs of sense are destroyed too; and the former is suppressed through the suppression of consciousness. ...

The best of men saw no self anywhere from the summit of existence downwards and came to tranquillity, like a fire whose fuel is burnt out, by the eightfold path of supreme insight, which starts forth and quickly reaches the desired point. ...

Pleasant breezes blew softly, the heaven rained moisture from a cloudless sky, and from the trees there dropped flowers and fruit out of due season as if to do him honour. ...

At that moment none gave way to anger, no one was ill or experienced any discomfort, none resorted to sinful ways or indulged in intoxication of mind; the world became tranquil, as though it had reached perfection.

The companies of deities, who are devoted to salvation, rejoiced; even the beings in the spheres below felt joy. Through the prosperity of the party who favoured virtue the *dharma* spread abroad and the world rose above passion and the darkness of ignorance. ...

Then for seven days, free from discomfort of body, he sat, looking into his own mind, his eyes never winking. The sage fulfilled his heart's desire, reflecting that on that spot he had obtained liberation.

Then the sage, who had grasped the principle of causation and was firmly fixed in the system of impersonality, roused himself, and, filled with great compassion, he gazed on the world with his Buddha-eye for the sake of its tranquillity.

Seeing that the world was lost in false views and vain efforts and that its passions were gross, seeing too that the law of salvation was exceeding subtle, he set his mind on remaining immobile.

Then remembering his former promise, he formed a resolution for the preaching of tranquillity. ...

Then, wishing to preach tranquillity in order to dispel the darkness of ignorance, as the rising sun the darkness, Gautama proceeded to the blessed city.

SOURCE: Asvaghosha, *Buddhacarita, or Acts of the Buddha*, trans. E. H. Johnson. New enlarged ed. Delhi: Motilal Banarsidass, 1984, pp. 188–217

Speculations Undeclared from the *Culamalunkya Sutta*

One of the Buddha's most notable teachings was his practical rejection of most metaphysical speculation. In this passage from the *Culamalunkya Sutta*, he teaches Mālunkyāputta, a disciple, that efforts to answer speculative questions such as whether the world is eternal are fruitless. They are like a man shot with an arrow who refuses to allow medical treatment until he is told the social caste of his attacker, his name, his size, his skin color, his home town, and the details of his weapon. Before he learned all this, he would die. The Buddha left such speculative metaphysics undeclared because they do not lead to the direct meditative experience of enlightenment that overcomes suffering.

Thus have I heard. On one occasion the Blessed One was living at Sāvatthī in Jeta's Grove, Anāthapindika's Park.

Then, while the venerable Mālunkyāputta was alone in meditation, the following thought arose in his mind:

"These speculative views have been undeclared by the Blessed One, set aside and rejected by him, namely: 'the world is eternal' and 'the world is not eternal'; 'the world is finite' and 'the world is infinite'; 'the soul is the same as the body' and 'the soul is one thing and the body another'; and 'after death a Tathāgata[2] exists' and 'after death a Tathāgata does not exist' and 'after death a Tathāgata both exists and does not exist' and 'after death a Tathāgata neither exists nor does not exist.' The Blessed One does not declare these to me, and I do not approve of and accept the fact that he does not declare these to me, so I shall go to the Blessed One and ask him the meaning of this." . . .

"Suppose, Mālunkyāputta, a man were wounded by an arrow thickly smeared with poison, and his friends and companions, his kinsmen and relatives, brought a surgeon to treat him. The man would say: 'I will not let the surgeon pull out this arrow until I know whether the man who wounded me was a noble or a brahmin or a merchant or a worker.' And he would say: 'I will not let the surgeon pull out this arrow until I know the name and clan of the man who wounded me; . . . until I know whether the man who wounded me was tall or short or of middle height; . . . until I know whether the man who wounded me was dark or brown or golden-skinned; . . . until I know whether the man who wounded me lives in such a village or town or city; . . . until I know whether the bow that wounded me was a long bow or a crossbow; . . . until I know whether the

---

2 Tathāgata—("transcendent one") one who has realized the truth.

bowstring that wounded me was fibre or reed or sinew or hemp or bark; . . . until I know whether the shaft that wounded me was wild or cultivated; . . . until I know with what kind of feathers the shaft that wounded me was fitted—whether those of a vulture or a crow or a hawk or a peacock or a stork; . . .

"All this would still not be known to that man and meanwhile he would die. . . .

"Mālunkyāputta, if there is the view 'the world is eternal,' the holy life cannot be lived; and if there is the view 'the world is not eternal,' the holy life cannot be lived. Whether there is the view 'the world is eternal' or the view 'the world is not eternal,' there is birth, there is ageing, there is death, there are sorrow, lamentation, pain, grief, and despair, the destruction of which I prescribe here and now. . . .

"Therefore, Mālunkyāputta, remember what I have left undeclared as undeclared, and remember what I have declared as declared. And what have I left undeclared? 'The world is eternal'—I have left undeclared. 'The world is not eternal'—I have left undeclared. 'The world is finite'—I have left undeclared. 'The world is infinite'—I have left undeclared. 'The soul is the same as the body'—I have left undeclared. 'The soul is one thing and the body another'—I have left undeclared. 'After death a Tathāgata exists'—I have left undeclared. 'After death a Tathāgata does not exist'—I have left undeclared. 'After death a Tathāgata both exists and does not exist'—I have left undeclared. 'After death a Tathāgata neither exists nor does not exist'—I have left undeclared.

"Why have I left that undeclared? Because it is unbeneficial, it does not belong to the fundamentals of the holy life, it does not lead to disenchantment, to dispassion, to cessation, to peace, to direct knowledge, to enlightenment, to Nibbāna.[3] That is why I have left it undeclared.

"And what have I declared? 'This is suffering'—I have declared. 'This is the origin of suffering'—I have declared. 'This is the cessation of suffering'— I have declared. 'This is the way leading to the cessation of suffering'—I have declared.

"Why have I declared that? Because it is beneficial, it belongs to the fundamentals of the holy life, it leads to disenchantment, to dispassion, to cessation, to peace, to direct knowledge, to enlightenment, to Nibbāna. That is why I have declared it.

"Therefore, Mālunkyāputta, remember what I have left undeclared as undeclared, and remember what I have declared as declared."

That is what the Blessed One said. The venerable Mālunkyāputta was satisfied and delighted in the Blessed One's words.

SOURCE: *The Middle Length Discourses of the Buddha*, trans. Bhikkhu Nanamoli and Bhikkhu Bodhi. Boston: Wisdom Publications, 1995, pp. 533–6

3 Nibbāna—*nirvana*.

Theravada

The Theravada (Teaching of the Elders) traditions are the traditions of
Buddhism as it spread south, to Sri Lanka (largely in the third century
CE), then to southeast Asia, to regions now called Myanmar, Malaysia,
Indonesia, and Cambodia (eleventh to fourteenth centuries). Theravada
adheres to early scriptures (*suttas*) and monastic renunciation. Its texts are drawn
from the Pali **Canon**, recorded in Sri Lanka as early as the first century BCE.
Theravadan meditation emphasizes stages of attainment and mindfulness or
Vipassana (insight) meditation. The ideal Buddhist is the *arhat*, a monk taking
refuge in the Buddha, an accomplished ascetic who attains *nirvana* (*nibbana* in Pali)
through self-effort.

Theravada
and a Relic

The Dhammapada

The *Dhammapada* (Teaching of the Verses) is a collection of 423 key Buddhist
verses of wide influence and importance. Teachers are often expected to conclude
a discourse with a key verse (*gatha*), and this text is a collection of such verses.
It urges a life of peace and non-violence, and teaches that hatred can never be
overcome by hatred, only by kindness. **Karmic** consequences follow from all
actions, and actions follow naturally from thoughts. This extract emphasizes the
importance of restraint and awakening to transcendence, rather than resorting
simply to a life of seclusion. The texts are recorded in Pali, Tibetan, Chinese, and
other languages.

Better than a thousand utterances, comprising useless words, is one single
   beneficial word, by hearing which, one attains peace. . . .

Though one should conquer a thousand times a thousand men in battle, he
   who conquers his own self, is the greatest of all conquerors. . . .

Ah, happily do we live without hate amongst the hateful; amidst hateful men
   we dwell unhating.

Ah, happily do we live in good health amongst the ailing; amidst ailing men
   we dwell in good health (free from the disease of passions).

Ah, happily do we live without yearning (for sensual pleasures) amongst
   those who yearn (for them); amidst those who yearn (for them) we
   dwell without yearning.

Ah, happily do we live, we who have no impediments. Feeders of joy shall
   we be even as the gods of the Radiant Realm.

Victory breeds hatred. The defeated live in pain. Happily the peaceful live,
   giving up victory and defeat.

There is no fire like lust, no crime like hate. There is no ill like the body, no
   bliss higher than Peace (Nibbana).

Hunger is the greatest disease. **Aggregates** are the greatest ill. Knowing this
   as it really is (the wise realize) Nibbana, bliss supreme.

Good health is the highest gain. Contentment is the greatest wealth.
   Trustworthy ones are the best kinsmen. Nibbana is the highest Bliss.

Having tasted the flavour of seclusion and the flavour of appeasement, free
    from anguish and stain becomes he, imbibing the taste of the joy of the
    Dhamma.
Happy is one, who beholds the holy ones. To live with the holy ones is ever
    pleasant. It would be pleasant if one never comes across a fool.
Truly, he who moves in company with fools grieves for a long time.
    Association with the foolish is ever painful as with a foe. Happy is
    association with the wise, even like meeting with kinsfolk.
Therefore: With the intelligent, the wise, the learned, the enduring, the
    dutiful and the Ariya[4]—with a man of such virtue and intellect should
    one associate, as the moon (follows) the starry path.

SOURCE: "The Thousands" and "Happiness," in *Dhammapada*, trans. Chng Tiak Jung and Tan Chade
Meng, verses 100, 103, 197–208
<http://www.serve.com/cmtan/Dhammapada/index.html>

Rejection of Birth Castes from the *Vasettha Sutta*

When the Buddha was living, there were several religious movements in India that
arose out of dissatisfaction with the external religious formalities and the rigid
social implications of the Hindu brahmanic caste system. Some protested against
this system by becoming wandering ascetics. The Hindu *Upanishads* literature grew
out of this movement, emphasizing renunciation and transcendental knowledge,
rather than ritual and caste. In northeastern India, less influenced by the brahmanic
traditions, arose several non-orthodox sects, including Buddhism. This extract,
from the *Vasettha Sutta*, is a Buddhist statement rejecting the belief that one
is born into one's social caste, and affirming that one's merit is determined by
one's actions.

One is not a brahmin by birth,
Nor by birth a non-brahmin.
By action is one a brahmin,
By action is one a non-brahmin.

For men are farmers by their acts,
And by their acts are craftsmen too;
And men are merchants by their acts,
And by their acts are servants too.

And men are robbers by their acts,
And by their acts are soldiers too;
And men are chaplains by their acts,
And by their acts are rulers too.

SOURCE: *The Middle Length Discourses of the Buddha*, trans. Bhikkhu Nanamoli and Bhikkhu Bodhi.
Boston: Wisdom Publications, 1995, p. 806

---

4 Ariya Buddhism—a path of liberation from the human condition using spiritual concentration and
intellectual catharsis, following the earliest teachings of the Buddha.

Mahayana

Mahayana (Large Vehicle) Buddhism is most prominent in Tibet, Mongolia, China, Korea, Vietnam, and Japan. The Mahayana *dharma* (teaching) emphasizes one's inherent wisdom and compassion for all sentient beings. The ideal practitioner (**bodhisattva**) honors the Pali Canon, yet delays his/her own *nirvana* in the effort to liberate other beings. Mahayana texts (*sutras*) emphasize the Buddha-nature (Buddhata) in all things and the importance of direct experience. The Buddha is not seen primarily as a historical person, as in Theravada, but is now conceived rather as a universal principle, a cosmic presence. Images of this Buddha-nature are common, although they are not to be conceived of as divinities. Two widespread *bodhisattvas* expressing compassion and mercy are Avalokiteshvara (masculine) and **Guanyin** (feminine). Mahayana *dharma* also teaches the emptiness of all things, in paradoxical language meant to take the mind beyond ordinary thought.

Emptiness by Nagarjuna

Sunyata (emptiness) is a basic element of Mahayana Buddhism. This is a subtle and debatable term, full of paradox. Early Buddhism initially rejected the brahmanic notion of the *atman*, or eternal soul, and opposed it with the *anatman*. For Buddhists, the five aggregates (**skandhas**) composing a human are empty of a permanent soul. This concept was soon extended to deny any permanent self-existing essence or substance in the universe. Buddhists emphasize that when we envision the independent existence of things, we cling to them. Seeing their basic emptiness permits us to release the clinging.

Nagarjuna was a major Buddhist philosopher who lived in India about 150 to 250 CE. His philosophy of emptiness has had enduring importance in subsequent Buddhist thought and is central to Mahayana's Prajnaparamita (Perfection of Wisdom) literature. The source of existence, he argues, cannot be described, but only realized meditatively, due to its undifferentiated nature. In *sunyata* all oppositions between earth and Heaven, *nirvana* and **samsara**, disappear. Worldly appearances, gods, and the self do have a conventional nature, but no independent substance, or self-existent thing-ness. Nagarjuna's "emptiness" is not the Western void of a hellish meaninglessness, or a denial of the world, but the very reason that the world exists.

An Analysis of a Self-Existent Thing

1   The production of a self-existent thing by a conditioning cause is not possible, [for,] being produced through dependence on a cause, a self-existent thing would be "something which is produced."
2   How, indeed, will a self-existent thing *become* "something which is produced"? Certainly, a self-existent thing [by definition] is "not-produced" and is independent of anything else.
3   If there is an absence of a self-existent thing, how will an other-existent thing come into being?

SOURCE: Frederick Streng, *Emptiness: A Study in Religious Meaning*. Nashville, TN: Abingdon Press, 1967, p. 199

The Heart Sutra

Monastic Life

The *Heart Sutra* comes from the Indian Prajnaparamita literature, about 350 CE, and is often chanted in Buddhist ceremonies. It distills the teachings on emptiness. The goal is to become a *bodhisattva*, seeking complete understanding, and dedicated to serving others by skillful means. Simultaneously, the realization is that there is no such thing as a *bodhisattva*, understanding, dedication, or attainment. To realize this emptiness is to approach perfection of wisdom.

Homage to the Perfection of Wisdom, the lovely, the holy!

Avalokita [Avalokiteshvara, a form of the Buddha emphasizing compassion], the holy Lord and Bodhisattva, was moving in the deep course of the wisdom which has gone beyond. He looked down from on high, he beheld but five heaps [aggregates], and he saw that in their own-being they were empty.

Here, O Sariputra [one of the Buddha's two principal followers], form is emptiness, and the very emptiness is form; emptiness does not differ from form, form does not differ from emptiness; whatever is form, that is emptiness, whatever is emptiness, that is form. The same is true of feelings, perceptions, impulses and consciousness.

Here, O Sariputra, all dharmas are marked with emptiness; they are not produced or stopped, not defiled or immaculate, not deficient or complete.

Therefore, O Sariputra, in emptiness there is no form, nor feeling, nor perception, nor impulse, nor consciousness; no eye, ear, nose, tongue, body, mind; no forms, sounds, smells, tastes, touchables or objects of mind; no sight-organ-element, and so forth until we come to: no mind-consciousness-element; there is no ignorance, no extinction of ignorance, and so forth until we come to: there is no decay and death, no extinction of decay and death; there is no suffering, no origination, no stopping, no path; there is no cognition, no attainment, and no non-attainment.

Therefore, O Sariputra, it is because of his indifference to any kind of personal attainment that a Bodhisattva, through having relied on the perfection of wisdom, dwells without thought-coverings. In the absence of thought-coverings he has not been made to tremble, he has overcome what can upset, and in the end he attains to Nirvana. All those who appear as Buddhas in the three periods of time fully awake to the utmost, right and perfect enlightenment because they have relied on the perfection of wisdom.

Therefore one should know the Prajnaparamita as the great spell, the spell of great knowledge, the utmost spell, the unequalled spell, allayer of all suffering, in truth—for what could go wrong? By the Prajnaparamita has this spell been delivered. It runs like this: *Gate! Gate! Paragate! Parasamgate! Bodhi Svaha!* (Gone! Gone! Gone beyond! Gone altogether beyond! O what an awakening!) All Hail! This completes the Heart of Perfect Wisdom.

SOURCE: Edward Conze, trans., *Buddhist Scriptures*. Harmondsworth, Middlesex: Penguin Books, 1986, pp. 162–4

Discovering Universal Emptiness by Dogen

Dogen was a leading Japanese Buddhist philosopher who lived 1200–53 in Kyoto and had a major influence on **Zen**. Orphaned at age seven, he joined a monastery at 13, then traveled to China, returned to Japan and founded the Soto Zen sect and the still-active Eiheiji temple. He struggled with questions such as whether enlightenment is gradual or instantaneous, and concluded that in all *zazen* (sitting meditation) one is in the midst of realizing Buddha-nature. Some said all things have the Buddha-nature, but he said that all things are the Buddha-nature, although this realization remains dormant until awakened in Buddhist practice. *Zazen* is the practice of non-thinking, which goes beyond ideas of good or bad, enlightenment or illusion, because universal emptiness is as close as your nose.

When we reflect upon our experience and practice of zazen we actualize the life of the Buddhas and Patriarchs and receive their right transmission which has been handed down from generation to generation. Our subject today is universal emptiness—the universal emptiness that is in our entire body, skin, flesh, bones and marrow. Universal emptiness has numerous meanings and interpretations—the 20 kinds, the 84,000 kinds and so on—[and if you can define it properly you can be said to be a Buddha or Patriarch].

Zen Master Shakyō Ezō once asked Zen Master Seidō Chizō, who was Shakyō's senior, "Do you know how to comprehend universal emptiness?" "Of course," Seidō answered. "How?" Shakyō wanted to know. Seidō grasped a handful of air. "Aha! You don't know how to grasp it then!" Shakyō exclaimed. Seidō challenged Shakyō to show him universal emptiness. Shakyō grabbed Seidō's nose and yanked it until he cried out in pain. "Now I've got it!" Seidō said. "Yes, now you know what it is," Shakyō agreed.

The purpose of Shakyō's initial question was to find whether or not our entire body is hands and eyes [i.e., universal emptiness]. Seidō's "Of course" was a defilement of Buddhism. To say you understand universal emptiness is to defile the truth—universal emptiness falls to the earth. When Shakyō asked Seidō how he understood universal emptiness he was asking him to show the "suchness" of universal emptiness; that is, show the true state of reality. However, we must be careful about this since circumstances are constantly changing the form of "suchness." When Seidō grabbed a handful of air it revealed that he understood only the head, but not the tail, of universal emptiness. Shakyō then saw that Seidō's understanding was limited and he could not even dream about universal emptiness. It was too profound and absolute for him. Therefore, Seidō asked Shakyō to show him universal emptiness. Half of the answer was already contained in Seidō's request but he had to discover the rest by himself. Shakyō grabbed his nose; he hid in Seidō's nostril so to speak. At that time universal emptiness in the form of Seidō and universal emptiness in the form of Shakyō were united and only universal emptiness remained. Prior to having his nose yanked

Seidō thought that universal emptiness existed outside himself, but now he
has cast off body and mind. Yet you must be careful not to cling to such a
discovery of universal emptiness—do not defile yourself but practice within
your own universal emptiness. Shakyō confirmed Seidō's understanding but
did not try to grasp universal emptiness with his hands—universal emptiness
cannot be grasped with our hands. After all, the entire world is universal
emptiness; there is absolutely no room for doubt. We can now see why this
koan[5] is so famous.

SOURCE: Dogen Zenji, *Shobogenzo (The Eye and Treasury of the True Law)*, trans. Kosen Nishiyama and
John Stevens. Sendai, Japan: Daihokkaikaku, 1975, vol. 1, pp. 130–1

Zen and Koans by Daisetz T. Suzuki

D. T. Suzuki (1870–1966), a major early popularizer of Zen in the United States,
taught Buddhist philosophy in Kyoto, Japan. He began Zen training at age 22, then
spent 13 years in the United States, translating and writing about Zen. He spoke to
Westerners in the language of ego ("we are too ego-centered"), love (which gives
us "a glimpse into the infinity of things"), and tragedy ("God gives tragedies to
perfect man"), as we can see in the first part of the extract below. In the second
part, Suzuki discusses the classic method of learning by the Zen *koan*, a riddle given
to a student by a Zen master. Classic *koans* are "What is the sound of one hand
clapping?" or "Show me your face before you were born." Such a riddle may
create a frustrating crisis for the student, but the Master strives to guide one past
the merely intellectual answer into the Buddha-mind.

We are too ego-centered. The ego-shell in which we live is the hardest thing
to outgrow. We seem to carry it all the time from childhood up to the time
we finally pass away. We are, however, given many chances to break
through this shell, and the first and greatest of them is when we reach
adolescence. This is the first time the ego really comes to recognize the
"other." I mean the awakening of sexual love. An ego, entire and undivided,
now begins to feel a sort of split in itself. Love hitherto dormant deep in his
heart lifts its head and causes a great commotion in it. For the love now
stirred demands at once the assertion of the ego and its annihilation. Love
makes the ego lose itself in the object it loves, and yet at the same time it
wants to have the object as its own. This is a contradiction, and a great
tragedy of life. This elemental feeling must be one of the divine agencies
whereby man is urged to advance in his upward walk. God gives tragedies
to perfect man. The greatest bulk of literature ever produced in this world is
but the harping on the same string of love, and we never seem to grow
weary of it. But this is not the topic we are concerned with here. What I
want to emphasize in this connection is this: that through the awakening of
love we get a glimpse into the infinity of things, and that this glimpse urges

---

5 *Koan*—a paradoxical riddle in Zen training, challenging the student to break through conventional
thought.

youth to Romanticism or to Rationalism according to his temperament and environment and education.

When the ego-shell is broken and the "other" is taken into its own body, we can say that the ego has denied itself or that the ego has taken its first steps towards the infinite. Religiously, here ensues an intense struggle between the finite and the infinite, between the intellect and a higher power, or, more plainly, between the flesh and the spirit. . . .

What is a koan? A koan, according to one authority, means "a public document setting up a standard of judgment," whereby one's Zen understanding is tested as to its correctness. A koan is generally some statement made by an old Zen master, or some answer of his given to a questioner. The following are some that are commonly given to the uninitiated:

1   A monk asked Tung-shan [**Pinyin**, Dong Shan],[6] "Who is the Buddha?" "Three *chin* [Pinyin, *jin*] of flax."
2   Yun-men [Pinyin, Yunmen] was once asked, "When not a thought is stirring in one's mind, is there any error here?" "As much as Mount Sumeru."
3   Chao-chou [Pinyin, Zhaozhou] answered, "*Wu!*" (*mu* in Japanese) to a monk's question, "Is there Buddha-nature in a dog?" *Wu* literally means "not" or "none," but when this is ordinarily given as a koan, it has no reference to its literal signification; it is "*Wu*" pure and simple.
4   When Ming the monk overtook the fugitive Hui-neng [Pinyin, Huineng], he wanted Hui-neng to give up the secret of Zen. Hui-neng replied, "What are your original features which you have even prior to your birth?"
5   A monk asked Chao-chou, "What is the meaning of the First Patriarch's visit to China?" "The cypress tree in the front courtyard."
6   When Chao-chou came to study Zen under Nan-ch'uan [Pinyin, Nanquan], he asked, "What is the Tao [Pinyin, Dao] (or the Way)?" Nan-ch'uan replied, "Your everyday mind, that is the Tao."
7   A monk asked, "All things are said to be reducible to the One, but where is the One to be reduced?" Chao-chou answered, "When I was in the district of Ch'ing [Pinyin, Qing] I had a robe made that weighed seven *chin.*"
8   When P'ang [Pinyin, Pang] the old Zen adept first came to Ma-tsu [Pinyin, Mazu] in order to master Zen, he asked, "Who is he who has no companion among the **ten thousand things** of the world?" Ma-tsu replied, "When you swallow up in one draught all the water in the Hsi Ch'iang [Pinyin, Xi Qiang], I will tell you."

6 Pinyin is the contemporary system of transliterating Chinese, replacing the earlier Wade-Giles system used in various extracts in this book. Within extracts we have indicated the Pinyin spelling in brackets at first occurrence; in other parts of the text Pinyin is used as the norm, with Wade-Giles shown once in parentheses so readers can recognize both forms of each word.

When such problems are given to the uninitiated for solution, what is the object of the master? The idea is to unfold the Zen psychology in the mind of the uninitiated, and to reproduce the state of consciousness, of which these statements are the expression. That is to say, when the koans are understood the master's state of mind is understood, which is *satori*[7] and without which Zen is a sealed book.

In the beginning of Zen history a question was brought up by the pupil to the notice of the master, who thereby gauged the mental state of the questioner and knew what necessary help to give him. The help thus given was sometimes enough to awaken him to realization, but more frequently than not puzzled and perplexed him beyond description, and the result was an ever-increasing mental strain or "searching and contriving" on the part of the pupil, of which we have already spoken in the foregoing pages. In actual cases, however, the master would have to wait for a long while for the pupil's first question, if it were coming at all. To ask the first question means more than half the way to its own solution, for it is the outcome of a most intense mental effort for the questioner to bring his mind to a crisis. The question indicates that the crisis is reached and the mind is ready to leave it behind. An experienced master often knows how to lead the pupil to a crisis and to make him successfully pass it. . . .

The worst enemy of Zen experience, at least in the beginning, is the intellect, which consists and insists in discriminating subject from object. The discriminating intellect, therefore, must be cut short if Zen consciousness is to unfold itself, and the koan is constructed eminently to serve this end.

SOURCE: D. T. Suzuki, *Zen Buddhism*, ed. William Barrett. New York: Doubleday, 1956, pp. 6–7, 134–7

Nothing to Do with Rules by Bankei

In a radical form Buddhism challenges one to live so fully from the Buddha-mind that rules and precepts would not be necessary to guide behavior. A sense of right-ness would so naturally flow that externally imposed rules would be superfluous. This is the view articulated here by the seventeenth-century Zen master Bankei (1622–93). Zen was becoming overly formalized in Japan in his time, so he insisted on spontaneity and such a clear everyday awareness of the Unborn Buddha Mind that precepts (the basic obligations undertaken by Buddhists) would be dispen-sable. In the West this view is echoed by Augustine's saying "Love and do what you will."

A certain master of the Precepts School asked: "Doesn't your Reverence observe the precepts?"

The Master said: "Originally, what people call the precepts were all for wicked monks who broke the rules; for the man who abides in the Unborn Buddha Mind, there's no need for precepts. The precepts were taught to

---

7 *Satori*—awakening, or enlightenment.

help sentient beings—they weren't taught to help buddhas! What everyone has from his parents innately is the Unborn Buddha Mind alone, so abide in the Unborn Buddha Mind. When you abide in the Unborn Buddha Mind, you're a living buddha here today, and that living buddha certainly isn't going to concoct anything like taking the precepts, so there aren't any precepts for him to take. To concoct anything like taking the precepts is not what's meant by the Unborn Buddha Mind. When you abide in the Unborn Buddha Mind, there's no way you can violate the precepts. From the standpoint of the Unborn, the precepts too are secondary, peripheral concerns; in the place of the Unborn, there's really no such thing as precepts."

SOURCE: *Bankei Zen: Translations from the Record of Bankei*, trans. Peter Haskel. New York: Grove Press, 1984, p. 7

Vajrayana

Vajrayana and Tibet

Vajrayana (Diamond Vehicle) Buddhism began in India, perhaps in Nagarjuna's time, and spread to Tibet. It encourages students to learn from both Theravada and Mahayana principles, then study Vajrayana. This school teaches that emptiness (*sunyata*) is complemented by the compassion of the *bodhisattva* (*karuna*), and also that the wisdom (*prajna*) of emptiness has an indestructible, diamond (*vajra*) quality that cuts through dualistic illusions. Compassion is the dynamic means (*upaya*) of acting in the world. Enlightenment emerges when wisdom and compassion are experientially discovered to be one. Further, physical-mental processes can also become vehicles for enlightenment. This approach is related to Hindu Tantric[8] ritual practices, and requires guidance from a compassionate teacher (*lama*). Rich in artistry, Vajrayana uses images of divinities, *mudras* (meditative gestures and postures), *mantras* (sacred syllables and phrases), and *mandalas* (sacred circular designs) as aids to meditation.

Love, Kindness, and Universal Responsibility
by the Dalai Lama

Many Tibetan Buddhists were forced into exile due to the communist Chinese takeover of Tibet in 1950. Some settled in Dharamsala, India, or Nepal. Others have spread Buddhism abroad with new monasteries in many countries. The current leader of Tibetan Buddhism, the Dalai Lama Tenzin Gyatso, has become a global spokesman for Vajrayana Buddhism. He has spoken with such peaceful integrity and wisdom that he was awarded a Nobel Peace Prize in 1989, for his adherence to Buddhist non-violence in the struggle with China. This is an extract from his Nobel Prize acceptance speech. He speaks of the dangers of the population

8 Tantra—esoteric spiritual practices of India, often involving emphasis on the feminine aspect of divinity.

and environmental crises, consumerism, religious intolerance, and the need for non-violence and compassion. In exile, he has attempted to shift his culture from a theocratic to a democratic government. A leader forcefully exiled from his country, still he inspires many by translating Buddhist principles of compassion and patience into contemporary application.

I believe that every individual has a responsibility to help guide our global family in the right direction. Good wishes alone are not enough; we have to assume responsibility. . . .

[In our era] we find that the world has grown smaller and the world's people have become almost one community. Political and military alliances have created large multinational groups, industry and international trade have produced a global economy, and worldwide communications are eliminating ancient barriers of distance, language and race. We are also being drawn together by the grave problems we face: over-population, dwindling natural resources and an environmental crisis that threatens our air, water and trees, along with the vast number of beautiful life forms that are the very foundation of existence on this small planet we share.

I believe that to meet the challenge of our times, human beings will have to develop a greater sense of universal responsibility. Each of us must learn to work not just for his or her own self, family or nation, but for the benefit of all mankind. Universal responsibility is the real key to human survival. It is the best foundation for world peace, the equitable use of natural resources, and through concern for future generations, the proper care of the environment. . . .

Whether we like it or not, we have all been born on this earth as part of one great human family. Rich or poor, educated or uneducated, belonging to one nation or another, to one religion or another, adhering to this ideology or that, ultimately each of us is just a human being like everyone else: we all desire happiness and do not want suffering. Furthermore, each of us has an equal right to pursue these goals.

Today's world requires that we accept the oneness of humanity. In the past, isolated communities could afford to think of one another as fundamentally separate and even existed in total isolation. Nowadays, however, events in one part of the world eventually affect the entire planet. Therefore we have to treat each major local problem as a global concern from the moment it begins. We can no longer invoke the national, racial or ideological barriers that separate us without destructive repercussion. In the context of our new interdependence, considering the interests of others is clearly the best form of self-interest.

I view this fact as a source of hope. The necessity for cooperation can only strengthen mankind, because it helps us recognize that the most secure foundation for the new world order is not simply broader political and economic alliances, but rather each individual's genuine practice of love and compassion. For a better, happier, more stable and civilized future, each of us must develop a sincere, warm-hearted feeling of brother- and sisterhood. . . .

I believe that despite the rapid advances made by civilization in this century, the most immediate cause of our present dilemma is our undue emphasis on material development alone. We have become so engrossed in its pursuit that, without even knowing it, we have neglected to foster the most basic human needs of love, kindness, cooperation and caring. If we do not know someone or find another reason for not feeling connected with a particular individual or group, we simply ignore them. But the development of human society is based entirely on people helping each other. Once we have lost the essential humanity that is our foundation, what is the point of pursuing only material improvement?. . . .

In particular, a tremendous effort will be required to bring compassion into the realm of international business. Economic inequality, especially that between developed and developing nations, remains the greatest source of suffering on this planet. Even though they will lose money in the short term, large multinational corporations must curtail their exploitation of poor nations. Tapping the few precious resources such countries possess simply to fuel consumerism in the developed world is disastrous; if it continues unchecked, eventually we shall all suffer. Strengthening weak, undiversified economies is a far wiser policy for promoting both political and economic stability. As idealistic as it may sound, altruism, not just competition and the desire for wealth, should be a driving force in business. . . .

One religion, like a single type of food, cannot satisfy everybody. According to their varying mental dispositions, some people benefit from one kind of teaching, others from another. Each faith has the ability to produce fine, warmhearted people and all religions have succeeded in doing so, despite their espousal of often contradictory philosophies. Thus there is no reason to engage in divisive religious bigotry and intolerance and every reason to cherish and respect all forms of spiritual practice. . . .

Throughout history, mankind has pursued peace one way or another. Is it too optimistic to imagine that world peace may finally be within our grasp? I do not believe that there has been an increase in the amount of people's hatred, only in their ability to manifest it in vastly destructive weapons. On the other hand, bearing witness to the tragic evidence of the mass slaughter caused by such weapons in our [era] has given us the opportunity to control war. To do so, it is clear we must disarm.

Disarmament can occur only within the context of new political and economic relationships. Before we consider this issue in detail, it is worth imagining the kind of peace process from which we would benefit most. This is fairly self-evident. First we should work on eliminating nuclear weapons, next, biological and chemical ones, then offensive arms, and, finally, defensive ones. At the same time, to safeguard the peace, we should start developing in one or more global regions an international police force made up of an equal number of members from each nation under a collective command. Eventually this force would cover the whole world. . . .

Our planet is blessed with vast, natural treasures. If we use them properly, beginning with the elimination of militarism and war, truly, every human being will be able to live a wealthy, well-cared-for life. . . .

I believe that the very process of dialogue, moderation and compromise involved in building a community of Asian states would itself give real hope of peaceful evolution to a new order in China. From the very start, the member states of such a community might agree to decide its defense and international relations policies together. There would be many opportunities for cooperation. The critical point is that we find a peaceful, nonviolent way for the forces of freedom, democracy and moderation to emerge successfully from the current atmosphere of unjust repression. . . .

I see Tibet's role in such an Asian Community as what I have previously called a "Zone of Peace": a neutral, demilitarized sanctuary where weapons are forbidden and the people live in harmony with nature. This is not merely a dream—it is precisely the way Tibetans tried to live for over a thousand years before our country was invaded. . . .

Another hopeful development is the growing compatibility between science and religion. Throughout the nineteenth century and for much of our [era], people have been profoundly confused by the conflict between these apparently contradictory world views. Today, physics, biology and psychology have reached such sophisticated levels that many researchers are starting to ask the most profound questions about the ultimate nature of the universe and life, the same questions that are of prime interest to religions. Thus there is real potential for a more unified view. In particular, it seems that a new concept of mind and matter is emerging. The East has been more concerned with understanding the mind, the West with understanding matter. Now that the two have met, these spiritual and material views of life may become more harmonized.

The rapid changes in our attitude towards the earth are also a source of hope. As recently as 10 or 15 years ago, we thoughtlessly consumed its resources, as if there was no end to them. Now, not only individuals but governments as well are seeking a new ecological order. . . .

I think we can say that, because of the lessons we have begun to learn, the [new] century will be friendlier, more harmonious, and less harmful. Compassion, the seed of peace, will be able to flourish. I am very hopeful. At the same time, I believe that every individual has a responsibility to help guide our global family in the right direction. Good wishes alone are not enough; we have to assume responsibility. Large human movements spring from individual human initiatives.

SOURCE: Tenzin Gyatso, *Love, Kindness and Universal Responsibility*. Delhi: Paljor Publications, n.d., pp. 50–71

Living Engaged Buddhism

How strong is the evidence that the Buddha fought for the common person against the establishment of his time, attempting to change society? He did oppose the birth caste system and the privileges of the brahmanic priestly caste. But his focus on individual consciousness does not seem like a direct critique of institutionalized social injustices. With the advent of modern technologies and increased resources far beyond those available during the Buddha's time, a renewed movement called Engaged Buddhism is emerging with a critique of social problems. The Dalai Lama is one leader critical of violence and consumerism, and others are applying Buddhist principles to rectify injustices in such areas as the environmental crisis and gender inequalities. Some of the traditional practices of Buddhism, such as monastic celibacy, are being called into question and modified in the global context of contemporary Buddhism.

Engaged Buddhism in Asia

by Christopher Queen and Sallie King

Christopher Queen and Sallie King, in their book *Engaged Buddhism: Buddhist Liberation Movements in Asia* (1996), show the growing influence of social activism among Asian Buddhists. There is a debate about whether Buddhism is essentially a withdrawn, reflective spiritual practice, focusing on overcoming one's own desires and attachments, or whether it also authentically includes a movement into social and political arenas to improve the situation of poor, oppressed peoples and victims of war. Queen, King, and others argue that traditional Buddhist teachings and the modern situation do justify a Buddhist movement toward changing not only individual consciousness, but also oppressive social structures.

To most people in the West, the term "Buddhism" means a religion of introspective withdrawal. Yet the reality of contemporary Asian Buddhism is often something very different. "Buddhism" in contemporary Asia means energetic engagement with social and political issues and crises at least as much as it means monastic or meditative withdrawal. . . .

In the socially engaged Buddhism of modern Asia, the liberation sought has been called a "mundane awakening" (*laukodaya*), which includes individuals, villages, nations, and ultimately all people (*sarvodaya*), and which focuses on objectives that may be achieved and recognized in this lifetime, in this world. George Bond has summarized the comprehensive nature of the liberative vision that inspires volunteers in the Sarvodaya Shramadana movement, including moral, cultural, spiritual, social, political, and economic dimensions. Thus, in addition to being a society based on the Buddhist precepts and offering opportunities for obtaining wisdom, happiness, and peace, Ariyaratna[9] and his colleagues have focused on the

---

9 Ariyaratna—E. T. Ariyaratna, *Buddhism and Sarvodaya: The Sri Lankan Experience*. Delhi: Sri Satguru Publications, 1996.

"ten basic human needs" that must be met for liberation to be possible: a clean and beautiful environment, an adequate and safe water supply, clothing, balanced diet, simple housing, basic health care, communication facilities, energy, education related to life and living, and free access to cultural and spiritual resources. The list is offered as a modern version of the Buddhist "middle way"—a balancing of the material and spiritual aspects of social change.

We may conclude that a profound change in Buddhist soteriology[10]— from a highly personal and other-worldly notion of liberation to a social, economic, this-worldly liberation—distinguishes the Buddhist movements in our study. The traditional conceptions of karma and rebirth, the veneration of the *bhikkhu sangha*,[11] and the focus on ignorance and psychological attachment to account for suffering in the world (the second Noble Truth) have taken second place to the application of highly rationalized reflections on the institutional and political manifestations of greed, hatred, and delusion, and on new organizational strategies for addressing war and injustice, poverty and intolerance, and the prospects for "outer" as well as "inner" peace in the world. . . .

Contemporary Buddhist liberation movements are as likely to apply their interpretive and organizational efforts to the critique and reform of social and political conditions as they are to propose and practice new spiritual exercises. The evils of war and genocide, of ethnic hatred and caste violence, and of economic disparity and degradation figure prominently in engaged Buddhist writings. On the other hand, the democratization, if not the transformation, of spiritual practices—for example, meditation and ritual initiations as now appropriated by lay practitioners—has been seen as an integral concomitant to the shift to mundane awakening.

To advance their vision of a new world, Buddhist liberation movements have harnessed modern methods of education, mass communication, political influence and activism, jurisprudence and litigation, and yes, even fund-raising and marketing. Many examples of these new "skillful means" may be cited.

If practical education is a basic human need, according to villagers in Sri Lanka, then the Buddhist liberation movements have concentrated major resources to this end. Among the first activities of the Buddhist women reformers in Sri Lanka at the turn of the century was the founding of primary schools for girls. . . .

"Buddhism is based on service to others," wrote Walpola Rahula, the eminent Sinhalese scholar-monk and activist, in 1946. . . .

Rahula's summary of the history of monastic engagement in the social and political life of Ceylon begins with a picture of the primitive sangha at the time of the Buddha. Here the founder and his followers are seen giving

---

10 Soteriology—doctrine of salvation from suffering.
11 *Bhikkhu sangha*—members of the Buddhist monastic communities.

practical advice to villagers who were "poor, illiterate, not very clean, and not healthy ... [who] needed simple moral ideas conducive to their material well-being and happiness rather than deep and sublime discourses on philosophy, metaphysics, or psychology as taught in the *Abhidhamma*. Such ideas, taken from early Pali scriptures (*suttas*) Rahula was well-qualified to interpret, included the view that crime and immorality in society are rooted in poverty (*Cakkavatti-sihanada-sutta*), that employment opportunities must be provided to ensure the common weal (*Kutadanta-sutta*), that merchants should be diligent, savvy, and scrupulous in their dealings and that laypersons should seek economic security, freedom from debt, good health, and wholesome associations (*Sigala-sutta; Anguttara-nikaya*), and that political leaders should observe the Ten Duties of the King, including liberality, morality, self-sacrifice, integrity, nonviolence, and so on (*Dhammapadatthakatha*). In short, "the Buddha and the *bhikkhus* taught such important ideas pertaining to health, sanitation, earning wealth, mutual relationships, well-being of society, and righteous government—all for the good of the people." ...

In his introduction to the writings of contemporary engaged Buddhists, Kenneth Kraft has noted their agreement that "the principles and even some of the techniques of an engaged Buddhism have been latent in the tradition since the time of its founder. Qualities that were inhibited in pre-modern Asian settings ... can now be actualized through Buddhism's exposure to the West, where ethical sensitivity, social activism, and egalitarianism are emphasized." When these principles and techniques, regardless of their provenance, are proclaimed and practiced in the name of the Awakened One, in accord with the teachings of wisdom and compassion, and in the spirit of the unbroken community of those seeking human liberation—that is, in harmony with the ancient refuges of Buddha, Dharma, and Sangha— then we may regard the catechism as authentically Buddhist. ...

Simply put, in keeping with the Middle Path, Buddhist principles mandate that the poor need more attention given to the material dimension of life than do those who have enough; those who have more than enough need their attention turned to that fact. ...

Buddhist liberation movements, collectively, constitute a major turning point in the development of Buddhism and will continue to play a role of substantial importance in the evolution of Buddhism into the foreseeable future.

SOURCE: Christopher S. Queen and Sallie B. King, eds., *Engaged Buddhism: Buddhist Liberation Movements in Asia*. Albany, NY: State University of New York Press, 1996, pp. ix, 9–33, 411–35

A Brief History of Buddhism in America by Serinity Young

Buddhism has long been a migrant religion, since it early left its original home in India and moved west and north. When it came to the Americas, it encountered a non-Asian industrial culture with a strong sense of human rights. Serinity Young, author of several books on Buddhism and women in religion, writes about the major dividing line among American Buddhists.

Buddhism has a long history in the United States beginning with the immigration of East Asians, such as the Chinese who came to California during the gold rush and brought their faith with them. Their Buddhism was a mix of Mahayana with the indigenous Chinese religions of Daoism and Confucianism. In contrast, the Japanese, who first immigrated mainly to Hawaii, were more institutionally organized. Their Buddhist Church of America, founded in 1899, follows the format of Protestant churches, for example by having Sunday morning worship. Additionally, Buddhism caught the interest of American intellectuals and philosophers, who believed non-European cultures had something to offer the West. As we shall see, from its very beginnings in America, Buddhism has been divided along racial lines: (a) the temples and centers created by and for Asian immigrants, and (b) centers created by and for Western converts. Five or six million Buddhists live in America, 80 percent of whom are of Asian descent.

In 1893 the World Parliament of Religion, an extraordinary meeting of representatives from almost all the world's great religions, was held in Chicago. This meeting was extensively covered by the press and it introduced many forms of world religions to Americans of European descent, or Euro-Americans. A young Theravada Buddhist monk from Sri Lanka, Anagarika Dharmapala (1864–1933), particularly caught the attention of the American public. Dharmapala had close ties to the Theosophical Society, though he later broke with it, and he became a leading force in reclaiming the main Buddhist pilgrimage sites in India— especially Bodh Gaya, which at that time was being run by a Hindu priest. He also converted the first Euro-American to Buddhism. Dharmapala devoted the remainder of his life to lecturing throughout America and the rest of the world, gaining many Euro-American converts and contributing to the revival of Buddhism in Asia, most particularly in Sri Lanka.

The Rinzai branch of Zen Buddhism also made an impression on the American public through its representative from the World Parliament of Religion, Shaku Soen, who was invited in 1905 to return to America to teach Zen. This led to the establishment of enduring Zen centers on the west coast and in New York City. The greatest influence, though, came from his disciple D. T. Suzuki, the primary interpreter of Zen in the West. In his writings and personal appearances, Suzuki argued that Zen was not limited to a Buddhist context, but that it could be practiced by anyone of any faith. This had great appeal to many Euro-Americans. Other Zen teachers, however, established meditation centers primarily for Westerners who followed strict Zen practices within a context of Buddhist values and morality. To name only one, the Zen Center of San Francisco was founded by Shunryu Suzuki-roshi in the early 1960s.

In America Tibetan Vajrayana Buddhism is dominated by Euro-Americans, although Tibetan monastics play an important part in it. Few American converts know any lay Tibetans; they know only monks and teachers. In part this is due to the very small number of Tibetan refugees who have been allowed into America and the fact that in Tibet practice is centered on monasteries; Tibetans living in the West do not necessarily practice in monasteries. Rather they practice at home through the maintenance of a shrine, or through private chanting and prayer. Most do not practice meditation. In Tibet, lay people rarely perform the more intensive Tantric practices, but in the United States Euro-American lay people are eager to participate in monastic Tantric practices.

Today Buddhism, in its many varieties, is an established religion in America with a strong institutional presence in the form of monasteries, retreat centers, and so on. Yet, for the most part, a breach remains between the Buddhism brought by Asian immigrants and that of Western practitioners. On the one hand, for people of Asian descent, Buddhism is part of their cultural heritage and they have little interest in reaching out to the larger Euro-American community. On the other hand, numerous Western Buddhists have taken Buddhist ideas completely out of context. For instance, they practice Buddhist meditation but ignore its moral and ethical teachings, or they divorce Buddhism from its cultural heritage and interpret the tradition freely. So Asian-Americans feel Euro-Americans neither respect nor understand Buddhism, while Euro-Americans feel Asian-Americans confuse Buddhism with Asian culture.

Both groups also read Buddhist history differently. Historically, Buddhism proved itself to be very adaptable to new environments as it spread throughout Asia. For Westerners, this means that Buddhism will once again adapt to its new home in America. Asian-Americans focus on another side of Buddhist history—the continual tendency to reform, to return to its roots. In the past there were kings who purified the monastic orders and renowned Chinese pilgrim-monks who made the difficult and dangerous journey to India to get the purest teachings of the Buddha. In recent decades, in response to the stresses of modernity and the ravages of war and revolution, Asian movements have developed a more socially meaningful Buddhism. Consequently, Asian-Americans feel that Buddhism must make an effort to remain true to its roots in America as it has elsewhere in Asia.

One important exception to the breach between Asian-American and Euro-American Buddhist practitioners can be seen in the work of Thich Nhat Hanh. As part of his protest against the Vietnam War, he made a trip to the United States to appeal for peace. At the end of this trip, neither of the warring regimes in Vietnam would allow him to return to his native land. He continues his work, living in exile and traveling the world, lecturing and writing books on the theme of Engaged Buddhism, which blends together the practice of meditation with social service. He has a large following among Westerners, many of whom live in the United States, but he also has a large following among Vietnamese refugees. As part of his practice of Engaged Buddhism, he holds meditation retreats for Vietnamese refugees and American Vietnam War veterans as a way for both sides to heal from the damage of war.

Another exception are two sects of Nichiren Buddhism, Soka Gakkai and Nichiren Shoshu, both of which have Asian and non-Asian members. In fact, Soka Gakkai is the only Buddhist group in America with a sizable African-American and Hispanic membership. The simplicity of its practice, chanting the name of the *Lotus Sutra*, makes it accessible to people from all walks of life. Its founder, the monk Nichiren (1222–82), established the predominance of the *Lotus Sutra* over all other Buddhist texts. He recommended repeating the *mantra "nam myoho renge kyo,"* which basically means "homage to the *Lotus Sutra*," as a means of salvation. Nichiren, too, lived through a period of political upheaval, foreign invasions, and natural disasters. He believed that it was the time of Degenerated Dharma and that only this simple practice could save people.

Although women have been prominent figures in establishing Buddhism in America from the nineteenth century to the present, gender is also a hot topic among Western converts. Quite a few are not comfortable with traditional Asian views of women's place, while some female converts feel feminism conflicts with their spiritual goals. Recent Western feminist interpretations of Tantric Buddhism, especially those of Miranda Shaw and Rita Gross, suggest it is a liberating spiritual path for Western women, which indeed it may well be, especially for women who are comfortable with vivid heterosexual imagery. Part of the appeal of Tantric Buddhism for feminists is its emphasis on practices that utilize, and thereby seem to affirm, the body—often the locus of negative views about women in other traditions—and on desire as a spiritually liberating force. Feminists or not, the fact remains that many Western women have successfully assumed leadership roles in various sects of American Buddhism, which in itself will chart a new course for American Buddhists.

Many Buddhist publishers are flourishing in the United States, and there is an enormous amount of information available on the Internet, all of which is having an impact on American Buddhism. Such availability was not possible until fairly recently, and marks a real break with Buddhist practice. One has to wonder what will happen to American Buddhism if students no longer enter into highly personal and highly charged relationships with their teachers but instead only participate electronically or through reading books.

SOURCE: Original article for this book by Serinity Young, 2006

Precepts for an Engaged Buddhism

by Thich Nhat Hanh

Thich Nhat Hanh on Mindfulness

After Vietnamese Zen master Thich Nhat Hanh's struggles against the 1960s war, he settled in exile in his "Plum Village" in France, where he teaches, writes, gardens, and helps other refugees. His several books have introduced many readers to a new brand of Buddhist activism. In his book *Being Peace* (1987) he outlines a number of new precepts for an Engaged Buddhism, "The Precepts of the Order of Interbeing." They clearly reflect careful study of both modern and ancient problems, such as religious intolerance, fanatical political ideology, and forceful indoctrination of children.

First: Do not be idolatrous about or bound to any doctrine, theory, or ideology, even Buddhist ones. All systems of thought are guiding means; they are not absolute truth. . . .

Second: Do not think that the knowledge you presently possess is changeless, absolute truth. Avoid being narrow-minded and bound to present views. Learn and practice non-attachment from views in order to be open to receive others' viewpoints. Truth is found in life and not merely in conceptual knowledge. Be ready to learn throughout your entire life and to observe reality in yourself and in the world at times. . . .

Third: Do not force others, including children, by any means whatsoever, to adopt your views, whether by authority, threat, money, propaganda, or even education. However, through compassionate dialogue, help others renounce fanaticism and narrowness. . . .

Fourth: Do not avoid contact with suffering or close your eyes before suffering. Do not lose awareness of the existence of suffering in the life of the world. Find ways to be with those who are suffering by all means, including personal contact and visits, images, sound. By such means, awaken yourself and others to the reality of suffering in the world. . . .

Fifth: Do not accumulate wealth while millions are hungry. Do not take as the aim of your life fame, profit, wealth, or sensual pleasure. Live simply and share time, energy, and material resources with those who are in need. . . .

Sixth: Do not maintain anger or hatred. As soon as anger and hatred arise, practice the meditation on compassion in order to deeply understand the persons who have caused anger and hatred. Learn to look at other beings with the eyes of compassion. . . .

Seventh: Do not lose yourself in dispersion and in your surroundings. Learn to practice breathing in order to regain composure of body and mind, to practice mindfulness, and to develop concentration and understanding. . . .

Eighth: Do not utter words that can create discord and cause the community to break. Make every effort to reconcile and resolve all conflicts, however small. . . .

Ninth: Do not say untruthful things for the sake of personal interest or to impress people. Do not utter words that cause division and hatred. Do not spread news that you do not know to be certain. Do not criticize or condemn things that you are not sure of. Always speak truthfully and constructively. Have the courage to speak out about situations of injustice, even when doing so may threaten your own safety. . . .

Tenth: Do not use the Buddhist community for personal gain or profit, or transform your community into a political party. A religious community should, however, take a clear stand against oppression and injustice, and should strive to change the situation without engaging in partisan conflicts. . . .

Eleventh: Do not live with a vocation that is harmful to humans and nature. Do not invest in companies that deprive others of their chance to life. Select a vocation which helps realize your ideal of compassion. . . .

Twelfth: Do not kill. Do not let others kill. Find whatever means possible to protect life and to prevent war. . . .

Thirteenth: Possess nothing that should belong to others. Respect the property of others but prevent others from enriching themselves from human suffering or the suffering of other beings. . . .

Fourteenth: Do not mistreat your body. Learn to handle it with respect. Do not look on your body as only an instrument. Preserve vital energies (sexual, breath, spirit) for the realization of the Way. Sexual expression should not happen without love and commitment. In sexual relationships be aware of future suffering that may be caused. To preserve the happiness of others, respect the rights and commitment of others. Be fully aware of the responsibility of bringing new lives into the world. Meditate on the world into which you are bringing new beings.

SOURCE: Thich Nhat Hanh, *Being Peace*. Berkeley, CA: Parallax Press, 1987, pp. 89–100

GLOSSARY

Aggregates *See Skandhas.*

Bodhisattva (Sanskrit, enlightenment being; Pali, **Bodhisatta**) In Theravada, an historical Buddha before Buddhahood was attained; in Mahayana, a compassionate being who vows to become a Buddha for all sentient beings.

Buddha In Theravada, the historical persons who awaken to truth, such as Gautama; in Mahayana, an enlightened person and a universal principle of all beings.

Canon The official list of books with authority in a religion, either because they are believed to be inspired or revealed, or have been so designated.

Dharma (Sanskrit; Pali, **Dhamma**) In Buddhism, cosmic law, the teachings of the Buddha, and the realization and practice of truth (the second of the Three Jewels: Buddha, *dharma, sangha*); in Hinduism, the universal cosmic law, duty.

Guanyin A widely beloved Buddhist goddess who embodies compassion. Known in China as Guanyin or Kuan Yin, her various names include Quan Âm in Vietnam, Kannon in Japan, and Kanin in Bali. Buddhists also see her as a form of Avilokiteshvara, *bodhisattva* of compassion and wisdom: she hears the sufferings of the world and devises ways to help.

Karma In Buddhism, the cosmic moral law of consequences for ethical actions and their effects from prior incarnations; *karma* can be altered by good or bad intentions, is not fatalistic, and can be changed at any time by meditative insight.

Mahayana (Sanskrit, Large Vehicle) The form of Buddhism from northern Asia that teaches the effort to liberate other beings; it emphasizes the Buddha-nature in all things and the importance of direct experience.

Nirvana (Sanskrit; Pali, **Nibbana**) A heavenly realm discovered after death and, in Mahayana teaching, a state of awakening during life: the discovery of the path beyond ego's desires and passions, the realization of the union of opposites, the transcendence of mind's limits. It is peace and tranquillity on earth, coming from beyond the duality of ordinary life.

Pinyin New romanized transcription of Chinese adopted in 1979, replacing 1859 Wade-Giles system.

Samsara In some Asian religions, cycles of birth and death through reincarnation involving the consequences of *karma*; the world of illusion to be escaped.

Skandhas The five aggregates that constitute a human appearance, such as sensation and consciousness; they are not fixed or substantial, but impermanent and co-dependently arising.

Sunyata (emptiness, or no-self; Sanskrit, **Anatman**) The lack of a permanent, self-existing soul in the *skandhas* and all reality.

Ten thousand things Chinese phrase indicating "everything."

Theravada (Pali, Teaching of the Elders) Form of Buddhism from southern Asia which adheres to early scriptures and monastic renunciation; its texts are the Pali Canon.

Vajrayana (Sanskrit, Diamond Vehicle) Form of Buddhism which teaches that emptiness is complemented by compassion and action. The Dalai Lama is its leader in the Tibetan tradition.

Vipassana (Pali, see clearly) The central focus of meditation in Theravada practice, which stresses mindfulness and tranquillity, leading to liberation.

Zen A Chinese and Japanese form of Buddhism emphasizing immediate experience. Of the two main schools, Rinzai, influenced by Hakuin, uses the *koan* to promote *satori* (awakening), while Soto, influenced by Dogen, uses more "silent illumination."

HOLY DAYS

Celebrating the Buddha Buddhist cultures celebrate the events and the meaning of the life of the Buddha in several ways.

1   Buddha's Day, or Visaka Puja in Theravada, is often the most holy day of the year, commemorating the birth, life, and death of the Buddha. It is usually celebrated at a full moon. Devotees gather at monasteries, have processions, chant, listen to sermons, water local *bodhi* trees, serve the poor and sick, honor relics such as the Buddha's eyetooth, and bathe Buddha images.

2   Relics, such as teeth or bones supposedly preserved from the Buddha's body, are commemorated as a way of participating in the magical power of his divine presence with rituals such as a procession and sprinkling holy water. Sometimes kings attempt to legitimate their rule by using such relics to empower and bless their state.

3   Honoring the *dharma* is celebrated by chanting sacred texts. In Tibet the Feast of the First Discourse is held at a full moon. Thais celebrate the Buddha's teaching this to his mother, and his establishing the core of the monastic discipline.

4   The founding of the *sangha/samgha*, or gathering community, of Buddhists is celebrated annually. The mirac unannounced gathering of 1, wandering *arhats* (in Therav evolved Buddhists) before th Rajagrha is recalled as the

of the first *sangha*. In Sri Lanka, thousands of people come to celebrate the arrival of Buddhism on the island, brought by Mahind, son of King Ashoka, and his sister Sanghamitta, who brought a branch of Buddha's sacred *bodhi* tree.

5   The saints of Buddhism are celebrated in annual festivals, honoring popular mythic events such as the Chinese Guanyin's birthday, enlightenment, and entry into *nirvana*. Holidays celebrate historical leaders such as Bodhidharma, the first Chinese Patriarch who brought Chan Buddhism to China, Hakuin, leader of the Rinzai Zen sect in Japan, and Padmasambhava, the leading missionary from India to Tibet.

Seasonal celebrations The Buddhist calendar incorporates festivals of seasonal changes, agricultural events, and human life and death rituals. New Year's Day is commonly celebrated, as are the origin of spring, the equinoxes, harvest thanksgiving, and festivals for the dead ancestors. These holidays are highly syncretic, blending Buddhist and ancient folk religion together. In Tibet, the New Year festival (Lo-gsar) combines the Buddhist miracle of Sravasti with the exorcism of the old year's evil and calling up good fortune for the new year. In Thailand the onset of the monsoon rains is the occasion of intensified monastic retreat activities, alongside New Year's sympathetic magic intended to ensure the new rains necessary for planting rice.

HISTORICAL OUTLINE

c. 563–483 BCE—life of Gautama Buddha

c. 258 BCE—King Ashoka spreads Buddhism outside India

200 BCE–200 CE—Theravada Buddhism develops

100 BCE—Theravada Pali Canon written down

c. 50 CE—Buddhism taken to China and East Asia

2nd century CE—Asvaghosha writes *Acts of the Buddha*

c. 100 CE—Mahayana Buddhism develops

c. 200 CE—Nagarjuna teaches emptiness

c. 500 CE—Buddhism taken to Japan

589–845 CE—peak of Chinese Buddhism

606 CE—Seng Can (Seng-tsan), third Buddhist Patriarch in China, dies

775 CE—Padmasambhava establishes first Buddhist monastery in Tibet

c. 1079–1153—Milarepa influences Tibetan Buddhism

13th century—Buddhism begins to lose influence in India

c. 13th century—Chan Buddhism taken from China to Japan, becomes Zen

c. 1250—Dogen founds Soto Zen Buddhism

c. 1750—Hakuin revitalizes Rinzai Zen Buddhism

1950—China annexes Tibet, Dalai Lama flees, Buddhism spreads to West

1966—Thich Nhat Hanh leaves Vietnam for the West

from 1970s—Dalai Lama teaches widely in the West

REVIEW QUESTIONS

1   What are the "middle path," the Four Noble Truths, the Eightfold Path? What does it mean to be free from delusions? Why is this important to Buddhists?
2   What questions did the Buddha leave undeclared? Why?
3   Describe the similarities and contrast the differences of the Theravada, Mahayana, and Vajrayana traditions, naming and quoting classic texts in each tradition.
4   What is a *koan*? What is its purpose? Give an example.

DISCUSSION QUESTIONS

1   What are the major similarities and differences between Hinduism and Buddhism?
2   Why is meditation so important to Buddhism?
3   What reality do Buddhists constantly refer to as most important, and how is it different from theism?

INFORMATION RESOURCES

Buddhaghosha. *Buddhaghosha's Parables*, trans. T. Rogers. London, 1870.

Buddhist Studies
<http://www.dharmanet.org>

Carter, Robert E. *The Nothingness Beyond God*. St. Paul, MN: Paragon House, 1997.

Chodron, Pema. *When Things Fall Apart*. Boston and London: Shambhala, 1997.

Conze, Edward, ed. *Buddhist Scriptures*. Harmondsworth, Middlesex: Penguin Books, 1986.

Cousins, L. S. "Buddhism," in *A New Handbook of Living Religions*, ed. John R. Hinnels. Oxford: Blackwell, 1997.

Goddard, Dwight, ed. *A Buddhist Bible*. Boston: Beacon Press, 1966.

Gross, Rita M. *Buddhism After Patriarchy*. Albany, NY: State University of New York Press, 1993.

Kapleau, Philip. *The Three Pillars of Zen*. Boston: Beacon Press, 1965.

Loori, John Daido. "The Precepts and the Environment," in *Mountain Record*. Vol. 14, no. 3, pp. 12–17. 1996.

Macy, Joanna. *World as Lover, World as Self*. Berkeley, CA: Parallax Press, 1991.

McGreal, Ian P. *Great Thinkers of the Eastern World*. New York: HarperCollins, 1995.

Nishitani, Keiji. *Religion and Nothingness*. Berkeley, CA: University of California Press, 1982.

Pilgrim, Richard. *Buddhism and the Arts of Japan*. Chambersburg, PA: Anima Press, 1993.

Powell, Andrew. *Living Buddhism*. Berkeley, CA, and Los Angeles: University of California Press, 1989.

Ramanan, K. Venkata. *Nagarjuna's Philosophy*. Delhi: Motilal Banarsidass, 1966.

Reynolds, Frank, and **Charles Hallisey**, *et al.* "Buddhism," in *Encyclopedia of Religion*, ed. Lindsay Jones. Vol. 2, pp. 1087–316. New York: Macmillan, 2005.

Reynolds, Frank, *et al.* "The Buddha and Buddhism," in *Encyclopedia Britannica*. Vol. 15, pp. 263–305. London, 1997.

Thurman, Robert. *The Tibetan Book of the Dead*. New York: Bantam, 1994.

Tricycle: the Buddhist Review
<http://www.tricycle.com>

CHAPTER 6

CONFUCIANISM

The ancient religious ways of China have developed into two distinct streams, known as Confucianism and Daoism. Confucianism is more humanistic and pragmatic; Daoism is more mystically inclined.

The stream known as Confucianism has developed from the ancient emphasis on veneration of ancestors and maintenance of proper rituals, or **li**, in order to stay in harmony with Heaven. Kong Qiu[1] (K'ung Ch'iu; c. 551–479 BCE), commonly known in the West by the latinized version of his name, Confucius, was an ardent proponent of the ancient rites as a practical base for an orderly and moral society. Born during a period of social chaos, he earnestly sought to advise rulers how to restore harmony. Failing to win their ear, he became a teacher of *li* and the arts of governance, so that his students might revive the ways of an idealized earlier period. The school of thought that he developed became the mainstream of Chinese philosophy for over two thousand years.

Confucian Virtues

Confucius focuses much of his attention on the development of human virtues within relationships with others. A man or woman whom he calls "noble" or "superior" is not one of high birth but one who manifests such virtues as humanity, or **ren** (*jen*), filial regard for one's parents, reverence toward ancestors, and observance of proprieties in human relationships, including benevolence in rulers and loyalty in their subjects. Confucius himself was from a prominent family which had been reduced to poverty, but he always maintained and encouraged gentlemanly behavior even in humble surroundings.

Whereas Confucius's ideas were not embraced by the rulers of his time, by the Han dynasty (206 BCE–220 CE) they were adopted as a way of uniting the people behind the ruler, who was portrayed as the link between Heaven and the populace. Study of the Confucian Classics became mandatory for public service. This requirement lasted until the twentieth century, when all religious practice was disrupted by Communism, but it has recently been revived, along with renewed interest in Confucian virtues as a guide to self-improvement.

---

1 Chinese words are transliterated here using the contemporary **Pinyin** system, with the earlier Wade-Giles transliteration given in parentheses at first occurrence; within extracts using Wade-Giles, the Pinyin version is shown in brackets.

The Confucian Classics

As promoted by Neo-Confucian scholars during the Song (Sung) dynasty (960–1279), the heart of Confucian teachings is found in the "Four Books"—*The Analects of Confucius*, *The Book of Mencius*, and two extracts from the ritual collections: "The Doctrine of the Mean" and "The Great Learning."

The Analects of Confucius

The **Analects**, or *Lunyu* (*Lun-yu*), are terse sayings of Kong Qiu, as collected by his students, some of whom are named.

Confucius said, "Is it not a pleasure to learn and to repeat or practice from time to time what has been learned? Is it not delightful to have friends coming from afar? Is one not a superior man if he does not feel hurt even though he is not recognized?"

Yü Tzu [Pinyin, Yuzi] said, "Few of those who are filial sons and respectful brothers will show disrespect to superiors, and there has never been a man who is not disrespectful to superiors and yet creates disorder. A superior man is devoted to the fundamentals [the root]. When the root is firmly established, the moral law [Dao] will grow. Filial piety and brotherly respect are the root of humanity."

Tseng-Tzu [Pinyin, Zengzi] said, "Every day I examine myself on three points: whether in counseling others I have not been loyal; whether in intercourse with my friends I have not been faithful; and whether I have not repeated again and again and practiced the instructions of my teacher."

Young men should be filial when at home and respectful to their elders when away from home. They should be earnest and faithful. They should love all extensively and be intimate with men of humanity. When they have any energy to spare after the performance of moral duties, they should use it to study literature and the arts.

Confucius said, "When a man's father is alive, look at the bent of his will. When his father is dead, look at his conduct. If for three years he does not change from the way of his father, he may be called filial."

Yü Tzu said, "Among the functions of propriety [*li*] the most valuable is that it establishes harmony. The excellence of the ways of ancient kings consists of this. It is the guiding principle of all things great and small. If things go amiss, and you, understanding harmony, try to achieve it without regulating it by the rules of propriety, they will still go amiss."

Confucius said, "The superior man does not seek fulfillment of his appetite nor comfort in his lodging. He is diligent in his duties and careful in his speech. He associates with men of moral principles and thereby realizes himself. Such a person may be said to love learning."

Confucius said, "A ruler who governs his state by virtue is like the north polar star, which remains in its place while all the other stars revolve around it."

Confucius said, "Lead the people with governmental measures and regulate them by law and punishment, and they will avoid wrongdoing but will have no sense of honor and shame. Lead them with virtue and regulate them by the rules of propriety, and they will have a sense of shame and, moreover, set themselves right."

Tzu-yü [Pinyin, Ziyu] asked about filial piety. Confucius said, "Filial piety nowadays means to be able to support one's parents. But we support even dogs and horses. If there is no feeling of reverence, wherein lies the difference?"

When Confucius offered sacrifice to his ancestors, he felt as if his ancestral spirits were actually present. When he offered sacrifice to other spiritual beings, he felt as if they were actually present. He said, "If I do not participate in the sacrifice, it is as if I did not sacrifice at all."

Confucius said, "If you set your mind on humanity, you will be free from evil."

Confucius said, "Wealth and honor are what every man desires. But if they have been obtained in violation of moral principles, they must not be kept. Poverty and humble station are what every man dislikes. But if they can be avoided only in violation of moral principles, they must not be avoided. If a superior man departs from humanity, how can he fulfill that name? A superior man never abandons humanity even for the lapse of a single meal. In moments of haste, he acts according to it. In times of difficulty or confusion, he acts according to it."

Confucius said, "A superior man in dealing with the world is not for anything or against anything. He follows righteousness as the standard."

Confucius said, "If one's acts are motivated by profit, he will have many enemies."

Confucius said, "The superior man understands righteousness; the inferior man understands profit."

Confucius said, "I transmit but do not create. I believe in and love the ancients . . ."

Confucius said, "Set your will on the Way. Have a firm grasp on virtue. Rely on humanity. Find recreation in the arts."

Confucius said, "With coarse rice to eat, with water to drink, and with a bent arm for a pillow, there is still joy. Wealth and honor obtained through unrighteousness are but floating clouds to me."

Confucius never discussed strange phenomena, physical exploits, disorder, or spiritual beings.

Confucius said, "Heaven produced the virtue that is in me; what can Huan Tui [Pinyin, Huan Dui][2] do to me?"

Confucius said, "The common people may be made to follow [the Way] but may not be made to understand it."

---

2 Huan Dui—a minister of war who attempted to kill Confucius when he was 59 by felling a tree on him.

Confucius said, "Have sincere faith and love learning. Be not afraid to die for pursuing the good Way. Do not enter a tottering state nor stay in a chaotic one. When the Way prevails in the empire, then show yourself; when it does not prevail, then hide. When the Way prevails in your own state and you are poor and in a humble position, be ashamed of yourself. When the Way does not prevail in your state and you are wealthy and in an honorable position, be ashamed of yourself."

Confucius wanted to live among the nine barbarous tribes of the East. Someone said, "They are rude. How can you do it?" Confucius said, "If a superior man lives there, what rudeness would there be?"

Chi-lu [Pinyin, Jilu] asked about serving the spiritual beings. Confucius said, "If we are not yet able to serve man, how can we serve spiritual beings?" "I venture to ask about death." Confucius said, "If we do not yet know about life, how can we know about death?"

Ssu-ma Niu [Pinyin, Sima Niu], worrying, said, "All people have brothers but I have none." Tzu-hsia [Pinyin, Zixia] said, "I have heard [from Confucius] this saying: 'Life and death are the decree of Heaven; wealth and honor depend on Heaven. If a superior man is reverential [or serious] without fail, and is respectful in dealing with others and follows the rules of propriety, then all within the four seas are brothers.' What does the superior man have to worry about having no brothers?"

Tzu-kung [Pinyin, Zigong] asked about government. Confucius said, "Sufficient food, sufficient armament, and sufficient confidence of the people." Tzu-kung said, "Forced to give up one of these, which would you abandon first?" Confucius said, "I would abandon the armament." Tzu-kung said, "Forced to give up one of the remaining two, which would you abandon first?" Confucius said, "I would abandon food. There have been deaths from time immemorial, but no state can exist without the confidence of the people."

Chi K'ang Tzu [Pinyin, Ji Kangzi] asked Confucius about government. Confucius replied, "To govern [cheng; Pinyin, zheng] is to rectify [cheng]. If you lead the people by being rectified yourself, who will dare not be rectified?"

Chi K'ang Tzu asked Confucius about government, saying, "What do you think of killing the wicked and associating with the good?" Confucius replied, "In your government what is the need of killing? If you desire what is good, the people will be good. The character of a ruler is like wind and that of the people is like grass. In whatever direction the wind blows, the grass always bends."

Confucius said, "If a ruler sets himself right, he will be followed without his command. If he does not set himself right, even his commands will not be obeyed."

Confucius said, "A man who is strong, resolute, simple, and slow to speak is near to humanity."

Confucius said, "The superior man understands the higher things [moral principles]; the inferior man understands the lower things [profit]."

Confucius said, "There are three kinds of friendship which are beneficial and three kinds which are harmful. Friendship with the upright, with the truthful, and with the well-informed is beneficial. Friendship with those who flatter, with those who are meek and who compromise with principles, and with those who talk cleverly is harmful."

Tzu-chang [Pinyin, Zizhang] asked Confucius about humanity. Confucius said, "One who can practice five things wherever he may be is a man of humanity." Tzu-chang asked what the five are. Confucius said, "Earnestness, liberality, truthfulness, diligence, and generosity. If one is earnest, one will not be treated with disrespect. If one is liberal, one will win the hearts of all. If one is truthful, one will be trusted. If one is diligent, one will be successful. And if one is generous, one will be able to enjoy the service of others."

Confucius said, "I do not wish to say anything." Tzu-kung said, "If you do not say anything, what will we little disciples ever learn to pass on to others?" Confucius said, "Does Heaven [*T'ien*, Nature; Pinyin, *Tian*] say anything? The four seasons run their course and all things are produced. Does Heaven say anything?"

SOURCE: Wing-tsit Chan, trans. and compiled, *A Source Book in Chinese Philosophy*. Princeton, NJ: Princeton University Press, 1963, pp. 18–47

The Book of Mencius

Mengzi (Meng-tzu; *c.* 390–305 BCE), generally known in the West by the latinized version of his name, Mencius, was a major commentator on the teachings of Confucius. Living during a period of extreme chaos in China, he nonetheless maintained a basic belief in the goodness of humanity. His teachings are conveyed via the convention of naming people such as Gaozi and Gongduzi, who engage him in dialogue.

II.A.2 Human Nature Is Basically Good Gaozi said, "Human nature is like swirling water. Open a passage to the east, and it flows east. Open a passage to the west, and it flows west. The basic indeterminacy of good and evil in human nature is just like the basic indeterminacy of east and west in the flow of water."

Mencius said, "Water certainly has no particular tendency to flow east or west, but can the same be said of flowing up or down? The basic goodness of human nature is just like the downward flow of water. . . .

"Now, with my hands or my feet I can splash water over my head; by channeling it, I can direct it all the way to the top of a hill. But is this the basic nature of water? No. These results are due to external force. The fact that people can be made to do evil reflects the same violation of their basic nature."

II.A.6 The Sprouts of Virtue Mencius said: "All persons have a heart which cannot bear to see the suffering of others. The Sage Kings had such a heart, and their governments did not permit the suffering of the people. In ruling the kingdom, if you manifest this heart to implement such a government, you can hold the world in the palm of your hand.

"What I mean by saying that 'all persons have a heart which cannot bear to see the suffering of others' is this: Anyone who suddenly came upon a toddler about to fall into a well would have a heart of alarm and concern. And we cannot say that this heart arises from wanting to be favored by the parents, or from seeking the praise of one's friends and community, or from hoping to avoid a reputation for callousness.

"Clearly, one who did not have the heart of concern would be inhuman. One who did not have the heart of shame for wrong-doing would be inhuman. One who did not have the heart which places others before oneself would be inhuman. And one who did not have the heart which distinguishes between right and wrong would be inhuman.

"The *heart of concern* is the sprout of *ren* (kindness). The *heart of shame* is the sprout of *yi* (morality). The *heart of yielding* is the sprout of *li* (propriety). The *heart of judgment* is the sprout of *zhi* (wisdom).

"Having these four 'sprouts' is like having arms and legs. If you say that you cannot act upon them, you are discrediting yourself, just as if you say that a ruler cannot act upon them, you are discrediting his rule. Anyone who has these four sprouts within themselves knows how to develop them and perfect them: they are like the initial spark of a fire, or the first waters of an open spring. If you can perfect them, you will be able to embrace the whole world with your virtue; if you do not perfect them, you will not even be able to serve your own parents."

III.A.5 The Natural Basis of Ancestor Veneration In ancient times there must have been people who did not bury their parents. When the parents died, they were thrown in the ditch. Then one day the sons passed the place and there lay the bodies, eaten by foxes and sucked by flies. A sweat broke out on their brows, and they could not bear to look. The sweat was not a put-on just for others to see: it was an outward expression of their innermost heart. They went home for baskets and shovels. Now, if it was right for them to bury the remains of their parents, then it must also be right for all dutiful children and benevolent persons to do the same.

VI.A.6 Many Hearts from the Start Gongduzi said, "Gaozi said that human nature is neither good nor evil. Others say that some persons can be made good while other persons can be made evil, which is why people were inclined to the good during the [righteous] reigns of Wen and Wu, and inclined to evil during the [unrighteous] reigns of Yü and Li. Still others say that some persons are naturally good while other persons are naturally evil, which is why Yao [a virtuous lord] could live under Xiang [an evil king], why Shun [a virtuous ruler] could have had a [morally] blind man as his father,[3] ... Now you

---

3 The examples illustrate that despite living under an evil king or father, individuals can retain their natural goodness.

claim that human nature is basically good. Does this mean that everyone else is wrong?"

Mencius said, "If he follows his natural inclinations, a man is capable of becoming good. That's what I mean by 'goodness.' Insofar as he does not do good, it is not a fault of his basic condition. All persons have the *heart of concern*. All persons have the *heart of shame*. All persons have the *heart of yielding*. All persons have the *heart of judgment....* *Ren, yi, li*, and *zhi* were not branded upon me from the outside; I possessed them from the start, even though I may not have known it. That's why it is said, 'You will find what you seek and lose what you cast aside.' People who are less virtuous—even by a factor of two, five, or a hundred—are so simply because they have not realized their full potential."

SOURCE: Original translation for this book by Randall Nadeau, 2006

The Doctrine of the Mean

"The Doctrine of the Mean" (the middle way) emphasizes conformity with the **Dao** (Tao), or way. This word is central to both Confucianism and Daoism, but is given different emphasis in the two traditions. In Confucianism, the Dao is the way of natural human sincerity, which reflects the Way of Heaven.

What Heaven (*T'ien*, Nature; Pinyin, *Tian*) imparts to man is called human nature. To follow our nature is called the Way. Cultivating the Way is called education. The Way cannot be separated from us for a moment. What can be separated from us is not the Way. Therefore the superior man is cautious over what he does not see and apprehensive over what he does not hear. There is nothing more visible than what is hidden and nothing more manifest than what is subtle. Therefore the superior man is watchful over himself when he is alone.

Before the feelings of pleasure, anger, sorrow, and joy are aroused it is called equilibrium (*chung*, centrality, mean; Pinyin, *zhong*). When these feelings are aroused and each and all attain due measure and degree, it is called harmony. Equilibrium is the great foundation of the world, and harmony its universal path. When equilibrium and harmony are realized to the highest degree, heaven and earth will attain their proper order and all things will flourish....

Confucius said, "I know why the Way is not pursued. The intelligent go beyond it and the stupid do not come up to it. I know why the Way is not understood. The worthy go beyond it and the unworthy do not come up to it. There is no one who does not eat and drink, but there are few who can really know flavor."...

"The Way of the superior man functions everywhere and yet is hidden. Men and women of simple intelligence can share its knowledge; and yet in its utmost reaches, there is something which even the sage does not know. Men and women of simple intelligence can put it into practice; and yet in its utmost reaches, there is something which even the sage is not able to put into practice. Great as heaven and earth are, men still find something in them with which to be dissatisfied. Thus with [the Way of] the superior man, if one speaks of its greatness, nothing in the world can contain it, and if one speaks of its smallness, nothing in the world can split it. The *Book of Odes*[4] says, 'the hawk flies up to heaven; the fishes leap in the deep.' This means that [the Way] is clearly seen above and below. The Way of the superior man has its simple beginnings in the relation between man and woman, but in its utmost reaches, it is clearly seen in heaven and on earth."

Confucius said, "The Way is not far from man. When a man pursues the Way and yet remains away from man, his course cannot be considered the Way. The *Book of Odes* says, 'In hewing an axe handle, in hewing an axe handle, the pattern is not far off.' If we take an axe handle to hew another axe handle and look askance from the one to the other, we may still think the pattern is far away. Therefore the superior man governs men as men, in accordance with human nature, and as soon as they change [what is wrong], he stops. Conscientiousness (*chung*) and altruism (*shu*) are not far from the Way. What you do not wish others to do to you, do not do to them.

"There are four things in the Way of the superior man, none of which I have been able to do. To serve my father as I would expect my son to serve me: that I have not been able to do. To serve my ruler as I would expect my ministers to serve me: that I have not been able to do. To serve my elder brothers as I would expect my younger brothers to serve me: that I have not been able to do. To be the first to treat friends as I would expect them to treat me: that I have not been able to do. In practicing the ordinary virtues and in the exercise of care in ordinary conversation, when there is deficiency, the superior man never fails to make further effort, and when there is excess, never dares to go to the limit. His words correspond to his actions and his actions correspond to his words. Isn't the superior man earnest and genuine?"...

Only those who are absolutely sincere can fully develop their nature. If they can fully develop their nature, they can then fully develop the nature of others. If they can fully develop the nature of others, they can then fully develop the nature of things. If they can fully develop the nature of things, they can then assist in the transforming and nourishing process of Heaven and Earth. If they can assist in the transforming and nourishing process of Heaven and Earth, they can thus form a trinity with Heaven and Earth....

The next in order are those who cultivate to the utmost a particular goodness. Having done this, they can attain to the possession of sincerity. As there is sincerity, there will be its expression. As it is expressed, it will become conspicuous. As it becomes conspicuous, it will become clear. As it becomes clear, it will move others. As it moves others, it changes them. As it

---

4 *Book of Odes*—a basic Confucian text of poems and songs for official functions, largely compiled from older traditions.

changes them, it transforms them. Only those who are absolutely sincere can transform others.

It is characteristic of absolute sincerity to be able to foreknow. When a nation or family is about to flourish, there are sure to be lucky omens. When a nation or family is about to perish, there are sure to be unlucky omens. These omens are revealed in divination and in the movements of the four limbs. When calamity or blessing is about to come, it can surely know beforehand if it is good, and it can also surely know beforehand if it is evil. Therefore he who has absolute sincerity is like a spirit.

Sincerity means the completion of the self, and the Way is self-directing. Sincerity is the beginning and end of things. Without sincerity there would be nothing. Therefore the superior man values sincerity. Sincerity is not only the completion of one's own self, it is that by which all things are completed. The completion of the self means humanity. The completion of all things means wisdom. These are the character of the nature, and they are the Way in which the internal and the external are united. Therefore whenever it is employed, everything done is right. . . .

Therefore absolute sincerity is ceaseless. Being ceaseless, it is lasting. Being lasting, it is evident. Being evident, it is infinite. Being infinite, it is extensive and deep. Being extensive and deep, it is high and brilliant. It is because it is extensive and deep that it contains all things. It is because it is high and brilliant that it overshadows all things. It is because it is infinite and lasting that it can complete all things. In being extensive and deep, it is a counterpart of Earth. In being high and brilliant, it is a counterpart of Heaven. In being infinite and lasting, it is unlimited. Such being its nature, it becomes prominent without any display, produces changes without motion, and accomplishes its ends without action.

The Way of Heaven and Earth may be completely described in one sentence: They are without any doubleness and so they produce things in an unfathomable way. The Way of Heaven and Earth is extensive, deep, high, brilliant, infinite, and lasting. The heaven now before us is only this bright, shining mass; but when viewed in its unlimited extent, the sun, moon, stars, and constellations are suspended in it and all things are covered by it. The earth before us is but a handful of soil; but in its breadth and depth, it sustains mountains like Hua and Yüeh without feeling their weight, contains the rivers and seas without letting them leak away, and sustains all things. The mountain before us is only a fistful of straw; but in all the vastness of its size, grass and trees grow upon it, birds and beasts dwell on it, and stores of precious things (minerals) are discovered in it. The water before us is but a spoonful of liquid, but in all its unfathomable depth, the monsters, dragons, fishes, and turtles are produced in them, and wealth becomes abundant because of it (as a result of transportation). The *Book of Odes* says, "The **Mandate of Heaven**, how beautiful and unceasing." This is to say, "This is what makes Heaven to be Heaven."

SOURCE: "The Doctrine of the Mean," in *A Source Book in Chinese Philosophy*, trans. and compiled Wing-tsit Chan. Princeton, NJ: Princeton University Press, 1963, pp. 98–110

Scholars' commentaries

Scholars were highly honored figures in traditional Confucianism. They assembled the teachings of Confucius, including his commentaries on ancient texts, and further developed his system of practical ethics.

The Great Commentary on the Book of Changes

The *Book of Changes*, or **Yijing** (*I Ching*), is an ancient compilation of Chinese wisdom which serves as foundational material for both Confucianism and Daoism. Its basic text gives terse, cryptic images referring to a system of divination by throwing stalks of yarrow or coins and observing and interpreting the patterns they form. The system is seemingly dualistic: the stalks are long or short, or the coins fall on one side or the other. This interplay of two basic states of being is often referred to as **yin** ("the cloudy") versus **yang** ("brightness"), or "the yielding" versus "the firm," or "the receptive" versus "the creative." But in Chinese tradition, the two states are not seen as being opposed; rather, their dynamic co-ordination is at work in the continual flux of the cosmos. Wisdom therefore lies in understanding and harmonizing oneself with this flux. The *Great Commentary* is thought to be based at least in part on Confucius's interpretation of the *Book of Changes*, as later compiled by Confucian scholars.

The Changes in the Universe and in the *Book of Changes*

1   Heaven is high, the earth is low; thus the Creative and the Receptive are determined. In correspondence with this difference between low and high, inferior and superior places are established.
Movement and rest have their definite laws; according to these, firm and yielding lines are differentiated.
Events follow definite trends, each according to its nature. Things are distinguished from one another in definite classes. In this way good fortune and misfortune come about. In the heavens phenomena take form; on earth shapes take form. In this way change and transformation become manifest.

2   Therefore the eight trigrams[5] succeed one another by turns, as the firm and the yielding displace each other.

3   Things are aroused by thunder and lightning; they are fertilized by wind and rain. Sun and moon follow their courses and it is now hot, now cold.

4   The way of the Creative brings about the male.
The way of the Receptive brings about the female.

5   The Creative knows the great beginnings.
The Receptive completes the finished things.

6   The Creative knows through the easy.
The Receptive can do things through the simple.

---

5 Trigrams—diagrams of some of the 64 possible throws of the yarrow stalks.

7   What is easy, is easy to know; what is simple, is easy to follow. He who is easy to know attains fealty. He who is easy to follow attains works. He who possesses attachment can endure for long; he who possesses works can become great. To endure is the disposition of the sage; greatness is the field of action of the sage.

8   By means of the easy and the simple we grasp the laws of the whole world. When the laws of the whole world are grasped, therein lies perfection.

On the Composition and the Use of the *Book of Changes*

1   The holy sages instituted the hexagrams,[6] so that phenomena might be perceived therein. They appended the judgments, in order to indicate good fortune and misfortune.

2   As the firm and the yielding lines displace one another, change and transformation arise.

3   Therefore good fortune and misfortune are the images of gain and loss; remorse and humiliation are the images of sorrow and forethought.

4   Change and transformation are images of progress and retrogression. The firm and the yielding are images of day and night. The movements of the six lines contain the ways of the three primal powers [heaven, earth, and humans].

5   Therefore it is the order of the Changes that the superior man devotes himself to and that he attains tranquillity by. It is the judgments on the individual lines that the superior man takes pleasure in and that he ponders on.

6   Therefore the superior man contemplates these images in times of rest and meditates on the judgments. When he undertakes something, he contemplates the changes and ponders on the oracles. Therefore he is blessed by heaven. . . .

The Deeper Implications of the *Book of Changes*

1   The Book of Changes contains the measure of heaven and earth; therefore it enables us to comprehend the *tao* [Pinyin, *dao*] of heaven and earth and its order.

2   Looking upward, we contemplate with its help the signs in the heavens; looking down, we examine the lines of the earth. Thus we come to know the circumstances of the dark and the light. Going back to the beginnings of things and pursuing them to the end, we come to know the lessons of birth and of death. The union of seed and power produces all things; the escape of the soul brings about change. Through this we come to know the conditions of outgoing and returning spirits [expanding and contracting phases].

3   Since in this way man comes to resemble heaven and earth, he is not in conflict with them. His wisdom embraces all things, and his *tao* brings

---

6 Hexagrams—diagrams of some of the 64 possible throws of the yarrow stalks.

order into the whole world; therefore he does not err. He is active everywhere but does not let himself be carried away. He rejoices in heaven and has knowledge of fate, therefore he is free of care. He is content with his circumstances and genuine in his kindness, therefore he can practice love. . . .

Tao in its Relation to the Light Power and to the Dark Power

1   That which lets now the dark, now the light appear is *tao*.

2   As continuer, it is good. As completer, it is the essence.

3   The kind man discovers it and calls it kind. The wise man discovers it and calls it wise. The people use it day by day and are not aware of it, for the way of the superior man is rare.

4   It manifests itself as kindness but conceals its workings. It gives life to all things, but it does not share the anxieties of the holy sage. Its glorious power, its great field of action, are of all things the most sublime.

5   It possesses everything in complete abundance; this is its great field of action. It renews everything daily: this is its glorious power.

6   As begetter of all begetting, it is called change.

7   As that which completes the primal images, it is called the Creative; as that which imitates them, it is called the Receptive.

8   In that it serves for exploring the laws of number and thus for knowing the future, it is called revelation. In that it serves to infuse an organic coherence into the changes, it is called the work.

9   That aspect of it which cannot be fathomed in terms of the light and the dark is called spirit.

SOURCE: "Ta Chuan [Pinyin, Da Zhuan]: The Great Commentary," trans. Richard Wilhelm, in the *Book of Changes*, ed. Cary F. Baynes. Princeton, NJ: Princeton University Press/Bollingen Foundation, 1950, 1967, pp. 280–301

Lessons for Women by Ban Zhao

Although the majority of Confucian scholars were men, there were also some female scholars. The most famous woman scholar was Ban Zhao (Pan Chao), who was historian for the imperial court of China in the first century CE. What follows is part of her advice to her daughters, and thus to women in general, on fulfilling their proper social roles.

Respect and Caution   As *Yin* and *Yang* are not of the same nature, so man and woman have different characteristics. The distinctive quality of the *Yang* is rigidity; the function of the *Yin* is yielding. Man is honored for strength; a woman is beautiful on account of her gentleness. Hence there arose the common saying: "A man though born like a wolf may, it is feared, become a weak monstrosity: a woman though born like a mouse may, it is feared, become a tiger."

Now for self-culture nothing equals respect for others. To counteract firmness nothing equals compliance. Consequently it can be said that the

Way of respect and acquiescence is woman's most important principle of conduct. So respect may be defined as nothing other than holding on to that which is permanent; and acquiescence nothing other than being liberal and generous. Those who are steadfast in devotion know that they should stay in their proper places; those who are liberal and generous esteem others, and honor and serve [them].

If husband and wife have the habit of staying together, never leaving one another, and following each other around within the limited space of their own rooms, then they will lust after and take liberties with one another. From such action improper language will arise between the two. This kind of discussion may lead to licentiousness. Out of licentiousness will be born a heart of disrespect to the husband. Such a result comes from not knowing that one should stay in one's proper place.

Furthermore, affairs may be either crooked or straight; words may be either right or wrong. Straightforwardness cannot but lead to quarreling; crookedness cannot but lead to accusation. If there are really accusations and quarrels, then undoubtedly there will be angry affairs. Such a result comes from not esteeming others, and not honoring and serving [them].

[If wives] suppress not contempt for husbands, then it follows [that such wives] rebuke and scold [their husbands]. [If husbands] stop not short of anger, then they are certain to beat [their wives]. The correct relationship between husband and wife is based upon harmony and intimacy, and [conjugal] love is grounded in proper union. Should actual blows be dealt, how could matrimonial relationship be preserved? Should sharp words be spoken, how could [conjugal] love exist? If love and proper relationship both be destroyed, then husband and wife are divided.

Womanly Qualifications   A woman [ought to] have four qualifications: (1) womanly virtue; (2) womanly words; (3) womanly bearing; and (4) womanly work. Now what is called womanly virtue need not be brilliant ability, exceptionally different from others. Womanly words need be neither clever in debate nor keen in conversation. Womanly appearance requires neither a pretty nor a perfect face and form. Womanly work need not be work done more skillfully than that of others.

To guard carefully her chastity; to control circumspectly her behavior; in every motion to exhibit modesty; and to model each act on the best usage, this is womanly virtue.

To choose her words with care; to avoid vulgar language; to speak at appropriate times; and not to weary others [with much conversation], may be called the characteristics of womanly words.

To wash and scrub filth away; to keep clothes and ornaments fresh and clean; to wash the head and bathe the body regularly, and to keep the person free from disgraceful filth, may be called the characteristics of womanly bearing.

With whole-hearted devotion to sew and to weave; to love not gossip and silly laughter; in cleanliness and order [to prepare] the wine and food for serving guests, may be called the characteristics of womanly work.

These four qualifications characterize the greatest virtue of a woman. No woman can afford to be without them.

SOURCE: Pan Chao, "Lessons for Women," in *An Anthology of Sacred Texts by and about Women*, ed. Serinity Young. New York: Crossroad Publishing, 1995, p. 359

Neo-Confucianism

As Buddhism spread within China, Confucianism was also revived. This "Neo-Confucianism," which became dominant after the tenth century CE, was more metaphysical than classical Confucianism, and it made extensive references to the *Book of Changes*.

The Great Ultimate   by Zhou Dunyi

The philosopher Zhou Dunyi (Chou Tun-i; 1017–73) is considered the pioneer of Neo-Confucianism. His "Explanation of the Diagram of the Great Ultimate," which follows, became the basic framework for Neo-Confucian metaphysics and cosmology.

The Great Ultimate through movement generates yang. When its activity reaches its limit, it becomes tranquil. Through tranquillity the Great Ultimate generates yin. When tranquillity reaches its limit, activity begins again. So movement and tranquillity alternate and become the root of each other, giving rise to the distinction of yin and yang, and the two modes are thus established.

By the transformation of yang and its union with yin, the Five Agents of Water, Fire, Wood, Metal, and Earth arise. When these five material forces (*ch'i*; Pinyin, **qi**) are distributed in harmonious order, the four seasons run their course.

The Five Agents constitute one system of yin and yang, and yin and yang constitute one Great Ultimate. The Great Ultimate is fundamentally the Non-ultimate. The Five Agents arise, each with its specific nature.

When the reality of the Ultimate of Non-being and the essence of yin, yang, and the Five Agents come into mysterious union, integration arises. *Ch'ien* (Pinyin, *Qian*; Heaven) constitutes the male element, and *K'un* (Pinyin, *Kun*; Earth) constitutes the female element. The interaction of these two material forces engenders and transforms the myriad things. The myriad things reproduce and reproduce, resulting in an unending transformation.

It is man alone who receives (the Five Agents) in their highest excellence, and therefore he is most intelligent. His physical form appears, and his spirit develops consciousness. The five moral principles of his nature (humanity or *jen* [Pinyin, *ren*], righteousness, propriety, wisdom, and truthfulness) are aroused by, and react to, the external world and engage in activity; good and evil are distinguished; and human affairs take place.

The sage settles these affairs by the principles of the Mean, correctness, humanity, and righteousness (for the way of the sage is none other than these four), regarding tranquillity as fundamental. (Having no desire, there will therefore be tranquillity.) Thus he establishes himself as the ultimate standard for man. Hence the character of the sage is identical with that of Heaven and Earth; his brilliancy is identical with that of the sun and moon; his order is identical with that of the four seasons; and his good and evil fortunes are identical with those of spiritual beings. The superior man cultivates these moral qualities and enjoys good fortune, whereas the inferior man violates them and suffers evil fortune.

Therefore it is said that "yin and yang are established as the way of Heaven, the weak and the strong as the way of Earth, and humanity and righteousness as the way of man." It is also said that "if we investigate the cycle of things, we shall understand the concepts of life and death." Great is the *Book of Changes*! Herein lies its excellence!

SOURCE: Chou Tun-i, "An Explanation of the Diagram of the Great Ultimate," in *A Source Book in Chinese Philosophy*, trans. and compiled Wing-tsit Chan. Princeton, NJ: Princeton University Press, 1963, pp. 463–5

The Western Inscription by Zhang Zai

Zhang Zai (Chang Tsai; 1020–77) was another of the leading developers of Neo-Confucian thought; his "Western Inscription" is one of its most famous treatises. It was inscribed on the west window of his lecture room.

Heaven is my father and Earth is my mother, and even such a small creature as I finds an intimate place in their midst.

Therefore that which fills the universe I regard as my body and that which directs the universe I consider as my nature.

All people are my brothers and sisters, and all things are my companions.

The greater ruler [the emperor] is the eldest son of my parents [Heaven and Earth], and the great ministers are his stewards. Respect the aged—this is the way to treat them as elders should be treated. Show deep love toward the orphaned and the weak—this is the way to treat them as the young should be treated. The sage identifies his character with that of Heaven and Earth, and the worthy is the most outstanding man. Even those who are tired, infirm, crippled, or sick; those who have no brothers or children, wives or husbands, are all my brothers who are in distress and have no one to turn to.

When the time comes, to keep himself from harm—this is the care of a son. To rejoice in Heaven and to have no anxiety—this is filial piety at its purest.

He who disobeys [the Principle of Nature] violates virtue. He who destroys humanity is a robber. He who promotes evil lacks [moral] capacity. But he who puts his moral nature into practice and brings his physical existence into complete fulfillment can match [Heaven and Earth].

One who knows the principles of transformation will skillfully carry forward the undertakings [of Heaven and Earth], and one who penetrates spirit to the highest degree will skillfully carry out their will.

Do nothing shameful in the recesses of your own house and thus bring no dishonor to them. Preserve your mind and nourish your nature and thus [serve them] with untiring effort. . . .

Wealth, honor, blessing, and benefits are meant for the enrichment of my life, while poverty, humble station, and sorrow are meant to help me to fulfillment.

In life I follow and serve [Heaven and Earth]. In death I will be at peace.

SOURCE: Chang Tsai, "The Western Inscription," in *A Source Book in Chinese Philosophy*, trans. and compiled Wing-tsit Chan. Princeton, NJ: Princeton University Press, 1963, pp. 497–8

Living Confucianism

During the twentieth century, Communism undercut the political, economic, and social base of Confucianism. However, Confucianism is not just a matter of past history, according to Confucian scholar Yao Xinzhong, Chairman of the Department of Religion, Ethics and Society at the University of Wales in Lampeter. He finds that even though Confucianism no longer molds Chinese social structure, its values continue to be significant in Chinese life.

Confucianism and the Twenty-first Century
by Yao Xinzhong

Will Confucianism go into the twenty-first century merely as a remnant of history? Or will it have much to offer and to contribute to a meaningful life in a rapidly changing society? What elements or parts of the Confucian tradition enable it not to be a dead culture, nor to be a tradition of the past, but continually to be a living organism comprehensively functioning in a multi-cultural society, emotionally and rationally motivating the people, and naturally making contributions to world peace and prosperity?

The Modern Relevance of Confucianism With the Confucian retreat from political, social and economic stages in East Asia since the end of last century, the Confucian influence has been limited to a small area of learning, seeming to be alive only among tradition-minded people and merely as a social and psychological background of their activities. The political and religious role of Confucianism in Mainland China[7] changed from being the orthodox ideology to a "doctrinal furnishing" of feudalism and aristocracy, and its values and ideals were severely undermined or demolished both by radical revolutionaries and by radical liberals. For most academics and non-academic people, Confucianism represented the shadow of the past, the symbol and the reason of a backward, disadvantaged and powerless China. As a result three irreversible changes took place in relation to Confucianism: Confucian organizations and institutions disappeared, Confucians lost their social identity, and Confucian rituals no longer had spiritual values. Confucianism seemed to have been reduced to being merely a theory or a doctrine without practical meaning, an old image without effect on modern life.

However, this is only one side of the story of Confucianism in the twentieth century. The umbilical cord between the Confucian tradition and modern China cannot be easily cut off. The elements in the Confucian heritage have travelled to the present, either hidden in both Nationalist and Communist doctrines, principles, ethics, public opinions and the system of a bureaucratic elite, etc., or implicitly underlying the whole structure of Chinese community (family, community, society and the state), whatever forms it may take, either capitalist or socialist, Nationalist or Communist. The link between the Three Principles of the People initiated by Sun Zhongshan and the Confucian vision of the Grand Commonwealth Society (*datong shehui*) is so strong that very few people would deny that there exists a succession from the latter to the former. And Communism inherited a great deal from the Confucian moral code, so much so that ... Communist ethics and Confucianism were not very different in practice.

After many years in which Confucianism suffered a setback, Confucianism is on the rise again in many states and areas of East Asia since the beginning of the 1980s, although the reasons and motives behind the Confucian popularity are quite different from one state to another. In any case, the revival of Confucianism is not simply a return to the tradition nor a wholesale restoration of the old practice and learning, but a renewal of the culture and a transformation of the heritage in order to redefine cultural identity and to guide social and economic development....

It is agreed among the scholars in Confucian Studies that while the social structure of old Confucianism has gone, its doctrinal and idealistic values are inherent in Chinese psychology and underlie East Asian peoples' attitudes and behaviour.

Despite criticism and caution about the relevance of Confucianism to modernization, Confucianism is nevertheless gradually regaining some of its lost place in people's lives and in intellectuals' minds. As a traditional organization Confucianism may not yet have obtained any new identity and

---

7 Mainland China—the current communist state of the People's Republic of China, as opposed to the Republic of China, which is the capitalist nationalist state in Taiwan.

those that are attached to old systems and old social structures may never be appreciated again. However, Confucian values have become functional once more and become more and more appealing to the people. For example, self-cultivation (*xiu shen*) as the basis for governing the state and bringing peace to the world has been partly accepted and deliberately adopted by this generation of students. The combination of Confucian values and modern qualities creates a new title for business leaders, "Confucian businessmen/women," praising the Confucian virtues of the industrial and commercial leaders, such as humaneness, trustfulness, sincerity and altruism in business dealings. Some people enthusiastically talk about "Marxist Confucianism" or "Confucian Marxism," while others see an opportunity in the economic experience of East Asia to merge Confucianism and the market economy, Capitalist Confucianism or Confucian Capitalism. Along with these new understandings of the nature and functions of Confucianism, efforts have also been made to rejuvenate and rehabilitate Confucian institutions, and interests in Confucian education, examination and academies are on the increase. For example, after the interval of more than half a century on the Mainland, the traditional civil service examination, which bears the hallmark of Confucianism, has partly been adopted as a modern means to recruit civil servants. Confucian academies are no longer regarded as "feudal institutes" but praised as centres for learning and education. In some Chinese communities in Hong Kong, Taiwan and South East Asia, a variety of Confucian organizations have been established aiming at restoring the spiritual functions of Confucianism; for example, the Confucian Academies, Confucian churches centred on the worship of Confucius, and even Confucian Sunday schools that take Confucian classics as their textbook. These may not be enough for Confucianism to reclaim the glorious image of its past. However, nobody would deny that it has become gradually relevant again to today's social/personal and religious life. There are obvious signs indicating that some aspects of the Confucian ethics are still useful and valuable, that the uniqueness of the Confucian religiosity is being recognized as an important dimension of human spirituality, and that the Confucian speculation on metaphysical views is considered conducive to the healthy growth of the global village. . . .

A Responsible Ethic Free choice is the foundation of modern society, and the pre-condition of market economy. However, freedom without responsibility would result in the collapse of the social network and in the conflict between individuals, and between individuals and society, and would lead to the sacrifice of the future in order to satisfy short-term needs. This has become a serious challenge to human wisdom and to human integrity. In this respect, Confucianism can make a contribution to a new moral sense, a new ecological view and a new code for the global village. Confucian ethics insists that the self be the centre of relationships, not in order to claim one's rights but to claim to be responsible; and that a sense of the community of trust must be modelled on the family, not in a way that excludes others but in a way that extends one's family affection to a wider world. According to a Confucian understanding, daily behaviour must be guided by an established ritual, not merely for restricting individuals, but more for cultivating the sense of holiness and mission in their heart. Education is essential for building up a good character, not primarily for building up one's physical power to conquer what is unknown, but for the ability to cooperate with others and to be in harmony with nature and the universe....

The early twentieth-century critics have drawn us a dim and depressing picture of Confucian education in which human nature is distorted and human knowledge is confined to memorizing a few outdated classics. Confucian education certainly has its flaws and is insufficient to cope with modern subjects, nor is it enough to equip the people with technological tools to deal with modern problems. It would therefore be naïve or even foolish to try to replace modern education with Confucian moral training, and unprofessional to credit too much to the traditional ways while rejecting modern methodology of education. Nonetheless, it is still legitimate to raise such a question as: "Are there any useful elements in Confucian education that may be drawn out to serve the goal of a comprehensive education?"...

The purpose of education is not only to transmit knowledge. It is also to transmit and apply values. In this sense, all traditional forms of education are relevant, and Confucian education can be a useful and valuable supplement to modern school education.... Confucian learning was never meant to be a merely scholarly exercise. It had practical extensions, one of which was to put into practice the doctrinal understanding of individual, family, community and society, the core of values fostering a spirit of self-discipline, family solidarity, public morality and social responsibility. Confucian education is fundamentally humanistic; its primary purpose is learning to be fully human and becoming a qualified member of the community of trust; and its primary tools are enhancing self-cultivation and developing one's inner strength of assuming responsibilities for oneself, for one's family and for society at large....

The Confucian faith is fundamentally humanistic, which lays the responsibility for a better world and for a secured future not in the hands of a supremely detached God, but in the hands of ordinarily engaged humans. In this sense, Confucianism provides us with an alternative way of dealing with the meaning of life and the meaning of death.... For a Confucian, the meaning of life can be realized only in learning and practice, in bringing oneself to the standard of a gentleman and the society to the standard of Great Unity: the destiny of a human can be fulfilled only in establishing words, merits and virtues for generations to come....

SOURCE: Yao Xinzhong, paper presented at First International Conference on Traditional Culture and Moral Education, Beijing, 1998

The Staying Power of Religion in China by Peng Liu

In contemporary China, there is considerable tension between the government and religions, because the Communist Party has long sought to eliminate any perceived threats to its ideological dominance. From the seventeenth century, the Confucian literati were opposed to Christianity, and even after the fall of the Manchu dynasty in 1911 and the resulting end of Confucianism as the state ideology, anti-Christian sentiments persisted in the form of nationalism and then communist atheism. Nevertheless, religions seem to be thriving in China today. Buddhist and Daoist temples, Catholic and Protestant churches, and Muslim mosques are full of worshippers, and many underground religious groups are growing outside the limitations that the government tries to impose. Peng Liu, a professor at the Institute of American Studies at the Chinese Academy of Social Sciences in Beijing, offers some observations about the government's pragmatic approach to this tension.

Within China, religion is considered quite differently. The ruling Communist Party views religion as a "backward" or even "superstitious" idealist ideology, opposed to and incompatible with Marxist "scientific" materialism. A Marxist government should propagate an atheistic worldview and must not encourage religious belief. At best, the state will tolerate religious teachings that focus on ethics and social service, playing down supernatural elements. China's leaders also view religion as a tool used by foreign powers to exercise undue influence within China. The introduction of the Chinese people to Christianity—Protestant, Roman Catholic and Orthodox—was closely connected with the unequal treaties of the nineteenth and early twentieth centuries, through which China lost control of its sovereignty, owing to its humiliating military defeats by the Western imperialist powers.

China's rulers recognize, however, that religion cannot be ignored or excluded altogether. The history of religion in China is a long one. Many Chinese practice some form of religion, and in some areas of China, religion is an integral part of the people's daily lives and communities. The culture of nearly all of China's ethnic minorities is profoundly influenced by religion. Thus religious issues cannot be separated from ethnic issues. Given these concerns, the party-state cannot easily or quickly eliminate religious belief, regardless of the preferences of China's leaders. Even according to Marxist theory, the predicted gradual death of religion is a protracted process.

Finally, most of the world's population has some kind of religious belief, and China's leaders have been forced to recognize the role religion plays in shaping international affairs. Thus religion and religious freedom and tolerance continually arise as foreign affairs issues that China must address. The state focuses on the practical import of religious diplomacy in the interests of trade and national security.

Given the resilience of religion in China and the pervasiveness of religious concerns in international affairs, the only practical thing for China to do is to shape religious practice and diplomacy into vehicles that serve the political purpose of building a socialist China. Jiang Zemin, as president of the People's Republic of China and general secretary of the Chinese Communist Party, speaking at national religious affairs conferences in 1991 and 2001, stressed that an overriding goal of both religious policy and religious regulations was "to guide religion to adapt to socialism." This statement summarizes the Chinese government's approach to religion; it is a political strategy to unite religious believers at home and overseas behind the Chinese Communist Party.

China's approach to religion drives the structure of its regulation of religion. Government institutions manage religious affairs according to the policies of the party-state, and religious groups have the duty to cooperate and carry out these policies. There are mechanisms for the religious groups to voice their concerns to the party and the government. For example, each religious group has representatives in the national and regional People's Political Consultative Conferences, in which they can talk things over with representatives of the party and the government, and there are periodic informal exchanges between national and local party and government heads and the various religious officials. These avenues only provide a way of exchanging opinions, however, and the concessions given to the religious groups have no legally binding force. The underlying premise of all the interaction and regulation is that the religious groups must accept the leadership of the government to the end of furthering the interests of the party-state. Foreign exchanges with religious groups are encouraged only when they are likely to serve this political purpose. . . .

Political elites in China are increasingly paying attention to and discussing religion, reversing their traditional tendency to ignore it altogether. In light of the party-state's continued fragmentation and weakening, coupled with the emergence of a more pluralistic society, there will most likely be increasing differences of approach to religion among the competing interest groups in society. The senior leaders of the Chinese Communist Party are mentally preparing for changes in religious polity. The conservative minority within the party, including the officials responsible for administration of religious affairs, along with the leaders of government-led religious organizations, are the main forces whose interests pit them against reform of current policies. There are other key actors, however, with different interests to which top leaders must pay attention. These include provincial and municipal authorities needing help with social services, local religious believers with increasing popularity and resources, and the educated urban middle stratum (including academic and polity experts in religion), who are interested in expanding all civil rights. The *de facto* loosening of the strict controls on believers' contacts with foreign coreligionists that emerges as society continues to open up fuels a growing awareness of religious rights and expectations of government respect and fair treatment. For all these reasons, efforts to maintain current religious policies will give way to the next generation of leaders' political need to win over the broadest internal and external support.

SOURCE: Peng Liu, "The Staying Power of Religion," in *God and Caesar in China*, eds. Jason Kindopp and Carol Lee Hamrin. Washington, DC: Brookings Institution Press, 2004, pp. 152–63

GLOSSARY

Analects The most revered scripture in Confucian tradition, a collection of the sayings of Master Kong (Confucius), probably compiled by the second generation of his disciples.

Dao (Tao) (the Way) The path of self-directing righteousness and harmony.

Li Ritual, propriety, etiquette, social norms.

Mandate of Heaven Confucian sense of transcendent rightness of the state, closer to religion than most Confucian ideas; may or may not be present in a ruler or a policy; drawn from Zhou dynasty's Duke of Zhou (d. 1094 BCE).

Pinyin New romanized transcription of

Chinese adopted in 1979, replacing 1859 Wade-Giles system.

Qi (Ch'i) The vital energy in the universe and in our bodies.

Ren (Jen) Benevolence, human-heartedness, humanistic love toward others; the highest Confucian virtue.

Yang The bright, assertive, "masculine" cosmic energy of *qi*, like a mountain.

Yijing (I Ching) (Book of Changes) A manual of ancient divination.

Yin The dark, receptive, "feminine" cosmic energy of *qi*, like a river.

HOLY DAYS

Explicitly Confucian holidays are celebrated in countries with remaining Confucian influence, such as Taiwan and South Korea.

Confucius's birthday September 28 is a state holiday in Taiwan, called "Teacher's Day," since Confucius advocated education not limited to aristocracy.

Domestic rites These are implicitly Confucian. In the People's Republic of China the ancient tradition of ancestor memorials is celebrated on Qing Ming (Ching Ming; Tomb Sweeping Day) in spring. Families clean and repair their ancestors' graves, place flowers, offer food, and burn paper money to send wealth to ancestors in the spirit world. In South Korea, Chusok is Thanksgiving Day, the most important national holiday. People visit

family tombs and present food offerings to their ancestors.

Dragon Boat Festival (Double Fifth Festival) Occurring on the fifth day of the fifth moon of the lunar calendar, it commemorates the Chinese scholar-statesman Zhu Yuan (Chu Yuan; 3rd century BCE). It is one of the three most important annual mainland Chinese festivals; the other two are the Autumn Moon Festival and Chinese New Year.

Sokchonje In March and September, traditional court orchestras play and costumed rituals are performed at Confucian shrines in South Korea. The best place to see this ceremony is at Sungkyunkwan University in Seoul.

HISTORICAL OUTLINE

c. 551–479 BCE—Confucius (Kong Qiu or K'ung Ch'iu)

c. 390–305 BCE—Mencius (Mengzi or Meng-tzu)

c. 300 BCE—birth of Xunzi (Hsun-tzu), who stressed the need for education

206 BCE–220 CE—Han dynasty, during which Confucius's teachings became the basis of the state educational system

1130–1200—Zhu Xi (Chu Hsi), Neo-Confucian scholar

1911—last of the imperial dynasties overthrown

1949—Mao Zedong (Mao Tse-tung) and his Communist Party take control of China

1966–76—Cultural Revolution in China

from 1990—Confucian revival in China

REVIEW QUESTIONS

1   Confucius said: "Wealth and honor are what every man desires. But if they have been obtained in violation of moral principles, they must not be kept." Is this a good basis for a social ethic?
2   Is Confucianism more optimistic or more pessimistic about human nature? How? What are the social implications of this belief?
3   How would the Confucian Way of Heaven and Earth work out in daily life?

DISCUSSION QUESTIONS

1   Is ancient Confucianism so feudal and patriarchal as to limit its relevance today?
2   Does ethical behavior need transcendent sources such as gods, goddesses, or a Mandate of Heaven to give it a motivating force?
3   Would Confucianism's stress on moderation and harmony stifle progressive corrections of social injustices? Would it help ecological consciousness?

INFORMATION RESOURCES

China Books and Periodicals
<http://www.chinabooks.com>

China Introduction
<http://www.warriortours.com>

Chinese Holidays
<http://www.index-china.com>

Confucian and Daoist Texts
<http://acc6.its.brookly.cuny.edu/~phalsall>

Csikszentmihalyi, Mark, et al. "Confucianism," in *Encyclopedia of Religion*, ed. Lindsay Jones. Vol. 3, pp. 1890–937. New York: Macmillan, 2005.

Lau, D. C., trans. *Confucius: The Analects.* London: Penguin Books, 1979.

Nadeau, Randall. *Confucianism and Taoism*, vol. 2 in *Introduction to the World's Major Religions*. Westport, CT: Greenwood Press, 2006.

Taylor, Rodney. *The Religious Dimensions of Confucianism*. Albany, NY: State University of New York Press, 1990.

Tu-Wei-ming. "Confucius and Confucianism," in *Encyclopedia Britannica*. Vol. 16, pp. 653–62. London, 1997.

CHAPTER 7

DAOISM

In contrast to the pragmatic logic of traditional Confucianism, the Daoist tradition is distinctly mystical. This mysticism actually had no name until scholars labeled it Daoism, lumping together ancient philosophical traditions and later religious sects which concentrate on the achievement of immortality.

Daoism is based on ancient Chinese ways and the teachings of **sages** whose remembrance is shrouded in the mists of time and legend. Most famous of these is Laozi (Lao-tzu),[1] who is thought to have lived some time between 600 and 300 BCE. To him is attributed the central scripture of Daoism, the **Dao de jing** (*Tao-te Ching*), which proposes a philosophical detachment, allowing things to take their own natural course without interference. By remaining quiet and receptive, one lives in harmony with the natural flow of life, with the **Dao** (Tao), the unnamable eternal Reality. Everything is to be accepted with equanimity, without preferences. The sage is like flowing water, which naturally flows into a valley from higher regions, makes its way around obstacles, and gently wears them down. He or she "does nothing," for the Dao if left to its own ways will express the underlying harmony in the universe. Energy is not to be wasted in artificial action, but may be expressed spontaneously and creatively when the natural energy is flowing in that direction. Daoist sages have traditionally withdrawn into the mountains to live contemplatively in nature.

The traditional canon

The *Dao de jing* has traditionally been attributed to Laozi, a curator of the royal library during the Zhou (Chou) dynasty. According to legend, he was leaving society to retire to the mountains at the age of 160, when a border guard requested him to share his wisdom. The terse five thousand characters thus inscribed have been translated more times than any book other than the Bible.

---

1 Chinese words are transliterated here using the contemporary **Pinyin** system, with the earlier Wade-Giles transliteration given in parentheses at first occurrence; within extracts using Wade-Giles, the Pinyin version is shown in brackets.

The Dao de jing by Laozi

The Dao

What we call "the Dao" is not the Dao forever.
Things named are not forever named.
"Non-being" is how we describe the origins of Heaven and Earth.
"Being" is how we describe the mother of the **ten thousand things**.
We employ "Eternal Non-Being" in observance of the subtleties of the Dao
And employ "Eternal Being" in observance of its fullest extent.
They are identical in origin, though differing in name.
But both may be called "mysterious,"
And in calling them mysterious they become even more mysterious—
The gate of all subtleties!

The Spirit of the Valley

The Spirit of the Valley is eternal; it is called "the mysterious female." The
gateway of the mysterious female is called the root of Heaven and Earth.
Though constantly flowing, it seems always to be present. Though used, it is
never used up.

Water

The most marvelous things are like water. Water can benefit the ten
thousand creatures without competing, and settle in places most people
despise. In these ways it is like the Dao.

Embracing the One

Can you carry the soul and embrace the One without letting go?
Can you concentrate your **qi** and attain the weakness of an infant?
Can you polish the mirror of mystery so as to make it spotless?
Can you practice **wu-wei** in loving the nation and governing the people?
   Can you adopt the role of the female when the gates of Heaven open
   and close?
Can you abandon all knowing even as your insight penetrates the universe?
   To give birth and to rear, to give birth but not to possess, to act but not
   to depend on the outcome, to lead but not to command: this is called
   "mysterious power."

Emptiness

Thirty spokes share a single hub; by virtue of its **Emptiness**, the hub is
useful to the cart. Clay is shaped to create a vessel; by virtue of its
Emptiness, a vessel has its use. Doors and windows are cut out to make a
room; by virtue of that Emptiness, a room has its use. So, to have something
may be beneficial, but it is in its Emptiness that it has its use.

Anti-Confucianism

When the Great Dao declined, the doctrines of *ren* and *yi* appeared. When
"knowledge" and "wisdom" emerged, there was great hypocrisy. It is only

when relatives can't get along that they talk about "filial children" and "loving parents," only when the state is in disorder that there are "loyal ministers."

Su and Pu

Abandon "sageliness" and "wisdom," and the people will benefit a hundredfold. Abandon *ren* and *yi,* and the people will again be obedient to their parents and loving towards their children. Abandon clever words and profit, and there will be no more thieves or robbers. Those things [which should be abandoned] are good in appearance, but insubstantial. So, let the people have something they can follow:

> manifest simplicity (**su**);
> embrace the uncarved block (**pu**);
> reduce selfishness;
> have few desires.

Floating in the Dark

Stop learning! You'll stop worrying. Is there really that much difference between "yes" and "no"? Is there really any difference at all between "good" and "evil"?

People are drunk with pleasure, as they are when eating a great feast or ascending a tower in the spring. I alone am quiet. I have left no sign, like an infant who has not yet smiled. I am weary, like a man with no home to return to.

Most people have more than they need. I alone seem to have too little. Mine is the mind of a fool—it's empty!

Common people show off their clarity. I alone am floating in the dark. Common people are committed to their investigations. I alone am all mixed up. I'm as calm as the sea, drifting with the wind.

Most people have a purpose. I alone am aimless and unsophisticated. I alone am different from other people, and value being fed by the Mother.

The Daoist Sage

He is whole because he's crooked, straight because he's bent, full because he's hollow, new because he's worn; he has because he lacks, he is amazed because there is so much.

This is why the sage embraces the One and becomes the model of the universe. He does not show himself, and so he is luminous. He does not consider himself right, and so he is revered. He does not claim credit, and so he is rewarded. He does not boast, and so he endures.

It is because he does not compete with anyone that no one under Heaven competes with him. When the ancients said, "He is whole because he is crooked," those were not empty words. Truly, he is whole to the end.

Dao

There is a thing, shaped by chaos, born prior to Heaven and Earth, silent and shapeless! It stands alone, unchanged by exterior forces. Its motion is circular, and it never tires. It is capable of being the Mother of everything under Heaven. I do not know its name, but if forced to, I'll call it "Dao"; if forced to, I'll name it "Great."

> Great, it is flowing.
> Flowing, it becomes distant.
> Distant, it returns.

Thus, the Dao is great, Heaven is great, Earth is great, and humankind is great. Among the four great things in the universe, humankind is counted as one of them. Humankind models itself on Earth, Earth on Heaven, and Heaven on the Dao. The Dao models itself on spontaneity.

The Role of the Female
Understand the male but keep to the role of the female, and you will be the river of the world. As the river of the world, your energy will be unsapped, like returning to infancy.

Understand the white but keep to the role of the black, and you will be the model of the world. As the model of the world, your energy will be restored, like returning to the unbounded.

Understand the honored but keep to the role of the humble, and you will be the valley of the world. As the valley of the world, your energy will be abundant, like returning to the uncarved block.

Reversion
Reversion is the way the Dao moves.
Weakness is what the Dao employs.
The ten thousand creatures under Heaven were born from Being,
   and Being was born from Non-Being.

Dao and *De*
When superior persons hear about the Dao, they do their best to put it into practice. When average persons hear about the Dao, they preserve it for a while, but then it disappears. When the lowest persons hear about the Dao, they laugh at it. If they didn't laugh, it wouldn't be the Dao. That's why it's been said,

> Brightening the Dao is more like darkening it;
> Advancing the Dao is more like pushing it back;
> Universalizing the Dao is more like differentiating things.
> Raising **de** is more like lowering it;
> Ennobling *de* is more like discrediting it;
> Enlarging *de* is more like diminishing it;
> Strengthening *de* is more like exhausting it;
> Witnessing for *de* is more like making a retraction.

A great square has no corners. A great vessel is completed only after a long time. A great note produces a weak sound. A great image has no shape. The Dao hides in namelessness. So, the Dao alone excels in endowing and in bringing things to completion.

Weakness and Strength

The weakest things under Heaven ride like a stallion over the hardest. The things which have no substance enter the places which have no space. Because of this, I understand the advantage of *wu-wei*. Few have the capacity to reach an understanding of the wordless teaching or of the advantage of *wu-wei*.

Wu wei er wu bu wei

In study, one learns more every day. But in acting in accordance with the Dao, one does less every day. One does less and less until finally there is *wu-wei*, and *wu wei er wu bu wei* (with *wu-wei* there is nothing that remains undone).

Speaking and Knowing

One who knows does not speak; one who speaks does not know.

    Block the opening;
    Shut the door;
    Blunt the sharpness;
    Untie the knot;
    Soften the brightness;
    Become like dust.

    This is what is meant by the "mysterious identity." So, it is impossible to be familiar with it, and yet it is also impossible to be separated from it. It is impossible to augment it, yet it is also impossible to diminish it. It is impossible to ennoble it, and yet it is also impossible to debase it. That is why it is valued throughout the world.

Water

Under Heaven, there is nothing softer or weaker than water. Yet, in attacking what is stubborn and strong, nothing can surpass it. That is why nothing can replace it. Everyone knows that the soft overcomes the stubborn, and the weak overcomes the strong, yet no one can put this into practice.

Utopia

Reduce the size of the state and the population. Let the weapons of war never be used. Let the people stay close to home because they do not take death lightly. Even though there are ships and chariots, there is no place to ride in them. Even though there are weapons and armor, there is no place to display them. Cause the people to revert to the use of knotted cords,[2] to regard their food as sweet and their clothing as beautiful, to be content in their homes and happy with their everyday lives. Though neighboring states can see one another, and the sounds of chickens and dogs can be heard from one state to the other, yet the people of each state will grow old and die without ever having had contact with one another.

SOURCE: Original translation for this book by Randall Nadeau, 2006

---

2 Knotted cords—an ancient general practice for calculation and writing worldwide.

The Great and Venerable Teacher by Zhuangzi

The second major book in the traditional Daoist canon is a compilation of the often humorous and ironic writings of the sage Zhuangzi (Chuang-tzu; c. 365–290 BCE). In the following passage, he refers to the ideal sage as the **True Man**.

He who knows what it is that Heaven does, and knows what it is that man does, has reached the peak. Knowing what it is that Heaven does, he lives with Heaven. Knowing what it is that man does, he uses the knowledge of what he knows to help out the knowledge of what he doesn't know, and lives out the years that Heaven gave him without being cut off midway— this is the perfection of knowledge.

However, there is a difficulty. Knowledge must wait for something to fix on to, and that which it waits for is never certain. How, then, can I know that what I call Heaven is not really man, and what I call man is not really Heaven? There must first be a True Man before there can be true knowledge.

What do I mean by a True Man? The True Man of ancient times did not rebel against want, did not grow proud in plenty, and did not plan his affairs. Being like this, he could commit an error and not regret it, could meet with success and not make a show. Being like this, he could climb the high places and not be frightened, could enter the water and not get wet, could enter the fire and not get burned. His knowledge was able to climb all the way up to the Way like this.

The True Man of ancient times slept without dreaming and woke without care; he ate without savoring and his breath came from deep inside. The True Man breathes with his heels; the mass of men breathe with their throats. Crushed and bound down, they gasp out their words as though they were retching. Deep in their passions and desires, they are shallow in the workings of Heaven.

The True Man of ancient times knew nothing of loving life, knew nothing of hating death. He emerged without delight; he went back in without a fuss. He came briskly, he went briskly, and that was all. He didn't forget where he began; he didn't try to find out where he would end. He received something and took pleasure in it; he forgot about it and handed it back again. This is what I call not using the mind to repel the Way, not using man to help out Heaven. This is what I call the True Man....

You hide your boat in the ravine and your fish net in the swamp and tell yourself that they will be safe. But in the middle of the night a strong man shoulders them and carries them off, and in your stupidity you don't know why it happened. You think you do right to hide little things in big ones, and yet they get away from you. But if you were to hide the world in the world, so that nothing could get away, this would be the final reality of the constancy of things.

You have had the audacity to take on human form and you are delighted. But the human form has ten thousand changes that never come to an end. Your joys, then, must be uncountable. Therefore, the sage wanders in the realm where things cannot get away from him, and all are preserved. He delights in early death; he delights in old age; he delights in the beginning; he delights in the end. If he can serve as a model for men, how much more so that which the ten thousand things are tied to and all changes alike wait upon!

The Way has its reality and its signs but is without action or form. You can hand it down but you cannot receive it; you can get it but you cannot see it. It is its own source, its own root. Before Heaven and earth existed it was there, firm from ancient times. It gave spirituality to the spirits and to God; it gave birth to Heaven and to earth. It exists beyond the highest point, and yet you cannot call it lofty; it exists beneath the limit of the six directions, and yet you cannot call it deep. It was born before Heaven and earth, and yet you cannot say it has been there for long; it is earlier than the earliest time, and yet you cannot call it old.

SOURCE: Chuang-tzu, *The Book of Chuang-tzu*, trans. Burton Watson. New York: Columbia University Press, 1968, pp. 77–83

Heaven's Gifts by Liezi

Traditionally attributed to the Daoist philosopher Liezi (Lieh-tzu, c. 475–221 BCE), who claimed metaphorically that he could ride on the wind, the *Book of Liezi* (*Classic of Complete Emptiness*) is the third old scripture in the Daoist canon. Using stories and parables, it describes the universe according to classical Chinese thinking as being essentially composed of *qi* (*ch'i*), meaning air or breath. This *qi* is itself insubstantial, but continually becomes more compacted and solid and then dissolves into nothingness.

The Book of the Yellow Emperor[3] **says:** "When a shape stirs, it begets not a shape but a shadow. When a sound stirs, it begets not a sound but an echo. When Nothing stirs, it begets not nothing but something."

That which has shape is that which must come to an end. Will heaven and earth end? They will end together with me. Will there ever be no more ending? I do not know. Will the Way end? At bottom it has had no beginning. Will there ever be no more of it? At bottom it does not exist.

Whatever is born reverts to being unborn, whatever has shape reverts to being shapeless. But unborn it is not the basically Unborn, shapeless it is not the basically Shapeless. That which is born is that which in principle must come to an end. Whatever ends cannot escape its end, just as whatever is born cannot escape birth; and to wish to live forever, and have no more of ending, is to be deluded about our lot. . . .

The thing which is shrinking there is swelling here, the thing which is maturing here is decaying there. Shrinking and swelling, maturing and

---

3 Yellow Emperor—a legendary ruler who is said to have ascended into Heaven on a great dragon and become one of the **Immortals**, who are certain humans said to have gained immortality, each with his or her own magical power.

decaying, it is being born at the same time that it is dying. The interval between the coming and the going is imperceptible; who is aware of it? Whatever a thing may be, its energy is not suddenly spent, its form does not suddenly decay; we are aware neither of when it reaches maturity nor of when it begins to decay. It is the same with a man's progress from birth to old age; his looks, knowledge and bearing differ from one day to the next, his skin and nails and hair are growing at the same time as they are falling away. They do not stop as they were in childhood without changing. But we cannot be aware of the intervals; we must wait for the fruition before we know.

There was a man of Ch'i [Pinyin, Qi] country who was so worried that heaven and earth might fall down, and his body would have nowhere to lodge, that he forgot to eat and sleep. There was another man who was worried that he should be so worried about it, and therefore went to enlighten him.

"Heaven is nothing but the accumulated air; there is no place where there is not air. You walk and stand all day inside heaven, stretching and bending, breathing in and breathing out; why should you worry about it falling down?"

"If heaven really is accumulated air, shouldn't the sun and moon and stars fall down?"

"The sun and moon and stars are air which shines inside the accumulated air. Even if they did fall down, they couldn't hit or harm anyone."

"What about the earth giving way?"

"The earth is nothing but accumulated soil, filling the void in all four directions; there is no place where there is not soil. You walk and stand all day on the earth, stamping about with abrupt spurts and halts; why should you worry about it giving way?"

The man was satisfied and greatly cheered; and so was the man who enlightened him.

When Ch'ang-lu-tzu [Pinyin, Chang luzi] heard of it, he said smiling:

"The rainbow, clouds and mist, wind and rain, the four seasons; these are formations in the accumulated air of heaven. Mountains and hills, rivers and seas, metal and stone, fire and wood; these are formations in the accumulated matter of earth. Knowing that they are accumulations of air and soil, how can we say that they will not perish? Heaven and earth are one tiny thing within the void, the largest among things that exist. It is no doubt true that it will be long before they reach their term and come to an end, and that it is no easy matter to estimate and predict when this will happen. To worry about them perishing is indeed wide of the mark; but to say they will never perish is also open to objection. Since heaven and earth are bound to perish, a time will come when they will perish. If we happen to be here when they do, why shouldn't we worry?"

When Lieh-tzu [Pinyin, Liezi] heard of it, he too smiled and said:

"It is nonsense to say either that heaven and earth will perish or that they will not. Whether they perish or not we can never know. However, from that side there is one point of view, from this side there is another. Hence the living do not know what it is like to be dead, the dead do not know what it is like to be alive. Coming, we do not know those who went before, going we shall not know those who came after. Why should we care whether they perish or not?"

Shun asked a minister:

"Can one succeed in possessing the Way?"

"Your own body is not your possession. How can you possess the Way?"

"If my own body is not mine, whose is it?"

"It is the shape lent to you by heaven and earth. Your life is not your possession; it is harmony between your forces, granted for a time by heaven and earth. Your nature and destiny are not your possessions; they are the course laid down for you by heaven and earth. Your children and grandchildren are not your possessions; heaven and earth lend them to you to cast off from your body as an insect sheds it skin. Therefore you travel without knowing where you go, stay without knowing what you cling to, are fed without knowing how. You are the breath of heaven and earth which goes to and fro; how can you ever possess it?"

SOURCE: *The Book of Lieh-tzu*, trans. A. C. Graham. London: John Murray/New York: Grove Press, 1960, pp. 22–31

Later developments

In addition to the philosophical system known as Daoism, as expressed in the preceding texts, from the second century CE onward various religious sects developed that are often referred to as "Immortals Daoism" or "Religious Daoism." Their relationship to the philosophical tradition is a

Daoist Immortality

matter of debate. These sects tend to focus on gods, spirits, magic, ritual, and **alchemical** efforts to achieve physical immortality.

A complex medical system developed in China regarding relationships between physical and spiritual aspects of the universe with reference to **yin** and **yang**, the receptive and active energies within the Dao. The *Huangdi Neijing Suwen* (*Huang Ti Nei Ching Su Wen*; *The Yellow Emperor's Classic of Internal Medicine*), compiled during the Han era (206 BCE–220 CE), illustrates the specificity of this system, in contrast to the more general philosophical nature of the Daoist **canon**.

Communication of the Force of Life with Heaven

from *Huangdi Neijing Suwen*

Yin and Yang, the two principles in nature, and the four seasons are the beginning and the end of everything and they are also the cause of life and death. Those who disobey the laws of the universe will give rise to calamities and visitations, while those who follow the laws of the universe remain free from dangerous illness, for they are the ones who have obtained Tao [Pinyin, Dao], the Right Way.

Tao was practiced by the sages and admired by the ignorant people. Obedience to the laws of Yin and Yang means life; disobedience means death. The obedient ones will rule while the rebels will be in disorder and confusion. Anything contrary to harmony (with nature) is disobedience and means rebellion to nature.

The Yellow Emperor said: "From earliest times the communication with Heaven has been the very foundation of life; this foundation exists between Yin and Yang and between Heaven and Earth and within the six points.[4] The (heavenly) breath prevails in the nine divisions,[5] in the nine orifices,[6] in the five viscera, and in the twelve joints; they are all pervaded by the breath of Heaven.

"Life has (the number) five, breath has (the number) three.[7] If people act contrary to these factors, then noxious influences will injure mankind. This (good conduct) is the foundation of long life. Just as the breath of the blue sky (is calm), so the will and the heart of those who are pure will be in peace, and the breath of Yang will be stable in those who keep themselves in harmony with nature. Even if there are noxious spirits they cannot cause injury to those who follow the laws of the seasons. Therefore the sages preserved the natural spirit and were in harmony with the breath of Heaven, and were thus in direct communication with Heaven. . . .

"The essence of the force of Yang protects the spirit, its gentleness protects the muscles. (If the atmosphere of Yang) cannot open and close, the cold air will follow and the result will be a great deformity. The deep pulse brings about ulcers which are transmitted to the flesh, and the breath of the ducts will become weakened, causing a propensity towards being easily frightened and startled. If the atmosphere of the (main) ducts is not harmonious with the system of the flesh, it will cause ulcers and swellings. Then the perspiration of the animal spirit is unable to reach out, one's body will be weakened, one's force of life will be melted, the '(acupuncture[8]) spots' will be closed, and there arise winds and intermittent fevers.

"Thus wind is the cause of a hundred diseases. When people are quiet and clear, their skin and flesh is closed and protected. Even a heavy storm, afflictions, or poison cannot injure those people who live in accord with the natural order.

"If a sickness lasts for a long time, there is danger that it might spread, then the upper and the lower (parts of the body) cannot communicate; and even skillful physicians are then not able to help.

---

4 The six points—the four points of the compass, the Zenith, and the Nadir.
5 The nine divisions of China established under Yu the Great.
6 The nine orifices: the eyes, the ears, the nostrils, and the mouth, corresponding to the male principle, and the two lower orifices, the anus and the urethra, corresponding to the female principle.
7 According to Wang Bing (Wang Ping), the three factors are: the heavenly climate, the subtle spirit of the earth, and good fortune.
8 Acupuncture—Chinese system of treating illness by means of needles inserted at specific points on the body.

"If Yang accumulates excessively one will die from the (resulting) disease. If the force of Yang is blocked, the blockage should be dispelled. If one does not drain it thoroughly and guide away the rough matter, there will be destruction. The force of Yang should move outwards every day."

SOURCE: *Huang Ti Nei Ching Su Wen* (*The Yellow Emperor's Classic of Internal Medicine*), trans. Ilza Veith. Berkeley, CA: University of California Press, 1972, pp. 105–9

Awakening to Perfection by Zhang Boduan

In Immortals Daoism, there are thought to be various means of ascending from earthly life to immortal heavenly glory. The Yellow Emperor is said to have ascended on a celestial dragon with heavenly escort; some adept practitioners simply vanish, and others leave their bodies while sitting in meditation and quaffing a highly poisonous elixir developed from transmutation of base metals. Some Daoist adepts use spiritual practices to develop within themselves an immortal "embryo" which can traverse the heavenly realms, while still others undertake spiritual practices designed to develop their subtler energies until they ultimately dissolve into the Dao. One of the most important texts about the processes of inner alchemy is the *Wuzhen pian* (*Awakening to Perfection*). It was written by Zhang Boduan (c. 983–1082) in 1075 to 1078. The text is highly metaphorical and has been interpreted on many different levels.

First take the power of heaven and earth and make them into your crucible;[9]
Then isolate the essences of the sun and the moon:
Urge the two things to return to the Tao [Pinyin, Dao] of the center:
Then work hard to attain the golden elixir[10]—how would it not come forth?

Secure your furnace, set up your crucible; always follow the power of
    heaven and earth.
Forge their essence and refine their innermost power, always keeping well
    in control of your yin and yang souls.
Congealing and dissolving, the incubating temperature produces
    transmutation.
Never discuss its mystery and wonder in idle conversation! . . .

Swallowing saliva and breathing exercises are what many people do,
Yet only with the method of this medicine can you truly transform life.
If there is no true seed in the crucible,
It is like taking water and fire and boiling an empty pot. . . .

"Empty the mind and fill the belly"—such profundity of meaning!
Just, to empty your mind, you must know it first.

---

9 Crucible—a vessel for melting at high temperatures, used in alchemy; a symbolic region of spirituality in inner alchemy.
10 Elixir—alchemical medical potion believed to bestow longevity.

Similarly, to refine your lead, you must first fill the belly:
Understand this to protect the mass of gold[11] that fills your halls within.

SOURCE: Zhang Boduan, "Awakening to Perfection," in *The Taoist Experience: An Anthology*, ed. Livia Kohn. New York: State University of New York Press, 1993, pp. 314–19

The Way of Perfect Truth by Wang Zhe

The new Daoist religious sects often freely mixed elements of Buddhism and Confucianism with Daoism, as these strands coexisted in Chinese culture without sharp demarcations. For example, the twelfth-century teacher Wang Zhe (Wang Che), also known as Wang Chongyang (Wang Ch'ung-yang, "Master Wang of Developed Yang"; 1112–70) had studied and practiced both Confucian and Buddhist ways before becoming a master of the Dao, living as a recluse in the mountains and attracting many followers to his "Perfect Truth" sect. He gave the sect these basic precepts for the spiritual life.

On Residence and Covering Sleeping in the open air would violate the sun and the moon, therefore some simple thatched covering is necessary. However, it is not the habit of the superior man to live in great halls and lavish palaces, because to cut down the trees that would be necessary for the building of such grand residences would be like cutting the arteries of the earth or cutting the veins of a man. Such deeds would only add to one's superficial external merits while actually damaging one's inner credits. It would be like drawing a picture of a cake to ward off hunger or piling up snow for a meal—much ado and nothing gained. Thus the Perfect Truth Taoist [Pinyin, Daoist] will daily seek out the palace hall within his own body and avoid the mundane mind which seeks to build lavish external residences. The man of wisdom will scrutinize and comprehend this principle.

On Companionship A Taoist should find true friends who can help each other in times of illness and take care of each other's burials at death. However he must observe the character of a person before making friends with him. Do not commit oneself to friendship and then investigate the person's character. Love makes the heart cling to things and should therefore be avoided. On the other hand, if there is no love, human feelings will be strained. To love and yet not to become attached to love—this is the middle path one should follow.

There are three dimensions of compatibility and three of incompatibility. The three dimensions of compatibility are an understanding mind, the possession of wisdom, and an intensity of aspiration. Inability to understand the external world, lack of wisdom accompanied by foolish acts, and lack of high aspiration accompanied by a quarrelsome nature are the three dimensions of incompatibility. The principle of establishing oneself lies in the grand monastic community. The choice of a companion should be motivated

---

11 Gold—an alchemical symbol for the spiritual treasure transformed from lead.

by an appreciation of the loftiness of a person's mind and not by mere feelings or external appearance.

On Sitting in Meditation Sitting in meditation which consists only of the act of closing the eyes and seating oneself in an upright position is only a pretense. The true way of sitting in meditation is to have the mind as immovable as Mount T'ai [Pinyin, Mount Tai][12] all the hours of the day, whether walking, resting, sitting, or reclining. The four doors of the eyes, ears, mouth, and nose should be so pacified that no external sight can be let in to intrude upon the inner self. If ever an impure or wandering thought arises, it will no longer be true quiet sitting. For the person who is an accomplished meditator, even though his body may still reside within this dusty world, his name will already be registered in the ranks of the immortals or free spirits and there will be no need for him to travel to far-off places to seek them out; within his body the nature of the sage and the virtuous man will already be present. Through years of practice, a person by his own efforts can liberate his spirit from the shell of his body and send it soaring to the heights. A single session of meditation, when completed, will allow a person to rove through all the corners of the universe.

On Pacification of the Mind There are two minds. One is quiet and unmoving, dark and silent, not reflecting on any of the myriad things. It is deep and subtle, makes no distinction between inner and outer, and contains not a single wandering thought. The other mind is that mind which, because it is in contact with external forms, will be dragged into all kinds of thoughts, pushed into seeking out beginnings and ends—a totally restless and confused mind. This confused mind must be eliminated. If one allows it to rule, then the Way and its power will be damaged, and one's Nature and Destiny will come to harm. Hearing, seeing, and conscious thoughts should be eliminated from all activities, from walking, resting, sitting, or reclining.

On Nurturing One's Nature The art of cultivating one's Nature is like that of playing on the strings of a musical instrument: too great a force can break the string, while too weak a pull will not produce any sound; one must find the perfect mean to produce the perfect note. The art of nurturing one's Nature is also like forging a sword: too much steel will make the sword too brittle while too much tin will make it too malleable. In training one's Nature, this principle must be recognized. When it is properly implemented, one can master one's Nature at will.

On Aligning the Five Primal Energies The Five Primal Energies are found in the Middle Hall. The Three Primal Energies are located at the top of the head. If the two are harmonized, then, beginning with the Green Dragon and the White Tiger [the supreme Yin–Yang pair], the ten thousand gods in the body will be arranged in perfect harmony. When this is

---

12 Mount Tai—a particularly sacred Chinese mountain.

accomplished, then the energy in the hundred veins will flow smoothly. Cinnabar[13] and mercury[14] will coalesce into a unity. The body of the adept may still be within the realm of men, but the spirit is already roving in the universe.

On the Union of Nature and Destiny Nature is spirit. Destiny is material energy. When Nature is supported by Destiny it is like a bird buoyed up and carried along by the wind—flying freely with little effort. Whatever one wills to be, one can be. This is the meaning in the line from the *Classic of the Shadowy Talismans*: "The bird is controlled by the air." The Perfect Truth Taoist must treasure this line and not reveal its message casually to the uninitiated. The gods themselves will chide the person who disobeys this instruction. The search for the hidden meaning of Nature and mind is the basic motif of the art of self-cultivation. This must be remembered at all times.

On the Path of the Sage In order to enter the path of the sage, one must accumulate patiently, over the course of many years, merit-actions and true practices. Men of high understanding, men of virtue, and men who have attained insight may all become sages. In attaining sagehood, the body of the person may still be in one room, but his Nature will already be encompassing the world. The various sages in the various Heavens will protect him, and the free spirits and immortals in the highest realm of the Non-Ultimate will be around him. His name will be registered in the Hall of the Immortals, and he will be ranked among the free spirits. Although his bodily form is in the world of dust, his mind will have transcended all corporal things.

On Transcending the Three Realms The Three Realms refer to the realms of desire, form, and formlessness. The mind that has freed itself from all impure or random thoughts will have transcended the first realm of desire. The mind that is no longer tied to the perception of objects in the object-realm will have transcended the realm of form. The mind that no longer is fixed upon emptiness will further transcend the realm of formlessness. The spirit of the man who transcends all three of these realms will be in the realm of the immortals. His Nature will abide forever in the realm of Jade-like Purity.

On Cultivating the Body of the Law The Body of the Law is formless form. It is neither empty nor full. It has neither front nor back and is neither high nor low, long nor short. When it is functioning, there is nothing it does not penetrate. When it is withdrawn into itself, it is obscure and leaves no trace: it must be cultivated in order to attain the true Way. If the cultivation is great, the merit will be great: if the cultivation is small, the merit will be small. One should not wish to return to it, nor should one be attached to this world of things. One must allow Nature to follow its own course.

---

13 Cinnabar—a heavy reddish ore of mercury, used in alchemical elixirs; a symbol for Nature.
14 Mercury—a liquid metal alchemical element, symbol for Destiny.

On Leaving the Mundane World Leaving the mundane world is not leaving the body; it is leaving behind the mundane mind. Consider the analogy of the lotus: although rooted in the mud, it blossoms pure and white into the clean air. The man who attains the Way, although corporally abiding in the world, may flourish through his mind in the realm of sages. Those people who presently seek after non-death or escape from the world do not know this true principle and commit the greatest folly.

The words of these 15 precepts are for our disciples of aspiration. Examine them carefully!

SOURCE: Wang Che, "The Way of the Taoist Tradition of Perfect Truth," in *Chinese Religion: An Anthology of Sources*, ed. Deborah Sommer. New York and Oxford: Oxford University Press, 1995, pp. 200–3

The Story of He Xiangu, a Female Immortal

In popular Daoism, many stories are told of the Eight Immortals, some of whom may have been based on historical figures. One of the Immortals is a female: He Xiangu (Ho Hsien Ku). The following story illustrates how her selfless virtue, as well as her asceticism, won her a place among the Immortals.

An old woman owned a small farm at the foot of Mi-Lo Shan [Pinyin, Milo Shan; Mount Milo]. She had never completed a full day's work and had no intention of doing so. As the years progressed she had become lazier and lazier, spending most of the day maliciously gossiping with her neighbours or giving abrupt orders to her servant.

Her latest servant was a young, beautiful and generous hearted girl called Ho Hsien Ku [Pinyin, He Xiangu]. However hard she worked the old woman was never satisfied. She continually harangued, scolded and punished the helpless girl. Ho Hsien Ku's day began at five o'clock in the morning and rarely finished before midnight.

Besides clearing the house and preparing the food she had to plant and reap the crops and feed and care for the animals. Ho Hsien Ku did this without complaint in return for food and lodgings, but at night, when she fell exhausted onto her straw mattress, she silently wept herself to sleep.

One day the old woman set off to visit her cousin, leaving the young girl to guard the house. Ho Hsien Ku placed a small wicker chair outside the front door and sat down with her sewing basket to repair the old woman's clothes.

Through the haze of the hot afternoon sun, she saw seven figures moving slowly towards her. As they drew closer, she saw their ragged clothes, gaunt faces and downcast eyes. The beggars eventually gathered around her. One stepped forward and in pleading tones addressed Ho Hsien Ku. "Could you please help us. We have not eaten a morsel of food in five days and now we are starving. Could you spare us a bowl of rice."

Ho Hsien Ku was moved by their distress. If she had had the choice, she would have given the beggars all the food in the house but she was hesitant. The old woman meticulously checked the amount of food in the house each day. If a handful of rice or a spoonful of oil was missing, she would beat the girl mercilessly. But Ho Hsien Ku could not turn the beggars away. She would rather be beaten black and blue than let these unfortunate ragged men starve by the roadside.

She beckoned the beggars to rest on the straw mats in front of the house then went into the kitchen to boil a pan of rice [noodles]. Ten minutes later each beggar had a bowl of rice in his hands which he devoured eagerly and gratefully. The rice gave them renewed strength and after thanking Ho Hsien Ku profusely, the beggars wandered in the direction of the nearest town. No sooner had they disappeared from view, when the old woman returned home. Without acknowledging Ho Hsien Ku, she marched straight into the kitchen to check the rice, noodles, eggs, fish, oil and wood. Ho Hsien Ku sat trembling outside the door and within a few minutes a piercing scream of anger came from the kitchen. The old woman ran from the kitchen brandishing a wooden broom.

"You thief, you ungrateful wretch! What have you done with my rice? Have you eaten it or sold it?" she demanded as she held the girl's arm with a vise-like grip.

Holding back her tears, Ho Hsien Ku recounted the whole story but the old woman had a heart like iron. "I have no pity for these dirty beggars. You either find them and bring them back to me or I will beat your legs till you can no longer walk."

The old woman loosened her grip on Ho Hsien Ku's arm, just enough for Ho Hsien Ku to break free and dash after the beggars. She eventually caught up with them as they were resting by the dusty road-side. Standing breathlessly before them she pleaded desperately.

"I am sorry to ask you this, but could you return with me to prove to my mistress that you ate the rice. If you do not come she will beat me black and blue."

The beggars were only too willing to help the girl who had taken pity on them and they returned home with her. The old woman was still in a furious temper when they arrived.

"How dare you eat the food that belongs to a poor old woman," she screamed. "I demand that you vomit every morsel on the floor in front of me. If you don't, I will make sure that nobody in this district offers you food or water. You deserve to starve."

The beggars had no choice but to do as they were told. One by one they vomited the noodles on to the packed earth floor in front of the house. The old woman then turned to Ho Hsien Ku and demanded vehemently, "Eat every single noodle that has been vomited. This is the price you have to pay for feeding dirty beggars."

She pushed the tearful and frightened Ho Hsien Ku to the floor and the helpless girl was forced to put a handful of the vomited noodles into her mouth. As soon as the noodles touched her tongue she felt her body become lighter and lighter. She felt her legs rise from the ground and her body began to float away from the spiteful old woman, away from the home where she had suffered so miserably.

The old woman began to panic and turned round to demand an explanation from the beggars, but they too had risen high above the house. She caught a last glimpse of the beggars before they disappeared into the clouds and her servant, Ho Hsien Ku, was in their midst.

The Seven Immortals had come to earth to test the young girl's character and she had proved herself worthy of immortality. Because she had endured suffering without complaint and given to the poor without thought for herself, she could work alongside the Immortals for eternity.

SOURCE: "The Story of Ho Hsien Ku," from Kwok Man Ho and Joanne O'Brien, *The Eight Immortals of Taoism*, in *An Anthology of Sacred Texts by and about Women*, ed. Serinity Young. New York: Crossroad, 1995, pp. 394–5

The Essence of Tai Ji by Al Chung-liang Huang

Today there is considerable global interest in Daoism, with many translations of the ancient texts being undertaken and some of the spiritual practices being taught to people from other societies. Even under atheistic communist rule, decades of Chinese have begun their days with **Taijiquan** (T'ai-chi-ch'uan) exercises for the sake of health and longevity. These slow, graceful movements were developed over two thousand years ago as a spiritual means of mental discipline and a physical aid to allowing the vital breath (*qi*) to flow freely through the body. In addition to the millions of people in East Asia who practice Taijiquan, Daoist masters such as Al Huang are teaching the practice to Westerners.

The yin/yang symbol is the interlocking, melting together of the flow of movement within a circle. The similar—and at the same time obviously contrasting—energies are moving *together*. Within the black area there is a white dot and within the white fish shape, there is a black dot. The whole idea of a circle divided in this way is to show that within a unity there is duality and polarity and contrast. The only way to find real balance without losing the centering feeling of the circle is to think of the contrasting energies moving together and in union, in harmony, interlocking. In a sense this is really like a white fish and a black fish mating. It's a union and flowing interaction. It's a kind of consummation between two forces, male and female, mind and body, good and bad. It's a very important way of living. People identify with this kind of concept in [Asia] much more than in our Western culture, where the tendency is to identify with one force and to reject the contrasting element. If you identify with only one side of the duality, then you become unbalanced. T'ai chi [Pinyin, **Tai Ji**] can help you to realize how you are unbalanced and help you to become centered again as you re-establish a flow between the two sides. So don't get stuck in a corner, because a circle has no corners. If you think in this way, you open up more, and you don't feel like you have to catch up with anything.

Someone said that the difference between an [Asian] man and a Western man is this: The [Asian] man is very empty and light up here in the head and very heavy down here in the belly and he feels very secure. The Western man is light in the belly and very heavy up here in the head, so he topples over. In our Western society so much is in the head, so much is in talking and thinking about things, that we can analyze everything to pieces and it's still distant from us, still not really understood. We have so many mechanical gadgets to do our work for us that our bodies are underemphasized. In order to regain balance we have to emphasize the body and we must work with the mind-body together.

Some people realize that their bodies need more work, so they run, jog, ride bicycles, swim, and then say "O.K. I have done my share of exercise." But this is still a separation of "body time" and "mind time," like the separation of work and play that most people experience. You work very hard so that you can take a vacation and come to a beautiful place to enjoy yourself. This brings a separation in your life. Working shouldn't be such a chore. Playing shouldn't be such a straining for fun, fun, fun. Work and play can combine. Non-verbal activities are a very important way to regain balance and find unity in your life. When you stop talking you have a chance to open up and become receptive to what is happening in your body and to what is going on around you.

T'ai chi is one of the many ways to help you to discipline your body and find a way to release that tension within you. T'ai chi can be a way of letting your body really teach you and be with you and help you to get through the conflicts you encounter every day. . . .

We work on a continuous flow. This is another aspect of t'ai chi, which ties in exactly with the *I Ching* [Pinyin, **Yijing**], the *Book of Changes*. Change is yin and constant is yang, or vice versa. So the constant thing is that we all can fit into the changing rise and fall. The change is constant; the constant is change. In movement, we learn to really understand this intellectual concept. Part of our everyday conflict is how to cope with the changes and how to be happy with the constant. We are usually bored with the constant, and we get frantic with the change. We have all kinds of gimmicks: "Meditate!" "Pull yourself together!" "Relax!" "Do therapy!" But these all boil down to one thing: Accept *both* the constant and the change. Learn how to be resilient and responsive to your surroundings, to time, and to yourself.

In t'ai chi practice, you move very slowly. By moving very slowly you have time to be aware of all the subtle details of your movement and your relationship to your surroundings. It's so slow that you really have no way of saying this is slower than that or faster than that. You reach a level of speed that is like slow motion, in which everything is just happening. You slow it to the point that you are fully involved in the process of each moment as it happens. . . .

Pay attention to the circular movement of your breathing. Allow the breathing pattern to really circulate inside of you, inside of your torso. Let it flow into your arms, up to your neck, to the top of your head, and down the backbone into your legs. Then energy can begin to expand to all directions at once. Feel all the energy from outside coming towards you, and your energy reaching out as your arms begin to lift. The rising of your arms is balanced by a sinking into your base, as the energy of the circle expands. Think of an expansion instead of a cut-and-dried hand-lift and knee-bend. . . . Think of that expansion into all directions from the center of your body and then the coming together, the collecting back to straight upright center support. Let that feeling of energy open you out into a curving yin/yang intertwining up/down flow as you expand in your arms and settle into your base. Then the outward energy curves and turns inward as your arms sink and your pelvis rises and you return to center. This energy must be a part of you; you must never move as an objective outsider observing. You must always be inside of it, with it. This is the only way you can do t'ai chi. . . .

Wherever you are, whatever you do, you can always come back to this marvelous sense of stillness, the feeling of yourself, very, very much *here*. This is your reference point; this is your stability. This is your life force that gives you balance. This is your home you carry around with you wherever you are. This is your powerhouse, your reservoir, your endless inexhaustible resource, that center you. . . . And the movement goes on and on and on.

SOURCE: Al Chung-liang Huang, *Embrace Tiger, Return to Mountain*. Moab, UT: Real People Press, 1973, pp. 12–19, 182–5

The Significance of Daoist Ethical Thought in the Building of a Harmonious Society by Zhou Zhongzhi

Although Daoism is an ancient spiritual way, practice of Daoist ideals may be of great relevance in contemporary China, according to Zhou Zhongzhi. He teaches Law, Economics, and Politics at Shanghai Normal University, is chief editor of the textbook *Ethics*, and has been deeply engaged in research pertaining to ethics in business, consumption, economics, globalization, and values education.

Daoism is an indigenous religion of China which has had a profound influence on Chinese traditional culture for thousands of years. Although what has prevailed in traditional China is Confucianism, Daoism nonetheless has its unique value that cannot be underestimated in that, as the whole society is concerned, Daoism and Confucianism complement each other. As China enters the twenty-first century, it enters an era calling to build a harmonious society. The author argues that the ethical thought of Daoism may play an important role in the building of a harmonious society in contemporary China. This will be shown in three ways, as follows.

1   According to the idea of the unification between man and universe,
Daoism believes that man, as the organic part of nature, is inalienable
from it, and emphasizes that "Dao follows the laws of its intrinsic
nature." That is to say, man should act in accordance with the laws of
nature, or he will be punished by nature. As a result of China's rapid
economic growth, the ecological environment in China is now at risk.
China's present effort in enhancing harmony between man and nature
should absorb the ethical nourishment of Chinese Daoist ecological
wisdom. Moreover, the Daoist School advocates avoiding selfishness and
limiting desire, and calls for upholding thriftiness and restraining
sumptuousness, which is evidently beneficial to the society of China in
refraining from consumerism and becoming environment-friendly with
lower consumption of resources.

2   In the Daoist opinion, the value of life is constituted not in the pursuit
of material benefit or personal fame, but in the respect for Dao—the
only thing to be desired to pursue—and the prize of virtue. People
should therefore have the sentiment of being content with their lot and
keep in good psychological condition. The development of a market
economy in contemporary China, on the one hand, can improve
people's living standards; while on the other hand, it may result in the
fact that most people, who are fickle and uneasy, will take maximizing
utility as the supreme aim of life. According to a survey conducted in
China, more than 70 percent of respondents say that their biggest desire
is to "get more money." The Daoist view on the value of life may urge
these people to reflect imperturbably upon what the worth of life is, to
maintain a harmony between material and spiritual life, and to seek the
equilibrium in their mind.

3   Aiming to build a perfect world of peace and tranquillity, Daoism
advocates loving others as well as loving oneself and encourages
everyone to accumulate merits and become a virtuous man. The Daoists
attach great importance to beneficence, which is regarded as critical to
the realization of the perfect world. In their opinion, beneficence is not
something for which people gain another's compliment but a duty they
should assume. In contemporary China, the gap between the rich and the
poor is widening, but the involvement in domestic charity is not as one
would wish because most of the rich are indifferent to it. To change this
situation, and hence to make different social classes get on well with each
other, the Daoist ethic of encouraging beneficence is of course helpful.

SOURCE: Zhou Zhongzhi, abstract of paper presented at Metanexus conference on Continuity and
Change: Perspectives on Science and Religion, Philadelphia, Pennsylvania, June 3–7, 2006

GLOSSARY

Alchemy In Chinese tradition, an external search for a potion for immortality; an internal quest for immortal soul by meditation, bodily control, and breathing.

Canon The official list of books with authority in a religion, either because they are believed to be inspired or revealed, or have been so designated.

Dao (Tao) (the Way) A term used by all Chinese schools of thought; in Daoism it means the ineffable, ultimate, universal reality, hidden behind existence.

Dao de jing (Tao-te Ching) (The Classic of the Way of Power) The primary text of Daoism, attributed to Laozi, addressed to a sage-king; condensed paradoxical poetry.

De Virtue, power, "what one has obtained from Dao," "the Dao manifested in individual things."

Emptiness (*wu*) The imperceptible, undifferentiated void giving birth to all existence; non-being, nothingness; lacking, without; intangible.

Immortals (Baxian, Pa-hsien) Eight Daoist perfected persons.

Pinyin New romanized transcription of Chinese adopted in 1979, replacing 1859 Wade-Giles system.

Pu Uncarved block, uncut tree.

Qi (Ch'i) The vital energy in the universe and in our bodies.

Sage A wise person, both scholar and teacher.

Su (white silk) Plainness, simplicity.

Tai Ji (T'ai Chi) The Great Ultimate (reality), which gives rise to *yin* and *yang*, drawn in a circle and embodied as a dance/exercise/meditation.

Taijiquan (T'ai-chi-ch'uan) (Power of the Great Ultimate) Stylized, graceful physical exercises practiced daily to enter into harmony with the universe, the Dao.

Ten thousand things Chinese phrase indicating "everything."

True Man (in Zhuangzi) Mythical perfect person who lives in perfect freedom, untroubled by the world.

Wu-wei Non-action, non-purposive action, no-ado.

Yang The bright, assertive, "masculine" cosmic energy of *qi*, like a mountain.

Yijing (I Ching) (Book of Changes) A manual of ancient divination.

Yin The dark, receptive, "feminine" cosmic energy of *qi*, like a river.

HOLY DAYS

Daoist priests share ritual feasts for initiation into the hierarchy, advancement in rank, or the consecration of an oratory. They meditate, practice abstinences, perform temple ceremonies to consult, appease, or drive off deities and ancestor spirits present in everyday events such as birth, marriage, burial, house construction, business affairs, and treatment of illness. In a trance, the priest may become the mouthpiece of a deity or deceased relative.

HISTORICAL OUTLINE

c. 1111–255 BCE—Zhou (Chou) dynasty

c. 600–300 BCE—Laozi (Lao-tzu) may have lived during this time

c. 475–221 BCE—Liezi (Lieh-tzu) may have lived during this time

c. 365–290 BCE—Zhuangzi (Chuang-tzu)

206 BCE–220 CE—Han dynasty

200–300 CE—Ge Hong (Ko Hung): writings on alchemy

364–370 CE—the visionary Yang Xi (Yang Hsi)

at the imperial court

c. 400–448 CE—Emperor Tai Wudi (T'ai Wu Ti) of Northern Wei dynasty declares Daoism official imperial religion

618–907 CE—Tang (T'ang) dynasty; Emperor Li Yuan, founder, claims descent from Laozi

1949—Zhang Enbu (Chang En-pu), 63rd Celestial Master, moves to Taiwan

from 1990—Daoist sects and temples re-established in China

REVIEW QUESTIONS

1   What is Emptiness for Laozi? Illustrate.
2   Explain Zhuangzi's "True Man."
3   Explain the meaning of the *yin/yang* circle.
4   Describe Taijiquan.

DISCUSSION QUESTIONS

1   Why do Daoists speak in paradoxical riddles? Explain some.
2   What are the goals of Daoist meditation?
3   What does Daoism have to offer Western culture?

INFORMATION RESOURCES

Al Chung-liang Huang. *Embrace Tiger, Return to Mountain: The Essence of T'ai Chi.* Moab, UT: Real People Press, 1973.

Bokenkamp, Stephen, *et al.* "Daoism," in *Encyclopedia of Religion,* ed. Lindsay Jones. 2nd ed. Vol. 4, pp. 2175–216, New York: Macmillan, 2005.

Chuang-tzu. *Basic Writings,* trans. Burton Watson. New York: Columbia University Press, 1964.

Huai-Chin Nan. *Tao and Longevity,* trans.

Wen Kuan Chu. Shaftesbury, Dorset: Element Books, 1988.

Kohn, Livia. *The Taoist Experience: An Anthology.* Albany, NY: State University of New York Press, 1993.

Seidel, Anna, and **Michael Strickmann**. "Daoism," in *Encyclopedia Britannica.* Vol. 28, pp. 383–96. London, 1997.

Young, Serinity, ed. *An Anthology of Sacred Texts by and about Women.* New York: Crossroad, 1995.

CHAPTER 8

JUDAISM

In the West, the oldest of the major global religions is Judaism. It is in fact the seminal tradition for the two largest existing world religions: Christianity and Islam. They all share a central belief in **monotheism**; all also refer back to the first Hebrew patriarch: Abraham. It is thought that he lived some time between 1900 and 1700 BCE. God is said to have called him to Canaan and made a **covenant** with him that he would be the father of a great nation. In addition, his first son, Ishmael, is considered the progenitor of the Muslim lineage.

Jewish tradition recognizes many later patriarchs and prophets. Moses is believed to have led the Israelites out of bondage in Egypt, to have spoken directly to God, and to have received God's commandments for the people. The revered King David united the kingdoms of Judah and Israel and established his capital in Jerusalem. His son Solomon (r. c. 967–928 BCE) increased the extent, wealth, and power of the kingdom of Israel and built the great Temple in Jerusalem for the priests to strengthen Hebrew piety. But the power of the nation diminished compared to surrounding empires until 586 BCE, when Babylonia captured Jerusalem, destroyed the Temple, and took many Jews into exile. Fifty years later some were allowed to return and rebuild the Temple, but the Hebrew kingdom had by then become a dispersed people (the **Diaspora**).

After the Second Temple was destroyed by the Roman occupiers in 70 CE, Judaism was maintained and shaped primarily by **rabbis**: teachers, decision-makers, and interpreters of the written and oral traditions. Outside Israel, Babylon became a center of Jewish theological activity; Jewish intellectual life also flourished in Spain, France, and Germany, and under Muslim rule in Baghdad. Despite their growing cultural and financial power, Jewish people were eventually oppressed by certain Christians in Western Europe, which led to large-scale massacres, ultimately including the murder of over a third of the world's Jews by Nazi Germany during World War II. In 1948 a special "homeland" for Jews was established in Palestine and given the ancient name of Israel, but it has never been free from tensions with the earlier and surrounding inhabitants of that area.

Today many people who are Jewish by birth do not practice the **Orthodox** tradition. Nevertheless, there is a renewal of interest in Judaism today, both among **Conservatives** and among **Reform** Jews who are re-interpreting their traditions to find their relevance to contemporary life.

The Jewish Bible: Tanakh

The Jewish Bible, written in the Hebrew language, is called the **Tanakh**, an acronym for its three parts:

1   The **Torah** ("teaching" or "law"), which is the first five books: Genesis, Exodus, Leviticus, Numbers, Deuteronomy. These are traditionally believed to have been given by God and written by Moses; they are also known as the **Pentateuch**, or "five scrolls." They contain the major founding traditions of the faith and the establishment of the Law.
2   The **Prophets** (*Nevi'im*) are a group of books ascribed to leading reformers such as Isaiah. The prophets spoke boldly and critically of the flaws in their society, but also promised a **Messiah** to free them and lead them to power.
3   The Wisdom Literature, or Writings (*Kethuvim*), is a diverse collection of texts, ranging from poetic Psalms to the nearly tragic drama of Job.

With many parts originating as oral tradition, the Tanakh was slowly written down over hundreds of years, particularly during the Exile, 586–535 BCE. It was translated into Greek from about 200 BCE. Following the destruction of Jerusalem in 70 CE the **canon** was gradually collected and finalized by rabbis.

The Torah

TORAH

The Five Books of Moses start with Genesis, which includes two stories of God's creation, Adam and Eve's disobedience, Noah's flood, and the lives of the patriarchs Abraham, Isaac, Jacob, and matriarchs Sarah, Rebekah, Leah, and Rachel, their wives. Exodus tells of God's liberation of the Hebrews from Egyptian slavery, led by Moses, his reception of the Torah's first Ten Commandments at the holy Mount Sinai, many later laws, and some historical accounts. Leviticus is a manual of rules for the ancient Hebrews. The movement of the tribes from Sinai to Canaan is recorded in Numbers. Deuteronomy includes a long farewell address from Moses and his death.

Since the nineteenth century, scholars have made historical and literary analyses of the Torah. They have found evidence that the Pentateuch is woven like a rope from strands of four different texts, from different historical periods: the **Yahwist**, the **Elohist**, the **Priestly**, and the **Deuteronomic**.

In the Beginning   from Genesis

The first book of the Torah begins with creation, which scholars divide into two sections. The first (a "Priestly" text) is the account of God's cosmic creation (Genesis 1:1–2:4). In six days, God created the universe from a void, the earth, vegetation, and humans, male and female in the divine image, giving humans responsibility for creation. On the seventh day he rested, which is why the Sabbath is kept as a holy day each week.

In the second creation account (Genesis 2:4–3:24, a "Yahwist" text), God first created one human, *ha'adam* ("earthling," from *ha'adamah*, "earth"). Later he made a second person, as the first one was lonely, and thus created *ish* and *ishshah*, man and woman (Adam and Eve). This is why "a man leaves his parents and cleaves to the woman and the two become one flesh." God then created vegetation and animals in the Garden of Eden. Eve, tempted by the serpent, took the fruit of the tree of knowledge of good and bad. She gave some to Adam; both ate. Their punishment was to labor—Eve in childbirth, Adam in the fields—and ultimately to die. This creation account is markedly different from the neighboring Babylonian *Enuma Elish*, in which many gods fight with each other until chaotic Tiamat is killed by heroic Marduk. However, the Genesis 6 flood story is very similar to the Babylonian *Epic of Gilgamesh* and Noah compares with Utnapishtim.

The First Creation Account in Genesis When God began to create heaven and earth—the earth being unformed and void, with darkness over the surface of the deep and a wind from God sweeping over the water—God said, "Let there be light"; and there was light. God saw that the light was good, and God separated the light from the darkness. God called the light Day, and the darkness He called Night. And there was evening and there was morning, a first day.

God said, "Let there be an expanse in the midst of the water, that it may separate water from water." God made the expanse, and it separated the water which was below the expanse from the water which was above the expanse. And it was so. God called the expanse Sky. And there was evening and there was morning, a second day.

God said, "Let the water below the sky be gathered into one area, that the dry land may appear." And it was so. God called the dry land Earth, and the gathering of waters He called Seas. And God saw that this was good. And God said, "Let the earth sprout vegetation: seed-bearing plants, fruit trees of every kind on earth that bear fruit with the seed in it." And it was so. The earth brought forth vegetation: seed-bearing plants of every kind, and trees of every kind bearing fruit with the seed in it. And God saw that this was good. And there was evening and there was morning, a third day.

God said, "Let there be lights in the expanse of the sky to separate day from night; they shall serve as signs for the set times—the days and the years; and they shall serve as lights in the expanse of the sky to shine upon the earth." And it was so. God made two great lights, the greater light to dominate the day and the lesser light to dominate the night, and the stars. And God set them in the expanse of the sky to shine upon the earth, to dominate the day and the night, and to separate light from darkness. And God saw that this was good. And there was evening and there was morning, a fourth day.

God said, "Let the waters bring forth swarms of living creatures, and birds that fly above the earth across the expanse of the sky." God created the great sea monsters, and all the living creatures of every kind that creep, which the waters brought forth in swarms, and all the winged birds of every kind. And God saw that this was good. God blessed them, saying, "Be fertile and increase, fill the waters in the seas, and let the birds increase on the earth." And there was evening and there was morning, a fifth day.

God said, "Let the earth bring forth every kind of living creature: cattle, creeping things, and wild beasts of every kind." And it was so. God made wild beasts of every kind and cattle of every kind, and all kinds of creeping things of the earth. And God saw that this was good. And God said, "Let us make man in our image, after our likeness. They shall rule the fish of the sea, the birds of the sky, the cattle, the whole earth, and all the creeping things that creep on earth." And God created man in His image, in the image of God He created him; male and female He created them. God blessed them and God said to them, "Be fertile and increase, fill the earth and master it; and rule the fish of the sea, the birds of the sky, and all the living things that creep on earth."

God said, "See, I give you every seed-bearing plant that is upon all the earth, and every tree that has seed-bearing fruit; they shall be yours for food. And to all the animals on land, to all the birds of the sky, and to everything that creeps on earth, in which there is the breath of life, [I give] all the green plants for food." And it was so. And God saw all that He had made, and found it very good. And there was evening and there was morning, the sixth day.

The heaven and the earth were finished, and all their array. On the seventh day God finished the work that He had been doing, and He ceased on the seventh day from all the work that He had done. And God blessed the seventh day and declared it holy, because on it God ceased from all the work of creation that He had done. Such is the story of heaven and earth when they were created. (Genesis 1:1–2:4)

The Second Creation Account in Genesis When the Lord God made earth and heaven—when no shrub of the field was yet on earth and no grasses of the field had yet sprouted, because the Lord God had not sent rain upon the earth and there was no man to till the soil, but a flow would well up from the ground and water the whole surface of the earth—the Lord God formed man from the dust of the earth. He blew into his nostrils the breath of life, and man became a living being.

The Lord God planted a garden in Eden, in the east, and placed there the man whom He had formed. And from the ground the Lord God caused to grow every tree that was pleasing to the sight and good for food, with the tree of life in the middle of the garden, and the tree of knowledge of good and bad.

A river issues from Eden to water the garden, and it then divides and becomes four branches. The name of the first is Pishon, the one that winds through the whole land of Havilah, where the gold is. (The gold of that land is good; bdellium[1] is there, and lapis lazuli.[2]) The name of the second river is

---

1 Bdellium—a tree whose resin is the basis for perfume.
2 Lapis lazuli—a deep blue semi-precious stone.

Gihon, the one that winds through the whole land of Cush. The name of the third river is Tigris, the one that flows east of Asshur. And the fourth river is the Euphrates.

The Lord God took the man and placed him in the garden of Eden, to till it and tend it. And the Lord God commanded the man, saying, "Of every tree of the garden you are free to eat; but as for the tree of knowledge of good and bad, you must not eat of it; for as soon as you eat of it, you shall die."

The Lord God said, "It is not good for man to be alone; I will make a fitting helper for him." And the Lord God formed out of the earth all the wild beasts and all the birds of the sky, and brought them to the man to see what he would call them; and whatever the man called each living creature, that would be its name. And the man gave names to all the cattle and to the birds of the sky and to all the wild beasts; but for Adam no fitting helper was found. So the Lord God cast a deep sleep upon the man; and, while he slept, He took one of his ribs and closed up the flesh at that spot. And the Lord God fashioned the rib that He had taken from the man into a woman; and He brought her to the man. Then the man said, "This one at last is bone of my bones and flesh of my flesh. This one shall be called Woman, for from man was she taken." Hence a man leaves his father and mother and clings to his wife, so that they become one flesh.

The two of them were naked, the man and his wife, yet they felt no shame. Now the serpent was the shrewdest of all the wild beasts that the Lord God had made. He said to the woman, "Did God really say: You shall not eat of any tree of the garden?" The woman replied to the serpent, "We may eat of the fruit of the other trees of the garden. It is only about fruit of the tree in the middle of the garden that God said: 'You shall not eat of it or touch it, lest you die.'" And the serpent said to the woman, "You are not going to die, but God knows that as soon as you eat of it your eyes will be opened and you will be like divine beings who know good and bad." When the woman saw that the tree was good for eating and a delight to the eyes, and that the tree was desirable as a source of wisdom, she took of its fruit and ate. She also gave some to her husband, and he ate. Then the eyes of both of them were opened and they perceived that they were naked; and they sewed together fig leaves and made themselves loincloths.

They heard the sound of the Lord God moving about in the garden at the breezy time of day; and the man and his wife hid from the Lord God among the trees of the garden. The Lord God called out to the man and said to him, "Where are you?" He replied, "I heard the sound of You in the garden, and I was afraid because I was naked, so I hid." Then He asked, "Who told you that you were naked? Did you eat of the tree from which I had forbidden you to eat?" The man said, "The woman You put at my side— she gave me of the tree, and I ate." And the Lord God said to the woman, "What is this you have done!" The woman replied, "The serpent duped me, and I ate." Then the Lord God said to the serpent, "Because you did this, more cursed shall you be than all cattle and all the wild beasts: on your belly shall you crawl and dirt shall you eat all the days of your life. I will put enmity between you and the woman, and between your offspring and hers; they shall strike at your head, and you shall strike at their heel." And to the woman, He said, "I will make most severe your pangs in childbearing; in pain shall you bear children, yet your urge shall be for your husband, and he shall rule over you." To Adam He said, "Because you did as your wife said and ate of the tree about which I commanded you, 'You shall not eat of it,' cursed be the ground because of you; by toil shall you eat of it all the days of your life: thorns and thistles shall it sprout for you. But your food shall be the grasses of the field; by the sweat of your brow shall you get bread to eat, until you return to the ground—for from it you were taken. For dust you are, and to dust you shall return."

The man named his wife Eve, because she was the mother of all the living. And the Lord God made garments of skins for Adam and his wife, and clothed them.

And the Lord God said, "Now that the man has become like one of us, knowing good and bad, what if he should stretch out his hand and take also from the tree of life and eat, and live forever!" So the Lord God banished him from the garden of Eden, to till the soil from which he was taken. He drove the man out, and stationed east of the garden of Eden the cherubim and the fiery ever-turning sword, to guard the way to the tree of life. (Genesis 2:4–3:24)

Abraham

Abraham's Covenant from Genesis

Essential to Judaism is the covenant. Like contracts made between individuals, states, and kings with their subjects, God made numerous covenants with Israel, such as "I shall be your God and you shall be my people" (Leviticus 26:12). Most notable are the covenants with:

1 Noah, signified by the rainbow, that God would never again destroy humanity with a flood (Genesis 9:8–17)
2 Abraham, signified by male circumcision, that God had chosen Israel as his people and that they would have the land that they "sojourn in" and be numerous (Genesis 17:1–21)
3 Moses, signified by the laws of the Torah, that, if Israel obeyed God's Law, they would be God's treasured "kingdom of priests and a holy nation" (Exodus 19:5–6)
4 King David, that he should build a temple in Jerusalem, and that his "throne shall be established forever" (II Samuel 7:5–16).

When Abram was ninety-nine years old, the Lord appeared to Abram and said to him, "I am El Shaddai. Walk in My ways and be blameless. I will establish My covenant between Me and you, and I will make you exceedingly numerous."

Abram threw himself on his face; and God spoke to him further, "As for Me, this is My covenant with you: You shall be the father of a multitude of nations. And you shall no longer be called Abram, but your name shall be Abraham, for I make you the father of a multitude of nations. I will make you exceedingly fertile, and make nations of you; and kings shall come forth from you. I will maintain My covenant between Me and you, and your offspring to come, as an everlasting covenant throughout the ages, to be God to you and to your offspring to come. I assign the land you sojourn in to you and your offspring to come, all the land of Canaan, as an everlasting holding. I will be their God." (Genesis 17:1–8)

The Mosaic Covenant from Exodus

Exodus records the heart of much of Jewish tradition, focusing on God's power to liberate the chosen people from unjust suffering. The Hebrews were slaves in Egypt, and the infant Moses was saved from Pharaoh's destruction to grow up a prince in Pharaoh's household. But he ran away, then returned to lead his people out of slavery after a great struggle with Pharaoh around 1250 BCE. At Sinai, the Hebrews were given the Ten Commandments, the first of the 613 laws of the Torah, when Moses ascended the holy mountain.

Moses led the people out of the camp toward God, and they took their places at the foot of the mountain. Now Mount Sinai was all in smoke, for the Lord had come down upon it in fire; the smoke rose like the smoke of a kiln, and the whole mountain trembled violently. . . .

God spoke all these words, saying:

I the Lord am your God who brought you out of the land of Egypt, the house of bondage: You shall have no other gods besides Me.

You shall not make for yourself a sculptured image, or any likeness of what is in the heavens above, or on the earth below, or in the waters under the earth. You shall not bow down to them or serve them. For I the Lord your God am an impassioned God, visiting the guilt of the parents upon the children, upon the third and upon the fourth generations of those who reject Me, but showing kindness to the thousandth generation of those who love Me and keep My commandments.

You shall not swear falsely by the name of the Lord your God; for the Lord will not clear one who swears falsely by His name.

Remember the sabbath day and keep it holy. Six days you shall labor and do all your work, but the seventh day is a sabbath of the Lord your God: you shall not do any work—you, your son or daughter, your male or female slave, or your cattle, or the stranger who is within your settlements. For in six days the Lord made heaven and earth and sea, and all that is in them, and He rested on the seventh day; therefore the Lord blessed the sabbath day and hallowed it.

Honor your father and your mother, that you may long endure on the land that the Lord your God is assigning to you.

You shall not murder.

You shall not commit adultery.

You shall not steal.

You shall not bear false witness against your neighbor.

You shall not covet your neighbor's house: you shall not covet your neighbor's wife, or his male or female slave, or his ox or his ass, or anything that is your neighbor's. (Exodus 19:17–18, 20:1–14)

An Eye for an Eye from Leviticus

For millennia the typical form of justice was clan vengeance. If someone killed a member of your clan, you were justified in killing a member of that clan. Neither was a sense of fair punishment for a crime common. So the Torah, along with other cultures' earlier legal documents, such as Hammurabi's Code in Babylon (1792–1750 BCE), attempted to set up fair punishment systems enacted by judges in court. Hammurabi's Code, inscribed on a stone pillar, listed among its laws "If a son has struck his father, his hands shall be cut off," and "If a man had destroyed the eye of another free man, his own eye shall be destroyed." This selection from Leviticus also shows the "eye for an eye" law. It represents an effort to limit excessive retaliation and revenge, which at the time was a refinement of justice.

And to the Israelite people speak thus: Anyone who blasphemes his God shall bear his guilt; if he also pronounces the name Lord, he shall be put to death. The whole community shall stone him; stranger or citizen, if he has thus pronounced the Name, he shall be put to death.

If anyone kills any human being, he shall be put to death. One who kills a beast shall make restitution for it: life for life. If anyone maims his fellow, as he has done so shall it be done to him: fracture for fracture, eye for eye, tooth for tooth. The injury he inflicted on another shall be inflicted on him. (Leviticus 24:15–20)

Jerusalem

Choose Life from Deuteronomy

In Deuteronomy the Mosaic Covenant is restated, emphasizing Israel's obligation to "choose life" by living by the Torah, taking moral responsibility, in order to fulfill the human side of the covenants. This condition stands in contrast with the Davidic Covenant's unconditional promise of a secure kingship in Jerusalem "forever."

I call heaven and earth to witness against you this day: I have put before you life and death, blessing and curse. Choose life—if you and your offspring would live—by loving the Lord your God, heeding His commands, and holding fast to Him. For thereby you shall have life and shall long endure upon the soil that the Lord your God swore to your ancestors, Abraham, Isaac, and Jacob, to give to them. (Deuteronomy 30:19–20)

The Davidic Covenant from II Samuel

"Further, say thus to My servant David: Thus said the Lord of Hosts: I took you from the pasture, from following the flock, to be ruler of My people Israel, and I have been with you wherever you went, and have cut down all your enemies before you. Moreover, I will give you great renown like that of the greatest men on earth. I will establish a home for My people Israel and will plant them firm, so that they shall dwell secure and shall tremble no more. Evil men shall not oppress them any more as in the past, ever since I appointed chieftains over My people Israel. I will give you safety from all your enemies.

"The Lord declares to you that He, the Lord, will establish a house for you. When your days are done and you lie with your fathers, I will raise up your offspring after you, one of your own issue, and I will establish his kingship. He shall build a house for My name, and I will establish his royal throne forever. I will be a father to him, and he shall be a son to Me. When he does wrong, I will chastise him with the rod of men and the affliction of mortals; but I will never withdraw My favor from him as I withdrew it from Saul, whom I removed to make room for you. Your house and your kingship shall ever be secure before you; your throne shall be established forever." (II Samuel 7:8–16)

PROPHETS

In the Ancient Near East, prophets were well-known cultic revealers of divine will. Known for their states of trance and ecstatic speaking, they performed miracles and symbolic actions. The biblical pre-classical prophets—Samuel, Nathan, Elijah, and Elisha—were renowned for foretelling events and working miracles, and were consulted by kings. The classical prophets—Isaiah, Jeremiah, Ezekiel, and the 12 minor prophets—also spoke in the name of God, beginning around 750 BCE. They emphasized ethical monotheism rather than cult activities and foretelling the future, criticizing their society's hypocrisies and injustices and pleading with Israel to repent. They also promised God's forgiveness and the coming of the Messiah.

The Prophecies of Isaiah

The Hebrew prophet Isaiah (c. 740–701 BCE) wrote during the difficult times when the great empires of Assyria and Babylonia (now Iraq) were attacking Israel and slowly conquering it. His text, chapters 1–35, is supplemented by two later writers in chapters 36–9 and 40–66. The people were extremely distressed and, since they believed in the Davidic Covenant in which God promised the land to them forever, they questioned how God could allow this. Prophets such as Isaiah spoke up and said that God was punishing the nation for insincere worship, belief in other gods, and social injustice. He compared it to the corrupt cities of Sodom and Gomorrah, whose destruction is described in Genesis 18–19. Isaiah said that God was even repulsed by the ancient rituals of sacrificial offerings of rams, bulls, lambs, and goats, and astrological calculations of new moons. This was a radical precursor to the abandonment of Temple sacrifices in favor of rabbinical teaching and learning. But, Isaiah assured the people, God promised that He would send a great leader, a Messiah, to save them later.

The prophecies of Isaiah son of Amoz, who prophesied concerning Judah and Jerusalem in the reigns of Uzziah, Jotham, Ahaz, and Hezekiah, kings of Judah.

Hear, O heavens, and give ear, O earth, For the Lord has spoken: "I reared children and brought them up—And they have rebelled against Me! An ox knows its owner, An ass its master's crib: Israel does not know, My people takes no thought."

Ah, sinful nation! People laden with iniquity! Brood of evildoers! Depraved children! They have forsaken the Lord, Spurned the Holy One of Israel, Turned their backs [on Him].

Why do you seek further beatings, that you continue to offend? Every head is ailing, and every heart is sick. From head to foot No spot is sound: All bruises, and welts, And festering sores—Not pressed out, not bound up, Not softened with oil. Your land is a waste, Your cities burnt down; Before your eye, the yield of your soil Is consumed by strangers—A wasteland as overthrown by strangers! Fair Zion is left Like a booth in a vineyard, Like a hut in a cucumber field, Like a city beleaguered. Had not the Lord of Hosts Left us some survivors, We should be like Sodom, Another Gomorrah.

Hear the word of the Lord, You chieftains of Sodom; Give ear to our God's instruction, You folk of Gomorrah! "What need have I of all your sacrifices?" says the Lord. "I am sated with burnt offerings of rams, And suet of fatlings, And blood of bulls; And I have no delight In lambs and he-goats. That you come to appear before Me—Who asked that of you? Trample my courts no more; Bringing oblations is futile, Incense is offensive to Me. New moon and sabbath, Proclaiming of solemnities, Assemblies with iniquity, I cannot abide. Your new moons and fixed seasons Fill me with loathing; They are become a burden to Me, I cannot endure them. And when you lift up your hands, I will turn My eyes away from you; Though you pray at length, I will not listen. Your hands are stained with crime—Wash yourselves clean; Put your evil doings Away from My sight. Cease to do evil; Learn to do good. Devote yourselves to justice; Aid the wronged. Uphold the rights of the orphan; Defend the cause of the widow.

"Come, let us reach an understanding,—says the Lord. Be your sins like crimson, They can turn snow-white; Be they red as dyed wool, They can become like fleece." If, then, you agree and give heed, You will eat the good things of the earth; But if you refuse and disobey, You will be devoured [by] the sword. For it was the Lord who spoke.
(Isaiah 1:1–20)

The people that walked in darkness Have seen a brilliant light; On those who dwelt in a land of gloom Light has dawned. You have magnified that nation, Have given it great joy; They have rejoiced before You As they rejoice at reaping time, As they exult When dividing spoil. . . . For a child has been born to us, A son has been given us. And authority has settled on his shoulders. He has been named "The Mighty God is planning grace; The Eternal Father, a peaceable ruler"—In token of abundant authority and of peace without limit Upon David's throne and kingdom, That it may be firmly established In justice and in equity Now and evermore. The zeal of the Lord of Hosts Shall bring this to pass. (Isaiah 9:1–2, 5–6)

WISDOM LITERATURE

Wisdom Literature was common in Ancient Near Eastern cultures. In the Tanakh it includes a diverse collection of texts, from songs sung in the Temple to the story of Job and the Song of Solomon. Proverbs is a collection of short oral sayings, while Ecclesiastes is a book skeptical of religion, raising many doubts. Job is a drama adapted from a Babylonian source in which Job's faith is tested by terrible suffering when he loses all his wealth and children and is stricken with illness. Here Psalm 23 and two quotes from Job have been selected, one showing a sense of ecological harmony with nature demonstrating God behind it all, and one showing God's grand cosmic answer to Job's suffering. The Psalms were songs sung in worship services in Jerusalem's Temple.

Psalm 23

A Psalm of David

The Lord is my shepherd; I lack nothing. He makes me lie down in green pastures; He leads me to water in places of repose; He renews my life; He guides me in right paths as befits His name.

Though I walk through a valley of deepest darkness, I fear no harm, for You are with me; Your rod and Your staff—they comfort me.

You spread a table for me in full view of my enemies; You anoint my head with oil; my drink is abundant. Only goodness and steadfast love shall pursue me all the days of my life, and I shall dwell in the house of the Lord for many long years.

The Earth Will Teach You from Job

But ask the beasts, and they will teach you; The birds of the sky, they will tell you, Or speak to the earth, it will teach you; The fish of the sea, they will inform you. Who among all these does not know That the hand of the Lord has done this? In His hand is every living soul And the breath of all mankind. (Job 12:7–10)

Where Were You When I Laid the Earth's Foundations?

from Job

Then the Lord replied to Job out of the tempest and said:

Who is this who darkens counsel, Speaking without knowledge? Gird your loins like a man; I will ask and you will inform Me.

Where were you when I laid the earth's foundations? Speak if you have understanding. Do you know who fixed its dimensions Or who measured it with a line? Onto what were its bases sunk? Who set its cornerstone When the morning stars sang together And all the divine beings shouted for joy? . . .

Have you ever commanded the day to break, Assigned the dawn its place, So that it seizes the corners of the earth And shakes the wicked out of it? . . .

Have the gates of death been disclosed to you? Have you seen the gates of deep darkness? Have you surveyed the expanses of the earth? If you know of these—tell Me. (Job 38:1–7, 12–13, 17–18)

SOURCE: Bible excerpts in this chapter are taken from *Tanakh: A New Translation of the Holy Scriptures.* Philadelphia, PA: Jewish Publication Society, 1985

Commentaries on the Tanakh

Over many centuries rabbis collected numerous interpretations and extrapolations of Jewish Law, adapting them to the era in which they lived. The **Midrash** are folklore elaborations, mainly concerned with interpreting Tanakh texts. The earliest Midrash may well be the Passover ritual **Haggadah**, now preserved in many versions. The **Mishnah** is a collection of laws originally handed down orally on festivals, marriage, damages, holy things, and purities, while the **Talmud** is the body of teachings commenting on earlier Mishnah.

Midrash

The first brief midrash below describes how God told Adam not to corrupt the world. The second demonstrates a strict versus a freer way of understanding the Tanakh: an unbeliever approached the influential rabbi Shammai (c. 50 BCE–30 CE), a strict interpreter of Torah, and then the sage Hillel, who lived at about the same time. He was a less rigorous interpreter of Torah who became president of the Sanhedrin, the supreme religious, political, and judiciary body of Israel.

Your World

In the hour when the Holy One, blessed be he, created the first man,

he took him and let him pass before all the trees of the garden of Eden, and said to him:

See my works, how fine and excellent they are!

Now all that I have created for you have I created.

Think upon this, and do not corrupt and desolate my world;
　　for if you corrupt it, there is no one to set it right after you.

The Rest is Commentary

Once a heathen came before Shammai. He said to him:
I will be converted, if you can teach me all the Torah while I stand on one leg.
Shammai pushed him away with the builder's measure he had in his hand.
The man came before Hillel. He converted him.
He said to him:
What is hateful to you, do not do to your fellow.
That is all the Torah. The rest is commentary—go and study.

SOURCE: Nahum N. Glatzer, ed., *Hammer on the Rock*. New York: Schocken, 1962, pp. 13, 80

Talmud

The Talmud is the large body of commentary on the Mishnah's oral traditions. The Jerusalem Talmud dates from about 500 CE, and the Babylonian Talmud was completed about 600 CE. The contents of the Talmud are notably historical, containing folklore, manners, customs, proverbs, prayers, ritual, and medical advice. The literary style is that of a discussion in an academy (*yeshivah*), led by scholars such as Ben Zoma. The visual format places a text in the middle of the page, and commentaries (*gemara*) are written around it. One third of the Talmud's two and a half million words is commentary on **Halakhah** (written, oral, and customary laws) and the rest concerns Haggadah, including the Passover Seder ritual.

Ben Zoma says: Who is a wise man? He that learns from all men, as it is said, *From all my teachers have I got understanding* (Psalm 119:99).

　　Who is a mighty man? He that subdues his evil impulse, as it is said, *He that is slow to anger is better than the mighty, and he that ruleth his spirit than him that taketh a city* (Proverbs 16:32).

　　Who is a rich man? He that is content with his portion, as it is said, *When thou eatest the labor of thy hands happy shalt thou be and it shall be well with thee* (Psalm 128:2): *Happy shalt thou be* in this world, *and it shall be well with thee* in the world to come.

　　Who is an honorable man? He that honors mankind, as it is said, *For them that honor me I will honor and they that despise me shall be lightly esteemed* (I Samuel 2:30).

A Wise Man: It is he who is ready to learn even from his inferiors. With such readiness, if his inferior should present him with a wise view, he will not be ashamed to accept it and will not treat his words with contempt. This was characteristic of David, King of Israel, who said, "I would pay attention to any man who came to teach me something."

　　The Gentile philosophers say that even if a person were to know everything [as it were], if he does not want to increase his knowledge, he is not a wise man but a fool.... On the other hand, one who passionately loves to increase his wisdom may be called a wise man even if he were to know nothing. Only this way can you attain true wisdom and discover the will of God.

SOURCE: Judah Goldin, ed. and trans., *The Living Talmud*. New Haven, CT: Yale University Press, 1957, p. 153

Prayer and ceremony

Prayer: Shema

Sabbath

Most important ancient instructions for prayer are spoken by Moses in the Torah. The first sentence is called the Shema after its opening Hebrew word, "*Shema Ysrael Adonai Elohainu Adonai Echad.*"

Hear O Israel! The Lord is our God, the Lord Alone. You shall love the Lord your God with all your heart and with all your soul and with all your might. Take to heart these instructions with which I charge you this day. Impress them upon your children. Recite them when you stay at home and when you are away, when you lie down and when you get up. Bind them as a sign on your hand and let them serve as a symbol on your forehead, inscribe them on the doorposts of your home and on your gates. (Deuteronomy 6:4–9)

And now O Israel, what does the Lord your God demand of you? Only this: to revere the Lord your God, to walk only in His paths, to love him and to serve the Lord your God with all your heart and soul, keeping the Lord's commandments and laws, which I enjoin upon you today, for your good. Mark, the heavens to their uttermost reaches belong to the Lord your God, the earth and all that is on it! Yet it was to your fathers that the Lord was drawn in His love for them, so that He chose you, their lineal descendants, from among all peoples—as is now the case. Cut away, therefore, the thickening about your hearts and stiffen your necks no more. For the Lord your God is God supreme and Lord supreme, the great, the mighty, and the awesome God, who shows no favor and takes no bribe, but upholds the cause of the fatherless and the widow, and befriends the stranger, providing him with food and clothing.—You too must befriend the stranger, for you were strangers in the land of Egypt. You must revere the Lord your God: only Him shall you worship, to him shall you hold fast, and by His name shall you swear. He is your glory and He is your God, who wrought for you these marvelous, awesome deeds that you saw with your own eyes. (Deuteronomy 10:12–21)

The Lord said to Moses as follows: Speak to the Israelite people and instruct them to make for themselves fringes on the corners of their garments throughout the ages; let them attach a cord of blue to the fringe at each corner. That shall be your fringe; look at it and recall all the commandments of the Lord and observe them, so that you do not follow your heart and eyes in your lustful urge. Thus you shall be reminded to observe all My commandments and to be holy to your God. I the Lord am your God, who brought you out of the land of Egypt to be your God: I, the Lord your God. (Numbers 15:37–41)

The Passover Story   from the Seder Meal Ceremony

The Jewish Passover Seder Meal is a major annual celebration of liberation from slavery in Egypt. "Passover" refers to God's angel of death coming to Egypt but passing over the Hebrew homes, thus freeing them. Unleavened *matzah* bread must be eaten, since the Hebrews escaping Egypt had no time to let their bread rise; it is called "the bread of affliction." The ceremonial plate at home always includes a shank bone (symbol of the sacrificial lamb), bitter herbs (*maror*), and a blend of fruit, spices, wine, and *matzah* meal (*charoset*) to symbolize the mortar made while slaves. Seder includes special prayers, reading the Haggadah text, from which we excerpt below, eating a festive meal, drinking wine, singing Passover songs, and finally saying "Next year in Jerusalem!"

Uncover the Matzah *and lift the plate for all to see. The recital of the Passover Story begins with the following words:* This is the bread of affliction which our ancestors ate in the land of Egypt. All who are hungry—let them come and eat. All who are needy—let them come and celebrate the Passover with us. Now we are here; next year may we be in the Land of Israel. Now we are slaves; next year may we be free.

    The plate is put down, the Matzah *is covered, and the second cup of wine is filled. The youngest present asks the Four Questions.*

The Four Questions How different is this night from all other nights? On all other nights we may eat either leavened or unleavened bread; on this night, only unleavened bread. On all other nights we may eat any vegetable; on this night we are required to eat bitter herbs. On all other nights we are not bidden to dip our vegetables even once; on this night we dip them twice. On all other nights we eat our meals in any manner; on this night, why do we sit around the table together in a ceremonial fashion?

    Uncover the Matzah *and begin the reply.*

The Answer "We were slaves of Pharaoh in Egypt," and the Lord our God brought us forth from there "with a strong hand and an outstretched arm." If the Holy One, blessed be He, had not brought forth our ancestors from Egypt, then we and our children, and our children's children, would still be enslaved to Pharaoh in Egypt. Therefore, even if we are all learned and wise, all elders and fully versed in the Torah, it is our duty nonetheless to retell the story of the Exodus from Egypt. And the more one dwells on the Exodus from Egypt, the more is one to be praised.

    Point to the shank bone: The Passover offering which our ancestors ate in Temple days, what was the reason for it? It was because the Holy One, blessed be He, passed over the houses of our ancestors in Egypt, as it is written: "And you shall say, 'It is the Passover offering to the Lord, Who passed over the houses of the children of Israel in Egypt, when He smote the Egyptians, and spared our houses.' And the people bowed their heads and worshipped."

Point to the Matzah: This *Matzah* which we eat, what is the reason for it? It is because there was not enough time for the dough of our ancestors to rise when the King of all kings, the Holy One, blessed be He, revealed Himself to them and redeemed them, as it is written: "And they baked the dough which they had brought out from Egypt into cakes of unleavened bread; for it had not leavened, because they were driven out of Egypt and they could not tarry; nor had they prepared any provisions for themselves."

Point to the bitter herbs: These bitter herbs which we eat—what is their meaning? It is because the Egyptians embittered the lives of our ancestors in Egypt, as it is written: "And they embittered their lives with hard labor, with mortar and bricks, and with every kind of work in the fields; all the work which they made them do was cruel."

In every generation one must see oneself as though having personally come forth from Egypt, as it is written: "And you shall tell your child on that day, 'This is done because of what the Lord did for me when I came forth, from Egypt.'" It was not our ancestors alone whom the Holy One, blessed be He, redeemed; He redeemed us too, with them, as it is written: "He brought us out from there that He might lead us to, and give us, the land which He had promised to our ancestors."

SOURCE: *Passover Haggadah*, trans. Nathan Goldberg. Hoboken, NJ: Ktav Publishing, 1949/1993, pp. 8–24

Evolving theology and spirituality

Jewish theology has continually elaborated and interpreted the principles of the faith in the light of contemporary life and thought. The philosopher Maimonides (c. 1135–1204), who was born in Spain and migrated to Egypt, blended Jewish theology with Greek and Muslim philosophy. His "Thirteen Principles of Faith" affirms his interpretation of the Creator, the Law, and the Messiah.

Thirteen Principles of Faith by Maimonides

1   I believe with perfect faith that the Creator, blessed be his name, is the Author and Guide of everything that has been created, and that he alone has made, does make, and will make all things.

2   I believe with perfect faith that the Creator, blessed be his name, is a Unity, and that there is no unity in any manner like unto his, and that he alone is our God, who was, is, and will be.

3   I believe with perfect faith that the Creator, blessed be his name, is not a body, and that he is free from all the accidents of matter, and that he has not any form whatsoever.

4 I believe with perfect faith that the Creator, blessed be his name, is the first and the last.

5 I believe with perfect faith that to the Creator, blessed be his name, and to him alone, it is right to pray, and that it is not right to pray to any being besides him.

6 I believe with perfect faith that all the words of the prophets are true.

7 I believe with perfect faith that the prophecy of Moses our teacher, peace be unto him, was true, and that he was the chief of the prophets, both of those that preceded and of those that followed him.

8 I believe with perfect faith that the whole Law, now in our possession, is the same that was given to Moses our teacher, peace be unto him.

9 I believe with perfect faith that this Law will not be changed, and that there will never be any other law from the Creator, blessed be his name.

10 I believe with perfect faith that the Creator, blessed be his name, knows every deed of the children of men, and all their thoughts, as it is said, It is he that fashioneth the hearts of them all, that giveth heed to all their deeds.

11 I believe with perfect faith that the Creator, blessed be his name, rewards those that keep his commandments and punishes those that transgress them.

12 I believe with perfect faith in the coming of the Messiah, and, though he tarry, I will wait daily for his coming.

13 I believe with perfect faith that there will be a resurrection of the dead at the time when it shall please the Creator, blessed be his name, and exalted be the remembrance of him for ever and ever.

SOURCE: Maimonides, "Thirteen Principles of Faith," trans. S. Singer, in *The Authorized Daily Prayer Book of the United Hebrew Congregations of the British Empire*. London: Eyre and Spottiswoode, 1912, pp. 89–90

From Strength to Strength by Baal-Shem Tov

The spiritual literature of Judaism expresses the experiences of the soul's mystical journey toward God. Mystical **Kabbalism** began during the Second Temple period and its esoteric teachings developed especially during the European Middle Ages. From it emerged complex images such as the *sefirot*, or aspects of God's being, drawn as a Tree of Life.

The founder of the mystical Jewish Hasidic sect in Eastern Europe in the eighteenth century was Rabbi Israel ben Eliezer (c. 1700–60), called the Baal-Shem Tov (Master of God's Name). Legends handed down about him tell of the longing of the Hasidim, who to this day strive to live the Torah with passionate mystical insight, guided by God's principles: Ecstasy (*Hitlahavut*), embracing God beyond time and space, Service (*Avoda*) to God in time and space, Intention (*Kavana*), the mystery of the soul directed to redeeming the world, and Humility (*Shiflut*). This legend tells how a bereaved youth is consoled by his lost friend who visits him from Heaven in a dream.

In the days of the Baal-Shem there lived two friends. They stood in that most beautiful time of youth when the last dawn still glows in heaven, enchanting and undefined: auroral dreams still hover near by, but soon the sun will draw near, the stern master, and his kingdom of forms will become visible.

Often the friends sat together, leaning against the bare wall of their little room, and talked of the meaning of life. To one of them the world was revealed through the word of the Baal-Shem. From each thing he received a message, and with every action he gave a response. He threw himself down on the green field, greeted the wind and the water and the beautiful animals that glided swiftly by, and his greeting was a prayer. Thus for him the meaning of life was founded in the Creator. His companion flew into a passion against him and declared that all this was a sin against the spirit of truth. For each thing has many surfaces and each creature many forms, but he who submits himself to a faith now sees of the multiple reality only one surface and one form; his way becomes at once secure and impoverished, and the search for truth, for the meaning of life, dies away in him. To this the other replied that in the world of enlightenment there are no surfaces and forms, rather each thing and creature stands there in its purity. Thus the friends often argued with each other.

Then it happened that a serious illness overtook that youth who was devoted to the Baal-Shem. In the pitiless intensity of the pain he recognized the message of a power which must bring his earthly life to its end. So he did not resist it, but rather yielded himself to the mighty element. Nonetheless, horror lay encamped on the road to that which would take place in the abyss of eternity. He let the Baal-Shem know that he was preparing himself for death, and when the master stood by his bed, he said, "Rabbi, how and by what means shall I proceed? A horror lies before me and disturbs my peace."

The Baal-Shem took the hand of the sick boy in his hands and said to him, "Child, recall: have you not always gone from strength to strength and from goal to goal? So you shall also move onward in the gardens of eternity." He touched the forehead of the sick boy and said to him, "Because the hour of the last dawn is still over you, and because you have lived in it genuinely and have not been afraid of its happiness, I shall write my sign on your forehead so that no one can terrify your way and hinder your path. So go hence, child, when death summons you." He bent over him, laid forehead to forehead, and blessed him.

When the master had gone, the other youth slipped into the room and knelt by the bed. He kissed the hand of the sick boy and said, "My beloved, they wish to take you away, and I know that you do not resist. Recall how we used to talk with each other among the birches of a summer evening, and finally you said only, 'Yes, it is,' and I said, 'No, it is not.' Now I am terribly frightened, for you are going away from me, are willingly going away with these, your eyes. My beloved, the birches are in your eyes, and also the summer evening. And everything says, 'Yes, it is.' I feel that it is, I myself say it, indeed, and know it too, for otherwise there were no meaning in everything, and yet you are going away from me. Whither are you going?" He sobbed over the hand of his friend and kissed it again and again.

The dying boy spoke, "Dear one, I go farther on the way. When I am on the way, I shall think of you and of our love. I will come to you to tell you of my path. Give me your hand."

Then the other cried out, "You shall not go, I shall keep you, you shall not go!"

But the dying boy spoke out of his peace, "Not so, you cannot strive against the Lord. You shall hold my hand until my pulse ceases to beat, and this is my promise to you that I shall return to behold the beautiful earth and you."

The gates of the firmament opened before the sign on his forehead and he ascended. He moved from goal to goal and from holiness to holiness and received the meaning of life. Time grew still and there was no space, only the way of becoming without place and lapse of time.

Suddenly his step was checked, time roared in his ears, and space struck him with cruel fists. Then he stood there in the midst of silent watchmen. He showed them the sign on his forehead. But they stared at him and shook their heads, and he knew that his forehead no longer bore a sign. Human despair threatened to overcome him, but he withstood it. Then he saw an old man before him who asked, "Why do you halt here?"

"I can go no farther," he answered. "This thing is not good," said the old man. "For if you tarry here, then the life of the spirit will abandon you and you will remain here as an unfeeling stone. For all the life of the world to come is this: to move from strength to strength unto the abyss of eternity."

"What can I do?" the youth asked him.

"I shall go into the sanctuary," replied the old man, "and find out why this has happened to you." He went, came back, and said, "You promised your friend that you would come to him and tell him of your way. You have forgotten to do this and have broken your promise. Therefore, the sign has been removed from your forehead and you have been prevented from entering the sanctuary of truth."

Then the youth beheld his friend on earth and grieved at having forgotten him. "What shall I do in order to free myself from my guilt?" he asked.

The old man answered, "Descend into the nightly dream of your friend and tell him what he desires to know."

The youth descended to earth and entered into the dream of his friend. He stroked the forehead of the sleeping man and whispered in his ear, "Dear one, I have come to tell you of my way. But do not be angry at me for having delayed so long. For how can one think of a man, even though he be the most beloved, in the midst of the terror of God's vortex that overflows all limits?"

But the other rose up in his sleep, pressed his hand to his eyes and hissed forth the words of his chagrin from out of clenched teeth, "Depart from me, lying image, I will no longer let myself be made a fool of by you. I have waited and waited, and the promised one did not come. And now my spirit is rotted by waiting so that night after night your phantom visits me. But now I will no longer let myself be made a fool of. I command you, dissolve and appear to me no more!"

Then the youth threw himself trembling on his companion and clung to him. "Truly, I am no phantom, but your friend," he said, "and I have come to you out of the world of being. Think how we sat among the birches of a summer evening. Think how our right hands clasped each other in the hour of my death."

But the dreamer shouted, "You say the same night after night, and you catch me and I lift myself to you, then you vanish into the shadows. So let go of me now. See, I free myself of you!"

Once more the dead youth strove with his friend and cried, "Did not you say yourself, 'Yes, it is'?"

But the other only laughed in a hard voice, "Indeed I spoke thus, and I also waited. But the promised one did not come, and now I know that I was the plaything in the hand of a cruel hour. It was this hour that enslaved me and shamed me and brought the yes of betrayal to my lips. But I cry out against you, 'No, it is not!'"

Then the youth yielded and turned to disappear, but a last hope came to him and out of the faint distance he called to his comrade, "Then I will return in broad daylight and bring you a sign."

In the upper world he hurried to the temple of truth, sought out the old man and questioned him, "Help me and say what sign I can bring my friend to show that it is really I?"

"On this too I shall give thee counsel, my son," answered the old man, "and God be with thee. At noon of every Sabbath the Baal-Shem preaches on the mysteries of the teaching in the house of study that stands in the heaven of holy knowledge. And at the third Sabbath meal which unites heaven and earth he preaches on these mysteries before the ears of men, after his word has received the consecration of the upper world. Therefore, go at noon of the Sabbath and listen to the speech of your master in heaven; then descend to your friend and report to him the speech. This then will serve him as a sign; he will come to the holy meal in the house of the Baal-Shem and receive the word out of his mouth."

The youth did as he was advised, he absorbed the speech of the master, descended, entered into the day-dream of his friend and poured out the word over him like a balm. After that he bent over him and kissed him, mouth on mouth, with the kiss of heaven. Then he fled.

The other arose at once, and it seemed to him as if he had experienced the unexperienceable. He went outside; there stood the birches in the midday sun. He sat for a long time under the birches like one who knows.

When the sun began to sink, he went to the house of the Baal-Shem, not out of doubt but out of yearning. Now he stood in the door and heard the words out of the mouth of the Baal-Shem. He bowed himself at the feet of the speaker and said, "Rabbi, bless me for I want to die. For what is there left for me here?"

"Not so," replied the master. "Go outside to the birches that again stand in the summer evening and speak to them in your joy, 'Yes, it is.' And I do indeed bless you, but not for death, rather that now and here you may move from goal to goal, from strength to strength, and thus for ever and ever."

SOURCE: Martin Buber, *The Legend of the Baal-Shem*, trans. Maurice Friedman. New York: Harper and Row, 1955, pp. 172–8

Branches of Judaism

There are several branches of modern Judaism, since there is no central authority. The majority of Jews form three major groups: the Orthodox, Conservative, and Reform. Jews feel less concerned about believing a list of dogmas than sincerely behaving according to religious laws, so there is a degree of flexibility and change in these groups.

Most non-assimilated Jews light candles on Sabbath (*Shabbat*) evening before dinner, participate in the Passover Seder, light Hanukkah candles, and celebrate high holidays: Rosh Hashanah and Yom Kippur. Many Jews have **Bar Mitzvahs** and Jewish weddings, go to summer camps, and support the nation of Israel.

More divisive are questions such as: should the Tanakh be read literally, or it is subject to scientific and historical criticism? Should Jews seek to maintain centuries-old traditions, such as speaking Yiddish and wearing a particular era's clothing, keep kosher food rules including avoiding pork, prohibit all work on the Sabbath, keep women separate in **synagogue**, and ordain only men to be rabbis? Should Jews have to marry only other Jews? Today such issues divide Jews into groups on a continuum, from strict Orthodox, through middle-ground Conservatives, to liberal Reform and more radical groups. One writer saw this process of questioning as the "de-ghettoization" of Judaism.

ORTHODOX

Many Orthodox Jews today are really Neo-Orthodox, holding mostly to nineteenth-century interpretations of literal reading of the Torah, speaking Yiddish, requiring men to wear beards and nineteenth-century Eastern European clothing, keeping women separate in synagogue and out of the rabbinate, eating strictly kosher meals, observing rigorous Sabbath practices, and requiring marriage to other Jews. Ultra-Orthodox Jews dominate Israel's politics and reject the validity of non-Orthodox rabbis and converts.

The Orthodox movement originated in a reaction against reformers in Germany, led notably by Rabbi Samson Raphael Hirsch (1808–88), a founder of modern Orthodoxy, who wrote the following.

Religion Allied to Progress   by Samson Hirsch

Now what is it that we want? Are the only alternatives either to abandon religion or to renounce all progress with all the glorious and noble gifts which civilisation and education offer mankind? Is the Jewish religion really of such a nature that its faithful adherents must be the enemies of civilisation and progress? ... We declare before heaven and earth that if our religion demanded that we should renounce what is called civilisation and progress we would obey unquestioningly, because our religion is for us truly religion, the word of God before which every other consideration has to give way. We declare, equally, that we would prefer to be branded as fools and do without all the honour and glory that civilisation and progress might confer on us rather than be guilty of the conceited mock-wisdom which the spokesman of a religion allied to progress here displays.

For behold whither a religion allied to progress leads! Behold how void it is of all piety and humanity and into what blunders the conceited, Torah-criticising spirit leads. Here you have a protagonist of this religion of progress. See how he dances on the graves of your forefathers, how he drags out their corpses from their graves, laughs in their faces and exclaims to you: "Your fathers were crude and uncivilised; they deserved the contempt in which they were held. Follow me, so that you may become civilised and deserve respect!" Such is the craziness which grows on the tree of knowledge of this "religion allied to progress"!

SOURCE: <http://www.ucalgary.ca/~elsegal/363_Transp/Orthodoxy/SRHirsch.html>

CONSERVATIVE

Middle-ground Conservative Jews embrace a wide range of practices, some close to Orthodoxy, some close to Reform. Most accept scientific study of the Tanakh and see it as written by inspired human hands, thus fallible and subject to interpretation as history progresses. But changes come through communal decision-making, not completely individual free choice. New York's Jewish Theological Seminary is the center of Conservative rabbinical education.

Shabbat and high holidays are celebrated, conversions are accepted, kosher food preparation is not required, dress rules are minimally decorous, some Hebrew is spoken in synagogue (and some Yiddish from Eastern Europe, as well) and is encouraged, but it is not required. Support for Israel as a nation is strong, but criticism of its politics may be heard. Women sit with men in synagogue and take synagogue leadership roles, including being counted in the *minyan* (minimum number required for worship). In 1983 the Jewish Theological Seminary opened its doors to women, allowing them to become Conservative rabbis. They are often active in community reform movements. This passage illustrates the Conservative view of revelation.

The Conservative Jewish Doctrine of Revelation

by Seymour Siegel

The basic question concerning Jewish law involves a doctrine of Revelation. All forms of Judaism accept the notion of God's communicating with man [sic] in general and the Jewish people in particular. Most Orthodox thinkers argue that the traditional doctrine of Torah MiSinai (the Torah coming from Sinai) posits that God literally commanded everything written in the Torah. This, in their view, makes Jewish law immutable, and change can take place only within the most narrow limits. The Reform thinkers believed that the moral and ethical demands of Judaism were revealed, and that the ritual laws (which means most of the corpus of Jewish law) were the products of human legislation, reflecting various social conditions of the time. This means that *halachah* [Jewish law] is not binding today.

In recent times, Conservative Judaism has tried to find a third way in which revelation could be taken seriously but not literally. Most thinkers have relied on the thinking of Franz Rosenzweig. Rosenzweig argued that revelation is not the transmittal of concrete directives. Revelation means that man and God have met each other. Revelation means the self-uncovering of the Divine in relation to man. It is the transmission to man of God's love and concern. It is a miracle that God does reveal Himself to man. . . .

Scripture and its interpretation in the rabbinic writings are not literally revelation. They are the human recordings of the experience of revelation. Therefore, Scripture is both divine and human. The words contain the divine initiative and the human response to it. In each word the two—the divine and the human—are joined and cannot be separated. Therefore, Scripture and Talmud are infinitely precious—for through them the divine is revealed. Scripture and Talmud contain the human response—and therefore are not infallible. . . . The history of Judaism is the history of the interpretation of revelation. In [Abraham] Heschel's striking sentence: "Judaism is a minimum of revelation and a maximum of interpretation." . . .

This, of course, means that there will be change and modification. It is true, for example, that God countenanced slavery, as is evident in Scripture, when there was no possibility of abolishing the institution. The aim of Jewish law was to humanize the institution until it could be abolished. Though God may have wanted slavery in antiquity, He certainly does not want it now. It is true that God once wanted the law of an "eye for an eye" to be applied literally. He certainly does not want it now. It is possible that God once wanted women to limit themselves to their roles as princesses whose grandeur consisted of being concealed. He probably does not want it now. Total subjectivity is avoided because of the presence of the community and because of the character of Catholic [the practicing community] Israel. The concrete laws are not to be viewed as if they were Platonic Ideas eternally residing in the world of Forms. They are dynamic concepts— subject to the dynamic voice of God, which encounters us anew at all times.

SOURCE: Seymour Siegel, ed., *Conservative Judaism and Jewish Law*. New York: The Rabbinical Assembly, 1977, pp. xx–xxi

REFORM

The Reform branch of Judaism developed in the nineteenth century, beginning in Germany, as the strongest movement to adapt to modern times. Reform Jews are more assimilated into their surrounding culture than Orthodox or Conservative. While honoring the Torah and much Jewish tradition, they seek to reconcile religion with science. Torah is interpreted using historical criticism, which sees many texts as humanly influenced by ancient times, and thus subject to being neglected or changed. They do not emphasize learning Hebrew or Yiddish and using them in worship services. They may or may not practice kosher dietary rules. While supporting Israel as a nation, Reform Jews respect voices of dissent about Israel's politics. They have been the leaders in opening doors for women in the synagogue and home, encouraging higher education, careers, equality with men, and ordination as rabbis. In 1972 the first American Jewish woman to be ordained was Sally Preisand, a Reform Jew. Members of this branch of Judaism are often active in social reform movements, as may be seen in Michael Lerner's *Tikkun* magazine.

The following Declaration of Principles, written by a group of American Reform rabbis by 1885 as part of the "Pittsburg Platform," represents the approach of Reform Judaism.

Declaration of Principles   from the "Pittsburg Platform"

1   We recognize in every religion an attempt to grasp the Infinite, and in every mode, source or book of revelation held sacred in any religious system the consciousness of the indwelling of God in man. We hold that Judaism presents the highest conception of the God-idea as taught in our Holy Scriptures and developed and spiritualized by the Jewish teachers, in accordance with the moral and philosophical progress of their respective ages. We maintain that Judaism preserved and defended midst continual struggles and trials and under enforced isolation, this God-idea as the central religious truth for the human race.

2   We recognize in the Bible the record of the consecration of the Jewish people to its mission as the priest of the one God, and value it as the most potent instrument of religious and moral instruction. We hold that the modern discoveries of scientific researches in the domain of nature and history are not antagonistic to the doctrines of Judaism, the Bible

reflecting the primitive ideas of its own age, and at times clothing its conception of divine Providence and Justice dealing with men in miraculous narratives.

3   We recognize in the Mosaic legislation a system of training the Jewish people for its mission during its national life in Palestine, and today we accept as binding only its moral laws, and maintain only such ceremonies as elevate and sanctify our lives, but reject all such as are not adapted to the views and habits of modern civilization.

4   We hold that all such Mosaic and rabbinical laws as regulate diet, priestly purity, and dress originated in ages and under the influence of ideas entirely foreign to our present mental and spiritual state. They fail to impress the modern Jew with a spirit of priestly holiness; their observance in our days is apt rather to obstruct than to further modern spiritual elevation.

5   We recognize, in the modern era of universal culture of heart and intellect, the approaching of the realization of Israel's great Messianic hope for the establishment of the kingdom of truth, justice, and peace among all men. We consider ourselves no longer a nation, but a religious community, and therefore expect neither a return to Palestine, nor a sacrificial worship under the sons of Aaron, nor the restoration of any of the laws concerning the Jewish state.

6   We recognize in Judaism a progressive religion, ever striving to be in accord with the postulates of reason. We are convinced of the utmost necessity of preserving the historical identity with our great past. Christianity and Islam, being daughter religions of Judaism, we appreciate their providential mission, to aid in the spreading of monotheistic and moral truth. We acknowledge that the spirit of broad humanity of our age is our ally in the fulfillment of our mission, and therefore we extend the hand of fellowship to all who cooperate with us in the establishment of the reign of truth and righteousness among men.

7   We reassert the doctrine of Judaism that the soul is immortal, grounding the belief on the divine nature of human spirit, which forever finds bliss in righteousness and misery in wickedness. We reject as ideas not rooted in Judaism, the beliefs both in bodily resurrection and in Gehenna and Eden (Hell and Paradise) as abodes for everlasting punishment and reward.

8   In full accordance with the spirit of the Mosaic legislation, which strives to regulate the relations between rich and poor, we deem it our duty to participate in the great task of modern times, to solve, on the basis of justice and righteousness, the problems presented by the contrasts and evils of the present organization of society.

SOURCE: <http://www.ucalgary.ca/~elsegal/363_Transp/PittsburgPlatform.html>

Living Judaism

Contemporary Jewish experience has been haunted by the question of how to respond to the Nazi **Holocaust**; it has been challenged by the rise of new women rabbis; and it has been enlivened by a renewal movement.

Surviving Auschwitz by Viktor Frankl

The systematic destruction of Jews and others from 1933 to 1945 by the Nazis—the Holocaust—killed six million Jews in concentration camps such as Auschwitz, Poland. Those lost are remembered annually on Holocaust Remembrance Day. A range of theological responses has followed from this immense tragedy. Some, like Richard Rubenstein, have declared God dead. Others have not lost their faith. One is the psychologist Viktor Frankl. While surviving Auschwitz, he observed that survivors of the death camps had to have a meaning, and he discovered four meanings that he found helped them make it: Love—even if his wife were dead, Frankl found solace in the love they shared; Art—the beauty of a sunset, flowers, music, prisoners' cabarets and jokes expressed their hope; Freedom—to choose one's response to suffering; and Faith in eternal life. He was moved by what one woman said about this just before she died.

1   "Love goes very far beyond the physical person of the beloved. It finds its deepest meaning in his spiritual being, his inner self; whether or not he is actually present, whether or not he is still alive at all, ceases somehow to be of importance . . . love is as strong as death."

2   "As the inner life of the prisoner became more intense, he also experienced the beauty of art and nature as never before . . . we were carried away by nature's beauty, which we had missed for so long."

3   "Man can preserve a vestige of spiritual freedom, of independence of mind, even in such terrible conditions of psychic and physical stress. We who lived in concentration camps can remember the men who walked through the huts comforting others, giving away their last piece of bread."

4   "This young woman knew that she would die in the next few days. But when I talked to her she was cheerful in spite of this knowledge. 'I am grateful that fate has hit me so hard,' she told me. 'In my former life I was spoiled and did not take spiritual accomplishments seriously.' Pointing through the window of the hut, she said, 'This tree here is the only friend I have in my loneliness.' Through that window she could see just one branch of a chestnut tree, and on the branch were two blossoms. 'I often talk to this tree,' she said to me. I was startled and didn't quite know how to take her words. Was she delirious? Did she have occasional hallucinations? Anxiously I asked her if the tree replied. 'Yes.' What did it say to her? She answered, 'It said to me, "I am here—I am life, eternal life."'"

SOURCE: Viktor Frankl, *Man's Search for Meaning*. Boston: Beacon, 1946/New York: Washington Square Press, 1994, pp. 58–90

Women in Jewish Life   by Ellen M. Umansky

The changing roles of Jewish women are described by Ellen M. Umansky of Fairfield University, Connecticut. Increasing numbers of educated Jewish women, women's rights, and persuasive feminist texts are dissolving many of the limits of ancient traditions.

The past hundred years have witnessed a tremendous change in the role of women in Jewish communal life. Up through the early nineteenth century, with generations of rabbis developing expectations and norms for Judaism as a way of life, women's religious roles were largely relegated to the home. To the rabbis, the destruction of the Second Temple in 70 CE led to the creation of two religious centers: the synagogue, which was largely the domain of men; and the home, largely the domain of women.

In addition to following most of the commandments encumbent upon men, women were seen as having three special commandments: baking *challah*, the braided loaf eaten on the Sabbath and holidays, in a ritually prescribed way; lighting the Sabbath candles (thereby ushering in the Sabbath); and following the laws of ritual purity, biblically based laws that regulated the times during which sexual relations between married couples were permitted. Today, many Jewish women continue to bake (or buy) ritually prepared *challah* and light candles on Friday night. Only the traditionally observant follow the laws of *niddah* (ritual purity). From the contemporary perspective of most non-Orthodox Jewish women, the laws of *niddah* are antiquated and thus rarely, if ever, followed. To Orthodox women, however, these laws, whether literally mandated by God or not, remain *halakhically* (legally) binding upon them. Indeed, some traditionally observant women today see these laws, which include immersing oneself in a ritual bath or *mikvah* after a set number of days following one's menstrual period or giving birth to a child, as a source of power. It is only when a woman has immersed herself in a *mikvah* that she and her husband can resume having sexual intercourse, thus enabling her husband to fulfill the obligation to be "fruitful and multiply."

Prior to the seventeenth century and the advent of modernity, Jewish women received a minimal religious education because of their exemption from the obligation to study. Consequently the Hebrew prayer book was inaccessible to most of them. While there were Jewish women throughout the Middle Ages who attended synagogue services, following the Hebrew or, by the sixteenth century, reading prayers in the vernacular written especially for them, most Jewish women cultivated a more private sense of spirituality. Those who became scholars were few and far between, always viewed as exceptions that proved the rule. Indeed, recognizing the fact that much of Jewish religious life is home-centered and well aware of the extent to which the continuation of Jewish life depended on them, it seems that prior to the nineteenth century, most Jewish women thought of their religious world as one which primarily, though again, not exclusively, centered around and within the home.

Since the end of the nineteenth century, and even more so, during the second half of the twentieth, women's roles in Jewish life have greatly expanded. In Europe and the United States, these changes have reflected the leadership roles assumed by women in many Protestant denominations and new nineteenth-century religious movements, including Christian Science, the Salvation Army, and the Seventh Day Adventists, founded, or co-founded by women; the creation of liberal or progressive Jewish religious movements, particularly Reform Judaism, founded in Germany in the early nineteenth century; Conservative Judaism, founded in the United States in 1886 with the opening of the Jewish Theological Seminary of America; and Reconstructionist Judaism, founded in New York in 1922 by Conservative rabbi Mordecai Kaplan. The expansion of Jewish women's roles within the synagogue and Jewish communal life have also been influenced by the second wave of American feminism, which began in the late 1960s, and has greatly, and perhaps irrevocably, changed women's expectations of what they want to achieve, and increasingly have achieved, not just in the United States but throughout the modern, largely Western world.

The first woman ordained as a rabbi was Regina Jonas. She was privately granted a rabbinic diploma in 1935 by Reform rabbi Max Dienemann of Offenbach, Germany, after the Talmud professor empowered with ordaining her from the Berlin Academy for the Scientific Study of Judaism, where she had studied, refused to do so on the grounds that she was a woman. Yet it wasn't until 1972 that Sally Preisand became the first woman ordained from a rabbinical seminary. Ordained in Cincinnati, Ohio, from the Reform movement's Hebrew Union College—Jewish Institute of Religion, she became the first of hundreds of women who have since been ordained in the United States, England, and Israel. While in 1985 the historic ordination of Amy Eilberg from the Jewish Theological Seminary of America led to a split in the Conservative movement, with some more traditional members arguing that women's ordination could not be justified within the framework of *halakhah* (rabbinic law), these traditionalists have since left the Conservative movement, which has increasingly followed Reform in investing women as cantors [Jews trained to lead the prayer service, noted for their musical and chanting skills], and, as in all of Judaism's more liberal branches, and some more traditionally religious congregations, encouraging them to serve as officers of congregations, including assuming the role of synagogue president.

For the past few decades, in Reform, Conservative, and Reconstructionist synagogues in the United States and in liberal synagogues throughout the world, women have been counted in the *minyan* (the quorum necessary for public worship), called to the Torah to recite the blessings before and after the Torah reading, and invited to read from the Torah itself. Women's increased educational and religious opportunities within these movements, including being called to the Torah as a **Bat Mitzvah**, at the age of 12 or 13 or, especially in the United States, as an adult *Bat Mitzvah* following a specific period of study, have helped facilitate such participation. Within many Conservative and Reconstructionist synagogues, and some Reform congregations as well, women have begun to wear *kippot* (skull caps) and *tallitot* (prayer shawls), traditionally worn only by Jewish men, and some women have begun to lay *tefillin* (leather straps wrapped around the arm, hand, and forehead during morning prayer) as well. These innovations have been influenced by Jewish feminism, which first arose in the United States as a short-lived national organization and has since led to the creation of smaller interest-based feminist groups that have called for, and in many cases helped institute, change.

Particularly noteworthy have been the creation of gender inclusive prayers in liberal congregations throughout the world, in which God is addressed "You" rather than "He" and invoked not only as the God of "our [biblical] fathers, Abraham, Isaac, and Jacob," but of "our [biblical] mothers, Sarah, Rebekah, Leah, and Rachel" as well. Equally significant have been the creation in all branches of Judaism of naming ceremonies for girls, frequently called a "Simchat Bat" (rejoicing in the birth of a daughter) or a "B'rit B'not" (covenant of the daughters, paralleling the term "B'rit Milah" which refers to the covenant of ritual circumcision of boys), and of *Rosh Chodesh* (New Moon) rituals created by and for women.

For several decades, women's Passover *seders* (ritual meals) have become communal gatherings of women that relive slavery and liberation through the lens of women's experiences. At these and family and synagogue *sedarim*, an increasing number of Jews, especially in the United States and Canada, have begun to place a "Miriam's Cup" of water on the table, along with the traditional Elijah's Cup of wine. Some have also begun to place an orange on the *seder* plate. According to Reconstructionist rabbi Rebecca Alpert, legend has it that this was instigated in the early 1980s by a group of Jewish feminists in response to a Hasidic (ultra-Orthodox) rabbi who declared that there was as much room for lesbians in Judaism as there was for leavened bread on the *seder* table. That is, no place at all. Initially these feminists placed bread on the table in protest. Moved by the ritual but uncomfortable with the bread, they soon substituted an orange which, like bread, traditionally has no place on a *seder* table but which, unlike bread, can be eaten during Passover. By the early 1990s, the story was retold as one in which a Jewish feminist was rebuked by a man who said that women rabbis had as much of a role in Judaism (or alternately, that women had as much of a place on the *bimah*, the stage or platform from which synagogue services are led) as oranges on a *seder* plate (Rebecca Alpert, *Like Bread on the Seder Plate*, pp. 2–3). Since then, many feminists have added an orange to their *seder* plates, to emphasize women's place in every facet of Jewish life.

Women's opportunities for full participation in the synagogue and greater roles of religious and communal leadership remain more limited in Orthodox

Judaism. Nonetheless, a small number of modern Orthodox synagogues in the United States have begun to hire women as teachers and leaders at women-only services and, alluded to previously, some modern Orthodox women are assuming such roles of public leadership as officers of synagogues and heads of communal organizations. The creation of the Jewish Orthodox Feminist Alliance (JOFA) in 1999, with the well-known writer and lecturer Blu Greenberg as its first president, and the publication of the quarterly *JOFA Journal*, have provided forums for Orthodox feminists throughout the world to voice concerns and suggested courses of action. By 2006, JOFA began to compile information about practices in Orthodox synagogues related to women. Firmly believing that women's equality and, thus, inclusivity, are overarching Jewish values, it hopes to serve as a resource for those seeking to join a synagogue and a reference for Orthodox congregations considering innovations that would create a more "welcoming environment for women in *shul* [synagogue]" (*JOFA Journal*, Summer 2006, p. 21).

Religious and political activism have come together in the actions of Women of the Wall, a group of Jewish women who since 1988 have gathered together in prayer at the *Kotel* (Western Wall) in Jerusalem on *Rosh Chodesh* and other holidays. Long facing opposition from Orthodox Israeli men who strenuously object to women's praying as a group at the wall, wearing *tallitot*, and holding and reading from the Torah, these women have faced several ongoing legal battles, arguing before the Israeli Supreme Court with varying degrees of success for women's religious rights at the *Kotel*.

Other Jewish women's groups, including synagogue auxiliary organizations throughout the world and such independent national or international organizations as the National Council of Jewish Women (in the United States), Hadassah, and Jewish Women International (formerly known as B'nai Brith women), have long fought for women's political, religious, and economic rights. Women continue to take an active role in Jewish philanthropy, through combined efforts with men and through separate women's divisions of such organizations as the United Jewish Appeal, the largest Jewish fund raising agency in the world. Some argue that a glass ceiling still exists for women at the top levels of Jewish organizational life. Yet if such a ceiling exists, it is on the verge of collapsing. Through the ongoing efforts of women and their male supporters and the growing impact of feminism on Judaism, equal access to roles within congregational and communal life, and with it the transformation of those roles by women, are increasingly becoming a reality, for as I have written elsewhere (see Arvind Sharma and Katherine Young, *Feminism and World Religions*, p. 208), "despite the fact that increasing opportunities and expectations undoubtedly create new internal and external conflicts, having tasted the fruit of the tree of knowledge, Jewish women are discovering that there is no road back to Eden."

SOURCE: Original article for this book by Ellen M. Umansky, 2006

Ten Commitments, Not Commandments

by Michael Lerner

The Ten
Commandments

Rabbi Michael Lerner is the editor of *Tikkun* magazine. *Tikkun* means "repair" in the cosmic sense. A philosopher and psychologist, he is an outspoken leader of a liberal Jewish renewal movement in our times. Advocating a sweeping renewal of Judaism rooted in Torah, he calls for a strong social conscience, a genuine sense of transcendence, and a vital Jewish community. He urges release from the silent pain inherited from the Holocaust and from a sense of victimization. He stands for liberation from sexism, homophobia, and ecological harm. Here he writes an interpretation of the traditional Ten Commandments in the biblical book of Exodus 20, generalizing so they make sense today.

Many of us find the notion of "commandments" oppressive and hierarchical. Yet we know that a community cannot be built on the principle of only doing what feels right at the moment—it requires a sense of responsibility to each other. So, we encourage our community to take on the following ten commitments, based roughly on a rereading of the Torah's ten commandments (and incorporating the framework and many specific ideas articulated by Rami Shapiro in his book *Minyan*).

Ten Commitments

1   YHVH, the Power of Transformation and Healing, is the Ultimate Reality of the Universe and the Source of Transcendent Unity   Aware of the suffering caused by not acknowledging the ultimate Unity of All Being, I vow to recognize every human being as a manifestation of the Divine and to spend more time each day in awe and wonder at the grandeur of Creation.

Aware of the suffering that is caused when we unconsciously pass on to others the pain, cruelty, depression, and despair that has been inflicted upon us, I vow to become conscious and then act upon all the possibilities for healing and transforming my own life and being involved in healing and transforming the larger world.

2   Idolatry   Aware of the suffering caused by taking existing social realities, economic security, ideologies, religious beliefs, national commitments, or the gratification of our current desires as the highest value, I vow to recognize only God as the ultimate, and to look at the universe and each part of my life as an evolving part of a larger Totality whose ultimate worth is measured by how close it brings us to God and to love of each other. To stay in touch with this reality, I vow to meditate each day for at least ten minutes and to contemplate the totality of the universe and my humble place in it.

3   Do not take God in Vain   Aware of the suffering caused by religious or spiritual fanaticism, I vow to be respectful of all religious traditions which preach love and respect for the Other, and to recognize that there are many possible paths to God. I vow to acknowledge that we as Jews are not better than others and our path is only one of the many ways that people have heard God's voice. I vow to remain aware of the distortions in our own traditions, and the ways that I myself necessarily bring my own limitations to every encounter with the Divine. So I will practice spiritual humility. Yet I will enthusiastically advocate for what I find compelling in the Jewish tradition and encourage others to explore that which has moved me.

4   *Observe the Sabbath*   Aware of the suffering produced by excessive focus on "making it" and obtaining material satisfactions, I vow to regularly observe Shabbat as a day in which I focus on celebrating the world rather than trying to control it or maximize my own advantage within it. I will build Shabbat with the Beyt Tikkun[3] community and enjoy loving connection with others. I will use some Shabbat time to renew my commitment to social justice and healing. I will also set aside significant amounts of time for inner spiritual development, personal renewal, reflection, and pleasure.

5   *Honor your Mother and Father*   Aware of the suffering caused by aging, disease, and death, I vow to provide care and support for my parents. Aware that every parent has faults and has inflicted pain on their children, I vow to forgive my parents and to allow myself to see them as human beings with the same kinds of limitations as every other human being on the planet. And I vow to remember the moments of kindness and nurturance, and to let them play a larger role in my memory as I develop a sense of compassion for them and for myself.

6   *Do not Murder*   Aware of the suffering caused by wars, environmental irresponsibility, and eruptions of violence, I vow to recognize the sanctity of life and not to passively participate in social practices that are destructive of the lives of others. I will resist the perpetrators of violence and oppression of others, the poisoners of our environment, and those who demean others or encourage acts of violence. Aware that much violence is the irrational and often self-destructive response to the absence of love and caring, I vow to show more loving and caring energy to everyone around me, to take the time to know others more deeply, and to struggle for a world which provides everyone with recognition and spiritual nourishment.

7   *Do not Engage in Sexual Exploitation*   Aware of the suffering caused when people break their commitments of sexual loyalty to each other, and the suffering caused by using other people for our own sexual purposes, I vow to keep my commitments and to be fully honest and open in my sexual dealings with others, avoiding deceit or manipulation to obtain my own ends. I will rejoice in my body and the bodies of others, will treat them as embodiments of Divine energy, and will seek to enhance my own pleasure and the pleasure of others around me, joyfully celebrating sex as an opportunity for encounter with the holy. I will do all I can to prevent sexual

---

3 Beyt Tikkun—the Tikkun school of interpretation of Jewish tradition.

abuse in adults and children, the spreading of sexually transmitted diseases, and the misuse of sexuality to further domination or control of others. I will respect the diversity of non-exploitative sexual expression and lifestyles and will not seek to impose sexual orthodoxies on others.

8   *Do not Steal*   Aware of the suffering caused by an unjust distribution of the world's resources, exploitation, and theft, I vow to practice generosity, to share what I have, and to not keep anything that should belong to others while working for a wise use of the goods and services that are available. I will not [hoard] what I have, and especially will not [hoard] love. I will support a fairer redistribution of the wealth of the planet so that everyone has adequate material well-being, recognizing that contemporary global inequalities in wealth are often the resultant of colonialism, genocide, slavery, theft, and the imposition of monetary and trade policies by the powerful on the powerless. In the meantime, I will do my best to support the homeless and others who are in need.

Aware that others sometimes contribute much energy to keeping this community functioning, I will give time and energy to the tasks of building the Beyt Tikkun community, and, when possible, will donate generously of my financial resources and my talents and time.

9   *Do not Lie*   Aware of the suffering caused by wrongful speech, I vow to cultivate a practice of holy speech in which my words are directed to increasing the love and caring in the world. I vow to avoid words that are misleading or manipulative, and avoid spreading stories that I do not know to be true, or which might cause unnecessary divisiveness or harm, and instead will use my speech to increase harmony, social justice, kindness, hopefulness, trust, and solidarity. I will be generous in praise and support for others. To heighten my awareness of this commitment, I will dedicate one day a week to full and total holiness of words, refraining from any speech that day which does not hallow God's name or bring joy to others.

10   *Do not Covet*   Aware of the suffering caused by excessive consumption of the world's resources, I vow to rejoice in what I have and to live a life of ethical consumption governed by a recognition that the world's resources are already strained and by a desire to promote ecological sustainability and material modesty. I vow to see the success of others as an inspiration rather than as detracting from my own sufficiency and to cultivate in myself and others the sense that I have enough and that I am enough and that there is enough for everyone.

SOURCE: *Tikkun* magazine, October 11, 2005
< http://www.tikkun.org>

GLOSSARY

Bar Mitzvah (son of the Commandment) An initiation for boys about 13 who have studied Judaism and ritually become responsible Jewish adult men.

Bat Mitzvah (daughter of the Commandment) An initiation for girls about 13 who have studied Judaism and ritually become responsible Jewish adult women, in some progressive congregations.

Canon The official list of books with authority in a religion, either because they are believed to be inspired or revealed, or have been so designated.

Conservative A moderate branch of modern Judaism, between Orthodox and Reform traditions.

Covenant A sacred contract between God and Israel, stipulating obligations such as circumcision and obedience to Torah on the part of Hebrews, and the promise of a great nation in Israel on the part of God.

Deuteronomic One of four strands of the Pentateuch, primarily Deuteronomy.

Diaspora (dispersion, exile) Jewish communities outside the land of Israel.

Elohist One of four strands of the Pentateuch, using "Elohim" to name God.

Haggadah The order of service for the Jewish Passover Seder.

Halakhah The written and oral Jewish Law.

Holocaust The destruction of many Jews in Germany, Poland, and other European countries by the Nazis before and during World War II.

Kabbalah The Jewish mystical tradition.

Messiah (the anointed one) Descendant of King David expected to restore the kingdom promised by the prophets; blended with apocalyptic expectations.

Midrash Interpretations of scriptures, the basis of much of the Talmud.

Mishnah A legal code based on the Torah, in oral traditions from around 200 CE.

Monotheism Belief in one supreme god only, in contrast with polytheism.

Orthodox The branch of a religious tradition that seeks to practice the original religion in its strictest form, in contrast with reform movements; a Jewish group, strong in Israel since 1948, that strives to preserve the ancient practices.

Pentateuch The first five books of the Hebrew Bible, also called "Torah": Genesis, Exodus, Leviticus, Numbers, and Deuteronomy.

Priestly One of four strands of the Pentateuch, written late, with ritual concerns.

Prophets Oracular seers in many religions, believed to channel divine messages; in Judaism, a group of such seers recorded in books such as Isaiah, Jeremiah, Ezekiel, and Daniel, who emphasized social injustices and promised the Messiah.

Rabbi (teacher) The Jewish leader of a congregation; the local synagogue leaders who replaced the priests of the old central Temple in Jerusalem.

Reform Progressive movement from the 19th century in Europe and the United States; accepts moral laws, rejects ritual laws inconsistent with modernity.

Synagogue A local center of worship, community and teaching; a focus that replaced the central Temple in Jerusalem during the Diaspora.

Talmud Body of commentary and discussion of interpretations of tradition.

Tanakh The complete Jewish scriptures: Torah, Prophets, and Writings.

Torah (teaching) Variously used to mean the first five scrolls of the Hebrew Scriptures (Pentateuch), all the Laws of Israel, or oral traditional law.

Yahwist (or Jahwist) One of four strands of the Pentateuch, using "YaHWeH" to name God.

HOLY DAYS

Shabbat (Sabbath) The seventh day of the week, when Jews abstain from work. It begins after dark on Friday. Synagogue services are held Friday nights and Saturdays.

Rosh Hashanah (New Year) Around the fall equinox, the spiritual year begins with the blowing of a ram's horn and prayers.

Yom Kippur (Day of Atonement) To renew God's covenant, a time of inner spiritual cleansing, forgiveness, and reconciliation.

Sukkot (Feast of Tabernacles) A fall harvest festival.

Hanukkah (Feast of Dedication) Around the winter solstice, eight candles are lit on a candle-holder (menorah), one each night, to commemorate two miracles.

Purim (Feast of Lots) A joyous remembrance of Esther and Mordecai's saving of Jews from destruction by Persians.

Pesach (Passover) The spring celebration of the liberation of Jews from Egyptian slavery by Moses; opens with an instructional, symbolic Seder meal.

Yom Hashoah Holocaust memorial day, honoring the victims.

Yom Haatzuma-ut Israel Independence Day, celebrating May 14, 1948, when Israel again became a sovereign state, after centuries of the Diaspora.

HISTORICAL OUTLINE

c. 1900–1700 BCE?—Abraham, the first patriarch

c. 1250 BCE—Exodus from Egypt led by Moses through Sinai to the promised land

c. 1010–970 BCE—King David unites northern and southern Israel in Jerusalem

c. 950 BCE—First Temple built by David's son, King Solomon

c. 750–250 BCE—age of classical prophets: Isaiah, Jeremiah, Ezekiel, and 12 minor prophets

722 BCE—fall of Northern Kingdom (Israel) to Assyria

586 BCE—fall of Southern Kingdom (Judah) to Babylon; First Temple destroyed; Jews taken into slavery

c. 535 BCE—exiles return from Babylon and rebuild Temple; Ezra and Nehemiah

168 BCE—successful Maccabean Revolt against Hellenistic rulers

70 CE—Romans destroy Jerusalem and Second Temple; end of sacrifices and priests at Temple, beginning of Diaspora and rabbinic leadership in synagogues

c. 90 CE—canon of Tanakh agreed by consensus

c. 200 CE—compilation of Mishnah

c. 1135–1204—Maimonides adapts Jewish theology to philosophy

c. 1200–1300—Zohar appears in Spain, contributes to Kabbalah

1470—Spanish Inquisition begins to purge Muslims, Jews, other non-Christians

1492—mass expulsion of Jews from Spain

c. 1555—ghettos built in Italy and Germany

c. 1700–60—Baal-Shem Tov in Eastern Europe begins Hasidism

1933–1945—Nazi Holocaust, reaching its climax during World War II

1948—state of Israel re-established after British rule

1950—Law of Return allows Jews to emigrate to Israel; beginning of rebuilding of culture, industry, and agriculture

1967–70—conflicts with Palestinians, Jordan, and Egypt erupt into war

1972—ordination of first Jewish (Reform) woman in U.S., Sally Preisand

1982—United Nations supports independent Palestinian state

1994—Vatican and Israel establish first diplomatic relations

2006—conflict between Lebanese Hezbollah and Israel

REVIEW QUESTIONS

1   What is a Jewish covenant? Describe three major covenants.
2   What major themes did Maimonides see as central to Jewish faith?
3   What does the Baal-Shem Tov teach about life after death?

DISCUSSION QUESTIONS

1   What are the two different creation stories in Genesis? Discuss major themes, different sequences of events (especially plant/human creation), mastery of nature, and gender issues. What do these differences in creation accounts tell us about how to interpret the Torah?
2   What are the important differences among the three major branches of contemporary Judaism? Which make most sense to you and why?
3   Compare the article "Women in Jewish Life" by Ellen Umanksy in this chapter with the article "The Image of God as Dominating Other" by Judith Plaskow in chapter 1. Do they agree with each other or differ markedly? How? What do you think?

INFORMATION RESOURCES

Bernstein, Ellen, ed. *Ecology and the Jewish Spirit*. Woodstock, VT: Jewish Lights Publishing, 1998.

Cohen, Arthur, and **Paul Mendes-Flohr**, eds. *Contemporary Jewish Religious Thought*. New York: Free Press/Macmillan, 1987.

Commentary Magazine
<http://www.Commentarymagazine.com>

Fackenheim, Emil. *God's Presence in History*. New York: New York University Press, 1970.

Gillman, Neil. *The Death of Death*. Woodstock, VT: Jewish Lights Publishing, 1997.

Glatzer, Nahum. *Hammer on the Rock: A Short Midrash Reader*, trans. Jacob Sloan. New York: Schocken, 1948/1962.

Heschel, Abraham. *The Prophets*. New York: Harper and Row, 1962.

Holz, Barry. *The Schocken Guide to Jewish Books*. New York: Schocken, 1992.

Janowitz, Naomi, and **Maggie Wenig**. "Sabbath Prayers for Women," in Carol Christ and Judith Plaskow, *Womanspirit Rising*. San Francisco: Harper and Row, 1992.

Jewish Film Archive Online
<http://www.Jewishfilm.com>

Jewish Links
<http://www.clas.ufl.edu/users/comenetz/jewishlinks.html>

Jewish Virtual Library
<http://www.jewishvirtuallibrary.org>

Jewishnet
<http://www.Jewishnet.net>

Kaplan, Mordecai. *Judaism as a Civilization: Toward a Reconstruction of Jewish Life*. Philadelphia, PA: Jewish Publication Society, 1934/1994.

Landman, Isaac, ed. *Encyclopedia Judaica*. 16 vols. New York: Macmillan, 1972.

Neusner, Jacob. *An Introduction to Judaism*. Louisville, KY: Westminster/John Knox Press, 1991.

Onishi, Norimitsu. "Reading Torah Women's Group Tests Tradition," in *The New York Times*, Feb. 16, 1997, Metro Section, pp. 43, 49.

Rubenstein, Richard L. *After Auschwitz*. Indianapolis, IN: Bobbs-Merrill, 1966.

Scholem, Gershom. *Major Trends in Jewish Mysticism*. New York: Schocken, 1946.

Silverman, Lou H., *et al.* "Judaism," in *Encyclopedia Britannica*. Vol. 22, pp. 379–456. London, 1997.

Swartz, Michael, *et al.* "Judaism," in *Encyclopedia of Religion,* ed. Lindsay Jones. 2nd ed. Vol. 7, pp. 4968–5022. New York: Macmillan, 2005.

CHAPTER 9

CHRISTIANITY

Christianity is such a widespread and influential religion that, around the world, dates are now commonly measured from the approximate birth date of Jesus, probably a few years before 1 CE. According to Christian tradition, he was born in Israel to a poor family under lowly circumstances, and his spiritual help was often offered to those who were neglected or rejected by society. When he began preaching openly at the age of about 30, he was sharply critical of religious hypocrisy. Himself a Jew, he upheld the spirit of the teachings of the Torah while pointing out their abuses by religious authorities. To his followers, however, he was not just a reformer. He was known as a miracle worker; many who came to him were healed. Some became convinced that Jesus was the Messiah for whom they had long been waiting.

Jesus spoke often about the kingdom of God, but it seems that he was referring to a spiritual rather than a political realm. Nonetheless, the religious authorities and the Roman rulers of the region ultimately had him crucified in Jerusalem. Three days later, according to varied accounts in the Bible, he was miraculously resurrected and appeared again in the flesh to his closest disciples, charging them to carry on his work. They, too, became great healers and preachers, despite persecution. One of the persecutors was reportedly transformed by a vision of Jesus, becoming the Apostle Paul. His extensive travels and writings were extremely influential in shaping Christianity as an organized religion and theology.

According to the biblical accounts, Jesus brought a message of love for all, especially the weak. He urged radical inner transformation and promised that God was forgiving to sinners who sincerely repented and turned toward him. Paul's teachings brought the additional beliefs that Jesus was the incarnation of God and that Jesus' death offered atonement for the sins of a believer of any nationality. With this understanding, many Christians feel that, while other religions may have their saints and prophets, only Jesus offers the way to receiving God's grace.

Christian belief is not unitary; on the contrary, those professing belief in Jesus have over time separated into some 21,000 different denominations in three major divisions: **Eastern Orthodox**, **Roman Catholic**, and **Protestant**. Today there are lively conservative and liberal movements throughout Christianity.

Jesus the Christ

Stories of the life and teachings of Jesus and their theological interpretation appear in the New Testament of the Christian Bible, written in Greek and some Aramaic (spoken by Jesus). The Christian Bible also includes a version of the Hebrew Bible, or Tanakh, labeled as the Old Testament. The New Testament begins with the four Gospels—Matthew, Mark, Luke, and John—and also includes material on the activities of Jesus' followers after his death, including letters from Paul to the newly developed Christian congregations.

The first three Gospels were written down between 70 and 90 CE. Mark is the oldest, and they all show evidence of earlier sources, oral and written. They are similar, and are thus called the **Synoptic** Gospels. But they also differ: Matthew has a genealogy of Jesus' family line, Mark has no appearances of the resurrected Christ, and Luke has a long birth narrative. The fourth Gospel, John (c. 95 CE), shows a more mystical and Greek influence (the Light, the Word). Paul's letters, or Epistles, were written between 48 and 64 CE, before the Gospels took their present form. Other New Testament books were written down as late as 150 CE. The following selections are taken from a mid-twentieth-century translation of the Bible, the **RSV**.

The Annunciation   from Luke

In the sixth month the angel Gabriel was sent from God to a city of Galilee named Nazareth, to a virgin betrothed to a man whose name was Joseph, of the house of David; and the virgin's name was Mary. And he came to her and said, "Hail, O favored one, the Lord is with you!" But she was greatly troubled at the saying, and considered in her mind what sort of greeting this might be. And the angel said to her, "Do not be afraid, Mary, for you have found favor with God. And behold, you will conceive in your womb and bear a son, and you shall call his name Jesus.

> He will be great, and will be called the Son of the Most High;
> and the Lord God will give to him the throne of his father David,
> and he will reign over the house of Jacob for ever;
> and of his kingdom there will be no end."

And Mary said to the angel, "How shall this be, since I have no husband?" And the angel said to her,

> "The Holy Spirit will come upon you,
> and the power of the Most High will overshadow you;
> therefore the child to be born will be called holy,
> the Son of God." (Luke 1:26–35)

The Magnificat   from Luke

And Mary said, "My soul magnifies the Lord, and my spirit rejoices in God my Savior, for he has regarded the low estate of his handmaiden. For behold, henceforth all generations will call me blessed; for he who is mighty has done great things for me, and holy is his name. And his mercy is on those who fear him from generation to generation. He has shown strength with his arm, he has scattered the proud in the imagination of their hearts, he has put down the mighty from their thrones, and exalted those of low degree; he has filled the hungry with good things, and the rich he has sent empty away. He has helped his servant Israel, in remembrance of his mercy, as he spoke to our fathers, to Abraham and to his posterity for ever." (Luke 1:46–55)

Jesus' Birth from Luke

Jesus' Birth

In those days a decree went out from Caesar Augustus that all the world should be enrolled. This was the first enrollment, when Quirinius was governor of Syria. And all went to be enrolled, each to his own city. And Joseph also went up from Galilee, from the city of Nazareth, to Judea, to the city of David, which is called Bethlehem, because he was of the house and lineage of David, to be enrolled with Mary, his betrothed, who was with child. And while they were there, the time came for her to be delivered. And she gave birth to her first-born son and wrapped him in swaddling cloths, and laid him in a manger, because there was no place for them in the inn.

And in that region there were shepherds out in the field, keeping watch over their flock by night. And an angel of the Lord appeared to them, and the glory of the Lord shone around them, and they were filled with fear. And the angel said to them, "Be not afraid; for behold, I bring you good news of a great joy which will come to all the people; for to you is born this day in the city of David a **Savior**, who is Christ the Lord. And this will be a sign for you: you will find a babe wrapped in swaddling cloths and lying in a manger." And suddenly there was with the angel a multitude of the heavenly host praising God and saying, "Glory to God in the highest, and on earth peace among men with whom he is pleased!" (Luke 2:1–14)

Jesus' Ministry Begins from Matthew

And he went about all Galilee, teaching in their synagogues and preaching the gospel of the kingdom and healing every disease and every infirmity among the people. So his fame spread throughout all Syria, and they brought him all the sick, those afflicted with various diseases and pains, demoniacs,[1] epileptics, and paralytics, and he healed them. And great crowds followed him from Galilee and the Decapolis[2] and Jerusalem and Judea and from beyond the Jordan. (Matthew 4:23–5)

---

1 Demoniac—person possessed by a demon.
2 Decapolis—Greek for "ten towns," a confederation of ten cities near the Sea of Galilee.

The Beatitudes from Matthew

Seeing the crowds, he went up on the mountain, and when he sat down his **disciples** came to him. And he opened his mouth and taught them, saying:

"Blessed are the poor in spirit, for theirs is the kingdom of heaven.
"Blessed are those who mourn, for they shall be comforted.
"Blessed are the meek, for they shall inherit the earth.
"Blessed are those who hunger and thirst for righteousness, for they shall be satisfied.
"Blessed are the merciful, for they shall obtain mercy.
"Blessed are the pure in heart, for they shall see God.
"Blessed are the peacemakers, for they shall be called sons of God.
"Blessed are those who are persecuted for righteousness' sake, for theirs is the kingdom of heaven.

"Blessed are you when men revile you and persecute you and utter all kinds of evil against you falsely on my account. Rejoice and be glad, for your reward is great in heaven, for so men persecuted the prophets who were before you." (Matthew 5:1–12)

Law from Matthew

"Think not that I have come to abolish the law and the prophets; I have come not to abolish them but to fulfill them. For truly, I say to you, till heaven and earth pass away, not an iota, not a dot, will pass from the law until all is accomplished. Whoever then relaxes one of the least of these commandments and teaches men so, shall be called least in the kingdom of heaven; but he who does them and teaches them shall be called great in the kingdom of heaven. For I tell you, unless your righteousness exceeds that of the scribes and Pharisees,[3] you will never enter the kingdom of heaven." (Matthew 5:17–20)

Sincerely Motivated Faith and Works from Matthew

"You have heard that it was said to the men of old, 'You shall not kill; and whoever kills shall be liable to judgment.' But I say to you that every one who is angry with his brother shall be liable to judgment; whoever insults his brother shall be liable to the council, and whoever says, 'You fool!' shall be liable to the hell of fire. So if you are offering your gift at the altar, and there remember that your brother has something against you, leave your gift there before the altar and go; first be reconciled to your brother, and then come and offer your gift." (Matthew 5:21–4)

---

3 Scribes and Pharisees—two major social groups in Israel in Jesus' time; scribes were temple-affiliated scholars, and Pharisees (after 160 BCE) stressed resurrection of the dead and the coming of the Messiah.

The Good Samaritan from Luke

[A lawyer said to Jesus:] "And who is my neighbor?" Jesus replied, "A man was going down from Jerusalem to Jericho, and he fell among robbers, who stripped him and beat him, and departed, leaving him half dead. Now by chance a priest was going down that road; and when he saw him he passed by on the other side. So likewise a Levite,[4] when he came to the place and saw him, passed by on the other side. But a Samaritan,[5] as he journeyed, came to where he was; and when he saw him, he had compassion, and went to him and bound up his wounds, pouring on oil and wine; then he set him on his own beast and brought him to an inn, and took care of him. And the next day he took out two denarii [about 40 cents] and gave them to the inn-keeper, saying 'take care of him; and whatever more you spend, I will repay you when I come back.' Which of these three, do you think, proved neighbor to the man who fell among the robbers?" He said, "The one who showed mercy on him." And Jesus said to him, "Go and do likewise." (Luke 10:29–37)

True Treasures from Matthew

"Do not lay up for yourselves treasures on earth, where moth and rust consume and where thieves break in and steal, but lay up for yourselves treasures in heaven, where neither moth nor rust consumes and where thieves do not break in and steal. For where your treasure is, there will your heart be also." (Matthew 6:19–21)

Healing the Blind from Matthew

And as Jesus passed on from there, two blind men followed him, crying aloud, "Have mercy on us, Son of David." When he entered the house, the blind men came to him; and Jesus said to them, "Do you believe that I am able to do this?" They said to him, "Yes, Lord." Then he touched their eyes, saying, "According to your faith be it done to you." And their eyes were opened. And Jesus sternly charged them, "See that no one knows it." (Matthew 9:27–30)

The Light of the World from John

In the beginning was the Word, and the Word was with God, and the Word was God. He was in the beginning with God; all things were made through him, and without him was not anything made that was made. In him was life, and the life was the light of men. The light shines in the darkness, and the darkness has not overcome it. (John 1:1–5)

---

4 Levites—a tribe of leading priests in Jerusalem's Temple, and later state officials.
5 Samaritans—inhabitants of Samaria; Jews not exiled to Babylon in the 6th century BCE, and therefore rejected by returning refugees because of intermarriage.

The Word (Logos)   from John

And the Word became flesh and dwelt among us, full of grace and truth; we have beheld his glory, glory as of the only Son from the Father. (John 1:14)

The Last Supper   from Mark

Then Judas Iscariot, who was one of the twelve [disciples], went to the chief priests in order to betray him to them. And when they heard it they were glad, and promised to give him money. And he sought an opportunity to betray him.

And on the first day of Unleavened Bread, when they sacrificed the passover lamb, his disciples said to him, "Where will you have us go and prepare for you to eat the passover?" . . . And the disciples set out and went to the city, and found it as he had told them; and they prepared the passover.

And when it was evening he came with the twelve. And as they were at table eating, Jesus said, "Truly, I say to you, one of you will betray me, one who is eating with me." They began to be sorrowful, and to say to him one after another, "Is it I?" He said to them, "It is one of the twelve, one who is dipping bread into the dish with me. For the Son of man goes as it is written of him, but woe to that man by whom the Son of man is betrayed! It would have been better for that man if he had not been born."

And as they were eating, he took bread, and blessed, and broke it, and gave it to them, and said, "Take; this is my body." And he took a cup, and when he had given thanks he gave it to them, and they all drank of it. And he said to them, "This is my blood of the covenant, which is poured out for many. Truly, I say to you, I shall not drink again of the fruit of the vine until that day when I drink it new in the kingdom of God." (Mark 14:10–12, 16–25)

The Crucifixion   from Mark

And Pilate again said to them, "Then what shall I do with the man whom you call the King of the Jews?" And they cried out again, "Crucify him." And Pilate said to them, "Why, what evil has he done?" But they shouted all the more, "Crucify him." So Pilate, wishing to satisfy the crowd, released for them Barabbas; and having scourged Jesus, he delivered him to be crucified.

And the soldiers led him away inside the palace (that is, the praetorium[6]); and they called together the whole battalion. And they clothed him in a purple cloak, and plaiting a crown of thorns they put it on him. And they began to salute him, "Hail, King of the Jews!" And they struck his head with a reed, and spat upon him, and they knelt down in homage to him. And when they had mocked him, they stripped him of the purple cloak, and put his own clothes on him. And they led him out to crucify him.

---

6 Praetorium—the official residence of the governor of the Roman province.

And they compelled a passer-by, Simon of Cyrene, who was coming in from the country, the father of Alexander and Rufus, to carry his cross. And they brought him to the place called Golgotha (which means the place of a skull). And they offered him wine mingled with myrrh; but he did not take it. And they crucified him, and divided his garments among them, casting lots for them, to decide what each should take. . . . So also the chief priests mocked him to one another with the scribes, saying, "He saved others; he cannot save himself. Let the Christ, the King of Israel, come down now from the cross, that we may see and believe." Those who were crucified with him also reviled him.

And when the sixth hour had come, there was darkness over the whole land until the ninth hour. And at the ninth hour Jesus cried with a loud voice, *"Elo-i, Elo-i, lama sabach-thani?"* which means, "My God, my God, why hast thou forsaken me?" And some of the bystanders hearing it said, "Behold, he is calling Elijah." And one ran and, filling a sponge full of vinegar, put it on a reed and gave it to him to drink, saying, "Wait, let us see whether Elijah will come to take him down." And Jesus uttered a loud cry, and breathed his last. And the curtain of the temple was torn in two, from top to bottom. . . .

. . . Joseph of Arimathea, a respected member of the council, who was also himself looking for the kingdom of God, took courage and went to Pilate, and asked for the body of Jesus. And Pilate wondered if he were already dead; and summoning the centurion, he asked him whether he was already dead. And when he learned from the centurion that he was dead, he granted the body to Joseph. And he bought a linen shroud, and taking him down, wrapped him in the linen shroud, and laid him in a tomb which had been hewn out of the rock; and he rolled a stone against the door of the tomb. (Mark 15:12–24, 31–8, 43–6)

The Resurrection   from Mark

Resurrection
Story

And when the sabbath was past, Mary Magdalene, and Mary the mother of James, and Salome, bought spices, so that they might go and anoint him. And very early on the first day of the week they went to the tomb when the sun had risen. And they were saying to one another, "Who will roll away the stone for us from the door of the tomb?" And looking up, they saw that the stone was rolled back—it was very large. And entering the tomb, they saw a young man sitting on the right side, dressed in a white robe; and they were amazed. And he said to them, "Do not be amazed; you seek Jesus of Nazareth, who was crucified. He has risen, he is not here; see the place where they laid him. But go, tell his disciples and Peter that he is going before you to Galilee; there you will see him, as he told you." And they went out and fled from the tomb; for trembling and astonishment had come upon them; and they said nothing to any one, for they were afraid. (Mark 16:1–8)

Paul's Conversion from Acts

But Saul, still breathing threats and murder against the disciples of the Lord, went to the high priest and asked him for letters to the synagogues at Damascus, so that if he found any belonging to the Way,[7] men or women, he might bring them bound to Jerusalem. Now as he journeyed he approached Damascus, and suddenly a light from heaven flashed about him. And he fell to the ground and heard a voice saying to him, "Saul, Saul, why do you persecute me?" And he said, "Who are you, Lord?" And he said, "I am Jesus, whom you are persecuting; but rise and enter the city, and you will be told what you are to do." The men who were traveling with him stood speechless, hearing the voice but seeing no one. Saul arose from the ground; and when his eyes were opened, he could see nothing; so they led him by the hand and brought him into Damascus. And for three days he was without sight, and neither ate nor drank.

... So Ananias departed and entered the house. And laying his hands on him he said, "Brother Saul, the Lord Jesus who appeared to you on the road by which you came, has sent me that you may regain your sight and be filled with the Holy Spirit." And immediately something like scales fell from his eyes and he regained his sight. Then he rose and was baptized, and took food and was strengthened.

For several days he was with the disciples at Damascus. And in the synagogues immediately he proclaimed Jesus, saying, "He is the Son of God." (Acts 9:1–9, 17–20)

Paul's letters to the new Christian churches

Paul traveled and wrote to the new Christian communities, helping interpret the meaning of Jesus for them. His writings show the universalizing of the new faith, by taking it outside the Jewish Law and opening it to any believers.

Paul on Faith and Works from Romans

For we hold that a man is justified by faith apart from works of law. Or is God the God of Jews only? Is he not the God of Gentiles also? Yes, of Gentiles also, since God is one; and he will justify the circumcised on the ground of their faith and the uncircumcised through their faith. Do we then overthrow the law by this faith? By no means! On the contrary, we uphold the law. (Romans 3:28–31)

---

7 The Way—an early understanding of followers of Jesus, not yet called "Christians."

Paul on Gender   from Galatians and I Corinthians

Paul's ideas on gender are varied and reflect both his society and the more univer-salizing contradictions to his society that the new faith presented to him.

There is neither Jew nor Greek, there is neither slave nor free, there is neither male nor female; for you are all one in Christ Jesus. (Galatians 3:28)

If there is anything they desire to know, let them ask their husbands at home. For it is shameful for a woman to speak in church. (I Corinthians 14:35)

Paul on Faith, Hope, and Love   from I Corinthians

If I speak in the tongues of men and of angels, but have not love, I am a noisy gong or a clanging cymbal. And if I have prophetic powers, and understand all mysteries and all knowledge, and if I have all faith, so as to remove mountains, but have not love, I am nothing. If I give away all I have, and if I deliver my body to be burned, but have not love, I gain nothing.

Love is patient and kind; love is not jealous or boastful; it is not arrogant or rude. Love does not insist on its own way; it is not irritable or resentful; it does not rejoice at wrong, but rejoices in the right. Love bears all things, believes all things, hopes all things, endures all things.

Love never ends; as for prophecies, they will pass away; as for tongues, they will cease; as for knowledge, it will pass away. For our knowledge is imperfect and our prophecy is imperfect; but when the perfect comes, the imperfect will pass away. When I was a child, I spoke like a child, I thought like a child, I reasoned like a child; when I became a man, I gave up childish ways. For now we see in a mirror dimly, but then face to face. Now I know in part; then I shall understand fully, even as I have been fully understood. So faith, hope, love abide, these three; but the greatest of these is love. (I Corinthians 13:1–13)

SOURCE: Bible excerpts in this chapter are taken from the Revised Standard Version. New York: Thomas Nelson, 1952. <http://goon.stg.brown.edu/bible_browser/pbform.shtml>

History and literature

A major biblical interpretive problem is how to differentiate between historical facts and literary images. When Jesus was healing two blind men he asked, "Do you believe that I am able to do this?" The history of Christianity has echoed with this question. What does it mean to believe that Christ was the Son of God on earth who can transform history? Does it mean that we are to interpret scripture as literally, factually true? Or, at the other extreme, should we read many biblical passages symbolically, understanding Jesus as healing the blindness of despair or bigotry? Or both? Christians have discussed these issues for two millennia.

The emphasis on the historical, factual side has been strengthened by ancient texts. The Jewish historian Josephus (c. 37–100 CE) wrote, "At about this time lived Jesus, a wise man ... He performed astonishing feats ... He attracted many Jews and many of the Greeks ... Upon an indictment brought by leading members of our society, Pilate sentenced him to the cross." In two Jewish commentaries, supplements to the Mishnah (compiled before 200 CE), are several references to Jesus, including: "It has been taught: On the even of Passover they hanged Yeshu ... because he practiced sorcery and enticed and led Israel astray" (Ian Wilson, *Jesus: the Evidence*, pp. 44–5).

But twentieth-century discoveries of other texts from biblical times have raised controversial and fascinating questions. The problem of how to interpret scripture is renewed by these religious texts, because they raise the question of the **canon**: how did the Bible come into history? Books not selected for the canon are called the **Apocrypha**. Protestants list many, but Roman Catholics and Eastern Orthodox Christians accept more as canonical.

EARLY NON-CANONICAL TEXTS

A number of spiritual writings were circulating among Jews and Christians in New Testament times; some are preserved in the Dead Sea Scrolls and the Nag Hammadi Library. However, they were not selected for inclusion in the biblical canon.

In 1945 Egyptian peasants discovered the first of many jars with scrolls, buried about 400 CE, written in the Coptic language and translated from Greek. These scrolls have given us a much better understanding of Gnosticism—a religious complex with roots in several faiths that blended with Christianity from the first century CE. Some Gnostics postulated a remote supreme divinity and an inferior, imperfect creator god. They stressed mystical, experiential *gnosis* (knowledge) as opposed to faith, and saw Jesus as more human than other Christians did. In the second and third centuries, Gnostics were rejected by the church as **heretics** on account of their theology, alleged elitism, opposition to church authority, and egalitarian view of women. However, as the following selections show, they were capable of highly poetic, paradoxical, and mystical insights.

The Gospel of Mary from the Nag Hammadi Library

The figure of Mary Magdalene in the Gospels has been a fascinating character in Christianity. She suffered the criticism of being called a prostitute by a medieval pope, with no biblical evidence. The discovery of the Nag Hammadi scrolls added fuel to this debate with the "Gospel of Mary" text. It does not use the word "Magdalene," but many take it to be she who saw a vision of the risen Christ and conveyed it to the Apostles, as indicated in this extract.

Mary Magdalene became the focus of the 2003 fictional novel *The Da Vinci Code* by Dan Brown. In it the medieval myth of her as Jesus' wife who carried their child to France and began their family line is connected to the mysterious legend of the Holy Grail, taken to symbolize the lost, repressed feminine aspect of Christianity. The book and its film version aroused a storm of controversy.

Peter said to Mary, "Sister, We know that the Savior loved you more than the rest of women. Tell us the words of the Savior which you remember—which you know (but) we do not nor have we heard them." Mary answered and said, "What is hidden from you I will proclaim to you." And she began to speak to them these words: "I," she said, "saw the Lord in a vision and I said to him, 'Lord, I saw you today in a vision.' He answered and said to me, 'Blessed are you, that you did not waver at the sight of me. For where the mind is, there is the treasure.' I said to him, 'Lord, now does he who sees the vision see it <through>[8] the soul <or> through the spirit?' The Savior answered and said, 'He does not see through the soul nor through the spirit, but the mind which [is] between the two—that is [what] sees the vision and it is [. . .].' (pp. 11–14 missing)

"The soul answered and said, 'What binds me has been slain, and what turns me about has been overcome, and my desire has been ended, and ignorance has died. In a [world] I was released from a world, [and] in a type from a heavenly type, and (from) the fetter of oblivion which is transient. From this time on I will attain to the rest of the time, of the season, of the aeon, in silence.'"

When Mary had said this, she fell silent, since it was to this point that the Savior had spoken with her.

SOURCE: "The Gospel of Mary," trans. George W. MacRae, in *The Nag Hammadi Library*, ed. James M. Robinson. San Francisco: Harper and Row, 1977, pp. 472–3

The Thunder, Perfect Mind from the Nag Hammadi Library

This text, in the voice of a woman, is similar in tone and style to some earlier Jewish Wisdom Literature and to Egyptian Isis goddess texts. Its antithetical character uses paradox to proclaim the absolute transcendence of its source, prior to opposites, whose greatness is unfathomable.

I was sent forth from the power, and I have come to those who reflect upon
    me, and I have been found among those who seek after me.
Look upon me, you who reflect upon me, and you hearers, hear me.
You who are waiting for me, take me to yourselves.
And do not banish me from your sight. . . .

I am the wife and the virgin. I am [the mother] and the daughter.
I am the members of my mother.
I am the barren one and many are her sons.
I am she whose wedding is great, and I have not taken a husband. . . .

---

8 < > pointed brackets indicate a corrected scribal omission or error in the original manuscript;
[ ] square brackets indicate a gap; ( ) parentheses indicate material supplied by modern editor or translator to clarify meaning.

I am the silence that is incomprehensible
　　and the idea whose remembrance is frequent.
I am the voice whose sound is manifold
　　and the word whose appearance is multiple.
I am the utterance of my name.
Why, you who hate me, do you love me, and hate those who love me?
You who deny me, confess me, and you who confess me, deny me. . . .

But I am she who exists in all fears and strength in trembling.
I am she who is weak, and I am well in a pleasant place.
I am senseless and I am wise.
Why have you hated me in your counsels?
For I shall be silent among those who are silent,
　　and I shall appear and speak. . . .

I am the one whose image is great in Egypt
　　and the one who has no image among the barbarians.
I am the one who has been hated everywhere
　　and who has been loved everywhere.
I am the one whom they call Life, and you have called Death.
I am the one whom they call Law, and you have called Lawlessness. . . .

I am she who does not keep festival,
　　and I am she whose festivals are many.
I, I am godless, and I am the one whose God is great. . . .
Come forward to childhood,
　　and do not despise it because it is small and it is little. . . .

For what is inside of you is what is outside of you,
　　and the one who fashions you on the outside
　　is the one who shaped the inside of you.
And what you see outside of you, you see inside of you;
　　it is visible and it is your garment. . . .

SOURCE: "The Thunder, Perfect Mind," trans. George W. MacRae, in *The Nag Hammadi Library*, ed. James M. Robinson. Rev. ed. San Francisco: HarperCollins, 1990, pp. 272–7

THEOLOGY, SPIRITUALITY, AND DIVISIONS

Christians have struggled with many of the age-old questions that life poses and religions strive to answer. Are heroic spiritual reformers like Jesus merely humans, or was Jesus actually God appearing in history? What is the nature of the evil apparently behind life's atrocities? How should we interpret the ancient and recurring frightening beliefs about the end of the world, or **Apocalypse**? What rational investigations can convince thinkers of religious truths? What is the meaning of mystical experiences of divine presence? How much authority is the social convention of the day, such as the role of women, to be given in religion? What is the significance of mysterious, poetic religious language? Does the ascetic life of a priest, monk, or nun take them closer to God? Can religion really replace painful grief with transcendent joy? Is the church a necessary mediator of God through sacraments, or does everyone have direct access to God? Why did the early church choose to reject some spiritual writings and give others divine status?

The Formation of the Canon by Athanasius

The process of selecting which of the numerous spiritual texts circulating about Jesus to include in the official Bible, the canon, took over 300 years. Church leaders had varying lists of their favorite books. The selection compiled in 367 CE by Athanasius (c. 296–373 CE), Bishop of Alexandria, is the oldest surviving one that approximates the current Christian Bible. The content of the Bible was roughly determined when a list very similar to that of Athanasius was proclaimed canonical by Pope Innocent I in 405 CE. Generally the year 400 CE is accepted as the point when the Christian canon reached consensus, as the Latin translation or Vulgate by Jerome (c. 347–419 CE) was circulating. Athanasius proposed the following biblical canon.

There are, then, of the Old Testament, 22 books in number; for, as I have heard, it is handed down that this is the number of the letters among the Hebrews; their respective order and names being as follows. The first is Genesis, then Exodus, next Leviticus, after that Numbers, and then Deuteronomy. Following these there is Joshua, the son of Nun, then Judges, then Ruth. And again, after these four books of Kings, the first and second being reckoned as one book, and so likewise the third and fourth as one book. And again, the first and second of the Chronicles are reckoned as one book. Again Ezra, the first and second are similarly one book. After these there is the book of Psalms, then the Proverbs, next Ecclesiastes, and the Song of Songs. Job follows, then the Prophets, the twelve being reckoned as one book. Then Isaiah, one book, then Jeremiah with Baruch, Lamentations, and the Epistle, one book; afterwards, Ezekiel and Daniel, each one book. Thus far constitutes the Old Testament.

Again it is not tedious to speak of the [books] of the New Testament. These are, the four Gospels, according to Matthew, Mark, Luke, and John. Afterwards, the Acts of the Apostles and Epistles (called Catholic), seven, viz. of James, one; of Peter, two; of John, three; after these, one of Jude. In addition, there are 14 Epistles of Paul, written in this order. The first, to the Romans; then two to the Corinthians; after these, to the Galatians; next, to the Ephesians; then to the Philippians; then to the Colossians; after these, two to the Thessalonians, and that to the Hebrews; and again, two to Timothy; one to Titus; and lastly, that to Philemon. And besides, the Revelation of John.

SOURCE: Philip Schaff, *Athanasius: Select Works and Letters*. New York: Christian Literature Publishing, 1892
<http://www.ccel.org/ccel/schaff/npnf204.xxv.iii.iii.xxv.html>

Eastern Orthodox Church

As the church developed historically, three major branches emerged that answered questions of theology and spirituality, sometimes in quite different ways. The Eastern Orthodox is the oldest, most Greek, and mystical, while the Western Roman Catholics worshipped in Latin and developed more legalistic traditions under the pope; conflicts led to a mutual separation in the year 1054. The most democratic branch—the Protestants—broke away in 1517.

The Eastern Orthodox Church focuses on the earliest days of Christianity. It held seven major councils that decided basic beliefs, such as the divinity of Jesus. Its theologians, among them Origen, wrote about how to interpret the Bible; its mystical monks include such figures as Gregory of Sinai.

How to Interpret Scripture by Origen

Jesus was known for stilling storms, feeding the hungry, healing the sick and blind, and raising the dead. From the beginning of the Christian faith, thinkers questioned the proper ways to interpret these reports. Here Origen, an Egyptian theologian (c. 185–254 CE), makes the important distinction between a literal, historical, factual ("bodily") reading and a symbolic, metaphoric, spiritual interpretation.

The right way, as it appears to us, of approaching the scriptures and gathering their meaning, is the following, which is extracted from the writings themselves. We find some such rule as this laid down by Solomon in the Proverbs concerning the divine doctrines written therein: "Do thou portray them threefold in counsel and knowledge, that thou mayest answer words of truth to those who question thee" (Proverbs 22:20–21).

One must therefore portray the meaning of the sacred writings in a threefold way upon one's own soul, so that the simple man may be edified by what we may call the flesh of the scripture, this name being given to the obvious interpretation; while the man who has made some progress may be edified by its soul, as it were; and the man who is perfect and like those mentioned by the apostle: "We speak wisdom among the perfect; yet a wisdom not of this world, nor of the rulers of this world, which are coming to naught; but we speak God's wisdom in a mystery, even the wisdom that hath been hidden, which God foreordained before the worlds unto our glory" (I Corinthians 2:6–7)—this man may be edified by the spiritual law (Romans 7:14), which has "a shadow of the good things to come" (Hebrews 10:1). For just as man consists of body, soul, and spirit, so in the same way does the scripture, which has been prepared by God to be given for man's salvation.

But since there are certain passages of scripture which, as we shall show in what follows, have no bodily [literal] sense at all, there are occasions when we must seek only for the soul and the spirit, as it were, of the passage.

That it is possible to derive benefit from the first, and to this extent helpful meaning, is witnessed by the multitudes of sincere and simple believers.

But if the usefulness of the law and the sequence and ease of the narrative were at first sight clearly discernible throughout, we should be unaware that there was anything beyond the obvious meaning for us to understand in the scriptures.

Now what man of intelligence will believe that the first and the second and the third day, and the evening and the morning existed without the sun and the moon and stars? And that the first day, if we may so call it, was even without a heaven (Genesis 1:5–13)? And who is so silly as to believe that God, after the manner of a farmer, "planted a paradise eastward in Eden," and set in it a visible and palpable "tree of life," of such a sort that anyone who tasted its fruit with his bodily teeth would gain life; and again that one could partake of "good and evil" by masticating the fruit taken from the tree of that name (Genesis 2:8–9)? And when God is said to "walk in the paradise in the cool of the day" and Adam to hide himself behind a tree, I do not think anyone will doubt that these are figurative expressions which indicate certain mysteries through a semblance of history and not through actual events (Genesis 3:8).

The aim of the divine power which bestowed on us the holy scriptures is not that we should accept only what is found in the letter; for occasionally the records taken in a literal sense are not true, but actually absurd and impossible, and even with the history that actually happened and the legislation that is in its literal sense useful there are other matters interwoven.

But someone may suppose that the former statement refers to all the scriptures, and may suspect us of saying that because some of the history did not happen, therefore none of it happened; and because a certain law is irrational or impossible when taken literally, therefore no laws ought to be kept to the letter; or that the records of the Savior's life are not true in a physical sense; or that no law or commandment of his ought to be obeyed. We must assert, therefore, that in regard to some things we are clearly aware that the historical fact is true ... [e.g.] that Jerusalem is the chief city of Judea, in which a temple of God was built by Solomon; and thousands of other facts.

For our contention with regard to the whole of divine scripture is, that it all has a spiritual meaning, but not all a bodily [literal] meaning; for the bodily meaning is often proved to be an impossibility. Consequently the man who reads the divine books reverently, believing them to be divine writings, must exercise great care.

SOURCE: "Origen on First Principles," in *Readings in Christian Thought*, ed. Hugh T. Kerr. Nashville, TN: Abingdon Press, 1966, pp. 45–7

The Nicene Creed

This is the ancient creed that is thought to have been worked out at the Council of Nicaea, organized by the Byzantine emperor Constantine in 325 BCE. Its main purpose was to unify the emerging church and oppose the Arian belief that Jesus was not the divine Son of God, but was human only. This is the English version said in many Eastern Orthodox churches' Divine Liturgy. It omits the phrase in brackets below [and the Son], which was not in the original version, but was added by the Roman Church later. Eastern Orthodox and Roman Catholic Christians generally recite it each Sunday, many Protestants less often.

I believe in one God, the Father, the Almighty, Creator of heaven and earth, and of all things visible and invisible.

And in one Lord, Jesus Christ, the only begotten Son of God, begotten of the Father before all ages. Light of Light, true God of true God, begotten, not created, of one essence with the Father, through whom all things were made. For us and our salvation, He came down from heaven and was incarnate by the Holy Spirit and the Virgin Mary and became man. He was crucified for us under Pontius Pilate, and He suffered and was buried. On the third day He rose according to the Scriptures. He ascended into heaven and is seated at the right hand of the Father. He will come again in glory to judge the living and the dead. His kingdom will have no end.

And in the Holy Spirit, the Lord, the Giver of Life, who proceeds from the Father [and the Son], who together with the Father and the Son is worshiped and glorified, who spoke through the prophets.

In one holy, catholic, and apostolic Church.

I acknowledge one baptism for the forgiveness of sins. I expect the resurrection of the dead. And the life of the age to come. Amen.

SOURCE: *The Divine Liturgy of Saint John Chrysostom*. Brookline, MA: Holy Cross Orthodox Press, 1985, pp. 18–19

Grief and Joy by Gregory of Sinai

The *Philokalia* (love of what is beautiful) is an ancient collection of Orthodox writings, ascetic and mystical, reflecting the monastic life of the Eastern Church. It has a wide influence on the modern Orthodox world, and new editions still add texts. This selection is from Gregory of Sinai, one of the bright lights of fourteenth-century Christianity. Born around 1265, he entered the monastic life at Sinai, then spent years at the famous Mount Athos monastery complex, perched precariously atop a remote mountain in Greece. Like other Orthodox Christians, he practiced repetition of the "Jesus Prayer"—"Jesus Christ, Son of God, have mercy on me"—to bring God into his heart. Here he discusses the depths of grief and the heights of joy in meditation.

Unless your life and actions are accompanied by a sense of inner grief you cannot endure the incandescence of stillness. If with this sense of grief you meditate—before they come to pass—on the many terrors that await us prior to and after death you will achieve both patience and humility, the twin foundations of stillness. Without them your efforts to attain stillness will always be accompanied by apathy and self-conceit. From these will arise a host of distractions and day-dreams, all inducing sluggishness. In their wake comes dissipation, daughter of indolence, making the body sluggish and slack and the intellect benighted and callous. Then Jesus is hidden, concealed by the throng of thoughts and images that crowd the mind....

For beginners prayer is like a joyous fire kindled in the heart; for the perfect is like a vigorous sweet-scented light. Or again, prayer is the preaching of the Apostles, an action of faith or, rather, faith itself, "that makes real for us the things for which we hope," active love, angelic impulse, the power of the bodiless spirits, their work and delight, the Gospel of God, the heart's assurance, hope of salvation, a sign of purity, a token of holiness, knowledge of God, baptism made manifest, purification in the water of regeneration, a pledge of the Holy Spirit, the exultation of Jesus, the soul's delight, God's mercy, a sign of reconciliation, the seal of Christ, a ray of the noetic[9] sun, the heart's dawn star.

SOURCE: Gregory of Sinai, *The Philokalia*, ed. G. E. H. Palmer, *et al.* London: Faber and Faber, 1995, vol. 4, pp. 236–7

Roman Catholic Church

The Roman Catholic Church is centered in Rome and is hierarchically organized under the pope, and his cardinals, whose offices are at the Vatican. This is a separate state within Rome, housing colleges, a museum, and the Renaissance-style St. Peter's Basilica. The largest branch of Christianity, Catholics are diverse worldwide, characterized by a strong celibate officially male priesthood. Mary, mother of Jesus, is greatly honored, as in the many French "Our Lady" cathedrals, such as Notre Dame in Paris. Roman Catholics emphasize the Eucharist in Mass, understanding it as Christ's saving grace coming through both the priest and the congregation.

The Eucharistic Prayer from the Roman Catholic Mass

The Eucharist is the high point of Christian liturgies, especially in the Orthodox and Catholic churches. Most Protestants celebrate Communion less often and stress the Word, or sermon. What follows

Eucharist

is a prayer said by English-speaking priests during the Roman Catholic Mass as part of the Eucharist, when bread and wine are shared as Jesus' body and blood.

Bless and approve our offering; make it acceptable to you, an offering in spirit and in truth. Let it become for us the body and blood of Jesus Christ, your only Son, our Lord. [Through Christ our Lord, Amen.]

The day before he suffered he took bread in his sacred hands and looking up to heaven to you, his almighty father, he gave you thanks and praise. He broke the bread, gave it to his disciples, and said:
Take this, all of you, and eat it: this is my body which will be given up for you.

---

9 Noetic—intellectual or abstract.

When supper was ended, he took the cup. Again he gave you thanks and praise, gave the cup to his disciples, and said:

Take this, all of you, and drink from it; this is the cup of my blood, the blood of the new and everlasting covenant. It will be shed for you and for all so that sins may be forgiven. Do this in memory of me.

SOURCE: *Today's Missal Large Print Ordinary.* Portland, OR: Oregon Catholic Press, 2004, vol. 71, no. 4, p. 94

The Confessions of Augustine by Augustine of Hippo

Augustine (354–430 CE), Bishop of Hippo in North Africa, wrote the first surviving Western autobiography showing an intense self-awareness. It describes in detail his transformation from a pleasure-enjoying youth, who fathered a child outside marriage, to a man awakened to deep spiritual realities. He struggled with the question of the nature of evil: is it a second cosmic force like God, as the **Manichaeans** believed (he was once a Manichaean), or is it a lack of God's goodness (*privatio boni*)? Augustine was persuaded by the Neoplatonists of a heavenly hierarchy, descending from an immaterial, eternal, and intelligible God down to earth. He wrote several influential books, including *The City of God* (426 CE), which criticizes "pagan" civic religions[10] as bankrupt. He wrote on the divine illumination of the intellect, the importance of introspection, and the need for God's **grace** to motivate morality.

My sins were being multiplied, and my concubine being torn from my side as a hindrance to my marriage, my heart which clave unto her was torn and wounded and bleeding. And she returned to Afric,[11] vowing unto Thee never to know any other man, leaving with me my son by her. But unhappy I, who could not imitate a very woman, impatient of delay, inasmuch as not till after two years was I to obtain her I sought, not being so much a lover of marriage as a slave to lust, procured another, though no wife, that so by the servitude of an enduring custom, the disease of my soul might be kept up and carried on in its vigour, or even augmented, into the dominion of marriage. Nor was that my wound cured, which had been made by the cutting away of the former, but after inflammation and most acute pain, it mortified, and my pains became less acute, but more desperate. . . .

And to Thee is nothing whatsoever evil: yea, not only to Thee, but also to Thy creation as a whole, because there is nothing without, which may break in, and corrupt that order which Thou hast appointed it. But in the parts thereof some things, because unharmonizing with other some, are accounted evil: whereas those very things harmonize with others, and are

---

10 Civic religion—a semi-religious nationalist cult of patriotism, pride, and identity with several qualities of traditional religions.
11 Afric—Africa, then referring only to the area of present-day Egypt, Libya, Algeria, and Morocco, as the rest of the continent was unknown to the Romans.

good; and in themselves are good. And all these things which harmonize not together, do yet with the inferior part, which we call Earth, having its own cloudy and windy sky harmonizing with it. . . .

But after Thou hadst soothed my head, unknown to me, and closed mine eyes that they should not behold vanity, I ceased somewhat of my former self, and my frenzy was lulled to sleep; and I awoke in Thee, and saw Thee infinite, but in another way, and this sight was not derived from the flesh.

And I looked back on other things; and I saw that they owed their being to Thee; and were all bounded in Thee: but in a different way; not as being in space; but because Thou containest all things in Thine hand in Thy Truth; and all things are true so far as they be; nor is there any falsehood, unless when that is thought to be, which is not. And I saw that all things did harmonize, not with their places only, but with their seasons. . . . And I enquired what iniquity was, and found it to be no substance, but the perversion of the will, turned aside from Thee, O God, the Supreme, towards these lower things, and casting out its bowels, and puffed up outwardly. . . .

I had found the unchangeable and true Eternity of Truth above my changeable mind. And thus by degrees I passed from bodies to the soul, which through the bodily senses perceives; and thence to its inward faculty, to which the bodily senses represent things external, whitherto reach the faculties of beasts; and thence again to the reasoning faculty, to which what is received from the senses of the body is referred to be judged. . . .

Then I sought a way of obtaining strength sufficient to enjoy Thee; and found it not, until I embraced that Mediator betwixt God and men, the Man Christ Jesus, who is over all, God blessed for evermore, calling unto me, and saying, I am the way, the truth, and the life, and mingling that food which I was unable to receive, with our flesh. For, the Word was made flesh, that Thy wisdom, whereby Thou createdst all things, might provide milk for our infant state. For I did not hold to my Lord Jesus Christ, I, humbled, to the Humble; nor knew I yet whereto His infirmity would guide us. For Thy Word, the Eternal Truth, far above the higher parts of Thy Creation, raises up the subdued unto Itself.

SOURCE: Augustine of Hippo, *The Confessions of Saint Augustine*, trans. Edward B. Pusey. New York: Washington Square Press, 1960, pp. 101, 119–22

A Medieval Argument for the Existence of God
by Anselm of Canterbury

Theologians explore questions such as what religious truths can be known by reason and which ones humans can know only by divine revelation. Thomas Aquinas (1225–74), for example, proposed five famous arguments that he thought could prove the existence of God by reason alone. But he concluded that some doctrines, such as the **Trinity** and **Incarnation**, can be known only by revelation.

Aquinas was preceded by Anselm of Canterbury (1033–1109) with his **onto-logical** argument of metaphysical proof that God exists. Anselm was a Benedictine monk and Archbishop of Canterbury (a major regional church official; later arch-bishops were leaders of the Anglican Church). His argument for the existence of God is the earliest ontological argument. He contends that the greatest or most perfect thing that can be thought is God and, because of its perfection, it must exist. German philosopher Immanuel Kant (1724–1804) argued that existence is no more proven by the concept of perfection than the existence of money is proven by the concept of money. Subsequent philosophical arguments became the onto-logical question asking, "What makes existence itself possible?"

Chapter 2: That God Really Exists   Therefore, Lord, you who give knowledge of the faith, give me as much knowledge as you know to be fitting for me, because you are as we believe and that which we believe. And indeed we believe you are something greater than which cannot be thought. Or is there no such kind of thing, for "the fool said in his heart, 'there is no God'" (Psalm 13:1, 52:1)? But certainly that same fool, having heard what I just said, "something greater than which cannot be thought," understands what he heard, and what he understands is in his thought, even if he does not think it exists. For it is one thing for something to exist in a person's thought and quite another for the person to think that thing exists. For when a painter thinks ahead to what he will paint, he has that picture in his thought, but he does not yet think it exists, because he has not done it yet. Once he has painted it he has it in his thought and thinks it exists because he has done it. Thus even the fool is compelled to grant that something greater than which cannot be thought exists in thought, because he understands what he hears, and whatever is understood exists in thought. And certainly that greater than which cannot be understood cannot exist only in thought, for if it exists only in thought it could also be thought of as existing in reality as well, which is greater. If, therefore, that than which greater cannot be thought exists in thought alone, then that than which greater cannot be thought turns out to be that than which something greater actually can be thought, but that is obviously impossible. Therefore something than which greater cannot be thought undoubtedly exists both in thought and in reality.

Chapter 3: That God Cannot be Thought Not to Exist   In fact, it so undoubtedly exists that it cannot be thought of as not existing. For one can think there exists something that cannot be thought of as not existing, and that would be greater than something which can be thought of as not existing. For if that greater than which cannot be thought can be thought of as not existing, then that greater than which cannot be thought is not that greater than which cannot be thought, which does not make sense. Thus that greater than which nothing can be thought so undoubtedly exists that it cannot even be thought of as not existing.

And you, Lord God, are this being. You exist so undoubtedly, my Lord God, that you cannot even be thought of as not existing. And deservedly, for if some mind could think of something greater than you, that creature would rise above the creator and could pass judgment on the creator, which is absurd. And indeed whatever exists except you alone can be thought of as not existing. You alone of all things most truly exist and thus enjoy existence to the fullest degree of all things, because nothing else exists so undoubtedly, and thus everything else enjoys being in a lesser degree. Why therefore did the fool say in his heart "there is no God," since it is so evident to any rational mind that you above all things exist? Why indeed, except precisely because he is stupid and foolish?

SOURCE: Anselm of Canterbury, *Proslogion*, trans. David Burr, in *Internet Medieval Sourcebook*, ed. Paul Halsall. <http://www.fordham.edu/halsall/source/anselm.html>

Everything Lives in God by Hildegard of Bingen

Hildegard (1098–1179) was a German nun of rare intelligence and originality. Beginning in childhood she had visions of God's light and angels and developed a spiritual wisdom based on her view that the Word of God is present in every living thing, expressed in its beauty. She pressed forward her conviction of the spiritual equality of men and women, and was able to establish an independent Benedictine convent. A popular public speaker in an age when women seldom preached, she gave sermons to crowds at cathedrals. Her wisdom was sought by many for personal counsel and healing.

Your eyes are not strong enough to look at God. Your mind is not strong enough to comprehend his mysteries. You can only see and know what God allows. Yet in your desire to see and know more, you engage in all manner of foolish speculations, which cause your soul to stagger. Just as water is absorbed by the heat of a burning forge, so your soul is absorbed by the restlessness of your thoughts, as you try to grasp what is beyond your grasp.

The Word of God regulates the movements of the sun, the moon and the stars. The Word of God gives the light which shines from the heavenly bodies. He makes the wind blow, the rivers run and the rain fall. He makes trees burst into blossom, and the crops bring forth the harvest.

The sky above us imitates God. Just as the sky has no beginning and no end, so God has no beginning and end. Just as the stars sparkle, so spiritual stars emanate from the throne of God, to sparkle within people's souls.

The Word of God spoke, and brought all creatures into being. God and his Word are one. As the Word spoke, so God's eternal will was fulfilled. The echo of the Word awakened life from inanimate dust.

When the Word of God spoke at the moment of creation, his sound was implanted in every creature, and gave life to every creature.

The love of God is symbolized by a leaping fountain. All who come near to it are showered by its sparkling waters. And they can see their own image in the pool below.

Everything lives in God, and hence nothing can truly die, since God is life itself. God is the wisdom that brought all things into being. He breathes life into all things.

In all creation—in trees, plants, animals and stones—there are hidden secret powers which no one can discern unless they are revealed by God.

SOURCE: Robert Van de Weyer, ed., *Hildegard*. London: Hodder and Stoughton, 1997, pp. 32–4

Protestant Churches

The Protestant Churches, beginning with Martin Luther in 1517, emphasize the priesthood of all believers, meaning that God's presence can be experienced directly by all believers, with no priest in between. Born in a time of growing literacy, they emphasize the authority of the Bible. Most allowed any Protestant to start a church, so numerous branches of Protestantism grew. All emphasize democratic governance, sermons, and congregational singing in varying degrees. They range from the Anglican, with King/Queen as leader of the state Church of England, with a fairly strong priesthood and Catholic-like liturgy, through mainstream Reformed Churches—Presbyterians, Methodists, Congregationalists, and Baptists—to more radical Free Churches—Mennonite, Quaker, Amish, Assembly of God—which usually reject government affiliation, military service, and any formal priesthood.

Baptism

Baptism from the Episcopal Church's *Book of Common Prayer*

This rite of initiation can be performed on infants or adults. Orthodox, Catholic, and Anglican churches prefer that a bishop administers baptisms, but sometimes a priest must do it and a deacon or lay leader may assist. For an infant the parents and possibly godparents are involved, as are the congregation ("people"). Adults being baptized speak for themselves. This selection combines both possibilities.

Celebrant [to parents and godparents, for a child] Will you be responsible for seeing that the child you present is brought up in the Christian faith and life?
Parents and godparents I will, with God's help.

Question [to candidates who can speak for themselves] Do you renounce Satan and all the spiritual forces of wickedness that rebel against God?
Answer I renounce them. . . .
Question Do you turn to Jesus Christ and accept him as your Savior?
Answer I do. . . .

Leader [to the congregation, about those being baptized] Deliver them, O Lord, from the ways of sin and death.
People Lord, hear our prayer.
Leader Open their hearts to your grace and truth.

People Lord, hear our prayer.
Leader Teach them to love others in the power of the Spirit.
People Lord, hear our prayer.

Celebrant [praying to God] Now sanctify this water, we pray you, by the power of your Holy Spirit, that those who here are cleansed from sin and born again may continue forever in the risen life of Jesus Christ our Savior. . . .

Each candidate is presented by name to the Celebrant, or to an assisting priest or deacon, who then immerses, or pours water upon, the candidate, saying
[Name], I baptize you in the Name of the Father, and of the Son, and of the Holy Spirit. Amen.

SOURCE: *The Book of Common Prayer, The Episcopal Church.* New York: Seabury Press, 1977, pp. 302–7

LUTHERAN CHURCH

The Protestant Reformation began with Martin Luther (1483–1546) in 1517. He argued for certain theological principles, most importantly **justification** by faith (salvation from sin through belief in God) not only works (good deeds), and the priesthood of all believers. These code phrases unraveled a number of the church's structures, and it was Luther who unintentionally splintered the church.

To deal with the issues raised by Protestants, Pope Paul III (r. 1534–49) organized the Council of Trent in 1545. This marked the start of the Roman Catholic Reformation (also called the Counter-Reformation), a movement of high spirituality that sought to revitalize the Catholic Church and oppose Protestantism.

Some of the social factors contributing to this century of religious reform were development of the printing press and spreading literacy, growth of the middle classes, expanding democracy and capitalism, rising European nationalism, and global exploration.

Faith Can Rule Only in the Inward Man
by Martin Luther

Luther was a German priest and taught at Wittenberg University. He proclaimed many of the principles of the Protestant Reformation, beginning with his "95 Theses"—his 1517 denunciation of the sale of indulgences (releases from spiritual punishment for sins). His inflammatory tracts resulted in his excommunication in 1521. In the following "Treatise on Christian Liberty" (1520) he argues for justification by faith rather than just by works. Luther said that God's grace and faith should lead to ethical action, but "religious" behavior alone is not sufficient to determine righteousness. Most basic was the priesthood of all believers, meaning that everyone has direct access to God, with no need for ecclesiastical intermediaries. Along with others, Luther proclaimed the Bible to be the authority in faith, and translated it into German (1534/45). He also opposed priestly celibacy, in 1525 marrying Catharine von Bora, a former nun.

One thing and one only is necessary for Christian life, righteousness and liberty. That one thing is the most holy Word of God, the Gospel of Christ. . . . The Word of God cannot be received and cherished by any works whatever, but only by faith. . . . When you have learned this, you will know that you need Christ, Who suffered and rose again for you, that, believing in Him, you may through this faith become a new man, in that all your sins are forgiven, and you are justified by the merits of another, namely, of Christ alone.

Since, therefore, this faith can rule only in the inward man, as Romans 10 says, "With the heart we believe unto righteousness"; and since faith alone justifies, it is clear that the inward man cannot be justified, made free and be saved by any outward work or dealing whatsoever, and that works, whatever their character, have nothing to do with this inward man. . . . yet he remains in this mortal life on earth, and in this life he must needs govern his own body and have dealings with men. Here the works begin; here a man cannot take his ease; here he must, indeed, take care to discipline his body by fastings, watchings, labors and other reasonable discipline, and to make it subject to the spirit so that it will obey and conform to the inward man and to faith, and not revolt against faith and hinder the inward man, as it is the body's nature to do if it be not held in check.

SOURCE: Martin Luther, "Treatise on Christian Liberty," letter to Pope Leo X, in *A History of Christianity*, ed. Clyde L. Manschreck. Englewood Cliffs, NJ: Prentice-Hall, 1964. Reprinted from *Works of Martin Luther, II*, trans. W. A. Lambert. Philadelphia, PA: Muhlenburg Press, 1943, pp. 25–7

The Living Cathedral: St. John the Divine

ANGLICAN CHURCH

The Protestant Church of England began when King Henry VIII of England (r. 1509–47) rejected the rule of the pope in 1533, 16 years after Luther's revolt. Adopting some of Luther's principles, he made the Church of England independent from Rome. The Anglican Church today is a worldwide communion, with a strong priesthood and formal liturgy. Parliament's Supremacy Act of 1534 made England's monarch the supreme head of the Anglican Church—a law still in effect.

The Supremacy Act of 1534

Albeit the king's majesty justly and rightly is and ought to be the supreme head of the Church of England, and so is recognized by the clergy of this realm in their Convocations, yet nevertheless for corroboration and confirmation thereof, and for increase of virtue in Christ's religion within this realm of England, and to repress and extirp all error, heresies, and other enormities and abuses heretofore used in the same; be it enacted by authority of this present Parliament, that the king our sovereign lord, his heirs and successors, kings of this realm, shall be taken, accepted, and reputed the only supreme head on earth of the Church of England called Anglicana Ecclesia.

SOURCE: "The Supremacy Act, 1534," in *A History of Christianity*, ed. Clyde L. Manschreck. Englewood Cliffs, NJ: Prentice-Hall, 1964, pp. 178–9

REFORMED CHURCH

John Calvin (1509–64) welcomed Luther's new principles and established a **theocracy** in Geneva, Switzerland. Calvin's church leaders effectively governed the city council. His theology became the basis of the Reformed Church, which led to the Churches of Christ, Presbyterian, Congregational, and other churches. He stressed the capacity of humans to experience God, the primary authority of the Bible, the depraved sinfulness of humanity, the salvation of a few only, and justification by faith in Jesus. Calvin's *Institutes of the Christian Religion* dates from 1559.

Institutes of the Christian Religion by John Calvin

We lay it down as a position not to be controverted, that the human mind, even by natural instinct, possesses some sense of a Deity (I.iii.1).... Good men, above all others Augustine, have laboured to demonstrate that we are not corrupted by any adventitious means, but that we derive an innate depravity from our very birth (II.i.5).... So the Scripture, collecting in our minds the otherwise confused notions of Deity, dispels the darkness, and gives us a clear view of the true God (I.vi.1).... Eternal life is foreordained for some, and eternal damnation for others (II.xxi.5).

SOURCE: John Calvin, *A Compend of the Institutes of the Christian Religion*, ed. Hugh Kerr. Philadelphia, PA: Westminster Press, 1964, pp. 7–129

FREE CHURCHES

The many varieties of independent Free Churches strongly oppose any government affiliation and do not practice infant baptism. Most Quakers still reject priests and sacraments, while the Amish withdraw from mainstream society. Baptists stress believers' baptism by total immersion. Two reformers from Zurich, Switzerland, formed the first Free Church or Anabaptist group in a nearby village; it later became the "Swiss Brethren." The classic statement of Free Church beliefs, adopted by the Swiss Brethren, is the 1527 Schlectheim Confession of Faith.

The Schlectheim Confession of Faith of 1527

Baptism shall be given to all those who have learned repentance and amendment of life, and who believe truly that their sins are taken away by Christ, and to all those who walk in the resurrection of Jesus Christ, and wish to be buried with him in death, so that they may be resurrected with Him, and to all those who with this significance request it [baptism] of us and demand it for themselves. This excludes all infant baptism, the highest and chief abomination of the pope.

SOURCE: "The Schlectheim Confession of Faith, 1527," in *A History of Christianity*, ed. Clyde L. Manschreck. Englewood Cliffs, NJ: Prentice-Hall, 1964, pp. 79–80

Living Christianity

Christian tradition encompasses dynamic movements that take many forms. The following excerpts illustrate some major themes: evangelical thought in 1989, Latin American Liberation Theology versus commercial development, Mother Teresa in India, a new Eastern Orthodox engagement with the environmental crisis, fresh evangelical concerns for global warming and political activism, the rising tide of evangelical megachurches, and Catholic struggles concerning women priests and child abuse.

An Evangelical Manifesto of 1989

The document excerpted below was drawn up in 1989 in Manila, Philippines, by three thousand representatives from 170 countries who consider themselves "progressive evangelicals." It was headed "Calling the whole church to take the whole gospel to the whole world." It set out 21 affirmations, 13 of which are reprinted here.

We affirm our continuing commitment to the Lausanne Covenant[12] as the basis of our cooperation in the Lausanne movement.

We affirm that in the Scriptures of the Old and New Testaments God has given us an authoritative disclosure of his character and will, his redemptive acts and their meaning, and his mandate for mission.

We affirm that the biblical gospel is God's enduring message to our world, and we determine to defend, proclaim and embody it.

We affirm that human beings, though created in the image of God, are sinful and guilty, and lost without Christ, and that this truth is a necessary preliminary to the gospel.

We affirm that the Jesus of history and the Christ of glory are the same person, and that this Jesus Christ is absolutely unique, for he alone is God incarnate, our sin-bearer, the conqueror of death and the coming judge.

We affirm that on the cross Jesus Christ took our place, bore our sins and died our death; and that for this reason alone God freely forgives those who are brought to repentance and faith.

We affirm that other religions and ideologies are not alternative paths to God, and that human spirituality, if unredeemed by Christ, leads not to God but to judgment, for Christ is the only way.

We affirm that we must demonstrate God's love visibly by caring for those who are deprived of justice, dignity, food and shelter.

We affirm that the proclamation of God's kingdom of justice and peace

---

12 Lausanne Covenant—proceedings of the International Congress on World Evangelization, Lausanne, Switzerland, 1971.

demands the denunciation of all injustice and oppression, both personal and structural; we will not shrink from this prophetic witness.

We affirm that we who claim to be members of the Body of Christ must transcend within our fellowship the barriers of race, gender and class.

We affirm that the gifts of the Spirit are distributed to all God's people, women and men, and that their partnership in evangelization must be welcomed for the common good.

We affirm that we who proclaim the gospel must exemplify it in a life of holiness and love; otherwise our testimony loses its credibility.

We affirm that God is calling the whole church to take the whole gospel to the whole world. So we determine to proclaim it faithfully, urgently and sacrificially until he comes.

SOURCE: "The Manila Manifesto," in Rowland C. Croucher, *Recent Trends Among Evangelicals*. 2nd ed. Heathmont, Australia: John Mark Ministries, 1991, pp. 103–4
<http://jmm.aaa.net.au/articles/9011.htm>

I've Seen the Promised Land by Martin Luther King, Jr.

Martin Luther King, Jr.

Martin Luther King, Jr. (1929–68), was the leader of the non-violent direct-action wing of the American civil rights movement. Born in Atlanta, he became a Baptist minister in Montgomery, Alabama, and soon earned his doctorate in theology. King traveled widely and spoke often against racial prejudice. He organized many protests, using carefully planned non-violent resistant tactics inspired by Mahatma Gandhi. Only after research, then negotiations, failed would he permit protests against unjust, racially prejudiced customs or laws. He prohibited protesters from fighting back while protesting, in order to demonstrate the moral motives for their cause. His "Letter from Birmingham Jail" (1963) and "I Have a Dream" speech (1963) articulated his principles and passions and won him the Nobel Peace Prize in 1964. He was assassinated in Memphis in 1968, shortly after he delivered the speech excerpted below.

Let us develop a kind of dangerous unselfishness. One day a man came to Jesus; and he wanted to raise some questions about some vital matters in life. At points, he wanted to trick Jesus, and show him that he knew a little more than Jesus knew, and through this, throw him off base. Now that question could have easily ended up in a philosophical and theological debate. But Jesus immediately pulled that question from mid-air, and placed it on a dangerous curve between Jerusalem and Jericho. And he talked about a certain man, who fell among thieves. You remember that a Levite and a priest passed by on the other side. They didn't stop to help him. And finally a man of another race came by. He got down from his beast, decided not to be compassionate by proxy, but with him, administered first aid, and helped the man in need. Jesus ended up saying, this was the good man, this was the great man, because he had the capacity to project the "I" into the "thou," and to be concerned about his brother. Now you know, we use our imagination a great deal to try to determine why the priest and the Levite didn't stop. At times we say they were busy going to church meetings—an ecclesiastical gathering—and they had to get on down to Jerusalem so they wouldn't be late for their meeting. At other times we would speculate that there was a religious law that "One who was engaged in religious ceremonials was not to touch a human body 24 hours before the ceremony." And every now and then we begin to wonder whether maybe they were not going down to Jerusalem, or down to Jericho, rather to organize a "Jericho Road Improvement Association." That's a possibility. Maybe they felt that it was better to deal with the problem from the causal root, rather than to get bogged down with an individual effort.

But I'm going to tell you what my imagination tells me. It's possible that these men were afraid. You see, the Jericho road is a dangerous road. I remember when Mrs. King and I were first in Jerusalem. We rented a car and drove from Jerusalem down to Jericho. And as soon as we got on that road, I said to my wife, "I can see why Jesus used this as a setting for his parable." It's a winding, meandering road. It's really conducive for ambushing. You start out in Jerusalem, which is about 1,200 . . . feet above sea level. And by the time you get down to Jericho, 15 or 20 minutes later, you're about 2,200 feet below sea level. That's a dangerous road. In the days of Jesus it came to be known as the "Bloody Pass." And you know, it's possible that the priest and the Levite looked over that man on the ground and wondered if the robbers were still around. Or it's possible that they felt that the man on the ground was merely faking. And he was acting like he had been robbed and hurt, in order to seize them over there, lure them there for quick and easy seizure. And so the first question that the Levite asked was, "If I stop to help this man, what will happen to me?" But then the Good Samaritan came by. And he reversed the question: "If I do not stop to help this man, what will happen to him?"

That's the question before you tonight. Not, "If I stop to help the sanitation workers, what will happen to all of the hours that I usually spend in my office every day and every week as a pastor?" The question is not, "If I stop to help this man in need, what will happen to me?" "If I do not stop to help the sanitation workers, what will happen to them?" That's the question.

Let us rise up tonight with a greater readiness. Let us stand with a greater determination. And let us move on in these powerful days, these days of challenge to make America what it ought to be. We have an opportunity to make America a better nation. And I want to thank God, once more, for allowing me to be here with you. . . .

And then I got into Memphis. And some began to say the threats, or talk about the threats that were out. What would happen to me from some of our sick white brothers?

Well, I don't know what will happen now. We've got some difficult days ahead. But it doesn't matter with me now. Because I've been to the mountaintop. And I don't mind. Like anybody, I would like to live a long life. Longevity has its place. But I'm not concerned about that now. I just want to do God's will. And He's allowed me to go up to the mountain. And I've looked over. And I've seen the promised land. I may not get there with you. But I want you to know tonight, that we, as a people will get to the promised land. And I'm happy, tonight. I'm not worried about anything. I'm not fearing any man. Mine eyes have seen the glory of the coming of the Lord.

SOURCE: Flip Schulke, ed., *Martin Luther King, Jr: A Documentary ... Montgomery to Memphis.* New York and London: Norton, 1976, pp. 222–3. Reprinted in James Melvin Washington, ed., *A Testament of Hope.* San Francisco: Harper and Row, 1986, pp. 284–6

Not Development, but Liberation by Gustavo Gutiérrez

In the late 1960s Liberation Theology arose from indignation at the poverty of the masses in South America, led by Roman Catholic village priests and theologians such as Gustavo Gutiérrez (b. 1928) in Peru. He opposed the destructive industrial world's surging "development" with a call to liberation. He argued that the poor need ethical and economic preference, because God raises up those who suffer. Liberation theologies have expanded into feminist theologies, black theologies, and indigenous world theologies in general. Gutiérrez points out that Jesus' saying, "The poor you will always have with you" (Matthew 26:11), assumes knowledge of its Deuteronomy 15:11 context: "For the poor will never cease out of the land; therefore I command you, You shall open wide your hand to your brother, to the needy, and to the poor in the land."

We can distinguish three reciprocally interpenetrating levels of meaning of the term *liberation*, or in other words, three approaches to the process of liberation.

In the first place, "liberation" expresses the aspirations of oppressed peoples and social classes, emphasizing the conflictual aspect of the economic, social, and political process which puts them at odds with wealthy nations and oppressive classes. In contrast, the word "development," and above all the policies characterized as developmentalist,[13] appear somewhat aseptic, giving a false picture of a tragic and conflictual reality. The issue of development does in fact find its true place in the more universal, profound, and radical perspective of liberation. It is only within this framework that "development" finds its true meaning and possibilities of accomplishing something worthwhile.

At a deeper level, "liberation" can be applied to an understanding of history. Man [sic] is seen as assuming conscious responsibility for his own

---

13 Developmentalist—Gutiérrez uses the word *desarrollista*, "making worse."

destiny. This understanding provides a dynamic context and broadens the horizons of the desired social changes. In this perspective the unfolding of all of man's dimensions is demanded—a man who makes himself throughout his life and throughout history. The gradual conquest of true freedom leads to the creation of a new man and a qualitatively different society. This vision provides, therefore, a better understanding of what in fact is at stake in our times.

Finally, the word "development" to a certain extent limits and obscures the theological problems implied in the process designated by this term. On the contrary the word "liberation" allows for another approach leading to the Biblical sources which inspire the presence and action of man in history. In the Bible, Christ is presented as the one who brings us liberation. Christ the Savior liberates man from sin, which is the ultimate root of all disruption of friendship and of all injustice and oppression. Christ makes man truly free, that is to say, he enables man to live in communion with him; and this is the basis for all human brotherhood.

SOURCE: David Batstone *et al.*, eds., *A Theology of Liberation: History, Politics, and Salvation.* Maryknoll, NY: Orbis, 1973, pp. 34–5

I Don't Want to Eat Any Sugar by Mother Teresa

Mother Teresa and Sister Emmanuel

Mother Teresa's life (1910–97) and work were exemplary. This Albanian Catholic nun in Calcutta picked up off the street and cared for thousands of dying people; she wore a sari worth about a dollar. She crawled past piles of manure into caves to help frightened people with leprosy. What gave her strength was faith and love. This is an extract from her 1979 Nobel Prize acceptance speech.

Jesus too suffered in order to love us. He still suffers. To be sure that we might remember his great love he became our bread of life to satisfy our hunger for his love, our hunger for God, because it was for this love that we were created. We were created to love and to be loved, and he became man to enable us to love him as he loves us. He has become one with the hungry, the naked, the homeless, the sick, the persecuted, the lonely, the abandoned ones. . . .

I was amazed when I learned that in the West so many young people are on drugs. I tried to understand the reason for this. Why? The answer is, "because in the family there is nobody who cares for them." Fathers and mothers are so busy they have no time. Young parents work, and the child lives in the street, and goes his own way. . . .

The poor are good people. They can teach us much. One day a man came to thank us: "You who practice chastity have taught us very well how to plan our family, because self-control is nothing but love of one for the other." I think he was right. And many times these are people who have nothing to eat, nor a house to live in, yet they know how to be great.

The poor are wonderful people. One evening we picked up four in the street; one was in pitiful condition. I told the other Sisters: "You take care of the other three; I will see about this weakest one." I did all that my love enabled me to do: I put her in a bed, and on her face there appeared a marvelous smile. She took my hand, and after saying just one word: "Thanks!" she died....

That is why we believe what Jesus said: "I was hungry, naked, homeless, unwanted, hated, nobody cared about me ... And you did this for me!" ...

There was a time in Calcutta when it was very difficult for us to get any sugar. I don't know how this came to the ears of the children, but a little four-year-old went home and said to his parents: "I don't want to eat any sugar for three days; I want to give it to Mother Teresa." Three days later his father and mother came to our house with the little fellow. I had never seen them before, and the child could hardly pronounce my name. But he knew very well why he had come: to share his love with others.

SOURCE: Lush Gjergji, *Mother Teresa: Her Life, Her Works*. New Rochelle, NY: New City Press, 1991, pp. 137–41

The Green Patriarch: Environmental Orthodoxy

by Melba Newsome

His Holiness Bartholomew I is the Ecumenical Patriarch, the leader of the world's Orthodox Christians. His office in the Cathedral of St. George in Istanbul over-looks the Bosporus, the seaway that links the Black Sea to the Mediterranean Sea, both suffering from overfishing and pollution. Like some leaders in the Roman Catholic Church and the Protestant churches, he is speaking up for the need for restraint and stewardship toward nature by Christians. Orthodox Christians have always loved nature, he says, and so he has organized several environmental forums, speeches, and trips. He sharply defines Christian moral responsibility for the environment, saying: "For humans to cause species to become extinct and to destroy the biological diversity of God's creation ... these are sins."

Throughout his tenure as Patriarch, Bartholomew I has made environmental protection his crusade. His considerable work to promote the sanctity of our world's natural resources has earned him the sobriquet the Green Patriarch. In November 1997 Bartholomew advanced his agenda significantly. During a tour of the United States—when he became only the fifth religious leader awarded the Congressional Gold Medal—he made a historic speech at a symposium on religion, science, and the environment in Santa Barbara, California. "To commit a crime against the natural world is a sin," the Patriarch told an audience of eight hundred. "For humans to cause species to become extinct and to destroy the biological diversity of God's creation; for humans to degrade the integrity of the earth by causing changes in its climate, by stripping the earth of its natural forests, or destroying its wetlands; for humans to contaminate the earth's waters, its land, its air, and its life with poisonous substances—these are sins."

This wasn't the first time a religious leader had spoken about our responsibility to safeguard the environment. In 1971 the Anglican church declared environmental abuse blasphemous (that is, irreverent or impious). In 1989 Pope John Paul II called the environmental crisis a symptom of a deeper moral crisis. But the Patriarch's pronouncement is believed to be the first time a leader of a major international religion has explicitly linked environmental problems with sinful behavior.

"The Orthodox believe that bread and wine acquire personal characteristics by being made the body and the blood of Christ, and so creation is sanctified and affirmed as being 'very good.' The central concern of Orthodoxy is to enact through the Eucharist this new mode of being in which death ceases to exist. Precisely because creation is 'very good' it is worth preserving. The development of a special ethos of the sanctity of creation springing up from the Eucharist is valuable in the formation of a new environmental consciousness." . . . Each of us has an obligation to God, who "placed the newly created human 'in the Garden of Eden to cultivate it and to guard it'" (Genesis 2:15). He imposed on humanity a stewardship role in relationship to the earth.

There is another aspect of personal responsibility that is close to the heart of Orthodoxy: *encratia*, or self-control, which is fundamental to Orthodox Christians. "Consuming the fruits of the earth unrestrained, we become consumed ourselves by avarice and greed. Asceticism is a corrective practice, a vision of repentance."

Voluntary restraint—and by implication, sustainable living—therefore is essential for practicing Orthodox Christians. "The Christian who harms the environment must start treating it for what it really is, namely, the extension of his or her own body, just as the church is the extension of Christ's physical body."

He has also made the Black Sea a priority. "The picture of the region is quite worrying," the Patriarch says, speaking about the long-term over-fishing and waste-dumping that have wrought havoc in the Black Sea; the last three monk seals spotted in 1996 now believed dead; the Black Sea's nutrient load, which has far exceeded the critical level; and the fishing fleets now idle. . . . "We call upon the world's leaders to take action to halt the destructive changes to the global climate that are being caused by human activity. We must be spokespeople for an ecological ethic that reminds the world that it is not ours to use for our convenience. It is God's gift of love to us, and we must return that love by protecting it and all that is in it. Let us renew the harmony between heaven and earth, and transfigure every detail, every particle of life."

SOURCE: Melba Newsome, "The Green Patriarch: Environmental Orthodoxy," interview with the Patriarch of Eastern Orthodoxy in *The Amicus Journal*, Winter 1999, vol. 20, no. 4, pp. 15–17

Macrowave: Taking Global Warming to Church

by David Batstone

A shift among evangelicals toward liberal social ethics has developed, illustrated by *Sojourners* magazine. This article on global warming, by David Batstone, a contributing editor, shows a change of emphasis from earlier evangelical conservatism. The next selection by Jim Wallis, the Editor-in-Chief, challenges false religion-politics alliances.

The Archbishop is making global warming a personal challenge

Global warming is not an abstract, future crisis. Human beings generate ever increasing amounts of greenhouse gases into the atmosphere, producing carbon dioxide and other gases that trap heat and keep it from escaping into space.

Our earth has arrived at a tipping point, and our own generation bears witness to the impact.

That point is worth emphasizing. A Time/ABC News poll shows that only 44 percent of the U.S. public understands global warming as "a serious problem" today. About 54 percent identify it as "a problem for the future."

To some degree, the mitigation of the crisis among the general public can be traced to a concerted campaign to sow doubt regarding the scientific validation of climate change. Lobby groups from the energy sector fund pseudo-research and ancillary public relations campaigns to promote the view that climate change is a "theory" that is highly contested in scientific circles. The journal *Science,* however, published in 2004 a survey of serious scientific studies addressing global warming. Of the 928 research studies that have been published on the subject in scholarly, peer-reviewed journals, "none of the papers disagreed with the consensus position" that our atmosphere is getting warmer, and the phenomenon is a consequence of human activity.

This past April Paul Krugman published in his *New York Times* column a leaked memo that emerged from a 1998 meeting of the American Petroleum Institute. Those assembled—major oil companies and their industry lobbyists—laid out a strategy to offer "logistical and moral support" to individuals and groups that raise doubts about global warming, "thereby raising questions and undercutting the 'prevailing scientific' wisdom."

The religious community is not in the media business, but it can do a tremendous amount to provide leadership and effective action to stem the rise of global warming. Local congregations could model new behaviors and make concrete a moral mandate to be good stewards of God's creation.

The Archbishop of Canterbury, Dr. Rowan Williams, proclaimed on BBC radio that the Christian church must do some serious soul-searching on the matter. "I think it's a profoundly immoral policy and lifestyle that doesn't consider those people who don't happen to share the present moment with us," said Williams.

The archbishop is making global warming a personal challenge. He drives a Honda Civic petrol-electric hybrid and has set up an environmental task force in the Anglican Church to review the carbon footprint that his national office and individual congregations are emitting.

"We are trying to walk the walk as well as talk the talk," Claire Foster, the Anglican Church's environmental officer, told *The Times* of London. "By 2008 we need to show a measurable reduction in consumption by church buildings themselves," she added.

A number of new tools can help religious communities to make global warming both personal and congregational. First off, it is helpful to realize how any one person contributes to carbon emissions. A California-based company, TerraPass, helps consumers measure the carbon footprint of the cars they drive. The company then offers for purchase a "green tag," which is an investment in a clean energy product like wind power—in equal amount to the amount of carbons emitted by an individual's vehicle.

Organizations can in like manner make every effort to cut their own carbon emissions, then offset the remaining pollutants with clean energy certificates. The grocery chain Whole Foods decided earlier this year to offset 100 percent of its energy consumption with alternative energy. Starbucks also has been on the forefront of the "green tag" movement. For 2006 the coffee company has promised to purchase 20 percent of its power from renewable sources. Of course, no single wind farm has the capacity to supply even a quarter of the 8,400 Starbucks shops across the U.S. But Starbucks does invest in a wind power company the equivalent of 20 percent of its energy consumption, and the wind power company uses that subsidy to offer competitive rates to local energy users. In effect, that is the model of "offset" investments.

Imagine if every religious community in developed nations made it a target to be carbon-neutral. The cumulative effect for alternative and renewable energy would be dramatic. Those efforts also would go a long way to illustrating to Jane and Joe in the pew that global warming is a present threat to our globe that demands immediate action.

SOURCE: *Sojourners* magazine, July 2006, vol. 35, no. 7, p. 31
<http://www.sojo.net/index.cfm?action=magazine.article&issue=Soj0607&article=060766>

Why Can't We Talk about Religion and Politics?
by Jim Wallis

Why can't we talk about religion and politics? These are the two topics you are not supposed to discuss in polite company. Don't break up the dinner party by bringing up either of these subjects! That's the conventional wisdom. Why? Perhaps these topics are too important, too potentially divisive, or raise the issues of core values and ultimate concerns that make us uncomfortable.

Sojourners magazine, where I serve as editor, commits the offense, in every single issue, of talking about faith, politics, and culture. Yet our subscriber and on-line lists are growing, especially among a younger generation. I am also on the road a lot, speaking almost every week to very diverse audiences of people. I hear and feel the hunger for a fuller, deeper, and richer conversation about religion in public life, about faith and politics. It's a discussion that we don't always hear in America today. Sometimes the most strident and narrow voices are the loudest, while more progressive, prophetic, and healing faith often gets missed. But the good news is about how all that is changing—really changing.

Abraham Lincoln had it right. Our task should not be to invoke religion and the name of God by claiming God's blessing and endorsement for all our national policies and practices—saying, in effect, that God is on our side. Rather, Lincoln said, we should pray and worry earnestly whether we are on God's side.

Those are the two ways that religion has been brought into public life in American history. The first way—God on our side—leads inevitably to triumphalism, self-righteousness, bad theology, and, often, dangerous foreign policy. The second way—asking if we are on God's side—leads to much healthier things, namely, penitence and even repentance, humility, reflection, and even accountability. We need much more of all these, because these are often the missing values of politics.

Of course, Martin Luther King Jr. did it best. With his Bible in one hand and the Constitution in the other, King persuaded, not just pronounced. He reminded us all of God's purposes for justice, for peace, and for the "beloved community" where those always left out and behind get a front-row seat. And he did it—bringing religion into public life—in a way that was always welcoming, inclusive, and inviting to all who cared about moral, spiritual, or religious values. Nobody felt left out of the conversation. I try to do that too in this book. . . .

The values of politics are my primary concern in this book. Of course, God is not partisan; God is not a Republican or a Democrat. When either party tries to politicize God, or co-opt religious communities for their political agendas, they make a terrible mistake. The best contribution of religion is precisely not to be ideologically predictable nor loyally partisan. Both parties, and the nation, must let the prophetic voice of religion be heard. Faith must be free to challenge both right and left from a consistent moral ground.

God's politics is therefore never partisan or ideological. But it challenges everything about our politics. God's politics reminds us of the people our politics always neglects—the poor, the vulnerable, the left behind. God's politics challenges narrow national, ethnic, economic, or cultural self-interest, reminding us of a much wider world and the creative human diversity of all those made in the image of the creator. God's politics reminds us of the creation itself, a rich environment in which we are to be good stewards, not mere users, consumers, and exploiters. And God's politics pleads with us to resolve the inevitable conflicts among us, as much as is possible, without the terrible cost and consequences of war. God's politics always reminds us of the ancient prophetic prescription to "choose life, so that you and your children may live," and challenges all the selective moralities that would choose one set of lives and issues over another.

SOURCE: Jim Wallis, *God's Politics: Why the Right Gets It Wrong and the Left Doesn't Get It.* New York: HarperCollins, 2005, pp. xv–xvii

The Rise of the Megachurch   from *The Week* magazine

Protestant "megachurches" began with the Crystal Cathedral in California, with about 10,000 members, and the Yodo Full Gospel Church in Korea, which seats 12,500. In the United States by 2005 there were more than 1,200 churches with over 2,000 people attending; about 4 percent were over the 10,000 mark. Megachurches tend to combine lively gospel or trendy Christian "praise" rock music with conservative theology.

The hottest sector of American religious life is the megachurch, where charismatic pastors preach to thousands of worshippers at once. Why are people flocking to these stadium-size houses of worship?

How big are megachurches? To be considered truly mega, a church must have a regular congregation of at least 2,000. But it's not just a matter of size. There are venerable Catholic churches with congregations in the tens of thousands and yet they aren't considered part of the same phenomenon. The term "megachurch" refers to a newer species of mammoth Protestant church defined as much by style as by head count. Megachurches attract their throngs the same way a business attracts customers: through marketing and friendly service, and by offering a compelling "product" that keeps people coming back for more. Sermons are typically delivered by a charismatic pastor through a top-notch sound system using video clips, live-music accompaniment, and even the occasional PowerPoint presentation. They tend to emphasize the upside of faith, such as how it can lead to personal growth and inner peace, while downplaying such unpleasant notions as burning in hell for all eternity.

How many megachurches are there? Suddenly, a lot. According to a 2005 survey by the Hartford Institute for Religion Research, the U.S. now has 1,210 churches with congregations larger than 2,000 souls, compared to just 350 in 1990. The boom started in the mid-1970s as a function of the same demographic forces that produced suburban sprawl and shopping malls. The father of the movement is generally considered to be Bill Hybels, pastor of the Willow Creek Church in South Barrington, Illinois. In 1975, Hybels conducted the first market-research survey of churchgoers, asking them how they felt about church and what could be done to make the experience more appealing. As a result, Hybels retooled his services with higher production values, and other churches copied the model. Hybels now preaches to a crowd of 20,000 each Sunday.

What are the other big ones? The most influential of the megachurches might be Saddleback in Lake Forest, California. It is the home church of Rick

Warren, an evangelical whose book *The Purpose Driven Life* has long been a fixture on the *New York Times* best-seller list, and whose book *The Purpose Driven Church* is considered the blueprint of the modern megachuch. Attendance at what has become known as "the Saddledome" routinely tops 20,000. Warren has unapologetically characterized his approach to church-building as removing "a lot of the religious trappings of Christianity." Another behemoth is Lakewood Church in Houston, a non-denominational Christian church where Joel Osteen preaches to 41,000 every weekend, in the building that used to be the home of the NBA's Houston Rockets. The demand is so great that in addition to traditional Sunday morning services, Osteen leads services on Sunday afternoons and Saturday evenings as well. Thanks to a widely telecast TV show, as well as his own best-seller—*Your Best Life Now*—the boyish, telegenic Osteen is often considered the public face of the megachurch movement.

Isn't this all just old-fashioned televangelism? In a literal sense, Osteen and Warren could be considered televangelists, since their sermons are broadcast by Christian television stations. But the megachurch movement has avoided the unsavory reputation for hucksterism that has tarnished many televangelists. Megachurches do encourage donations, but many have no mandatory membership dues, and most don't even have a collection plate. Revenues are very healthy, though, thanks to the range of other services megachurches offer. The campus of a full-blown megachurch might include a bank, pharmacy, its own Wi-Fi network, tennis courts, rock-climbing walls, martial-arts classes, restaurants, and gourmet coffee bars. A person might head to their megachurch for AA meetings, job training, a singles group, or classes in auto repair. Some megachurches even house McDonald's franchises—which may be fitting, considering that detractors of megachurches often disparage them as "McChurches."

What don't the critics like? Some traditionalists say that in their zeal to appear welcoming and nonjudgmental, megachurches deliver a bland "Christianity Lite" that glosses over some of the less comfortable truths of the Bible's message. The perennially upbeat Osteen, for instance, is fond of telling his congregation that "God is not mad at you," which some would argue is questionable, given the sheer number of potential miscreants in his audience. Moreover, most megachurches are essentially non-denominational, and therefore are seen in some quarters as diminishing the influence of the mainstream churches. Although roughly two-thirds do have a nominal tie to one of the branches of American Protestantism—usually Southern Baptist—most downplay these connections in order to project a spirit of inclusiveness.

So who's in the pews? Actually, for the most part, pews are out—chairs, often comfortably upholstered, are in. As for who's filling them, megachurch congregants tend to be relatively young and economically diverse. The average age is about 38, and an estimated 60 percent are women. And though most congregations are predominantly white, that has been changing. Osteen's Houston church is said to be 40 percent Caucasian, 30 percent African-

American, and 30 percent Hispanic. The relative anonymity of megachurches, insiders say, encourages people who are uncertain about their faith to drop by. "It's easy to slip in and hang out and experiment, and see what it's like," said Scott Thumma, a sociologist who has studied megachurches. "It's much harder to slip in when there are only 25 other folks in the church."

The Next Little Thing In an attempt to recapture the feeling of neighborhood churches, megachurches encourage members to form smaller groups, or "cells," within the main congregation. A cell will typically meet midweek for Bible study, emotional support, or simple conversation. In recent years, however, hundreds of these cells have split off from the main church and are going it alone, as so-called "home churches" or "mini-churches." Frank Viola, who attends a home church in Florida, says that without the trappings of the "modern institutional church," worshippers take a more active role in their own spiritual journeys. "I don't believe you are going to see the fullness of Jesus Christ expressed, just sitting in a pew listening," Viola says. While the megachurch explosion shows no signs of slowing down, experts say "big-building Christianity" has driven thousands to explore more intimate alternatives. Many of these megachurch refugees are fond of quoting Jesus when he said, "For where two or three are gathered together in my name, there am I."

SOURCE: *The Week* magazine, April 28, 2006
<http://www.theweekmagazine.com/article.aspx?id=1436>

Roman Catholic Womenpriests

The Roman Catholic Church restricts the priesthood to men, arguing that Jesus and his disciples were male. Women today, qualified by seminary education and church leadership roles, have been denied the position, but some have been ordained priests or deacons by supportive bishops. Ordinations of over 24 women have been performed in Europe and North America since 1970. This article from the Catholic Womenpriests movement explains.

Mission The goal of the group "RC Womenpriests" (Roman Catholic Womenpriests) is to bring about the full equality of women in the Roman Catholic Church. At the same time we are striving for a new model of Priestly Ministry.

The movement "RC Womenpriests" does not perceive itself as a counter-current movement against the Roman Catholic Church. It wants neither a schism nor a break from the Roman Catholic Church, but rather wants to work positively within the Church.

Myths and Truths Myth: Women (by virtue of their sex) cannot image Christ. Truth: It is the call of every female and male Christian to image Christ; and it is the call of every female and male Christian to see Christ in every person.

Myth: Roman Catholic women have never been ordained. Truth: Epigraphic evidence exists of women bishops. Until at least the ninth century the Church gave women the full sacramental ordination of deacons. Women priests existed in the West during the fourth and fifth centuries according to literary evidence, and according to epigraphic evidence.

Myth: Roman Catholic women have not been ordained deacons or priests in the modern era. Truth:

Ludmila Javorova, ordained priest, December 28, 1970, among other women ordained

Christine Mayr Lumetzberger, ordained priest 2002, Danube. Ordained a bishop, 2003

Gisela Forster, Ph.D., ordained priest 2002, Danube. Ordained a bishop, 2003

Ida Raming, Ph.D., ordained priest 2002, Danube

Iris Mueller, Ph.D., ordained priest 2002, Danube

Sr. Adelinde Theresia Roitinger, ordained priest 2002, Danube

Pia Brunner, ordained priest 2002, Danube

Dagmar Braun Celeste, ordained priest 2002, Danube

Patricia Fresen, Ph.D., ordained priest 2004, Spain

Deacons ordained 2004, Danube: Genevieve Beney Michele Birch Conery, Ph.D., Jane Via, Ph.D., Astrid Indrican, Victoria Rue, Ph.D., Monica Wyss.

Nine ordinations of women deacons and priests took place on the St. Lawrence Seaway, July 2005. Over 60 women are currently enrolled worldwide in the preparation program of RC Womenpriests.

Myth: These ordinations as women priests are not recognized or valid. Truth: The group "RC Womenpriests" receives its authority from Roman Catholic bishops who stand in full Apostolic Succession. These bishops bestowed sacramentally valid ordinations on the women listed above. All the documents pertaining to these ordinations have been attested and notarized. All minutes of the ordinations, including data about persons, Apostolic Succession, and rituals, together with films and photos, are deposited with a Notary Public.

Myth: Mandatory celibacy goes back to the earliest days of the church. Truth: Scripture citations refer to the marriage of Simon Peter. Citations also refer to married bishops and deacons in the earliest Christian churches.

1   Jesus heals Simon Peter's mother-in-law Matthew 8:14; Mark 1:30; Luke 4:38.
2   I Timothy 3:2 A bishop must be irreproachable, married only once. I Timothy 3:4 A bishop must manage his own household well, keeping his children under control with perfect dignity.
3   I Timothy 3:12 Deacons may be married only once and must manage their children and their households well.

SOURCE: <http://www.romancatholicwomenpriests.org>

Child Abuse Struggles: Facts, Myths and Questions
by Thomas J. Reese

The Roman Catholic Church has struggled with accusations of child sexual abuse by priests. Such abuse also occurs in other religious institutions, and the rate of abuse in society in general is much higher. Numerous churches have been closed and a few dioceses have gone bankrupt. Pope John Paul II (r. 1978–2005) called this crisis an appalling sin, and said that "there is no place in the priesthood and religious life for those who would harm the young." Pope Benedict XVI (r. 2005–) instituted stricter controls to prevent potentially abusive men from becoming priests. Bishops have also expressed profound sorrow for the pain inflicted. Thomas J. Reese is a Jesuit and Editor-in-Chief of *America* magazine.

For those who have been following the sexual abuse crisis in the American Catholic Church since the mid-1980s, the reports by the John Jay College of Criminal Justice and the National Review Board for the Protection of Children and Young People provided confirmation of hunches and the destruction of myths. At the same time, they left many questions unanswered.

The myths have been promoted by people on both sides of the debate— those who want to beat up on the church and those who want to downplay the crisis. But what are the facts reported in this study of sexual abuse in the church between 1950 and 2002?

Myths About the Priests Myth: Less than 1 percent of the clergy are involved in sexual abuse. Fact: 4,392 priests, or 4 percent of the total number of members of the Catholic clergy between 1950 and 2002, have had allegations made against them.

Myth: Much of the abuse was not really serious. Fact: All incidents reported to John Jay involved more than verbal abuse or pornography. Only 3 percent of the acts involved only touching over the victim's clothes. On the other hand, 57 percent of the acts involved touching under the victim's clothes, 27 percent involved the cleric performing oral sex, and 25 percent involved penile penetration or attempted penetration.

Myth: Most of the abusers were serial offenders. Fact: 56 percent of priests had only one allegation against them. The 149 priests who had more than 10 allegations against them were responsible for abusing 2,960 victims, thus accounting for 27 percent of the allegations.

Myth: These offending priests were "dirty old men." Fact: Half the priests were 35 years of age or younger at the time of the first instance of alleged abuse.

Myth: Many of the abusive priests had been victims of sexual abuse as children. Fact: Fewer than 7 percent of the priests were reported to have experienced physical, sexual or emotional abuse as children.

Myth: Celibacy caused the sex abuse crisis. Fact: 96 percent of priests (all of them obliged by celibacy) were not involved in sexual abuse.

Myth: Homosexuality caused the abuse crisis: Fact: No one knows the exact percentage of priests who are homosexual. Estimates have ranged from 10 percent to 60 percent. In any case, most homosexual priests were not involved in the sexual abuse of minors.

Myth: Most abuse was done under the influence of alcohol or drugs when the priest did not know what he was doing. Fact: Although 19 percent of the accused priests had alcohol or substance abuse problems, only 9 percent used drugs or alcohol during the alleged instances of abuse.

Myths About the Victims Myth: There were 60,000 to 100,000 victims of sexual abuse. Fact: While we know only the number of victims who reported their abuse to bishops, it is difficult to see how there could be 6 to 10 times as many victims as the number (10,667) who came forward.

Myth: The victims did not approach the church but sent their lawyers. Fact: Only 20 percent of the allegations were reported to the church by lawyers representing victims. Almost 50 percent of the allegations were reported by victims, plus another 14 percent by parents or guardians.

Myth: Most of the abuse occurred with older teenagers. Fact: Only 15 percent of the victims were 16 to 17 years of age; 51 percent were between the ages of 11 and 14.

Myth: Abusers targeted children of single mothers. Fact: Only 11 percent of victims were living with their mothers only. Almost 79 percent of the victims had both parents living at home.

Myth: Most abusers threatened their victims. Fact: Only 8 percent of victims were threatened by their abuser. Most abusers indulged in "grooming," a premeditated behavior intended to manipulate the potential victim into complying with the sexual abuse; 39 percent of the clerics offered alcohol or drugs to their victims.

Myths About the Church Myth: The abuse is a result of the seminary training after the Second Vatican Council (1963–5). Fact: Almost 70 percent of the abusive priests were ordained before 1970, after attending pre-Vatican II seminaries or seminaries that had had little time to adapt to the reforms of Vatican II.

Myth: This problem is unique to the Catholic Church. Fact: The John Jay report notes that in the period 1992–2000, the number of substantiated sexual abuse cases in American society as a whole has been between 89,355 and 149,800 annually. At a minimum, this number for one year is eight times the total number of alleged abuses in the church over a period of 52 years.

Myth: The abuse is still going on at the same rate. Fact: The number of alleged abuses increased in the 1960s, peaked in the 70s, declined in the 80s, and by the 90s had returned to the levels of the 1950s.

Myth: The Catholic Church has been slower to respond to this crisis than the rest of American society. Fact: The John Jay study reports that for the country as a whole the number of substantiated sexual abuse cases peaked at approximately 149,800 in 1992 and declined by 2 percent to 11 percent per year through 2000. Since sexual abuse in the church appears to have peaked in the 1970s and declined in the 80s and 90s, the church seems to have been ahead of the rest of American society.

Myth: Billions of dollars have been spent by the church dealing with this crisis. Fact: Though the cost may eventually reach a billion dollars, the figure reported by John Jay was $472,507,094.

Myth: The church is spending more money on treating priests and hiring lawyers than on the victims. Fact: 83 percent of the amount spent by the church went to compensation for victims; another 4 percent went to treatment for victims.

Myth: The church knew about these allegations from the very beginning. Fact: According to the John Jay report, one-third of the accusations were made in the years 2002–3. Two-thirds have been reported since 1993. "Thus, prior to 1993, only one-third of cases were known to church officials," says the report.

Myth: The bishops should leave this problem to the criminal justice system. Fact: When allegations were made known to the police, only one in three accused priests was charged with a crime; only 3 percent of all priests with allegations served prison time. There seems to be no correlation between the severity of the offense and whether the alleged victim contacted the police or whether the priest was ultimately charged or convicted, according to the report.

Myth: The abusive priests always/never received treatment. Fact: Nearly 40 percent of priests alleged to have committed sexual abuse participated in treatment programs. The more allegations a priest had, the more likely he was to participate in treatment, according to the report.

SOURCE: *America* magazine, March 22, 2004
<http://www.americamagazine.org/gettext.cfm?articleTypeID=1&textID=3497&issueID=478>

GLOSSARY

Apocalypse Belief that the end of the world, or end times, are coming soon; an ancient and recurring belief expressed in the Noah's Ark story, that God will punish evil-doers but save the good; symbolizes anxiety about the end of an era, such as the destruction of Jerusalem by Rome in New Testament times.

Apocrypha (hidden things) Non-canonical books associated with the Bible.

Canon The official list of books with authority in a religion, either because they are believed to be inspired or revealed, or have been so designated.

Disciples The 12 companions of Christ, the first followers of his teachings.

Eastern Orthodox Branch of Christianity, once Church of the Byzantine Empire; broke with Roman Church in 1054; especially strong in Russia and Greece.

Grace God's freely given, unmerited love and forgiveness.

Heresy, heretic Belief contrary to the orthodox doctrines of Christianity; a follower of such beliefs.

Incarnation God (the Word) made flesh in the person of Jesus Christ.

Justification God's saving of humans from sin by grace through sacraments (Catholic) or faith (Protestant).

Manichaeism Third-century Iranian religion founded by Mani, with a dualistic faith opposing God and matter; apostles of light fight powers of darkness.

Ontology Reflection on ultimate reality behind appearances.

Orthodox The branch of a religious tradition that seeks to practice the original religion in its strictest form, in contrast with reform movements.

Protestant Branch of Christianity that began with Martin Luther in 1500s; stresses authority of Bible, priesthood of all believers, justification by faith; many denominations.

Roman Catholic Branch of Christianity centered in Rome, led by pope; priests officially male and celibate, Mary honored, opposed to abortion.

RSV Revised Standard Version of the Bible: American English translation, using twentieth-century language (1946/52); the New RSV is more gender-inclusive (1989/95).

Savior Christians focus on Jesus as the Messiah or *Christos* (Greek), a human appearance of God who brings salvation; some hoped for political leadership, but Jesus stressed spirituality.

Synoptic The similar gospels of Matthew, Mark, and Luke, whose contents can be compared side-by-side in synopsis fashion.

Theocracy Rule of the state by a religious organization.

Trinity Doctrine of One God in three persons: Father, Son, and Holy Ghost or Holy Spirit.

HOLY DAYS

Epiphany January 6, celebration of the three kings' visit to the baby Jesus.

Ash Wednesday The beginning of Lent; ashes on the forehead initiate a 40-day period of self-restraint and reflection before Easter.

Palm Sunday The Sunday before Easter; begins Holy Week, commemorating Christ's ride into Jerusalem.

Maundy Thursday The Thursday before Easter; remembering the Last Supper and the betrayal of Christ by Judas.

Good Friday Christ's crucifixion.

Easter Sunday Christ's resurrection; Catholic and Protestant date is the Sunday after the full moon after the spring equinox; Orthodox celebrate later.

Ascension Christ's withdrawal into Heaven 40 days after his resurrection.

Pentecost or **Whitsun** The Holy Spirit descends on the Apostles.

The Assumption August 15; Roman Catholic feast, Virgin Mary taken body and soul into Heaven when she died; declared dogma by Pope Pius XII in 1950.

All Saints' Day November 1; memorial for all saints and deceased, with requiem masses in Roman Catholic Church.

Immaculate Conception December 8; Roman Catholic celebration of dogma of Mary's freedom from original sin.

Christmas December 25, celebration of Christ's birth; absorbed festive atmosphere of Roman Saturnalia; Eastern Orthodox date is January 6.

HISTORICAL OUTLINE

c. 4 BCE–0 CE—Jesus born

c. 27–33 CE—Jesus crucified

c. 37–100 CE—Josephus

c. 48–64 CE—letters of Paul

c. 70–95 CE—Gospels written down

c. 150 CE—last of New Testament writings; Gnostic syncretism of Jewish, Iranian, and Platonic mysticism emerges

c. 185–254 CE—Origen

296–373 CE—Athanasius

325 CE—Nicene Creed; Council of Nicaea affirms divinity of Jesus

354–430 CE—Augustine

392 CE—Roman Empire adopts Christianity as official religion

c. 400 CE—canon of Bible set

800–1300—consolidation of papal power

950–1350—Crusades

1054—division between Western Roman Catholic and Eastern Orthodox churches

1098–1179—Hildegard of Bingen

1182–1226—Francis of Assisi

1225–74—Thomas Aquinas

1412–31—Joan of Arc

1453—Gutenberg Bible published

1478—Spanish Inquisition established

1491–1547—King Henry VIII, English founder of Anglican Church

1505–72—John Knox, Scottish leader in Presbyterian tradition

1509–64—John Calvin, French founder of "Reformed" traditions

1517—Protestantism begins with Martin Luther's "95 Theses"; Luther excommunicated four years later

1527—Free Church Schlectheim Confession

1545–63—Council of Trent: Roman Catholic Reformation; rejection of sale of indulgences

1624–91—George Fox, English founder of Quakers (Friends)

1707–88—John Wesley, founder of Methodism

1825–1921—Antoinette Brown Blackwell, first Christian woman ordained

1910–97—Mother Teresa

1929–68—Martin Luther King

1945—Nag Hammadi Library discovered

1947—first of Dead Sea Scrolls found

1962—Vatican II brings more democracy to Catholic Church

2002—seven women claim ordination as Roman Catholic priests

2003—priestly child abuse conflicts expand; U.S. Episcopalians ordain Gene Robinson

2005—Pope John Paul II dies; Joseph Ratzinger elected Pope Benedict XVI

REVIEW QUESTIONS

1   What is the significance of the Resurrection?
2   Summarize Anselm's ontological argument. Does it convince you?
3   How did Martin Luther King relate the Good Samaritan to death?

DISCUSSION QUESTIONS

1   Outline the main themes of Jesus' teachings. How are they similar to and different from those of other major religions?
2   What were the main principles of the Protestant Reformation? Why did they stimulate such a violent reaction?
3   Do you think Christianity can be reconciled with contemporary Western science? How?

INFORMATION RESOURCES

Barrett, David, George Kurian, and Todd M. Johnson, eds. *World Christian Encyclopedia*. 2 vols. Oxford: Oxford University Press, 2001.

Berry, Jason. *Lead Us Not into Temptation: Catholic Priests and the Sexual Abuse of Children*. New York: Doubleday/Champaign, IL: University of Illinois Press, 1992.

Bishop Accountability
<http://www.Bishop-Accountability.org>

Cone, James, and Gayraud Wilmore, eds. *Black Theology: A Documentary History*. 2 vols. Maryknoll, NY: Orbis, 1993.

Cross, F. L., ed. *The Oxford Dictionary of the Christian Church*. Oxford: Oxford University Press, 1997.

Dillenberger, John, ed. *Martin Luther*. Garden City, NY: Anchor Doubleday, 1961.

Ferme, Deane W., ed. *Third World Liberation Theologies: A Primer*. Maryknoll, NY: Orbis, 1986.

Fox, Matthew. *The Coming of the Cosmic Christ*. San Francisco: Harper and Row, 1988.

Freedman, David N., ed. *The Anchor Bible Dictionary*. 6 vols. Garden City, NY: Doubleday, 1992.

Furlong, Monica. *Visions and Longings: Medieval Women Mystics*. Boston: Shambhala, 1996.

Harrington, Daniel. "Introduction to the Canon," in *The New Interpreter's Bible*. Vol. 1, pp. 7–21. Nashville, TN: Abingdon Press, 1994.

Hartford Seminary for Religion Research
<http://hirr.hartsem.edu/org/faith_megachurches_research.html>

Haskins, Susan. *Mary Magdalene: Myth and Metaphor*. New York: Riverhead Books, 1993.

Kavanaugh, Kieran, ed. *John of the Cross: Selected Writings*. New York: Paulist Press, 1987.

Keck, Leander, ed. *The New Interpreter's Bible*. 12 vols. Nashville, TN: Abingdon Press, 1994.

King, Karen L. *The Gospel of Mary of Magdala: Jesus and the First Woman Apostle*. Santa Rosa, CA: Polebridge Press, 2003.

Küng, Hans, et al. *Christianity and the World Religions*. Garden City, NY: Doubleday, 1986.

Lampman, Jane. "Megachurches' way of worship is on the rise," in the *Christian Science Monitor*, Feb. 6, 2006.
<http://www.csmonitor.com/2006/0206/p13s01-lire.html>

Leith, John. *Creeds of the Churches*. Louisville, KY: John Knox Press, 1963.

LeLoup, Jean-Ives. *The Gospel of Mary Magdalene*. Rochester, VT: Inner Traditions, 1997/2002.

Lindler, Eileen. "Megachurches: How Do they Count?" in her *Yearbook of American and Canadian Churches 2003*. Nashville, TN: Abingdon Press, 2003.

Lossy, Vladimir. *The Mystical Theology of the Eastern Church*. Crestwood, NY: St. Vladimir's Seminary Press, 1976.

Marty, Martin, et al. "Christianity," in *Encyclopedia Britannica*. Vol. 16, pp. 251–366. London, 1997.

McGrath, Alister, ed. *The Blackwell Encyclopedia of Modern Christian Thought*. Oxford: Blackwell, 1993.

Merton, Thomas. *Thomas Merton: Spiritual Master*, ed. Lawrence Cunningham. New York: Paulist Press, 1992.

Pagels, Elaine. *The Gnostic Gospels*. New York: Random House, 1979.

Pelikan, Jaroslav, et al. "Christianity," in *Encyclopedia of Religion*, ed. Lindsay Jones. 2nd ed. Vol. 3, pp. 1661–756. New York: Macmillan, 2005.

Plaskow, Judith, and Carol Christ. *Weaving the Visions*. San Francisco: Harper and Row, 1989.

Ruether, Rosemary, and Rosemary Keller, eds. *Women and Religion in America*. 3 vols. San Francisco: Harper and Row, 1981.

Tillich, Paul. *A History of Christian Thought*. New York: Harper and Row, 1968.

Walker, Williston, Richard Norris, Robert Handy, and David Lotz. *A History of the Christian Church*. New York: Scribner, 1985.

Wilson, Ian. *Jesus: the Evidence*. New York: Harper and Row, 1984.

Zefferelli, Franco, dir. *Jesus of Nazareth*. Videorecording. RAI/ITC Entertainment, Ltd., 1977/DVD Artisan Entertainment, 2000.

CHAPTER 10

ISLAM

الله

In the sixth century CE, another great spiritual messenger appeared: the Prophet Muhammad. Although illiterate, he said he received revelations from an angel of God, and recited them in language so beautiful that to this day people weep when they hear It. Many of the revelations concern the absolute oneness of the deity, who has many names according to his attributes (such as the Merciful, the All-Knowing) but who is generally referred to with love and awe by the name of Allah. The most important virtue is submission to the will of Allah. This is one derivation of the word "Islam," which also means "peace."

The Prophet Muhammad is not considered divine, for in Islam worship is to be directed only toward Allah. Nevertheless, his life is considered a beautiful model for humanity, and his sayings and doings have been lovingly recorded. Muslims consider him the last in a series of great prophets of monotheism, beginning with Abraham and the other Jewish patriarchs, and including Jesus. They thus tend to regard Judaism, Christianity, and Islam as a single evolving tradition which was renewed, corrected of historical distortions, and sealed by the Prophet Muhammad.

After early opposition in **Mecca** and subsequent migration to Medina in 622 CE (1 AH),[1] the Prophet Muhammad became a strong political leader, returned triumphantly to Mecca, and made it a great center of monotheistic worship—which it remains to this day. Pilgrimage to Mecca's holy sites at least once in one's life is incumbent upon all Muslims, even though today they are spread around the world, forming the second largest and fastest-growing of all world religions. They are expected to regard all humanity as a single family, without racial distinctions, and to share the Prophet's message in a non-coercive way with non-Muslims so that they, too, may embark upon the straight path that leads to heavenly bliss, rather than the path of non-believers, which leads to hellish torments.

After Muhammad's death, conflicts over leadership divided Muslims into major groups. The Sunni (at present about 80 percent of all Muslims) elect their caliph leaders. The Shi'a (adj. Shi'ite) recognize not elected Sunni caliphs, but a series of

---

1 The Muslim (AH) calendar is based on lunar years starting from the **Hijrah** (migration to Medina). Compared to the solar calendar used for calculating Common Era (CE) dates, which are based on the approximate birth year of Jesus, there are 11 days fewer in a lunar calendar, so the difference between CE dates and AH dates is continually changing.

12 hereditary Imams (leaders, guides) following Muhammad. The **Sufis** form a third, overlapping group which pursues esoteric, contemplative prayer, meditation, and dance (the "Whirling Dervish" Mevlevi Order).

Non-Muslims commonly think of Islam as an attempt to create Muslim-dominated societies ruled by Muslim law, a desire which has spawned passionate revolutionary movements in many parts of the world. However, Islam has also given birth to great mystics and great intellectuals over the centuries, and its rich spirituality continues to coexist today with more politicized versions of the faith.

The Prophet Muhammad

The Prophet Muhammad was born in 570 CE into an Arabic culture of clans who lived by farming, herding, and camel caravan trade between Asia and the Mediterranean, carrying valuables such as silks, cinnamon, and pepper. Their religions were polytheistic and nature-oriented; their ethics were tribally centered, the societies largely patriarchal. Prophecy was often practiced, involving trance visions and behavioral guidelines. Contact with nearby Jews and Christians was commonplace, and their religions were known to Muhammad's society. Many traditions of the actions and words of the Prophet, outside the Qur'an, were collected in **Hadith** (reports of the Prophet's actions). Two of the most important Hadith concerning the faith tell of the Prophet's first revelations around 610 CE, and his **Night Journey** to the seventh heaven. They are from *Sahih Muslim*, chapters 74 and 75.

The Beginning of Muhammad's Revelation

from *Sahih Muslim*

'A'isha, the wife of the Apostle of Allah (may peace be upon him), reported: The first (form) with which was started the revelation to the Messenger of Allah was the true vision in sleep. And he did not see any vision but it came like the bright gleam of dawn. Thenceforth solitude became dear to him and he used to seclude himself in the cave of Hira', where he would engage in *tahannuth* (and that is a worship for a number of nights) before returning to his family and getting provisions again for this purpose. He would then return to **Khadija** and take provisions for a like period, till Truth came upon him while he was in the cave of Hira'. There came to him the angel and said: Recite, to which he replied: I am not lettered. He took hold of me [the Apostle said] and pressed me, till I was hard pressed; thereafter he let me off and said: Recite. I said: I am not lettered. He then again took hold of me and pressed me for the second time till I was hard pressed and then let me off and said: Recite, to which I replied: I am not lettered. He took hold of me and pressed me for the third time, till I was hard pressed and then let me go and said: Recite in the name of your Lord Who created, created man from a clot of blood. Recite. And your most bountiful Lord is He Who taught the use of pen, taught man what he knew not (Qur'an 96:1–4). Then the Prophet returned therewith, his heart was trembling, and he went to Khadija and said: Wrap me up, wrap me up! So they wrapped him till the fear had left him. He then said to Khadija: O Khadija! what has happened to me?—and he informed her of the happening, saying: I fear for myself. She replied: It can't be. Be happy. I swear by Allah that He shall never humiliate you. By Allah, you join ties of relationship, you speak the truth, you bear people's burden, you help the destitute, you entertain guests, and you help against the vicissitudes which affect people. Khadija then took him to Waraqa b. Naufal b. Asad b. 'Abd al-'Uzza, and he was the son of Khadija's uncle, i.e. the brother of her father. And he was the man who had embraced Christianity in the Days of Ignorance (i.e. before Islam) and he used to write books in Arabic and, therefore, wrote Injil in Arabic as God willed that he should write. He was very old and had become blind. Khadija said to him: O uncle! listen to the son of your brother. Waraqa b. Naufal said: O my nephew! what did you see? The Messenger of Allah (may peace be upon him), then, informed him what he had seen, and Waraqa said to him: It is *namus*[2] that God sent down to Musa. Would that I were then (during your prophetic career) a young man. Would that I might be alive when your people would expel you! The Messenger of Allah (may peace be upon him) said: Will they drive me out? Waraqa said: Yes. Never came a man with a like of what you have brought but met hostilities. If I see your day I shall help you wholeheartedly.

This hadith has been narrated on the authority of 'A'isha with another chain of narrators like the one transmitted by Yunus, i.e. the first thing with which the revelation was initiated with the Messenger of Allah (may peace be upon him) except the words: By Allah, Allah would never humiliate you, and Khadija said: O son of my uncle! listen to the son of your brother.

This hadith has been reported from 'A'isha by another chain of transmitters and the words are: He (the Holy Prophet) came to Khadija and his heart was trembling. The rest of the hadith has been narrated like one transmitted by Yunus and Ma'mar, but the first part is not mentioned, i.e. the first thing with which was started the revelation to the Holy Prophet was the true vision. And these words like those transmitted by Yunus are mentioned thus: By Allah, Allah would never humiliate you. And there is also mention of the words of Khadija: O son of my uncle! listen to the son of your brother.

SOURCE: *Sahih Muslim*, trans. 'Abdul Hamid Siddiqi. Lahore, Pakistan: Sh. Muhammad Ashraf, 1973, vol. 1, pp. 96–8

Night Journey

The Night Journey from *Sahih Muslim*

It is narrated on the authority of Anas b. Malik that the Messenger of Allah (may peace be upon him) said: I was brought al-Buraq who is an animal white and long, larger than a donkey

---

2 *Namus*—the angel entrusted with divine secrets.

but smaller than a mule, who would place his hoof at a distance equal to the range of vision. I mounted it and came to the Temple (Bait-ul-Maqdis[3] in Jerusalem), then tethered it to the ring used by the prophets. I entered the mosque and prayed two rak'ahs in it, and then came out and Gabriel brought me a vessel of wine and a vessel of milk. I chose the milk, and Gabriel said: You have chosen the natural thing. Then he took me to heaven.

Gabriel then asked the (gate of the heaven) to be opened and he was asked who he was. He replied: Gabriel. He was again asked: Who is with you? He (Gabriel) said: Muhammad. It was said: Has he been sent for? Gabriel replied: He has indeed been sent for. And (the door of the heaven) was opened for us and lo! we saw Adam. He welcomed me and prayed for my good. Then we ascended to the second heaven. Gabriel (peace be upon him) asked the door of the heaven to be opened, and he was asked who he was. He answered: Gabriel; and he was again asked: Who is with you? He replied: Muhammad. It was said: Has he been sent for? He replied: He has indeed been sent for. The gate was opened. When I entered Isa b. Maryam and Yahya b. Zakariya (peace be upon both of them), cousins from the maternal side, welcomed me and prayed for my good. Then I was taken to the third heaven and Gabriel asked for the opening (of the door). He was asked: Who are you? He replied: Gabriel. He was (again) asked: Who is with you? He replied: Muhammad (may peace be upon him). It was said: Has he been sent for? He replied: He has indeed been sent for. (The gate) was opened for us and I saw Yusuf (peace of Allah be upon him) who had been given half of (world) beauty. He welcomed me and prayed for my well-being. Then he ascended with us to the fourth heaven. Gabriel (peace be upon him) asked for the (gate) to be opened, and it was said: Who is he? He replied: Gabriel. It was (again) said: Who is with you? He said: Muhammad. It was said: Has he been sent for? He replied: He has indeed been sent for. The (gate) was opened for us, and lo! Idris was there. He welcomed me and prayed for my well-being. (About him) Allah, the Exalted and the Glorious, has said: "We elevated him (Idris) to the exalted position" (Qur'an 19:57).

Then he ascended with us to the fifth heaven and Gabriel asked for the (gate) to be opened. It was said: Who is he? He replied: Gabriel. It was (again) said: Who is with thee? He replied: Muhammad. It was said: Has he been sent for? He replied: He has indeed been sent for. (The gate) was opened for us and then I was with Harun (Aaron—peace of Allah be upon him). He welcomed me and prayed for my well-being. Then I was taken to the sixth heaven. Gabriel (peace be upon him) asked for the door to be opened. It was said: Who is he? He replied: Gabriel. It was said: Who is with thee? He replied: Muhammad. It was said: Has he been sent for? He replied: He has indeed been sent for. (The gate) was opened for us and there I was with Musa (Moses—peace be upon him). He welcomed me and prayed for

3 Bait-ul-Maqdis—"The Much Frequented House"; the Dome of the Rock.

my well-being. Then I was taken up to the seventh heaven. Gabriel asked the (gate) to be opened. It was said: Who is he? He said: Gabriel. It was said: Who is with thee? He replied: Muhammad (may peace be upon him). It was said: Has he been sent for? He replied: He has indeed been sent for. (The gate) was opened for us and there I found Ibrahim (Abraham—peace be upon him) reclining against the Bait-ul-Ma'mur and there enter into it seventy thousand angels every day, never to visit (this place) again.

Then I was taken to Sidrat-ul-Muntaha[4] whose leaves were like elephant ears and its fruit like big earthenware vessels. And when it was covered by the Command of Allah, it underwent such a change that none amongst the creation has the power to praise its beauty. Then Allah revealed to me a revelation and He made obligatory for me fifty prayers every day and night. Then I went down to Moses (peace be upon him) and he said: What has your Lord enjoined upon your **Ummah**? I said: Fifty prayers. He said: Return to thy Lord and beg for reduction (in the number of prayers), for your community shall not be able to bear this burden, as I have put to test the children of Isra'il and tried them (and found them too weak to bear such a heavy burden). He (the Holy Prophet) said: I went back to my Lord and said: My Lord, make things lighter for my Ummah. (The Lord) reduced five prayers for me. I went down to Moses and said: (The Lord) reduced five (prayers) for me. He said: Verily thy Ummah shall not be able to bear this burden, return to thy Lord and ask Him to make things lighter. I then kept going back and forth between my Lord Blessed and Exalted and Moses, till He said: There are five prayers every day and night, O Muhammad, each being credited as ten, so that makes fifty prayers. He who intends to do a good deed and does not do it will have a good deed recorded for him; and if he does it, it will be recorded for him as ten; whereas he who intends to do an evil deed and does not do, it will not be recorded for him; and if he does it, only one evil deed will be recorded. I then came down and when I came to Moses and informed him, he said: Go back to thy Lord and ask Him to make things lighter. Upon this the Messenger of Allah remarked: I returned to my Lord until I felt ashamed before Him.

It is narrated on the authority of Anas b. Malik that the Messenger of Allah (may peace be upon him) said: (The angels) came to me and took me to the Zamzam[5] and my heart was opened and washed with the water of Zamzam and then I was left (at my place).

Anas b. Malik reported that Gabriel came to the Messenger of Allah (may peace be upon him) while he was playing with his playmates. He took hold of him and lay him prostrate on the ground and tore open his breast and took out the heart from it and then extracted a blood-clot out of it and said: That was the part of Satan in thee. And then he washed it with the

---

4 The Sidr is the Arabian *lote* tree, known for its abundant shade.
5 Zamzam or Zumzum—("abundant water") the legendary sacred spring at Mecca near the Ka'ba stone, opened by Gabriel to save Hajira and Ismail from dying of thirst.

water of Zamzam in a golden basin and then it was joined together and restored to its place. The boys came running to his mother, i.e. his nurse, and said: Verily Muhammad has been murdered. They all rushed towards him (and found him all right). His colour was changed. Anas said: I myself saw the marks of needle on his breast.

SOURCE: *Sahih Muslim*, trans. 'Abdul Hamid Siddiqi. Lahore, Pakistan: Sh. Muhammad Ashraf, 1973, vol. 1, pp. 100–3

Islamic scripture: the Qur'an

The Qur'an

The Holy Book of Islam, the Qur'an (Koran), was revealed to Muhammad and was written down by aides. Unlike the Jewish Tanakh, which was assembled over a thousand-year period, the Qur'an was recorded by the year 650 CE, a scant 18 years after Muhammad died. It has a stronger historical basis than many sacred texts of world religions, since it was written down more recently than most. Its original language—Arabic—has been carefully preserved, and it is felt that the Holy Qur'an cannot be translated properly from Arabic into any other language. Nonetheless, English translations have been attempted for the sake of those who do not understand Arabic. None of them is able to capture the musical, soulful quality of the Arabic, but they give some idea of the scripture's content. There follows a selection of passages, beginning with the **Fatiha** or opening chapter, and covering topics such as right behavior, the family, and **jihad** as well as figures familiar from other religions—Adam, Abraham, Moses, Mary, and Jesus.

Fatiha

In the name of God, Most Gracious, Most Merciful.
Praise be to God, the Cherisher and Sustainer of the Worlds;
Most Gracious, Most Merciful; Master of the Day of Judgment.
Thee do we worship, And Thine aid we seek.
Show us the straight way, The way of those on whom
Thou hast bestowed Thy Grace,
Those whose (portion) is not wrath, and who go not astray. (**Sura** 1)

Allah

There is no god but He; That is the witness of Allah, His angels, and those endued with knowledge, standing firm on justice. There is no god but He, the Exalted in Power, the Wise. (3:18)

He it is Who created the heavens and the earth in Six Days, and is moreover firmly established on the Throne (of Authority). He knows what enters within the earth and what comes forth out of it, what comes down from heaven and what mounts up to it. And He is with you wheresoever ye may be. And Allah sees well all that ye do. (57:4)

To Allah belongeth all that is in the heavens and on earth. Whether ye show what is in your minds or conceal it, Allah calleth you to account for it. He forgiveth whom He pleaseth, and punisheth whom he pleaseth, for Allah hath power over all things. (2:284)

To Allah belong the East and the West: Whithersoever ye turn, there is the presence of Allah. For Allah is all-Pervading, all-Knowing. (2:115)

He is the First and the Last, and the Outward and the Inward; and He is Knower of all things. (57:3)

He is the One Who sends to His Servant Manifest Signs, that He may lead you from the depths of Darkness into the Light and verily Allah is to you most kind and Merciful. (57:9)

Messengers

Muhammad is not more than an Apostle; many were the Apostles that passed away before him. (3:144)

We have sent thee inspiration, as We sent it to Noah and the Messengers after him: We sent inspiration to Abraham, Isma'il, Isaac, Jacob, and the Tribes, to Jesus, Job, Jonah, Aaron, and Solomon, and to David We gave the Psalms. (4:163)

Say: "We believe in Allah, and in what has been revealed to us and what was revealed to Abraham, Isma'il, Isaac, Jacob, and the Tribes, and in (the Books) given to Moses, Jesus, and the prophets, from their Lord: We make no distinction between one and another among them, and to Allah do we bow our will (in Islam)." (3:84)

O mankind! The Apostle hath come to you in truth from God: believe in him; it is best for you. (4:170)

People of the Book

Mankind was one single nation, and Allah sent Messengers with glad tidings and warnings; and with them He sent the Book in truth, to judge between people in matters wherein they differed; but the People of the Book, after the clear Signs came to them, did not differ among themselves, except through selfish contumacy.[6] Allah by His Grace guided the believers to the Truth, concerning that wherein they differed. For Allah guides whom He will to a path that is straight. (2:213)

Say: "O People of the Book! come to common terms as between us and you: That we worship none but Allah; that we associate no partners with him; that we erect not, from among ourselves, Lords and patrons other than

---

6 Contumacy—stubborn rebellion.

Allah." If then they turn back, say ye: "Bear witness that we (at least) are Muslims (bowing to Allah's Will)." (3:64)

Those who believe (in the Qur'an), and those who follow the Jewish (scriptures), and the Christians and the Sabians,[7] any who believe in Allah and the Last Day, and work righteousness, shall have their reward with their Lord; on them shall be no fear, nor shall they grieve. (2:62)

Unity of Humanity

And hold fast, all together, by the Rope which God stretches out for you, and be not divided among yourselves; and remember with gratitude God's favor on you; for ye were enemies and He joined your hearts in love, so that by His Grace, ye became brethren. (3:103)

Righteousness

Those who believe, and do deeds of righteousness, and establish regular prayers and regular charity, will have their reward with their Lord: on them shall be no fear, nor shall they grieve. (2:277)

Allah hath promised to Believers, men and women, gardens under which rivers flow, to dwell therein, and beautiful mansions in gardens of everlasting bliss. But the greatest bliss is the good pleasure of Allah: that is the supreme felicity. (9:72)

O ye who believe! Eat not up your property among yourselves in vanities: But let there be amongst you Traffic and trade by mutual good-will: Nor kill (or destroy) yourselves: for verily Allah hath been to you Most Merciful! (4:29)

They ask thee concerning wine and gambling. Say: "In them is great sin and some profit for men; but the sin is greater than the profit." (2:219)

Mecca

We see the turning of thy face (for guidance) to the heavens: now shall We turn thee to a Qibla[8] that shall please thee. Turn then thy face in the direction of the sacred Mosque: wherever ye are, turn your faces in that direction. (2:144)

For **Hajj** are the months well known. If any one undertakes that duty therein, Let there be no obscenity, nor wickedness, nor wrangling in the Hajj. And whatever good ye do, (be sure) Allah knoweth it. And take a provision (with you) for the journey, but the best of provisions is right conduct. So fear Me, o ye that are wise. (2:197)

---

7 Sabians (or Mandaeans)—a small monotheistic sect from southern Iraq with ancient roots which practices baptism and Babylonian astrology; their holy book is the *Ginza Rba*.
8 Qibla—the direction faced in prayer (toward Mecca).

Jihad

Not equal are those believers who sit (at home) and receive no hurt, and those who strive and fight in the cause of God with their goods and their persons. God hath granted a grade higher to those who strive and fight. (4:95)

Fight in the cause of God those who fight you, but do not transgress limits; for God loveth not transgressors. (2:190)

And fight them on until there is no more tumult or oppression, and there prevail justice and faith in God; but if they cease, let there be no hostility except to those who practice oppression. (2:193)

And if any strive (with might and main), they do so for their own souls: for Allah is free of all needs from all creation. (29:6)

Let there be no compulsion in religion: Truth stands out clear from Error: whoever rejects evil and believes in Allah hath grasped the most trustworthy hand-hold, that never breaks. And Allah heareth and knoweth all things. (2:256)

Gender, Family

O mankind! reverence your Guardian-Lord, who created you from a single person, created, of like nature, his mate, and from them twain scattered (like seeds) countless men and women; reverence Allah, through whom ye demand your mutual (rights), and (reverence) the wombs (that bore you); for Allah ever watches over you. (4:1)

Men are the protectors and maintainers of women, because God has given the one more (strength) than the other, and because they support them from their means. Therefore the righteous women are devoutly obedient, and guard in (the husband's) absence what God would have them guard. As to those women on whose part ye fear disloyalty and ill-conduct, admonish them (first), (next), refuse to share their beds, (and last) beat them (lightly); but if they return to obedience, seek not against them means (of annoyance): For God is Most High, Great (above you all). (4:34)

Do not marry unbelieving women (idolaters), until they believe: A slave woman who believes is better than an unbelieving woman, even though she allures you. Nor marry (your girls) to unbelievers until they believe: A man slave who believes is better than an unbeliever, even though he allures you. Unbelievers do (but) beckon you to the Fire. But Allah beckons by His Grace to the Garden (of bliss) and forgiveness, and makes His Signs clear to mankind: That they may celebrate His praise. (2:221)

If ye fear that ye shall not be able to deal justly with the orphans, marry women of your choice, two or three or four; but if ye fear that ye shall not be able to deal justly (with them), then only one, or (a captive) that your right hands possess, that will be more suitable, to prevent you from doing injustice. (4:3)

If a wife fears cruelty or desertion on her husband's part, there is no blame on them if they arrange an amicable settlement between themselves; and such settlement is best; even though men's souls are swayed by greed. But if ye do good and practice self-restraint, Allah is well-acquainted with all that ye do. (4:128)

So if a husband divorces his wife (irrevocably), he cannot, after that, remarry her until after she has married another husband and he has divorced her. In that case there is no blame on either of them if they re-unite, provided they feel that they can keep the limits ordained by Allah. (2:23)

If any do deeds of righteousness—be they male or female—and have faith, they will enter heaven, and not the least injustice will be done to them. (4:124)

Self-restraint

O ye who believe! Fasting is prescribed to you as it was prescribed to those before you, that ye may (learn) self-restraint.... Ramadan is the (month) in which was sent down the Qur'an, as a guide to mankind, also clear (signs) for guidance and judgment (between right and wrong). So every one of you who is present (at his home) during that month should spend it in fasting, but if any one is ill, or on a journey, the prescribed period (should be made up) by days later. (2:183, 185)

Adam

He said: "O Adam! Tell them their names." When he had told them, Allah said: "Did I not tell you that I know the secrets of heaven and earth, and I know what ye reveal and what ye conceal? And behold, We said to the angels: "Bow down to Adam" and they bowed down. Not so Iblis: he refused and was haughty: He was of those who reject Faith.

We said: "O Adam! dwell thou and thy wife in the Garden; and eat of the bountiful things therein as (where and when) ye will; but approach not this tree, or ye run in harm and transgression."

Then did Satan make them slip from the (garden), and get them out of the state (of felicity) in which they had been. We said: "Get ye down, all (ye people), with enmity between yourselves. On earth will be your dwelling-place and your means of livelihood—for a time."

Then learnt Adam from his Lord words of inspiration and his Lord turned towards him; for He is Oft-Returning, Most Merciful. (2:33–7)

Abraham

And remember that Abraham was tried by his Lord with certain commands, which he fulfilled: He said: "I will make thee an **Imam** to the Nations." He pleaded: "And also (Imams) from my offspring!" He answered: "But My Promise is not within the reach of evil-doers." (2:124)

Moses

We sent an inspiration to Moses: "Travel by night with my servants, and strike a dry path for them through the sea, without fear of being overtaken (by Pharaoh) and without any other fear." Then Pharaoh pursued them with his forces, but the waters completely overwhelmed them and covered them up. Pharaoh led his people astray instead of leading them aright. O ye Children of Israel! We delivered you from your enemy, and We made a Covenant with you on the right side of Mount Sinai, and We sent down to you manna and quails. (22:77–80)

Mary

Behold! the angels said: "O Mary! Allah hath chosen thee and purified thee—chosen thee above the women of all nations. . . . Behold! the angels said: "O Mary! Allah giveth thee glad tidings of a Word from Him: his name will be Christ Jesus, the son of Mary, held in honour in the world and the Hereafter and of (the company of) those nearest to Allah; He shall speak to the people in childhood and in maturity. And he shall be (of the company) of the righteous." She said: "O my Lord! How shall I have a son when no man hath touched me?" He said: "Even so: Allah createth what He willeth: When He hath decreed a plan, He but saith to it, 'Be,' and it is!" (3:42–7)

Jesus

Then will Allah say: "O Jesus the son of Mary! Recount My favour to thee and to thy mother. Behold! I strengthened thee with the holy spirit, so that thou didst speak to the people in childhood and in maturity. Behold! I taught thee the Book and Wisdom, the Law and the Gospel and behold! thou makest out of clay, as it were, the figure of a bird, by My leave, and thou breathest into it and it becometh a bird by My leave, and thou healest those born blind, and the lepers, by My leave. And behold! thou bringest forth the dead by My leave. And behold! I did restrain the Children of Israel from (violence to) thee when thou didst show them the clear Signs, and the unbelievers among them said: 'This is nothing but evident magic.'" (5:110)

Christ the son of Mary was no more than a messenger; many were the messengers that passed away before him. His mother was a woman of truth.

They had both to eat their (daily) food. See how Allah does make His signs clear to them; yet see in what ways they are deluded away from the truth! (5:75)

That they said (in boast), "We killed Christ Jesus the son of Mary, the Messenger of Allah"; but they killed him not, nor crucified him, but so it was made to appear to them, and those who differ therein are full of doubts, with no (certain) knowledge, but only conjecture to follow, for of a surety they killed him not: Nay, Allah raised him up unto Himself; and Allah is exalted in Power, Wise. (4:157–8)

They say: "Allah hath begotten a son." Glory be to Him.—Nay, to Him belongs all that is in the heavens and on earth: everything renders worship to Him. (2:116)

If only they had stood fast by the Law, the Gospel, and all the revelation that was sent to them from their Lord, they would have enjoyed happiness from every side. There is from among them a party on the right course: but many of them follow a course that is evil. (5:66)

From those, too, who call themselves Christians, We did take a covenant, but they forgot a good part of the message that was sent them: so We estranged them, with enmity and hatred between the one and the other, to the day of judgment. And soon will Allah show them what it is they have done. (5:14)

The Day of Judgment

Then, on the Day of Judgment, He will cover them with shame, and say: "Where are My 'partners' concerning whom ye used to dispute (with the godly)?" Those endued with knowledge will say: "This Day, indeed, are the Unbelievers covered with shame and misery (namely) those whose lives the angels take in a state of wrong-doing to their own souls." Then would they offer submission (with the pretence), "We did no evil (knowingly)." (The angels will reply), "Nay, but verily Allah knoweth all that ye did; So enter the gates of Hell, to dwell therein. Thus evil indeed is the abode of the arrogant." To the righteous (when) it is said, "What is it that your Lord has revealed?" they say, "All that is good." To those who do good, there is good in this world, and the Home of the Hereafter is even better and excellent indeed is the Home of the righteous, Gardens of Eternity which they will enter: beneath them flow (pleasant) rivers: they will have therein all that they wish: thus doth Allah reward the righteous, (namely) those whose lives the angels take in a state of purity, saying (to them), "Peace be on you; enter ye the Garden, because of (the good) which ye did (in the world)." (16:27–32)

SOURCE: Qur'an excerpts are taken from *The Holy Qur'an*, trans. with a commentary by Abdullah Yusuf Ali. Beirut, Lebanon: Dar Al Arabia, 1968 <http //www.usc.edu/dept/MSA/quran>

Hadith

"Hadith," as we have seen, means "report" on the actions and words of the Prophet, outside the Qur'an, as told by his companions. Hadith range from grand revelations from Allah to descriptions of the Prophet's life, rules of war, marriage, **mosque** conduct, and personal behavior. Like all religious guidelines, they reflect their cultural environment. They are the second basis, after the Qur'an, for Islamic law, or **Shari'ah**. They contain references to their sources and seek to establish an authoritative chain (**isnah**) of transmission. Reporting on one Hadith on Jihad, Abdullah Suhrawardy (1882–1935) wrote in *The Sayings of Muhammad*: "The most excellent Jihad is that for the conquest of self." Traditionally, the most authoritative and famous Hadith collections are the *Sahih* ("the Authentic") *of Muhammad Ibn Ismail al-Bukhari* (d. 870 CE, called "Bukhari") and the *Sahih of Abu-l-Husayn Muslim ibn al-Hajjaj* (d. 875 CE, called "Muslim"). The following are from *Sahih Muslim* (volumes and pages or websites given).

Allah's Mercy

Allah's Messenger (may peace be upon him) said: When Allah created the creation He put down in his Book, which is with Him upon the Throne: Verily, My mercy predominates My wrath. (Arabic 4939)

SOURCE: *Sahih Muslim*
<http://hadith.al-islam.com/Bayan/Display.asp?Lang=eng&ID=1571>

Allah is a Light

It is narrated on the authority of Abu Dharr: I asked the Messenger of Allah (may peace be upon him): Did you see thy Lord? He said: He is a Light: how could I see Him? (I:341)

  Abu Musa reported: The Messenger of Allah (may peace be upon him): was standing among us and he told us five things. He said: Verily, the Exalted and Mighty God does not sleep, and it does not befit him. He lowers the scale and lifts it. The deeds of the day are taken up to Him before the deeds of the night. His veil is the light. In the Hadith narrated by Abu Akr (instead of the word "light") it is fire. If he withdraws it (the veil) the splendour of His countenance would consume His creation so far as His sight reaches. (I:343)

Seeking Consent for Marriage

Abu Huraira (Allah be pleased with him) reported Allah's Messenger (may peace be upon him) as having said: A woman without a husband (or divorced or a widow) must not be married until she is consulted, and a virgin must not be married until her permission is sought. They asked the Prophet of Allah (may peace be upon him): How her (virgin's) consent can be solicited? He (the Holy Prophet) said: That she keeps silent. (II:714)

Fighting of Women Side by Side with Men

It has been narrated on the authority of Anas that, on the Day of Hunain, Umm Sulaim took out a dagger she had in her possession. Abu Talha saw her and said: Messenger of Allah, this is Umm Sulaim. She is holding a dagger. The Messenger of Allah (may peace be upon him) asked (her): What for are you holding this dagger? She said: I took it up so that I may tear open the belly of a polytheist who comes near me. The Messenger of Allah (may peace be upon him) began to smile (at these words). She said: Messenger of Allah, kill all those people—other than us—whom thou hast declared to be free (on the day of the Conquest of Mecca). (They embraced Islam because) they were defeated at your hands (and as such their Islam is not dependable). The Messenger of Allah (may peace be upon him) said: Umm Sulaim, God is sufficient (against the mischief of the polytheists) and He will be kind to us (so you need not carry this dagger).

It has been narrated on the authority of Anas b. Malik who said that the Messenger of Allah (may peace be upon him) allowed Umm Sulaim and some other women of the Ansar to accompany him when he went to war; they would give water (to the soldiers) and would treat the wounded. (III:1001)

Prohibition of Killing Women and Children in War

It is narrated on the authority of 'Abdullah that a woman was found killed in one of the battles fought by the Messenger of Allah (may peace be upon him). He disapproved of the killing of women and children.

It is narrated by Ibn 'Umar that a woman was found killed in one of these battles; so the Messenger of Allah (may peace be upon him) forbade the killing of women and children. (IV:946)

Compel not your Slave-girls to Prostitution

Jabir reported that 'Abdullah b. Ubayy b. Salul used to say to his slave-girl: Go and fetch something for us by committing prostitution. It was in this connection that Allah, the Exalted and Glorious, revealed this verse: "And compel not your slave-girls to prostitution when they desire to keep chaste in order to seek the frail goods of their world's life, and whoever compels them, then surely after their compulsion Allah is Forgiving, Merciful" (xxiv:33).

Jabir reported that 'Abdullah b. Ubayy b. Salul had two slave-girls; one was called Musaika and the other one was called Umaima and he compelled them to prostitution (for which 'Abdullah b. Ubayy b. Salul compelled them). They made a complaint about this to Allah's Messenger (may peace be upon him) and it was upon this that this verse was revealed: "And compel not your slave-girls to prostitute" up to the words: "Allah is Forgiving, Merciful." (IV:1555)

Removal of the Idols from the Vicinity of the Ka'ba

It has been narrated by Ibn 'Abdullah who said: The Holy Prophet (may peace be upon him) entered Mecca. There were three hundred and sixty idols around the Ka'ba. He began to thrust them with the stick that was in his hand saying: "Truth has come and falsehood has vanished. Lo! falsehood was destined to vanish" (xvii:8). Truth has arrived, and falsehood can neither create anything from the beginning nor can it restore to life. (III:978)

The Merits of Jesus Christ (Peace Be Upon Him)

Abu Huraira reported Allah's Messenger (may peace be upon him) as saying: I am most akin to the son of Mary among the whole of mankind and the Prophets are of different mothers, but of one religion, and no Prophet was raised between me and him (Jesus Christ). (IV:1260)

It is Forbidden to Commit Oppression

Abu Dharr reported Allah's Messenger (may peace be upon him) as saying that Allah, the Exalted and Glorious, said: My servants, I have made oppression unlawful for Me and unlawful for you, so do not commit oppression against one another. (IV:1365)

SOURCE: *Sahih Muslim*, trans. 'Abdul Hamid Siddiqi. Lahore, Pakistan: Sh. Muhammad Ashraf, 1973–5, vol. 1, p. 113, to vol. 4, p. 1555

Shari'ah

Muslim law is called Shari'ah ("the path leading to the watering place"). Since the Qur'an could not be a guide for all future developments, the Hadith were collected to help prescribe behavior. But even more guidelines were needed. The third source of sacred authority in Islam is Shari'ah, or the law, elaborated for unforeseen situations. It is based upon the Qur'an and Hadith and interpreted by judges (*qadi*) using practical reasoning as well. Fundamental to Shari'ah are the Five Pillars of Islam: (1) Pronouncing the confession of faith, (2) Performing *salaat* prayers, (3) Fasting during the month of Ramadan, (4) *Zakat*, or charity, and (5) Hajj, or spiritual pilgrimage to Mecca. There are five types of law: (1) obligatory, (2) meritorious, (3) indifferent, (4) reprehensible, and (5) forbidden. Shari'ah includes dietary prohibitions (such as pork and alcohol) and guidelines for dress (no sexually provocative clothing); it also commands further legal rights for women (divorce, owning property, making a will). In medieval times, when tribal loyalty and customs were uppermost, Shari'ah began to restrict destructive practices such as infanticide, drunkenness, and gambling.

On Pictures and Images

Iconoclasm, which prohibits images of divinity, is an example of Shari'ah. To emphasize the ineffable transcendence of Allah, and in reaction against the numerous images of divinities in the polytheistic world, and in agreement with the Jewish prohibition against portraying divinity, Muhammad banned all human and animal images. Consequently most Muslim art incorporates only calligraphy or plant life, as in the Taj Mahal in India. But not all Muslim cultures were strict about this rule. Persian (now Iranian) art illustrates Muhammad's Night Journey, for example. This Shi'a Hadith records an account of the Prophet's rejection of imagery.

Rafi' b. Ishaq, who was the freedman of Shifa', reported: I and 'Abd Allah b. Abi Talhah went together to Abu Sa'id Khudri to see him in his illness. Abu Sa'id said: The Apostle of Allah (may peace be upon him) told me that angels did not enter a house where there were pictures and images.

SOURCE: Malik, *Muwatta Imam Malik*, trans. with notes by Muhammad Rahimuddin. Lahore, Pakistan: Sh. Muhammad Ashraf, 1980, p. 409

Hajj: Asceticism and Social Leveling
by Maulana Muhammad Ali

Mecca

Hajj, the fifth Pillar of Islam's primary prescriptions, is centered on the revered Ka'ba, which is traditionally considered to date from the time of Abraham and his son Ishmael. Under the guidance of the Qur'an, the pilgrimage became a means of ascetic practice and social equality. This explanation was provided by the founder of the Pakistan-based missionary society Ahmadiyya Anjuman Isha'at Islam.

Islam discourages asceticism in all its aspects. . . . Yet Islam lays the greatest stress upon the spiritual development of man [sic], and in its four main institutions—prayer, *zakat* [charity], fasting, and hajj—introduces workable ascetic formulae into the daily life of man—an asceticism which is quite in keeping with the secular side of life. The five daily prayers require the sacrifice of a small part of his time and, without in any way interfering with his everyday life, enable him to realize the Divine that is within him. The institution of *zakat* demands the giving up of a small portion of his wealth without interfering with his right to property. Fasting requires the giving up of food and drink but not in such a manner as to make him unfit for carrying on his regular work or business. It is only in hajj that asceticism assumes a marked form, for the pilgrim is required not only to give up his regular work for a number of days for the sake of the journey of Makkah [Mecca], but he must, in addition, give up many other amenities of life, and live, more or less, the life of an ascetic. The hajj is, however, a function which generally comes only once in a lifetime, and, therefore, while leading a man through the highest spiritual experience, it does not interfere in any appreciable degree with the regular course of his life. . . .

No other institution in the world has the wonderful influence of the hajj in leveling all distinctions of race, colour and rank. Not only do people of all races and all countries meet together before the Holy House of God as His servants, as members of one Divine family, but they are clad in one dress—in two white sheets—and there remains nothing to distinguish the high from the low. There is a vast concourse of human beings, all clad in one dress, all moving in one way, all having but one word to speak, *labbaika Allah-umma labbaika*, meaning "here are we, O Allah! Here are we in Thy Presence." It is hajj alone that brings into the domain of practicality what would otherwise seem impossible, namely, that all people, to whatever class or country they belong, should speak one language and wear one dress. Thus is every Muslim made to pass once in his life through that narrow gate of equality which leads to broad brotherhood. All men are equal in birth and death; they come into life and pass out of it in the same way, but hajj is the only occasion on which they are taught how to live alike, how to act alike and how to feel alike.

SOURCE: Maulana Muhammad Ali, *The Religion of Islam*. 6th ed. Delhi: Motilal Banarsidass, 1994, pp. 386–7

How to Perform Salaat

Salaat (the second Pillar) is ritual worship of the community at a mosque, especially on Friday noon, but also five times daily. Worshippers wash ritually, then bow repeatedly facing the direction of Mecca (*qibla*), which is marked in a mosque by a niche (*mihrab*). A leader (*imam*) leads prayers, all spoken in Arabic; a prayer rug (*sajjada*) defines the sacred space for bowing. This is the first portion:

Before *Salaat*:
Body, clothes and place of prayer must be clean.
Perform *wudu*[9] if needed.
Traditionally, women cover their hair.
Face the *Qibla*, the direction of Mecca.
Stand erect, head down, hands at sides, feet evenly spaced.
Recite *Iqama* (private call to prayer):
    Allaahu Akbar (4×)
    Ashhadu an la ilaaha illa-Lah (2×)
    Ash Hadu anna Muhamadar rasuulullah (2×)
    Hayya' alas Salaah (2×)
    Hayya' ala Falaah (2×)
    [*Fajr* only: *A-Salaatu Khayrun Mina-Naum* (2×)]
    Qad qaamitis Salaah (2×)
    Allaahu Akbar (2×)
    Laa ilaaha illa-Lah

9 *Wudu*—ritual ablution.

God is the most great.

I bear witness that there are no gods but God.

I bear witness that Muhammad is the Messenger of God.

Come to prayer.

Come to felicity.

[Prayer is better than sleep.]

Our prayers are now ready. Our prayers are now ready.

God is the most great.

There is no deity save God.

Express intent to perform *Salaat* (*niyyat*):

I intend to offer the____*rakats*[10] of the____prayer, and face the *Qibla* for the sake of Allah and Allah alone.

(For example: "I intend to offer the 4 *rakats* of the *Isha* prayer and face the *Qibla* for the sake of Allah and Allah alone.")

Salaat

Niyyat: Stand in respect and attention; put the world behind you.

Bring hands to ears, palms forward, thumbs behind earlobes.

Allahu Akbar/God is the most great.

Qiyam: Place right hand over left, men below navel, women at chest level; look at the ground in front of you.

Opening Supplication (optional):

Subhaanaka alahumma wa bihamdik
wa tabaaraka smuka wa ta'aalaa jadduka
wa laa ilaaha ghairuk

Glory to You, O Allah, and Yours is the praise.

And blessed is Your Name, and exalted is Your Majesty.

And there is no deity to be worshipped but You.

A'uudhu billaahi minash shaitaan ar-Rajeem
I seek refuge in Allah from Satan, the accursed. . . .

[Repetitions of bowing and more prayers . . . conclusion:]

Look over right shoulder (toward the angel recording your good deeds), then the left (toward the angel recording your wrongful deeds); say each time:

As Salaamu 'alaikum wa rahmatulaah
Peace and blessings of God be upon you.

Say personal prayers with hands cupped and palms up at chest level.

Wipe face with palms.

If praying in a group, stand and greet each other individually, saying: "May God receive our prayers."

SOURCE: <http://www.sufism.org/society/salaat/salaat.html>

---

10 *Rakat*—one cycle of bowing and praying.

Reason and revelation

The Qur'an serves as the basis of the Muslim's search for truth that guides the actions of believers. Thus the theological debates that developed are concerned with establishing with certainty the moral and ethical responsibility of the individual in relation to Allah.

The rationalist Mu'tazilah school (ninth century CE) emphasized the capacity, when aided by reason, to act in accordance with God's unity and justice. In response the more spiritual Ash'arites (tenth century CE), in asserting the omnipotence of Allah, attempted to shift the focus back to the Qur'an as the starting point of all ethical knowledge. The incorporation and translation of inspiring Greek ideas into Muslim ideals by subsequent philosophers refined Muslim philosophy. Logic, reason's tool, became instrumental in developing the moral and ethical system of Islamic law.

Rationalism by Ibn Sina (Avicenna)

Ibn Sina (980–1037 CE), the Persian philosopher, followed others such as al-Kindi (b. 800 CE?) and al-Razi (d. 926 CE). But it was the theories of logic, metaphysics, and politics of al-Farabi (d. 950 CE) that set the foundations for Ibn Sina's causal scheme. In Ibn Sina's Neoplatonist system, God's self-knowledge evokes a First Intelligence, then successive intelligences. Of these, the Active Intelligence produces all theoretical knowledge where logic, as well as the rational consideration of self-evident intuitive concepts, provides demonstrations of God's existence. Only prophets receive these principles directly, and they speak symbolically in their imaginative faculty so that believers can easily understand them.

Here, like al-Farabi, Ibn Sina holds that religion is the imitation of philosophy. But Ibn Sina's philosophical interpretations of his belief in the oneness of God and the prophethood of Muhammad were considered unacceptable by al-Ghazali, his foremost critic.

That person upon whom the First Intelligence gazes, so that he or she becomes refined, cultivated, subtle, beautiful, brave, and perfect in intellect, becomes a prophet. The First Intelligence becomes for this person as our intellect (is for us). And intellect for him or her is on the level of our soul. Just as the soul that grasps a truth from the intellect is learned, the intellect that grasps from the First Intelligence is a prophet.

But this state varies. Either it occurs in sleep, since in wakefulness the preoccupations of the senses and the multitude of activities become a hindrance; or it occurs in wakefulness, since in sleep the imaginative faculty predominates; or in each it is full and true. The motion and repose of this person is pure in legislative function. It never admits abrogation or distortion. This person is free of worldly distractions and secular controls and is devoted to the affairs of the Necessary Existent. The First Intelligence nourishes his or her soul from itself. This nourishing is called sanctification. As the Qur'an states, "We have supported him with the Holy Spirit." (The

First Intelligence) reveals itself to this person so that through (its) good auspices he or she comprehends. When he or she fully understands the universal,[11] he or she attains knowledge of the included particulars,[12] since this person does not need time or delay (to understand matters). Thus (Muhammad) said, "My Lord instructed me; and how well was my instruction; and I instructed 'Ali, and I instructed him well." Similarly (the Qur'an) said, "And We taught him knowledge from Us.".... That which becomes clear from this summons is religion. And the law of that religion is religious creed. The acceptance of all this is faith. The name of that which prophets receive is revelation. When it is united with a human, and the Holy Spirit opens his or her way to itself and becomes governor of that disposition, it makes (that person) lofty in aspiration, and slight in greed, rancourless, without envy. Whatever this person does is through that Holy Power. Just as is (found) in the (prophetic) tradition, "I ask of you a faith that my heart touches."

Thus the Holy Spirit is the noblest of all souls, for all (other) souls are subordinate to the Universal Intelligence. The Holy Spirit, however, is that which is the intermediary between the Necessary Existent and the First Intelligence. The faith of that Power is the prophet, who is the messenger and bearer of the Holy Emanation. That Power is the fruit of proximity to the First Intelligence....

Faith consists of two parts: real and metaphorical, the husk and the core. Prophets have real faith, the core, for they bear the core and the truth. Ordinary people bear the husk, the form. Their faith is sensible, not intelligible. With the aid of the (intellectual) faculty, (the prophet) draws down the Holy Spirit. As he said, "I feel the breath of the Merciful from the Yemen." This Holy Spirit is a divine faculty. It is not a body, nor a substance, nor an accident. It is the pure divine Command; "Indeed, His is the Command and the Creation." The intent of (the word Command) is not (physical) speech and expression. People who do not consider this appropriate and consider the Holy Spirit to be a result of the Command do so because they do not know the reality of Command. There is no nobility greater than a soul joined to the divine Command.... The Qur'an says, "A day in which the Spirit and the angels arise in a row."

When these preliminaries are known, it should (also) be known that reason comprehends truth through itself, while prophethood comprehends truths through Holy Support. Just as speech is not reason, reason is not summons, and summons is not prophethood. Recollection[13] stands between speech and reason, and apostleship between prophethood and summons.

---

11 Universals—global principles, such as truth, justice, faith, or parenthood, e.g. Plato's ideas and Jung's archetypes.
12 Particulars—specific, individual, existing things or phenomena; instances of universals, such as an act of justice or a parent.
13 Recollection—a Platonic concept: the eternal soul's recalling universals known in Heaven.

Hence, whatever rational concepts that the intellect wishes to convey to the senses, it does so by means of recollection. (The latter then) formulates it in sensible sounds and unites (it) with speech, so that hearing apprehends.

SOURCE: Peter Heath, *Allegory and Philosophy in Avicenna (Ibn Sina)*. Philadelphia, PA: University of Pennsylvania Press, 1992, pp. 118–19

Istanbul-style
Mosques

Mysticism by al-Ghazali

Al-Ghazali (1058–1111) was an Ash'ari theologian, jurist, and mystic who criticized the rationalism of al-Farabi and Ibn Sina. Following a spiritual crisis, al-Ghazali concluded that systematic reasoning could not yield the insights of mysticism. In his treatise "The Incoherence of the Philosophers" (1095), he attacks philosophical theories that oppose religious principles. His metaphysics was "occasionalistic" and was clearly irreconcilable with the uniformly rational, causal order of Ibn Sina, which took power away from God and did not permit miracles. However, al-Ghazali believed that logic was not tied to any metaphysical system, and was thus a neutral tool that could be used in expounding ethical rules of conduct. His criticism of Ibn Sina had two effects: first, in clarifying Ibn Sina's study of logic, he popularized it; second, he thus made Greek modes of thinking more accessible.

When I had finished with these sciences, I next turned with set purpose to the method of mysticism (or Sufism). I knew that the complete mystic 'way' includes both intellectual belief and practical activity; the latter consists in getting rid of the obstacles in the self and in stripping off its base characteristics and vicious morals, so that the heart may attain to freedom from what is not God and to constant recollection of Him. . . .

I apprehended clearly that the mystics were men [sic] who had real experiences, not men of words, and that I had already progressed as far as was possible by way of intellectual apprehension. What remained for me was not to be attained by oral instruction and study but only by immediate experience and by walking in the mystic way. . . .

Next I considered the circumstances of my life, and realized that I was caught in a veritable thicket of attachments. I also considered my activities, of which the best was my teaching and lecturing, and realized that in them I was dealing with sciences that were unimportant and contributed nothing to the attainment of eternal life.

After that I examined my motive in my work of teaching, and realized that it was not a pure desire for the things of God, but that the impulse moving me was the desire for an influential position and public recognition. I saw for certain that I was on the brink of a crumbling bank of sand and in imminent danger of hell-fire unless I set about to mend my ways. . . .

For nearly six months beginning with Rajab[14] 488 AH [July 1095 CE], I

---

14 Rajab—the month during which Muhammad ascended to Heaven.

was continuously tossed about between the attractions of worldly desires and the impulses towards eternal life. In that month the matter ceased to be one of choice and became one of compulsion. God caused my tongue to dry up so that I was prevented from lecturing. One particular day I would make an effort to lecture in order to gratify the hearts of my following, but my tongue would not utter a single word nor could I accomplish anything at all.

This impediment in my speech produced grief in my heart, and at the same time my power to digest and assimilate food and drink was impaired; I could hardly swallow or digest a single mouthful of food. My powers became so weakened that the doctors gave up all hope of successful treatment. "This trouble arises from the heart," they said, "and from there it has spread through the constitution; the only method of treatment is that the anxiety which has come over the heart should be allayed."

Thereupon, perceiving my impotence and having altogether lost my power of choice, I sought refuge with God most high as one who is driven to Him, because he is without further resources of his own. He answered me, He who "answers him who is driven (to Him by affliction) when he calls upon Him" (Qur'an 27:63). He made it easy for my heart to turn away from position and wealth, from children and friends.

In due course I entered Damascus, and there I remained for nearly two years with no other occupation than the cultivation of retirement and solitude, together with religious and ascetic exercises, as I busied myself purifying my soul, improving my character and cleansing my heart for the constant recollection of God most high, as I had learnt from my study of mysticism. I used to go into retreat for a period in the mosque of Damascus, going up the minaret of the mosque for the whole day and shutting myself in so as to be alone.

At length I made my way from Damascus to the Holy House (that is, Jerusalem). There I used to enter into the precinct of the Rock every day and shut myself in.

Next there arose in me a prompting to fulfil the duty of the Pilgrimage, gain the blessings of Mecca and Medina, and perform the visitation of the Messenger of God most high (may peace be upon him).

I continued at this stage for the space of ten years, and during these periods of solitude there were revealed to me things innumerable and unfathomable. This much I shall say about that in order that others may be helped: I learnt with certainty that it is above all the mystics who walk on the road of God; their life is the best life, their method the soundest method, their character the purest character; indeed, were the intellect of the intellectuals and the learning of the learned and the scholarship of the scholars, who are versed in the profundities of revealed truth, brought together in the attempt to improve the life and character of the mystics, they would find no way of doing so; for to the mystics all movement and all rest, whether external or internal, brings illumination from the light of the lamp of prophetic revelation; and behind the light of prophetic revelation there is no other light on the face of the earth from which illumination may be received.

SOURCE: W. Montgomery Watt, *The Faith and Practice of Al-Ghazali*. London: George Allen and Unwin, 1953, pp. 54–61

Two Truths   by Ibn Rushd (Averroes)

Ibn Rushd (1126–98), physician, philosopher, and judge, came from a stimulating philosophical movement in Spain, which also included Ibn Bajjah (Avempace, d. 1138) and Ibn Tufayl (d. 1185). Ibn Rushd's commentaries on Aristotle greatly influenced medieval Latin philosophy. His famous reply to al-Ghazali ("The Incoherence of the Incoherence", c. 1180) is a legal, theological, and philosophical defense of an Aristotelian causal view; it contests al-Ghazali's Ash'ari conception of divine causality as well as Ibn Sina's Neoplatonism. The West hailed Ibn Rushd as the originator of the theory of "two truths," where the higher truth was located in revelation. Rational truth was for philosophers, and religious truth for the masses. In Spain, Ibn Rushd was followed by Ibn 'Arabi.

Now since this religion is true and summons to the study which leads to knowledge of the Truth, we the Muslim community know definitely that demonstrative study does not lead to [conclusions] conflicting with what Scripture has given us; for truth does not oppose truth but accords with it and bears witness to it.

This being so, whenever demonstrative study leads to any manner of knowledge about any being, that being is inevitably either unmentioned or mentioned in Scripture. If it is unmentioned there is no contradiction, and it is in the same case as an act whose category is unmentioned, so that the lawyer has to infer it by reasoning from Scripture. If Scripture speaks about it, the apparent meaning of the words inevitably either accords or conflicts with the conclusions of demonstration about it. If this [apparent meaning] accords there is no argument. If it conflicts there is a call for allegorical interpretation of it. The meaning of "allegorical interpretation" is: extension of the significance of an expression from real to metaphorical significance, without forsaking therein the standard metaphorical practices of Arabic, such as calling a thing by the name of something resembling it or a cause or consequence or accompaniment of it, or other things such as are enumerated in accounts of the kinds of metaphorical speech.

SOURCE: "Philosophy Contains Nothing Opposed to Islam," in Averroes, *On the Harmony of Religion and Philosophy*, trans. George F. Hourani. London: Luzac and Co., 1967, p. 50
<http://www.muslimphilosophy.com/ir/fasl/htm>

Sufi mysticism

Sufis

Muslims who seek direct mystical experiences of Allah are known as Sufis. Initially Sufis lived simply, wore a coarse woolen garment, and practiced asceticism. Today many Muslims are associated with variations of Sufism, some emphasizing its uniquely Muslim quality, some its universalism. Techniques such as *dhikr* (prayer), *sama* (music), or dance (the "Whirling Dervishes") are customs used to induce trance states and thus refine spiritual awareness of Allah.

One notable Sufi, Ibn 'Arabi, perceived that in the world there is actually nothing but God, transcendent yet manifested on earth. Two other great Sufis, quoted below, were Rabi'a and Rumi. The Sufi Order of the West, founded in London in 1910 by Hazrat Inayat Khan (1882–1927; see chapter 13), furthered the universal theme of Sufism, seeking the unity of religions and relevance to the modern world.

The Rarest Treasure by Rabi'a

Rabi'a al-Adawiyya (713–801 CE) was born into a poor family and sold into slavery, but later freed. She devoted herself to a life of prayer, poverty, and seclusion. Her asceticism and pure love of God banished hatred and inspired many Sufis thereafter. She believed that one should not love out of desire for paradise or fear of hell, but for love of God alone.

"Doorkeeper of the Heart"

Your hope in my heart is the rarest treasure
Your Name on my tongue is the sweetest word
My choicest hours
Are the hours I spend with You—

O God, I can't live in this world
Without remembering You—
How can I endure the next world
Without seeing Your face?

I am a stranger in Your country
And lonely among Your worshippers:
This is the substance of my complaint.

"Dream Fable"

I saw myself in a wide green garden, more beautiful than I could begin to understand. In this garden was a young girl. I said to her,

"How wonderful this place is!"

"Would you like to see a place even more wonderful than this?" she asked. "Oh yes," I answered. Then taking me by the hand, she led me on until we came to a magnificent palace, like nothing that was ever seen by human eyes. The young girl knocked on the door, and someone opened it.

Immediately both of us were flooded with light. God alone knows the inner meaning of the maidens we saw living there. Each one carried in her hand a serving-tray filled with light. The young girl asked the maidens where they were going, and they answered her, "We are looking for someone who was drowned in the sea, and so became a martyr. She never slept at night, not one wink! We are going to rub funeral spices on her body."

"Then rub some on my friend here," the young girl said.

"Once upon a time," said the maidens, "part of this spice and the fragrance of it clung to her body—but then she shied away."

Quickly the young girl let go of my hand, turned, and said to me:

> "Your prayers are your light;
> Your devotion is your strength;
> Sleep is the enemy of both.
> Your life is the only opportunity that life can give you.
> If you ignore it, if you waste it,
> You will only turn to dust."

Then the young girl disappeared.

> In love, nothing exists between breast and Breast.
> Speech is born out of longing,
> True description from the real taste.
> The one who tastes, knows;
> The one who explains, lies.
> How can you describe the true form of Something
> In whose presence you are blotted out?
> And in whose being you still exist?
> And who lives as a sign for your journey?

SOURCE: *Rabi'a*, trans. Charles Upton. Brattleboro, VT: Threshold Books, 1988

The Sound of Love by Rumi

Jalal ad-Din ar-Rumi (1207–73) was one of the greatest of Muslim mystics. Living in Persia and Turkey, he founded the order of the Mevlevi—the "Whirling Dervishes"—known for their spinning, ecstatic dances. His belief in reincarnation, his universalism, and his Platonic influence went beyond Islamic orthodoxy, but have been neglected in view of his strong influence otherwise.

With every breath the sound
of love surrounds us,
and we are bound for the depths
of space, without sightseeing.
We've been in orbit before
and know the angels there.
Let's go there again, Master,

for that is our land.
Yet we are beyond all that
and something more than angels.
Out beyond duality,
we have a home, and it is Glory.
That pure substance is
different from this dusty world.
What kind of place is this?
We once came down, soon we'll return.
A new happiness befriends us
as we work at offering our lives.
Muhammad, an ornament to the world,
is our caravan's chosen guide.
The sweetness we breathe on the wind
is from the scent of his hair,
and the radiance of this thought
is from the light of his day.
His face once split the moon in two—
she couldn't endure the sight of him.
Yet how lucky she was,
she who humbly received him.
Look into our hearts and see
the splitting moon in each breath.
Having seen that vision,
how can you still dream?
When the wave of *Am I not?* struck,
it wrecked the body's ship;
when the ship wrecks once more,
it will be the time of union.

SOURCE: William C. Chittick, *The Sufi Path of Love: The Spiritual Teachings of Rumi*. Albany, NY: State University of New York Press, 1983, pp. 36–7

Between the Yea and the Nay by Ibn 'Arabi

Ibn 'Arabi Muhyi al-Din (1165–1240) was born in Spain. As a young man at a party in Seville, he heard a strange voice say: "O Muhammad, it was not for this that you were created." Disturbed, he retreated and had a vision in which he saw Moses, Jesus, and Muhammad. He studied with several spiritual masters, began traveling, and eventually wrote over 700 books, influencing many Sufis. He considered all prophets to be teachers of a primordial religion: "There is no knowledge except that taken from God." He taught a **monism** in which Being is essentially one: "There is nothing in Being but God." Ibn 'Arabi performed the pilgrimage to Mecca in 1202, then settled in Damascus in 1223 until his death. In this passage he tells of his meeting with the great Ibn Rushd.

I spent the day in Cordoba at the house of Abu al-Walid Ibn Rushd. He had expressed a desire to meet me in person, since he had heard of certain revelations I had received while in retreat and had shown considerable astonishment concerning them. In consequence my father, who was one of his closest friends, took me with him on the pretext of business, in order to give Ibn Rushd the opportunity of making my acquaintance. I was at the time a beardless youth. As I entered the house, the philosopher rose to greet me with all the signs of friendliness and affection, and embraced me. Then he said to me "Yes," and showed pleasure on seeing that I had understood him. I, on the other hand, being aware of the motive for his pleasure, replied "No." Upon this Ibn Rushd drew back from me, his colour changed and he seemed to doubt what he had thought of me. He then put to me the following question, "What solution have you found as a result of mystical illumination and divine inspiration? Does it coincide with what is arrived at by speculative thought?" I replied, "Yes and no. Between the Yea and the Nay the spirits take their flight beyond matter, and the necks detach themselves from their bodies."

At this Ibn Rushd became pale, and I saw him tremble as he muttered the formula "there is no power save from God." This was because he understood my allusion . . . After that he sought from my father to meet me in order to present what he himself had understood: he wanted to know if it conformed with or was different from what I had. He was one of the great masters of reflection and rational consideration. He thanked God that in his own time he had seen someone who had entered into the retreat ignorant and had come out like this—without study, discussion, investigation or reading.

SOURCE: Muhyi al-Din Muhammad ibn 'Ali Ibn al-'Arabi, *Sufis of Andalusia*. London: George Allen and Unwin, 1971/Northleach, Gloucestershire: Beshara Publications, 1988, p. 23

Living Islam

Islam today is expanding and encountering the impact of technological culture. Often this creates a conflict with Muslim ethics. Three of the outstanding areas of debate are women, ecology, and violence in the name of religion.

Women and Islam

Rights of Women: Qur'anic Ideals Versus Muslim Practice by Riffat Hassan

Extensive research is currently being done to determine the legal position of women according to Muslim tradition. There are many sources of the tradition, the most important of which is the Qur'an. It is considered the Word of God, as transmitted to the Prophet Muhammad through the angel Gabriel. Other sources include sayings attributed to the Prophet, decisions of schools of law, and the Shari'ah, or code of law. Feminist scholar Riffat Hassan, at the University of Louisville, has carefully researched the rights of women granted by the Qur'an but notes that these are not necessarily upheld.

Muslim men never tire of repeating that Islam has given more rights to women than has any other religion. Certainly, if by "Islam" is meant "Qur'anic Islam" the rights that it has given to women are, indeed, impressive. Not only do women partake of all the "General Rights" mentioned in the foregoing pages [rights to life, respect, justice, freedom, knowledge, sustenance, work, privacy, protection from slander and ridicule, development of one's aesthetic sensibilities and enjoyment of God's bounties, leaving one's homeland when there is oppression, and the "good life"], they are also the subject of much particular concern in the Qur'an. Underlying much of the Qur'an's legislation on women-related issues is the recognition that women have been disadvantaged persons in history to whom justice needs to be done by the Muslim Ummah. Unfortunately, however, the cumulative (Jewish, Christian, Hellenistic, Bedouin, and other) biases which existed in the Arab-Islamic culture of the early centuries of Islam infiltrated the Islamic tradition and undermined the intent of the Qur'an to liberate women from the status of chattels or inferior creatures and make them free and equal to men.

A review of Muslim history and culture brings to light many areas in which—Qur'anic teaching notwithstanding—women continued to be subjected to diverse forms of oppression and injustice, often in the name of Islam. While the Qur'an, because of its protective attitude toward all downtrodden and oppressed classes of people, appears to be weighted in many ways in favor of women, many of its women-related teachings have been used in patriarchal Muslim societies against, rather than for, women. Muslim societies, in general, appear to be far more concerned with trying to control women's bodies and sexuality than with their human rights. Many Muslims, when they speak of human rights, either do not speak of women's rights at all,[15] or are mainly concerned with how a woman's chastity may be protected.[16] (They are apparently not worried about protecting men's chastity.)

Women are the targets of the most serious violations of human rights which occur in Muslim societies in general. Muslims say with great pride that Islam abolished female infanticide; true, but it must also be mentioned that one of the most common crimes in a number of Muslim countries (e.g., in Pakistan) is the murder of women by their husbands. These so-called "honor-killings" are, in fact, extremely dishonorable and are frequently used to camouflage other kinds of crimes.

Female children are discriminated against from the moment of birth, for it is customary in Muslim societies to regard a son as a gift, and a daughter as a trial, from God. Therefore, the birth of a son is an occasion for celebration while the birth of a daughter calls for commiseration, if not lamentation. Many girls are married when they are still minors, even

---

15 For example, R. A. Jullundhri, "Human Rights in Islam," in *Understanding Human Rights*, ed. A. D. Falconer. Dublin: Irish School of Ecumenics, 1980.
16 For example, A. A. Maududi, *Human Rights in Islam*. Lahore, Pakistan: Islamic Publications, 1977.

though marriage in Islam is a contract and presupposes that the contracting parties are both consenting adults. Even though so much Qur'anic legislation is aimed at protecting the rights of women in the context of marriage,[17] women cannot claim equality with their husbands. The husband, in fact, is regarded as his wife's gateway to heaven or hell and the arbiter of her final destiny. That such an idea can exist within the framework of Islam—which, in theory, rejects the idea of there being any intermediary between a believer and God—represents both a profound irony and a great tragedy.

Although the Qur'an presents the idea of what we today call a "no-fault" divorce and does not make any adverse judgments about divorce,[18] Muslim societies have made divorce extremely difficult for women, both legally and through social penalties. Although the Qur'an states clearly that the divorced parents of a minor child must decide by mutual consultation how the child is to be raised and that they must not use the child to hurt or exploit each other,[19] in most Muslim societies, women are deprived both of their sons (generally at age 7) and their daughters (generally at age 12). It is difficult to imagine an act of greater cruelty than depriving a mother of her children simply because she is divorced. Although polygamy was intended by the Qur'an to be for the protection of orphans and widows,[20] in practice Muslims have made it the Sword of Damocles which keeps women under constant threat. Although the Qur'an gave women the right to receive an inheritance not only on the death of a close relative, but also to receive other bequests or gifts during the lifetime of a benevolent caretaker, Muslim societies have disapproved greatly of the idea of giving wealth to a woman in preference to a man, even when her need or circumstances warrant it. Although the purpose of the Qur'anic legislation dealing with women's dress and conduct[21] was to make it safe for women to go about their daily business (since they have the right to engage in gainful activity as witnessed by Surah 4: An-Nisa':32 without fear of sexual harassment or molestation), Muslim societies have put many of them behind veils and shrouds and locked doors on the pretext of protecting their chastity, forgetting that according to the Qur'an,[22] confinement to their homes was not a normal way of life for chaste women but a punishment for "unchastity."

Woman and man, created equal by God and standing equal in the sight of God, have become very unequal in Muslim societies. The Qur'anic description of man and woman in marriage: "They are your garments/And you are their garments" (Surah 2: Al-Baqarah:187), implies closeness,

---

17 For instance, see Surah 4: An-Nisa':4, 19; Surah 24: An-Nur:33; Surah 2: Al-Baqarah:187; Surah 9: At-Tawbah:71; Surah 7: Al-A'raf:189; Surah 30: Ar-rum:21.
18 For instance, see Surah 2: Al-Baqarah:231, 241.
19 The reference here is to Surah 2: Al-Baqarah:233.
20 The reference here is to Surah 4: An-Nisa':2–3.
21 For instance, see Surah 24: An-Nur:30–1; Surah 33: Al-Ahzab:59.
22 The reference here is to Surah 4: An-Nisa':15.

mutuality, and equality. However, Muslim culture has reduced many, if not most, women to the position of puppets on a string, to slave-like creatures whose only purpose in life is to cater to the needs and pleasures of men. Not only this, it has also had the audacity and the arrogance to deny women direct access to God. It is one of Islam's cardinal beliefs that each person—man or woman—is responsible and accountable for his or her individual actions. How, then, can the husband become the wife's gateway to heaven or hell? How, then, can he become the arbiter not only of what happens to her in this world but also of her ultimate destiny? Such questions are now being articulated by an increasing number of Muslim women and they are bound to threaten the existing balance of power in the domain of family relationships in most Muslim societies.

However, despite everything that has gone wrong with the lives of countless Muslim women down the ages due to patriarchal Muslim culture, there is hope for the future. There are indications from across the world of Islam that a growing number of Muslims are beginning to reflect seriously upon the teachings of the Qur'an as they become disenchanted with capitalism, communism, and western democracy. As this reflection deepens, it is likely to lead to the realization that the supreme task entrusted to human beings by God, of being God's deputies on earth, can only be accomplished by establishing justice which the Qur'an regards as a prerequisite for authentic peace. Without the elimination of the inequities, inequalities, and injustices that pervade the personal and collective lives of human beings, it is not possible to talk about peace in Qur'anic terms. Here, it is of importance to note that there is more Qur'anic legislation pertaining to the establishment of justice in the context of family relationships than on any other subject. This points to the assumption implicit in much Qur'anic learning, namely, that if human beings can learn to order their homes justly so that the human rights of all within its jurisdiction—children, women, and men—are safeguarded, then they can also order their society and the world at large justly. In other words, the Qur'an regards the home as a microcosm of the Ummah and the world community, and emphasizes the importance of making it "the abode of peace" through just living.

SOURCE: Excerpted from Riffat Hassan, "Are Human Rights Compatible with Islam?"
<http://religiousconsultation.org/hassan2.htm>

Ecology: A Sacred Science by Seyyed H. Nasr

The ecology crisis will not be solved simply by social engineering, new technologies, or by creating an ethics expanded to include the non-human, argues Seyyed Nasr, who teaches Islamic Studies at Washington University. What is needed is a *scientia sacra*, a sacred science that brings out our suppressed sense of the interconnected-ness of all beings. We cannot bestow sacredness on nature, because it is already there. The major world religions have forgotten this, although the indigenous sacred ways of tribal peoples have long remembered it. Religions need also to respect the varied sacred ways of each other's traditions. Muslims in India, for example, need to respect the Hindu sense of the sacredness of the Ganges River. Awakening to the signature of God in everything will be the foundation of a new ecological ethic.

The Earth is bleeding and the natural environment suffering in an unprecedented manner from the onslaught of man [sic]. The problem is now too evident to deny, and the solutions proposed are many but for the most part insufficient. Earth will not be healed by some kind of social engineering or changes in a technology that cannot but treat the world of nature as pure quantity to be manipulated for human needs whether they be real or imaginary. All such actions are no more than cosmetics with an effect that is of necessity only skin deep.

What is needed is a rediscovery of nature as sacred reality and the rebirth of man as the guardian of the sacred, which implies the death of the image of man and nature that has given birth to modernism and its subsequent developments. It does not mean the "invention of a new man" as some have claimed, but rather the resurfacing of the true man, the pontifical man whose reality we still bear within ourselves. Nor does it mean the invention of a sacred view of nature, as if man could ever invent the sacred, but rather the reformulation of the traditional cosmologies and views of nature held by various religions throughout history. It means most of all taking seriously the religious understanding of the order of nature as knowledge corresponding to a vital aspect of cosmic reality and not only subjective conjectures or historical constructs. There must be a radical restructuring of the intellectual landscape to enable us to take this type of knowledge of nature seriously, which means to accept the findings of modern science only within the confines of the limitations that its philosophical suppositions, epistemologies,[23] and historical development have imposed upon it, while rejecting completely its totalitarian claims as *the* science of the natural order. It means to rediscover a science of nature that deals with the *existence* of natural objects in their relation to Being, with their subtle as well as gross aspects, with their interrelatedness to the rest of the cosmos and to us, with their symbolic significance and with their nexus to higher levels of existence leading to the Divine Origin of all things.

Furthermore, in speaking of the religious view of the order of nature we must now do so in a global context reflecting the global character of the problem at hand. It is necessary to delve into religions as different as the Shamanic and Hindu, Buddhist and Abrahamic, without a relativization that would destroy the sense of the sacred in each tradition. There are perspectives and schools within most religions that have not paid much attention to the domain of nature, as seen especially in Western Christianity, but within every integral tradition there *are* those schools that have dealt

---

23 Epistemologies—theories of knowledge.

with the domain of nature both in its spiritual and cosmic reality. It is those schools that must be sought and studied across religious frontiers in a manner so as to preserve the authenticity of each tradition while bringing out the spiritual significance of nature in a universal fashion. . . .

On a more practical level, it is necessary to create respect on behalf of the followers of a particular religion for what is held to be sacred in another religion not only in the domain, say, of sacred art and architecture but also in the world of nature. A Muslim in Benares does not consider the Ganges to be sacred for himself but must accept its sacredness for the Hindus and respect it, as was done for Hindu holy places by traditional Muslims of Benares for centuries and vice versa as far as Muslim holy places were concerned; this mutual respect has continued for the most part and still survives to some extent despite recent communal tragedies. The respect accorded to manmade sites possessing religious significance must also be extended to natural ones despite difficulties that come about when two or three religions claim the same site or land as holy, as we find in Palestine and Israel, or when the economic considerations of a more powerful people confront the belief system of others who consider a particular forest, river, or mountain to be sacred. The despicable record of the modern world in overlooking the claims of others to the sacred not only in an abstract manner but also concretely, such as land, rivers, forests, etc.—as seen in the destruction of much of the habitat of the Native American peoples—has been itself a major cause of the present environmental crisis and cannot any longer act as a model for future dealings among peoples. In evoking the religious understanding of the order of nature, this sense of respect for the religious teachings concerning nature of religions other than our own must be strengthened in the same way that respect for other human beings or houses of worship of other faiths is encouraged, at least by the majority of those concerned with religion and spirituality on a global scale today.

Religions serve as the source of both an ethics involving the environment and a knowledge of the order of nature. They can abet and strengthen one another in both domains if authentic religious teachings are not compromised and diluted in the face of secularism. This is particularly true of Western Christianity, which for so long has tried to identify itself with a civilization that has grown more secular every day. Traditional Christian teachings even in the domain of nature are in fact much closer to those of other religions than to the modern secularist philosophies of the West, as witnessed by questions concerning the sanctity of life and abortion. . . .

Finally, every being in the world of nature not only issues from the Divine Principle or the One, but also reflects Its Wisdom and, to use theistic language, sings the praises of the Lord. The religious understanding of the order of nature, which we can share only on the condition of conforming ourselves to the world of the Spirit, enables us to read the signatures of God upon the face of things and hear their prayers. It thereby re-creates a link between us and the world of nature that involves not only our bodies and psyches but also the Spirit within us and our final end. It enables us to see the sacred in nature and therefore to treat it not only with respect but also as part of our greater self. It reminds us how precious is each being created by God and how great a sin to destroy wantonly any creature that by virtue of its existence bears the imprint of the Divine and is witness to the One who is our Origin and End.

SOURCE: Seyyed H. Nasr, *Religion and the Order of Nature*. New York and Oxford: Oxford University Press, 1996, pp. 286–9

Muslim
Resurgence in
Tatarstan

Islam and the West: So, are Civilisations at War?
Interview with Samuel Huntington

Are we caught in a war against terror, or the "clash of civilizations" predicted in 1993 by Harvard political scientist Samuel Huntington? Interviewed here by Michael Steinberger of the *New York Times*, he answers critics who fear that his generalizations fuel conflict.

Is this the clash of civilisations you have been warning about for nearly a decade?

Clearly, Osama bin Laden wants it to be a clash of civilisations between Islam and the West. The first priority for our government is to try to prevent it from becoming one. But there is a danger it could move in that direction. The administration has acted exactly the right way in attempting to rally support among Muslim governments. But there are pressures here in the United States to attack other terrorist groups and states that support terrorist groups. And that, it seems to me, could broaden it into a clash of civilisations.

Were you surprised the terrorists were all educated, middle-class individuals?

No. The people involved in fundamentalist movements, Islamic or otherwise, are often people with advanced educations. Most of them do not become terrorists. But these are intelligent, ambitious young people who aspire to put their educations to use in a modern economy, and they become frustrated by the lack of opportunity. They are cross-pressured as well by the forces of globalisation and what they regard as Western imperialism and cultural domination. They are attracted to Western culture, but also repelled by it.

You have written that "Islam has bloody borders". What do you mean by this?

If you look around the borders of the Muslim world, you find a whole series of local conflicts involving Muslims and non-Muslims: Bosnia, Kosovo, the Caucasus, Chechnya, Tajikistan, Kashmir, India, Indonesia, the Philippines, North Africa, the Palestinian–Israeli conflict. Muslims also fight Muslims, and much more than the people of other civilisations fight each other.

So are you suggesting Islam promotes violence?

I don't think Islam is any more violent than any other religions, and I suspect if you added it all up, more people have been slaughtered by

Christians over the centuries than by Muslims. But the key factor is the demographic factor. Generally speaking, the people who go out and kill other people are males between the ages of 16 and 30.

During the 1960s, 70s and 80s there were high birth rates in the Muslim world, and this has given rise to a huge youth bulge. But the bulge will fade. Muslim birth rates are going down; in fact, they have dropped dramatically in some countries. Islam did spread by the sword originally, but I don't think there is anything inherently violent in Muslim theology.

Islam, like any great religion, can be interpreted in a variety of ways. People like bin Laden can seize on things in the Koran as commands to go out and kill infidels. But the Pope did exactly the same thing when he launched the Crusades.

Should the United States do more to promote democracy and human rights in the Middle East?

It would be desirable but also difficult. In the Islamic world there is a natural tendency to resist the influence of the West, which is understandable given the long history of conflict between Islam and Western civilisation.

Obviously, there are groups in most Muslim societies that are in favour of democracy and human rights, and I think we should support those groups. But we then get into this paradoxical situation: many of the groups arguing against repression in those societies are fundamentalists and anti-American. We saw this in Algeria. Promoting democracy and human rights are very important goals for the United States, but we also have other interests.

President Carter was committed to promoting human rights, and when I served on his National Security Council, we had countless discussions about this. But nobody ever mentioned the idea of trying to promote human rights in Saudi Arabia, and for a very obvious reason.

Apart from our closest allies, no country has lined up more solidly behind the United States than Russia. Is this when Russia turns decisively to the West?

Russia is turning to the West for pragmatic reasons. The Russians feel threatened by Muslim terrorists and see it as in their interest to line up with the West and to gain some credit with the United States in the hope we will reduce our push for NATO expansion into the Baltic states and missile defence. It's a coincidence of interests, but we shouldn't blow it up into a big realignment. But I think they are very worried about the rise of China, and this will turn them to the West.

India and China, two countries you said would be at odds with the United States, have joined in this war on terrorism. Instead of the West versus the rest, could the clash become Islam versus the rest?

Conceivably. You have Muslims fighting Westerners, Orthodox Christians, Jews, Hindus, Buddhists. But there are a billion Muslims in the world, stretching across the Eastern hemisphere from western Africa to eastern Indonesia, and they interact with dozens of different people. So they have more opportunity to clash with others.

The most frequent criticism leveled against you is that you portray entire civilisations as unified blocks.

That is totally false. The major section on Islam in my book is called "Consciousness Without Cohesion", in which I talk about all the divisions in the Islamic world, about Muslim-on-Muslim fighting. Even in the current crisis, they are still divided. You have a billion people, with all these sub-cultures, the tribes. Islam is less unified than any other civilisation. The problem with Islam is the problem Henry Kissinger expressed with regard to Europe: "If I want to call Europe, what number do I call?" If you want to call the Islamic world, what number do you call? If there was a dominant power in the Islamic world, you could deal with them. Now what you see is the different Islamic groups competing with each other.

SOURCE: *The Observer,* October 21, 2001
<http://observer.guardian.co.uk/islam/story/0,,577982,00.html>

The United States and Islam

God in a World of Christians and Muslims
by Martin Forward

In contrast to the "clash of civilizations" scenario proposed by Samuel Huntington, Martin Forward gave the following sermon shortly after 9/11, drawing on his extensive personal experience of both Christianity and Islam. He is now the Executive Director of the Wackerlin Center for Faith and Action at Aurora University. Previously he was the Academic Dean of Wesley House and a member of the Faculty of Divinity at Cambridge University. An ordained British Methodist minister and also an ordained deacon in the Church of South India, he has traveled extensively and has written numerous books and articles on Christianity, Islam, and inter-religious dialogue.

When I think of Islam and Muslims, four people come readily to mind. Mohammed Alam is British, born in Pakistan. We met when I sought a person to teach me Urdu, the Muslim language of North India and Pakistan. His family and mine became fast friends. He once told me of a dream of his. Muslims hope to die with the name of God being whispered in their ear. In his dream, I was there to fulfill that role for him. Alam's a large, humorous, warm man. I love him dearly.

The second person? Over a quarter of a century ago, I lived in India and struggled to learn Arabic from Hayath Khan, prayer-leader at Malakpet, a suburb of the city of Hyderabad, which, in my dreams, is still my city. In appearance, he was many people's idea of a Muslim: white coat and trousers, long white beard, black cap on his head. In our lessons, as he recited words from the Koran, Islam's holy scripture, in a Muslim's view the exact words of God, tears flowed down cheeks and into his beard. I caused him problems. He liked me. He knew that I respected Islam, and loved some Muslims, but that I'd no intention of converting to Islam. So he worried and fretted lest, in the life of the world to come, I should be among the losers and miss out on paradisal joys. Like lots of religious people, Hayath Khan had to make a choice about whether God loved the many or the few. His heart told him one thing; bits of his tradition taught him something else. I remember him with much affection.

Sabiha Latifi was also a Muslim friend from my Indian days. She was a frail woman, who worried about my health, not hers. She often fed me, gave me a wonderful recipe for lentil curry and, if she had a sin, it was an overwhelming love for chocolate. In later years, whenever I visited India from England, I had to bring lots of chocolate for her and hope that it wouldn't melt under the glare of the Indian sun and of customs officials. Sabiha was a saintly woman, whom I mourned greatly when she died. May she rest in peace and rise in glory.

Last, but not least, I remember my father. In one sense, he provided me with my love of Islam, since, due to his work, I lived in Aden when I was nine through eleven years old. Aden: that entrancing, barren heap of land at the heel of the Arabian peninsula, where I met Muslims, saw them at prayer, and had my imagination and respect kindled for a faith that gave much to its practitioners and demanded a great deal of them. Years after I began my long acquaintance with the world of Islam, my dear old dad told me that he almost became a Muslim when he fought alongside Arabs in the Second World War, so taken was he with their life and faith.

There are other forms of Islam than that observed, with gratitude and delight, by my father, and those practiced by Mohammed Alam, Hayath Khan and Sabiha Latifi. I expect that, on September 11, the pilots of the hijacked planes died thinking that they'd done a religious deed, and with the words "*Allahu akbar*" on their lips, which mean "God is greater"; greater, presumably, than, in their judgment, America, the great Satan.

The thing is: all religions are complex realities, offering a variety of choices to believers as they reflect upon them and live by them. Am I, a Christian, compelled to approve the deeds of the Inquisition in the late medieval and early modern eras, which expelled Muslims and Jews from Christian lands, or even tortured or killed them in the name of the prince of peace? Absolutely not: I prefer to make very different choices from my religious past

If I were a Muslim, I would be aware of the fact that Islam was, in its origins, the most successful of religions. After the Prophet Muhammad's death on June 8, 632, the Muslims quickly overthrew the Persian Empire and reduced the Eastern Roman Empire, Byzantium, to a shadow of its former self. Christian and Jewish heartlands fell before Muslim invaders. Jerusalem, Alexandria, North Africa, Spain: all succumbed to the Arab invaders, fueled by their fervent belief in the One God and the last and greatest of his prophets, Muhammad. Exactly one hundred years after the death of Muhammad, in 732, Muslim forces were defeated by the Christian Charles Martel at the battle of Poitiers, in south-western France. It's fascinating to speculate what would have happened had the battle taken a different turn. Europeans today would likely be Muslims, and history would have taken rather a different course than it has.

For one thousand years, Europeans lived in fear of Muslim conquest. No wonder, then, that Muslims have filled the European imagination with fear. The fall of Constantinople to Muslim Turks in 1453 ended Christian rule in Eastern Europe for almost half a millennium. As late as 1683, Ottoman Muslims laid siege to the gates of Vienna. Such events led to deadly suspicion between Christian and Muslim in the Balkans, which, always liable to be fanned into a conflagration, has engulfed Kosovo and elsewhere, appallingly, in the last decade.

Islam is not, however, entirely or even mostly a violent religion. The largest Muslim-population country in the world is Indonesia. There, most people were converted to Islam by traders from abroad, traders who preferred mysticism to market-forces and bartering to battering. Even when Islam has countenanced and practiced violence, its scholars have, for the most part, emphasized defensive struggle rather than aggressive and offensive wars.

Of course, Muslims fear Christian militarism, too. The crusades are but one example, when violent, oversexed, landless and fanatical soldiers of faith set off to rescue the Christian Holy Land from infidel Muslims, and killed lots of Jews and different sorts of Christians before ever they reached the Middle East and saw a Muslim. That's one sort of Christianity, but let's not go there, for God's sake.

For the sake of God: not, let me underline, for the sake of religion. Contrary to much popular opinion, religions, the one or the many, are not God. They are human creations, attempting to map out as best they can, in mortal life, the ways of the immortal God among his creatures. At their best: religions are porous to the divine presence, they provide us with homes within which the human spirit can flourish, and help us grow in holiness. At their worst: well, think of the Aztecs who, for all their remarkable accomplishments, raided other nations for youngsters to kill as human sacrifices. They would hold up the still beating heart of their victim as an offering to God.

The prophet Muhammad made choices from his religious past. He rejected polytheism, the worship of many gods, and, building on the belief in one God that a few Arabs followed, he brought Islam to people. Islam means submitting to the one God and, in submitting, finding peace and meaning. Jesus also made choices from his religious past. He said: "You have heard that it was said, 'You shall love your neighbor and hate your enemy.' But I say to you, Love your enemies and pray for those who persecute you."

Muhammad and Jesus made choices from the religion of their day, rejecting some things and accepting others. So, also, like all people, whether we admit it or not, like it or hate it, we have to choose elements from our religious heritage upon which to construct our life. On what basis do we make our choices? No doubt, personal factors come into play, but I reckon it's best done on the basis of what the majority of the evidence seems to suggest. Remarkably, most religions argue, suggest or just assume that Transcendent reality presses down upon us, beckons us, allures us into hearing and following what he has to say. In other words, God reveals himself to us: not always with the clarity we would like; but I guess that's a deliberate attempt to get us thinking about and engaging with what she desires for our good.

When some Christian tells us that September 11 was God's wake-up call to America, commanding us to get rid of gays, new agers, Muslims, feminists or whomever, I remind myself that it's more important to attempt to hear God's word than the comments of one of his self-appointed spokespersons who, instead of listening to God, project onto him all their unpleasant stuff.

If God speaks through the scriptures of the great religions, as I believe him to do, then I am entranced by Jesus' teaching of the fatherhood of God, who is not some unpleasant, bossy patriarch but a loving parent. I'm mindful that every chapter of the Muslim scripture bar one begins "in the name of God, the merciful one, the source of mercy." Scriptures don't always provide an edifying read. We can find bad temper in most scripture, or the emphatic assertion or casual assumption of a cultural practice that has now passed its sell-by date, or illogical reasoning, or a pile of other irritating or even offensive things.

Scriptures, too, like religion, are liable to be confused by many people with Transcendent reality. I prefer to invoke the Daoist image that it's the foolish man who mistakes the finger pointing to the moon for the moon itself. The finger may be a little crooked and uncertain, but the reality to which it points is sublimely real.

The choices we should make are not eccentric, or self-serving. They are ones that have been sifted by time and found to work. Christians, by and large, know that God is love, even though it's usually best to get them to leave the statement there and not hear all the qualifications they make, which usually betray their pride and prejudice rather than their wisdom. Muslims fundamentally know that God is merciful, even though, again, they often hedge it round with reservations that tell us more about them than about God. Oddly, most people find it easier to deal with an ornery God than a gracious one, but we shouldn't succumb to that ease. Religions are most amazing when they tell us that the one who made the stars is wonderfully kind rather than as crabby as we are.

My father, of blessed memory, nearly became a Muslim. I have never wanted to make that choice but, in a world more closely bound yet more complex than ever before, we need to respectfully learn about the other, not to undermine but to understand. Islam is too important to be left to Muslims, and Christianity too complicated to yield its secrets only to Christians. We can learn from the other, even about ourselves.

We are brought face-to-face with true religion when, just occasionally, we meet a goodly and a godly person, Christian or Muslim or whomever. Then I am reminded of a favorite saying of mine, by William Penn. He was a difficult man, to be sure, hardly saintly, but certainly a wrestler with God. He wrote:

> The humble, meek, merciful, just, pious and devout souls are everywhere of one religion, and when death has taken off the mask, they will know one another though the diverse liveries they wear here make them strangers.

SOURCE: <http://www.aurora.edu/cfa/published/muslims.htm>

GLOSSARY

'A'isha Muhammad's youngest wife, who was the source of many Hadith.

Fatiha The first Sura of the Qur'an.

Hadith A traditional report about the Prophet's sayings or actions.

Hajj The holy pilgrimage to Mecca, taken at least once in a lifetime if affordable.

Hijrah (or **Hegira**) The journey of the Prophet from Mecca to Medina in 622 CE.

Iconoclasm Prohibition of images in art to prevent distortion of Allah's reality, sometimes leading to the destruction of images.

Imam A Muslim prayer leader, and a Shi'ite religious leader.

Isnah Authoritative chain of transmission of a Hadith.

Jihad The Muslim term for struggle, with two meanings: an inner struggle against evil, and an outer struggle for a Muslim social order.

Khadija Muhammad's first wife, who supported him when he received prophecies.

Mecca The holy city of Islam whose Ka'ba is the goal of Hajj pilgrimages.

Monism The philosophy that ultimately only one substance exists underneath the multiplicity of appearances.

Mosque Sacred building for Muslim worship, usually an open-roofed rectangle with towers (minarets) for calling to prayer.

Night Journey Muhammad's visionary journey to Jerusalem and up through seven heavens to Allah to receive revelations.

Salaat Islamic prayer five times a day, and especially ritual worship at mosque on Friday noon.

Shari'ah The divine law, as interpreted by judges, based on Qur'an and Hadith.

Sufi Muslim mystical tradition; some say Islamic only, some say universal.

Sura A chapter in the Qur'an.

Ummah The Muslim community as a whole.

HOLY DAYS

Friday Mosque Worship

10th of Muharram New Year

12th of Rabi'al-Awwai The Prophet's Birthday

27th of Rajab Muhammad's Ascension

Ramadan Month of Fasting

27th of Ramadan Night of Power

1st of Shawwal Breaking of the Fast; Pilgrimage Season

Dhu al-Qa'da Pilgrimage Season

8th–13th of Dhu al-Hihha Hajj: Pilgrimage to Mecca

HISTORICAL OUTLINE

570 CE—birth of Muhammad

c. 610 CE—revelations of Qur'an begin

622 CE—migration from Mecca to Medina (Hijrah)

c. 630 CE—Muhammad converts southern Arabian tribes

632 CE—death of Muhammad; election of Abu Bakr as first caliph

633 CE—spread of Islam begins, expanding to northern Egypt, Palestine, Iran

650 CE—canon of the Qur'an set

691 CE—Dome of the Rock in Jerusalem completed

750 CE—Islam spreads to Spain, southern Russia, Afghanistan

750–1258—Islam reaches its peak under Abbasid caliphs: control of Indonesia, India, Middle East, Egypt, Turkey, Balkans, Spain; much cultural development

by 870 CE—Muhammad Ibn Ismail al-Bukhari writes authoritative Hadith (*Sahih Bukhari*)

by 875 CE—Abu-l-Husayn Muslim writes authoritative Hadith (*Sahih Muslim*)

980–1037—Ibn Sina (Avicenna), major rationalist philosopher

1058–1111—Al-Ghazali, leading mystical philosopher

1126–98—Ibn Rushd (Averroes), important philosopher of "two truths"—revelation and reason

1165–1240—Ibn 'Arabi, influential mystical philosopher

1171—Salah-al-Din recaptures Jerusalem from Crusaders

1300–1400s—Christians fight to retake Spain using Inquisition

1453—Turks conquer Constantinople, renaming it Istanbul

1556—Akbar becomes the Muslim Mughal emperor in India

1800–1900s—many Muslim colonies come under European control

1910—Sufi Order of the West founded by Hazrat Inayat Khan

1947—Muslim-majority Pakistan separates from Hindu-majority India

1970s—oil-wealthy Muslim nations start OPEC; Muslim resurgence begins

2001—September 11 attacks in United States

2003—United States and allies invade Iraq

REVIEW QUESTIONS

1 Based on the readings, what kind of society did Muhammad encounter?
2 What views of women, children, and divorce does the Qur'an teach?
3 Describe how three major Islamic philosophers saw the relation between reason and revelation.
4 What is Sufism? Describe the thoughts of three major Sufis.

DISCUSSION QUESTIONS

1 Why do you think that of all possibilities, "submission" is the major theme of Islam? What various forms does it take?
2 Do you think that Islam promotes violence more or less than any other religion?
3 How has Islam shaped its place in geography and history, and how has it been shaped by these factors?

INFORMATION RESOURCES

Ahmed, Leila. *Women and Gender in Islam*. New Haven, CT: Yale University Press, 1992.

Ask, Karen, and **Marit Tjomsland**, eds. *What is Islam?* New York: Oxford University Press, 1998.

Athar, Shahid. *What is Islam?* <www.islam-usa.com>

Bayat, Mojedh, and **Mohammad Ali Jamnia**. *Tales from the Land of the Sufis*. Boston and London: Shambhala, 1994.

Beck, Lois, and **Nikki Deddie**, eds. *Women in the Muslim World*. Cambridge, MA: Harvard University Press, 1982.

Ernst, Carl W. *The Shambhala Guide to Sufism*. Boston and London: Shambhala, 1997.

Fakhry, Majid. *A History of Islamic Philosophy*. 3rd ed. New York: Columbia University Press, 2004.

Glasse, Cyril. *The Concise Encyclopedia of Islam*. San Francisco: Harper and Row, 1989.

Hixon, Lex. *Heart of the Koran*. Wheaton, IL, and London: Theosophical Publishing House, 1988.

Jomier, Jacques. *How to Understand Islam*. New York: Crossroad, 1991.

Lawrence, Bruce B. *Defenders of God: The Fundamentalist Revolt Against the Modern Age*. San Francisco: Harper and Row, 1989.

Lester, Toby. "What is the Koran?" in *The Atlantic Monthly*, Jan. 1999, pp. 43–56.

Martin, Richard C. *Islamic Studies: A History of Religions Approach*. Upper Saddle River, NJ: Prentice-Hall, 1982/1996.

Mernissi, Fatima. *Beyond the Veil: Male–Female Dynamics in a Modern Muslim Society*. New York: Wiley, 1975.

Mevlevi Order <http://www.hayatidede.org>

Nasr, Seyyed Hossein. *Ideals and Realities of Islam*. London: George Allen and Unwin/Harper, 1966.

Rahman, Fazlur, *et al.* "Islam," in *Encyclopedia of Religion*, ed. Lindsay Jones. 2nd ed. Vol. 7, pp. 4560–726. New York: Macmillan, 2005.

Schimmel, Annemarie. *Islam: An Introduction*. Albany, NY: State University of New York Press, 1992.

Shah, Idries. *The Way of the Sufi*. New York: Dutton, 1970.

Smith, Huston. *Islamic Mysticism: The Sufi Way*. Videorecording. Cos Cob, CT: The Hartley Film Foundation, 1997.

Stern, S. M., Albert Hourani, and **Vivian Brown**, eds. *Islamic Philosophy and the Classical Tradition*. Columbia, SC: University of South Carolina Press, 1972.

Universal Islamic Declaration of Human Rights, Islamic Council of London, 1981. <http://www.alhewar.com/ISLAMDECL.html>

Wadud-Muhsin, Amina. *Qur'an and Woman*. Kuala Lumpur: Penerbit Fajar Bakti Sdn. Bhd, 1992.

Watt, W. Montgomery, *et al.* "Muhammad and the Religion of Islam," in *Encyclopedia Britannica*. Vol. 22, pp. 1–43. London, 1997.

CHAPTER 11

SIKHISM

From 1469 to 1708, not one but a continuous series of ten prophets appeared in North India, developing a tradition that has come to be known as Sikhism. In the Punjabi language of the founders, *sikh* means "student." And according to contemporary understanding of the religion, those who are known as Sikhs are students not only of the Ten Sikh **Gurus** but also of the founders and saints of other traditions. Even more so, Sikhs are those who love God, try to remember God in everyday life, and attempt to serve God in the world.

The first of the Sikh Gurus became known as Guru Nanak (1469–1539). He was born into a Hindu family but in his eleventh year, when the time came for him to be invested with the traditional sacred thread, he refused. He explained in inspired verse that the thread would wear out, in contrast to eternal spiritual virtues which should be inwardly cultivated. This preference for inward transformation and closeness to God rather than outward rituals is evident in many stories told about his life. Guru Nanak spent much of his adult life on long journeys, preaching to Hindus and Muslims alike about spiritual truth. During his last 20 years, he developed a unique village in which land was owned in common, people pooled their labor, and the food was offered to everyone freely in a **langar**—a communal kitchen. He praised women, cut through the caste system, and declared manual work holy, thereby challenging prejudices that had developed within Hindu society. He offered a straightforward path to God-realization: work hard to support yourself by honest means, share with others, and always recite the Name of God.

The mystical teachings, new social order, and practicality of Guru Nanak's path were continued and developed by his nine successors. Their spiritual power and the devotion of their followers were construed as threatening by the Mughal rulers, as well as the Hindu hill chiefs, and from time to time the Gurus and their Sikhs had to face armed attacks. The saintly Fifth and Ninth Gurus were martyred. Ultimately, the powerful Guru Gobind Singh (1666–1708), tenth of the Sikh masters, transformed his intimidated people into **Khalsa**, extraordinarily courageous warrior-saints pledged to protect people of all religions and castes from oppression. Sacrificing his entire family and ultimately himself, Guru Gobind Singh instructed his followers thenceforth to regard as their master the sacred scriptures compiled by the Gurus: the **Guru Granth Sahib**.

Guru Nanak at Mecca

Amritsar, Guru
Nanak

Many stories are told about miracles occurring in the Gurus' lives. This one concerns Guru Nanak's journey to Mecca, the holy city to which only Muslims are allowed to travel.

The Guru after a fairly long sojourn at Kapurthala started for Mecca and joined a party of faqirs.[1] The Guru wore a long yellow robe on which were impressed some words and carried a staff such as a Haji[2] carried.

The faqirs watched him and one day asked, "What is your religion?"

"I belong to the religion of those who follow the path of God," replied the Guru.

The faqirs pressed him to confess that he was a Muslim but the Guru refused to do so. The faqirs were greatly troubled. They were not sure whether they were right in having with them a man who was an infidel. The Guru read their hearts and disappeared from amongst them with his two attendants. They noticed that a cloud that used to protect them from the scorching rays of the sun also disappeared with him.

The faqirs thought that travelling by himself he would never reach Mecca. They were astonished when they found that the Guru had already arrived with his two attendants. They were even more puzzled when they were told that the Guru had been there for several days. They were convinced that he was some great soul and begged him to forgive them for their suspicions about him.

The keeper of the Kaaba[3] one night discovered that he was sleeping with his feet towards the Kaaba. It was time for prayers so he informed the priest that a pilgrim was committing a great sacrilege by turning his feet towards the house of God. The priest in high dudgeon rushed to where the Guru was sleeping.

"Wake up, you stupid fool," he exclaimed, "and rub your face on the ground and beg to be forgiven for turning your feet towards the house of God."

The Guru did not move, but said, "Turn my feet towards the place where God does not dwell."

The priest could no more control himself and ordered the keeper to take him by the feet and turn him right about in the other direction. The door keeper obeyed but whichever direction they turned the Guru's feet they say that the Kaaba turned with them. The priest stood spell-bound. He saw that the house of God was in all directions.

The Guru rose and looked at the priest with eyes full of compassion. "Your eyes have been opened just for a moment," he said. "Don't forget what you have seen. The entire space is nothing but God's dwelling place."

---

1 Faqir—Muslim ascetic.
2 Haji—a pilgrim to Mecca.
3 Kaaba—the revered central cubic stone structure of the great mosque in Mecca.

The priest bowed before the Guru and then told his Chief of what had happened. The Chief was a seeker after truth. He hastened to the Guru in the hope of getting some glimpses of the eternal light.

He respectfully saluted, the Guru returned the salute, and then he sat down beside him.

"You are a godly man from all appearance," said Rukin-ud-Din, for this was his name, "but tell me to what religion you belong."

"I believe in the religion of Him, who is the master of all that is visible and invisible," answered the Guru.

"What do you mean by Him?" asked Rukin-ud-Din.

"He who is without a second," said the Guru, "to whom birth and death are not known. Who is beyond all change, and who pervades everywhere, lands, seas, air and skies."

"So you believe in one God; you must be a Muslim."

"I accept no creed," said the Guru. "I am His slave and slaves have not even their own will. How can they accept any creed who yield unwavering obedience to the Lord?"

"God as you have described Him, is the same God of which our Kalma[4] speaks," repeated Rukin-ud-Din. "Why not acknowledge yourself to be a Muslim?"

"The Vedas too speak of one God, the supreme God of all," said the Guru. "Then why should not I declare myself a Hindu? Truth remains Truth. It is the coloured lenses of the self that reflect it in various colours. A servant of God, aware of His presence, cannot accept creeds, which imprison truth and impose on it their own limitations."

"How do you make this out?" asked Rukin-ud-Din.

"You have an example before your eyes. You call this sacred temple a house of God. If you were a true believer, you would find there is no place where the house of God does not exist. Further, you say you believe in one God. Then why don't you recognize in men of diverse creeds a brother? If this truth dwelt in your heart, you would act in its light."

SOURCE: Jogendra Singh and Daljit Singh, *The Great Humanist Guru Nanak*. Patiala, Punjab: Languages Department Punjab, 1970, pp. 52–3

Daily prayers

Traditional Sikhs spend several hours each day in reciting prayers composed under inspiration by the Gurus, in addition to trying always to recite the Name of God inwardly. The day begins early in the morning with prayer and recitation of five hymns. Another long prayer is recited at dusk, and another at bedtime. Repeated recitation of the prayers is a way of training the mind in thinking spiritually, and of increasing one's faith in and awareness of God. Excerpts from some of these prayers are offered here.

---

4 Kalma—profession of faith in one God and in Muhammad as Messenger.

JapJi by Guru Nanak

JapJi (a title based on the verb meaning "to recite") sets forth the essence of Sikh philosophy. It is the first of the morning prayers.

There is one God
His Name is Truth
He is the Creator
He is without fear
He is without hate
Immortal is His form
He is not born to die or be born again
By the Guru's grace, He is obtained.

He was true before time began and He was the Truth when time began.
True He is even now and true He shall be hereafter.

By thinking alone one cannot know Him
  though one may think a hundred thousand times.
One cannot obtain peace of mind
  by keeping silent and remaining absorbed in Him.
The hunger for knowing Him can neither be appeased by remaining hungry,
  nor by accumulating all the good things of life.
No, by none of these, nor by a hundred thousand other devices
  can God be reached.
How then shall the truth be known
  and how the veil of false illusion torn?
Only by obeying, O Nanak! the will of the Lord.

By His will all forms are created, but His will we do not know.
By His will are all beings infused with life
  and by His will some achieve greatness.
By His will some are made high, some low,
  and by His will some get pleasure, some get pain.
By His will some are saved, others doomed to die, relive, and die again.
All are subject to His will, no one is exempt from it.
O Nanak! he who knows His will has no ego or pride. . . .

True is the master, True is His name and His speech is unbounded love.
His creatures ever cry, "Give, O give,"
  and He, the bounteous, never says "no."
What then should we offer at His feet so that we may see His court?
What should we speak, by hearing which He may give us His love?
In the sweet hours of the early morning, meditate on His greatness.
By good action this body is obtained, by His grace we get salvation.
Know then, that the True one is all by Himself.

SOURCE: *JapJi: The Morning Prayer*, trans. Bhagat Singh and G. P. Singh. Delhi: Hemkunt Press, 1986, pp. 9–13

Jaap Sahib by Guru Gobind Singh

Jaap Sahib is the second morning prayer. In wave after wave of negative and positive epithets, it paints a vast picture of the Formless God.

Salutations to the Eternal, Salutations to the Merciful.
Salutations to the Formless, Salutations to the Peerless....

Salutations to the One beyond deeds,
Salutations to the One beyond creeds.
Salutations to the One beyond names,
Salutations to the One beyond any fixed locale.

Salutations to the Unconquerable,
Salutations to the Fearless.
Salutations to the Unshakeable,
Salutations to the Invincible.

Salutations to the One without colour or hue,
Salutations to the One who hath no beginning.
Salutations to the One who is impenetrable,
Salutations to the One who is unfathomable....

Salutations to the Absolute One,
Who is yet manifest in myriad forms.
Salutations to the One beyond physical elements,
Salutations to the One beyond all bonds....

Salutations to the One who is ever steady,
Salutations to the One beyond physical elements.
Salutations to the One who cannot be seen,
Salutations to the One beyond sorrow or grief....

Salutations to the Divine Reveller,
Salutations to the Divine Ascetic.
Salutations to the Lord, without any hue,
Salutations to the Lord, ever Indestructible....

Salutations to the One who hath no caste,
Salutations to the One who hath no lineage.
Salutations to the One beyond confines of religions,
Salutations to the One who is wonderful....

Salutations to the Destroyer of all,
Salutations to the Creator of all.
Salutations to the Annihilator of all,
Salutations to the Preserver of all.

Salutations to the Lord of Light and Truth,
Salutations to the Lord, ever mysterious.

Salutations to the Lord, ever unborn,
Salutations to the Lord of beauty.

Salutations to the Lord, immanent everywhere,
Salutations to the Lord, who pervades everything.
Salutations to the Lord, manifest in all colours,
Salutations to the Lord, who destroys everything. . . .

Salutations to Thee,
Wielder of weapons and Pride of arms,
Perfect of knowledge and Mother of all.

O Lord,
Having Thy domain in all quarters,
Thou art the Reveller everywhere.
Self-created, compassionate and auspicious,
Thou art ever united with everyone.
Destroyer of bad times,
Thou art the Embodiment of Compassion.
Ever so close to everyone,
Everlasting is the treasure of Thy glory and power.

SOURCE: Guru Gobind Singh, *Jaap Sahib*, trans. Surendra Nath. Delhi: Gobind Sadan, 1991, rev. 1996, pp. 20–33, 174

Sukhmani Sahib by Guru Arjun Dev

Sukhmani Sahib ("The Song of Greatest Spiritual Bliss"), composed by the Fifth Guru, takes over an hour to recite, and thus it is not part of all Sikhs' daily practice. Nevertheless, it contains many important concepts, including the passage given here, a description of the *Brahm-giānī*, a God-realized being who lives in the world to help society but is not entangled in worldliness. This is the Sikh spiritual ideal.

The brahm-giānī is always uncontaminated,
Like the lotus, which is unaffected by muddy water.

The brahm-giānī is ever free from sins and remains pious;
(He burns others' sins), just as the sun burns and dries up things.

The brahm-giānī sees all men as equal;
Just as the wind blows on the rich and the poor without any distinction.

The brahm-giānī remains uniformly patient;
Like the earth, whether one digs it up or another smears it with precious
    sandal.[5] . . .

Divine knowledge is the (spiritual) food of the brahm-giānī.
The brahm-giānī meditates on God alone, (says) (Gurū) Nānak.

---

5 *Sandal*—the fragrance of sandalwood.

The brahm-giānī has his hopes (only) on One.
The brahm-giānī shall never perish.

The brahm-giānī is steeped in humility.
The brahm-giānī takes joy in doing good to others.

The brahm-giānī is not entangled in worldly matters.
The brahm-giānī controls his wandering mind.

To the brahm-giānī, whatever is done (by God), is the best.
The brahm-giānī obtains the fruit of his human life.

In the company of the brahm-giānī, all are saved.
With the help of the brahm-giānī, the whole world worships and remembers
    God, (says) (Gurū) Nānak.

The brahm-giānī keeps love for One Supreme Being in his heart.
God lives with the brahm-giānī. . . .

The Lord of Supreme joy resides in the heart of the brahm-giānī.
The heart of the brahm-giānī is full of joy.

In the life of the brahm-giānī every event is spontaneous.
The teachings of the brahm-giānī are pure.

He becomes brahm-giānī, whom God makes so.
The glory of the brahm-giānī is great.

Who can estimate the greatness of the brahm-giānī?
Only a brahm-giānī knows the divine spiritual state of the brahm-
    giānī . . . .

The brahm-giānī is the helper of the helpless.
The brahm-giānī extends his hand over all.

The brahm-giānī owns the whole world.
The brahm-giānī is himself the Formless One. . . .

SOURCE: Guru Arjun Dev, *Sacred Sukhmani*, trans. Harbans Singh Doabia. Amritsar, Punjab: Singh Brothers, 1979, pp. 83–91

Sikh scripture: the Guru Granth Sahib

Sikhs treat their scripture with great reverence. It is a vast collection of mystical devotional poetry—some 5,867 hymns sung in classical musical forms. They were composed by seven of the Sikh Gurus and also by numerous Hindu and Muslim saints of all castes. The overarching theme is devotion to God and inner detachment from worldly concerns. Living by the instructions of the Guru and remembering God's Holy Name are prescribed as antidotes to worldliness. A few selections from this unique inter-religious scripture are given here.

HYMNS OF THE SIKH GURUS

"Oh honey-bee, thou art lost in worldly flowers"

by Guru Nanak (the First Guru)

.... O my soul, thou honey-bee,
Buzzing around the blossoms to rifle their sweets,
Hear me, thy sorrow is great:
I asked the Guru in so many words
"What is the true path?"
And the Guru in so many words answered me:
O honey-bee, thou art lost in worldly flowers,
When the sun rises after death,
Thy soul will suffer as a body scalded by oil.

Without the Word of the Guru
Man is stupid and cannot find his way,
He dieth and forever suffereth agony.
Forget not God, O heart of a fool, O honey-bee:
On the other road lieth death,
On the other road lieth destruction, saith Nānak.

My soul thou art not a native of this world,
Wherefore then get caught in the net?
Entertain within thyself the Holy Name of God.
The fish like the human soul is ensnared in the net of death,
It weeps and gasps in agony,
And now she knows that life ever pleasant was a delusion.
Adore and cherish the Lord
And cast out baseless fears.
Pay heed, O my soul, to this admonition of Nānak:
My soul, thou art not native to this place,
In thine inner depths cherish the true Lord.

As streaming rivers that start from the same source
Are separated but meet in the Ocean,
So do souls meet in the Infinite,
One in a million knows
That age upon age
The world's illusions enchant and poison the soul.
Those that contemplate the Guru
Learn easily and realize God.

Those who do not cherish the Lord's Name
Wander, deceived and bewildered;
Without such cherishing of the Lord's Name,
Without the love of His Eternal Being,

Man can have no destiny except remorse and anguish.
Nānak utters a truth:
Through the Word of the Guru
The long estrangement of the soul and God end in meeting.

"Oh my mind, remember the Holy Name"
by Guru Amar Das (the Third Guru)

If the mind is unclean, all else is unclean;
And ceremonial washings cannot wash the mind.
This world is the realm of illusion:
There are few who grasp the Real.
O my mind, remember the Holy Name![6]
That is the precious gift of the Guru to men.
Were a man to learn all the postures of the most austere Yogis,
And mortify all his senses,
Not so would he cleanse the mind, or discard self-will.
There is no cure for the mind's sickness
But taking shelter at the Guru's feet.
To meet the Guru is to experience
A change of outlook that cannot be described.
Saith Nānak: From the mind of him who dies to self
Through meeting the Guru, and is reborn through the Guru's Word,
All uncleanness is removed.

"My eyes are wet with the Lord's nectar"
by Guru Ram Das (the Fourth Guru)

My eyes are wet with the Lord's nectar; my soul is drenched in his Love.
He tested my heart with His touchstone: He found it pure
Through the Guru my soul and body are dyed as with deep crimson.
Nānak, the slave, has made himself fragrant with musk:
My earthly life is blessed.

The hymn of the Lord's love is like a pointed arrow,
That hath pierced deep in my heart: who feels love's pain knows it
And he that dies to this life even while living
Has obtained his deliverance even in this life.
Saith Nānak: By meeting the True Guru
Life's dangerous ocean is crossed.

Ignorant and a fool though I am, I seek thy sanctuary.
May I attain to the love of my Beloved!

---

6 Holy Name—*nam*, remembrance of God by inner or outer recitation of one of God's names, a central Sikh practice.

I reached God through the perfect Guru: may I seek nothing but His service.
My mind and body are soothed, O Lord, by Thy Word:
I repeat Thy Holy Name with thrilling delight.
Through meeting the saints and seeking Truth in their company
Nānak has attained to God.

Hear my prayer, O Thou who hast pity on the wretched!
I seek my shelter in the Name: I long for the Name to be on my lips.
O Lord, it is Thy Greatness to love Thy Saints and save the honour.
Humble Nānak has taken Thee as his stronghold:
Thy Name has helped him to cross the dangerous ocean.

"The true Guru is an ocean of pearls"
by Guru Arjun Dev (the Fifth Guru)

That man is blind within and blind without,
Though he pretendeth to sing of the Lord
And performeth ritual washings and puts on caste-marks,
If in his heart he runneth after Mammon.
He cannot remove his inner dirt of self-sense.
In births he comes and goes,
Overwhelmed by sleep, played by lust,
And uttereth the name of God.
Though he call himself a Vaishnav,[7]
Since self-will is the goad of his actions
What can he hope to gain?
Pretended holiness is like thrashing empty husks,
Or like the crane who sits among the swans,
Is still on the watch for fish. The swans find him an intruder.
They live upon pearls and precious stones, the crane on frogs,
And finally the poor crane flies away
In fear that the swans might spot his true nature.
Men do as God wills. Why should we blame anyone?
When anything happens, God wills that it should.
The True Guru is an ocean-wide lake of pearls:
The sincere seeker after his pearls shall find them.
The True Guru is the holy lake of Mansrover,[8]
And his Sikhs are there gathered like his swans.
The lake is full of pearls and precious stones;
However many the swans eat, they will not be exhausted.
The Sikhs are like swans who remain at the lake for ever
And banquet for ever on jewels. God has so willed it.
Nānak, blessed is the disciple who comes to the Guru:

---

7 Vaishnav—an ascetic devoted to some form of Lord Vishnu, such as Krishna.
8 Lake Mansrover—a holy lake high in the Himalayas.

The Guru will save him, save his family,
Nay, in the end he will save the whole world!

"The one who mingles with God"
by Guru Tegh Bahadur (the Ninth Guru)

That man who in the midst of grief is free from grieving,
And free from fear, and free from the snare of delight,
Nor is covetous of gold that he knows to be dust,
Who is neither a backbiter nor a flatterer,
Nor has greed in his heart, nor vanity, nor any worldly attachment,
Who remains at his centre unmoved by good and ill fortune,
Who is indifferent to the world's praise and blame
And discards every wishful fantasy
Accepting his lot in a disinterested fashion,
Not worked upon by lust or by wrath,
In such a man God dwelleth.
The man on whom the Grace of the Guru alights
Understands the way of conduct:
His soul, O Nānak, is mingled with the Lord
As water mingles with water!

HYMNS OF THE HINDU AND MUSLIM SAINTS

In addition to hymns of the Sikh Gurus, the Guru Granth Sahib includes compositions by numerous Hindu and Muslim saints and musicians who lived before the Sikh Gurus. Many were of a low caste, illustrating the Sikh conviction that the heights of spiritual realization transcend caste distinctions. Nam Dev (1270–1350) was a low-caste Hindu tailor.

"God is the object of the yearning of my soul" by Nam Dev

As water is precious
To the traveller in Marwar,
As the hungry camel
Yearns for the creeper,
As the wild deer at night
Hearken enrapt
To the hunter's bell,
So God is the object
Of the yearning of my soul!

Thy Name is beauty,
Thy Form is beauty,
Thy Hues are beauty,
O my living Lord!

As the dry earth yearneth
In thirst for the raindrops,
As the honey-bee yearneth
For the scent of the flowers,
As the kokil[9] loves the mango-tree,
So I long for the God.

As the sheldrake
Longs for sunrise,
As the swan yearneth
For Mansrover Lake,
As the wife pines
For her husband,
So God is the object
Of the yearning of my soul!

As the babe yearneth
For his mother's breast-milk,
As the chatrik[10] who drinketh
Only the raindrops
Yearneth for the rain,
As the stranded fish
Yearneth after water,
So God is the object
Of the yearning of my soul!

All seekers, sages, teachers
Yearn, O Lord, after Thee.
How few of them have seen Thee!
As Thy Name is yearned after
By Thy whole vast creation,
So for Nama God is the object
Of the yearning of his soul!

"How can there be any difference between me and Thee?"

by Ravi Das

Ravi Das was a fourteenth- to fifteenth-century Hindu saint who was an extremely low-caste hide-tanner and shoemaker.

Between Thee and me, between me and Thee,
How can there be likeness or difference?
Likeness or difference as between gold
And a bracelet made of it, as between water

---

9 Kokil—a type of bird.
10 Chatrik—a type of bird, said to drink only raindrops.

And the waves that move on its surface!
Were I not a sinner, O Eternal Lord,
How couldst Thou have the title of Redeemer of Sinners?
Thou, O Lord, art the Searcher of hearts.
Through God, the Master, we know the saints, His Servants:
Through the servants of God, we know God.
Grant me O Lord that my body may be Thy shrine.
Few, O Ravi Das, see God in everything.

SOURCE: Hymns from the Guru Granth Sahib are taken from *Selections from the Sacred Writings of the Sikhs*, trans. Trilochan Singh *et al*. New York: Samuel Weiser, 1973, standard pagination pp. 438, 558, 448, 633, 393, 93

"Pray crow, peck not these eyes, so that I may see the Beloved" by Sheikh Farid, with commentary by Guru Nanak

The mystical poetry of several Muslim saints is lovingly included in the Guru Granth Sahib. One is the great Sufi dervish, Sheikh Farid (1175–1265). His burning ardor for his Beloved is tempered by a commentary from Guru Nanak.

Mighty river, erode not thy banks; thou too to thy maker art answerable.
What power is in the river to flow this way or that?
God's Will guides its course.
Farid, thy days have been sorrow-filled, thy nights in suffering passed.
Now towards the close the Pilot shouts:
"Thy boat's in jaws of storm."
Life's long river flows on, bringing down the sandy banks;
Yet is the boat safe from the storm, if the Pilot be attentive.
Farid, scores profess to be my friends; but true friends see I nowhere.
For one true friend my heart yearns as in smouldering fire.
Farid, the body keeps ever a tumult, who will bear its suffering for ever?
Let me plug my ears,
Blow storm never so loud.
Farid, this life is like ripe dates and rivers of honey.
With each passing day comes closer the grip of death.
Farid, penance has left my body a skeleton;
Crows peck at my soles.
God still has not revealed Himself—
Such is my destiny.

Thou crow pecking at my emaciated body, eating away its flesh,
Pray touch not these two eyes, so I have sight of the Beloved.
Pray crow, peck not at my body; fly off from where thou art settled.
Swallow not the flesh of this body wherein is lodged the Beloved.
Farid, the lowly grave makes call to homeless man to come to his real
    abode—
Saying, come to me thou must; fear not death.

With these eyes have I beheld the vast world vanish into eternity.
Each in his own trials is caught;
Nor am I free from mine.

In separation from God my body burns like the oven;
My bones flame like firewood;
To find union with the Beloved
Could I walk till my feet be tired,
Would walk on my head.

Theme continued by Guru Nanak
Thou needst not burn thyself like the oven nor put in flames thy bones:
Why torture thy poor limbs? Behold the Beloved in thy own heart.

SOURCE: Sheikh Farid, with commentary from Guru Nanak, *Sri Guru Granth Sahib*, trans. Gurbachan Singh Talib. Patiala, Punjab: Punjabi University Publication Bureau, 1990, pp. 2761–4

Writings of the Tenth Guru: Dasam Granth

When Guru Gobind Singh undertook the final compilation of the Guru Granth Sahib, including in it the poetry of his father, the martyred Guru Tegh Bahadur (1621–75), he included only one of his own compositions. However, the literature attributed to Guru Gobind Singh is vast and complex. It includes lengthy descriptions of "Hindu" deities, discipline for the Khalsa, a powerful letter to the tyrannical Muslim ruler Aurangzeb (r. 1658–1707), his spiritual autobiography (*Bacchitar Natak*), and *Akal Ustat*, assertions of the oneness of all religions and the unity of humankind. Portions from the last two are given below.

"This is the purpose for which God sent me"
by Guru Gobind Singh

I now relate my own story,
How while doing "Tapasya"[11] I had to come to earth.
There is a mountain by the name of Hemkund,
Which is adorned by seven peaks.

There I remained in deep meditation and performed "Tapasya"
worshipping the timeless and mighty God who transcends death.
In consequence of this "Tapasya,"
from the dual state, I became One with God.

Then under command of God,
I took birth in Kali Yug,[12]

---

11 Tapasya—austere meditation.
12 Kali Yug, or Kali Yuga—the last and darkest of the four ages which continually recur, according to Indian thought.

My heart did not really wish to come down,
because I was totally immersed in meditation at the feet of the Lord.
He then explained to me His purpose,
and sent me here with His command.

Lord (Akal Purukh) said:
"You are my chosen and cherished son
whom I have installed for strengthening faith and religion.
Go down to earth and propagate righteousness
and guide mankind away from wickedness."

This is the purpose for which Lord sent me
and in consequence I took birth on this earth.
I shall speak (and act) as directed by Lord
and shall not bear enmity to anyone.
But any people who address me as God,
will be consigned to the cauldron of hell.
Regard me only as the humble servant of God.
Let there be no doubt or mystery on this score.
I am the servant of the Supreme Lord,
come to earth to watch His play.
I shall utter on earth the word of Lord,
and shall not remain silent in this mortal world.

SOURCE: Guru Gobind Singh, *Bacchitar Natak*, in *Jap*, trans. Surendra Nath. Delhi: Gobind Sadan, n.d., pp. xv–xvi

"Let all humanity be recognized as one"

by Guru Gobind Singh

There are monks with shaven heads; there are many kinds of yogis, celibates, and ascetics, Hindus, Turks, Shi'ite Muslims, and Sunni Muslims.
But know that all of humanity is recognized as one race.
The Creator and the Beneficent One are the same; the Provider and the Merciful One are the same;
Let no one make the mistake of thinking there is a difference.
There is not one God for Hindus and another for Muslims.
Worship the one God who is the divine Preceptor for all, the One Form whose Light suffuses all.
Temples and mosques are the same,
Hindu worship and Muslim prayer are the same,
All people are the same.
It is only through erroneous thinking that they appear different.
Deities and demons, Muslims and Hindus wear their regional garb,
But all people have the same eyes, the same ears, the same body, the same composition of earth, air, fire, and water.

Allah and Abekh[13] are the same, the messages of the Puranas[14] and Qur'an
are the same.

All are alike; one God created all.

As from one fire millions of sparks arise separately and then unite again in
the fire,

As from one dustheap many dust particles fill the air and then resettle,
blending with the dust,

As in one stream millions of waves are produced, but being made of water,
become water again,

So from God's Form all non-sentient and sentient things are manifested, and
springing from God, all shall be united in God again.

SOURCE: Guru Gobind Singh, *Manas ki jaat*, from *Akal Ustat*, trans. Gobind Sadan, Delhi (unpublished)

Living Sikhism

In 1999, Sikhs around the world jubilantly celebrated the three-hundredth
anniversary of Guru Gobind Singh's creation of the Khalsa. In the process,
many people proclaimed the idealistic and universalist nature of the Gurus'
mission.

The Sikh Gurus' Vision of an Ideal Society
by Dharam Singh

Dharam Singh, who teaches at Punjabi University in Patiala and specializes in Guru
Gobind Singh's social philosophy, asserts that the Sikh Gurus' mission included
measures designed to develop an ideal classless society.

Besides caste which is peculiar to Indian society, the economic factor is
equally responsible for stratification of society into different classes all over
the world. In such a set-up, the affluent and the haves generally adopt an
oppressive and exploitative attitude towards the poor and the have-nots: this
is equally true in the case of individuals as well as nations. This gulf between
the two classes widens further as a result of the pace of social, material
progress being different for these different classes. Since the economic factor
comes to determine human social relations, man [sic] becomes unduly more
unmindful of moral and ethical values in this struggle for economic
betterment. Sikhism, however, believes in the universal brotherhood of
mankind, and therefore holds everyone an equal claimant to the natural
resources provided them by the universal Father. Any attempt to deny one's
share in that heritage would amount to sacrilege against God. The ethics of
the kingdom of God as taught in the Sikh scripture are the ethics of a
classless society.

---

13 Abekh—a Name of God, meaning "without garb."
14 Puranas—Sanskrit sacred writings.

An important socio-religious directive for the Sikhs is to earmark a tithe[15] of their income for philanthropic purposes. Every Sikh, when he visits a *gurdwara*[16] to pay obeisance to the Guru Granth Sahib, offers some cash. There is no lower or higher limit on this offer and, in fact, it is not even obligatory if one is

The Gurdwara

not in a position to offer any. This offer of cash, though made with religious faithfulness, is not to please the Guru or God: it is an individual's modest contribution towards general, communal purposes. . . .

Besides caste and class, religion is another very potent factor which divides mankind into diverse groups of different religious denomination. At the time Sikhism was born and during the period of its ascendancy, persecution of man in the name of religion was quite common. The Sikh Gurus felt it an insult to the divine essence in man, and declared that all human beings, irrespective of their religious denominations, are one. Guru Gobind Singh in his *Akal Ustat* refers to the diversity of religions followed by people of the world, and declares emphatically that followers of diverse religions are one. Religious labels are temporary and wither away with the bodily vesture whereas it is the worth of deeds done by man that is the criterion of judgment both in this world and the Divine Court. Guru Amar Das confers equal validity on all religions in helping man realize the ultimate end of life. The role of religion is not that of scissors that tears asunder but that of a needle that sews together the torn fabric of human society. . . .

The concept of the equality of mankind includes the womenfolk as well. Woman occupies a subordinate position in the patriarchal society, but her position becomes worse in the poor societies, especially in India where she suffers oppression as a woman and as a member of the oppressed caste or class. The Indian woman of Guru Nanak's time was a victim of this sexist discrimination and oppression, and was completely denied an independent personality of her own. Infanticide, child marriage, malnutrition and *sati*[17] were some of the evils resulting from this *Weltanschauung*.[18] Sikhism makes no distinction between man and woman, and considers both as the equal manifestation of the Divine. Man and woman are equal but distinct because of the functional distinction they have in the historical order. Even if none of the Gurus was a woman, there is no inferiority for woman in the orthodox Sikh ecclesiology. Guru Nanak was perhaps the first personage in the religious history of mankind to raise his voice against her discrimination.

The Sikh Gurus not only provided ideational basis in their hymns for the socio-religious rehabilitation of women but also undertook and advised to undertake some widespread and practical steps in this direction. As a result

---

15 Tithe—a proportion, originally a tenth.
16 *Gurdwara*—a Sikh temple.
17 *Sati, suttee*—the Hindu custom of a widow's self-immolation on her husband's funeral pyre.
18 *Weltanschauung*—philosophy, literally "world view" (German).

of this, she came to occupy a place equal to man and play an active role in the socio-religious life. That the women were quite active as missionaries of Sikh faith during the Guru-period is confirmed by a *hukumnama*[19] issued by Guru Tegh Bahadur to the *sangat*[20] of Patna wherein he refers among others to one Bebe Peri Bai. The role played by Mai Bhago[21] during the pontificate of Guru Gobind Singh is common knowledge. Sikh tradition, supported by the *Rahitnama*[22] literature, lays injunctions against female infanticide, *purdah*[23] and *sati*. It also permits widow remarriage for her rehabilitation in social life. The *Rahitnamas* denounce any kind of marginalization of woman. Chastity and fidelity, two important constituents of the sanctity of the family life as well as of social relations, are no more the virtues expected of woman alone: they apply to women as much as they apply to men and even to the rulers. . . . The Sikhs in their daily supplication (*ardas*) seek the welfare of all—*sarbat da bhala*. . . .

There is no priestly class as such in Sikhism and anybody can lead the congregation. . . . In the appointment of leaders of congregation, caste, class and status are given no consideration, and the only criterion of merit is the incumbent's spiritual and moral state. . . .

In the *gurdwara*, everybody is welcome irrespective of his social or economic status, and none is favoured or discriminated against on any count. Here the prince and the pauper sit together and pray.

Meals for All

When membership of the *sangats* and the frequency of their visits to the *dharamsalas*[24] increased, it was considered imperative to arrange food for the devotees. The institution of *langar* or *Guru-ka-Langar* (free community kitchen) started with a view to meeting this requirement. The institution became popular during the pontificate of Guru Angad Dev. . . . Guru Amar Das further consolidated the institution and made it mandatory for every visitor, high or low, to partake of food in the *langar* before seeing the Guru. Each successive Guru contributed to the consolidation of this institution, and today we find *langar* an integral part of almost every *gurdwara* or the Sikh place of worship the world over.

In the *langar*, the food is prepared communally, without anybody asking for the caste or class of the volunteer lending a helping hand. *Seva*[25] or service in the *langar* has been accepted as highly meritorious. All the visitors sit in *pangat* (row) without any distinction of caste, class or creed, and take their food. There is an injunction against providing a special seat or special food for anyone whosoever. The Sikh history stands witness that here

19 *Hukumnama*—spiritual instructions taken from opening the Guru Granth Sahib at random.
20 *Sangat*—Sikh congregation.
21 Mai Bhago—great female warrior and martyr in Sikh history.
22 *Rahitnama*—disciplines prescribed for Sikhs.
23 *Purdah*—veiling and separation of women.
24 *Dharamsala*—holy place.
25 *Seva*—voluntary service in devotion to God.

princes have sat alongside peasants. This has been a very important step in translating the principle of equality into practice—more so, in a society where rigidity of casteism and sectarianism segregated people from one another. It has also served as a medium of social integration between the king and the commoner, the prince and the peasant. . . .

The desire for *seva* is born of the feeling of love for others. Love is, as we have said earlier, the natural corollary of the Sikh precept of the universal brotherhood of mankind and universal fatherhood of God. All men, whatever their caste, clan or creed, are the children of God and all are spiritually united to each other and to the Creator-Lord. That is why, like *seva*, love has also been declared a very potent means of reaching God. . . .

Love for all as equal members of the universal brotherhood of mankind and social service and other altruistic deeds done with humility and with absolutely no selfish motives naturally lead to the establishment of a social order which is marked by justice, communal harmony and peaceful co-existence. These social conditions are all the more needed in the modern social phenomena which are experiencing rapid socio-cultural transformations that do not, however, occur at a uniform pace. Consequently, the economically poor and the socially backward are in the world today at odds with the affluent and the socially and politically advanced. These inequalities cause personal and social insecurity, distrust and hatred in personal and social relations and gross violation of human rights and a widespread sense of fear and frustration. . . . It was to overcome these and such other negative tendencies that the Sikh Gurus preached a distinct metaphysical theory and then made it the *vis-a-tergo*[26] of their vision of an ideal social structure marked by humanitarian outlook.

According to the Sikh thought, *kirt karna* (to earn one's bread with the sweat of one's brow), *nam japna* (remember the Divine Name; . . . feeling and realizing His presence in all beings and at all places), and *wand chhakna* (to share with others what one earns through honest means) are the three cardinal values in the Sikh vision of an ideal society.

SOURCE: Dharam Singh, *Sikhism: Norm and Form*. Patiala, Punjab, and Delhi: Vision and Venture, 1997, pp. 120–9

---

26 *Vis-a-tergo*—(Latin) literally "push from behind."

GLOSSARY

Guru A teacher of religious knowledge and spiritual insight, a channel of divine understanding.

Guru Granth Sahib The collection of Sikh sacred scriptures.

Khalsa Sikh warrior-saints pledged to protect people of all religions and castes from oppression.

Langar Free community kitchen.

HOLY DAYS

Sikh celebrations usually include continuous reading of the entire Guru Granth Sahib over a period of 48 hours, followed by offering of a large communal meal. Dating of holy days has traditionally followed the lunar calendar, but now some organizations are attempting to fix the dates according to the solar calendar.

January 14 Maghi, celebration of the martyrdom of 40 Immortals at Muktsar in Guru Gobind Singh's last battle against the Mughal forces.

April 13 or 14 Baisakhi, anniversary of the creation of the Khalsa, often including initiation of new members of the Khalsa with *amrit* (holy water stirred with a double-edged sword as the Sikh prayers are recited).

[June] 4th day of the lunar month of Jeth Martyrdom of Guru Arjun Dev by heat torture, commemorated by offering of a cooling drink to all passers-by.

[October–November] Full moon of the lunar month of Kartik Traditional celebration of Guru Nanak's birthday (although scholarship has placed the true date at April 15).

[November] 5th light part of the lunar month of Maghar Martyrdom of Guru Tegh Bahadur.

[December–January] 7th light part of the lunar month of Poh Birthday of Guru Gobind Singh.

HISTORICAL OUTLINE

1469–1539—life of Guru Nanak, the first Sikh Prophet

1563–1606—life of the Fifth Guru, Arjun Dev, tortured to death by the Mughal emperor Jahangir

1621–75—life of the Ninth Guru, Tegh Bahadur, who offered his life to protect Hindus' freedom of religion

1666–1708—life of Guru Gobind Singh, the Tenth Guru, who turned his followers into courageous saint-soldiers

1699—Guru Gobind Singh initiates the order of Khalsa

1708—at his death, Guru Gobind Singh installs the Guru Granth Sahib as the Guru

1780–1839—Maharaja Ranjit Singh rules a strong Sikh kingdom with regard for all religions

1848—British move into Punjab, Sikh rule falls

1919—bloody massacre by the British in Amritsar

1947—in India/Pakistan partition, two and a half million Sikhs are compelled to leave Pakistan for India

1984—Indian army storms the Golden Temple to dislodge Sikh separatists; prime minister Indira Gandhi assassinated by Sikh bodyguards, starting widespread Hindu violence against Sikhs

1999—millions of Sikhs converge on Anandpur Sahib to celebrate the 300th anniversary of the Khalsa

REVIEW QUESTIONS

1   What are the three cardinal values in the Sikh vision of an ideal society?

2   How does Sikh theology reflect its environment? Discuss, for example, *karma*, caste, one formless God. How is Sikh theology and practice different from its environment?

3   Is Sikh faith focused on monastic retreats or active work? What view of society does this reflect?

DISCUSSION QUESTIONS

1   What does Sikh history illustrate about reforming religions?

2   How do Sikh Gurus differ from rabbis, priests, ministers, caliphs, or imams?

3   What do you think of the problem seen by some Sikhs that a majority of Sikhs are so by birth only and lack the commitment of conversion by choice?

INFORMATION RESOURCES

Cole, W. Owen, and **Piara Singh Sambhi**. *The Sikhs: Their Religious Beliefs and Practices*. London: Routledge, 1985.

———. *A Popular Dictionary of Sikhism*. Richmond, Surrey: Curzon Press, 1990.

Duggal, K. S. *Sikh Gurus: Their Lives and Teachings*. Delhi: UBS Publishers' Distributors, 1993.

Gobind Sadan
<http://www.gobindsadan.org>

Institute of Sikh Studies
<http://www.sikhstudies.org>

Kohli, Surindar Singh. *The Life and Ideals of Guru Gobind Singh*. Delhi: Munshiram Manoharlal Publishers Pvt., 1986.

Macauliffe, Max Arthur. *The Sikh Religion: Its Gurus, Sacred Writings, and Authors*. Oxford: Oxford University Press/Delhi: S. Chand and Company, 1963.

Singh, Harbans, ed. *The Encyclopedia of Sikhism*. Patiala, Punjab: Punjabi University, 1992–9.

Singh, Nikky-Guninder Kaur. *The Feminine Principle in the Sikh Vision of the Transcendent*. Cambridge: Cambridge University Press, 1993.

———. "Sikhism," in *Encyclopedia of Religion*, ed. Lindsay Jones. 2nd ed. Vol. 12, pp. 8393–8. New York: Macmillan, 2005.

CHAPTER 12

NEW RELIGIOUS MOVEMENTS

From time immemorial, there have been many visionaries and philosophers pro-claiming spiritual truth. Some with particular abilities of leadership and spiritual qualities have attracted followers; those who have been especially successful in doing so are still honored today as the founders of the world's major living reli-gions. Others are now forgotten. This process continues in the present, with thousands of new religious movements emerging since World War II and others withering away.

New religious movements have always been regarded skeptically by previously established religions. In general, most religions claim to be the best, perhaps the exclusive carriers of authentic spiritual truth. Whether institutionalization or human waywardness is the cause, people may drift away from the initial fervor of their religion. Spiritual renewal may then arise either within the religion as a reform movement or without, as a new religious movement which nonetheless is likely to have some links with past tradition.

New religious movements may be perceived not only as threats to earlier move-ments, but also as threats to their followers' mental health and personal safety. In our times, there have been group suicides by members of movements anticipating doomsday or even trying to be picked up by unidentified flying objects. Some groups have encouraged their followers to withdraw from their communities and families to develop a non-worldly lifestyle. Such behaviors have led to negative branding of new religious movements as **cults** or **sects**, and have led to vigorous anti-cult organiz-ations in some parts of the world. However, the word "cult" is value-neutral and could be applied to some existing religions; it connotes a religion that is centered upon devotion to a single person or deity. Similarly, "sect" connotes a branch of a larger tradition. The term "new religious movements" is preferred today by scholars of religion. Below are examples of some types of new religious movements that are popular today.

Offshoots of older religions

Not infrequently a new religion is an offshoot that seeks to return to an earlier, purer version of an old tradition. One of the fastest-growing religions today, the Mormon Church—the Church of Jesus Christ of Latter-day Saints—is an American offshoot of Christianity that originated in 1822 near Palmyra, New York, and is now centered in Salt Lake City, Utah. *The Book of Mormon* includes the founding tradition of the ancient Mormon journey from Israel to America extracted below. In 1822 Joseph Smith (1805–44) discovered buried gold tablets, as told in "Moroni's Visit."

The Mormon Journey by Sea to the Promised Land

from *The Book of Mormon*

And it came to pass that they did worship the Lord, and did go forth with me; and we did work timbers of curious workmanship. And the Lord did show me from time to time after what manner I should work the timbers of the ship. Now I, Nephi, did not work the timbers after the manner which was learned by men, neither did I build the ship after the manner of men. And I, Nephi, did go into the mount oft, and I did pray oft unto the Lord; wherefore the Lord showed unto me great things. And it came to pass that after I had finished the ship, according to the word of the Lord, my brethren beheld that it was good, and that the workmanship thereof was exceeding fine; wherefore, they did humble themselves again before the Lord. And it came to pass that the voice of the Lord came unto my father, that we should arise and go down into the ship.

And it came to pass that on the morrow, after we had prepared all things, much fruits and meat from the wilderness, and honey in abundance, and provisions according to that which the Lord had commanded us, we did go down into the ship, with all our lading and our seeds, and whatsoever thing we had brought with us, everyone according to his age; wherefore we did all go down into the ship, with our wives and our children.

And now, my father had begat two sons in the wilderness; the elder was called Jacob and the younger Joseph. And it came to pass after we had all gone down into the ship, and had taken with us our provisions and things which had been commanded us, we did put forth into the sea and were driven forth before the wind towards the promised land. . . .

And it came to pass that after we had sailed for the space of many days we did arrive at the promised land; and we went forth upon the land, and did pitch our tents; and we did call it the promised land.

And it came to pass that we did begin to till the earth, and we began to plant seeds; yea, we did put all our seeds into the earth, which we had brought from the land of Jerusalem. And it came to pass that they did grow exceedingly; wherefore, we were blessed in abundance. And it came to pass that we did find upon the land of promise, as we journeyed in the wilderness, that there were beasts in the forests of every kind, both the cow and the ox, and the ass and the horse, and the goat and the wild goat, and all manner of wild animals, which were for the use of man [sic]. And we did find all manner of ore, both of gold, and of silver, and of copper.

And it came to pass that the Lord commanded me, wherefore I did make plates of ore that I might engrave upon them the record of my people. (I Nephi 18:1–8, 23–5, 19:1)

SOURCE: *The Book of Mormon*. Salt Lake City, UT: The Church of Jesus Christ of Latter-day Saints, 1830/1963, pp. 38–41

Moroni's Visit from the *Testimony of the Prophet Joseph Smith*

Joseph Smith, the founder of the Mormon Church, reports how the angel Moroni revealed to him where to find the buried gold tablets mentioned above in I Nephi 19. Smith dug them up. On them were written God's words, he claimed, and he translated and published them in 1830. They were said to tell of the lost tribes of Israel who came to America. Most died in conflict, and only Mormon (who wrote on the tablets) and his son Moroni (who buried them) survived.

Persecution continued as Joseph refused to deny that he had seen God. On 21 September 1823 after retiring to bed, Joseph prayed to know his standing before the Lord. The angel Moroni appeared to him.

On the evening of the above-mentioned twenty-first of September, after I had retired to my bed for the night, I betook myself to prayer and supplication to Almighty God for forgiveness of all my sins and follies, and also for a manifestation to me, that I might know of my state and standing before him; for I had full confidence in obtaining a divine manifestation, as I previously had one.

Three years after Joseph Smith's First Vision, God sent the angel Moroni to instruct Joseph about restoring the gospel of Jesus Christ.

While I was thus in the act of calling upon God, I discovered a light appearing in my room, which continued to increase until the room was lighter than at noonday, when immediately a personage appeared at my bedside, standing in the air, for his feet did not touch the floor.

He had on a loose robe of most exquisite whiteness. It was a whiteness beyond anything earthly I had ever seen; nor do I believe that any earthly thing could be made to appear so exceedingly white and brilliant. His hands were naked, and his arms also, a little above the wrist; so, also, were his feet naked, as were his legs, a little above the ankles. His head and neck were also bare. I could discover that he had no other clothing on but this robe, as it was open, so that I could see into his bosom.

Not only was his robe exceedingly white, but his whole person was glorious beyond description, and his countenance truly like lightning. The room was exceedingly light, but not so very bright as immediately around his person. When I first looked upon him, I was afraid; but the fear soon left me.

He called me by name, and said unto me that he was a messenger sent from the presence of God to me, and that his name was Moroni; that God had a work for me to do; and that my name should be had for good and evil among all nations, kindreds, and tongues, or that it should be both good and evil spoken of among all people.

He said there was a book deposited, written upon gold plates, giving an account of the former inhabitants of this continent, and the source from whence they sprang. He also said that the fulness of the everlasting Gospel was contained in it, as delivered by the Savior to the ancient inhabitants.

Also, that there were two stones in silver bows—and these stones, fastened to a breastplate, constituted what is called the Urim and Thummim[1]—deposited with the plates; and the possession and use of these stones were what constituted "seers" in ancient or former times; and that God had prepared them for the purpose of translating the book. . . .

SOURCE: <http://www.lds.org/library/display/0,4945,104-1-3-6,00.html>

Esoteric wisdom

There have long been people who claim to be privy to deeper secrets of religion that have been hidden from the general public. A famous nineteenth-century proponent of this idea was the Russian Madame Helena Blavatsky (1831–91). She said that she had received higher initiations by hidden Ascended Masters, some of them from Eastern religions, and proposed that the eternal truths they revealed to her were the key to harmonizing all religions. The global Theosophical Society is an outgrowth of her teachings. The dialogue below is between an Enquirer and a Theosophist.

The Wisdom-Religion Esoteric in All Ages
by Helena Blavatsky

THEO. [Ammonius[2]] was born a Christian, but never accepted Church Christianity. As said of him by [Mosheim]:

"He had but to propound his instructions according to the ancient pillars of Hermes, which Plato and Pythagoras[3] knew before, and from them constituted their philosophy. Finding the same in the prologue of the Gospel

---

1 Urim and Thummim—an ancient Hebrew priestly device for telling oracles, worn on a breastplate.
2 Ammonius Saccas (175–242 CE)—a philosopher of Alexandria, Egypt, whose most famous pupils were Origen and Plotinus.
3 Plato, Pythagoras—ancient Greek philosophers.

according to St. John, he very properly supposed that the purpose of Jesus was to restore the great doctrine of wisdom in its primitive integrity. The narratives of the Bible and the stories of the gods he considered to be allegories illustrative of the truth, or else fables to be rejected." Moreover, as says the *Edinburgh Encyclopedia*, "he acknowledged that Jesus Christ was an excellent *man* and the 'friend of God,' but alleged that it was not his design entirely to abolish the worship of demons (gods), and that his only intention was to purify the ancient religion."

ENQ. Since Ammonius never committed anything to writing, how can one feel sure that such were his teachings?

THEO. Neither did Buddha, Pythagoras, Confucius, Orpheus, Socrates, or even Jesus, leave behind them any writings. Yet most of these are historical personages, and their teachings have all survived. The disciples of Ammonius (among whom were Origen and Herennius) wrote treatises and explained his ethics. Certainly the latter are as historical, if not more so, than the Apostolic writings. Moreover, his pupils—Origen, Plotinus, and Longinus (counsellor of the famous Queen Zenobia[4])—have all left voluminous record of the Philaletheian System[5]—so far, at all events, as their public profession of faith was known, for the school was divided into **exoteric** and **esoteric** teachings.

ENQ. How have the latter tenets reached our day, since you hold that what is properly called the Wisdom-Religion was esoteric?

THEO. The Wisdom-Religion was ever one, and being the last word of possible human knowledge, was, therefore, carefully preserved. It preceded by long ages the Alexandrian Theosophists, reached the modern, and will survive every other religion and philosophy.

ENQ. Where and by whom was it so preserved?

THEO. Among Initiates of every country; among profound seekers after truth—their disciples; and in those parts of the world where such topics have always been most valued and pursued: in India, Central Asia, and Persia.

ENQ. Can you give me some proofs of its esotericism?

THEO. The best proof you can have of the fact is that every ancient religious, or rather philosophical, cult consisted of an esoteric or secret teaching, and an exoteric worship. Furthermore, it is a well-known fact that the Mysteries of the ancients comprised with every nation the "greater" (secret) and "Lesser" (public) Mysteries—e.g., in the celebrated solemnities called the *Eleusinia*,[6] in Greece. From the Hierophants[7] of Samothrace, Egypt, and the initiated Brahmins of the India of old, down to the later Hebrew Rabbis, all preserved,

---

4 Zenobia (d. c. 274 CE)—queen of Palmyra in Syria.
5 Philaletheian System—an esoteric philosophical system of knowledge.
6 Eleusinian Mysteries—in ancient Greece, rites sacred to Demeter, goddess of fruitfulness and the harvest.
7 Hierophant—an interpreter of sacred mysteries.

for fear of profanation, their real *bona fide* beliefs secretly. The Jewish Rabbis called their secular religious series the *Mercavah* (the exterior body), "the vehicle," or, "the covering which contains the hidden soul"—i.e., their highest secret knowledge. Not one of the ancient nations ever imparted through its priests its real philosophical secrets to the masses, but allotted to the latter only the husks. Northern Buddhism has its "greater" and its "lesser" vehicle, known as the *Mahayana*, the esoteric, and the *Hinayana*, the exoteric, Schools. Nor can you blame them for such secrecy; for surely you would not think of feeding your flock of sheep on learned dissertations on botany instead of on grass? Pythagoras called his *Gnosis* "the knowledge of things that are," and preserved that knowledge for his pledged disciples only: for those who could digest such mental food and feel satisfied; and he pledged them to silence and secrecy. Occult alphabets and secret ciphers are the development of the old Egyptian hieratic[8] writings, the secret of which was, in the days of old, in the possession only of the Hierogrammatists, or initiated Egyptian priests. Ammonius Saccas, as his biographers tell us, bound his pupils by oath not to divulge his higher doctrines except to those who had already been instructed in preliminary knowledge, and who were also bound by a pledge. Finally, do we not find the same even in early Christianity, among the Gnostics,[9] and even in the teachings of Christ? Did he not speak to the multitudes in parables which had a two-fold meaning, and explain his reasons only to his disciples? "To you," he says, "it is given to know the mysteries of the kingdom of heaven; but unto them that are without, all these things are done in parables" (Mark 4:11). "The Essenes[10] of Judea and Carmel made similar distinctions, dividing their adherents into neophytes, brethren, and the perfect, or those initiated." Examples might be brought from every country to this effect.

ENQ. Can you attain the "Secret Wisdom" simply by study? Encyclopedias define Theosophy pretty much as Webster's Dictionary does, i.e., as "supposed intercourse with God and superior spirits, and consequent attainment of superhuman knowledge by physical means and chemical processes." Is this so?

THEO. I think not. Nor is there any lexicographer capable of explaining, whether to himself or others, how superhuman knowledge can be attained by physical or chemical processes. Had Webster said "by metaphysical and alchemical processes," the definition would be approximately correct: as it is, it is absurd. Ancient Theosophists claimed, and so do the modern, that the infinite cannot be known by the finite—i.e., sensed by the finite Self—but that the divine essence could be communicated to the higher Spiritual Self in a state of ecstasy. This condition can hardly be attained, like hypnotism, by "physical and chemical means."

---

8 Hieratic—priestly; relating to the Egyptian hieroglyphic sacred texts.
9 Gnostics—early Christian sect that embraced a mystical perception of spiritual knowledge.
10 Essenes—a Jewish sect of c. 200 BCE–100 CE who lived in ascetic, monastic communities in the region of the Dead Sea in Palestine.

ENQ. What is your explanation of it?

THEO. Real ecstasy was defined by Plotinus as "the liberation of the mind from its finite consciousness, becoming one and identified with the infinite." This is the highest condition, but not one of permanent duration, and it is reached only by the very very few. It is, indeed, identical with that state which is known in India as *Samadhi*. The latter is practised by the Yogis, who facilitate it physically by the greatest abstinence in food and drink, and mentally by an incessant endeavour to purify and elevate the mind. Meditation is silent and unuttered prayer, or, as Plato expressed it, "the ardent turning of the soul toward the divine; not to ask any particular good (as in the common meaning of prayer), but for good itself—for the universal Supreme Good" of which we are a part on earth, and out of the essence of which we have all emerged. Therefore, adds Plato, "remain silent in the presence of the divine ones, till they remove the clouds from thy eyes and enable thee to see by the light which issues from themselves, not what appears as good to thee, but what is intrinsically good."

ENQ. Theosophy, then, is not, as held by some, a newly devised scheme?

THEO. Only ignorant people can thus refer to it. It is as old as the world, in its teachings and ethics, if not in name, as it is also the broadest and most catholic system among all.

SOURCE: H. P. Blavatsky, *The Key to Theosophy*. Los Angeles, CA: The United Lodge of Theosophists, 1920, pp. 5–9

Apocalyptic expectations

Throughout human history, there have been widespread expectations that life is about to come to a dramatic end. Expectations of an **apocalypse** have taken many forms, including the movement known as "Jehovah's Witnesses." It is based on a literal interpretation of Bible passages about the coming kingdom of God, as developed starting in the 1870s by Charles Taze Russell. It now has a world headquarters in Brooklyn, New York, and some six and a half million members worldwide, all of whom go from door to door offering their neighbours literature such as the following tract, which is also available on the Internet.

Life in a Peaceful New World by Jehovah's Witnesses

Life in God's New World God's Kingdom will bring earthly benefits beyond compare, accomplishing everything good that God originally purposed for his people to enjoy on earth. Hatreds and prejudices will cease to exist, and eventually everyone on earth will be a true friend of everyone else. In the Bible, God promises that he will "make wars to cease to the extremity of the earth." "Nation will not lift up sword against nation, neither will they learn war anymore"—Psalm 46:9; Isaiah 2:4.

The whole earth will eventually be brought to a gardenlike paradise state. The Bible says: "The wilderness and the waterless region will exult, and the desert plain will be joyful and blossom as the saffron.... For in the wilderness waters will have burst out, and torrents in the desert plain. And the heat-parched ground will have become as a reedy pool, and the thirsty ground as springs of water"—Isaiah 35:1, 6, 7.

There will be every reason to be happy in the Paradise earth. Never again will people hunger for lack of food. "The earth itself will certainly give its produce," the Bible says (Psalm 67:6; 72:16). All will enjoy the fruits of their own labor, as our Creator promises: "They will certainly plant vineyards and eat their fruitage.... they will not plant and someone else do the eating"—Isaiah 65:21, 22.

In God's new world, no longer will people be crammed into huge apartment buildings or run-down slums, for God has purposed: "They will certainly build houses and have occupancy.... They will not build and someone else have occupancy." The Bible also promises: "They will not toil for nothing" (Isaiah 65:21–3). Thus people will have productive, satisfying work. Life will not be boring.

In time, God's Kingdom will even restore the peaceful relations that existed in the garden of Eden between animals, and between animals and humans. The Bible says: "The wolf will actually reside for a while with the male lamb and with the kid the leopard itself will lie down, and the calf and the maned young lion and the well-fed animal all together; and a mere little boy will be leader over them"—Isaiah 11:6–9; Hosea 2:18.

Just imagine, in the Paradise earth all sicknesses and physical infirmities will also be healed! God's Word assures us: "No resident will say: 'I am sick'" (Isaiah 33:24). "[God] will wipe out every tear from their eyes, and death will be no more, neither will mourning nor outcry nor pain be anymore. The former things have passed away"—Revelation 21:4.

How It Is Possible for You   Surely your heart must be moved by the promises of God regarding life in his new world of righteousness. And while some may consider the realizing of such blessings too good to be true, they are not too good to come from the hand of our loving Creator—Psalm 145:16; Micah 4:4.

Of course, there are requirements to be met if we are to live forever in the coming Paradise on earth. Jesus showed a principal one, saying in prayer to God: "This means everlasting life, their taking in knowledge of you, the only true God, and of the one whom you sent forth, Jesus Christ"—John 17:3.

So if we truly want to live in God's new world, we must first learn God's will and then do it. For it is a fact: This "world is passing away and so is its desire, but he that does the will of God remains forever," to enjoy eternally the blessings to be showered down by our loving Creator— I John 2:17.

SOURCE: Jehovah's Witnesses Official Website, from "Life in a Peaceful New World" <http://www.watchtower.org/library/t15/peaceful.htm>

Following a charismatic leader

Charismatic leadership often attracts converts to new religious movements. During the twentieth century, many young people were drawn to give up their possessions and adopt a self-sacrificing lifestyle for the sake of others, while regarding a Korean former Christian Sunday school teacher, Sun Myung Moon, as the promised second coming of Christ. He teaches that Jesus' mission was incomplete, and that he and his wife have come to fulfill God's original plan as the "True Parents" of humankind.

The Lord of the Second Advent and the Ideal of True Parents by Sun Myung Moon

Mary, when she was engaged to Joseph, received from the Archangel Gabriel the surprising message that the Messiah would be born through her (Luke 1:31). In those days, if an unmarried woman became pregnant, she would be killed. But Mary accepted the will of God with absolute faith, saying, "Behold, I am the handmaid of the Lord; let it be to me according to your word" (Luke 1:38).

Mary consulted with the priest Zechariah, who was her relative and was highly respected. In this way, God let Mary, Zechariah, and Elizabeth know about the birth of the Messiah before anybody else. All of them had the absolutely crucial mission of following the will of God and serving Jesus. Zechariah's family let Mary stay in their house. Jesus was conceived in the house of Zechariah.

For the first time in history, there could be born on earth, free of satanic accusation and through a prepared womb, the seed of the Son of God—the seed of the True Father. In this way, the only begotten Son of God, the owner of the first love of God, was born for the first time in history.

Although the Son of God could be born on earth, he needed a wall of protection to grow up safely in the satanic world and fulfill the will of God. God had hoped that these three people in the family of Zechariah would establish that protective foundation.

Jesus was viewed as an illegitimate son, and lacking the protection of Zechariah's family and the love of Joseph, he grew up with an indescribable loneliness in his heart.

Jesus was aware of his path as the Messiah, and he lamented by himself these lonely circumstances and the serious obstacle they presented to fulfilling the will of God. The Messiah is the True Parent. And to fulfill that mission he needed to receive his substantial bride.

If Zechariah and Elizabeth, who had received the revelation and spiritual support from God, had maintained absolute faith, they would have served Jesus as the Son of God and as the Messiah and would have received God's will through Jesus and would have followed him absolutely. Also, John the

Baptist was born to serve Jesus and should have brought his followers to believe in Jesus and receive salvation. But unfortunately, although Zechariah, Elizabeth and John the Baptist testified at first to Jesus as the Son of God, there is no evidence that they served him as such. The respected priest Zechariah was simply a spectator. John the Baptist stood separate from Jesus. These circumstances blocked the people from following Jesus and made his path very difficult. And once this family lost faith in Jesus, looking at him through human eyes, there was no room for them to help him receive his bride.

Faced with the opposition of Mary, Zechariah, Elizabeth and finally John the Baptist, Jesus gave up hope for their protection as he sought to fulfill his mission. Therefore, Jesus left his home in search of a new spiritual foundation to restart the Providence of Salvation.

Now without a family and household, Jesus lamented, "Foxes have holes, and birds of the air have nests; but the Son of man has nowhere to lay his head" (Matthew 8:20). With his family-level foundation lost, Jesus sought to replace it. That was his three-year course.

In the end, as people disbelieved and the disciples lost faith, Jesus took Satan's attack. And as his foundation crumbled, he went the way of the cross.

Originally, Jesus came to the earth as the Messiah to give blessings to his disciples and all humankind. He was to build the sinless Kingdom of Heaven. But because of the lack of faith in him, he could not receive his bride, he could not become the True Parent and he could not accomplish his mission. This is why he promised to return.

The Lord of the **Second Advent** comes to perfect the foundation of God's Providence of Restoration left uncompleted by Jesus. That is to say, he comes as the seed of the original True Child to complete the ideal of creation. He comes to complete the idea of True Parents, who are the origin of the True Love, True Life and the True Lineage of God. He comes on the victorious foundation of the fundamental providence of God's side up to the time of Jesus. He also stands upon the victorious foundation of Jesus' life and finds the bride that Jesus could not find. Together they become the True Parents to save all humankind.

SOURCE: Sun Myung Moon, "The True Family Movement that will Save Mankind," Founder's Address. Washington, DC: Fourth Congress of the Inter-Religious Federation for World Peace, 1997

Spiritual psychotherapy

In today's individualistic milieu, many people are looking for help for their personal problems. A number of psychological self-help movements have sprung up to meet the demand. One is called *A Course in Miracles*. Its founders were professors of medical psychotherapy. One of them, Helen Schucman, discovered an inner Voice which dictated *A Course in Miracles* to her over a period of seven years. The course has become the basis for study groups and retreat centers. The following explanation of the content of *A Course in Miracles* was itself received through inner dictation, according to Helen Schucman.

A Course in Miracles Summarized by Helen Schucman

Nothing real can be threatened. Nothing unreal exists. Herein lies the peace of God.

This is how *A Course in Miracles* begins. It makes a fundamental distinction between the real and the unreal; between knowledge and perception. Knowledge is truth, under one law, the law of love or God. Truth is unalterable, eternal and unambiguous. It can be unrecognized, but it cannot be changed. It applies to everything that God created, and only what He created is real. It is beyond learning because it is beyond time and process. It has no opposite; no beginning and no end. It merely is.

The world of perception, on the other hand, is the world of time, of change, of beginnings and endings. It is based on interpretation, not on facts. It is the world of birth and death, founded on the belief in scarcity, loss, separation and death. It is learned rather than given, selective in its perceptual emphases, unstable in its functioning, and inaccurate in its interpretations. . . .

When you have been caught in the world of perception you are caught in a dream. You cannot escape without help, because everything your senses show merely witnesses to the reality of the dream. God has provided the Answer, the only Way out, the true Helper. It is the function of His Voice, His Holy Spirit, to mediate between the two worlds. He can do this because, while on the one hand He knows the truth, on the other He also recognizes our illusions, but without believing in them. It is the Holy Spirit's goal to help us escape from the dream world by teaching us how to reverse our thinking and unlearn our mistakes. Forgiveness is the Holy Spirit's great learning aid in bringing this thought reversal about. However, the Course has its own definition of what forgiveness really is just as it defines the world in its own way.

The world we see merely reflects our own internal frame of reference—the dominant ideas, wishes and emotions in our minds. "Projection makes perception." We look inside first, decide the kind of world we want to see and then project that world outside, making it the truth *as we see it*. We make it true by our interpretations of what it is we are seeing. If we are using the perception to justify our own mistakes—our anger, our impulses to attack, our lack of love in whatever form it may take—we will see a world of evil, destruction, malice, envy and despair. All this we must learn to forgive, not because we are being "good" and "charitable," but because what we are seeing is not true. We have distorted the world by our twisted defenses, and are therefore seeing what is not there. As we learn to recognize our perceptual errors, we also learn to look past them or "forgive." At the same time we are forgiving ourselves, looking past our distorted self-concepts to the Self that God created in us and as us.

Sin is defined as "lack of love." Since love is all there is, sin in the sight of the Holy Spirit is a mistake to be corrected, rather than an evil to be punished. Our sense of inadequacy, weakness and incompletion comes from the strong investment in the "scarcity principle" that governs the whole world of illusions. From that point of view, we seek in others what we feel is wanting in ourselves. We "love" another in order to get something ourselves. That, in fact, is what passes for love in the dream world. There can be no greater mistake than that, for love is incapable of asking for anything.

Only minds can really join, and whom God has joined no man can put asunder. It is, however, only at the level of Christ Mind that true union is possible, and has, in fact, never been lost. The "little I" seeks to enhance itself by external approval, external possessions and external "love." The Self that God created needs nothing. It is forever complete, safe, loved and loving. It seeks to share rather than to get; to extend rather than project. It has no needs and wants to join with others out of their mutual awareness of abundance. . . .

Perception is a function of the body, and therefore represents a limit on awareness. Perception sees through the body's eyes and hears through the body's ears. It evokes the limited responses which the body makes. The body appears to be largely self-motivated and independent, yet it actually responds only to the intentions of the mind. If the mind wants to use it for attack in any form, it becomes prey to sickness, age and decay. If the mind accepts the Holy Spirit's purpose for it instead, it becomes a useful way of communicating with others, invulnerable as long as it is needed, and to be gently laid by when its use is over. Of itself it is neutral, as is everything in the world of perception. Whether it is used for the goals of the ego or the Holy Spirit depends entirely on what the mind wants.

The opposite of seeing through the body's eyes is the vision of Christ, which reflects strength rather than weakness, unity rather than separation, and love rather than fear. The opposite of hearing through the body's ears is communication through the Voice for God, the Holy Spirit, which abides in each of us. His Voice seems distant and difficult to hear because the ego, which speaks for the little, separated self, seems to be much louder. This is actually reversed. The Holy Spirit speaks with unmistakable clarity and overwhelming appeal. No one who does not choose to identify with the body could possibly be deaf to His messages of release and hope, nor could he fail to accept joyously the vision of Christ in glad exchange for his miserable picture of himself.

Christ's vision is the Holy Spirit's gift, God's alternative to the illusion of separation and to the belief in the reality of sin, guilt and death. It is the one correction for all errors of perception; the reconciliation of the seeming opposites on which this world is based. Its kindly light shows all things from another point of view, reflecting the thought system that arises from knowledge and making return to God not only possible but inevitable. What was regarded as injustices done to one by someone else, now becomes a call for help and for union. Sin, sickness and attack are seen as misperceptions calling for remedy through gentleness and love. Defenses are laid down because where there is no attack there is no need for them. Our brothers' needs become our own, because they are taking the journey with us as we go to God. Without us they would lose their way. Without them we could never find our own. . . .

Through forgiveness the thinking of the world is reversed. The forgiven world becomes the gate of Heaven, because by its mercy we can at last forgive ourselves. Holding no one prisoner to guilt, we become free. Acknowledging Christ in all our brothers, we recognize His Presence in ourselves. Forgetting all our misperceptions, and with nothing from the past to hold us back, we can remember God. Beyond this, learning cannot go. When we are ready, God Himself will take the final step in our return to Him.

SOURCE: Helen Schucman, Preface to *A Course in Miracles*, April 1999
<http://64.77.6.149/about_acim_section/what_it_says.html>

Nature spirituality

In urbanized, industrialized cultures, many people now feel a longing to re-embrace nature-oriented and goddess-centered spiritual ways, such as those practiced by indigenous societies. Not being directly connected with such cultures, some are now freely adapting spiritual practices that regard the cosmos as sentient and sacred, forming a movement often known as **Neo-paganism**.

The Goddess and Women's Spirituality
by Charlene Spretnak

Charlene Spretnak teaches at the California Institute for Integral Studies in San Francisco. In this selection from her first book, *The Politics of Women's Spirituality* (1982), she criticizes patriarchal religions as beyond reform and calls for a reawakening of the goddess tradition as the best path to the divine for women. Her subsequent books have been *The Spiritual Dimension of Green Politics* (1986), *States of Grace: The Recovery of Meaning in the Postmodern Age* (1991), *The Resurgence of the Real* (1997), and *Missing Mary: The Queen of Heaven* (2004).

The underlying rationale for patriarchal societies is patriarchal religion. Christianity, Judaism, Islam, and Hinduism all combine male godheads with proscriptions against woman as temptress, as unclean, as evil. We were all made to understand that Eve's act of heeding the word of the serpent caused the expulsion of the human race from the Garden of Eden. We were made to understand that, as a result of her act, it was decreed by God that woman must submit to the dominance of man. We were all raised in cultures that reflect this decree: men enjoy the secular and spiritual positions of power; women cook and clean for them and supply them with heirs.

Most of the four billion people currently living in accordance with the patriarchal order do not question it: things have been this way for a long time; it must be the natural order. But what if the patriarchy is only a few thousand years old? What if, for tens of thousands of years before that, societies were built around the concept of the Great Goddess? If this is the case, our entire overview of history is altered: We once passed through a very long phase of matrifocal[11] culture; we are now passing through a phase of patriarchal culture (which appears to be self-destructing after a relatively brief run); and the future phase is ours to design.

Manifestations of our reclaimed spirituality   *Anat, Aphrodite, Artemis, Asherah, Astarte, Athena, Attor, Au Set, Blodeuwedd, Britannia, Britomaris, Changing Woman, Demeter, Dictynna, Gaia, Hathor, Hecate, Hera, Ananna, Ishtar, Isis, Ix Chel, Kali, Kuan Yin, Magna Mater, Nut, Pandora, Persephone, Rhea, Rhiannon, Saraswati, Selene, Tara, Themis, White Goddess.*

Ours is the oldest spiritual tradition on Earth. Now we understand the symbolism in patriarchal myths wherein Apollo slays the python at Delphi, wherein evil comes to weak-willed Eve in the form of a snake, wherein Saint George fiercely slays the giant snake-like dragon, wherein Saint Patrick rids Ireland of the snakes—for in matrifocal spirituality snakes were a widespread symbol of cyclical renewal and regeneration, continually growing and shedding their skins. We understand why the animal declared unclean by the Judaic fathers was the pig, which had long been held sacred to Demeter[12] and other Mediterranean forms of the Goddess for its prolificacy.

The great silence has been broken at last. Women are coming together to cultivate the powers that can result from exploring matrifocal heritage, personal and collective mythology, natural healing, meditation, dreamwork, celebrating the cycles of nature (i.e., our surroundings and our own bodies), and ritual. As we all bear scars from having been raised under patriarchy, the ability to heal ourselves and each other psychically and physically is essential to the growth of women's culture. Ritual can generate and

---

11 Matrifocal—focused on women as the leaders of society.
12 Demeter—Greek goddess of fecundity and plenty.

transform tremendous fields of force. That energy is always there for us to tap and manifest. Rituals created within a framework of women's spirituality differ in form and content from the empty, hierarchically imposed, patriarchal observances with which most of us grew up. They involve healing, strengthening, creative energy that expands with spontaneity from a meaningful core of values. . . .

SOURCE: Charlene Spretnak, ed., *The Politics of Women's Spirituality*. New York: Anchor/Doubleday, 1982, pp. 394–5. Reprinted from *Chrysalis: A Magazine of Women's Culture*, no. 6, November 1978

Witchcraft by Diane Mariechild

Some Neo-pagans from the West draw particularly on ways that were thought to exist in pre-Christian Europe. Diane Mariechild, who leads rituals in the Boston area, offers this explanation and guided meditation.

Feminists, working to reclaim a positive image of female consciousness, are digging back to our roots. These excavations have led us into matriarchal time, a time when our foremothers had a very strong and valuable effect on each other, themselves and society. It was a time when women's values were the predominant values, a time when ancient women walked in harmony with their inner, cyclical natures, a time when women valued their intuitions and dreams.

One of humankind's oldest religions is Wicca, craft of the wise. Wise Ones—or witches, as they are more commonly known—worship the female creative force in the form of the Great Mother. The Great Mother, revered Creatress of Life, was the dominant figure for thousands of years. The worship of the Great Mother spanned the world and Her names were legion: Nut, Isis, Ishtar, Inanna, Diana, Hecate, Artemis, Selene, Demeter, Astarte, Hathor, Aphrodite, Kali, Bellona, Harmonia, Shin Moo, Rhea, Luna, Cybele, Trivia, Cerridwen.

The male force was secondary and was introduced much later as the son/lover. He was her consort; she the immortal mother of a mortal son. The horned god appeared as a later personification of nature, but the female principle, the Moon Goddess, was the Queen of Heaven. In all ancient Babylonian and Sumerian creation myths women and men were created together in pairs by the Goddess. Female and male values were not polarized then. The male was part of the female, and female and male doubled in power by manifesting side by side.

The witches' concept of a god is the life force of the universe. Feminist witches worship this life force as a triune Goddess—Artemis, Selene and Hecate—the maiden, the mother and the crone. The three-formed Goddess has also been identified with the three phases of the moon: Artemis, the waxing; Selene, the full; and Hecate, the waning. Each phase represents another manifestation of the life energy, so that the generating, the organizing and the destructive aspects are all included.

The female principle is an agent of transformation: she is both creator and destroyer. Hatred of the female principle stems from a fear of death. When we come to realize that death is only a transformation, not an end, it will no longer hold any fear. Witches do not accept death as a finality, nor do they conceive of any heaven or hell in the Christian sense. They accept, as do many other ancient religions, the reincarnational process.

Witches believe in magic. Magic is knowing that the world consists of more than a physical reality. Magic does not work against nature: rather it is a deep understanding of the highest workings of nature and a movement in accordance with it. The object of magic is not to tell the future, to communicate with the spirits or to make one's will work for various ends. These are only the means. A witch develops her powers of magic in order to develop herself. Magic requires that we begin to change the world by first changing ourselves.

Witches, acknowledging that the world is composed of more than physical reality, realize that humans also possess more than the five senses. The sixth sense, the psychic sense, which is latent in all of us, enables us to connect with the world beyond the physical.

To learn the craft of the wise is to develop the powers of the deep mind. As these powers are developed, one has access to spiritual and psychic information and energy. Psychic sensitivity alone, however, will not develop the powers of the mind. Self-control and a strength of character must be combined with psychic awareness.

Witchcraft is more than a religion and the practice of magic. It is a philosophy, a way of life. Witchcraft offers us a beautiful synthesis of female and male energies. It integrates thought, feelings and intuition and provides a meaningful connection between the material and non-material worlds.

Witches celebrate each month when the moon is full, a time of great psychic energy. These celebrations are called "esbats." *Lady of Silver Magic* is a guided fantasy which enables you to create and experience a full moon ritual or esbat. . . .

Lady of Silver Magic Relax, deepen and protect yourself. Float down now to a deserted beach. Here on this quiet beach lighted by the moon you sit and watch the moonbeams sparkling and shimmering across the water. The sparkling beams dancing on the waters carry you even deeper. And you begin a slow and steady walk. Winding your way along the shoreline, your path guided by the moon. And you feel once again that irresistible pull that draws you to her, Lady of Silver Magic.

And that magical force shows you that you are in her presence. Whisper to her, lovely Lady of Silver Magic. And in so doing, you, her faithful daughter, find joy, serenity and peace in her presence.

Feeling that force rising within you, your pace quickens and you are pulled along, pulled as the tides are pulled, drawn back to the time of the great matriarchies, an age that is past, present and future all in one.

And ahead of you is a small grove of trees. Entering that grove now you remember a time when you were one of the wise ones and that time is now. The trees seem to part and there in the clearing is the space where your sisters gather once in the month "when the moonswell fills to brimming."

Together you silently gather the stones and begin to mark off the circle and build the small altar in the north corner.

And drawing the circle from east to north, the women, each in turn, enter the circle.

The fire is lit and facing the altar you speak: "My Lady of Silver Magic, I do build this circle, a space sacred and apart, in your honor."

Taking a torch and lighting the east you say, "Beautiful Lady of the Winds, the skies are yours. May I become as free as you."

Taking the torch and lighting the south you say, "Oh Goddess of warmth and fire, the seasons are yours. May each spring bring forth the richness of the natural world."

Taking the torch and lighting the west you say, "Oh, Lovely One, the sparkling waters are yours. May the streams and rivers continue to flow clean and pure."

Taking the torch and lighting the north you say, "Oh, fertile lush Goddess of the earth, ancient mother who nourishes, who gives birth to all living things, the earth is yours. May it stay fertile and rich and free from spoil."

Facing the altar once again you speak, "Beautiful Ancient One, bless your daughters with your presence. Fill us with your light and love." All gathered now meditate on Her presence. *Pause about three minutes.*

Face the north and slowly extinguish the torch thanking the Goddess for Her presence.

Face the west and slowly extinguish the torch thanking the Goddess for Her presence.

Face the south and slowly extinguish the torch thanking the Goddess for Her presence.

Face the east and slowly extinguish the torch thanking the Goddess for Her presence.

And facing the altar a final time you thank the Goddess for strengthening you with Her presence and slowly extinguish the fire.

Share farewells with your sisters and then quietly leave the grove, returning to the beach. And winding your way along the shoreline you move up and back to your usual waking reality. Return relaxed, refreshed and filled with energy. Take your time and then open your eyes and stretch your body.

SOURCE: Diane Mariechild, *Mother Wit: A Feminist Guide to Psychic Development*. Trumansburg, NY: The Crossing Press, 1981, pp. 125–9

The fate of new religious movements

No matter how successfully a new prophet has gathered followers, the continuation of his or her mission depends upon what happens after he or she dies. J. Gordon Melton, co-founder of the Center for Studies on New Religions, director of the Institute for the Study of American Religion, and one-time United·Methodist pastor, discusses the organizational matters that come into play after the prophet's death.

After the Founder's Death by J. Gordon Melton

In simple terms, the average founder of a new religion, especially one that shows some success during the first generation, is obviously an important factor in the growth and development of his/her movement. The movement is initially an extension of the founder's ideas, dreams, and emotional make-up. The leader may be valued as a teacher and/or venerated as a cosmic being or even divine entity. However, once the founder articulates the group's teachings and practices, they exist independently of him/her and can and do develop a life of their own. Once the follower experiences the truth of the religion, that experience also exists independently. Once a single spokesperson for the founder arises, the possibility of transmitting the truth of the religion independently of the founder has been posited. If a leader has developed a religious vision with the depth to gain a significant following during his/her lifetime, it will be a religion in which the role of the individual who created the religion, however important, will be but one element, not the overwhelming reality. Just as the disconfirmation of a prophecy rarely alters the direction of a group, so the death of the founder rarely proves fatal or leads to drastic alteration in the group's life. But what does happen when the founder dies? Generally the same thing that happens in other types of organizations, that is, very simply, power passes to new leadership with more or less smoothness depending upon the extent and thoroughness of the preparation that has been made ahead of time.

    . . . When a new religion dies, it usually has nothing to do with the demise of the founder; it is from lack of response of the public to the founder's ideas or the incompetence of the founder in organizing the followers into a strong group. Most new religions will die in the first decade, if they are going to die.

    In the overwhelming majority of cases, however, if a new religion finds some response and survives its initial phases of organization to attain a relative stability (the more so if it becomes fairly successful, with multiple centers and a mature leadership), the death of the founder will be experienced as a sad event but not a fatal or even traumatic one. In years past, the passing of a founder has often led to a power struggle, with the loser breaking away and taking some supporters to establish a rival organization. Such power struggles are a clear sign that leadership was allowed to develop in the group, though the final choice among several possible successors was postponed until after the founder's death.

Such power struggles, while momentarily important, are no more significant than any other issues that threaten schism. The more preparation is made for a smooth transition, the more likely an orderly succession is to occur. . . .

One important factor that has served to further lessen the impact of succession problems on new religions is the control of property. In past years, the single leader of a group could have complete control of the group's assets. If no clear successor was named, the property was the bounty to be won by rivals. However, that concern has increasingly become a non-issue. . . . In the United States, almost all new religions are organized as corporations under the leadership of boards of directors who have formal legal control of the corporate assets. . . . Given the collective nature of the board leadership, it is not subject to the disturbances caused by the death of any single person, including a founder, in a leadership position. Imposed for tax purposes, the corporate structure has as a by-product given new religious groups an additional stability that no single leader could bequeath.

In Conclusion As we rid ourselves of the myths about new religions, we lose our naïveté about their seriousness and the fullness of their religious life. We also can discard the inappropriate list of superlatives frequently used to describe new religions as totalistic societies under the absolute control of their charismatic leaders. Such talk is more rhetoric than reality and more polemic than analysis. While we observe the adulation of religious leaders in ritual setting, we also experience the ability of members to distance themselves emotionally when away from the presence of the guru. As the myths drop away, we become free to explore the rich storehouse of data available to us in the experience and operation of first-generation religion. Normal, creative people form new religious structures, and the continued generation of new religions is to be expected as a sign of health in any open society.

New religions as first-generation religions, whether a new orthodox Christian movement such as eighteenth-century Methodism, or a new Hindu group built around a recently arrived guru, share many characteristics. During the first generation, the founder, whose new ideas led to the formation of the group, places a definitive stamp upon it. The first members are self-selected because of their initial confidence in the leader and/or their agreement with the leader's program. The first generation is also a time of experimentation and rapid change. The leader must discover the right elements to combine in a workable program, generate solutions to unexpected obstacles, choose and train capable leaders, and elaborate upon the initial ideas or vision that motivated the founding of the group in order to create a more complete theology. The group formally or informally gives feedback in the form of approval or disapproval of the leader's actions. The most successful leaders are continually adjusting and reacting to that feedback.

Over time, the choices open to the leader are narrowed. Structures (and expectations) develop. As the movement grows, and especially as branches are established, the leader has to work through intermediaries, and the lines of authority and communication become more impersonal. The leader's real ability to change structures, should s/he desire such adjustments, meets greater and greater resistance. Though the leader may retain some important pieces of control, the real task of managing the organization and administering the organization's affairs increasingly passes to the second and third echelon [of] leadership. The analogy between religious and secular corporations, however much it offends religious sensibilities, is both appropriate to and informative of religious group dynamics.

Just as different religious groups will believe and act differently when their founders are alive, different groups will bring all of their unique experiences as new religions to bear in their responses to the leaders' deaths and to filling the vacuums created by those losses. . . . The problem of succession is not the determinative trauma it has often been considered to be and it in no way cuts off options limiting the group's determination of its own future course. Groups will tend to react to their leaders' deaths as they have previously reacted to other situations, and will make the necessary decisions in much the same way they have made decisions in the past.

SOURCE: J. Gordon Melton, Introduction to *When Prophets Die: The Postcharismatic Fate of New Religious Movements*, ed. Timothy Miller. New York: State University of New York Press, 1991, pp. 8–12

GLOSSARY

Apocalypse Belief that the end of the world, or end times, are coming soon; an ancient and recurring belief expressed in the Noah's Ark story, that God will punish evil-doers but save the good; symbolizes anxiety about the end of an era, such as the destruction of Jerusalem by Rome in New Testament times.

Charismatic Extraordinary personal magnetic appeal of a person, or speaking in a strange language.

Cult A religious group devoted to a single person or deity.

Esoteric Knowledge understood only by a restricted small group.

Exoteric Knowledge understood by a large group.

Neo-paganism A variety of religions reawakening ancient nature mysticism.

Second Advent The Second Coming of Jesus.

Sect A religious group different from an orthodox tradition, with a charismatic leader, strict rules of conduct, a sense of elite privilege, and restrictions on individuality.

REVIEW QUESTIONS

1   Is Sun Myung Moon's belief in the true parents and the bride of the returning Jesus an extension of Jesus' biblical teaching? Does it matter whether it is an extension or not?
2   Can we distinguish between the psychological and spiritual themes in *A Course in Miracles*? Discuss perception, projection, defenses, ego, truth, illusion, sin, forgiveness, God, Christ, Holy Spirit, divinity in each person.
3   How does the new witchcraft movement differ from traditional stereotypes of witches? Do you think conventional consciousness will accept this change?

DISCUSSION QUESTIONS

1   Should any legal limits be placed on new religions? If so, by what criteria? If not, why?
2   Do you think that parents should have the legal right to hire "de-programmers" to kidnap their children under 18 who have joined what they consider a deceptive, manipulative, brainwashing "cult"? Why?
3   Can you envision qualities and beliefs that would constitute a positive new religion?

INFORMATION RESOURCES

Academic Info New Religious Movements and Alternative Spirituality
<http://www/academicinfo.net/nrms.html>

Bowker, John, ed. "New Religious Movements," in *Oxford Dictionary of World Religions*. Oxford: Oxford University Press, 1997.

Campion, Jane, dir. *Holy Smoke*. Videorecording/DVD. U.S.A: Miramax Films, 1999.

Cults
<http://www.Religioustolerance.org/cults.htm>

Fisher, Mary Pat. *Religion in the Twenty-first Century.* Upper Saddle River, NJ: Prentice-Hall, 1999.

Religious Movements Page
<http://religiousmovements.lib.Virginia.edu>

Wessinger, Catherine, *et al.* "New Religious Movements," in *Encyclopedia of Religion,* ed. Lindsay Jones. 2nd ed. Vol. 10, pp. 6513–82. New York: Macmillan, 2005.

CHAPTER 13

RELIGION IN A NEW ERA

In the new era of the twenty-first century, global population growth and emigration are exploding, and new technologies are bringing cultures more closely in contact. Culture clashes have emerged, and the United Nations is calling for peaceful cultural dialogue. The ecology crisis brought about by industrial society has challenged religions to rethink their sanctions for humans dominating the earth. Fundamentalism has resurfaced as a reaction against modern industrial-commercial society. It is a conservative, sometimes even violent movement, seeking certain truth in traditional religion and social roles. By contrast, liberal believers are moving toward universalism, seeking to find interfaith understanding or a common core in all faiths.

Globalization

Christianity, the largest world religion, followed by about 32 percent of the global population, is decreasing in its share, while Islam, the second-largest religion, with about 20 percent of the world's population, is increasing its share. Hinduism is stable at about 13 percent; likewise Buddhism at about 6 percent. Some predict that Islam will overtake Christianity as the largest global religion, since its population growth rate (about 2.9 percent) exceeds that of both Christianity and the world (about 2.6 percent). Now most of Christianity's believers live in the earth's southern hemisphere, as Philip Jenkins, Professor of History and Religious Studies at Pennsylvania State University, shows.

The Next Christendom by Philip Jenkins

We are currently living through one of the transforming moments in the history of religion worldwide. Over the past five centuries or so, the story of Christianity has been inextricably bound up with that of Europe and European-derived civilizations overseas, above all in North America. Until recently, the overwhelming majority of Christians have lived in White nations, allowing theorists to speak smugly, arrogantly, of "European Christian" civilization. Conversely, radical writers have seen Christianity as an ideological arm of Western imperialism. Many of us share the stereotype of Christianity as the religion of the "West" or, to use another popular metaphor, the global North. It is self-evidently the religion of the haves. To adapt the phrase once applied to the increasingly conservative U.S. electorate of the 1970s, the stereotype holds that Christians are un-Black, un-poor, and un-young. If that is true, the growing secularization of the West can only mean that Christianity is in its dying days. Globally, the faith of the future must be Islam.

Over the past century, however, the center of gravity in the Christian world has shifted inexorably southward, to Africa, Asia, and Latin America. Already today, the largest Christian communities on the planet are to be found in Africa and Latin America. If we want to visualize a "typical" contemporary Christian, we should think of a woman living in a village in Nigeria or in a Brazilian *favela* [urban shanty town]. As Kenyan scholar John Mbiti has observed, "the centers of the church's universality [are] no longer in Geneva, Rome, Athens, Paris, London, New York, but Kinshasa, Buenos Aires, Addis Ababa, and Manila."[1] Whatever Europeans or North Americans may believe, Christianity is doing very well indeed in the global South—not just surviving but expanding.

This trend will continue apace in coming years. Many of the fastest-growing countries in the world are either predominantly Christian or else have very sizable Christian minorities. Even if Christians just maintain their present share of the population in countries like Nigeria and Kenya, Mexico and Ethiopia, Brazil and the Philippines, there are soon going to be several hundred million more Christians from these nations alone. Moreover, conversions will swell the Christian share of world population. Meanwhile, historically low birth rates in the traditionally Christian states of Europe mean that these populations are declining or stagnant. In 1950, a list of the world's leading Christian countries would have included Britain, France, Spain, and Italy, but none of these names would be represented in a corresponding list for 2050.

Christianity should enjoy a worldwide boom in the new century, but the vast majority of believers will be neither white nor European, nor Euro-American. According to the respected *World Christian Encyclopedia*, some 2 billion Christians are alive today, about one-third of the planetary total. The largest single bloc, some 560 million people, is still to be found in Europe. Latin America, though, is already close behind with 480 million. Africa has 360 million, and 313 million Asians profess Christianity. North America claims about 260 million believers. If we extrapolate these figures to the year 2025, and assume no great gains or losses through conversion, then

---

1 John Mbiti is quoted in Kwame Bediako, *Christianity in Africa*. Edinburgh University Press/Orbis, 1995, p. 154.

there would be around 2.6 billion Christians, of whom 633 million would live in Africa, 640 million in Latin America, and 460 million in Asia. Europe, with 555 million, would have slipped to third place.[2] Africa and Latin America would be in competition for the title of most Christian continent. About this date too, another significant milestone should occur, namely that these two continents will together account for half the Christians on the planet. By 2050, only about one-fifth of the world's 3 billion Christians will be non-Hispanic Whites.[3] Soon, the phrase "a White Christian" may sound like a curious oxymoron, as mildly surprising as "a Swedish Buddhist." Such people can exist, but a slight eccentricity is implied.

This global perspective should make us think carefully before asserting "what Christians believe" or "how the church is changing." All too often, statements about what "modern Christians accept" or what "Catholics today believe" refer only to what the ever-shrinking remnant of *Western* Christianity and Catholics believe. Such assertions are outrageous today, and as time goes by, they will become ever further removed from reality. The era of Western Christianity has passed within our lifetimes, and the day of Southern Christianity is dawning. The fact of change itself is undeniable; it has happened, and will continue to happen.

SOURCE: Philip Jenkins, *The Next Christendom: The Coming of Global Christianity*. Oxford and New York: Oxford University Press, 2002, pp. 1–3

Ecology and nature spirituality

The devastating impact of industrial society has become evident in global warming, species destruction, the spread of toxic wastes, reduction in valuable resources; the list goes on and on. The role of religions in sanctifying the exploitation of nature is being challenged. More believers are seeking to solve ecological problems, from Christians condemning gas-guzzling and polluting vehicles, saying in church and the mass media: "What would Jesus drive?" to radical critiques of the basic foundations of industrial culture, such as the command in Genesis to humans to have dominion over earth. The common middle ground promoting "stewardship" of the earth is not moving industrial devastation out of its path. More sweeping criticism has emerged in religious circles, from calls for serious nature mysticism to witchcraft's return to Neo-pagan respectful participation in nature, loving it so we will not want to damage it so. This is a challenge to traditional Christian theology, which stresses the heavenly transcendence of God and the archaic historicity of Jesus, rather than the immanent presence of the divine in nature. The "sustainability" movement stresses the need to examine every area, from resource use to

---

2 David B. Barrett, George T. Kurian, and Todd M. Johnson, *World Christian Encyclopedia*. 2nd ed. New York: Oxford University Press, 2001, pp. 12–15.
3 The figures here for Asia should be regarded with some skepticism.... I stress here the large disparities [underestimates] that separate estimates about the size of Christian populations, especially in countries where the religion is officially disapproved.

faith in "progress," in order to move back to living a sustainable lifestyle that does not use up the world's reserves and destroy the human habitat. Re-awakening our perceptions of the sacred in the environment is a fundamental re-visioning of religions that long ago rejected nature spirituality.

Sacred Whispers in the World by Lee W. Bailey

Of all the recent books about religion and nature, the most striking to me is *The Hand of God*, a picture book showing stunning photographs of deep space taken from satellite cameras. They have shown us the incredible vastness of the universe, the awesome immensity of about 150 billion visible galaxies—150 billion!—colorful nebulae clouds, rings around planets, huge balls of nuclear fire, and enough dazzling visions of outer space to awaken a newfound wonder at this astonishing spectacle. Our planet is just a tiny blue dot in the disk of the Milky Way galaxy, one hundred thousand light years across (590,000 trillion miles—6,400,000 trips from earth to the sun), with 100 to 200 billion stars.

All this new scientific awareness is shaping a new cosmology, broadening our sense of who we are in the cosmos. We inhabit a precious planet gifted with the right conditions for life—just the right temperatures, gravity, oxygen, water, that seem to be rare. Our neighbor planets are deadly cold or hot, with toxic atmospheres or oceans. Mercury's day can rise to 873°F hot and sink to −303°F cold at night. Jupiter, which could be filled with a thousand earths, is covered with a vast ocean of liquid hydrogen. Venus has a dense atmosphere of carbon dioxide and sulfuric acid that traps heat in a greenhouse effect of about 900°F—hot enough to melt lead.

All this could make us feel incredibly blessed to be given life on such a rarely fruitful planet in such a huge universe. But do we look up at the stars and thank the mysterious power that created us and turn back to earth with great respect and careful stewardship of our resources? Or do we carelessly poison the waters, overfish the oceans, overheat the atmosphere, drive species to extinction, pollute the air we breathe, and exploit our resources as fast as we can? You know. But why? If our instincts for power and pleasure are released in the frenzy to conquer the planet, don't our religions urge restraint and care of nature? They offer guidance for social justice and moral behavior, spiritual peace in troubled times, and life after death. But even though they may also have embedded messages about respect for all life, these have had precious little actual impact on the way we relate to nature.

Western religions have almost totally left nature out of their theologies and ethics, and are seeing ecological devastation as a result. Western-invented nuclear energy is spreading cancerous radiation across the globe. Hinduism, which sees Brahman in all the world, still cannot control the overpopulation of its land and the accompanying ecological disaster. The sacred Ganges, a holy place for bathing, is terribly polluted. Japan has a beautiful sense of preserving nature expressed in its mountain pilgrimages and gardens, but its industrial development is having harsh effects. Its huge fishing fleets are overfishing oceans and ignoring world calls for restraint in whaling.

We are all ignoring global warming when we refuse to give up our fossil-fuel electric generation plants and smoky transportation systems that daily send tons of dangerous gases into the atmosphere. The damaging march of technological "progress" listens to precious few calls for restraint, and not many of them are from religions. The worldviews and cosmologies of our traditional religions are not being called upon to deal with the ecological crisis, and some cling fiercely to archaic creation myths and familiar but old traditions that ignore our urgent environmental predicament. We desperately need a new sense of the sacred in nature and our holy obligations to live in harmony with our environment. We urgently need to hear and attend to the ecological implications of the sacred whispers that fill the cosmos.

Ancient religions (and their surviving indigenous peoples) saw sacred spirits in nature. Some were ancestor spirits, others spirits of vegetation, birth, and death, and they were all respected. The numerous southwestern American Pueblo *kachinas*, for example, are ritual images of supernatural beings between humans and gods, both helpful and harmful. Some are believed to be spirits of departed ancestors. *Kachina* dolls are very popular gifts for Pueblo children and are sold to tourists. Hopi *kachinas* represent the spirits behind nature and society: the solstice, cactus, flowers, eagles, bears, buffalo, sheep, snow, rain, thunder, corn, and an earth god, as well as brides, chiefs, mothers, clowns, and warriors. Each has its sacred ways and requires respect for them. Men wear *kachina* masks and dance in ceremonies at *mesa* villages (villages on level desert mountaintops) several times a year, such as for the solstices. Have you seen the sacredness in the rain, the thunder, the solstice, the flowers, the animals, the stars?

Major world religions retain remnants of ancient beliefs about nature. In the biblical book of Job the question is asked, who made the world, and answered:

> But ask the beasts, and they will teach you,
> Ask the birds of the air to inform you,
> or tell the creatures that crawl to inform you,
> and the fish of the sea to instruct you.
> Who does not come to know from all these
> that the hand of the Lord has done this?
> In his hand are the souls of all that live,
> The spirits of every human being. (Job 12:7–10)

This nature spirituality has come to mean a sense of God as the remote creator, rather than the sacred spirit always present in the "Book of Nature." Nature theology is part of Western religions, but it plays a minor role. Humanity instead dwells on the outdated Genesis command to "fill the earth and subdue it, have dominion over the fish in the sea, the birds of the air, and every living thing that moves on the earth" (Genesis 1:28).

Western science of course assumes the metaphysical desacralization of the world in order to analyze it fearlessly. Humans need little encouragement to dominate, but religion and science have combined to permit a massive project of domination. During the long dawn of human history, when people suffered greatly from hunger, wild animals, cold, and hard work, domination made sense. But now we are coming to the end of the era when careless, unrestrained domination over nature, irrational and immoral, can continue, given the massively destructive weapons available and the widespread pollution poisoning our nest. We need a major shift in consciousness and priorities to take us away from thoughtless domination and bring us into careful harmony with our delicate home.

The first step in this urgently needed shift in awareness can arrive with a spiritual opening to sacred whispers from the world. The world is not overtly sacred, since it contains suffering and evil, and is not eternal. But there are quiet moments and glorious spectacles when the sense of sacredness floats forth. We need to discern these.

First we must differentiate the sacred in nature from technological wonders. Space rockets thundering aloft are awesome human accomplishments, but are only tiny bursts of power compared to the cosmic gravitation of the sun that holds our planet in its annual cycle around the sun. Computers are wonderful accomplishments of human reasoning, but are merely partial, artificial extensions of the incredible brains that we are given at birth, perhaps the most complex organs in the known universe. Cell phones are delightful ways to communicate wirelessly, but they pale in comparison to the very existence of the organic ear itself, the language we share, and the electromagnetic radio waves that we have learned to use. There are large natural and cultural phenomena of great antiquity and wide power that our clever technologies simply share.

We can think of ourselves as "taking advantage" of natural phenomena like these, or gratefully, thankfully sharing in their wonders harmoniously and respectfully, remembering our place in the grand sacred scheme, rather than grabbing for all the power we can get and running from the consequences. Our technologies are enchanting and exciting, powerful and welcome reliefs from suffering. But they simply rest upon the vast store of water, oil, steel, silicon, electricity, and other resources that make them possible—the cosmic furnaces that generated the atoms, the oceans that nourished the molecules and cells, the species that evolved into life's wondrous variations. This all has a sacred dimension, not just for human use, but in itself. We are not atop a hierarchy of beings that we should dominate. We depend on a vast network of subatomic forces, electromagnetic fields, gravitational pulls, life-supporting air, earth, water, food, and endless reproducing species of plants and animals. The mystery of the origin and finely tuned structure of all this has an incredible sacredness.

A new consciousness would say "thank you" instead of "gimme"—thanks to our home universe, galaxy, sun, planet, oceans, atmosphere, foods, medicines, fellow creatures on earth, our inner feelings, and our varieties of social developments.

Our spirituality and traditional religions have a great task, the challenge of developing ways to experience the sacredness in nature, to honor it, and to work out the many ethical implications for living sustainably on earth—reducing resource consumption, pollution, and population growth as well as social injustice. We can and must shift our spiritual beliefs and practices so that they inspire not the vision of humans standing above nature, exploiting it just for the ego's pride, power, and pleasures. Promoting the "prosperity gospel" and ethnic-group population growth, for example, are not consistent with sacred whispers in the world. Sharing the sacred wonders of the sunrise and sunset, the seasonal round, the powers of life's sustaining reproduction patterns, and the beautiful gifts of our home planet's land, plants, animals, and fellow humans living around the globe—this is feeling the sacred whispers in the world. Our eco-spirituality goal is to learn to live in tune with the sacredness inherent around us and within us. This would be the start of a truly significant sacred earth ethic, a new dimension that we urgently need to cultivate.

SOURCE: Original article for this book by Lee W. Bailey, 2006

Violence and religion

Down the ages, warriors have sought, and usually received, religious blessing. Since weapons of mass destruction have spread, however, more people are questioning the validity of calling on God to sanction often thinly concealed base motives, such as greed for land, power, and oil. Some religious texts teach loving peace in certain passages and bloody violence in others. Jack Nelson-Pallmeyer, who teaches Justice and Peace Studies at the University of St. Thomas in Minnesota, argues in his book *Is Religion Killing Us?* (2003) that religious blessings of violence should be seen not as distorted additions, but as inherent parts of the holy books.

Is Religion Killing Us? by Jack Nelson-Pallmeyer

The Hebrew Scripture, the Christian New Testament, and the Qur'an contain stories urging compassionate living, social justice, and ethical conduct. The collective weight of *all* passages in these texts that advocate ethical behavior or present evidence of a loving, compassionate God cannot, however, overcome the violent images and expectations of God that overwhelm these "sacred" texts. God's violence or human violence justified in service to God is sometimes understood to be the principal means to justice in, or at the end of, history. At other times, ethical conduct is urged under the threat of God's punishing violence. God's violence is at times so pervasive, unpredictable, vindictive, or destructive that it reflects a deep and troubling pathology. In such cases, we can say that if human beings acted as God does or as God tells them to act, they would rightfully be considered certifiably insane. Religious violence prevalent among the followers of monotheistic faith traditions is not primarily a problem of believers distorting their "sacred" texts. It is, rather, a problem rooted in the violence-of-God traditions that lie at the heart of these "sacred" texts. . . .

Violence today is God, the one and only functional God at the heart of most ideologies, whether capitalist, Marxist, anarchist, revolutionary, reactionary, or religious. In the secular world, superior violence is God because violence is presumed to be the only and ultimate means to security or victory or revenge. . . .

The good news is that there is an alternative conception of power rooted in love, and it is, as Gandhi says, effective. Gandhi's experiments in truth revealed that one instrument of effective power is active nonviolence.[4] If we are to be saved from the spiral of violence that threatens us, then we must have sufficient doubt to challenge the authority of the Bible and the Qur'an that offer distorted images of God and wrongfully associate divine and human power with superior violence and defeat of enemies. . . .

It is foolish to grant authority to the violence-of-God traditions at the heart of the Bible and the Qur'an. It is time to learn from our enemies, run with our doubts, and embrace the power of nonviolence. The world clamors for a constituency of nonviolent peacemakers willing to dedicate their lives to building a world of compassion and justice. It remains to be seen whether Jews, Christians, and Muslims can heed the call and overcome violence "legitimated" by our "sacred" texts. If we reject violence and re-envision human and divine power, then a joyous cry will be heard throughout the earth: "Thanks be to God."

SOURCE: Jack Nelson-Pallmeyer, *Is Religion Killing Us?* New York and London: Continuum, 2003, pp. 92–3, 136, 130, 148

Fundamentalism and universalism

Religious fundamentalism and universalism are extremes on a continuum of shifting religious forces. Naïve fundamentalism is an ancient, simplistic way following religious authorities unquestioningly and accepting religious stories, symbols, and texts as literally true. Modern fundamentalism is a more complex phenomenon. When some believers come into contact with the modern individualism, rationalism, and scientific thought that ignores or rejects religion, they are frustrated with the loss of transcendence in the modern worldview and reject its seamier side, although they use many of its technologies. Some foresee the apocalyptic end of the world coming soon, in a cataclysm that will take the righteous faithful to

---

4 See Homer A. Jack, ed., *The Gandhi Reader*. New York: Grove Press, 1956.

Heaven and destroy or send to hell all others. Many are patriarchal, repressive about sexuality, and enforce the rule of men over women. They admire charismatic, authoritarian leaders. Varieties of ultra-conservative fundamentalists can be found in any major world religion.

Universalists are liberal religious believers who are open to accepting truths in all religions, rather than just one, who appreciate many cultural differences in religions and seek to find the best in each—even a common core of truth that they share. They actively work to improve human rights for all genders and races, and explore new ways of experiencing the sacred, as in nature mysticism.

The Battle for God by Karen Armstrong

One of the most startling developments of the late twentieth century has been the emergence within every major religious tradition of a militant piety popularly known as "fundamentalism." Its manifestations are sometimes shocking. Fundamentalists have gunned down worshippers in a mosque, have killed doctors and nurses who work in abortion clinics, have shot their presidents, and have even toppled a powerful government. It is only a small minority of fundamentalists who commit such acts of terror, but even the most peaceful and law-abiding are perplexing, because they seem so adamantly opposed to many of the most positive values of modern society. Fundamentalists have no time for democracy, pluralism, religious toleration, peacekeeping, free speech, or the separation of church and state. Christian fundamentalists reject the discoveries of biology and physics about the origins of life and insist that the Book of Genesis is scientifically sound in every detail. At a time when many are throwing off the shackles of the past, Jewish fundamentalists observe their revealed Law more stringently than ever before, and Muslim women, repudiating the freedoms of Western women, shroud themselves in veils and *chadors*. Muslim and Jewish fundamentalists both interpret the Arab–Israeli conflict, which began as defiantly secularist, in an exclusively religious way. Fundamentalism, moreover, is not confined to the great monotheisms. There are Buddhist, Hindu, and even Confucian fundamentalisms, which also cast aside many of the painfully acquired insights of liberal culture, which fight and kill in the name of religion and strive to bring the sacred into the realm of politics and national struggle.

This religious resurgence has taken many observers by surprise. In the middle years of the twentieth century, it was generally taken for granted that secularism was an irreversible trend and that faith would never again play a major part in world events. It was assumed that as human beings became more rational, they either would have no further need for religion or would be content to confine it to the immediately personal and private areas of their lives. But in the late 1970s, fundamentalists began to rebel against this secularist hegemony[5] and started to wrest religion out of its

---

5 Hegemony—the dominating influence of one group's worldview over another.

marginal position and back to center stage. In this, at least, they have enjoyed remarkable success. Religion has once again become a force that no government can safely ignore. Fundamentalism has suffered defeats, but it is by no means quiescent. It is now an essential part of the modern scene and will certainly play an important role in the domestic and international affairs of the future. It is crucial, therefore, that we try to understand what this type of religiosity means, how and for what reasons it has developed, what it can tell us about our culture, and how best we should deal with it.

SOURCE: Karen Armstrong, *The Battle for God: A History of Fundamentalism.* New York: Ballantine Books, 2001, pp. xi–xii

God Will Break All the Barriers! by Baba Virsa Singh

Baba Virsa Singh is a revered teacher from Sikh tradition. Under his inspiration, celebrations of the major holy days of all religions have long been held in his communities in India and the United States, known as Gobind Sadan. As Sikhs, Hindus, Muslims, and Christians gathered joyously on December 28, 1996 at his community outside Delhi to celebrate the birthdays of both Jesus and Guru Gobind Singh, Baba Virsa Singh made the following prophetic statement.

One day, when Gobind Sadan was facing many problems, I was sitting on a sofa, feeling very serene and joyous. My mind was neither asleep nor awake. Great rays of light awoke me and in a vision drew my attention to this very place where we are sitting. Jesus was standing right here [a place near the dairy where now a statue of Jesus has been erected], with his arms outspread. Speaking as loud as thunder, he said, "Blesssss!" His voice seemed to echo through the cosmos. For an hour and a quarter, Jesus kept blessing and speaking about the things which were weighing on my mind. Just by his words, they were all resolved.

Even before that, I did not think that Jesus was separate from other prophets. Whatever slight sectarian boundary that existed in my mind was completely demolished then. It was not a matter of faith or pride on my part. It was by his wish that I saw him standing here in vision. I fully believe that after this happened, indescribable blessings came to Gobind Sadan.

These spiritual Powers are not only for one country, one community, one fortified institution. I feel that they are meant to bring enlightenment to the whole cosmos. Their light spreads everywhere. Our attempts to divide the Light into different countries and sects have caused us great trouble. The Light cannot be broken into pieces. It is everyone's right to celebrate whenever the holy day of any prophet, messiah, or messenger of God occurs. It is our right to welcome them in all places. I feel that if we all mold our minds like this, the light of the prophets will manifest in everyone's minds, throughout the world.

Guru Gobind Singh said, "Listen everyone, for I speak the truth: Only those who have deeply loved God have realized God." What is God? Love.

Guru Gobind Singh, who called God his Father, said, "My Father is spreading light throughout the cosmos, giving blessings to the entire Creation." Jesus likewise said, "If you want to see the Power of my Father, the Creation of my Father, look at the flowers, the rivers, the trees, the animals. There is no place where my Father's light is not doing its work of blessing."

At present, our problem is that we take the name of religion without having faith in religion. Love is one, truth is one, and God is one. Then why are there divisions? If a person speaks ill of one messenger and praises another, he can never receive enlightenment. We must believe that light appeared when they came, that they were bestowing light, and that their light is here even today.

Today you yourself may be feeling inexplicable happiness, inexplicable peace. Why? Because we have been celebrating both Jesus' birthday and Guru Gobind Singh's birthday. Our feeling is that we have been moving through light all day, with light falling all around us. My firm faith is that God has filled each one with love, each to his own mind's capacity for love. Those who have come here have learned something new: that Jesus has come to a gurdwara [Sikh temple]. What is a gurdwara? The house of God. And Jesus is His son; he must come to his house. And we are loving him— what else?

Don't go near people who are critical of such things, for they are far from the Light. All of us should come beneath the Light. When you shall see one Form in all the prophets, your mind's tendency to hate will turn into kindness. Your mind will rise above the tendency to create boundaries.

I can say from full inner wisdom that these boundaries will be broken, that all these barriers will be removed, because God wants it so. He has been looking at these barriers, confined within these boundaries for a very long time, and now He feels, "I can no longer live within these boundaries." God wants to enjoy Himself, and God wants you to enjoy yourselves. Now you will see: God will break all these forts. We will all be happy, for then His blessings will fall upon us all. When a person breaks out of confinement, he breathes fresh air and moves freely through nature. When he remains in confinement, he feels suffocated.

We have been in confinement for a long time, but God now wants to break the barriers. At last He will now manifest His Light. I have full faith that the minds of the whole world will change. The public will be happy, but the religious authorities may experience some difficulties. They may be disappointed with God: "We were enjoying ourselves—What have You done now? We have concealed You until now, but now You are in the open." God will laugh: "I waited for a very long time, but you did not allow Me to come out of the boundaries, so now I am going to manifest Myself." He will say, "Let the Light go forth! Such a long time has passed while you 'authorities' were keeping a curtain between the Light and the people...."

I pray, "Oh God, please make Your priests understand, for they have become very rigid and exclusive. You are the King of the Spirit. Please refresh their minds and make them understand. The public is very good; they will follow whatever they are told." Today our prayer has reached God, and now He will send a bit of His Love to His priests. He can make them understand through their dreams, through visions. We leave it to God to decide how to make them understand, but He will surely do so.

Today is a day of great happiness, of great blessings, of great mercy. I have never spoken like this in the past, but today He has said, "Speak!" and I have done so. Today is a day of great celebration. It is a day for dancing. All of you dance!

SOURCE: Baba Virsa Singh, "God Will Break All the Barriers!" Talk given at Gobind Sadan, Delhi, on December 28, 1996

A New Revelation from the Unifier by Bahá'u'lláh

Baha'i is a major universalizing religion founded by Bahá'u'lláh (1817–92) from Iran, who offered belief in one God worldwide. It has spread to embrace five million members who believe in the harmony of the teachings of major religious prophets such as Moses, Jesus, Muhammad, Krishna, and Buddha. Baha'i seeks concord with science, equality, education, gender equity, peace, and the overcoming of poverty.

This is the Day in which God's most excellent favors have been poured out upon men, the Day in which His most mighty grace hath been infused into all created things. It is incumbent upon all peoples of the world to reconcile their differences, and, with perfect unity and peace, abide beneath the shadow of the Tree of His care and loving-kindness. It behoveth them to cleave to whatsoever will, in this Day, be conducive to the exaltation of their stations, and to the promotion of their best interests....

Beseech ye the one true God to grant that all men [sic] may be graciously assisted to fulfil that which is acceptable in Our sight. Soon will the present-day order be rolled up, and a new one spread out in its stead. Verily, thy Lord speaketh the truth, and is the Knower of things unseen.

This is the Day whereon the Ocean of God's mercy hath been manifested unto men, the Day in which the Day Star of His loving-kindness hath shed its radiance upon them, the Day in which the clouds of His bountiful favor have overshadowed the whole of mankind. Now is the time to cheer and refresh the down-cast through the invigorating breeze of love and fellowship, and the living waters of friendliness and charity.

They who are the beloved of God, in whatever place they gather and whomsoever they may meet, must evince, in their attitude towards God, and in the manner of their celebration of His praise and glory, such humility and submissiveness that every atom of the dust beneath their feet may attest the depth of their devotion....

It is incumbent upon every man, in this Day, to hold fast unto whatsoever will promote the interests, and exalt the station, of all nations and just governments. Through each and every one of the verses which the

Pen of the Most High hath revealed, the doors of love and unity have been unlocked and flung open to the face of men. We have erewhile declared—and Our Word is the truth—: "Consort with the followers of all religions in a spirit of friendliness and fellowship." Whatsoever hath led the children of men to shun one another, and hath caused dissensions and divisions amongst them, hath, through the revelation of these words, been nullified and abolished. From the heaven of God's Will, and for the purpose of ennobling the world of being and of elevating the minds and souls of men, hath been sent down that which is the most effective instrument for the education of the whole human race. The highest essence and most perfect expression of whatsoever the peoples of old have either said or written hath, through this most potent Revelation, been sent down from the heaven of the Will of the All-Possessing, the Ever-Abiding God. Of old it hath been revealed: "Love of one's country is an element of the Faith of God." The Tongue of Grandeur hath, however, in the day of His manifestation proclaimed: "It is not his to boast who loveth his country, but it is his who loveth the world." Through the power released by these exalted words He hath lent a fresh impulse, and set a new direction, to the birds of men's hearts, and hath obliterated every trace of restriction and limitation from God's holy Book.

SOURCE: Bahá'u'lláh, *Gleanings from the Writings of Bahá'u'lláh*, trans. Shoghi Effendi. 2nd ed. Wilmette, IL: Baha'i Publishing Trust, 1976, pp. 6–7, 94–6

The Essential Truth is One by Hazrat Inayat Khan

Mystics of all religions find underlying unity in their spirituality, which transcends the externals of religions. The following passage is from a great Sufi mystic from India who brought a universal spiritual message to the West early in the twentieth century.

Perhaps a person belongs to the best religion in the world. He does not live it, belongs to it. He says that he is a Muslim, or a Christian, or a Jew. He is sure it is the best religion, but at the same time he does not care to live it—he just belongs to it, and thinks that belonging to a certain religion, which is an accepted religion, is all that is needed. And people of all different religions have made it appear so, owing to their enthusiasm, and forced by their mission in life. For they have made facilities for those who belong to their particular religion, saying that by the very fact of their belonging to that particular religion they will be saved on the Day of Judgment, while others, with all their good actions, will not be saved, because they do not belong to that particular religion. This is a man-made idea, not God-made. God is not the Father of one sect; God is the Father of the whole world, and all are entitled to be called His children, whether worthy or unworthy. And in fact it is man's [sic] attitude toward God and Truth which can bring him closer to God, who is the idea of every soul. And if this attitude is not developed, then, whatever a man's religion be, he has failed to live it. Therefore, what is important in life is to try and live the religion to which one belongs, or that one esteems, or that one believes to be one's religion.

But one must always know that religion has a body and has a soul. Whatever body of religion you may touch, you touch the soul; but if you touch the soul, you touch all its bodies, which are like its organs. And all the organs constitute one body, which is the body of *the* religion, the religion which is the religion of Alpha and Omega, which was and which is and which will always be. Therefore the dispute, "I am right and you are wrong," in the path of religion is not necessary. We do not know what is the heart of man. If outwardly he seems to be a Jew, a Christian, a Muslim, or a Buddhist, we are not the judge of his religion, for every soul has a religion peculiar to itself, and no one else is entitled to judge its religion. There may be a person in a very humble garb, without any appearance of belief in God, or of piety or orthodoxy, and he may have a religion hidden in his heart which not everybody can understand. And there may be a person who is highly evolved, and his outward conduct, which alone manifests to people's views, may appear to be altogether contrary to their own way of looking at things, and they may accuse him of being a materialist or an unbeliever, or someone who is far from God and Truth. And yet we do not know; sometimes appearances are merely illusions; behind them there may be the deepest religious devotion or the highest ideal hidden, of which we know very little.

. . . Those who, with the excuse of their great faith in their own religion, hurt the feeling of another and divide humanity, whose Source and Goal is the same, abuse religion, whatever be their faith. The Message, whenever, at whatever period it came to the world, did not come to a certain section of humanity; it did not come to raise only some few people who perhaps accepted the faith, the Message, or a particular organized Church. No, all these things came afterwards. The rain does not fall in a certain land only; the sun does not shine upon a certain country only. All that is from God is for all souls. If they are worthy, they deserve it; it is their reward; if they are unworthy, they are the more entitled to it. Verily, blessing is for every soul; for every soul, whatever be his faith or belief, belongs to God. . . .

Every child is born in life a pupil, one who is willing to learn and willing to believe. As the Prophet Muhammad says: "Every soul is born on earth a believer; it is only afterwards that he turns into an unbeliever." It is certain that if one had not been born a believer one would never have learned the language of one's country, because if anyone had tried to teach the words and one had refused to accept the teachings as true, one would never have learned the names and character of things. For instance, if it were said, "This is water," and one had not believed it, and had thought, "It is fruit," then one would never really have known what was water and what fruit. A child is born with the tendency to believe and learn what it is taught.

The divine life has a certain capability to give life, and it gives this life as teaching to the children of earth, and this teaching is called *Dharma*, religion. Religions are many and different from one another, but only in form. Water is one and the same element, and formless, only it takes the shape of the channel which holds it and which it uses for its accommodation; and so the name water is changed into river, lake, sea, stream, pond, etc. So it is with religion; the essential truth is one, but the aspects are different. Those who fight about external forms will always fight, those who recognize the inner truth will not disagree, and thus will be able to harmonize the people of all religions.

Dharma has been given from time to time to the world, at times quietly, and sometimes with a loud voice; but it is a continual outpouring of the inner knowledge, of life, and of divine blessing.

SOURCE: Hazrat Inayat Khan, *The Unity of Religious Ideals*. New Lebanon, NY: Sufi Order Publications, 1979, pp. 5–8

Interfaith initiatives

Similarities and differences are evident in world religions. Many teach detachment from worldly possessions, power, and pleasures, and urge love for others. With increasing education and travel, more people are aware of other traditions, and people from different faith traditions are more often joining in dialogue and spiritual relationships seeking understanding. Interfaith initiatives come from seekers who remain in their religious traditions but seek to find common ground with other traditions, such as the golden rule.

At the other extreme, some people claim that their faith justifies the most horrendous violence in the name of ethnic cleansing, feelings of victimization, or even blatant quests for wealth. Some claim exclusive truth, require animal sacrifice, or sanctify political patriotism.

Yet the finest principles of religions bring people together in peace and seek to solve divisive problems. For example, at the 2004 Parliament of the World's Religions in Barcelona, Spain, the Sikhs set up a large tent and fed large crowds free lunches daily (as they commonly do), and this stimulated a large amount of goodwill.

Can We Share in Others' Spiritual Traditions?

by Marcus Braybrooke

Beyond the level of comparing different religions in a spirit of mutual tolerance, is it possible that people from different religions can enter into the spiritual experiences of others on a deeper level? Marcus Braybrooke, a retired Anglican minister, is Chairman of the International Interfaith Centre in Oxford, England, and is one of the long-time leaders of the interfaith movement.

The life of faith is nourished in a particular faith community. Such a community has its beliefs, its symbols, its pattern of worship, its expected behavior. These are interwoven and cannot easily be unraveled. There is a particularity about the life of faith. To what extent are we able to enter into another tradition's spiritual experience or do we impose our own meaning on it? This is partly a question of understanding the other at depth but also of whether another's spiritual occasion can become for us an encounter with the Divine. . . .

> Dr. Jonathan Sacks[6] says: "A multicultural mind can use Zen for inwardness, Hasidic tales for humour, liberation theology for politics, and nature mysticism for environmental concern. But that is a little like gluing together slices of da Vinci, Rembrandt, Van Gogh, and Picasso and declaring the result a composite of the best in Western art."

Each religious tradition has its own integrity and I am not suggesting such pasting together. But if we have been shaped by and treasure Western music, may we not also learn to appreciate the beauties of Indian music? Indeed there are now musical works which draw upon both traditions. Can we not admire both the great Gothic cathedrals of Western Europe and the mosques of India? I believe that just as we can come to speak a language that is not our native tongue or appreciate a culture that is not our own, so we can to some extent enter the spiritual life of another faith community. Because this is the heart of the religious life, it is the most vital aspect of interreligious fellowship, even if it is the most sensitive. Here we begin to appreciate the other in the depths of his or her spirituality.

"Take off your shoes, for the place where you are standing is holy ground." God's words to Moses are a warning to all who approach the sanctuary of another faith. There is much that we shall not understand: the sacred language, the mythology, the music, the age-old gestures and ritual movements. Yet if we believe in the Oneness of God and the unity of the human family, then despite all the splendid difference and variety, there is "the selfsame aching" for God in every human heart. The attempt to enter sympathetically into the spiritual life of other traditions is a vital contribution to human unity, for such meeting is at the deepest level of our being.

It may be also that not only do we begin to appreciate the other's spirituality, but that our own also is enriched. While our regular spiritual diet will continue to be that of our faith community, it will be deepened by our discoveries, just as many peoples' traditional meals have been added to by dishes from overseas. There are some who draw from several spiritual traditions, but do not count themselves members of any particular faith community—some call themselves seekers or even universalists. . . .

Whatever our background and approach, there are moments when the gift of togetherness blinds us to our labels. . . . In some interfaith services that I have attended or helped to arrange there has been an experience of oneness felt by almost everyone present. At one service, held at Christ Church, Bath, we invited the readers to select a passage from their tradition about forgiveness and reconciliation. These were not texts from sacred writings but stories which told of recent experiences. As we listened

---

6 Jonathan Sacks—Chief Rabbi of Great Britain.

together, the sources of the stories did not matter, for their messages spoke
to us all. . . .

Interfaith worship attracts strong opposition because it is the most
powerful symbolic expression of the interfaith vision. . . . Interfaith worship
is not a substitute for the regular life of prayer and worship of a particular
faith community, but it is a powerful symbolic reminder of our unity in the
presence of the Holy One. In the Bible, all people are said to be descended
from common ancestors, namely Adam and Eve. If we are to live together
in one world, we need to recognize that we are one family, children of
One God.

SOURCE: Marcus Braybrooke, *Faith and Interfaith in a Global Age*. Grand Rapids, MI: CoNexus
Press/Oxford: Braybrooke Press, 1998, pp. 114–19

Global Imperatives for the Third Millennium
by Robert Muller

Robert Muller is a leading optimist about the possibility that humankind will
develop a global consciousness. For decades he was Assistant to the Secretary-
General of the United Nations, and he is now Chancellor Emeritus of the University
for Peace created by the United Nations in Costa Rica. His World Core Curriculum
earned him the UNESCO Peace Education Prize in 1989; more recently he received
the Albert Schweitzer International Prize for the Humanities and the Eleanor
Roosevelt Man of Vision Award.

. . . . In my view, from all perspectives—scientific, political, social, economic,
and ideological—humanity finds itself in the pregnancy of an entirely new
and promising age: the global, interdependent, universal age; a truly
quantum jump; a cosmic event of the first importance that is perhaps
unique in the universe: the birth of a global brain, heart, senses and soul to
humanity, of a holistic consciousness of our place in the universe and on
this planet, and of our role and destiny in them.

Much of this new consciousness is enhanced by the prodigious advances
in sciences and technology. Yet most people, governments and
institutions—including religions—are bewildered by this phenomenon.
They have difficulty adapting to it with understanding and creativity; they
were not educated for it. They see the future with anxiety. Many of them
turn and cling to the past or look inwards to the nation, ethnic group
or religion which they know and where they feel secure. As a result,
the world seems at a loss and is badly equipped and organized globally
and politically.

But we will make it. We are learning. Once aware of our problems and
errors, we are beginning to correct them. The *Encyclopedia of World Problems
and Human Potential*, published by the International Union of International
Associations in Brussels, lists more than 11,400 world problems but even
more potentials to solve them. One progress is happening after another: the

decolonization of the planet in less than 40 years; no world war in half a century; the end of the cold war; the end of apartheid; a substantial decrease in child mortality; the eradication of major epidemics; the increase in human longevity, both in poor and in rich countries; a universal organization of nations; one world conference after the other, attended by more and more heads of states (the first world conference on the environment in 1972 in Stockholm was attended by only two heads of states; the second conference 20 years later in Rio de Janeiro was attended by 140); the creation of free trade areas and regional communities; and I could go on with this list. . . .

Nevertheless, one important dimension has been missing from this extraordinary journey of humanity in recent times, a dimension lamented by Secretaries-General Dag Hammarskjöld, U Thant and Javier Perez de Cuellar: the *spiritual* dimension, the highest, deepest, most common, universal and binding dimension of all. What science, politics, economics and sociology were trying to achieve, the religions knew long ago by virtue of transcendence, of elevated consciousness and union with the universe and time. This dimension is still missing, yet it is urgently needed in world affairs. . . .

The crucial task of the world's religious and spiritual traditions and interfaith organizations is restoring a sense of spirituality to all that we do. The common heritages and institutional authority of the religions, combined with an emerging global spirituality, can make enormous contributions to the challenges and details of creating a better world. Though an atheist, André Malraux has said that "the third millennium will be spiritual or there will be no third millennium." Dag Hammarskjöld, a rational economist and world observer whom the UN transformed into a mystic, said, "I see no hope for permanent world peace. We have tried and failed miserably. Unless the world has a spiritual rebirth, civilization is doomed."

The religions are still accused of hindering peace, human progress and brotherhood. How often have I heard, after one of my speeches, "Mr. Muller, we agree with most of what you said, except one: forget about religions. They are one of the main troublemakers and dividing factors in the world." But I continue to preach about the spiritual and religious dimension. The new age we are entering will be an age of communities and of cooperation: it will be an age of family (celebrated by the UN in 1994), and of the family of nations. The family of religions cannot be absent; its absence could mean the retrocession and evanescence of religions, left behind by rapidly growing political, economic, scientific, ecological and sociological globalizations of the world. . . .

May I express my own overpowering conviction, born from five decades as a world servant? It is this:

At this crucial point of human history, on the eve of the third millennium, the main duty of the religions is not to propagate their dogmas and rituals or to try to increase their memberships. Their main *spiritual* duty is to give the world a desperately needed Renaissance from the extreme materialism and moral decay into which we have fallen. The issue is *not* whether we should pray standing or kneeling, our heads covered or uncovered; it is whether we will pray—period; whether we will be *good Samaritans* to those in need; whether we can give renewed hope to youth; whether we will revitalize the sacredness of life-giving, belief in the soul, marriage and fidelity. The main duty of religions must be to inspire love for all human brothers and sisters, especially the downtrodden, the poor, the handicapped, abandoned children, the homeless, the refugees, the innocent victims of violence. . . .

May we enter the twenty-first century consciously choosing to live in love, togetherness and fulfillment on this beautiful and miraculous celestial body—endowed with life and perhaps unique in the fathomless and mysterious universe.

SOURCE: Robert Muller, "Preparing for the Next Millennium," in *A SourceBook for Earth's Community of Religions*, ed. Joel D. Beversluis. Rev. ed. Grand Rapids, MI: CoNexus Press/New York: Global Education Associates, 1995, pp. 2–4

Declaration on the Elimination of All Forms of Intolerance and of Discrimination Based on Religion or Belief
by the United Nations

The following declaration was adopted by the General Assembly of the United Nations on November 25, 1981.

The General Assembly
Considering that one of the basic principles of the Charter of the United Nations is that of the dignity and equality inherent in all human beings, and that all Member States have pledged themselves to take joint and separate action in co-operation with the Organization to promote and encourage universal respect for and observance of human rights and fundamental freedoms for all, without distinction as to race, sex, language or religion,

Considering that the Universal Declaration of Human Rights and the International Covenants on Human Rights proclaim the principles of nondiscrimination and equality before the law and the right to freedom of thought, conscience, religion and belief,

Considering that the disregard and infringement of human rights and fundamental freedoms, in particular of the right to freedom of thought, conscience, religion or whatever belief, have brought, directly or indirectly, wars and great suffering to mankind, especially where they serve as a means of foreign interference in the internal affairs of other States and amount to kindling hatred between people and nations,

Considering that religion or belief, for anyone who professes either, is one of the fundamental elements in his conception of life and that freedom of religion or belief should be fully respected and guaranteed,

Considering that it is essential to promote understanding, tolerance and respect in matters relating to freedom of religion and belief and to ensure that the use of religion or belief for ends inconsistent with the Charter, other relevant instruments of the United Nations and the purposes and principles of the present Declaration is inadmissible,

Convinced that freedom of religion and belief should also contribute to the attainment of the goals of world peace, social justice and friendship among peoples and to the elimination of ideologies or practices of colonialism and racial discrimination,

Noting with satisfaction the adoption of several, and the coming into force of some, conventions, under the aegis of the United Nations and of the specialized agencies, for the elimination of various forms of discrimination,

Concerned by manifestations of intolerance and by the existence of discrimination in matters of religion or belief still in evidence in some areas of the world,

Resolved to adopt all necessary measures for the speedy elimination of such intolerance in all its forms and manifestations and to prevent and combat discrimination on the grounds of religion or belief,

Proclaims this Declaration on the Elimination of All Forms of Intolerance and of Discrimination Based on Religion or Belief:

Article 1

1   Everyone shall have the right to freedom of thought, conscience and religion. This right shall include freedom to have a religion or whatever belief of his choice, and freedom, either individually or in community with others and in public or private, to manifest his religion or belief in worship, observance, practice and teaching.
2   No one shall be subject to coercion which would impair his freedom to have a religion or belief of his choice.
3   Freedom to manifest one's religion or beliefs may be subject only to such limitations as are prescribed by law and are necessary to protect public safety, order, health or morals or the fundamental rights and freedoms of others.

Article 2

1   No one shall be subject to discrimination by any State, institution, group of persons or person on the grounds of religion or other beliefs. . . .

Article 3

Discrimination between human beings on the grounds of religion or belief constitutes an affront to human dignity and a disavowal of the principles of the Charter of the United Nations, and shall be condemned as a violation of the human rights and fundamental freedoms proclaimed in the Universal Declaration of Human Rights and enunciated in detail in the International Covenants on Human Rights, and as an obstacle to friendly and peaceful relations between nations.

Article 4

1   All States shall take effective measures to prevent and eliminate discrimination on the grounds of religion or belief in the recognition, exercise and enjoyment of human rights and fundamental freedoms in all fields of civil, economic, political, social and cultural life.

2   All States shall make all efforts to enact or rescind legislation where necessary to prohibit any such discrimination, and to take all appropriate measures to combat intolerance on the grounds of religion or other beliefs in this matter.

Article 5

1   The parents or, as the case may be, the legal guardians of the child have the right to organize the life within the family in accordance with their religion or belief and bearing in mind the moral education in which they believe the child should be brought up.

2   Every child shall enjoy the right to have access to education in the matter of religion or belief in accordance with the wishes of his parents or, as the case may be, legal guardians, and shall not be compelled to receive teaching on religion or belief against the wishes of his parents or legal guardians, the best interests of the child being the guiding principle.

3   The child shall be protected from any form of discrimination on the grounds of religion or belief. He shall be brought up in a spirit of understanding, tolerance, friendship among peoples, peace and universal brotherhood, respect for freedom of religion or belief of others, and in full consciousness that his energy and talents should be devoted to the service of his fellow men. . . .

Article 7

The rights and freedoms set forth in the present Declaration shall be accorded in national legislations in such a manner that everyone shall be able to avail himself of such rights and freedoms in practice.

SOURCE: Reprinted in Joel D. Beversluis, ed., *A SourceBook for Earth's Community of Religions*. Rev. ed. Grand Rapids, MI: CoNexus Press/New York: Global Education Associates, 1995, pp. 167–9

Ground Rules for Interfaith Dialogue by Leonard Swidler

Serious attempts to explore differences and similarities between religions may require a certain mindset. Leonard Swidler, Christian theologian, editor of *The Journal of Ecumenical Studies*, and a veteran of many interfaith conferences, proposes some basic ground rules to facilitate such dialogues.

Dialogue of course is conversation between two or more persons with differing views, the primary purpose of which is for each participant to learn from the other so that both can change and grow. . . .

But that is not what dialogue is. Dialogue is *not* debate. In dialogue each partner must listen to the other as openly and sympathetically as possible, in an attempt to understand the other's position as precisely and, as it were, as much from within, as possible. Such an attitude automatically includes the assumption that if at any point we might find the partner's position persuasive, we—our integrity being at stake—would have to change....

The following are some basic ground rules of interreligious, interideological dialogue that must be observed if dialogue is actually to take place. These are not theoretical rules given from "on high," but ones that have been learned from hard experience.

First Rule: *The primary purpose of dialogue is to learn—that is, to change and grow in the perception and understanding of reality, and then to act accordingly*. We come to dialogue that we might learn, change, and grow, not that we might induce change in the *other*, as one hopes to do in debate—a hope realized in inverse proportion to the frequency and ferocity with which debate is entered into. On the other hand, because in dialogue *all* partners come with the intention of learning and changing themselves, one's partner in fact will also change. Thus the intended goal of debate, and much more, is accomplished far more effectively by dialogue.

Second Rule: *Interreligious, ideological dialogue must be a two-sided project— within each religious or ideological community, and between religious or ideological communities*. Because of the "corporate" nature of interreligious, interideological dialogue, and because the primary goal of dialogue is that each partner learn and change, it is also necessary that each participant enter into dialogue not only with partners across a faith line—Catholics with Protestants, for example—but also with coreligionists, with fellow Catholics or fellow Protestants, to share with them the fruits of interreligious dialogue. Only thus can the whole community eventually learn and change, moving toward an ever more perceptive insight into reality.

Third Rule: *Each participant must come to the dialogue with complete honesty and sincerity*. It should be made clear in what direction the major and minor thrusts of the tradition move, what the future shifts might be, and, if necessary, where the participants have difficulties with their own traditions. No false fronts have any place in dialogue.

Conversely, *each participant must assume complete honesty and sincerity in the other partners*. Not only will the absence of sincerity prevent dialogue from happening, the absence of the assumption of one's partners' sincerity will do so as well. In brief: no trust, no dialogue.

Fourth Rule: *In interreligious, interideological dialogue, we must not compare our ideals with our partner's practice*, but rather our ideals with our partner's ideals, our practice with our partner's practice.

Fifth Rule: *All participants must define themselves*. Only the Jew, for example, can define from the inside what it means to be a Jew. The rest can only describe what it looks like from the outside. Moreover, because dialogue is a dynamic medium, as Jewish participants learn, they will change and hence continually deepen, expand, and modify their self-definition as Jews—being careful to remain in continual dialogue with fellow Jews. Thus it is mandatory that all dialogue partners define what it means to be an authentic member of their own tradition.

Conversely, *the interpreted must be able to recognize themselves in the interpretation.* This is the golden rule of interreligious, interideological hermeneutics.[7] ... For the sake of understanding, dialogue participants will naturally attempt to express for themselves what they think is the meaning of the partners' statements; the partners must be able to recognize themselves in that expression. ...

Sixth Rule: *Each participant must come to the dialogue with no hard-and-fast assumptions as to points of disagreement.* Rather, each partner should not only listen to the other partner with openness and sympathy, but also attempt to agree with the dialogue partner as far as possible, while still maintaining integrity with one's own tradition. Where one absolutely can agree no further without violating personal integrity, precisely there is the real point of disagreement—which most often turns out to be different from the point of disagreement assumed ahead of time.

Seventh Rule: *Dialogue can take place only between equals.* ... Both must come to learn from each other. Therefore, if, for example, the Muslim views Hinduism as inferior, or if the Hindu views Islam as inferior, there will be no dialogue. If authentic interreligious, interideological dialogue between Muslims and Hindus is to take place, then both the Muslim and the Hindu must come mainly to learn from each other; only then it will be "equal with equal."

Eighth Rule: *Dialogue can take place only on the basis of mutual trust.* Although interreligious, interideological dialogue must occur with some kind of "corporate" dimension—that is, the participants must be involved as members of a religious or ideological community—for instance, as Marxists or Taoists [Pinyin, Daoists]—it is also fundamentally true that it is only *persons* who can enter into dialogue. But a dialogue among persons can be built only on personal trust. Hence it is wise not to tackle the most difficult problems in the beginning, but rather to approach first those issues most likely to provide some common ground, thereby establishing the basis of human trust. Then, gradually, as this personal trust deepens and expands, the more thorny matters can be undertaken. Thus, just as in learning we move from the known to the unknown, so in dialogue we proceed from commonly held matters—which, given our mutual ignorance resulting from centuries of hostility, will take us quite some time to discover fully—to discuss matters of disagreement.

Ninth Rule: *Persons entering into interreligious, interideological dialogue must be at least minimally self-critical of both themselves and their own religious or ideological tradition.* A lack of such self-criticism implies that one's own

---

7 Hermeneutics—the branch of knowledge dealing with interpretation of texts.

tradition already has all the correct answers. Such an attitude makes dialogue not only unnecessary, but even impossible, because we enter into dialogue primarily so that *we* can learn—which obviously is impossible if our tradition has never made a misstep, if it has all the right answers. To be sure, in interreligious, interideological dialogue one must stand within a religious or ideological tradition with integrity and conviction, but such integrity and conviction must include not exclude healthy self-criticism. Without it there can be no dialogue—and, indeed, no integrity.

Tenth Rule: *Each participant eventually must attempt to experience the partner's religion or ideology "from within."* A religion or ideology is not merely something of the head, but also of the spirit, heart, and "whole being," individual and communal. John Dunne here speaks of "passing over" into another's religious or ideological experience and then coming back enlightened, broadened, and deepened.

SOURCE: Leonard Swidler, "Interreligious and Interideological Dialogue: The Matrix for All Systematic Reflection Today," in *Toward a Universal Theology of Religion*, ed. Leonard Swidler. Maryknoll, NY: Orbis, 1988, pp. 6, 13–16

REVIEW QUESTIONS

1   What is ironic about the globalization of Christianity? Go into detail.
2   Contrast the meaning of Pueblo *kachinas* with the Genesis command for humans to dominate the earth.
3   Does Nelson-Pallmeyer see violence as a distortion of religions' sacred texts?
4   Does the United Nations declaration on religious freedom support fundamentalism?

DISCUSSION QUESTIONS

1   What are the implications of the major trends in the globalization of religions?
2   What can religions contribute to solving the ecological crisis?
3   Do you think any religious sanctions for violence in sacred texts and traditions are valid? Why?
4   Organize a classroom debate between fundamentalists and universalists, requiring that each side support their arguments with research.

INFORMATION RESOURCES

GLOBALIZATION

Beyer, Peter. *Religion and Globalization*. London: Sage Publishing, 1994.

——. "Globalization and Religion," in *Encyclopedia of Religion*, ed. Lindsay Jones.

2nd ed. Vol. 5, pp. 3497–504. New York: Macmillan, 2005.

The Globalist
<http://www.theglobalist.com/DBWeb/Community.aspx?FeatureId=113>

Swatos, William. "Globalization," in *Encyclopedia of Religion and Society*. Alta Mira Press. <http://hirr.hartsem.edu/ency/globa.htm>

Thurow, Lester. *Fortune Favors the Bold: What We Must Do to Build a New and Lasting Global Prosperity*. New York: HarperCollins, 2003.

A World Connected: Globalization and Religion <http://www.aworldconnected.org/article.php/601.html>

ECOLOGY

The Forum on Religion and Ecology <http://environment.harvard.edu/religion>

Fox, Matthew. *Creation Spirituality*. San Francisco: HarperSanFrancisco, 1991.

Gottlieb, Roger, ed. *This Sacred Earth: Religion, Nature, and Environment*. New York and London: Routledge, 1996.

Taylor, Bron, ed. *Encyclopedia of Religion and Nature*. 2 vols. London and New York: Continuum Publishers, 2006. <http://www.religionandnature.com>

Tucker, Mary E., and **John Grim**. "Ecology and Religion," in *Encyclopedia of Religion*, ed. Lindsay Jones. 2nd ed. Vol. 4, pp. 2605–68. New York: Macmillan, 2005.

VIOLENCE

Bellinger, Charles, ed. *Religion and Violence: A Bibliography*. <http://www.wabashcenter.wabash.edu/Internet/hedgehog_viol_bib.htm>

Cline, Austin. *Top 10 Recently Reviewed Books on Religion, Violence, and Terrorism*. <http://atheism.about.com/cs/productreviews/tp/TopRecentTerr.htm>

Ellens, Harold, ed. *The Destructive Power of Religion: Violence in Judaism, Christianity, and Islam*. 4 vols. Westport, CT: Greenwood Press, 2004.

Graf, Fritz. "Violence," in *Encyclopedia of Religion*, ed. Lindsay Jones. 2nd ed. Vol. 14, pp. 9595–600. New York: Macmillan, 2005.

FUNDAMENTALISM

Brasher, Brenda. *The Encyclopedia of Fundamentalism*. New York: Routledge, 2001.

Fundamentalism <http://religiousmovements.lib.Virginia.edu/nrms/fund.html>

Marty, Martin, and **Scott Appleby**, eds. *The Fundamentalism Project*. 5 vols. Chicago: University of Chicago Press, 1991–5.

UNIVERSALISM

The Baha'is <http://www.bahai.org/>

Fox, Matthew. *One River, Many Wells*. New York: Tarcher/Putnam, 2000.

Hick, John. *God Has Many Names*. Philadelphia, PA: Westminster Press, 1980.

Koster, Rich, ed. *Universalist Herald*. <http://www.universalist-herald.net.html>

Krieger, David. *The New Universalism*. Maryknoll, NY: Orbis, 1991.

Smith, Huston. *Forgotten Truth: The Primordial Tradition*. New York: Harper and Row, 1976.

Thich Nhat Hanh. *Living Buddha, Living Christ*. New York: Riverhead/Putnam, 1995.

Unitarian-Universalist Association <http://www.uua.org/>

INTERFAITH ISSUES

Bowker, John, ed. "Dialogue," in *The Oxford Dictionary of World Religions*. Oxford: Oxford University Press, 1997.

Braybrooke, Marcus. *Pilgrimage of Hope: One Hundred Years of Global Interfaith Dialogue*. New York: Crossroad, 1992.

Council for a Parliament for the World's Religions <http://www.cpwr.org/index.html>

Gobind Sadan <http://www.gobindsadan.org>

Institute for World Spirituality <http://www.worldspirit.org>

Interfaith Center of New York <http://www.interfaithcenter.org>

International Interfaith Centre, U.K. <http://interfaith-centre.org>

Panikkar, Raimon. *The Intra-religious Dialogue*. New York: Paulist Press, 1978.

Stokes, Allison. *Shalom, Salaam, Peace*. New York: United Methodist Church, Global Ministries, 2006.

LITERARY ACKNOWLEDGMENTS

Laurence King Publishing wish to thank those who have kindly allowed their copyright material to be reproduced in this book, as listed below. Every effort has been made to contact or trace copyright holders prior to publication, but should there be any errors or omissions, the publishers would be pleased to insert the appropriate acknowledgment at the earliest opportunity.

CHAPTER 1
pp. 3–7 Lee W. Bailey: "The Study of World Religions," original article for this book, © Lee W. Bailey, 2006.
pp. 7–9 Harcourt, Inc.: From *The Sacred and the Profane: The Nature of Religion* by Mircea Eliade, translated by Willard R. Trask (New York: Harcourt Brace Jovanovich, 1959), © 1959 by Harcourt Brace Jovanovich, Inc.
pp. 9–10 Doubleday Broadway Publishing Group: From *The Future of an Illusion* by Sigmund Freud (New York: Doubleday, 1961).
p. 11 International Publishers, Inc.: From *On Religion* by Karl Marx and Friedrich Engels (Moscow: Foreign Languages Publishing House, 1955).
p. 12 Penguin Group (USA): *The Gay Science* from *The Portable Nietzsche*, edited and translated by Walter Kaufmann (New York: Viking, 1994), translation © 1954 by The Viking Press, renewed © 1982 by Viking Penguin, Inc.
p. 13 Rabbi Fritz A. Rothschild: From *Between God and Man: An Interpretation of Judaism* by Abraham Heschel, edited by Fritz A. Rothschild (New York: Simon and Schuster, 1998), © 1959 by Fritz A. Rothschild.
pp. 14–15 David L. Miller: From *The New Polytheism: Rebirth of the Gods and Goddesses* by David L. Miller (New York: Harper and Row, 1974).
p. 16 Dharma Publishing: From *Openness Mind* by Tarthang Tulku (Berkeley, CA: Dharma Publishing, 1978).
pp. 17–19 Prima Publishing: From *God: The Evidence* by Patrick Glynn (Rocklin, CA: Prima Publishing, 1997).
pp. 20–22 Ashgate Publishing: From *Scientism: Science, Ethics and Religion* by Michael Stenmark (Aldershot, Hampshire: Ashgate Publishing, 2001).
pp. 23–5 Princeton University Press: From *The Archetypes and the Collective Unconscious*, 2nd edition, by C. G. Jung (Princeton, NJ: Princeton University Press, 1968), © 1959 by Bollingen Foundation, Inc.
pp. 25–6 Celeste Federico: "The Ominous Sphere: A Transforming Dream," original article for this book, © Celeste Federico, 2006.
pp. 26–9 Princeton University Press: From *The Hero with a Thousand Faces* by Joseph Campbell (Princeton, NJ: Princeton University Press, 1949; 2nd edition, 1968), © 1949 by Bollingen Foundation, Inc.
pp. 30–1 HarperCollins Publishers: From *Standing Again at Sinai: Judaism from a Feminist Perspective* by Judith Plaskow (San Francisco: HarperSanFrancisco, 1990), © 1990 by Judith Plaskow.
pp. 32–4 University of Chicago Press: "The Lost Dimension in Religion" by Paul Tillich, from *The Essential Tillich*, edited by F. Forrester Church (New York: Macmillan Publishing Company/Collier Books, 1987), © 1987 by F. Forrester Church.

CHAPTER 2
pp. 38–44 Penguin Books: From *Of Water and Spirit: Ritual, Magic, and Initiation in the Life of an African Shaman* by Malidoma Patrice Somé (New York: G. P. Putnam's Sons, 1994), © Malidoma Patrice Somé, 1994.
pp. 44–7 Georges Niangoran-Bouah: "The Talking Drum: A Traditional African Instrument of Liturgy and of Mediation with the Sacred," from *African Traditional Religions in Contemporary Society*, edited by Jacob K. Olupona (New York: Paragon House, 1991), © 1991 by International Religious Foundation.
pp. 47–8 Shambhala Publications, Inc.: From *Oya: In Praise of the Goddess* by Judith Gleason (Boston: Shambhala Publications, 1987).
pp. 48–9 University of Minnesota Press: From *Daughters of the Dreaming*, 2nd edition, by Diane Bell (Minneapolis, MN: University of Minnesota Press, 1993).
pp. 52–5 University of Nebraska Press: From *The Sixth Grandfather: Black Elk's Teachings Given to John G. Neihardt* by John G. Neihardt, edited by Raymond J. DeMallie (Lincoln, NE: University of Nebraska Press, 1984), © 1984 by the University of Nebraska Press.
pp. 55–6 Kalpulli Chaplin: From *Nahui Mitl: The Journey of the Four Arrows* by Tlakaelel (Chaplin, CT: Mexicayotl Productions, 1998).
pp. 56–7 HarperCollins Publishers: "Seeing with a Native Eye: How Many Sheep Will it Hold?" by Barre Toelken, from *Seeing with a Native Eye: Essays on Native American Religion*, edited by Walter Holden Capps (New York: Harper and Row, 1976), © 1976 by Walter Holden Capps.
p. 58 <http://www.alphacdc.com/banyacya/un92.html>: From "The Hopi Message to the United Nations General Assembly" by Thomas Banyacya, Kykyotsmovi, Arizona (December 10, 1992).

CHAPTER 3
pp. 63–4 Motilal Banarsidass: From *The Hymns of the Rgveda*, new revised edition, translated by Ralph T. H. Griffith (Delhi: Motilal Banarsidass, 1976, 1986), © Motilal Banarsidass.
p. 65 Low Price Publications: From *Mundaka Upanishad*, in *The Upanishads*, 2nd edition, translated by Bibek Debroy and Dipavali Debroy (Delhi: Books For All, 1995).
pp. 66–8 Nilgiri Press: From *Bhagavad Gita*, translated by Eknath Easwaran (Delhi: Arkana/Penguin Books, 1986), © 1985 The Blue Mountain Center of Meditation, California.
pp. 68–70 Bharatiya Vidya Bhavan: From *Ramayana*, 27th edition, by C. Rajagopalachari (Mumbai: Bharatiya Vidya Bhavan, 1990), © Bharatiya Vidya Bhavan.
pp. 70–1, 72–3 Columbia University Press: From *Sources of Indian Tradition*, volume 1, edited by William Theodore de Bary (New York: Columbia University Press, 1958), © 1958 Columbia University Press.
pp. 73–4 Sivananda Yoga Vedanta Center: From *Meditation and Mantras*, edited by Swami Vishnu Devananda (New York: Om Lotus Publishing Company, 1975).
pp. 75–6 Motilal Banarsidass: From *Siva Purana*, translated and annotated by a board of scholars (Delhi: Motilal Banarsidass, 1970), © Motilal Banarsidass.
pp. 76–7 Columbia University Press: From *Bhagavata Purana*, in *Sources of Indian Tradition*, volume 1, edited by William Theodore de Bary (New York: Columbia University Press, 1958), © 1958 Columbia University Press.
pp. 77–8 Shiromani Gurdwara Parbandhak Committee: From *Guru Granth Sahib*, 3rd edition, adapted from English translation of Manmohan Singh (Amritsar, Punjab: Shiromani Gurdwara Parbandhak Committee, 1989).
pp. 78–9 Columbia University Press: "Worship Him in Silence" by Lalla, in *Sources of Indian Tradition*, volume 1, edited by William Theodore de Bary (New York: Columbia University Press, 1958), © 1958 Columbia University Press.
p. 79 Motilal Banarsidass: From *The Devotional Poems of Mirabai*, translated by A. J. Alston (Delhi: Motilal Banarsidass, 1980), © Motilal Banarsidass.
pp. 82–3 Self-Realization Fellowship: From *Autobiography of a Yogi*, 2nd edition, by Paramahansa Yogananda (Mumbai: Jaico Publishing House, 1975/Los Angeles: Self-Realization Fellowship, 1998), © 1946 Paramahansa Yogananda, © renewed 1974 Self-Realization Fellowship.
pp. 83–4 Navajivan Trust: From *The Message of Mahatma Gandhi* by Mahatma Gandhi, edited by U. S. Mohan Rao (Delhi: Publications Division, Ministry of Information and Broadcasting, Government of India, 1968).
pp. 85–6 Columbia University Press: From "Hindutva" by V. D. Savarkar, in *Sources of Indian Tradition*, volume 2, edited by S. Hay (New York: Columbia University Press, 1988).
pp. 86–8 *Vidyajyoti Journal*: "The Secular Face of Hinduism" by Joseph Vellaringatt, from *Vidyajyoti Journal*, volume 65, no. 9 (September 2001), 4/A, Raj Niwas Marg, Delhi 110054.
pp. 89–90 Mata Amritanandamayi: From "The Awakening of Universal Motherhood," an address to A Global Peace Initiative of Women Religious and Spiritual Leaders, Geneva (October 7, 2002).

CHAPTER 4
pp. 95–7 Manas Publications: From *Spiritual Masters from India* by Shashi Ahluwalia (Delhi: Manas Publications, 1987).
pp. 98–9 Columbia University Press: From *Akaranga Sutra*, in *Sources of Indian Tradition*, volume 1, edited by William Theodore de Bary (New York: Columbia University Press, 1958), © 1958 Columbia University Press.
pp. 104–7 Indian Books Centre: From "The Renunciate Life of Sādhvi Vicakṣaṇa," in *The Unknown Pilgrims: The Voice of the Sādhvis* by N. Shanta, translated by Mary Rogers (Delhi: Sri Satguru Publications, 1997). All rights reserved.
pp. 107–8 Kund-Kund Bharati: From *Barasa Anuvekkha* by Acharya Kund-Kund (Delhi: Kund-Kund Bharati, 1990).
pp. 109–10 Jain Publishing Company: From *Life Force: The World of Jainism* by Michael Tobias (Berkeley, CA: Asian Humanities Press, 1991), <http://www.jainpub.com>.

CHAPTER 5
pp. 114–17 Motilal Banarsidass: From *Buddhacarita, or Acts of the Buddha* by Asvaghosha, new enlarged edition, translated by E. H. Johnson (Delhi: Motilal Banarsidass, 1984), © Motilal Banarsidass.
pp. 117–18, 120 Wisdom Publications: From *The Middle Length Discourses of the Buddha: A Translation of the Majjhima Nikaya*, translated by Bhikkhu Nanamoli and Bhikkhu Bodhi (Boston: Wisdom Publications, 1995), © 1995, 2001 Bhikkhu Bodhi, <http://www.wisdompubs.org>, 199 Elm Street, Somerville, MA 02144, USA.
pp. 119–20 <http://www.serve.com/cmtan/Dhammapada/index.html>: "The Thousands" and "Happiness," in *Dhammapada*, translated by Chng Tiak Jung and Tan Chade Meng.

p. 122 Penguin Group (UK): From *Buddhist Scriptures*, translated by Edward Conze (London: Penguin Classics, 1959), © Edward Conze, 1959.

pp. 123–4 Daihokkaikaku Publishing Company: From *Shobogenzo*, volume 1, by Dogen Zenji, translated by Kosen Nishiyama and John Stevens (Sendai, Japan: Daihokkaikaku, 1975), © 1975 by Kosen Nishiyama and John Stevens.

pp. 124–6 Doubleday Broadway Publishing Group: From *Zen Buddhism* by D. T. Suzuki, edited by William Barrett (New York: Doubleday, 1956).

pp. 126–7 Grove/Atlantic, Inc.: From *Bankei Zen: Translations from the Record of Bankei* by Peter Haskel (New York: Grove Press, 1984), © 1984 by Peter Haskel and Yoshito Hakeda.

pp. 128–30 Office of the Dalai Lama: From *Love, Kindness and Universal Responsibility* by Tenzin Gyatso (New Delhi: Paljor Publications, n.d.), © Tenzin Gyatso, the XIV Dalai Lama.

pp. 131–3 State University of New York Press: From *Engaged Buddhism: Buddhist Liberation Movements in Asia*, edited by Christopher S. Queen and Sallie B. King (Albany, NY: State University of New York Press, 1996), © 1996, State University of New York. All rights reserved.

pp. 134–6 Serinity Young: "A Brief History of Buddhism in America," original article for this book, © Serinity Young, 2006.

pp. 137–8 Parallax Press: From *Being Peace* by Thich Nhat Hanh, edited by Arnold Kotler (Berkeley, CA: Parallax Press, 1987), © 1987, 1996 by Thich Nhat Hanh.

CHAPTER 6

pp. 143–6 Princeton University Press: From *The Analects of Confucius*, in *A Source Book in Chinese Philosophy*, translated and compiled by Wang-tsit Chan (Princeton, NJ: Princeton University Press, 1963), © 1963, renewed 1991 by Princeton University Press.

pp. 146–8 Randall Nadeau: From *The Book of Mencius*, original translation for this book, © Randall Nadeau, 2006.

pp. 148–50 Princeton University Press: "The Doctrine of the Mean," in *A Source Book in Chinese Philosophy*, translated and compiled by Wang-tsit Chan (Princeton, NJ: Princeton University Press, 1963), © 1963, renewed 1991 by Princeton University Press.

pp. 151–3 Princeton University Press: From "Ta Chuan: The Great Commentary," in the *Book of Changes*, translated by Richard Wilhelm, rendered into English by Cary F. Baynes (Princeton, NJ: Princeton University Press/Bollingen Foundation, 1950, 1967), © 1967, renewed 1977 by Princeton University Press.

pp. 153–5 The Crossroad Publishing Company: From "Lessons for Women" by Pan Chao, in *An Anthology of Sacred Texts by and about Women*, edited by Serinity Young (New York: The Crossroad Publishing Company, 1995), © 1993 by Serinity Young.

pp. 155–6, 156–7 Princeton University Press: "An Explanation of the Diagram of the Great Ultimate" by Chou Tun-i, and "The Western Inscription" by Chang Tsai, in *A Source Book in Chinese Philosophy*, translated and compiled by Wang-tsit Chan (Princeton, NJ: Princeton University Press, 1963), © 1963, renewed 1991 by Princeton University Press.

pp. 157–60 Yao Xinzhong: From "Confucianism and the Twenty-first Century," paper presented at First International Conference on Traditional Culture and Moral Education, Beijing (1998), reprinted in *Journal of Beliefs and Values: Studies in Religion and Education*, volume 20, no. 1, under the title "Confucianism and its Modern Values: Confucian moral, educational and spiritual heritages revisited" (London: Taylor and Francis Group/Carfax Publishing, 1999).

pp. 161–2 Peng Liu: "The Staying Power of Religion," from *God and Caesar in China*, edited by Jason Kindopp and Carol Lee Hamrin (Washington, DC: Brookings Institution Press, 2004).

CHAPTER 7

pp. 166–9 Randall Nadeau: From *Dao de jing* by Laozi, original translation for this book, © Randall Nadeau, 2006.

pp. 170–1 Columbia University Press: From "The Great and Venerable Teacher" by Chuang-tzu, from *The Book of Chuang-tzu*, translated by Burton Watson (New York: Columbia University Press, 1968), © 1964 Columbia University Press.

pp. 171–3 John Murray (Publishers) Ltd.: From *The Book of Lieh-tzu*, translated by A. C. Graham (London: John Murray/New York: Grove Press, 1960).

pp. 173–5 University of California Press: From *Huang Ti Nei Ching Su Wen/The Yellow Emperor's Classic of Internal Medicine*, translated by Ilza Veith (Berkeley, CA: University of California Press, 1972), © 1947, 1975 Ilza Veith.

pp. 175–6 State University of New York Press: From "Awakening to Perfection" by Zhang Boduan, from *The Taoist Experience: An Anthology*, edited by Livia Kohn (Albany, NY: State University of New York Press, 1993), © 1993, State University of New York. All rights reserved.

pp. 176–9 Simon and Schuster, Inc.: "The Way of the Taoist Tradition of Perfect Truth" by Wang Che, from *Chinese Civilization and Society: A Sourcebook* by Patricia Buckley Ebrey (New York: The Free Press, 1981), © 1981 The Free Press, a division of Macmillan, Inc.; reprinted in *Chinese Religion: An Anthology of Sources*, edited by Deborah Sommer (New York: Oxford University Press, 1995).

pp. 179–81 Penguin Group (USA): "The Story of Ho Hsien Ku," from *The Eight Immortals of Taoism* by Kwok Man Ho and Joanne O'Brien (New York: New American Library, 1990), © 1990 by Kwok Man Ho and Joanne O'Brien.

pp. 181–2 Celestial Arts: From *Embrace Tiger, Return to Mountain* by Al Chung-liang Huang (Berkeley, CA: Celestial Arts, 1997), © 1987, 1997 by Al Chung-liang Huang; originally published by Real People Press, 1973.

pp. 183–4 Zhou Zhongzhi: "The Significance of Daoist Ethical Thought in the Building of a Harmonious Society," abstract of paper delivered at the conference "Continuity and Change: Perspectives on Science and Religion," Philadelphia (June 3–7, 2006), a program of the Metanexus Institute, <http://www.metanexus.net>.

CHAPTER 8

pp. 189–98, 200–1 The Jewish Publishing Society: From *Tanakh: A New Translation of the Holy Scriptures* (Philadelphia, PA: The Jewish Publication Society, 1985), © 1985 by The Jewish Publication Society.

pp. 198–9 Judith Glatzer Wechsler: From *Hammer on the Rock*, edited by Nahum N. Glatzer, translated by Jacob Sloan (New York: Schocken Books, 1962), © 1948, 1962 by Schocken Books, Inc.

pp. 199–200 Yale University Press: From *The Living Talmud*, edited and translated by Judah Goldin (New Haven, CT: Yale University Press, 1957).

pp. 201–2 Ktav Publishing House: From *Passover Haggadah*, revised edition, translated by Rabbi Nathan Goldberg (Ktav Publishing House, 1993), © 1949, 1956, 1966, 1993 by Asher Scharfstein.

pp. 204–7 Balkin Agency, Inc.: From *The Legend of the Baal-Shem* by Martin Buber, translated by Maurice Friedman (Schocken Books, 1969), © 1955, 1969, 1987 The Estate of Martin Buber.

pp. 209–10 The Rabbinical Assembly: From *Conservative Judaism and Jewish Law*, edited by Seymour Siegel (New York: The Rabbinical Assembly, 1977).

pp. 213–16 Ellen M. Umansky: "Women in Jewish Life," original article for this book, © Ellen M. Umansky, 2006.

pp. 217–19 Michael Lerner: "Ten Commitments, Not Commandments," in *Tikkun* magazine (October 11, 2005), © *Tikkun* magazine, <http://www.tikkun.org>.

CHAPTER 9

pp. 224–31 National Council of Churches of Christ in the USA: From *The Holy Bible: Revised Standard Version* (New York: Thomas Nelson, 1952), <http://goon.stg.brown.edu/bible_browser/pbform.shtml>.

pp. 233, 233–4 HarperCollins Publishers: From "The Gospel of Mary" and "The Thunder, Perfect Mind," translated by George W. MacRae, in *The Nag Hammadi Library*, edited by James M. Robinson (San Francisco: Harper and Row, 1977; revised edition HarperCollins, 1990).

pp. 236–7 Abingdon Press: "Origen on First Principles," from *Readings in Christian Thought*, edited by Hugh T. Kerr (Nashville, TN: Abingdon Press, 1966), © 1966 by Abingdon Press.

pp. 240–1 Simon and Schuster, Inc.: From *The Confessions of Saint Augustine*, translated by Edward B. Pusey (New York: Washington Square Press, 1960), © 1951, by Washington Square Press, Inc.

pp. 242–3 <http://www.fordham.edu/halsall/source/anselm.html>: *Proslogion* by Anselm of Canterbury, translated by David Burr, in *Internet Medieval Sourcebook*, edited by Paul Halsall.

pp. 243–4 Hodder and Stoughton Ltd.: From *Hildegard*, edited by Robert Van de Weyer (London: Hodder and Stoughton, 1997), © 1997 Robert Van de Weyer.

pp. 248–9 John Mark Ministries: "The Manila Manifesto," 1989, from *Recent Trends Among Evangelicals*, 2nd edition, by Rowland C. Croucher (Heathmont, Australia: John Mark Ministries, 1991).

pp. 249–51 Writers House: From "I've Seen the Promised Land" by Martin Luther King, from *A Testament of Hope: The Essential Writings of Martin Luther King, Jr.*, edited by James Melvin Washington (San Francisco: Harper and Row, 1986), © 1986 by Coretta Scott King, Executrix of the Estate of Martin Luther King, Jr.

pp. 251–2 Orbis Books: From "Not Development, but Liberation" by Gustavo Gutiérrez, from *A Theology of Liberation: History, Politics, and Salvation*, edited by David Batsone et al. (Maryknoll, NY: Orbis Books, 1973, 1988).

pp. 252–3 New City Press: From *Mother Teresa: Her Life, Her Works* by Lush Gjergji (New Rochelle, NY: New City Press, 1991).

pp. 253–4 Melba Newsome: "The Green Patriarch: Environmental Orthodoxy," interview with the Patriarch of Eastern Orthodoxy, from *The Amicus Journal*, volume 20, no. 4 (Winter 1999).

pp. 255–6 David Batstone: "Macrowave: Taking Global Warming to Church," in *Sojourners* magazine, volume 35, no. 7 (July 2006), <http://www.sojo.net/index.cfm?action=magazine.article&issue=Soj060 7&article=060766>.

pp. 256–8 HarperCollins Publishers: From *God's Politics: Why the Right Gets It Wrong and the Left Doesn't Get It* by Jim Wallis (New York: HarperCollins, 2005).

pp. 258–60 *The Week* magazine: "The Rise of the Megachurch" (April 28, 2006), <http://www.theweekmagazine.com/article.aspx?id=1436>.

pp. 260–1 <http://www.romancatholicwomenpriests.org>: "Catholic women's ordinations."

pp. 262–4 Thomas J. Reese: "Child Abuse Struggles: Facts, Myths and Questions," in *America* magazine (March 22, 2004), <http://www.americamagazine.org>.

CHAPTER 10

pp. 269–70, 270–3, 280–2 Sh. Muhammad Ashraf: From *Sahih Muslim*, volume 1, translated by 'Abdul Hamid Siddiqi (Lahore, Pakistan: Sh. Muhammad Ashraf, 1973), © Sh. Muhammad Ashraf, Lahore.

pp. 273–9 Dar Al Arabia: From *The Holy Qur'an: Text, Translation and Commentary* by Abdullah Yusuf Ali (Beirut, Lebanon: Dar Al Arabia, 1968), © 1968 by Khalil Al-Rawaf, <http://www.usc.edu/dept/MSA/quran>.

pp. 283–4 Ahmadiyya Anjuman Isha'at Islam: From *The Religion of Islam*, 6th edition, by Maulana Muhammad Ali (Delhi: Motilal Banarsidass, 1994), © Ahmadiyya Anjuman Isha'at Islam.

pp. 284–5 <http://www.sufism.org/society/salaat/salaat.html>: "How to Perform Salaat."

pp. 286–8 University of Pennsylvania Press: From *Allegory and Philosophy in Avicenna (Ibn Sina)* by Peter Heath (Philadelphia, PA: University of Pennsylvania Press, 1992), © 1992 by the University of Pennsylvania Press.

pp. 288–90 W. Montgomery Watt: From *The Faith and Practice of Al-Ghazali* by W. Montgomery Watt (London: George Allen and Unwin, 1953).

pp. 291–2 The Threshold Society: "Doorkeeper of the Heart" and "Dream Fable," from *Rabi'a*, translated by Charles Upton (Brattleboro, VT: Threshold Books, 1988).

pp. 292–3 State University of New York Press: From *The Sufi Path of Love: The Spiritual Teachings of Rumi* by William C. Chittick (Albany, NY: State University of New York Press, 1983), © 1983, State University of New York. All rights reserved.

p. 294 George Allen and Unwin Ltd.: From *Sufis of Andalusia: The Ruh Al-Quds and 'Al-Durrat al-Fakhirah* by Muhyi al-Din Muhammad ibn al-'Arabi (London: George Allen and Unwin, 1971).

pp. 295–7 Riffat Hassan: From "Are Human Rights Compatible with Islam?" <http://religiousconsultation.org/hassan2.htm>.

pp. 298–300 Oxford University Press, Inc.: From *Religion and the Order of Nature: The 1994 Cadbury Lectures at the University of Birmingham* by Seyyed Hossein Nasr (New York: Oxford University Press, 1996), © 1996 by Seyyed Hossein Nasr.

pp. 300–2 *The Observer*: "Islam and the West: So, are Civilisations at War? Interview with Samuel Huntington, in *The Observer* (October 21, 2001, <http://observer.guardian.co.uk/islam/story0,,577982,00html>.

pp. 302–6 Martin Forward: "God in a World of Christians and Muslims" by Martin Forward, <http://www.aurora.edu/cfa/published/muslims.htm>.

CHAPTER 11

pp. 310–11 Languages Department Punjab: From *The Great Humanist Guru Nanak* by Sir Jogendra Singh and Raja Sir Daljit Singh (Patiala, Punjab: Languages Department Punjab, 1970).

p. 312 Hemkunt Press: From *JapJi: The Morning Prayer*, translated by Bhagat Singh and G. P. Singh (Delhi: Hemkunt Press, 1986), © 1986 Hemkunt Press.

pp. 313–14 Gobind Sadan Institute and Surendra Nath: From *Jaap Sahib* by Guru Gobind Singh, revised edition, translated by Surendra Nath (Delhi: Gobind Sadan, 1996).

pp. 314–15 Singh Brothers: From *Sacred Sukhmani* by Guru Arjun Dev, translated by Harbans Singh Doabia (Amritsar, Punjab: Singh Brothers, 1979).

pp. 316–21 George Allen and Unwin Ltd.: Hymns from the Guru Granth Sahib, in *Selections from the Sacred Writings of the Sikhs*, translated by Trilochan Singh *et al.* (London: George Allen and Unwin, 1960/New York: Samuel Weiser, 1973).

pp. 321–2 Punjabi University: "Pray crow, peck not these eyes, so that I may see the Beloved" by Sheikh Farid, with commentary by Guru Nanak, in *Sri Guru Granth Sahib*, translated by Gurbachan Singh Talib (Patiala, Punjab: Punjabi University Publication Bureau, 1990), © Punjabi University, Patiala.

pp. 322–3, 323–4 Gobind Sadan Institute: From *Bacchitar Natak* by Guru Gobind Singh, in *Jap*, translated by Surendra Nath (Delhi: Gobind Sadan, n.d.); from *Manas ki jaat* by Guru Gobind Singh, from *Akal Ustat*, translated by Gobind Sadan Institute, previously unpublished.

pp. 324–7 Vision and Venture: From *Sikhism: Norm and Form* by Dharam Singh (Patiala, Punjab, and Delhi: Vision and Venture, 1997), © 1997, The Author.

CHAPTER 12

pp. 331–2, 332–3 The Church of Jesus Christ of Latter-day Saints: From *The Book of Mormon* by Joseph Smith (Salt Lake City, UT: The Church of Jesus Christ of Latter-day Saints, 1830/1963); "Testimony of the Prophet Joseph Smith: Moroni's Visit" (1823), <http://www.lds.org/library/display/O,4945,104-1-3-6,00.html>.

pp. 336–7 Watch Tower Bible and Tract Society of New York, Inc.: "Life in a Peaceful New World," <http://www.watchtower.org/library/t15/peaceful.htm>.

pp. 338–9 The Inter-Religious Federation for World Peace: "The True Family Movement that will Save Mankind" by Sun Myung Moon, Founder's Address to Fourth IRFWP Congress, Washington, DC (November 25–30, 1997), © IRFWP, 1997.

pp. 340–2 Foundation for *A Course in Miracles*: From Preface to *A Course in Miracles* by Helen Schucman (April 1999), © 1975, 1992 Foundation for Inner Peace, <http://64.77.6.149/about_acim_section/what_it_says.html>.

pp. 343–4 Charlene Spretnak: From "The Politics of Women's Spirituality," from *Chrysalis: A Magazine of Women's Culture*, no. 6 (November 1978), © Charlene Spretnak, 1978.

pp. 344–6 The Crossing Press: From *Mother Wit: A Feminist Guide to Psychic Development* by Diane Mariechild (Trumansburg, NY: The Crossing Press, 1981), © 1981, Diane Mariechild.

pp. 347–9 State University of New York Press: From Introduction, by J. Gordon Melton, to *When Prophets Die: The Postcharismatic Fate of New Religious Movements*, edited by Timothy Miller (Albany, NY: State University of New York Press, 1991), © 1991, State University of New York. All rights reserved.

CHAPTER 13

pp. 351–3 Oxford University Press, Inc.: From *The Next Christendom: The Coming of Global Christianity* by Philip Jenkins (New York: Oxford University Press, 2002).

pp. 354–7 Lee W. Bailey: "Secret Whispers in the World," original article for this book, © Lee W. Bailey, 2006.

pp. 357–8 The Continuum International Publishing Group: From *Is Religion Killing Us?* by Jack Nelson-Pallmeyer (New York and London: Continuum, 2003).

pp. 359–60 Random House, Inc.: From *The Battle for God: A History of Fundamentalism* by Karen Armstrong (New York: Ballantine Books, 2001).

pp. 360–2 Gobind Sadan Institute: "God Will Break All the Barriers!" by Baba Virsa Singh, talk given at Gobind Sadan, Delhi (December 28, 1996).

pp. 362–3 Baha'i Publishing Trust: From *Gleanings from the Writings of Bahá'u'lláh*, 2nd edition, translated by Shoghi Effendi (Wilmette, IL: Baha'i Publishing Trust, 1976), copyright 1939, 1952, © 1976 by the National Spiritual Assembly of the Baha'is of the United States. All rights reserved.

pp. 363–5 Sufi Order Publications: From *The Unity of Religious Ideals* by Hazrat Inayat Khan (New Lebanon, NY: Sufi Order Publications, 1979), © 1979 by Sufi Order. All rights reserved.

pp. 365–7 CoNexus Press and Braybrooke Press: From *Faith and Interfaith in a Global Age* by Marcus Braybrooke (Grand Rapids, MI: CoNexus Press/Oxford: Braybrooke Press, 1998), © 1998 Marcus Braybrooke.

pp. 367–9 CoNexus Press and Global Education Associates: From "Preparing for the Next Millennium" by Robert Muller, in *A SourceBook for Earth's Community of Religions*, revised edition, edited by Joel D. Beversluis (Grand Rapids, MI: CoNexus Press/New York: Global Education Associates, 1995).

pp. 371–4 Orbis Books: From "Interreligious and Interideological Dialogue: The Matrix for All Systematic Reflection Today" by Leonard Swidler, in *Toward a Universal Theology of Religion*, edited by Leonard Swidler (Maryknoll, NY: Orbis Books, 1988), © 1987 by Leonard Swidler.

INDEX